P9-CJC-892

Dictionary of Economics

Dictionary of Economics

Donald Rutherford

1268350

ROUTLEDGE

London and New York

Riverside Community College
Library
4800 Magnolia Avenue
Riverside, California 92506

OCT '94

First published in 1992
by Routledge
11 New Fetter Lane, London EC4P 4EE

Simultaneously published in the USA and Canada
by Routledge
a division of Routledge, Chapman and Hall, Inc.
29 West 35th Street, New York, NY 10001

© Donald Rutherford 1992

Printed in England by Clays Ltd, St Ives plc

All rights reserved. No part of this book may be reprinted or reproduced or
utilized in any form or by any electronic, mechanical or other means, now
known or hereafter invented, including photocopying and recording, or in any
information storage or retrieval system, without permission in writing from the
publishers.

British Library Cataloguing in Publication Data
A catalogue record for this book is available from the British Library.

Library of Congress Cataloging-in-Publication Data
A catalog record for this book is available on request.

ISBN 0-415-06566-6

Contents

Preface

Economics, the Queen of the Social Sciences, has now established itself as a major subject in dialogue with the physical sciences, law and the arts. There are few aspects of human behaviour that do not have an economic dimension and little of current affairs can be understood without a knowledge of economic principles. It is, therefore, not surprising that it is a major discipline in schools, colleges and universities throughout the world, studied annually by millions and the topic of conversation of millions more.

The *Dictionary of Economics* has as its concerns as many issues as the subject Economics now covers. The breadth can be appreciated by considering the subject classifications used by the Journal of Economic Literature (USA) and the Economic Journal (UK). The related specialties of economic history, commercial law, and econometric and statistical techniques are all within its ambit. However, to prevent a subject dictionary becoming encyclopedic, a lexicographer can follow the useful convention of taking from sister disciplines only what is regularly used in mainstream economic literature. For example, from law, it is customary to emphasize competition, fiscal and banking law more than constitutional or criminal law. This interpretation of economics in the broad sense makes a dictionary of this kind more of a dictionary *for* economists, rather than a dictionary *of* economics with terms peculiar to the subject.

Even if a dictionary takes a broad view of its subject matter, it is usually addressed to a particular audience, such as first-year undergraduates. This is an approach that I have wanted to avoid, as there is a substantial heterogeneity of economics courses and students often need to research some areas of the subject in more depth than others. Also, it can be patronizing to the general reader to regard all of his or her knowledge to date as rudimentary. Even the reader of daily newspapers who never looks at an economics textbook will encounter the most complex of ideas, chaos theory for example.

To produce a dictionary of this kind, I started with an assortment of basic textbooks and many current newspapers and journals. I soon discovered that about a thousand concepts are common to all the textbooks, for example notions of cost, economic systems and banking. From general textbooks I moved to a perusal of specialist books on the diverse divisions of the subject. The areas of economics encompassed obviously have to reflect current concerns; many environmental concepts are included and the 'male' character of many economics works has been partially avoided by including biographies of several leading female economists. Newspapers and journals provide a modern guide to current economic discourse. There is no foreseeable end to the creation of economic neologisms – major events such as the deregulation of financial markets and the political developments in Eastern Europe, which have changed the nature of many economies, have produced an expansion of new terms. Some terminology is ephemeral but many words that start as slang, such as 'yuppy', have a surprising longevity. I have taken the optimistic view that numerous catchwords and catchphrases will render linguistic service for many years.

The entries in this *Dictionary* are sequenced alphabetically, letter by letter: for example, *discounted share price* precedes *discount house*, which precedes *discounting*. The standard form for each item included begins with a headword and one or more three-digit codes to indicate the branch or branches of economics that most frequently use that term. As it is important to ensure that all entries are immediately comprehensible and independent of others, the text of each entry begins with a short definition before any discussion is included. Where related entries can profitably be read in conjunction, reference is made to them. Standard diagrams are included in the entries that require them. For the longer or more difficult entries, references to other works that either indicate the original use of that idea or provide a modern discussion of it are given.

A dictionary is a solace for the perplexed, a guide for the scholar and a map of a new terrain for the general reader. I hope that this *Dictionary of Economics* is all of these.

Acknowledgements

The resources of the National Library of Scotland and of Edinburgh University Library have been invaluable to me in the compilation of this *Dictionary*. I am particularly indebted to the reference librarians of the University, especially Margaret Dowling, John Green and Lorna Cheyne for their energetic eagerness to help me at all times.

Writing a dictionary oneself is a daunting and solitary task so I am deeply grateful for the encouragement received, both within the University and outside it, from Stuart Sayer, Gordon Hughes, Michael Anderson, Gavin Reid, Brian Main, Gordon Miller, William Cameron, Graham Richardson, Duncan Spiers, Owen Dudley Edwards, Richard McAllister, John Berry, Andrew Roberts, Colin Tate and, of course, my dear mother.

The publishers and I would also like to thank the editors of the *Economic Journal* and its publisher, Blackwell Publishers, for permission to use the subject classification system that has been adopted throughout the *Dictionary*.

I shall always recall with appreciation the expertise and guidance of all at Routledge who have worked on this project, especially Liz Fidlon, Wendy Morris, Emma Waghorn, Christine Sharrock and, in particular, Mark Barragry who, like a games master, always kept me running around the track.

Dictionary of Economics

A

AAA (310)
The top credit rating of the securities issued by corporations and companies, as judged by the US rating agency **Standard & Poor**. This rating is based on the view that default is likely to be minimal.

See also: **BB**; **BBB**; **C**; **D**; **DDD**; **Prime-1**.

abatement (010, 720)
See: **marginal cost of abatement**.

ability to pay (320)
1 The principle of taxation that persons with equal incomes and equal capacity to pay a tax should be taxed the same. This alternative to a **benefit tax** was suggested as early as in the **mercantilist** period because it appears to be a 'just' approach. John Stuart **Mill** argued that equality in taxation meant equality of sacrifice: this is ambiguous as the sacrifice may be in absolute, proportional or marginal terms. As sacrifice means loss of utility, the theory can only work if different persons' **utilities** can be compared.

2 An employer's stance in wage bargaining of making offers according to a firm's financial state.

abortive benefits (320, 910)
Social benefits which fail to achieve their purpose. There is no net increase in a recipient's income as the benefits are outweighed by income taxation. Proposals for a **negative income tax**, which would merge benefits and taxation into a single system, attempt to ensure that benefits raise net income.

above the line (320, 520, 540)
1 A type of expenditure or revenue of a government or a firm. In the case of British budgets from 1947 to 1963 it referred to spending and receipts relating to current tax revenue; for a firm it means expenditure on direct advertising.

2 The items in the summary British **balance of payments** which are within the current and capital balances.

See also: **below the line**.

Abramovitz, Moses, 1912– (030)
Educated at Harvard and Columbia universities. He was on the staff of the **National Bureau of Economic Research** from 1938 to 1942 and Director of Business Cycles Study from 1946 to 1948; he was principal economist of the War Production Board in 1942 before serving in the US Army and was a member of the faculty of Columbia University, 1940–2 and 1946–8, and of Stanford University, 1948–77. After early work on price theory, he turned to a study of inventories and business cycles. Later he examined explanations of long swings in growth, considering changes in the supply of factors of production and the influence of an initial level of productivity on subsequent economic progress.

Abramovitz, M. (1950) *Inventories and Business Cycles*, New York: National Bureau of Economic Research.

Abramovitz, M. (ed.) (1958) *Capital Formation and Economic Growth*, Princeton, NJ: Princeton University Press.

absenteeism (830)
A form of industrial unrest often used instead of a **strike**. Workers dissatisfied with their conditions take days off work, without pay. Some industries have been noted for this practice, e.g. the British coalmining industry. It is one of the forms of expressing a grievance available to non-unionized workers.

See also: **exit voice**.

absolute advantage (410)
An early theory of trade which states that a country enters into trade with another because it has a greater productivity than the other country in certain industries, e.g. its cotton industry is more productive than the foreign cotton industry. Adam Smith

advanced this as the reason for trade, stating that a nation, like a household, should specialize.

See also: **comparative advantage.**

absolute concentration (610)
See: **aggregate concentration.**

absolute income hypothesis (020)
A theory of the **consumption function** which states that consumption is a function of current personal disposable income. This was **Keynes**'s original view, later refined by **Tobin** and Smithies. The consumption function is non-linear because the **marginal propensity to consume** declines as national income increases. Keynes asserted that 'men are disposed, as a rule and on average, to increase their consumption as their income increases, but not by as much as the increase in their income'. The early approach was superseded by the **relative income, permanent income** and **life-cycle hypotheses.**

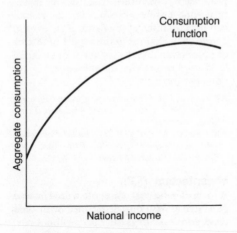

absolute poor (160, 910)
Persons whose income is below what is needed to maintain a minimum standard of nutrition.

See also: **poverty; subsistence.**

absolute scarcity (720)
The limited non-renewable nature of some resources, notably metals and fossil fuels.

absolute surplus value (010)
See: **surplus value.**

absolute tax incidence (320)
The burden of a particular tax compared with a situation in which there are no taxes or governmental expenditures.

See also: **tax incidence.**

absorption approach (430)
A method of analysing a country's **balance of payments** by comparing its total output with its 'absorption', i.e. its domestic expenditure on goods and services. There will only be an improvement in a country's balance of payments if its total output is greater than its absorption of its own output. By the use of price elasticities and a **multiplier**, it is possible to examine the effects on output and absorption of the **devaluation** of a currency.

Kyle, J.F. (1976) *The Balance of Payments in a Monetary Economy*, Princeton, NJ: Princeton University Press.

See also: **price elasticity of demand.**

absorptive capacity (640)
The limit to the amount of investment which is physically possible because of the decline in **productivity** as the rate of investment increases; the extent to which a country can increase investment without depressing returns to its investment.

Adler, J. (1965) *Absorptive Capacity: the Concept and its Determinants*, Washington, DC: Brookings Institution.

abstinence (010)
A justification for the payment of interest, first advanced by Nassau **Senior**. An individual who abstains from current consumption is rewarded with interest for adding to the capital stock. Abstinence explains the supply of savings; that supply, together with the demand for capital, forms a theory of the interest rate.

Senior, N.W. (1836) *An Outline of the Science of Political Economy.* Reprinted New York: Augustus M. Kelly, 1965.

abstract labour (810)
Labour which is abstracted from expenditures of human labour-power. **Marx** regarded abstract labour as the creator of exchange values.

See also: **concrete labour.**

AC (110)
Advanced country.

ACAS (830)
See: **Advisory, Conciliation and Arbitration Service (UK)**.

Accelerated Cost Recovery System (320, 520)
US Federal tax allowance introduced in 1981 but modified in subsequent years. Capital goods were mostly assumed to have a life of three, five or ten years; as many were more durable, this system was a means of cutting corporate taxation. An example of **supply-side economics**.

accelerated depreciation (320, 520)
Depreciation in excess of the annual wear and tear of a fixed capital asset allowed at the beginning of its life. Thus, if an asset has an expected life of ten years, under the straight-line method of depreciation the value of the asset would be deemed to depreciate by 10 per cent per year. But if accelerated depreciation were permitted, then for example the value of the asset could be depreciated by 20 per cent in the first year. Governments have used this fiscal device to encourage private sector investment.

acceleration clause (310)
A clause in many mortgage agreements making the **principal** and interest immediately payable on the occurrence of an event, e.g. failure to make payments due or failure to keep a covenant.

accelerator principle (140, 520)
A major theory of investment which asserts that the amount of net investment in a given time period will be equal to a coefficient approximating to the amount of capital needed to produce another unit of output multiplied by the change in income. One of the earliest writers to make use of this principle was Aftalion in *Les Crises périodiques de surproduction* (1913) but it has been more powerfully applied by Lundberg, **Harrod**, **Samuelson**, **Hicks** and Goodwin in their investment equations. The basic principle, expressed in the equation

$$I = \alpha \Delta Y_t$$

where I is net investment in year t, α is the accelerator coefficient and ΔY is the annual change in income, has been modified to take into account different reaction times to a change in income and the existence of **excess capacity**:

$$I = \alpha \Delta Y_{t-1}$$

where ΔY_{t-1} is the change in income in the previous year;

$$I = \alpha \Delta Y_t - \beta K_t$$

where β is the proportion of the capital stock which is excess capacity and K is the capital stock in year t.

In combination with the **multiplier, ceilings** and **floors**, the accelerator plays an important role in the explanation of **business cycles**, and is prominent in **Harrod–Domar** models.

Hicks, J.R. (1950) *A Contribution to the Theory of the Trade Cycle*, Oxford: Clarendon Press (reprinted 1978).
Knox, A.D. (1952) 'The acceleration principle and the theory of investment: a survey', *Economica*, New Series 19: 269–97.
Lundberg, E. (1937) *Studies in the Theory of Economic Expansion*, Oxford: Basil Blackwell (reprinted 1955).

accepting house (310)
A British **merchant bank** which, by approving a commercial **bill of exchange**, creates a short-term marketable asset. In the past such accepting was the major activity of many of these banks but now they have diversified into other activities, including corporate finance and portfolio management. In 1981, the Bank of England ended their special status as endorsers of bills: the Bank of England now regards other **commercial paper** as eligible for purchase.

The seventeen members of the Accepting Houses Committee are Arbuthnot Latham, Baring Brothers, Brown Shipley, Charterhouse Japhet, Robert Fleming, Guinness Mahon, Hambros, Hill Samuel, Kleinwort Benson, Lazard Brothers, Samuel Montagu, Morgan Grenfell, Rea Brothers, N.M. Rothschild, J. Henry Schroeder Wagg, Singer & Friedlander and S.G. Warburg.

access differential (160)
A difference in access to goods and services

and the institutions which produce them. This is used as an alternative to income differentials in planned economies, e.g. higher ranking officials can use shops, schools and clinics not open to the rest of society.

accession tax (320)
A tax on the gifts and bequests received by heirs.

accommodating credit (310, 430)
A form of automatic credit, especially in international trade, which consists of the seller (exporter) financing the purchase by a buyer (importer).

account (310)
1 A financial statement expressed in words and sums of money.

2 A standard time period used on the **International Stock Exchange** for settling payments and delivering securities, referring to a fortnight (or three weeks if there is a public holiday). During an account, stocks and shares can be bought and sold without any cash settlement.

account days (310)
The days on which **International Stock Exchange** transactions have to be settled, usually the second Monday after the end of an account.

See also: **rolling settlement**.

accounting (540)
The recording of the economic activities of firms and national economies. As early as 1494, double-entry bookkeeping, the basis of modern accounting, was explained in Pacioli's 'The Method of Venice', although civilizations as early as the Babylonian practised intricate accounting. In the nineteenth century, the development of joint stock companies and corporations necessitated auditing greatly expanding the role of the accountant. Accounting has moved from **financial accounting** (the historical recording of past activities) to **management accounting** (the frequent presentation of information to managers to help them in current decision-making).

Bull, R.J. (1984) *Accounting in Business*, 5th edn, London: Butterworth.

Chatfield, M. (1977) *A History of Accounting Thought*, rev. edn, Huntington, NY: Robert E. Krieger.

accounting balance of payments (430)
A record of all the financial transactions between the residents of one country and the residents of foreign countries in a given time period (usually a quarter or a whole year).

accounting costs (540)
All the costs of producing a good or service recorded in the accounts of a firm. These include most economic costs but are likely to omit the cost of the owner's time and the **opportunity cost** of the financial capital used in the firm.

accounting cycle (540)
The period from the start to finish of an operational sequence. Accountants typically consider periods of a month, three months, six months or a year.

accounting identity (540)
A balance which makes each side of an equation equal to the other because of the accounting definitions used. In economics such an identity is usually contrasted with equilibrium conditions. Thus, in basic macroeconomics, the accounting equations $Y = C + I$ and $Y = C + S$ entail that $I \equiv S$ but planned saving and investment may diverge (Y is national income, C is aggregate consumption, I is net investment and S is aggregate saving).

accounting profit (010, 540)
The excess of total revenue over the costs and expenses of a productive activity in a given time period. Contrast with **economic profit**.

accrual accounting (540)
Accounts based on transactions when they occur, as opposed to when the cash is received or paid. Contrast with **cash flow accounting**.

accrual interest rate (310)
The rate at which interest accrues on a loan as distinct from the rate at which it is actually paid. This accrual rate can be the

current market rate or the rate originally set when the loan was made.

accrued expense (010, 540)
An expense incurred in a particular time period but not yet paid.

accrued income (010, 540)
Income which has been earned in a particular time period but has not yet been received in cash.

ACH (310)
See: **automated clearing house**.

acid-test ratio (520, 540)
Liquid assets divided by current liabilities: a measure of a company's ability to pay immediate liabilities.

ACM (420)
See: **Andean Common Market; Arab Common Market**.

ACP (130)
African, Caribbean and Pacific; the sixty-three countries that signed the **Lomé Convention** with the **European Community** in 1975.

ACRS (320, 520)
See: **Accelerated Cost Recovery System**.

ACT (320)
See: **Advance Corporation Tax**.

active fiscal policy (140, 320)
Frequently used discretionary **fiscal policy**. Instead of relying on **automatic stabilizers** alone to achieve a desired level of aggregate demand, a government makes many changes in its spending and taxation.

activist (310, 320)
An economic policy adviser who believes in the use of discretionary monetary and fiscal instruments for **fine-tuning** the economy.

activity analysis (210)
See: **linear programming**.

activity rate (810)
Official UK term for the **labour force participation rate**. If the female population is 100 million but the female labour force is only 55 million, then the female activity rate will be 55 per cent.

activity ratio (540)
An accounting measure of the amount of activity of a firm. (Standard hours for actual output/standard hours for budgeted output) x 100; net sales divided by total assets or net fixed assets; accounts receivable divided by daily credit sales.

actual budget (320)
National taxation and expenditure accounts of a government which may be in balance, in surplus or in deficit: this is contrasted with a **full-employment budget**.

actual deficit (320)
See: **primary deficit**.

Adam Smith Institute (010)
Free market economics policy research think tank based in London, UK. It was founded in 1977 by a group of like-minded graduates of St Andrews University, Scotland. It has published a series of reports on economic policies since 1979.

In Eastern Europe there are now several separate Adam Smith Institutes with a similar philosophy.

adaptive expectations (010, 210)
The expected value of an economic variable at a future date measured by the weighted average of all previous values of the variable. The concept was first applied to the study of investment behaviour and the **consumption function** and later to inflation. The narrowness of this approach to expectations (first advanced by Cagan), although easy for economic model builders, has been criticized because forecasters often take into account information other than the past behaviour of the variable being studied.

Cagan, P. (1956) 'The monetary dynamics of hyperinflation', in M. Friedman (ed.) *Studies in the Quantity Theory of Money*, Chicago, IL: University of Chicago Press.

AD–AS (020)
Aggregate demand–aggregate supply macroeconomic model.

ADB (130, 310)
See: **Asian Development Bank**.

adding-up controversy (020)

A dispute concerning the ways of solving the problem of ensuring that the amount of income going to factors of production is equal to the national income. From P.H. Wicksteed's *An Essay in the Coordination of the Laws of Distribution* (1894) onwards, many attempts to solve the problem have been limited to the special case of a long-run perfectly competitive equilibrium.

See also: **Euler's theorem; perfect competition**.

additional facilities (430)

Extra credit arrangements of the **International Monetary Fund** to ease the balance of payments difficulties of member countries. These include:

- 1963 Compensatory Financing Facility to provide compensation for a shortfall in export earnings
- 1969 Buffer Stock Financing Facility
- 1974–5 Oil Facility
- 1974 Extended Fund Facility
- 1974 Supplementary Financing Facility
- 1986 Structural Adjustment Facility.

additional-worker hypothesis (010)

The assertion that unemployment will encourage more labour force participation amongst **secondary workers** and thus will increase the size of the labour force. This often occurs when there is a shift from heavy to light industry. If those made redundant in the heavy industries are males but the jobs available in the light industries are predominantly suitable for females, then male unemployment will coincide with women joining the labour force.

Cann, G.G. (1967) 'Unemployment and the labor force participation of secondary workers', *Industrial and Labor Relations Review* 20: 275–97.

See also: **discouraged worker hypothesis; labour force participation rate**.

adjustable peg (430)

A **fixed exchange rate** which can occasionally be altered according to certain rules. The best example is the Bretton Woods system which permitted revaluations and devaluations of up to 10 per cent without the permission of the **International Monetary Fund**. An adjustable peg has the disadvantage of requiring the costly accumulation of foreign exchange reserves and can be unstable as every rumour about a currency change may provoke speculation necessitating an adjustment. A currency can be pegged to another single currency (often the US dollar) or to a basket of currencies such as a **special drawing right** or a basket chosen to reflect the trade structure of the country.

See also: **Bretton Woods Agreement**.

adjustable-rate mortgage (310)

A **mortgage** bearing an interest rate which fluctuates according to market interest rates. These are popular with savings institutions as they have less **interest risk** and with individuals and households because they offer lower initial interest rates.

adjusted claim (310)

See: **note issuance facility**.

adjustment cost (010)

The cost to an economic agent (e.g. a firm or a household) of a change in the value of a variable crucial to its decisions. If, for example, a firm were to change its capital stock by embarking on an investment programme, it incurs costs of research, planning, installation of equipment and training of workers.

adjustment gap (710)

The ratio of international to domestic food prices. The greater the amount of farm support, the greater the gap. In the 1980s, the ratio for the **European Community** was about one-third.

adjustment speed (520)

The time it takes a price to adjust to **excess demand** or **excess supply** in a particular market. It is important to consider this when studying the behaviour of money wage rates, product prices, interest rates and nominal exchange rates.

administered inflation (150)

Inflation that is brought about by firms increasing the profit mark-up on their products; a form of **cost-push inflation**.

See also: **mark-up pricing**.

administered pricing (520)

The practice of setting prices according to a formula irrespective of the short-run forces of demand and supply. The market power of monopolistic and oligopolistic firms makes it possible to adopt this approach to pricing. As it is expensive to change prices (e.g. new catalogues have to be printed) and as there is always the possibility of adverse consumer reaction, there is a tendency for prices to be more rigid when administered. As part of an anti-inflation programme, especially in wartime, governments will administer major prices, i.e. prices of goods and services which are prominent in most consumers' budgets; in these circumstances the rules for increasing prices are strictly laid down. Most administered prices are calculated by adding a profit margin to average cost.

Means, G.C. (1935), 'Industrial prices and their relative inflexibility,' *Senate Document No. 13*, Washington, DC: US Government Printing Office.

See also: **mark-up pricing**.

administration lag (310, 320)
See: **implementation lag**.

administrative cost (320, 520)

1 The personnel and equipment costs of collecting taxes (public finance).

2 Costs incurred to manage an enterprise (managerial economics).

See also: **transaction cost**.

administrative costs of regulation (610)

All the costs of employing officials and running the offices of regulatory agencies. These are to be contrasted with **compliance costs.**

ADR (310)
See: **American Depository Receipt**.

ad valorem tax (320)

An **indirect tax** which is levied as a percentage of the value of a transaction. **Sales taxes**, **excise duties** and **value-added taxes** are major examples. In calculating such taxes, either the final price of the good or service or the value added at a particular stage of production is the basis. This tax reduces the amount of revenue that a firm obtains from the sale of a good or a service.

See also: **unit tax**.

advance (310)

A bank loan or an overdraft which has a term of less than three years, usually less than one year. When a bank creates money, it does so by allowing advances to its customers, i.e. permitting them to draw on the extra bank deposits created for them. An overdraft is a permission to 'overdraw' up to a certain amount for a specified period but a loan results in an immediate crediting of the borrower's account.

Advance Corporation Tax (320)

An interim settlement of UK corporation tax. If a company makes a qualifying distribution of earnings, e.g. by distributing a dividend, during its accounting period, it pays a proportion of the amount of the dividend as an advanced payment of tax which will later be deducted from its tax liability for that period. The proportion which has been levied varies from year to year: in most years it has been about 30 per cent.

advanced organic economy (110)

An **economy** which reaches a considerable level of real income by using agricultural products, especially wood, for energy and raw materials. A pre-industrial economy.

Wrigley, E.A. (1988) *Continuity, Chance and Change*, ch. 2, Cambridge: Cambridge University Press.

adverse selection (520)

A problem of insurance which arises when the insurer does not know whether or not an insured person is at risk, with the consequence that the same premium is charged, irrespective of whether that individual is likely to claim. This can occur, for example, if an applicant for life insurance does not disclose all his health details.

See also: **asymmetric information**.

adverse supply shock (010)

A change in a factor price, e.g. the price of

energy or labour, which reduces **aggregate supply** at each price level. In the short term, the macroeconomic consequences of a shock are an increase in the price level and a fall in output.

advertising (530)

A communication activity used to influence potential buyers, voters or others who can help the advertiser to reach defined goals. The theory of **monopolistic competition** was the first major economic theory to incorporate considerations of advertising. In the case of firms, it is a selling cost incurred with the hope of increasing sales. Advertising increases the amount of information available in a market but it also helps to create monopoly situations as it can be a **barrier to entry**. By advertising, **oligopolists** can create wants and markets, escaping the strictures of **consumer sovereignty**. The annual amount of a firm's advertising expenditure is often determined by an arbitrary ratio of advertising expenditure to sales revenue and frequently has the effect, not of enlarging total expenditure on a particular good or service, but of redistributing demand among the firms of an industry and adding to their costs.

Although large advertising expenditures are associated with **market economies**, advertising has a role in **command economies**, particularly to increase consumer demand for products new to the market or in excess supply.

Reekie, W.D. (1981) *The Economics of Advertising*, London: Macmillan.
Schmalensee, R. (1972) *The Economics of Advertising*, Amsterdam: North-Holland.

Advisory, Conciliation and Arbitration Service (830)

The central UK body, set up in 1974 under the **Trade Union and Labour Relations Act**, to promote an improvement in industrial relations, to encourage an extension of collective bargaining and its reform through advice, conciliation, enquiries and arbitration, and to run the **Central Arbitration Committee**. An important aspect of its activities has been the publication of Codes of Practice in industrial relations.

AEA (010)

See: **American Economic Association**.

AFBD (310)

Association of Futures Brokers and Dealers (London): a **self-regulatory organization**.

AfDB (310)

See: **African Development Bank**.

AFDC (910)

See: **Aid to Families with Dependent Children**.

Affärsvälden General Index (310)

The price index of the leading shares traded on the Stockholm Stock Exchange.

affinity card (310)

A **credit card** linked with a charity which receives donations in proportion to the amount spent by the user of that card.

affirmative action (820)

A series of actions taken by an employer or educational authority to advance the opportunities of disadvantaged groups, especially ethnic minorities, to increase their representation particularly in employment.

See also: **reverse discrimination**.

AFL–CIO (830)

American Federation of Labor and Congress of Industrial Organizations: a merger of two rival labor federations of the USA in 1955 which brought back the breakaway industrial unions that had separated from their colleagues in craft unions. Not all US labor unions are affiliated to the AFL–CIO.

See also: **craft union; general union; industrial union**.

African Development Bank (430)

A bank which began operations in 1966: it finances investment projects in Africa and raises capital throughout the world. By 1985, it had fifty African and twenty-five non-African countries as members, including the UK, the USA, Germany and Japan.

See also: **development bank**.

after-hours dealings (310)

Dealings in stocks and shares after the

International Stock Exchange closes for the day. Such **bargains** are recorded as the next day's business. In the past these dealings were at less attractive prices to both buyer and seller because of the greater risk of trading when market opinion was unknown; now, long hours of electronic dealing have removed this price differential.

See also: **twenty-four-hour trading**.

aftermarket (310)
The trading in securities immediately after they have been issued.

AG (510)
Aktiengesellschaft: a public company of Germany or Switzerland.

age–earnings profile (850)
A graph plotting earnings against age. Such profiles are frequently used in **human capital** analysis to show the financially beneficial effects of education. More education usually raises the profile to a new plateau; other determinants of the profile's shape include rules for salary structures and seniority. The frequently used method of constructing a profile from cross-section data provides a poor estimate if age differentials in earnings change. **Longitudinal data** provide a more accurate picture of life-time earnings.

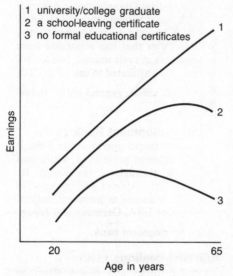

1 university/college graduate
2 a school-leaving certificate
3 no formal educational certificates

ageing population (840)
1 A population with an increasing proportion of its population in older age groups, often because a large group born in a period of high birth rate is maturing.

2 A population with a rising **median** age. In developed countries, a decline in the birth rate since the 1960s has added to this demographic effect. A slower growth in **gross national product** of a nation can encourage emigration of the young, with the consequence that the remaining population 'ages'. A typical pattern of consumption and saving is associated with each age group and hence, when a population 'ages', it changes its demand for particular goods and services in the private and public sectors; also, innovation may be affected and the size of the **multiplier** for the whole economy may change.

Clark, R.L. and Spengler, J.J. (1980) *The Economics of Individual and Population Ageing*, Cambridge and New York: Cambridge University Press.
Clark, R.L., Kreps, J. and Spengler, J.J. (1978) 'Economics of aging: a survey', *Journal of Economic Literature* 16 (September): 919–62.
Lee, R.D., Arthur, W.B. and Rodgers, G. (eds) (1989) *Economics of Changing Age Distributions in Developed Countries*, Oxford: Oxford University Press.

See also: **grey society**; **life-cycle hypothesis**.

ageism (820)
Treating people who have reached a particular age, the customary age of retirement in that society or even younger, as of little value and excluding them from employment and many other activities. This form of **discrimination** is being fought by senior citizens' lobbies in the USA and elsewhere. Increasing shortages of young workers in developed countries in the late twentieth century have diminished some of this discrimination. Also, firms which have waived age rules have discovered that many older workers have lower absenteeism and higher numeracy and literacy than younger workers.

agency broker (310)
A stockbroker who buys and sells shares of companies from **market-makers**. It is argued that agency brokers have the advantage of being able to find better prices than an

individual market-maker can offer and of providing more confidentiality.

agency cost (010, 510)

A cost arising from a contractual relationship between a principal and an agent. These costs include the expenses of drawing up and enforcing a contract, as well as **transaction costs**, **moral hazard** costs and **information costs**. Agency costs are major determinants of how firms are organized and how their staff are remunerated.

agency relationship (510)

See: **agency theory**.

agency shop (830)

A voluntary **union shop**, extensively present in the US public sector, under which employees pay the equivalent of union dues in return for that union acting as a bargaining agent. It is used to evade the ban on **closed shops** in **right-to-work states**.

agency theory (020, 510)

A theory of the firm which explores the relationships between **property rights** and financial structures. The central concept used is the 'agency relationship', i.e. the contractual relationship between a principal person(s) and others who render services as agents, e.g. between the stockholders of a corporation and the managers they appoint to run that firm. The costs of the agency include the costs to the principal of monitoring the agreement and any loss if the agent's decisions fail to maximize his welfare; the agent often incurs the costs of putting up a bond as a guarantee of not harming the principal. This theory can be applied to many other aspects of cooperative behaviour.

Jensen, M.C. and Meckling, W.H. (1976) 'Theory of the firm: managerial behavior, agency costs and ownership structure', *Journal of Financial Economics* 3: 305–60.

agent bank (310)

A bank which arranges with a consortium of banks a credit facility for a borrower.

agent de change (310)

See: **specialist**.

agglomeration diseconomy (930)

An external **diseconomy of scale** caused by the growth of a town or city. For example, the population growth of a city often results in increased pollution and congestion.

agglomeration economy (010, 930)

An external **economy of scale** brought about by the massing of a population in one place. As the population of a town or city increases, a more complex infrastructure is possible and a greater division of labour can be achieved than in a smaller settlement. The larger the settlement, the more likely it is to have a full range of transport, shopping, cultural and health facilities.

aggregate concentration (610)

The **concentration** of the economic activity of a nation or an industry in the hands of a few giant firms. Also called absolute concentration.

See also: **concentration ratio; relative concentration**.

aggregate demand (010)

The total amount of national planned expenditure by firms, households, governments and other nations at each price or income level.

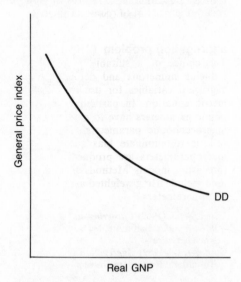

aggregate output (010, 220)

An output measure of the **national income**

which is calculated by summing the amount of **value added** by each industry. This aggregate is measured at **factor cost**.

aggregate supply (010)

1 The total output which all the producers of an economy are willing to supply at each price level.

2 Total output as a function of the amount of labour.

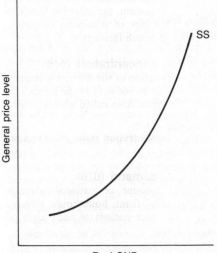

Real GNP

aggregation problem (210)

The choice of a suitable procedure for reducing numerous and detailed data to aggregate variables for use in an econometric equation. In particular, microeconomic **parameters** have to be expressed in macroeconomic parameters. The difficult task is to eliminate bias so that stable macroparameters are produced of use in forecasting models. Methods of aggregation used include using weighted averages of the microparameters.

Fisher, W.D. (1969) *Clustering and Aggregation in Economics*, Baltimore, MD: Johns Hopkins University Press.

Gupta, K.L. (1969) *Aggregation in Economics*. Rotterdam: Rotterdam University Press.

agio theory of interest (020)

An explanation for interest being paid. Interest is paid to allow money or goods to be obtained now because they are desired more in the present than in the future. 'Agio' literally means 'ease or convenience'.

AGM (510)

Annual General Meeting. The meeting of the shareholders of a company or corporation at which its accounts are approved and directors are elected or re-elected.

AGNP (220)

See: **augmented GNP**.

agribusiness (610, 710)

A large organization which processes or distributes agricultural products. It benefits from **economies of scale** and is run as an industrial firm with all the customary managerial functions, including personnel, marketing, finance and production.

Davis, J.H. and Goldberg, R.A. (1957) *A Concept of Agribusiness*, Cambridge, MA: Harvard University Press; London: Barley & Swinfen.

Agricultural Adjustment Act 1933 (710)

The basis of US Federal support to farmers which has provided price support to maintain farm incomes. It created the **Commodity Credit Corporation** to execute its policy.

agricultural household (010, 710)

A farm whose labour force is provided by residents of a household. This economic institution, analysed as both a firm and a household, was the basic economic unit of Ancient Greece and is widespread today in large sectors of less developed countries.

See also: **Ancient Greeks; villa economy**.

agricultural policy (710)

Price and income support schemes designed mainly to stabilize or increase farmers' incomes. Although consumers of food suffer through having to pay higher prices under most agricultural policies, it is unlikely that developed countries with highly productive agricultural sectors will allow a market in unsubsidized agricultural products as the votes of farmers are needed to keep governments in power. The **General Agreement on Tariffs and Trade** has become increasingly concerned with world trade in agricultural products, with the consequence that national agricultural policies may be harmonized more in the future.

Moyer, H.W. and Josling, T.E. (1990) *Agricultural Policy Reform. Politics and Process in the EC and USA*, Hemel Hempstead: Harvester Wheatsheaf.

See also: **Agricultural Adjustment Act 1933; Common Agricultural Policy; Uruguay Round**.

AHC Banks (310)

The sixteen members of the Accepting Houses Committee of London (UK).

See also: **accepting house**.

AIBD (310)

See: **Association of International Bond Dealers**.

aid (430)

See: **foreign aid**.

Aid and Trade Provisions (430)

UK governmental assistance to exporters to make their contractual terms more attractive. Some of the 'aid' goes to the richer developing countries instead of the poorest. This government financial help is paid as a subsidy to companies and not directly to its ultimate beneficiaries.

Aid to Families with Dependent Children (910)

The US federal welfare program, originally 'Aid to Dependent Children' which was inaugurated under Title IV of the 1935 Social Security Act. It enabled states to provide financial assistance to needy dependent children: the states had the tasks of planning and supervising the use of these federal grants. When it began in 1936, there were about half a million recipients; by 1987 the average number of monthly recipients was 11 million.

Originally it was intended to enable female heads of households to stay at home to rear their children; in 1967, the scheme was amended to encourage mothers to join the labour force: this was done by reducing the implicit tax rate on earnings from 100 per cent to 67 per cent.

ALC (310)

See: **Australian Loan Council**.

alienation (010, 830)

Workers' estrangement from their work which they do not control, from their products which are appropriated, from other men who are capitalists, from the human species as man becomes a mere animal, according to **Marx**. Adam **Smith** noted that increasing the subdivision of labour would have unfortunate effects on workers as repetitive simple work dulls the brain and can cause a variety of occupational health problems.

Allais, Maurice, 1911– (030)

Educated at the Ecole Polytechnique and the Ecole Supérieure des Mines. After service in the army, 1943–8, Director of the Bureau of Mines Documentation and Statistics, Paris; from 1944, Professor of Economic Analysis at the Ecole Supérieure des Mines. Awarded the **Nobel Prize for Economics** in 1988.

Influenced by **Walras**, **Pareto** and **Fisher**, he was concerned with the synthesis of real and monetary phenomena and the relationship between economics and the other social sciences in his great work of 1943, *In Quest of an Economic Discipline*, Part 1, *Pure Economics*, which was followed by five other volumes. Later work has involved the theory of choice under uncertainty (which included survey work to investigate cardinal utility) and comparative international studies of real income.

allocative efficiency (010)

The selection of factor inputs which minimizes the cost of producing goods and services to satisfy given wants, subject to resource and technological constraints. This efficient allocation includes efficiency of both production and distribution.

Welfare economics has been concerned with setting out the conditions for efficiency, including the appropriate set of prices. Increasingly the recognition of **indivisibilities** and **externalities** has required departures from a **neoclassical** approach.

See also: **Pareto optimality**.

All Ordinaries Index (310)

The price index of leading Australian shares.

allotment letter (310)
A letter confirming the purchase of newly issued shares.

All Share Index (310)
See: **Financial Times Actuaries All Shares Index.**

alpha stock (310)
A stock of the **International Stock Exchange** which is one of those most actively traded, and hence is always quoted on the **Stock Exchange Automated Quotation system.** There are usually ten or more **marketmakers** for each share. In 1990, the ISE had about 110 such stocks.

See also: **beta stock; gamma stock; delta stock.**

alternative economic strategy (310, 320, 420)
See: **new Cambridge economics.**

altruism (010, 070)
Seeking the good of others; the basis for a society or economy which rejects self-interest as the major motive for economic activity. Many schemes of idealistic socialism rest on this principle. Adam **Smith** used the concept of the **invisible hand** to show that unconscious altruism can occur in an economy based on the principle of self-interest.

Collard, D.A. (1978) *Altruism and Economy*, Oxford: Martin Robertson; New York: Oxford University Press.

See also: **non-profit enterprise.**

ambient standard (720)
A standard for air quality set in the USA by the **Environmental Protection Agency.**

See also: **primary standard; secondary standard.**

American Depository Receipt (310)
A share certificate or **bearer security** which entitles the person with that security to shares of a non-US company which have been deposited in a bank located outside the USA. This US financial instrument, originally devised in 1927, is now traded on both the US and UK stock exchanges.

American Economic Association (010)
The leading US professional association of academic and other economists, founded in 1885 and based at Evanston, IL (now at Nashville, TN). From its earliest years it has sought to promote economic research, particularly by publishing its prestigious *American Economic Review*, a core journal of economics, from 1911 and *Journal of Economic Literature* from 1963. The AEA currently has over 25,000 members.

Coats, A.W. (1985) 'The American Economic Association and the economics profession', *Journal of Economic Literature* 23: 1697–727.

American Federation of Labor (830)
See: **AFL–CIO.**

American Stock Exchange (310)
Previously the New York Curb Market and then the New York Curb Exchange, tracing its ancestry back to trading in the streets of lower Manhattan in 1793. It acquired its current name in 1953 and was incorporated in 1971; by 1987 it had 661 regular members with 60 per cent of its business with private clients and 40 per cent with institutional investors. It ended fixed commissions on dealings in 1975 and from 1985 has been linked to the Toronto Stock Exchange.

See also: **New York Stock Exchange.**

AMEX (310)
See: **American Stock Exchange.**

amortization (010, 520)
Gradually extinguishing a liability or debt by allocating the cost of it to a number of time periods. Major examples are the **depreciation** of an asset and the repayment of a loan by regular instalments to cover the amount advanced and the interest.

AMU (430)
See: **Arab Maghreb Union.**

analysis of variance (210)
The decomposition of the **variance** in a dependent variable into the variance explained by the regression and the residual variance.

See also: **linear regression**.

anarchism (010, 610)

The political doctrine which asserts that economic and social life should not be subject to any governmental control. The leading early exponents of this view were Pierre Proudhon (1809–65) and Mikhail Bakunin (1815–76). In practice, anarchism has been applied to industrial organization in the form of workers' syndicates but experiments of this nature in France and Spain in the early twentieth century were short lived. Although anarchists share with socialists a dislike of capitalism, with **laissez-faire** economists a mistrust of the state and with members of the cooperative movement a belief that firms should be managed by labour, they are more extreme, especially in wanting the abolition of private property and being prepared to risk the abandonment of systems of law and order.

Ritter, A. (1980) *Anarchism: A Theoretical Analysis*, Cambridge: Cambridge University Press.

anchor tenant (930)

The leading commercial tenant of an office block who influences its design and has its logo on the façade in return for leasing a large portion of the building, thereby making the return on the property developer's investment more secure. Sometimes the anchor tenant is given a marketable share in the equity of the building.

Ancient Greeks (030)

One of the earliest groups of writers on economic problems who, despite living in an underdeveloped economy mainly agrarian in character, discussed value, money, comparative property systems, the division of labour, exchange controls and public finance.

Finley, M.I. (1985) *The Ancient Economy*, 2nd edn, London: Hogarth.
Gordon, B. (1975) *Economic Analysis before Adam Smith*, London: Macmillan.
Laistner, M.L.W. (1923) *Greek Economics*, London: Dent; New York: Dutton.
Lowry, S.T. (1979) 'Recent literature on Ancient Greek economic thought', *Journal of Economic Literature* 17 (March): 65–86.

See also: **Aristotle**; **Plato**; **villa economy**; **Xenophon**.

Andean Common Market (420, 430)

An association of Bolivia, Chile, Columbia, Ecuador and Peru set up in 1969 to coordinate responses to overseas investors and to organize a common market.

Anderson, James, 1739–1808 (030)

The Scottish farmer and agricultural economist who was the first to expound a clear theory of **differential rent** in his *An Inquiry into the Nature of the Corn Laws* (Edinburgh, 1777), regarding rent as a payment for using land superior in fertility. This was to inspire **Malthus** and **Ricardo**. His other major work of economic interest was *Observations on the National Industry of Scotland* (1775). In addition, he proposed schemes for developing the Scottish Highlands and edited *The Bee*, a weekly journal with articles on literature and current affairs, from 1790 to 1794. As his professional papers are reputed to have been used by his widow to scorch chickens, research on his work is difficult.

Mullet, C.F. (1968) 'A village Aristotle and the harmony of interests: James Anderson of Monks Hill', *Journal of British Studies* 8: 94–118.

See also: **differential theory of rent**.

angel (310)

An investor in a stage production. This high risk type of investment can yield, if successful, very high returns. In London, for example, there are several hundred 'angelic' investors.

animal spirits (010, 520)

Keynes's description of the whimsical investment attitudes of entrepreneurs, sometimes optimistic, sometimes pessimistic; an approach much emphasized by Joan **Robinson**.

announcement burden of a tax (320)

The loss of **producer's** and **consumer's surpluses** as a consequence of a tax change. The announcement has the effect of adjusting taxpayers' behaviour, e.g. in supplying labour.

Pigou, A.C. (1928) *A Study in Public Finance*, Part II, ch. 5, London: Macmillan.

announcement effect (310, 320)

The immediate effect on household and firms of a government's statement of a change in monetary or fiscal policy. Unlike the other effects of policy changes, there is no time lag. The first effects are felt in financial markets as security prices can be adjusted immediately.

annualized-hours system (820)

An alternative to the standard working week by which a worker contracts to work for a year of working weeks. The annual number of hours is calculated by aggregating the previous weekly hours, less leave. It is a useful system for avoiding substantial overtime and other premium payments. Continuous-process industries were among the first to use this system.

annual percentage rate (of interest) (310, 920)

Actual annual cost of borrowing. The Truth in Lending Act (USA) and Britain's Consumer Credit Act 1974 have made it mandatory for all lenders to state the true cost of borrowing. This annual rate (in per cent) is calculated by using the formula

$$APR = 100 \left(\frac{1 + \text{total charge for credit}}{\text{amount of credit}} \right)^{1/t}$$

where t is the number of years of the loan.

annuity (310)

An amount of money paid annually or at other regular intervals. Major examples include life assurance premiums, pensions, rent payments and instalment payments. An annuity certain has a fixed term, unlike a perpetuity whose payments continue indefinitely (e.g. an unredeemable government stock). An annuity contingent depends on an uncertain event, e.g. the death of a person. The purchase price, or present value V, of an annuity depends on the rate of interest used in the calculation.

$$V = A \frac{1 - (1 + i)^{-n}}{i}$$

where i is the rate of interest (expressed as a decimal) and n is the number of periods that the annuity is paid.

ANOVA (210)

See: **analysis of variance**.

antagonistic growth (110)

1 Tensions, often of a social nature, in the growth process because of the trade-offs between growth, stability and equity.

2 The deliberate creation of disequilibria to bring about new economic activities, e.g. an infrastructure deficiency which stimulates the growth of a transport industry.

anticipatory pricing (520)

The practice of including expected cost increases in the make-up of prices. Firms adopting this policy hope that it will stabilize their prices as prices will not have to fluctuate with every change in costs. The **menu-costs of inflation** are therefore reduced.

anticompetitive practices (610)

Corporate behaviour in a market which attempts to increase a firm's market power, e.g. licensing agreements, special selling conditions and other measures which stop short of being monopolization or cartelization.

See also: **antitrust; competition policy**.

Anti-Injunction Act (830)

See: **Norris–La Guardia Act**.

antitrust (610)

US policy beginning with the Sherman Act 1890 to prevent monopolistic practices in interstate commerce. There is also legislation at the state level which is able to deal with production industries. Although national competition policies are common in **Organization for Economic Cooperation and Development** countries, few are as tough, with criminal sanctions, as is the US antitrust legislation administered by the Department of Justice and the Federal Trade Commission. The Federal policy is for the most part stated in five major statutes: **Sherman Act 1890, Clayton Act 1914, Federal Trade Commission Act 1914, Robinson Patman Act 1936** and **Celler Kefauver Antimerger Act 1950**.

Blair, R.D. and Kaserman, D.L. (1985) *Antitrust Economics*, Homewood, IL: Richard D. Irwin.

Neale, A.D. and Goyder, D.G. (1980) *The Antitrust Laws of the USA*, 3rd edn, Cambridge: Cambridge University Press.

APACS (310)

Association for Payment Clearing Services (UK): a cheque clearing house owned by the major banks.

APB (540)

Accounting Principles Board (UK).

APC (010)

See: **average propensity to consume**.

apprenticeship (810, 850)

A period of training in a firm which enables a trainee to learn a craft under the supervision of a skilled worker. The length of the apprenticeship varies from trade to trade and country to country. Adam **Smith** noted that in ancient times the period was commonly seven years, even in universities for studying for a Master of Arts degree. Apprenticeships have long been a major method of providing technological education and of transmitting sophisticated manual skills from one generation to another. But critics have viewed them as a union restrictive practice as they have been used to limit the number in a trade, and hence to increase average earnings. Recurrent skilled labour shortages in engineering have been attributed to the system.

appropriate technology (620)

Labour-intensive small-scale methods of production using renewable energy. A technology advocated for Third World countries.

Dunn, P. (1978) *Appropriate Technology: Technology with a Human Face*, London: Macmillan.
Jequier, N. (ed.) (1976) *Appropriate Technology: Problems and Promises*, Paris: Development Centre of the Organization for Economic Cooperation and Development.

See also: **Schumacher**.

appropriation bill (320)

A US federal legislative bill which authorizes expenditure for a particular purpose, e.g. defence. It has to be passed by both the House of Representatives and the Senate. Annually all the bills are expected to be reconciled by a Reconciliation Bill by the end of June; if reconciliation is impossible, then a continuing resolution is passed which permits Departments to continue at their current expenditure levels.

APR (310, 920)

See: **annual percentage rate (of interest)**.

Aquinas, St Thomas, 1225–74 (030)

The leading medieval economic and social thinker and theologian, the most prominent of the Schoolmen. His interpretation of the teaching of **Aristotle** and the early Christian Fathers is set out in his massive *Summa Theologica*. He formulated the doctrine of the **just price**, permitted the charging of interest (when there was a risk that the lender would not be paid on time) and supported the institutions of private property and trade (if the public good is promoted).

Baldwin, J.W. (1959) *The Mediaeval Theories of the Just Price*, Philadelphia, PA: American Philosophical Society.
Gordon, B. (1975) *Economic Analysis before Adam Smith*, London: Macmillan.
Worland, S.T. (1967) *Scholasticism and Welfare Economics*, Notre Dame, IN: University of Notre Dame Press.

Arab Common Market (420)

A **common market** set up in 1964 with the aims of free movement of labour and capital, free trade and unimpeded transport access among the member countries which, originally, were Jordan, Kuwait, Morocco, Syria and the United Arab Republic (Egypt and Syria).

Arab Maghreb Union (420)

An economic union of Morocco, Algeria, Tunisia, Mauritania and Libya set up in 1989. Progress towards free mobility of labour and capital and the creation of a common or single currency have been slow.

arb (310)

Arbitrageur, especially a speculator in the stocks of companies likely to be taken over by others.

arbitrage (010, 310, 430)

An investment strategy which takes the form

of a simultaneous purchase of an item in one market and sale of it in another with the expectation of a positive return. It is common in currency and commodity markets and is a force that produces price equalization, after allowing for transport and **transaction costs** and risk. Profits are often made from small differences in price. In the case of a currency, this occurs and continues until the cross exchange rates are consistent. For example, if initially US$1 = DM4, DM1 = 2 guilders and US$1 = 6 guilders, the correct cross-rate should be DM1 = 1.5 guilders. The arbitrageur sells spot and buys forward if he believes that the value of a currency is falling: he benefits from the difference between two prices, with the forward contract protecting him from a fall in the exchange rate.

arbitration (520, 830)

Settlement of a dispute by referral to a third party, used in industrial relations and in many commercial disagreements. The arbitrator may be a court of law, an independent arbitrator chosen by the parties in dispute or a permanent government body, e.g. the **Advisory, Conciliation and Arbitration Service** in the UK. As arbitration is either voluntary or imposed, it can be binding, compulsory, mandatory or unilateral. Landlord and tenant, shipping and building contracts often use this method of resolving conflicts. Private arbitration, which may be instituted in advance by a contractual term, is cheaper and quicker than resort to litigation.

See also: **pendulum arbitration**.

arc elasticity (210)

The **elasticity of demand** over a portion of a demand curve or the elasticity of supply over a section of a supply curve. It is calculated from the midpoint between old and new prices and quantities on the curve, using the ratio of the percentage change in quantity to the percentage change in price, i.e.

$$\text{elasticity} = \frac{\Delta Q/(Q_1 + Q_2)}{\Delta P/(P_1 + P_2)}$$

where P_1 and Q_1 are the price and quantity originally and P_2 and Q_2 are the price and quantity after the change. It provides an average of **point elasticities**.

Ariel (310)

See: **Automated Real-time Investment Exchange**.

ARIMA (210)

Autoregressive integrated moving-average model. A model of a time series whose underlying stochastic process changes over time.

See also: **stochastic term**.

Aristotle, 384–322 BC (030)

One of the earliest writers on economics who anticipated many later debates on value, money and economic systems. In the *Nichomachean Ethics*, Book V, he discussed the nature of value in the context of a discussion of justice; in *Topica*, he anticipated subsequent ideas of value based on utility. He supported the idea of private property on the grounds that it leads to increased production and clearly saw that money has the important functions of serving as a unit of account, a medium of exchange and a store of value.

Gordon, B. (1975) *Economic Analysis before Adam Smith*, London: Macmillan.

Soudek, J. (1952) 'Aristotle's theory of exchange: an inquiry into the origin of economic analysis', *Proceedings of the American Philosophical Society* 96: 45–75.

arithmetic mean (210)

The sum of a set of values divided by the number of values in that set.

See also: **geometric mean; harmonic mean**.

arithmetic progression (210)

A series of numbers increasing by a constant increment, called a common difference, e.g. 2, 4, 6, 8. **Malthus** asserted that the means of subsistence increases arithmetically.

See also: **geometric progression**.

ARM (310)

See: **adjustable-rate mortgage**.

ARMA (210)

Autoregressive moving-average model. This model of a stationary random process, i.e. a process whose mean is constant over time, recognizes that a combination of moving-average and autoregressive models is necessary.

Box, G.E.P. and Jenkins, G.M. (1970) *Time Series Analysis: Forecasting and Control*, San Francisco, CA: Holden-Day.

See also: **ARIMA**.

Arrow, Kenneth Joseph, 1921– (030)

US economist, educated at City College, New York, and Columbia University and professor at Stanford University from 1953 to 1968, and from 1979, with an interlude at Harvard from 1968 to 1979. His study of social choice led him to formulate the **impossibility theorem**, his most famous contribution to economics. Also, he and **Debreu** proved in an *Econometrica* article of 1954 that a multimarket equilibrium under perfect competition required the existence of forward markets for all goods and services. His work on risk aversion and on growth theory (particularly learning-by-doing) is also notable. In 1972, he shared the **Nobel Prize for Economics** with **Hicks**. The range of his contribution to economic theory and his interest in the functioning of a **general equilibrium** system are evident in his *Collected Papers*. He shows how he developed the ideas in Hicks's *Value and Capital* to explain what it means to be better off. His analysis of **voting procedures** advanced the study of social choice. Also, he has written much on the economics of information.

Leading works include the following:
Arrow, K.J. (1966) *Social Choice and Individual Values*, New York: Wiley.
—— (1984–5) *Collected Papers of Kenneth J. Arrow*, vols I–V, Oxford: Basil Blackwell.
Arrow, K.J. and Hahn, F. (1971) *General Competitive Analysis*, San Francisco, CA: Holden-Day; Edinburgh: Oliver & Boyd.
Feiwel, G.R. (ed.) (1987) *Arrow and the Ascent of Modern Economic Theory*, Basingstoke and London: Macmillan.

See also: **social choice theory**.

Arrow–Debreu model (020)

An economic theory concerned with establishing the existence of an equilibrium for an integrated model of production, exchange and consumption. The two theorems produced by the authors were that (1) a competitive equilibrium exists if every individual has initially some positive quantity of every commodity available for sale and (2) there are individuals capable of supplying a positive amount of at least one type of labour with positive usefulness in the production of desired commodities.

Arrow, K.J. and Debreu, G. (1954) 'The existence of an equilibrium for a competitive economy', *Econometrica* 22: 265–90.

See also: **general equilibrium**.

artificial barrier to entry (610)

A **barrier to entry** of firms into a market or industry erected by a government or the existing firms and not by natural market forces. Governments may insist on licensing new entrants; firms may refuse to provide access to existing technology.

artificial currency (430)

A currency unit used either as a common unit of account for international transactions or as an international reserve asset. Principal examples of these are **special drawing rights**, **European currency units**, **European units of account** and, in general, baskets of currencies. Such currencies are very useful for international accounting in times of volatile exchange rates.

See also: **gold franc**.

ASEAN (420)

See: **Association of South East Asian Nations**.

A share (310, 520)

Usually a non-voting share of the equity capital of a British company. These shares have been created to retain most of the control of a company in the hands of the founders. A shares trade at lower prices than **B shares** as they are useless to other companies attempting to gain control. Gradually these shares are being given voting rights as the International Stock Exchange regards them as unfair.

Asian Development Bank (430)

Founded in 1966 with capital provided by Asian countries, the USA, Canada, the UK and West Germany on the recommendation of the United Nations Economic Commission for Asia and the Far East. It covers half of the world's population. It is based in

Manilla, the Philippines, and is dominated by the Japanese, the largest contributor of its capital. Its conservative lending policy has chiefly favoured loans for specific projects, e.g. to build ports, roads and bridges, rather than sectoral lending to restructure troubled economies. It has increased its lending to the private sector and has a joint venture with commercial banks, the Asian Finance and Investment Corporation (AFIC).

Asiatic mode of production (070, 710)

The most primitive form of production, according to Marx, in which self-sufficient agricultural communities are despotically governed. The state, through taxation, appropriates the economic surplus of the agricultural sector to finance the building of the country's infrastructure. The concept was developed in the 1950s and 1960s to examine more aspects of state formation and the formation of classes in primitive communities.

Krader, L. (1975) *The Asiatic Mode of Production*, Assen, Netherlands: Van Gorcum.

Marx, K. (1964) *Pre-capitalist Economic Formations*, ed. by E. Hobsbawm, London: Lawrence & Wishart.

O'Leary, B. (1989) *The Asiatic Mode of Production: Oriental Despotism, Historical Materialism and Indian History*, Oxford: Basil Blackwell.

asset (010)

1 A resource with a market value.

2 A unit of wealth capable of earning an income.

3 A stream of future services.

Real (or tangible) assets include land and machinery; intangible assets include goodwill and patents; financial assets include cash and stock market securities.

See also: **national wealth; wealth**.

asset motive (310)

A motive for holding money. To avoid risky investments, persons are prepared to sacrifice high returns by keeping their portfolios in a liquid or near-liquid form.

See also: **speculative demand for money**.

asset specificity (010)

The unique character of a durable asset, e.g. a machine, a skilled worker or a production site, which means that it has a low return in other uses. For many specific assets the cost of employing them is in the nature of a **sunk cost**.

See also: **economic rent; transfer earnings**.

asset stripping (520)

The sale of parts of a company which, in many cases, has recently been taken over by another company. In this way large holding companies have been built up in the past as each stripping provides resources for another company acquisition. By selling off parts of the company undervalued in the past, finance for the making of further acquisitions is obtained.

asset sweating (310, 520)

Raising bank finance on the security of the property owned by a company. Sweating can also be effected by **securitization** of the property.

assisted area (940)

A region or smaller area of a country eligible for grants and **soft loans** under the regional policy conditions of a national government or the **European Community**. The criteria for an area's being assisted include its rate of unemployment, the decay of its infrastructure and its part in a larger plan to achieve interregional balance.

Association of International Bond Dealers (310)

An association of 850 dealing firms, three-quarters outside the UK. Under new rules in force from 1987, inter-dealer brokers are only able to deal with reporting dealers. Every evening there is electronic reporting of closing bids, offered quotations and that day's highest and lowest prices for each bond in which it trades.

Association of South East Asian Nations (420)

The trading association of Brunei, Indonesia, Malaysia, the Philippines, Singapore and Thailand founded in 1967. Its principal task has been to arrange preferential import tariff rates on trade between these countries.

Although 19,000 products are given preference, they have little impact on freeing trade as the major items (about 95 per cent of trade) are excluded from the list. It hopes by the year 2000 to free most of intra-association trade and be more than an association representing this area in international negotiations. Industrial **joint ventures** with non-Asian countries, a new insurance company and improved transportation arrangements are likely to promote further economic integration. It was agreed in 1987 that goods at present enjoying preferential tariffs should have the preference increased to 50 per cent of the tariff and goods enjoying preference for the first time should have 25 per cent of the tariff.

asymmetric information (010, 820)
Information possessed by one side of a market only. If, for example, buyers but not sellers have relevant information, they will be at an advantage. In labour markets, employers usually know more about the present and future financial state of their firms than trade unions and thereby have a bargaining advantage in wage negotiations. This view of information has also been incorporated into models of industrial organization and the valuation of **public goods**.

See also: **lemons market**.

ATM (310)
1 An **automated teller machine**.

2 In transport economics, an ATM is an air transport movement, a landing or a takeoff.

atomistic competition (010)
Similar to **perfect competition** in that there are a large number of buyers and sellers, each with no significant influence on the market, behaving like atoms – very small but with a joint importance. This view of competition is based on an individualistic view of economic activity.

ATP (430)
See: **Aid and Trade Provisions**.

ATS (310)
1 Automated transfer from a savings (bank) account to another account.

2 Automatic transfer service account.

auction (010, 530)
A type of selling in which a system of bidding determines the price and the successful buyer. **Walras** showed the crucial role of auction models in his discussion of *tâtonnement*, using the idea of an auction to describe the movement of a market to equilibrium with supply equal to demand.

Englelbrecht-Wiggins, R., Shubik, M. and Stark, R.M. (eds) (1983) *Auctions, Bidding and Contracting: Uses and Theory*, New York: New York University Press.
McAfee, R.F. and McMillan, J. (1987) 'Auctions and bidding', *Journal of Economic Literature* 25 (June): 699–738.
Smith, C.W. (1989) *Auctions: The Social Construction of Value*, Hemel Hempstead: Harvester Wheatsheaf.

See also: **Dutch auction; English auction; first price auction; second price auction; hybrid auction**.

auctioneer (010)
A person who conducts an auction, stating when a buyer and a seller have concluded a deal at a particular price.

See also: **auction**.

augmented-GNP (220)
Gross national product plus the value of public goods and services of all kinds, whether marketed or not. This measure takes into account the criteria for a good environment by measuring 'goods' net of 'bads'.

See also: **measure of economic welfare; public good**.

Australian Industries Preservation Acts 1906–50 (610)
Commonwealth of Australia statutes modelled on the **Sherman Act** of the USA which have created a **competition policy** for Australia. The difficulty of successfully prosecuting firms under them has caused antitrust actions to be more a concern of the individual Australian states.

Australian Loan Council (310)
An agency of federal government, founded in 1928, to raise loans for state governments and for public utilities.

Austrian School (030)

A prominent school of economics which has provided an opposing view to much of mainstream economics since it was founded by Carl **Menger** in the 1870s. At its inception, the School shared with **Jevons** and **Walras** an interest in expounding a subjective theory of value based on **marginal utility** but it did not use a mathematical approach as it sought to deal with essences and not quantities. The 'Austrians' opposed the popular contemporary **German Historical School**, partly because they took the view that economic laws are based on simple elements such as needs and satisfaction expressed as invariable sequences not influenced by time and space.

Menger's leadership of the school was taken over by **Böhm-Bawerk** and von Weiser. **Böhm-Bawerk** extended the analysis of consumer valuation to explain costs, prices, interest rates and economic growth. However, he is chiefly known for his time analysis of capital as a **roundabout method of production** and his interest rate theory. Von Weiser used his broad knowledge as an economist, sociologist and historian to examine all social phenomena with an attitude to economic policy which transcended both *laissez-faire* and interventionist approaches. His idea that the chief importance of prices is to provide information on all economic conditions was to inspire both Mises and **Hayek**; his concept of entrepreneurial leadership was followed by **Schumpeter** in the latter's theory of development. Both Mises and Schumpeter were members of Böhm-Bawerk's celebrated seminar.

After the collapse of the Austro-Hungarian empire at the end of the First World War, the members of the School dispersed to the UK, USA and Germany. Prominent new members of it included **Haberler** and **Machlup**. Present-day leaders include **Hayek** and Ludwig Lachmann. Later Austrians have attempted to use the basic concepts of radical subjectivism, human purpose and a spontaneous market order to contribute to modern debates about expectations, competition and economic welfare. Their policy concerns have included the relationship between monetary policy and the **trade cycle**, **free banking** and criticism of socialism.

Grassl, W. and Smith, B. (1986) *Austrian Economics*, London: Croom Helm.

Hicks, J.R. and Weber, W. (eds) (1973) *Carl Menger and the Austrian School of Economics*, Oxford: Oxford University Press.

Lachmann, L. (1976) 'From Mises to Shackle: an essay on Austrian economics and the Kaleidic Society', *Journal of Economic Literature* 14: 54–62.

Littlechild, S. (1990) *Austrian Economics*, 3 vols, Aldershot: Edward Elgar.

autarky (010, 410)

1 Self-sufficiency.

2 A completely closed economy which does not engage in international trade. Although many economies have wanted such independence from the rest of the world as a means of increasing employment, their enthusiasm has been tempered by an examination of the other effects of **protection**.

authoritative contracting (820)

See: **employment contract**.

autocorrelation (210)

The state of an econometric relation such that some or all of the explanatory variables are highly correlated with each other. This often arises because of poor specification of the relationship between variables in the regression equation.

auto-economy (070)

That part of an economy, according to **Hicks**, which finances itself from its own stock of liquid assets.

Hicks, J. (1974) *The Crisis in Keynesian Economics*, ch. 2, Oxford: Basil Blackwell.

autogestion (070)

A French approach to **workers' participation** in the running of enterprises, proposed after the 1968 uprisings in France. This philosophy of management holds that enterprises should be less hierarchical, with all employees participating directly in decision-making, especially about work organization, employment procedures (e.g. promotion), technology and methods of production. This democratization would include a new framework for discussions between enterprises.

Chauvey, D. (1970) *Autogestion*, Paris: Editions du Seuil.

See also: **syndicalism**.

automated clearing house (310)

An organization for the electronic matching of cheques drawn on different banks so that interbank indebtedness can be settled.

See also: **CHAPS; CHIPS**.

Automated Real-time Investment Exchange (310)

A computerized arrangement for dealing in shares set up by **merchant banks** in the City of London in 1974 to bypass the **International Stock Exchange** and thus save brokers' commission. It never attracted a high proportion of the London trading volume.

automated teller machine (310)

A cash-dispensing machine of a bank or other financial institution, e.g. a building society, which accepts deposits from the public. The machine allows customers continuous access to their bank deposits. Other services provided by automated teller machines include the production of bank statements.

automatic stabilizer (320)

A built-in feature of tax structures and public expenditure programmes which reduces fluctuations in an economy, making it respond more easily to shocks. Prominent examples of stabilizers include **progressive taxes** (which prevent post-tax income rising at the same rate as pre-tax income) and unemployment insurance (which prevents personal income from falling below a predefined 'floor'). The **gold standard** was a major type of automatic stabilizer. All these stabilizers have the characteristic that they prevent the rise or fall of national income, and consequently employment, being as great as it would be in the absence of a government with an active fiscal policy. It is the experience of most countries that these stabilizers are insufficient in themselves to stabilize an economy and so discretionary changes in taxation and public expenditure are also used as policy instruments.

See also: **fine-tuning**.

autonomous consumption (010)

Consumption unrelated to the level of income. At zero income, in the short run, there can be autonomous consumption to maintain physical existence; it is financed by borrowing and the liquidation of assets.

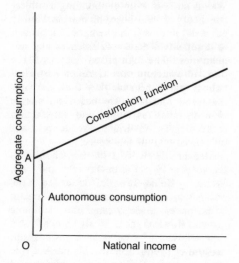

autonomous expenditure (010)

Expenditure independent of the level of income, often because of its necessary character.

autonomous investment (010)

Investment independent of the level of income. It can be affected by changes in

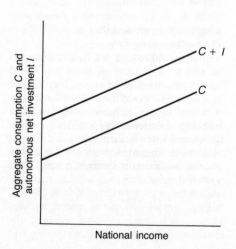

interest rates and in the **'animal spirits'** of entrepreneurs. It is shown by a parallel shift in the aggregate demand schedule.

Autumn Statement (320)

UK statement on public expenditure plans which is made separately from the budget statement in the following March.

availability thesis (420)

The view that a high proportion of international trade is an exchange between goods which are only available in one or a few countries. **Elasticity of supply** in one country and inelasticity of supply in another gives rise to trade. Often, new products are only available in some countries, partly because of the nature of the patent protection for them.

Kravis, I.B. (1956) 'Availability and other influences on the commodity composition of international trade', *Journal of Political Economy* 64: 143–55.

average (210)

A value which shows the central tendency of a set of data and is often used as a way of comparing that set with others; for example, the average age of the Finnish population is compared with the average age of the Romanian population.

See also: **mean; median; mode**.

average deviation (210)
See: **mean deviation**.

average incremental cost (010)

Change in total cost divided by change in output; an approximation to **marginal cost**, necessary because marginal cost is associated with such small quantity changes that in the real world it is difficult to measure it. In the 1978 guidelines for British **nationalized industries** it was used as a measurable alternative to marginal cost. Because it is a rough approximation, it fails to give precise guidance for the expansion of integrated systems.

HMSO (1978) *White Paper on Nationalised Industries*, Cmnd 7131.

average propensity to consume (010)

The ratio of a consumer's total consumption to his or her total income. For low income groups the average propensity to consume is unity, or close to unity, as there is no surplus over expenditure available for saving. As income rises and basic consumer goods have been purchased, the average propensity to consume declines. The average propensity to consume varies over the life cycle (see **life-cycle hypothesis**). If a graph of the **consumption function** passes through the origin, the average propensity to consume (C/Y) equals the **marginal propensity to consume** ($\Delta C/\Delta Y$) at all levels of income and is unity; a consumption function with a constant slope has the same **marginal propensity to consume** at all income levels.

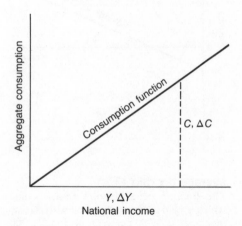

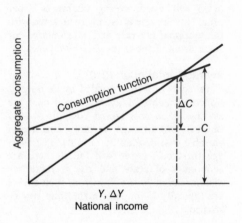

average propensity to save (010)

Total savings as a proportion of total income. This proportion is likely to be negative at low levels of income as poor households often need to borrow to finance basic consumption; at higher income levels, households can afford to save because their consumption needs have been met. The average propensity to save for a national economy will depend on its income distribution and average level of income.

See also: **savings**; **savings ratio**.

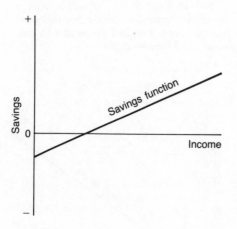

average tax rate (320)

The fraction of a person's total income which is paid in taxes. A person with a gross income of £50,000 per year, paying £10,000 in tax, will have an average tax rate of 20 per cent. This tax rate is usually contrasted with the **marginal tax rate** and is calculated for some or all of the taxes paid by a person.

average total cost (010)

Total costs of a firm divided by its output. Subcomponents of average total cost are average fixed cost (**fixed cost** divided by output) and average variable cost (total variable cost divided by output). The average total cost curve will fall if there are **economies of scale** and rise if there are **diseconomies**. In the short run, such curves are typically U-shaped; in the long run L-shaped.

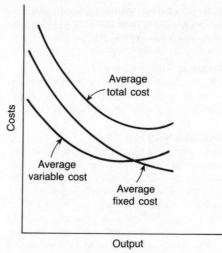

Averch–Johnson effect (610)

The misallocation in resources that results from regulatory agencies relating price levels to a 'fair' rate of return. Averch and Johnson asserted that **regulation** of this kind would fail to minimize social cost as a firm would not equate marginal rates of factor substitution to the ratio of factor costs and that firms would have an incentive to move into other regulated markets where they would be able to operate at a loss and drive out the lowest cost producers.

Averch, H.A. and Johnson, L.L. (1962) 'Behavior of the firm under regulatory constraint', *American Economic Review* 52: 1052–69.

axioms of preference (010)

The assumptions which must hold for a consumer to be rational. These are the assumptions of completeness, transitivity, reflexivity and non-satiation.

Ayres, Clarence Edwin, 1891–1972 (030)

A leading US **institutionalist** economist who was educated at Brown and Chicago universities. He taught philosophy at Chicago, Amherst and Reed universities from 1917 to 1930 and was Professor of Economics, University of Texas, from 1930 to 1968. His thinking was considerably influenced by **Veblen** and the philosopher Dewey. His powerful analysis of economic progress asserted that the technology which makes industrialization possible is constantly in conflict with established institutions which approve of ceremony to protect vested interests. Ayres' work has made a great impact on development economics.

Breit, W. and Culbertson, W.P., Jr (1976) *Science and Ceremony: The Institutional Economics of C.E. Ayres*, Austin, TX: University of Texas Press.

B

backwardation (310)

1 The charge made on a stock exchange for carrying the settlement of a **bargain** into the next accounting period.

2 In commodity markets, it is the amount by which a **spot price** and the cost of carrying a commodity over time exceeds the forward price. The opposite is **contango**.

backward-bending labour supply curve (810)

A curve plotting the supply of labour against wage rates which becomes negatively sloped at higher wage rates as proportionately less labour is supplied. This phenomenon is caused by the relative size of the **income** and **substitution effects** of the wage-rate change. As an increase in the wage rate also represents an increase in the price of leisure, this price effect can be divided into a substitution effect (the effect on the number of hours of leisure chosen of an increase in its price) and an income effect (the effect of an increased wage rate that a given income is reached with fewer hours of work – in the figure, beyond point A higher real wages discourage workers from supplying more hours of work). A negative income effect greater than zero or a positive substitution effect will produce the backward bend in the labour supply curve.

Buchanan, J.M. (1971) 'The backbending supply curve of labour: an example of doctrinal retrogression', *History of Political Economy* 3: 383–90.

backward linkage (110, 940)
See: **linkage**.

backward shifting (320)
See: **shifting of taxes**.

backwash effect (940)

The unfavourable effect of economic growth in a region on other regions in the same national economy. The growing region

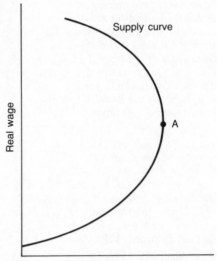

attracts capital and labour from other regions, bringing about a concentration in economic activity and regional economic differentials. This effect has been noted in the context of the study of the **core** and **periphery** of a country.

See also: **spread effect**.

BACS (310)
Banks Automated Clearing System (UK).

bad (010, 720)

An output from economic activity which does not benefit consumers. Most cases are external costs associated with production, e.g. pollution and other health hazards. Bads must be taken into account when measuring the welfare conferred by a particular level of the national income.

See also: **economic welfare; externality; illth; measure of economic welfare**.

badge engineering (530)

Production of a range of car models with similar characteristics to create a number of distinct **brands**.

Bagehot, Walter, 1826–77 (030)

Nineteenth-century economic and political journalist who was the first editor of *The Economist* (1861–1977) and inventor of the **treasury bill**, still used by the UK Treasury as a source of short-term finance. After his début as an economics writer with a review of John Stuart **Mill**'s *Principles of Political Economy* (first published in 1848) he quickly showed his ability to distil economic truth from a mass of evidence. In *Lombard Street* (1873) he acutely analysed the British banking system and money market showing the crucial role of the Bank of England and the importance of confidence as the basis of credit.

Bagehot, W. (1965–78) *The Collected Works of Walter Bagehot*, ed. by N. St John-Stevas, London: Economist.

baht (430)

The currency of Thailand.

Bailey, Samuel, 1791–1870 (030)

A major opponent of the Ricardian theory of value, mainly known for his *A Critical Dissertation on the Nature, Measures and Causes of Value: Chiefly in Reference to the Writings of Mr Ricardo and his Followers* (1825) in which he equated value with 'esteem' and emphasized its essentially relative nature. In his attack on intrinsic and labour theories of value, he stressed the importance of the forces of supply and demand as determinants of relative value. His entire career was spent on the Sheffield Town Trust (a quasi-governmental agency), although he attempted to gain membership of parliament in the elections of 1832 and 1835.

Bailey, S. (1825, reprinted 1931) *Critical Dissertation on the Nature, Measures, and Causes of Value: Chiefly in Reference to the Writings of Mr Ricardo and his Followers*, London: Series of Scarce Tracts in Economic and Political Science, No. 7.
Rauner, R.M. (1961) *Samuel Bailey and the Classical Theory of Value*, London: G. Bell.
Seligman, E.R.A. (1905) 'On some neglected British economists', *Economic Journal* 13: 335–63, 511–35.

Bain, Joe Staten, 1912– (030)

An American economist educated at the University of California at Los Angeles and Harvard, and a professor of economics for thirty years at Berkeley, California, until his retirement in 1975. He is particularly famous for his study of **barriers to entry** as a cause of monopoly power. Also, he has provided a detailed examination of the relationship between **concentration ratios** and profitability.

Bain, J.S. (1956) *Barriers to Entry*, Cambridge, MA: Harvard University Press.
—— (1972) *Essays on Price Theory and Industrial Organisation*, Boston, MA: Little, Brown.

Baker plan (430)

US plan for easing the Third World debt problem, proposed by US Secretary for the Treasury James Baker at the annual meeting of the **World Bank** and the **International Monetary Fund** (IMF) in Seoul, South Korea, October 1985. It proposed that once the debtor countries have put together 'supply-side packages' (liberalizing trade and relying more on the price mechanism to allocate resources) and service their debts on time, money will be available in the form of loans from the World Bank, the IMF and commercial banks. It was not enthusiastically received among debtor countries (except for Mexico which reached a preliminary agreement in July 1986 to obtain US$7 billion of money as a loan). The Plan has been criticized because it tries to solve a debt problem by creating more debt; it gives time for procrastination and fails to deal with the root problem – that the rate of growth of Third World exports has been slower than the rate of interest on dollar loans since 1981.

It was proposed in 1986 that the World Bank would lend a net US$20 billion over three years to a selected group of fifteen countries with a combined foreign debt of US$430 billion; it was difficult to persuade the commercial banks, who are lending less to these countries, to match the generosity of the World Bank.

See also: **world debt problem**.

balanced budget (320)

A government budget which equates revenue with expenditure. This prudent approach to fiscal policy has long been advocated by conservative finance ministers but has frequently been attacked by **Keynesians** who regard it as an inflexible rule which is followed whatever the level of aggregate demand and unemployment. A government surplus will increase public sector saving; a government deficit will require borrowing. It has often been feared that unbalanced budgets will result in **crowding-out** or long-term insolvency of a country (if the national debt is financed at a rate of interest in excess of the country's rate of growth) or inflation (if a country increases its money supply to finance its borrowing).

Balanced Budget and Emergency Deficit Control Act 1985 (320)
See: **Gramm–Rudman–Hollings Act**.

balanced budget multiplier (010, 320)
A measure of the expansion or contraction of **national income** which occurs despite an equal change in the revenue and expenditure of a government. An expansion in national income is possible because the **propensity to consume** of a government is greater than that of the private sector. If the government taxed £100 million of personal income at 30 per cent, it would have revenue of £30 million which, if spent in its entirety, would be a greater addition to total demand than if the tax was not raised but was left with persons who habitually saved 20 per cent of their incomes.

balanced growth (110)
1 Growth of different sectors of an economy at the same rate. This has been advocated by many development economists as a strategy; for example Ragnar Nurske propounded the view that growth should take the form of the coordinated and simultaneous application of capital to a wide range of industries so that the national economy would not be a mixture of expanding, declining and stationary sectors.

2 **Steady state growth** such that the real variables of the economy, including output and employment, grow at the same negative or positive rates.

Rosenstein-Rodan, P.N. (1943) 'Problems of industrialization of Eastern and south-eastern Europe', *Economic Journal* 53: 202–11.

Balance for Official Financing (430)
The current balance of the balance of payments + capital transfers + investment transactions + **balancing item**.

See also: **balance of payments**.

balance of payments (430)
The record of the transactions between the residents of one country and the rest of the world in a given time period; credits and debits in international transactions. The balance of payments is divided into a current account which records trade in goods and services and a capital account. In accounting terms the balance of payments always 'balances', as a surplus or deficit has to be offset by loans granted or received, but the balance does not indicate whether there is an equilibrium between a domestic economy and rest of the world demand. A balance of payments may be in deficit in the 'stock' sense of a country switching from cash balances into stocks of commodities, or in the 'flow' sense of a country spending more than its income, a more serious type of deficit. There have been changes in the presentation of the UK balance of payments accounts. Before 1970, the equation used was

visible + invisible
balance   = current balance + balance of long-term capital
     = basic balance + balancing item + balance of monetary movements
     = 0.

From 1970–80, it was

visible + invisible
balance   = current balance + balance of private and other autonomous capital flows + balancing item
     = total currency flow + allocation of special drawing rights – gold subscription to the IMF + total official financing
     = 0.

After 1980, it has been

visible + invisible

balance = current balance + total investment and other capital transactions + balancing item + allocation of special drawing rights – gold subscription to the IMF
= total official financing + methods of financing
= 0.

The US balance of payments consists of

exports of goods and services +

transfer of goods and services under US military grants net –

imports of goods and services –

US military grants of goods and services net –

unilateral transfers (excluding military grants) net –

US assets abroad net (increase/capital outflow) +

foreign assets in the USA net (increase/capital inflow) +

allocations of special drawing rights +

balances of the above subaccounts.

Central Statistical Office (annual) *UK Balance of Payments*, London: HMSO.

Stern, R.M. (1973) *The Balance of Payments: Economic Theory and Policy*, London: Macmillan.

Thirlwall, A.P. (1986): *Balance of Payments Theory and the United Kingdom Experience*, London: Macmillan.

See also: **accounting balance of payments; balance of payments equilibrium; fundamental equilibrium; market balance of payments**.

balance of payments equilibrium (430)

A balance within the overall **accounting balance of payments**. The equilibria most frequently examined are in the current account, in the visible trade account or in the current and long-term capital accounts combined. The balance chosen for examination depends on the purpose of the analysis; for example, if the performance of industry is being considered, then the balance of trade

will be examined, but the capital accounts merit attention if a foreign exchange market is under scrutiny.

balance of trade (430)

See: **trade balance**.

balance sheet (540)

A statement of the assets and liabilities of a firm or other organization which possesses property. The assets show what the firm owns, and what the firm owes is indicated by its liabilities. For a bank, the management of its balance sheet from day to day is a central part of its business tasks.

balancing item (430)

Part of the **Balance for Official Financing** which takes into account statistical discrepancies.

bancor (430)

An international currency proposed by **Keynes** at **Bretton Woods** as part of his **International Clearing Union** scheme. It was hoped that this new currency would be the medium for settling inter-country indebtedness. As Keynes's recommendation was not accepted, the US dollar assumed the role designed for bancor.

bank advance (310)

See: **advance**.

bank capital (310)

Assets of a bank which constitute its ultimate means of meeting its creditors. It consists of both the stockholders' equity in a bank and funds obtained by selling bonds and notes with a maturity of more than seven years on average. This capital is necessary to reduce the demands made on **deposit insurance** organizations, e.g. the **Federal Deposit Insurance Corporation**, and on uninsured deposit-holders. As definitions of this capital (e.g. whether to include both stock and equity) vary from country to country, in January 1987 the Bank of England and the US banking authorities created a common system for measuring the capital strength of UK and US banks. The system introduced the concept of **primary capital** and assigned a weight to each asset or off-balance-sheet item so that a risk–asset ratio can be calculated.

See also: **risk–asset system**.

bank charges (310)

The charges that retail banks make to their customers for bank advances or for various transactions, including the transfer of funds, the purchase of foreign currency and accounting facilities. They tend to be greatest in countries with high inflation and consequently high and variable nominal interest rates and where there are many regulations restricting the types of financial mediation. As both the UK and the US economies have had these characteristics, there has been great scope in their banking sectors for a reduction in charges.

See also: **Islamic banking**.

Bank Charter Act 1844 (040, 310)

British statute which was the last major nineteenth-century attempt to regulate the British banking system by the creation of new rules for the operation of the Bank of England, particularly through control of the note issue. The Bank was divided into an Issue Department responsible for the note issue and a Banking Department for other bank activities. The Bank's note issue was limited to a 'fiduciary issue' of £14 million (backed by government securities) and the remainder was backed by gold which rose and fell in amount according to international transactions. The Act also regulated the seventy-two country banks which had rights of note issue: not until 1921 did the Bank have a monopoly of note issue in England and Wales (Scotland retained its separate banking system with a number of banks having the power to issue banknotes after the Act of Union in 1707). The rigidity of the Act necessitated its suspension during several trade depressions. However, it did represent a triumph for the thinking of the **Currency School**.

bank deposits (310)

The liabilities of banks which constitute the major part of the money supply of modern national economies. They have the character of liabilities: banks as the holders of deposits can transfer them by cheque to other banks who then have a claim on the original bank. Such deposits are created by an individual or firm giving an asset to a bank, e.g. coin and banknotes, or a promise to repay a loan at a future date.

See also: **current account**; **demand deposit**; **NOW account**; **sight deposit**.

bank efficiency (310)

A measure of a bank's effectiveness in using the money available to it. This can be assessed by the 'mark-up' between interest rates, i.e. either the ninety-day bank time deposit day rate minus the **prime rate of interest** or the bank demand deposit rate minus the bank prime rate. Mark-ups are similar within one country but differ between countries.

banker's turn (310)

The margin between the rate of interest a bank pays to depositors and the rate it receives for money lent out.

See also: **endowment effect**.

Bank for International Settlements (430)

Founded in Basle, Switzerland, in 1930 by Belgium, Britain, Germany, Italy and Japan. Since 1945 it has continued to arrange currency swaps between European central banks. It is also the agent for the **European Monetary Cooperation Fund** and other European institutions.

bank holding company (310)

A company which owns one or more banks and, often, firms engaged in non-banking activities. The development of such companies in the USA in the twentieth century made the expansion of banking possible, despite the existence of **unit banking**.

Bank Holding Company Act 1956 (310)

US Federal statute which defined a bank holding company as one which directly or indirectly owns or holds power to vote 25 per cent or more of the shares of two or more major banks. Previously, bank holding companies were only mildly controlled by the Banking Act 1933 if they were member banks of the **Federal Reserve System**. In 1966, the Act was amended to apply **antitrust** law to the chartering and acquisitions of these companies. The 1956 Act prohibited the companies from participation in non-banking activities; amendments to the Act in 1970 permitted the Board of Governors of the Federal Reserve System to authorize many non-banking activities, which have included leasing, insurance, mortgage banking, community development and data processing.

banking (310)

Money-changing originally; after the Church permitted the charging of interest, primarily money-lending. Banks began producing money by issuing banknotes and then expanded credit by creating bank deposits, which became the major part of the broadly defined money supply. The power to create credit made banks key institutions in modern economies, influencing the level of economic activity.

In the twentieth century banks have increased in size through mergers and joint operations (e.g. in the UK through mergers in the 1920s and 1960s, and in the USA through the growth of bank holding companies), internationalization of their operations and an extension of the range of their services. In a sense, every major commercial bank of today aims to be a financial conglomerate supplying every form of credit, financial advice and service.

Lewis, M.K. and Davis, K.T. (1987) *Domestic and International Banking*, Deddington: Philip Allan.

See also: **branch banking; domestic banking system; fractional reserve banking; free banking; investment banking; Islamic banking; laser banking; merchant bank; offshore banking; unit banking; usury**.

Banking Act 1933 (310)

See: **Glass–Steagall Act**.

Banking Act 1979 (310)

The aims of this UK statute were to regulate deposit-taking business and to confer on the Bank of England the functions of controlling such businesses. It defined 'deposit-taking business' as the receiving of deposits of money and then lending to others, or as being financed out of the capital or interest received by way of deposit. The Act also set up a Deposit Protection Board to manage a deposit protection fund.

Banking Act 1987 (310)

This UK statute extended the amount of regulation of deposit-taking business under the **Banking Act 1979**, gave the Bank of England exclusive powers to authorize the business of deposit-taking and to revoke such powers, instructed the Bank of England to establish a Board of Banking Supervision and regulated financial advertisements.

Banking School (030, 310)

A group of British economists, led by Thomas Tooke and John Stuart **Mill**, who argued that there could never be an excess note issue as notes were only issued to cover real transactions. Also, they wanted the Bank of England to have higher reserves and the growing importance of bank deposits to be incorporated into monetary theory.

See also: **Bank Charter Act 1844; Currency School; Free Banking School; real bills doctrine**.

banknote (310)

Paper currency issued by a bank. Although the first known notes were issued by Chinese banks in the eleventh century, it was not until the eighteenth and nineteenth centuries that they substantially replaced coinage and bills of exchange. In London, banknotes took the form, originally, of receipts for bullion stored with goldsmiths and then became a form of bank advance when banks discovered their power to create money. When countries were on the **gold standard**, it was possible to convert banknotes into bullion; since 1931 notes have been **fiat money**. In most countries the only note issue today is that of the **central bank** (the limited power of Scottish banks to issue notes is exceptional).

See also: **Bradbury**.

Bank of England (310)

The UK's **central bank** which received its first charter in 1694. Although originally a privately owned bank, it administered the national debt from 1752. In a series of statutes culminating in the **Bank Charter Act** 1844, it was increasingly subjected to government regulation, particularly in its note-issuing powers. After the collapse of the **gold standard** in 1931, it operated exchange controls from 1939 to 1979 and from 1945 was more and more involved in supervising the UK banking sector. It was nationalized in 1946. It conducts **monetary policy** through **open market operations** and by influencing market interest rates. The note issue is now entirely **fiduciary** but the monetary assets backing the note issue are used for the Bank's daily interventions in government security and money markets. Also, the Bank holds accounts for about 130 overseas central banks, the **International Monetary Fund** and some private and public individuals. It acts, too, as the Registrar of government stocks of the UK, several Commonwealth countries and British local authorities.

Geddes, P. (1987) *Inside the Bank of England*, London: Boxtree.
Sayers, R.S. (1976) *The Bank of England, 1891–1944*, Cambridge: Cambridge University Press.

See also: **bank rate; Competition and Credit Control; corset; minimum lending rate**.

bank rate (310)

The lowest rate charged by the Bank of England prior to September 1971 for discounting high quality short-term **bills** presented by financial institutions to preserve their liquidity. It was replaced by the **minimum lending rate**.

bank run (310)

See: **run on a bank**.

bankruptcy (520)

A legal action which leads to the control of the property of an insolvent debtor for the benefit of creditors. After the court has appointed a receiver, the debtor can make an offer to his/her creditors.

bank settlement system (310)

An electronic means of transferring deposits between banks to settle their mutual indebtedness. In the USA, Fed Wire is the Federal Reserve's system, Bank Wire is a system for domestic payments and **CHIPS** is a system for payments between New York banks. Japan has the Zenyin system for interbank transfers. The UK has **CHAPS** for the clearing banks, as well as **BACS**.

Baran, Paul, 1910–64 (030)

Leading US Marxist economist of Russian descent who was educated at the universities of Berlin and Harvard. During 1940–7, he worked in the US Office of Strategic Services and was Professor of Economics at Stanford University, 1948–64. His exposition of Marxist economics included theories of **monopoly capital** and **dependency**.

Baran, P. (1957) *The Political Economy of Growth*, New York: Monthly Review Press.
Baran, P. and Sweezy, P.M. (1966) *Monopoly Capital: An Essay on the American Economic and Social Order*, New York: Monthly Review Press.

Barber boom (310, 320)

The period from 1971 to early 1974 in the UK when Anthony Barber as Chancellor of the Exchequer overstimulated the economy with inevitable inflationary consequences. In the property market, in particular, there was appreciable inflation, e.g. between 1970 and 1973 commercial property prices almost tripled.

Barclays index (310)

The price index of the leading New Zealand shares.

bargain (310)

1 A good or service supplied at a lower than expected price.

2 A sale or purchase of stocks or shares on the **International Stock Exchange** at the price agreed, not necessarily at a low price as would be the case outside the Stock Exchange.

bargaining (010)

Negotiation between parties with opposing interests with the hope of an agreement which takes the form of a compromise or a victory for one of the parties. If there is a failure to agree, conflict may ensue. From earliest times, bargaining has been a major activity of markets as a means of reconciling the opposing interests of buyers for low prices and of sellers for high prices. This is a method of coordinating an **economy** which is the alternative to **planning**, although even under central planning the managers of different enterprises bargain with government officials to bring about the allocation of goods and services. In the labour market, the advent of trade unions has transformed individual bargaining into **collective bargaining**.

See also: **game theory**; **Nash bargaining**.

bargaining theory of wages (820)

An attempt to model the wage negotiating process to show how wages are determined. **Hicks** was one of the first economists to model wage bargaining. In the figure, OZ is the wage rate an employer would have paid if unconstrained by a trade union and OA is the highest wage union negotiators can obtain from the employer. The union, as shown by the downward-sloping resistance curve, will begin by asking a high wage rate knowing little of the employer's position; the employer will gradually increase his offer to avoid a costly strike. This famous model of *collective bargaining* was invented by Hicks in his *Theory of Wages*.

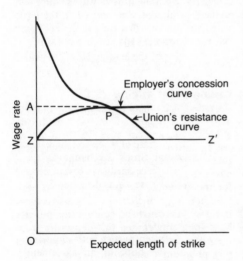

Hicks, J.R. (1963) *The Theory of Wages*, ch. 7, London: Macmillan; New York: St Martin's Press.

bargaining unit (830)

The group of US workers represented by a labor union. The rules for the boundaries of the unit have been built up by the **National Labor Relations Board** under the provision of the **Wagner** and **Taft–Hartley Acts** with a view to making them homogeneous units which reflect local needs and further **collective bargaining**.

barometric firm leadership (610)

The price leadership of an oligopolistic firm which makes price changes first to act as a 'barometer' to test the market. Often a small firm is chosen for this role, as happened when British clearing banks changed their bank charges.

barrier to entry (010)

A principal method of creating or preserving a monopoly position. Such barriers can be legal (governments only permit certain qualified persons to enter the market), technological (only large-scale production is possible, as is the case with steel mills and the mass production of consumer durables), financial (a large amount of capital is required to set up a business) or based on customers' loyalty (through **product differentiation**). In the labour market, trade unions and professional associations (e.g. medical associations) limit the number of entrants to an occupation to preserve the income and employment of their members.

Bain, J.S. (1956) *Barriers to New Competition*, Cambridge, MA: Harvard University Press.

See also: **artificial barrier to entry**; **barrier to exit**.

barrier to exit (610)

The costs or forgone profits of a firm which will occur if it leaves an industry and thus make it reluctant to do so. Barriers to exit are less common than barriers to entry, except in cases when a government, to prevent increased unemployment, keeps in existence a large organization threatened with financial collapse; specialized assets may also deter a firm from leaving an industry.

Caves, R.E. and Porter, M.E. (1977) 'From entry barriers to mobility barriers: conjectural decisions and contrived deterence to new competition', *Quarterly Journal of Economics* 91: 241–62.

See also: **barrier to entry**.

barter (010, 420)

The most primitive form of exchange as

commodities are directly exchanged for each other. An exchange is possible when two persons mutually desire each other's production. It is more cumbersome than when money is used as a medium of exchange as the bartering parties have to search for each other, without the advantage of an intermediary. Nevertheless, in modern times countries short of foreign exchange, e.g. the USSR, have used this form of trade. If trade bartering is used, there can be a balance at a point of time or over a few years, e.g. Finland and the USSR have used the method of balancing the value of their bilateral trade over a five-year period.

See also: **countertrade**.

barter economy (010)

One of the earliest forms of an **economy** in which goods are directly changed for other goods and money is not used as a medium of exchange. Prices are expressed in relative terms, e.g. X amount of A = Y amount of B. Transactions can be expensive as high search costs can be incurred in the pursuit of trading partners. However, to avoid taxation and create employment, in some areas of, for example, Canada and the UK the exchange of services has replaced the usual market.

base capital (310)

The capital of a securities house which is required to protect it against a fall in its profitability.

base rate (310)

The rate of interest that a British clearing bank uses as the basis of its structure of interest rates for lending and receiving deposits. Lending rates are above, and rates on deposits below, base rate. Only large and creditworthy institutions borrow close to the base rate. This system came into force in 1971; despite the abolition of their interest rates cartel, few clearing banks are out of line with their competitors.

basic commodity (010)

One which directly or indirectly enters into the production of all commodities. A concept introduced by **Sraffa**.

Sraffa, P. (1960) *Production of Commodities by Means of Commodities: Prelude to a Critique*

of Economic Theory, Cambridge: Cambridge University Press.

basic industry (930)

An industry which exports its products to other regions, thus being a major determinant of its own region's prosperity. Contrast with **non-basic industry**.

Alexander, J. (1954) 'The basic–nonbasic concept of urban economic functions', *Economic Geography* 30: 246–61.

basic relief (320)

Income tax relief for all taxpayers irrespective of their marital and other personal characteristics.

basic wage (820)

The common element in all Australian wages to which **margins** are added to produce a differentiated wage structure. The basic wage is not merely a national wage but a general component of all wages which can in itself be altered. An increase in the basic wage will be awarded only if the economy has the economic capacity to pay for it.

See also: **over-award payment**.

basing point pricing (520)

A system of uniform pricing which includes a transport charge from an arbitrarily chosen geographical base. In the USA, it was first used to sell steel at Pittsburgh prices plus freight charges from Pittsburgh to consumer (hence the name 'Pittsburgh-Plus' for the system). The system has also been used in Europe, including the British cement industry. **Antitrust** and **competition policies** have long condemned this departure from price competition. Under it, some customers pay phantom charges for journeys which were never undertaken and the pattern of plant location will be distorted by the incentive to be where one receives the benefit of paying less in freight charges.

See also: **Robinson–Patman Act 1936**.

Basle Concordat on Banking Supervision (310, 430)

An international pact, drawn up in 1975 by the **Bank for International Settlements**, to supervise banking activities.

bastard Keynesianism (030)

This expression was invented by Joan **Robinson** to describe the imposition of **neoclassical** thinking on the theories of **Keynes**. She complained that the concept of **effective demand** had been abandoned and that there was less concern for the meaning of capital than for its measurement. In particular, she was angry that modern theorists had distorted Keynes by stating that, given a level of savings, the government ensures that there is enough investment, a view little different from the classical assertion that savings determine investment, ignoring the effect of **distribution** on consumption and investment. **Hicks** with his IS–LM analysis, **Patinkin** and her US opponents in the **Cambridge controversies** were included in the ranks of the illegitimate.

Robinson, J. (1979) 'What has become of the Keynesian revolution?', in *Collected Economic Papers*, vol. V, pp. 168–77, Oxford: Basil Blackwell.

BAT (720)

See: **best available technology**.

batch production (510)

The production of a limited quantity of a particular product, rather than continuous mass production.

Bauer, Peter Thomas, 1915– (030)

A prominent development economist born in Budapest, Hungary, and professor at the London School of Economics from 1960 to 1983. He was created a Life Peer on retirement. After early field work in Malaysia and West Africa, he progressed to a general study of economic development, emphasizing the superiority of markets as a method of allocation. He has long been a trenchant critic of many forms of economic aid and central economic planning. Michael Lipton calls him 'a classical economist' in that he sees enterprise, trade and the enlargement of markets as crucial to development. Bauer does not rely on the maximizing claims of the **neoclassicals** and is therefore opposed to barriers to trade, investment and migration.

Bauer, P.T. (1948) *The Rubber Industry*, Cambridge, MA: Harvard University Press.
—— (1954) *West African Trade*, Cambridge: Cambridge University Press.
—— (1957) *Economic Analysis and Policy in Underdeveloped Countries*, Durham, NC: Duke University Press.
—— (1971) *Dissent on Development Studies and Debates in Development Economics*, London: Weidenfeld & Nicolson.
—— (1984) *Reality and Rhetoric: Studies in the Economics of Development*, London: Weidenfeld & Nicolson; Cambridge, MA: Harvard University Press.

Baumol, William Jack, 1922– (030)

US economist, educated at City College, New York, and London University; he was a professor at Princeton University from 1954 to 1971. He is famous for his economic analysis of management science, particularly his research finding that businesses set out to maximize their sales subject to minimum profit targets. Also, his 'unbalanced growth' model demonstrates that the different opportunities for technical progress in the various sectors of an economy lead to chronic problems in the financing of cities, medical care, educational systems and the performing arts. Recently he has been concerned with the environmental implications of welfare economics and **contestable markets**.

Baumol, W.J. (1977) *Economic Theory and Operations Analysis*, 4th edn, Englewood Cliffs, NJ: Prentice Hall.
—— (1966) *Performing Arts, the Economic Dilemma: a Study of Problems Common to Theatre, Opera, Music and Dance*, New York: Twentieth Century Fund.
Baumol, W.J. and Oates, W.E. (1975) *The Theory of Environmental Policy*, Englewood Cliffs, NJ, and London: Prentice Hall.
Baumol, W.J., Willig, R.D. and Panzar, J.S. (1982) *Contestable Markets and the Theory of Industry Structure*, New York: Harcourt Brace Jovanovich.

Bayesian method (210)

A method of revising the probability of an event's occurring by taking into account experimental evidence. The usefulness of this approach depends on the size of the sample used in an experiment. Bayes's theorem of 1763 originally stated that the probability of q conditional on H (prior information) and p (some further event) varies as the probability of q on H times the probability of p, given q and H.

Cyert, R.M. (1987) *Bayesian Analyses and*

Uncertainty in Economic Theory, London: Chapman and Hall.

BB (310)

Standard & Poor credit rating of securities which designates them as speculative.

See also: **AAA**; **BBB**; **C**; **D**; **DDD**.

BBB (310)

Standard & Poor credit rating of securities which states that they are of medium grade.

See also: **AAA**; **BB**; **C**; **D**; **DDD**.

b/d (720)

Barrels per day: the rate of oil production or outflow.

BDI (830)

Bundesverrand der deutschen Industrie: a major employers' association in Germany. Founded in 1949 by grouping together thirty-nine national industrial federations. Today it has separate sections for leading sectors and secondary sectors.

BDR (310)

See: **British Depository Receipt**.

BEA (220)

See: **Bureau of Economic Analysis**.

bear (310 430)

A market speculator who, believing that prices will fall, sells securities (for example) now and purchases them later to effect delivery of them. A profit is made by the difference between the selling and buying prices. This reversal of the normal sequence of transactions is possible on stock exchanges where the year is divided into a number of account periods during which stocks sold do not have to be delivered. Also, there is speculation of this nature in currency and commodity markets where there is a choice between spot and future transactions. If the bear already possesses what is being sold, he is 'protected' or 'covered'; if not, he is selling short.

See also: **bull**; **stag**.

bearer bond (310)

A bond owned by the person currently in possession of it. As no endorsement is needed to transfer such bonds, there is no central register of the owners of any particular bearer bond issue. The **Eurobond** is a major example of such bonds.

bearer security (310)

See: **bearer bond**; **bearer share**.

bearer share (310)

A company share owned by the person holding it at a particular time.

Becker, Gary Stanley, 1930– (030)

US economist, educated at Princeton and Chicago, who was a professor at Columbia from 1960 to 1970 and has been a professor at Chicago since 1970. His major contributions to economics have been: an extension of the study of racial and sexual **discrimination** in labour markets by the inclusion in the utility functions of employers and employees of a 'taste for discrimination'; the formalization of the study of **human capital** by an examination of the investment-like nature of schooling and on-the-job training; the analysis of crime as an occupation with expected benefits and expected costs (if caught); and a new economics of the family as a multi-person production unit practising division of labour amongst its members. His work has extended economic study into areas previously the preserve of sociologists, psychologists and anthropologists.

Becker, G.S. (1968) 'Crime and punishment: an economic approach', *Journal of Political Economy* 76: 169–217.
—— (1971) *Economics of Discrimination*, 2nd edn, Chicago, IL: University of Chicago Press.
—— (1975) *Human Capital: a Theoretical and Empirical Analysis, with Special Reference to Education*, New York: Columbia University Press.
—— (1977) *The Economic Approach to Human Behaviour*, Chicago, IL, and London: University of Chicago Press.
—— (1981) *Treatise on the Family*, Cambridge, MA: Harvard University Press.
Shackleton, J.R. (1981) 'Gary S. Becker: the economist as empire-builder', in J.R. Shackleton and G. Locksley (eds) *Twelve Contemporary Economists*, London and Basingstoke: Macmillan.

bed and breakfast (310)

1 A sale and purchase of securities within

twenty-four hours to accumulate tax-deductible losses.

2 Tourist accommodation for one night with a breakfast included in the tariff.

beggar-my-neighbour policy (420)

A **protectionist** foreign trade policy which attempts to improve the domestic economy at the expense of foreign countries. This policy was at the heart of much of **mercantilist** thinking and was later practised in the 1930s by many countries. Predominantly agricultural economies resorted to it first; then it was adopted by the UK, USA, France, the Netherlands and Switzerland. Post-1945, currency devaluations have embodied this principle. A policy of this type has always been criticized because of its self-defeating character: domestic industries, being able to ignore foreign competition, become more inefficient and export industries, the victims of retaliation on the part of foreign countries, have a reduced output and often higher unit costs which make them even more uncompetitive in world markets.

See also: **General Agreement on Tariffs and Trade**.

behavioural economics (030, 610)

The varied approaches to the study of economic behaviour, including decision-making in firms and other organizations, a psychological approach to the study of consumers and a multidisciplinary 'technological economics' with some of the assumptions of the **post-Keynesians**. Much of this school of economics is concerned with microeconomic issues but it also has macroeconomic interests, e.g. in an examination of inflation and unemployment. Behavioural economics has flourished to the extent of having specialist journals – the *Journal of Behavioral Economics* and the *Journal of Economic Behavior and Economics*.

Earl, P.E. (ed.) (1988) *Behavioral Economics*, 2 vols, Aldershot: Edward Elgar.
Gilad, B. and Kaish, S. (eds) (1986) *Handbook of Behavioral Economics*, vols A and B, Greenwich, CT: JAI Press.
Loasby, B. (1976) *Choice, Complexity and Ignorance: An Inquiry into Economic Theory and the Practice of Decision-Making*, Cambridge: Cambridge University Press.

See also: **economics and psychology**; **evolutionary theory of the firm**.

behaviour line (010)

An **indifference curve**.

below the line (320, 520, 540)

1 In the UK budgets of 1947–63 it referred to receipts and expenditure relating to borrowed funds or the servicing of the national debt.

2 For a firm, it refers to expenditure on sales promotion other than on direct advertising.

3 In the UK balance of payments, below the line refers to official financing.

See also: **above the line**.

benefit approach to taxation (320)

The levying of taxation so as to match the burden of taxation with the amounts of public goods received by each taxpayer. The principle was first enunciated by Hobbes, Grotius and Locke. In essence there is an exchange between taxpayers and a government of taxes for services. Since public goods are collectively provided and taxes are individually paid, a taxation system on this basis will always be criticized. For example, it would be difficult to allocate charges for the maintenance of external defence to individuals in proportion to their consumption. Until governments know more of the preferences of taxpayers it will be impossible to apply the principle exactly.

benefit tax (320)

A tax linked to the provision of a government service, e.g. a bridge toll, fuel tax or a charge to use a swimming bath. The principle followed is 'he who benefits should pay'.

See also: **ability to pay**; **user charge**.

Benelux (730)

Customs union of Belgium, the Netherlands and Luxemburg. In 1943, the three countries signed a monetary convention for controlling payments between them after the Second World War. In 1944, they agreed to a customs union which came into force in 1948: this abolished tariffs within Benelux and set a **common external tariff**. The aims of Benelux include the free movement of goods and factors of production, the coordination of economic, financial and social policies to attain a satisfactory employment level and the highest standard of living, and a joint trade policy.

Bentham, Jeremy, 1748–1832 (030)

Legal philosopher and writer on many economic, constitutional and prison reform issues; founder of the British utilitarian school of philosophy. Educated at Westminster School, the Queen's College, Oxford (which he hated, which led him to found University College London in 1832), and Lincoln's Inn, London, where he read for the English Bar. He is most famous for his exposition of **utilitarianism**, the principle that there should be a 'felicific calculus', i.e. that a course of action should aim to promote the greatest happiness for the greatest number. This inspired **Jevons** in his subjective value theory of exchange. John Stuart **Mill**, who was much under Bentham's influence in his youth, rebelled against the cold rationality of utilitarianism.

Bentham studied political economy from 1786 to 1804, between the ages of 38 and 56, when he was at his intellectual peak. A reading of Smith's *The Wealth of Nations* was decisive for his economic thinking, although he had an earlier interest in unemployment. With an atomistic view of social life, it was not surprising that he used induction as his principal approach and only resorted to mathematics as a convenient method of expression. His first work on economics, *Defence of Usury* (1787) was inspired by a rumour that the legal maximum for interest was to fall from 5 per cent to 4 per cent: Bentham recommended that there should be free determination of interest rates. Although the work did not advance a theory of the rate of interest, it was nevertheless widely praised in Britain, France and the USA.

He was against artificial attempts to increase trade, e.g. by having colonies, because he believed that trade is limited by capital. His *Manual of Political Economy* (1793–5) dealt with international trade. He took to public finance in *Supply without Burthen* (1795) in which he combined a minimal view of the state with a new proposal to raise the small amount of taxation still necessary – the public auction of all properties in vacant possession because no relatives were alive to inherit. Further, in *A Plan for Augmentation of the Revenue* (1794–5), he proposed a reduction in the national debt by the use of government-run lotteries and government dealings in life annuities. His *Proposal for the Circulation of a New Species of Paper Currency* (1795–6) argued that a government monopoly on the issue of paper currency is a cheaper means for the government to borrow than the issue of interest-bearing bills. *Circulating Annuities* (1800) also suggested a new type of paper currency, and in *True Alarm* (1801) he contributed to the raging bullion debate of the period by tracing the effects of excessive country bank issues on prices, as well as enunciating a theory of value based on utility. *Of the Balance of Trade* (1801) attacked **mercantilism**; *Defence of a Maximum* (1801) advocated price controls for grain and *Institute of Political Economy* (1801–4) set out his views on the role and limits of government policy, as well as discussing whether political economy is an art or a science.

Dinwoody, J. (1989) *Bentham*, Oxford: Oxford University Press.
Stark, W. (1955) *Jeremy Bentham's Economic Writings*, London: Allen & Unwin.

BERD (420)

French for **European Bank for Reconstruction and Development**.

Bergson, Abram, 1914– (030)

US economist educated at Johns Hopkins and Harvard universities. After wartime experience from 1942 to 1945 as chief of the Russian Economic Subdivision of the US Office of Strategic Services, he returned to academic life and has been a professor at Harvard since 1956. In 1938, he created the new welfare economics by asserting that a social welfare function can be established by attaching weights to each individual's welfare function: this rejected the earlier **cardinal utility** approach. Also, he introduced the distinction between 'efficiency' and 'equity', applying it to an analysis of the individual income effects of economic change. He has applied his welfare analysis to many areas of economics, including **market socialism** and monopoly. Also, he became a leading US authority on the Soviet economy.

Bergson, A. (1964) *Economics of Soviet Planning*, New Haven, CT: Yale University Press.
—— (1966) *Essays in Normative Economics*, Cambridge, MA: Harvard University Press.
—— (1982) *Welfare, Planning and Employment: Selected Essays in Economic Theory*, Cambridge, MA: MIT Press.

Bergson social welfare function (010)

The welfare of a community in a given time period expressed as a function of the amounts of consumer goods produced, the amounts of labour and non-labour factor inputs and the production unit for which the work is performed. Bergson, in his approach, intended to challenge the view that a community's welfare is the sum of individuals' welfare.

Bergson, A. (1938) 'A reformulation of certain aspects of welfare economics', *Quarterly Journal of Economics* 52: 310–34.

Bernoulli hypothesis (030)

The hypothesis, named after Daniel Bernoulli (1700–82), that in a gamble an individual will participate according to the personal **utilities** he attaches to the probabilities. This approach is prominent in the economics of **risk** and **uncertainty**.

Pearson, K. (1978) *The History of Statistics in the 17th and 18th Centuries*, New York: Macmillan.

Bertrand duopoly model (020)

A development of **Cournot's duopoly model** which uses price adjustments to bring about an equilibrium. At equilibrium, neither firm would benefit from charging a different price and so the price becomes equal to marginal cost.

best available technology (720)

A technique of production which reduces pollution levels by using the cleanest available method.

beta (310)

The ratio of a change in the return on a security to a change in the returns on all securities of a particular stock market. Beta is unity if the changes in the individual share and in the whole of the market are the same. Betas are positive if the individual and market returns move in the same direction, and negative if they move in opposite directions.

See also: **Sharpe**.

beta stock (310)

Five hundred or so stocks and shares which are the most actively traded on the **Stock Exchange Automated Quotation** system after **alpha stocks**.

See also: **gamma stock**; **delta stock**.

Beveridge, William Henry (Lord), 1879–1963 (030)

In many senses, the founder of the British **welfare state**. After an education at Balliol College, Oxford, he was a Law Fellow at University College, Oxford, from 1902 to 1909 as well as subwarden of Toynbee Hall, London, from 1903 to 1905, where he investigated casual labour and unemployment in the London docks. As Director of Labour Exchanges at the UK Board of Trade from 1909 to 1915 he created a national system of employment exchanges. In 1919 as Permanent Secretary of the Ministry of Food he completed a national food rationing scheme. From 1919 to 1937 he was Director of the London School of Economics and expanded the range of its activities, attracting scholars such as **Hayek** and **Hicks**, as well as encouraging empirical studies. Returning to University College, Oxford, as Master (1937–44) he headed a committee which drew up the Beveridge Report on social security in 1942; this was expanded in 1944 into the celebrated *Full Employment in a Free Society*, a report which laid the foundations for much of postwar British welfare policies.

Harris, J. (1977) *William Beveridge: a Biography*, Oxford: Clarendon Press.
Williams, K. and Williams, J. (eds) (1987) *A Beveridge Reader*, London: Unwin Hyman.

bidding technique (210)

Estimation of consumers' valuation of benefits using questionnaires.

See also: **contingent valuation**.

bid price (310)

The selling price for **unit trust** units or shares of companies.

bid rent (930)

The amount of money a household will offer a landowner for space which provides a particular level of **utility**.

Wheaton, W. (1977) 'A bid rent approach to housing demand', *Journal of Urban Economics* 4: 200–17.

BIDS (310)

See: **British Institute of Dealers in Securities**.

bid vehicle (720)

A proposed means of payment based on surveys to make a **contingent valuation**, e.g. the amount of cash charged to obtain a permit to hunt wildlife.

Big Bang (310)

The **deregulation** of the London Stock Exchange on 27 October 1986 which involved the ending of minimum dealing commissions and the distinction between dealers and jobbers. Under the fierce gale of competition, smaller firms found it difficult to survive and even the larger firms withdrew from market-making by 1990. Firms anxious to be ahead of their rivals offered grossly inflated salaries to prospective staff and the best of existing staff, making the volume of consequent redundancies greater.

The seeds of the recent changes were sown in the early 1970s when British **competition policy** was extended to cover the provision of services as well as goods; the present changes were forced on the Stock Exchange when, to avoid investigation under the restrictive trade practices legislation, it agreed in 1983 to abolish minimum commissions within three years. The abolition of British **exchange controls** in 1979 made internationalization of the London market inevitable. The first stage of these changes was on 1 March 1986 when financial institutions such as banks and insurance companies were allowed to acquire holdings in firms of stockbrokers and stockjobbers. In the USA the equivalent set of changes took place on 1

May 1975 and the consequences of these were the formation of many new **financial conglomerates**.

Three years of preparation enabled London to adjust quickly to the new regime. The high volume of trading in the early months made it easier for firms to adjust to lower commissions and to cope with the huge costs of setting up new dealing systems. Instead of the old practice of charging clients on the basis of price plus commission, the majority of deals are quoted at prices net of commission. The next step will be to use the London system to enable brokers throughout the world to quote prices to each other. It has been estimated (in 1987) that the cost of regulating the City of London will be about £120 million per year. In the period 1986–9, the volume of stocks traded in London fell by a third and the number of jobs fell by 35,000 but much of this decline was the consequence of the **Black Monday** stock market crash.

Thomas, W.A. (1986) *The Big Bang*, Deddington: Philip Allan.
—— (1989) *The Securities Market*, London: Philip Allan.

See also: **Mayday**.

'Big Board' (310)

The nickname for the New York Stock Exchange situated at 11 Wall Street and established in 1792. Its importance is such that 60 per cent of world trading in securities and 85 per cent of the USA's volume is conducted by it.

big push (110)

A theory of simultaneous economic development in several sectors. Rosenstein-Rodan asserted that for economic development to succeed there should be, as a minimum, several large investment projects in different industries in order to secure increasing returns from indivisibilities in production. It was hoped that the scale of such development would reduce divergences between private and social products. However, the lack of resources of many Third World countries made it unlikely that so ambitious a scheme would be implemented.

Rosenstein-Rodan, P. (1943) 'Problems of industrialization in Eastern and south-eastern Europe', *Economic Journal* 53: 202–11.

bilateral aid (430)

Aid which flows between a particular donor country and a particular recipient; often **tied aid**.

See also: **foreign aid; multilateral aid**.

bilateral monopoly (010)

A market consisting of a **monopolist** and a **monopsonist**. In many national economies there are examples of this form of monopoly in the public sector, e.g. when a state education employer faces a single teachers' **union** in the labour market. To analyse bilateral monopoly, as is the case with **duopoly**, the interaction of both sides, buyer and seller, has to be considered.

bill (310)

1 A short-term monetary asset.

2 An invoice stating the amount owed for the supply of goods or services.

See also: **bill of exchange; commercial bill; trade bill; treasury bill**.

bill of exchange (310, 430)

A short-term financial instrument, usually of ninety days' duration, which is now used to finance foreign trade, although in the nineteenth century it had a wider usage as a commercial bill. The Bills of Exchange Act 1882 legally defined it as 'an unconditional order in writing, addressed by one person to another, signed by the person giving it, requiring the person to whom it is addressed to pay on demand or at a fixed or determinable future time a sum certain in money to or to the order of a specified person, or to bearer'.

bimetallism (040, 310)

The use of two metals, usually gold and silver, in a fixed ratio as the standard of value and ultimate means of payment. This currency system met with the approval of Adam **Smith**. It was argued in favour of it that each metal would be more stable in value if connected with the other, that the low production levels of gold caused falling prices and trade recession and that it would make possible fixed exchange rates between countries on a pure gold standard and those on a pure silver standard. The system was practised in the nineteenth century in the USA and in Europe in the Latin Union. (The Latin Union was the monetary alliance of France, Belgium, Switzerland, Italy, Greece and Romania formed in 1865 and abandoned in 1873 as a consequence of the large amount of Nevada silver and Germany's conversion from a silver to a gold standard.)

bimodal frequency curve (210)

A **frequency curve** with two maxima.

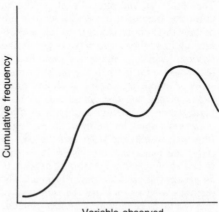

Variable observed

binomial charge (010)

A **two-part tariff** which consists of a fixed payment that allows a consumer access to the service and variable payments related to the use made of the service, e.g. a telephone rental and telephone call charges.

See also: **price discrimination**.

bioeconomics (010, 720)

1 The application of sociobiology to economics, first suggested by **Becker** in 1979. It is argued that competitiveness and self-interest, not selfishness and collectivism, when built into human genes produce an effective economic system of the capitalist type.

2 The economics of renewable natural resources.

See also: **altruism; economic man; homo economicus; homo sovieticus**.

BIS (430)

See: **Bank for International Settlements**.

blackboard trading (310)

A method of trading in small quantities which involves buyers writing their bids on one side of the blackboard and sellers their offers on the other side. When agreement is reached, it is noted on the sales panel as a binding future contract. This method is used on the Chicago Mercantile Exchange for dealings in agricultural commodities. When trading is heavy, the method has to be abandoned.

black economy (010)

The unofficial, and often illegal, part of an **economy**. It consists of persons who do not declare their entire incomes to tax authorities, and also those who produce goods and services illegally. Companies participating in this sector falsify their accounts by omissions or inaccurate entries. Rich and poor, capitalist and socialist economies all have black sectors. Numerous countries are often cited as examples, including India, Portugal, Italy – as well as the USA and the UK. In Italy, the black economy is so large that estimates of its size range from 10 per cent to 50 per cent of gross domestic product. The methods used to measure the total size of this sector's economic activities include comparing national income with national expenditure (not the best of methods since both sets of estimates have always been subject to error) and examining discrepancies between household income and spending in household expenditure surveys to calculate undisclosed incomes. Also, changes in the ratio of cash transactions to total transactions indicate that many in a national economy would prefer methods of trading which are less detectable. It is difficult for tax authorities to track down the participants in the black economy and tax them for certainty of taxation would be such a disincentive to work that little extra revenue for the government might be obtained.

Heertje, A., Allen, M. and Cohen, A. (1982) *The Black Economy*, London: Pan.
Smithies, E. (1984) *The Black Economy in England since 1914*, Atlantic Highlands, NJ: Humanities Press; Dublin: Gill & Macmillan.

black gold (720)

1   Coal (originally).

2   Oil when it became a more important source of energy than coal.

blackleg (830)

A worker who reduces the effectiveness of a **strike** by continuing to work during a period of an industrial dispute. Police protection has often been needed for such dissenters.

black market (010, 530)

An unauthorized market with transactions contrary to governmental regulations. Markets of this kind are usually found when there are price or exchange controls or the restriction of trading to a list of authorized dealers. Soviet-type economies were characterized by these markets.

Black Monday (310)

Stock market crash in New York and London of 19 October 1987. In London the FT-SE index dropped by 500 points.

Bose, M. (1988) *The Crash*, London: Mandarin Paperback.

See also: **Brady Commission**.

Blaug, Mark, 1927– (030)

Leading historian of economic thought, education economist and biographer of the economics profession. Born in the Netherlands and educated at Columbia University. After working as a statistician at the US Department of Labor, he was assistant professor of economics at Yale University (1954–62) before becoming Professor of the Economics of Education at the University of London Institute of Education; since 1984 he has been consultant professor at the University of Buckingham, England. He has both written extensively on human capital theory and manpower forecasting and moved from an early interest in Ricardian economics to wide-ranging writing and editing of major works on the history of economic thought.

Blaug, M. (1958) *Ricardian Economics: A Historical Study*, New Haven, CT: Yale University Press.
—— (1970) *An Introduction to the Economics of Education*, London: Allen Lane.
—— (1985) *Economic Theory in Retrospect*, 4th edn, Cambridge: Cambridge University Press.
—— (1986) *Who's Who in Economics*, 2nd edn, Brighton: Wheatsheaf.

See also: **Ricardian theory of value**.

bliss point (010)

An optimal combination of **private** and **public goods**. This combination is derived from a **social welfare function**. In the figure W_1, W_2 and W_3 are different social welfare functions, BB is a grand utility maximization frontier, P is the bliss point, U_x and U_y are ordinal preference functions and $W = W(U_x, U_y)$ is a social welfare function. At the bliss point P, social welfare is at a maximum because BB touches the highest welfare function contour.

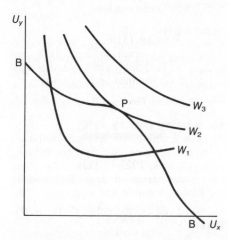

Bator, F.M. (1957) 'The simple analysis of welfare maximization', *American Economic Review* 47: 22–59.

bloc grant (320)

The revenue transferred by the US Federal Government to a state or local government so that the lower level government has sufficient revenues to provide a service, e.g. education, at the standard desired by central government.

blocked development (110)

Economic **development** which is deliberately impeded by developed countries. It has been asserted that dominant countries of the world have blocked the development of Third World countries, permitting them only '**peripheral capitalism**'.

Amin, S. (1976) *Unequal Development: An Essay on the Social Formations of Peripheral Capitalism*, Hassocks: Harvester Press; New York: Monthly Review Press.

block of shares (310)

Any block of more than 10,000 shares, according to the New York Stock Exchange Rule 390. With few exceptions, this rule requires that listed stocks must be traded on the floor of the Exchange, even if sold in 'blocks'.

block trade (310)

See: **put-through**.

Blue Book (220)

1 The annually published national income and expenditure accounts of the UK.

2 The document setting out the terms and conditions of a firm agreed through **collective bargaining** or unilaterally imposed by an employer, e.g. the Ford agreement.

blue chip (310)

A stock issue by a company or corporation with a high standing because of its earnings record. Such shares are chosen as a basis for the Financial Times, Dow-Jones and other share indices. The term is taken from the game of poker as the highest value chips used are blue.

blue-collar worker (810)

US expression for a person engaged in manual employment; usually contrasted with a **white-collar worker**. **De-industrialization** and the increasing education of the labor force has reduced the number of these workers and, also, labor union membership.

blue economy (070)

The official economy, known to and recorded by government. The term is derived in the UK from the term 'Blue Book', the annual summary of national income accounts.

See also: **black economy**; **informal economy**; **unofficial economy**.

blue return (320)

A self-assessment business income tax system recommended by the **Shoup Mission** to Japan in 1949 for collecting taxes from small and medium-sized firms. This system was intended to encourage smaller businesses to maintain minimal accounting systems.

blue-sky laws (310)

US Securities Act 1933 and other US statutes which regulate and supervise the securities industry so that persons do not attempt to sell something which they do not possess, e.g. part of the sky, to another person or otherwise organize fraudulent investment schemes.

See also: **bubble; Securities and Exchange Commission**.

BOF (430)

See: **Balance for Official Financing**.

Böhm-Bawerk, Eugen von, 1851–1914 (030)

Leading economist of the **Austrian School** and disciple of **Menger**. He read law at Vienna University and then economics at Heidelberg, Leipzig and Jena universities; his student contemporary was von Weiser. From 1889 to 1893 he was a civil servant working on income tax and currency reform. On three occasions (1893, 1896–7 and 1900–4) he was Minister of Finance of Austria; in 1902 he was appointed professor by the University of Vienna. In his economic writings, he began with a theory of value based on **marginal utility** and then proceeded to a theory of interest and capital. His lengthy exposition of the **roundabout method of production**, possible through the use of capital, is central to his work. More capitalistic production has on average a longer period of production. He rejected explanations for the payment of interest on the grounds of either productivity or exploitation and asserted that interest is paid because present goods have a higher subjective value than future goods.

Böhm-Bawerk, E. von (1959) *Capital and Interest*, 3 vols, translated by G.D. Huncke and H.F. Sennholz, South Holland, IL: Libertarian Press.

Kuenne, R.E. (1971) *Eugen von Böhm-Bawerk*, New York and London: Columbia University Press.

bond (310)

1 A promise under seal to pay money.

2 A fixed interest security issued by a government, corporation or company.

See also: **deep discount bond; government bond; junk bond; straight bond**.

bond fund (310)

A fund established to receive the proceeds of a bond issue and to make subsequent disbursements. Funds of this kind are often set up by local authorities.

bonding cost (520)

The cost to an agent of putting up a **bond** as a guarantee of meeting losses. Bonding is common amongst travel agents and insurance underwriters.

bond market (310)

A market which raises long-term capital in the form of bonds that bear a fixed rate of interest for governments and firms and organizes the trading of bonds that have already been issued.

bond rating agency (310)

An agency which rates the creditworthiness of the governments, municipalities and corporations issuing bonds. Standard & Poor and Moody's are the leading US agencies of this kind.

See also: **AAA; BB; BBB; C; D; DDD; Prime-1**.

bonus issue (310)

An issue to existing shareholders of extra shares in proportion to existing holdings. If issued without charge, known as a **scrip issue**.

book value (540)

The value of an asset as recorded in the books or accounts of a firm or other organization. Often this valuation is made at the time that assets are originally purchased with the consequence that changes in value due to inflation are not taken into consideration.

See also: **inflation accounting**.

boom (140)

A peak in economic activity, a turning point in the **business cycle**. Booms, the opposite of **recessions**, are characterized by high output, low unemployment, speculative investment and many short **strikes**.

bootblack economy (070)
A derogatory term for an **economy** dominated by **labour-intensive** service industries. Bootblacking is manual and non-exportable, unlike the products of modern technologically advanced and internationally oriented service industries, e.g. banking and accounting.

See also: **services**.

border trade (420)
Importing and exporting across a border which is often **intra-industry trade** as, if the border is long, the products exported over one part of a border will also be imported over another, e.g. building materials over the USA–Canada border.

bottleneck (010)
A shortage in the supply of a **factor of production** which, if not remedied, can add to inflationary pressures. Lack of an appropriate **infrastructure** has often been a major bottleneck impeding the development of less developed countries. An economy with full employment suffers many bottlenecks.

bottom-line accounting (540)
Accounting which is especially concerned with net profit or earnings that appears at the bottom of a profit and loss account.

bottom-up linkage model (730)
An interregional model of a national economy which aggregates the values of regional variables. The quality of these models is affected by shortages of regional data in many countries.

Ballard, K.P., Gustely, R.D. and Wendling, R. (1980) *NRIES: Structure, Performance and Applications of a Bottom-up Interregional Econometric Model*, Washington, DC: Bureau of Economic Analysis.

bought deal (310)
The purchase of a stock issue or a portfolio of investments by one or more financial institutions for resale in whole or part. Offloading parts of an acquired portfolio has become easier as there are now so many types of financial instrument. As these deals cut dealing costs, they provide a popular method for acquiring **investment trusts**.

Boulding, Kenneth Ewart, 1910– (030)
A polymath economist, born in the UK, who has made diverse contributions to many areas of US economics. He was educated at Oxford, Chicago and Harvard universities. His career, which began as an assistant lecturer at Edinburgh University, has been spent chiefly in American universities where he has been professor at Michigan from 1949 to 1977 and subsequently at Colorado. His long writing career began with an article in the *Economic Journal* in 1932 on displacement cost; subsequently he has written another 300 articles and more than twelve books. His major textbook, *Economic Analysis*, blends together **Keynesianism** and **neoclassical** economics. In 1950, in *A Reconstruction of Economics*, he urged a theoretical switch from **flows to stocks**, from incomes to assets, and from the prices of labour and capital to their national income shares. His close examination of equilibrium links price and ecological equilibria. His study of social organization contrasts the exchange system and its threat system of war with the integrative system of a **grants economy**.

Boulding, K.E. (1945) *Economics of Peace*, New York: Prentice Hall.
—— (1950) *A Reconstruction of Economics*, New York: Wiley.
—— (1966) *Economic Analysis*, 4th edn, New York: Wiley.
—— (1978) *Ecodynamics*, Beverly Hills, CA, and London: Sage.
—— (1981) *A Preface to Grant Economics: The Economy of Love and Fear*, New York: Praeger.
Kernan, C.E. (1974) *Creative Tension: The Life and Thought of Kenneth Boulding*, New York: Basic Books.

Boulwareism (830)
A substitute for **collective bargaining**, named after Lemuel Boulware, the vice-president for industrial relations at General Electric, which consisted of the company making a unilateral offer based on research into the union's demands. It was held by the US Supreme Court in 1969 that this was not US 'bargaining in good faith' as intended by the **Taft–Hartley Act**.

boundary constraint (210)

The limit to the value of a variable, e.g. 0 or positive.

See also: **Tobit model**.

bounded rationality (010)

A theory of decision-making which takes into account the capacities of the human mind and has become a central theme of behavioural economics. It asserts that the rational choice of a decision-maker is subject to cognitive limits as human beings lack knowledge and have only a limited ability to forecast the future.

Cyert, R.M. and March, J.G. (1975) *A Behavioral Theory of the Firm*, 2nd edn, Englewood Cliffs, NJ: Prentice Hall.

Simon, H.A. (1982) *Models of Bounded Rationality*, 2 vols, Cambridge, MA: MIT Press.

See also: **cognitive dissonance**; **economics and psychology**; **Simon**.

bourgeoisie (510)

The capitalist middle class created by the Industrial Revolution and regarded as a group of exploiters by **Marx**. The bourgeoisie was accused of wrongly appropriating **surplus value** from the product of the **proletariat**.

bourse (310)

Stock market of a European country. The term is derived from the Bruges commodity exchange founded in 1360 in front of the home of Chevalier van de Buerse.

Box–Jenkins (210)

A methodological approach to the study of time series which has improved short-term economic forecasting by following the method of identification of economic relationships and then estimation of them and diagnostic checking.

Box, G.E.P. and Jenkins, G.M. (1970) *Time Series Analysis: Forecasting and Control*, San Francisco, CA: Holden-Day.

BOY (540)

Beginning of the year, or of an accounting period.

boycott (820)

Stopping trade either by refusing to deal with a particular country or supplier or, as a form of **trade (labor) union** action, preventing a firm from distributing its goods as a means of forcing it to concede union demands. This form of protest, first used against Ireland's landlords in the nineteenth century, has been used against South Africa and in many trade disputes. However, industrial relations legislation has increasingly made it an illegal form of union action, as has **antitrust** law in the USA.

See also: **economic sanctions**.

bracket creep (320)

The movement of income tax payers into higher tax brackets as the inevitable consequence of the growth of money incomes with the income bands for each rate of income tax remaining the same. The results of this are higher marginal and average tax rates. The **Tax Reform Act 1986** (USA) attempted to eliminate this creep by indexing tax brackets and reducing the number of tax brackets.

See also: **indexation**; **Rooker–Wise Amendment**.

Bradbury (310)

British Treasury note of £1 or 10 shillings issued in the period from 1914 to 1928 after the withdrawal of gold coins in 1914. These were named after John Bradbury, Permanent Secretary to the Treasury, and were also known as Treasury notes or British currency notes. The Bank of England's dislike of small denomination notes necessitated issue by the Treasury. The smallest Bank of England note until 1928 was a £5 note; in that year, £1 and 10 shilling notes were included in the Bank of England issue.

See also: **banknote**.

Brady Commission (310)

US presidential commission which reported in 1988 on the Wall Street stock market crash of October 1987. Its principal recommendations were that one institution, preferably the **Federal Reserve System**, should have the task of coordinating financial regulation; that clearing systems should be unified as a means of reducing financial risk; that there should be better information, including the trade, time of trade and ultimate customer in each major market; that there should be a harmonization of rules on margins; and that 'circuit breakers' should be coordinated across markets.

See also: **circuit breaker mechanism**.

brain drain (840)

International migration of highly qualified persons, e.g. surgeons, physicians, scientists and engineers, from low income countries to more prosperous economies, especially the USA. Differences in salaries and research facilities, together with the over-supply of specialized graduates in less developed countries, has brought about this increase in the **human capital** stock of advanced countries.

See also: **immigration**; **migration**.

branch banking (310)

A system of banking which permits a banking institution to operate at many locations. This eighteenth-century Scottish invention was slow to be copied by other countries: the USA began to adopt it in 1933. The advantage of this type of banking is that it reduces the risk that a bank is too committed to the financial needs of a particular area. It has permitted the major British banks, especially Barclays and National Westminster, to grow to their present large sizes. The considerable growth of US branch banking in the second half of the twentieth century is a result of the liberalization of state banking laws, the growth of suburbs, the difficulty of reaching banks in congested city centres and the movement of industry to peripheral locations.

branch economy (070, 940)

A national or regional **economy** substantially controlled elsewhere because many of its businesses are foreign-owned subsidiaries. The Scottish economy and others that also have regional policy incentives that attract inward foreign investment are the principal examples of this type of economy.

branding (010, 530)

Product differentiation that establishes for a particular product an image gives it individuality. A producer hopes thereby to gain a measure of monopoly power through reducing the amount of substitution

between its products and those of its competitors.

See also: **monopolistic competition**.

brand loyalty (530)

A consumer's continued purchasing of the same differentiated good for a considerable period of time. As firms benefit from a stable regular demand, they will make it an objective of their advertising to achieve this goal. Brand loyalty lowers the elasticity of demand for a good and gives firms a measure of **monopoly power**.

See also: **monopolistic competition**.

Brandt Commission (430)

The Independent Commission on International Development chaired by Willy Brandt, previous Chancellor of West Germany, and subsequently chaired by Julius Nyerere after he retired from the office of President of Tanzania. Its first report, *North–South: a Programme for Survival* (1980) failed to produce any action; its second report *Common Crisis: North–South Cooperation for World Recovery* (1983) responded to the **Third World** debt problem by recommending the **amortization** of old debts.

breakeven analysis (210)

A graphical representation of the relation-

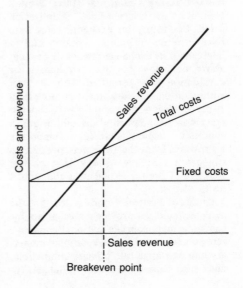

ship between total costs and total revenue with breakeven taking place where total cost is equal to total revenue (i.e. average cost is equal to average revenue).

breakeven level of income (010)
The level of income at which all income is consumed and no debts are incurred.

breakeven pricing (520)
A firm's policy of setting prices equal to average total costs with the consequence that neither **supernormal profits** nor losses are made. This was the original pricing policy laid down for British **nationalized industries**.

breakthrough (620)
A major technological change which can consist of a new method of production, a new product or a new market.

See also: **innovation**.

Bretton Woods Agreement (430)
An agreement signed in Bretton Woods, New Hampshire, USA, in 1944 which created the **International Monetary Fund** (IMF). It set rules for exchange rate behaviour and created a pool of **common currencies**, thereby making the IMF the world's 'lender of last resort'. The agreement which was achieved was a compromise between **Keynes**'s proposals for an **International Clearing Union** and Harry White's plan for an International Stabilization Fund. Par values for exchange rates were fixed in terms of gold. A country had to intervene if its exchange rate was 1 per cent above or below par but revaluation or devaluation was permitted without IMF authorization. An adjustment of more than 10 per cent was permitted if the IMF thought there was a fundamental disequilibrium (a condition vaguely defined). Temporary borrowings from the IMF were possible to support a currency. The gold exchange standard of Bretton Woods was abandoned on 15 August 1971.

Critics of Bretton Woods noted that the agreement did not provide a mechanism for changing inappropriate national exchange rate policies, failed to make national monetary and exchange rate policies compatible, and discouraged frequent changes in exchange rate parities. However, this international monetary regime was in force from 1944 to 1971. Its demise was hastened by the problems created in the US economy by the Vietnam War. In practice, it was a **dollar standard** as most countries fixed their currencies against the US dollar.

Dormael, A. van (1978) *Bretton Woods: Birth of a Monetary System*, London: Macmillan.

bridge financing (310)
See: **bridging**.

bridging (310)
Short-term lending in anticipation of more permanent finance becoming available. This is often done to effect a major purchase such as a house or to enable an adjustment in the investment portfolio of a person or an institution. This type of financing is often necessary as a purchaser is awaiting the proceeds from the sale of another asset.

Bridlington rules (830)
Trade union recruitment rules agreed by the British Trades Union Congress in 1939 at their Bridlington Conference to prevent trade unions competing with each other for potential members in the same occupational group.

BRITE (620)
Basic research in industrial technologies for Europe. A successful **European Community** series of transfrontier programmes linking industries and universities in projects to rejuvenate traditional industries. The success of BRITE 1 (1985–8) brought about BRITE 2 (1988–92).

British depository receipt (310)
A means of purchasing US treasury **bonds** in New York and settling in London which was introduced in 1984.

See also: **American depository receipt**.

British Institute of Dealers in Securities (310)
UK regulatory body of the securities industry. Its rulebook includes liquidity requirements for **market-makers**, the details which must be published before a company's shares may be traded and, in order to protect private investors, rules for dealing arrange-

ments and compensation funds. Larger dealers in over-the-counter trading are also included.

See also: **over-the-counter market**.

'British problem' (420)
The continuing problem in the **European Community** of meeting the demands of the British Government for lower contributions to Community budgets.

broad money (310)
M2 or **M3**.

brokered deposit (310)
A deposit obtained for a bank by stockbrokers in order to increase its liquidity. As such deposits are made where there is the highest yield, these deposits are highly volatile and consequently unreliable as liquid assets.

broker loan rate (310)
US money market rate, usually 1–1½ per cent below the US prime rate, charged on the debit balances of margin traders. It is often regarded as an indicator of future changes in the **prime rate of interest**.

Brookings Institution (010, 140)
An independent centre founded in 1927 in Washington, DC, for research into economics, government, foreign policy and other social sciences. It is famous for its forecasting model of the US economy and for its influential studies of major economies, including those of Japan and the UK. Taxation, international economics, growth and stabilization have been major research concerns.

Fromm, G. and Klein, I.R. (1975) *The Brookings Model: Perspectives and Recent Developments*, Amsterdam: North-Holland.

brown good (010, 630)
A consumer durable used for leisure purposes, e.g. a television set or a compact disc player.

Brundtland Report (110, 710, 720)
The 1987 report of the World Commission on Environment and Development. This 880-page report recommended that **Third World** development projects should take into account environmental issues such as the destruction of forests and overfarming which ruins agricultural land for a long time. In future, the **World Bank** will take into account the environmental implications of proposed development projects.

World Commission on Environment and Development (1987) *Our Common Future*, Oxford: Oxford University Press.

B share (310, 520)
An ordinary share of a British company with voting rights.

See also: **A share**.

bubble (010, 310)
1 An asset price which continues to rise to a high level until it collapses.

2 A speculative venture. Famous bubbles include the Dutch tulip mania of 1625–37 and the South Sea Bubble in England of 1720. Unless there is an infinite number of traders, a bubble is irrational in nature.

Blanchard, O.J. and Watson, M.W. (1982) 'Bubbles, rational expectations and financial markets', in P. Wachtel (ed.) *Crises in the Economic and Financial Structure*, Lexington, MA: Lexington Books.
Carswell, J. (1960) *The South Sea Bubble*, London: Cresset Press.
Kindleberger, C. (1978) *Manias, Panics and Crashes*, New York: Basic Books; London: Macmillan.

bubble policy (720)
A policy which allows emitters of pollutants to discharge more at one source if there is an equivalent reduction at other sources. An example would be a firm with two plants which can increase its emissions at A if it reduces them at B.

Buchanan, James McGill, 1919– (030)
US economist, educated at the universities of Tennessee and Chicago and professor of economics since 1956 at various universities of Virginia, who became University Distinguished Professor and General Director of the Centre for the Study of Public Choice, Virginia Polytechnic Institute, in 1969. He is famous for founding **public choice theory** which unites the theory of market exchange and the theory of the functioning of political

markets. Inspired by a year in Italy (1955), where he read nineteenth-century European classics of **public finance**, he developed the concept of a democratic government receiving taxes from consenting citizens in return for governmental services by establishing constitutional rules to maintain majority consensus. His wide-ranging critique of public sector economics relies on the notion that costs are basically subjective, and he departs from the doctrine of the marginal cost pricing of public utilities. His analysis of choice is extended to cover the behaviour of politicians, legislators and bureaucrats.

Although a leader of the school of public choice economics, he recognized the early contribution of **Wicksell** who discussed the distribution of the costs of proposed public expenditure. Having Frank **Knight** and Henry **Simons** as his mentors when he was a postgraduate student at Chicago, it is not surprising that his work has been loyal to the principles of capitalism and individualism. In 1986, he was awarded the **Nobel Prize for Economics** for his work on public choice theory.

Buchanan, J.M. (1966) *Public Finance in a Democratic Process: Fiscal Institutions and Individual Choice*, Chapel Hill, NC: University of North Carolina.
—— (1972) *Theory of Public Choice: Political Applications of Economics*, Ann Arbor, MI: University of Michigan Press.
Buchanan, J.M. and Tullock, G. (1962) *The Calculus of Consent*, Ann Arbor, MI: University of Michigan Press.
Reisman, D. (1990) *The Political Economy of James Buchanan*, Basingstoke: Macmillan.

bucket shop (310, 610)

An agency selling goods, services or securities at a discount. The main examples of these 'shops' are those selling the portion of share issues not immediately taken up by the public, and also travel agents offering at low prices air-tickets for scheduled services of airlines which are operating with a high proportion of unoccupied seats.

Buddhist economics (110)

Economic growth which takes into account spiritual development and does not squander **natural resources** so that all have a 'right livelihood'.

Buiter, W. (1989) *Principles of Budgetary and Financial Policy*, Hemel Hempstead: Harvester Wheatsheaf.
Schumacher, E.F. (1973) *Small is Beautiful: a Study of Economics as if People Mattered*, ch. 4, London: Blond & Briggs.

budgetary policy (320)

The principles underlying the revenue and expenditure accounts of a governmental or other organization. The accounts used in a budget will reflect the responsibilities of that organization and its relationships with others, e.g. a state budget will show its financial relationship with the federal government of that country. In those accounts will be stated the sources of revenue and objects of expenditure, a reflection of the taxing and other fund-raising carried out and the spending programmes chosen by that government or firm. It is usual to divide budgets into current and capital budgets. An overall budgetary policy can be summarized by whether it is balanced, in surplus or in deficit. Until **Keynesian** policy ideas influenced governments, government budget deficits were regarded as a sign of financial recklessness: now budget deficits are regarded as a fiscal policy option by most governments.

Report of the President's Commission on Budget Concepts, Washington, DC: US Government Printing Office, 1967.

See also: **fiscal policy**.

budget constraint (010)

A line showing the maximum amount of

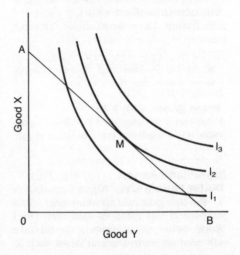

goods, in different combinations, which a consumer can obtain from his income. It is drawn in combination with **indifference curves** to indicate the maximum utility which can be obtained from a particular level of real income. In the figure, if AB is the budget line and I_1, I_2 and I_3 are indifference curves, then M is the combination of quantities of goods X and Y at which this consumer maximizes utility.

budget cutting (320)
Proposals to reduce planned public expenditure. In the USA, this has been a prominent feature of recent **supply-side economics** and has taken the form of attempts to reduce federal outlays for civil purposes. A major cut proposed has been in social transfer payments, on the grounds that such payments discourage the supply of labour.

budget incidence (320)
The total effect on a household of the taxation and expenditure policies of a government.

See also: **tax incidence**.

budget line (010)
A line used extensively in consumer analysis to express the total real income of a consumer. Its slope measures the relative prices of the goods in which income is expressed. As real income rises, this line moves away from the origin of a diagram with two axes.

Budget Resolution (320)
The statement passed by the US Senate and House of Representatives which details spending outlays and authorizes the future expenditure of moneys for specific purposes.

budget year (320)
The fiscal year chosen by national finance ministries and treasuries. In the UK the year runs from 5 April to 4 April of the next year; in the USA it runs from 1 October to 30 September of the following year.

buffer stock (420, 710)
1 An accumulation of a commodity for the purpose of stabilizing its world price. The stock built up provides a method of intervention, particularly in the markets for

metals, oil and agricultural produce. Buffer stock managers buy in the commodity in times of falling prices and sell when prices are rising. But there are limits to the amount of stabilization possible by the use of buffer stocks – for example, the major price fall of tin in 1985 was so cataclysmic that the managers were unable to prevent it. Governments have financed many of these stocks to maintain the incomes and employment of primary producers.

2 Money in the sense that a cash balance can absorb unexpected variations in expenditure and income.

Laidler, D. (1984) 'The buffer stock notion in monetary economics', *Economic Journal* (*Supplement*) 94 : 17–34.

building and loan association (310)
US cooperative association whose stockholders offer mortgage loans for the purchase or building of houses.

See also: **building society; savings and loan association**.

Building Societies Act 1986 (310)
UK statute which liberalized the operating rules for British building societies and brought them more into line with other financial institutions. The societies can now lend to individuals who are not their members, hold and develop land as a commercial asset and invest in corporate bodies, including companies. They can diversify into banking, insurance, investment, trusteeship and executorship, and land management services. Liquid assets are not allowed to be more than a third of a society's assets. Instead of being required to keep 90 per cent of their loans secured by property, building societies are permitted to reduce that proportion to 75 per cent by 1992, enabling them to diversify their investments. A new Building Societies Commission regulates the building societies.

Building Societies Association (310, 930)
UK association of building societies which jointly represents their interests. It was once a powerful **cartel** when it fixed common mortgage interest rates.

building society (310)

A British financial institution primarily concerned with raising, through members' deposits, a stock or fund for making advances to them secured on land and buildings for residential use, according to the Building Societies Act 1986. As they stand between those who save and those who ultimately borrow money, they act as financial intermediaries. All of them were founded as local non-profit-making institutions, the earliest dating from the 1840s. Through mergers some societies, especially the Halifax, have acquired a power rivalling that of the major banks and, like the latter, offering a wide range of financial services. In 1900, there were 2,286 building societies; in 1990, 105. A further decline in their numbers is expected through mergers between building societies or between building societies and banks or insurance companies. The Building Societies Act 1986 has freed them from many restrictions, changing their character from organizations with social aims to competitive firms with a commercial orientation.

See also: **thrift**.

built-in stabilizer (320)

See: **automatic stabilizer**.

bulge-bracket firm (310)

A top investment bank of the USA, one of the leading oligopolists of the US securities industry. The separation of commercial from investment banking under the **Glass–Steagall Act** protects their privileged position.

bull (310, 430)

A speculator who, expecting prices of shares, commodities or currencies to rise, will buy now and sell after prices have risen, thereby making a capital gain. The opposite is a **bear**.

bulldog issue (310)

A long-term sterling bond issue, mostly purchased by UK **institutional investors**.

bullion (310)

Gold or silver ingots or bars used as bank reserves and as private stores of wealth.

See also: **gold bullion standard**.

Bullionist controversy (030)

A major debate in classical monetary theory from 1797 to 1825 wnich was occasioned by the suspension of cash payments, i.e. the inconvertibility of the pound sterling during the Napoleonic Wars. The Bullionists, named after the supporters of the Bullion Committee's report of 1810 to the House of Commons, included **Ricardo**: they recommended that as soon as it was possible to do so, convertibility should be restored. During the period of suspension, the Bank of England was accused of over-issuing banknotes and creating much of the wartime inflation. However, Henry **Thornton**, a commercial banker, in his brilliant *Paper Credit*, took a broader view of money and the banking system.

See also: **Currency School**.

Bullock Committee (830)

UK governmental committee which reported in 1977 on workers' participation in the management of companies. The committee, headed by the historian Lord Bullock and consisting of trade unionists, employers and industrial relations experts, was asked to assume that there is a need for a radical expansion of industrial democracy through trade union representation. The majority, consisting of the trade unionists and academic experts, recommended that for UK companies with more than 2,000 employees there should be a reconstitution of their boards of directors according to a '$2x + y$' principle of equal numbers of employee and shareholder representatives ($2x$) and co-opted directors (y). This was intended to be an extension of **collective bargaining** into the boardroom. The minority report recommended two-tier (supervisory and executive) boards following the European example of West Germany. Neither the majority nor minority recommendations were embodied in legislation.

Committee of Inquiry on Industrial Democracy (1977) *Report*, London: HMSO, Cmnd 6706.

bunch map (210)

A set of lines from the origin of a graph with

each line measuring a coefficient between two variables. These maps have been used to check for the presence of **multicollinearities** in the data used.

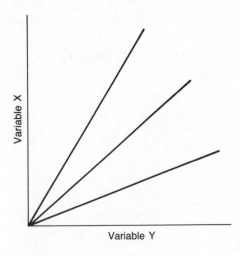

Variable Y

Bundesbank (310)

Germany's **central bank** which replaced the Reichsbank in 1957. It has the central aim of safeguarding the value of the currency by regulating the quantities of money in circulation and of credit in the economy. Although expected to support the government's general economic policy, it is independent of instructions from the government. The Bank's president chairs fortnightly meetings of the Bank Council on which bank directors and presidents from the Federal States sit; the council fixes interest rates and credit policy. Also, the Bundesbank decides on the size of the note issue, is custodian of the nation's gold and foreign currency reserves and is in charge of official dealings in foreign exchange markets. The Bundesbank's contribution to low German inflation in the past has been praised but critics have accused the Bank of setting money market interest rates which were too high on several occasions, risking recession in the economy.

bundled deal (010)

See: **interlinked transaction**.

bundling (530)

The sale of two or more goods or services in a package deal. The seller benefits from reacting to consumers who differ in their willingness to buy.

Adams, W.J. and Yellen, J.L. (1976) 'Commodity bundling and the burden of monopoly', *Quarterly Journal of Economics* 90: 475–98.

See also: **mixed bundling; pure bundling**.

buoyant tax (320)

A tax with a rising yield because the **tax base**, e.g. income or property values, keeps increasing in value.

Bureau of Economic Analysis (220)

The branch of the US Department of Commerce responsible for assembling and publishing US national income accounts.

See also: **National Income and Product Accounts**.

Bureau of the Budget (320)

A US Federal Bureau created within the US Treasury by the Accounting Act 1921 to provide operational control over expenditure programmes. In 1939 it was transferred to the President's Office, at which time it changed its function increasingly to ensuring managerial efficiency.

See also: **Office of Management and Budget**.

Burns, Arthur Frank, 1904–87 (030)

An Austro-Hungarian who emigrated to the USA in 1914. He was educated at Columbia University where he was professor from 1944 to 1965. The most distinguished periods of his life were when he was engaged in business cycle research at the National Bureau of Economic Research, Washington, DC, from 1930 to 1944 and his periods of public service as Chairman of the Board of Governors of the US Federal Reserve System, from 1970 to 1978 (where he was noted for his conservative monetary beliefs), and as US Ambassador to West Germany (1981–5), in which office he negotiated the German Treaty in 1982 to provide more German logistic support for US troops. He spent his closing years writing at the American Enterprise Institute. His leading work on business cycle theory

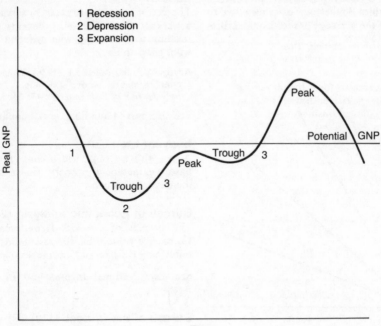

1 Recession
2 Depression
3 Expansion

Time

(written jointly with Wesley Mitchell) drew up a selection of economic indicators which became the basis of business cycle forecasting in the USA after 1945. He calculated 'reference cycles' as the single indicator of turning points of cycles. In addition, he was famous for his fervent criticisms of Keynesian policy recommendations.

Burns, A.F. (1946) *Economic Research and the Keynesian Thinking of Our Times*, Washington, DC: National Bureau of Economic Research.
—— (1954) *Frontiers of Economic Knowledge*, Princeton, NJ: Princeton University Press.
—— (1969) *The Business Cycles in a Changing World*, New York: National Bureau of Economic Research.
Burns, A.F. and Mitchell, W.C. (1946) *Measuring Business Cycles*, Washington, DC: National Bureau of Economic Research.
Mullineux, A. (1990) *Business Cycles and Financial Crises*, Hemel Hempstead: Harvester Wheatsheaf.

business cycle (140)

'A type of fluctuation found in the aggregate economic activity of nations that organize their work mainly in business enterprises: a cycle consists of expansions occurring at about the same time in many economic activities, followed by similarly general recessions, contractions, and revivals which merge into the expansion phase of the next cycle; this sequence of changes is recurrent but not periodic; in duration business cycles vary from more than one year to ten or twelve years' (Mitchell).

Previously these were known as periodic 'commercial crises'. The **National Bureau of Economic Research** has studied these cycles since 1920. **Haberler** in an extensive survey of business cycle research noted the variety of suggested causes of the cycles, including credit changes, over-investment, costs of production, under-consumption, mass psychology, variations in harvests, the interaction of the **multiplier** and the accelerator and international influences. More recently, the cycle of elections in democratic countries has been associated with fluctuations in national economies. (See figure above.)

Bowers, D.A. (1985) *An Introduction to Business Cycles and Forecasting*, Reading, MA, and Wokingham: Addison Wesley.
Burns, A.F. and Mitchell, W.C. (1946) *Measuring Business Cycles*, New York: National Bureau of Economic Research.

Haberler, G. (1958) *Prosperity and Depression. A Theoretical Analysis of Cyclical Movements*, 3rd edn, London: Allen & Unwin.

Mitchell, W.C. (1927) *Business Cycles: The Problem and its Setting*, New York: National Bureau of Economic Research; London: Pitman.

See also: **accelerator principle**; **Juglar cycle**; **Kitchin cycle**; **Kondratieff cycle**; **Kuznets cycle**; **political business cycle**.

Business Expansion Scheme (310, 520)

UK investment scheme introduced in 1981 to encourage small businesses, especially by giving them access to the finance provided by the **Unlisted Securities Market**. Tax incentives are available to investors in these businesses.

business organization (510)

A particular legal arrangement for owning a **firm**. The principal forms are sole traders, partnerships and companies/corporations. They are distinguished from each other by the degree of liability for the firm's debts on the part of the owners and by the number of individuals who share in the ownership. There is limited liability for the shareholders of companies and corporations but unlimited liability for sole traders and the members of partnerships.

business studies (510)

The multidisciplinary analysis of the problems of business, using economic, accounting, psychological, legal and statistical methods. The distinctive discipline developed within the ambit of the subject has been organization theory. It became a subject as a consequence of the establishment of business schools, especially the Wharton School of Finance and Commerce in Philadelphia in 1881 and the Henley Administrative Staff College (UK) in 1947. The growth of business schools, which are the chief practitioners of business studies, in the twentieth century has reduced many managerial inefficiencies, which used to be regarded as the principal cause of **diseconomies of scale**.

Butskellism (310, 320)

The similar economic policies pursued by Hugh Gaitskell and R. A. Butler as British Chancellors of the Exchequer in the early 1950s. The techniques of demand management that they employed were based on a mixture of planning and market freedom.

See also: **mixed economy**.

butterfly effect (210, 310, 430)

The large differences in the values of dependent economic variables which result from minuscule differences in inputted economic variables. The effect has been noted in foreign exchange markets. As a consequence of it, policymakers can never be sure of the effects of their decisions.

See also: **chaos theory**.

buyers' market (530)

A market in which buyers have the dominant influence on price because of excess supply. Contrast with **sellers' market**.

C

C (010, 310)

1 Total consumer expenditure of a national economy. This is shown as a function of national income in the **consumption function**.

2 The lowest quality of security, according to Standard & Poor, as such securities have no interest paid on them.

See also: **AAA**; **BB**; **BBB**; **D**; **DDD**.

C-20 (430)
See: **Committee of Twenty**.

CA (210, 540)
1 **Confluence analysis**.

2 Chartered accountant (UK).

cable (430)
A foreign exchange trading term for transactions between the dollar and sterling.

cabotage (630)
1 Coastal and commercial navigation between ports.

2 Permission for an air carrier of a foreign country to pick up passengers or freight in another country for transport to a third country.

CAC (830)
The price index of the leading shares traded on the Paris bourse.

See also: **Central Arbitration Committee**.

cadastral survey (320, 710)
A survey, usually undertaken for taxation purposes, of the ownership, extent and value of land.

Cairn's Group (710)
The group of major agricultural exporting countries founded in 1986 and based in Australia. It consists of Argentina, Australia, Brazil, Canada, Chile, Colombia, Fiji, Hungary, Indonesia, Malaysia, New Zealand, the Philippines, Thailand and Uruguay. Its aims are to liberalize trade in agricultural products, especially by reductions in agricultural export subsidies and barriers to consumer markets, entailing changes in national agricultural policies. The Group also acts as the representative of these countries in **General Agreement on Tariffs and Trade** talks.

call (310)
An order to pay a further instalment of cash for the purchase of shares.

call money (310)
Money lent within the City of London by **clearing banks** to **discount houses** for short periods, sometimes only overnight, and immediately payable on demand. After cash and deposits with the Bank of England, this is the most liquid asset of the UK clearing banks as they can recall it at any time.

call option (310)
The right to buy a stock exchange security at the current price within a specified period, normally three months.

Cambridge Circus (030)
Several young economists who debated with **Keynes** in the early 1930s the development of his ideas in *A Treatise of Money* (1930) into the theories central to *The General Theory of Employment, Interest and Money*. The group included Joan **Robinson**, Roy **Harrod**, Richard **Kahn**, James **Meade** and Piero **Sraffa**.

Keynes, J.M. (1985) *Collected Works*, vols XIII and XXIX, London: Macmillan.

Cambridge controversies (020)
Disputes between economists in Cambridge, England (Joan **Robinson** and **Kaldor**), and Cambridge, MA (**Solow** and **Samuelson**), about the nature of **capital**. In particular, the English contestants have attacked the

neoclassical assumptions of their trans-atlantic opponents by questioning the existence of the aggregate **production function**. Also, they debated the theory of profits and capital, the determination of savings and the interest rate, aggregate capital and the reswitching of techniques.

Blaug, M. (1975) *The Cambridge Revolution. Success or Failure?*, rev. edn, London: Institute of Economic Affairs.
Harcourt, G.H.C. (1972) *Some Cambridge Controversies in the Theory of Capital*, Cambridge: Cambridge University Press.

Cambridge Economic Policy Group (030)

A group of Cambridge economists led by Wynne Godley who recommended an expansionary fiscal policy and import controls in order to alleviate British unemployment after 1974. They opposed the use of demand management and incomes policies as central instruments for determining the level of aggregate demand.

See also: **new Cambridge economics**.

Cambridge School (030)

Successive generations of economists at Cambridge University, particularly after the establishment of the separate Economics Tripos in 1903. The School was founded by **Marshall** and was made famous in the 1930s by **Keynes**, its intellectual leader. In the post-war period its prominent leaders have included **Kaldor**, Joan **Robinson**, **Sraffa** and Wynne Godley. A succession of ideas has occupied the School in the post-war period: in the 1950s, the refinement of Keynesian ideas; in the 1960s, 'the **Cambridge controversies**' about **capital**; and, more recently, an examination of the nature of markets to show that **market clearing** is so poor that **disequilibrium** is a major economic problem.

See also: **new Cambridge economics**.

Canal Age (040)

The period 1757–1830 in Britain when a network of 4,250 miles of navigable rivers and canals was created to transport agricultural produce and the manufactures of the Industrial Revolution. Railways superseded canals as the major transport system.

canons of taxation (320)

Adam Smith's criteria for taxes – equality (based on a person's ability to pay), certainty (the time for payment, manner of payment and quantity to be paid should be clear), convenience (payable at the time the taxpayer is in receipt of income) and economy in collection.

Smith, A. (1776) *The Wealth of Nations*, ed. by R.H. Campbell and A.S. Skinner, Book V, ch. II, pt II, Oxford: Clarendon Press, 1976.

Cantillon, Richard, c.1680–c.1734 (030)

Irish-born banker and economist who spent much of his life in France where he made a large personal fortune after the collapse of John Law's Mississippi Company. His writings on economics, other than the *Essai sur la Nature du Commerce en Général*, appear to have perished with him when his house in Albemarle Street, London, was burnt down. His remarkable *Essai* showed his keen reading of several economists, including **Petty**, and his immense practical knowledge of banking. In many senses he anticipated **Quesnay** and other **Physiocrats** by setting out a model of the economy with villages, market towns and cities engaged in mutual exchanges. Also, he powerfully explained the role of the **entrepreneur** in economic activity, with a more plausible explanation than Smith's **invisible hand** postulate. His analysis of exchange rates, open market operations and the **bank** credit multiplier gives his work a modern focus.

Cantillon, R. (1755) *Essai sur la Nature du Commerce en Général*, English translation by H. Higgs, London: Macmillan for the Royal Economic Society, 1931.
Murphy, A.E. (1986) *Richard Cantillon, Entrepreneur and Economist*, Oxford: Clarendon Press.

Cantillon effect (320)

The differential impact of an increase in the money supply brought about because different recipients of extra cash have different uses for the cash, thus affecting relative demand for goods and services and their relative prices.

cap (310)

The maximum interest rate paid on a floating rate security by its issuer. The seller gives funds to cover interest payments over a specified rate.

See also: **collar; floor**.

CAP (420, 710)
See: **Common Agricultural Policy**.

capacity (640)
1 The maximum output that a firm or an economy can produce from its existing supply of factors of production. Thus, to increase its capacity, a firm must enlarge its labour force or its capital stock.

2 The maximum amount of money which a financial institution can lend.

See also: **capital utilization**.

capacity charge (610, 640)
A component of the price of the goods or services of **public enterprises** which is expected to cover the costs of fixed capital.

capacity ratio (540)
See: **volume ratio**.

capacity utilization (640)
The ratio of the actual output of a firm, industry or national economy to its maximum output at a point in time. This ratio will fluctuate cyclically and a high degree of utilization will be a signal for more **net investment**.

See also: **accelerator principle; trade cycle**.

capital (010)
1 Durable goods capable of producing a stream of goods or services over a period of time.

2 A factor of production distinct from land, the entrepreneur and labour currently being used.

3 A sum of money which is invested in a business enterprise.

4 Accumulated expenditures giving rise to higher subsequent incomes, as in **human capital**.

5 Wealth.

6 Stored-up labour; exchange value which is becoming wealth, according to **Marx**.

See also: **Cambridge controversies; capital theory**.

capital account (430)
One of the **balance of payments** accounts which records the sales and purchases of financial assets of a particular country. The rates of interest in force throughout the world will have a major influence on a country's capital account, as capital mobility is stimulated by differences in the rates of return to financial assets throughout the world.

capital accumulation (110, 520)
Increasing the capital stock by undertaking investment in excess of what is necessary as **replacement investment**. This accumulation has been viewed alternately as the expansion of the productive potential of the economy and that adjustment of the amount of capital to the equilibrium level which will bring about an optimal allocation of scarce resources. Adam **Smith** attributed this investment to a person's desire for betterment; **Marx** to the innate greed of capitalists. Today, the principal motivation is to achieve a desired rate of economic growth.

capital asset pricing model (310)
A model which demonstrates that the reward for holding a risky security which is part of a well-diversified portfolio is based on its **beta** risk. It is assumed that the securities market is in a state of frictionless **perfect competition**, that investors invest for the same length of time and have identical expectations concerning the probable returns from securities invested then and that investors can borrow or lend unlimited amounts of money at a risk-free rate of interest. The publication of **beta** statistics for many shares has often enabled investors to increase the overall return to their portfolios. Criticisms of the model are directed chiefly at its assumptions.

Levy, H. and Sarnat, M. (eds) (1977) *Financial Decision Making under Uncertainty*, New York: Academic Press.

Merton, R.C. (1973) 'An intertemporal capital asset pricing model', *Econometrica* 41: 867–87.

capital-augmenting technical progress (620)
Technical progress which increases output

even though the rate of investment remains the same, as measured in machine hours.

capital budgeting (540)
Appraising the financial implications of investment plans using techniques such as calculating **discounted cash flow, net present value** and **rates of return**. As major investments are risky and irreversible, capital budgeting is a crucial managerial activity of firms.

capital consumption (220, 520)
Depreciation. Since fixed assets have only a limited life-span, it is necessary to add to the annual costs of an enterprise or a national economy an estimate of the amount notionally spent on the wear and tear of such assets. Capital consumption is deducted from the gross national product to obtain the net national product, or **national income**.

capital deepening (110)
Investment which results in an increase in a **capital–labour ratio**, because the capital stock grows at a faster rate than the labour force.

See also: **capital widening**.

capital flight (430)
A capital outflow from a particular country. It can be broadly defined as all purchases of foreign assets (other than to increase official reserves), together with the errors and omissions item of a **balance of payments**; narrowly, it can be regarded as short-term capital outflows ('hot money') plus errors and omissions. A refined measure would be to limit the 'flight' to the proportion of a country's foreign assets which does not yield investment income.

capital gains tax (320)
A tax based on the increase in capital value of an asset between its purchase and its sale. This tax discourages investors from adjusting their portfolios and reduces business for stockbrokers.The country with the highest rate of tax is Australia (50.25 per cent) followed by the UK and the USA.

capital income tax (320)
A tax levied on the returns from investments or capital. Often such a tax is levied at a higher rate than taxes on employment incomes.

capital intensive (010, 610)
A form of production which uses much physical capital per unit of labour input. The degree of factor intensity is usually measured by the slope of an **isoquant**.

See also: **capital deepening; labour intensive**.

capitalism (050)
1 A socioeconomic system of production using **roundabout methods of production**.

2 An **economy** based on private enterprise.

3 The use of markets and not planning to allocate economic resources.

4 Production motivated by the profit motive.

The **Physiocrats** and classical economists such as **Smith** regarded capitalism as the natural form of economic organization based upon man's propensity to truck and barter and likely to be the most successful in increasing economic welfare. **Marx** criticized many definitions of capitalism for being timeless, ignoring the different historical forms it takes, and for the institution of private property, which prevents the reconciliation of individual and general interests, causing the alienation of workers. Marxists have classified capitalism into different stages, namely agricultural capitalism, merchant capitalism, industrial capitalism and state capitalism.

See also: **creative destruction; fundamental contradiction of capitalism; industrial capitalism; late capitalism; lemonade-stand capitalism; merchant capitalism; monopoly capitalism; peripheral capitalism; personal capitalism; popular capitalism; socialism; state capitalism; state monopoly capitalism**.

Dobb, M. (1946) *Studies in the Development of Capitalism*, London: Routledge.

Graham, D. and Clarke, P. (1986) *The New Enlightenment: The New Birth of Liberalism*, London: Macmillan.

Hirschman, A.O. (1982) 'Rival interpretations of market society: civilizing, destructive, or feeble?', *Journal of Economic Literature* 20 (December): 1463–84.

Tribe, K. (1981) *Genealogies of Capitalism*, London: Macmillan.

Wallerstein, I. (1979) *The Capitalist World-Economy*, Cambridge: Cambridge University Press.

capitalist class (070)
See: **bourgeoisie**.

capitalist imperialism (070, 610)
The exercise of power by major capitalist countries over less developed countries, often through the medium of **multinational corporations**. It is argued by Marxists and others that the declining rate of profit on home production forced capitalists to expand overseas.

Owen, R. and Sutcliffe, B. (eds) (1972) *Studies in the Theory of Imperialism*, London: Longman.

capitalization (310)
The conversion of an interest payment or a liquid asset into permanent capital. A company can capitalize its cash reserves by the issue of shares (a free, **bonus** or **scrip issue**). A debtor, even a nation, can capitalize interest payments by adding them to the original sum borrowed.

See also: **securitization**.

capitalization effect of a tax (320)
The reduced value of an asset resulting from the imposition of a tax on the income from the asset, e.g. a tax on the imputed income from owner-occupied housing depresses the value of houses.

capital–labour ratio (010)
The amount of physical capital employed by each worker which is usually measured by dividing the value of the capital stock by the size of the labour force. These ratios are frequently referred to in the theories of growth and of **comparative advantage**.

See also: **capital deepening**; **capital intensive**; **capital widening**.

capital market (310)
A market for raising long-term capital for industry by the issue of securities.

See also: **primary market**; **secondary market**.

capital–output ratio (010, 620)
The amount of capital divided by the amount of output produced by it. This is used as a measure of capital intensity and is central to an understanding of the **accelerator principle**.

capital reswitching (010)
A return to more **capital-intensive** methods of production because a technique has become more profitable through an increase in the marginal product of capital or a fall in the rate of interest.

See also: **Cambridge controversies**.

capital tax (320)
A tax based on the value of assets. Such taxes, which are very costly to collect because of valuation problems, rarely constitute a large proportion of a country's total tax revenue but are imposed for distributional reasons, i.e. to increase the relative tax burden of the rich. In practice, governments often reduce the effective rate of capital taxes by a variety of allowances, e.g. to allow for depreciation, life insurance and pensions.

See also: **wealth tax**.

capital theory (020)
A theory which links the theories of production, growth, value and distribution to explain why capital produces a return which keeps capital intact but yields interest (or profit) which is permanent. Over the past 200 years the notion of capital has varied greatly – to many of the **classical economists** it was to a large extent the raw materials and the **wages fund**; then it was viewed as a physical **intermediate good**. To **Marx** capital was a social mode of production; to the **Austrian School** time was crucial to the concept; to **Fisher** capital was a stock which produced a stream of income with its value determined by relative preference for future rather than present goods. There has been much debate about the relationship between the **rate of interest** and the value of capital, as well as discussion of the notion of aggregate capital. As there are many important subspecies of capital, including **human capital** and **equity** capital, specialist theories of capital are also propounded. The theory expanded its concerns in the 1960s within the context of growth theory discussions of capital accumulation. A major issue discussed then was the method of measuring

aggregate or social capital to achieve a value independent of distribution and prices. Joan **Robinson** suggested using labour time as a measure; Champernowne introduced a **chain index method**.

Harcourt, H.G. (1972) *Some Cambridge Controversies in the Theory of Capital*, Cambridge: Cambridge University Press.

Kregel, J.A. (1976) *Theory of Capital*, London: Macmillan.

See also: **Cambridge controversies**.

capital transfer tax (320)
UK tax introduced in 1975 on transfers of wealth payable by the donor or recipient during life or at death. This tax replaced estate duty which was in force from 1894 to 1975.

capital utilization (640)
The extent to which the fixed capital, i.e. buildings and machinery, of a firm is used. Thus, if machinery is worked for only half of a time period, the capital utilization rate will be 50 per cent. It is also measured as output as a percentage of output at a reference date.

See also: **capacity utilization**.

capital value (540)
A valuation of an asset broadly measured either by discounting the future income expected from the asset or by capitalizing the expected income.

See also: **discounting; net present value**.

capital widening (110)
An increase in the real capital stock which does not change the **capital–labour ratio** as the capital stock and the labour force grow at the same rate.

See also: **capital deepening**.

capitation tax (320)
See: **poll tax**.

CAPM (310)
See: **capital asset pricing model**.

capping an interest rate (310)
Separating the part of interest payments in excess of real interest payments and then capitalizing it by adding it to the long-term debt.

capture theory (010, 610)
See: **regulatory capture**.

CAR (310)
Compounded annual rate (of interest, gross or net of tax).

carbon tax (320, 720)
A tax related to the carbon content of coal, natural gas or oil, which is imposed to improve environmental conditions. The tax can take the form of a fixed amount per ton of carbon embodied in each fuel or be an *ad valorem* tax. The level of the tax is related to the emission reduction target chosen.

See also: **effluent fee; environmental tax; marketable discharge permit**.

cardinal utility (010)
The satisfaction obtained from consumption, or engaging in an economic activity, which is directly measurable in monetary or other units. The cardinalist argues that it is possible to compare, e.g. in **utils**, the relative amount of satisfaction from consuming different quantities of the same or other goods. Thus, the law of **diminishing marginal utility** could be described as follows: a woman obtains 10 utils from the first glass of champagne, 8 utils from the second, 6 utils from the third etc. Proxy measures of utility, e.g. the amount of money which a person is prepared to give up to obtain x amount of a good, have all met with objections for being too indirect.

Majumdar, T. (1961) *The Measurement of Utility*, London and New York: Macmillan.

See also: **ordinal utility; revealed preferences; utility**.

Caribbean Basin Initiative (420)
An arrangement agreed in 1984 to give exports of countries of the Caribbean region tariff-free access to the USA.

Caribbean Community (420)
Founded in 1973 as a common market with agricultural and industrial integration in succession to the Caribbean Free Trade Area. The members are Antigua, Barbados, Belize, Dominica, Grenada, Guyana, Jamaica, Montserrat, St Kitts-Nevis, Anguilla,

St Lucia, St Vincent, Trinidad and Tobago.

Caribbean Development Bank (310)
Development bank founded in 1970 consisting of seventeen member countries from the Caribbean region with Canada and the UK.

CARICOM (420)
See: **Caribbean Community**.

CARIFTA (420)
Caribbean Free Trade Area, founded in 1968 and replaced in 1973 by the **Caribbean Community**.

caring society (910)
See: **altruism; welfare state**.

carry-back, carry-forward system (320)
A tax system which permits businesses to carry net operating losses back or forward against past or future gains in income or capital appreciation.

carrying capacity (640, 840)
The ability of a particular area to sustain a population at a specified level of **subsistence**, usually specified as the number of persons per unit of land.

cartalist (310)
Someone who believes that the value of a currency depends on the power of the issuing authority and not on its intrinsic value or its convertibility into gold.

See also: **Banking School; fiat money; metallist**.

carte à mémoire (310)
French for **smart card**.

cartel (610)
An association of producers who agree to fix common prices and output quotas in an oligopolistic market. As the aim of a cartel is to prevent competition, there is a tendency for the producers to strive to maintain existing market shares, with the consequence that a firm can only increase its output if market demand rises. The device of a cartel has long been used as a method of restricting competition: Adam **Smith** acknowledged the existence of cartels in the eighteenth century – 'People of the same trade seldom meet together, even for merriment and diversion, but the conversation ends in a conspiracy against the public or in some contrivance to raise prices.' Firms afraid of the effects of recession are eager to join such associations, e.g. in the 1880s in the US economy and in Germany in the interwar period. Increasingly tough legislation in the USA and Western Europe has outlawed many cartels. The **Organization of Petroleum Exporting Countries** has some of the characteristics of a cartel.

cash (310)
The most **liquid** of **assets**, consisting of coin and banknotes; often defined as a zero-interest asset, although Goodhart and others have suggested that interest could be paid by running a national lottery on the serial numbers of the notes. Government banks also regard deposits at the 'central' bank as cash.

Goodhart, C.A.E. (1986) 'How can non-interest bearing assets co-exist with safe interest-bearing assets?', *British Review of Economic Issues* 8: 1–12.

cash budgeting (540)
Predicting the cash flows of a business.

See also: **cash flow; cash flow accounting**.

cash crop (710)
Agricultural produce marketed for cash, rather than retained for the use of the farmer's household.

See also: **agricultural household**.

cash–deposits ratio (310)
The ratio of a bank's holdings of **cash** to its total deposits, sometimes used as a measure of control over the banking system to guarantee its liquidity. In the past few decades, **liquid asset** ratios have been preferred as a method of controlling the total volume of bank deposits.

cash dispenser (310)
A machine provided by a bank or other deposit-taking institution, often at its premises, to dispense cash through the insertion of a card to account-holders of that bank or a bank in association with it. Usage of dispensers varies from country to coun-

try. In Britain and France they are particularly popular: by 1985, there were 6,886 in Britain and 7,172 in France but only 2,000 in West Germany. There is likely to be a single European system in the 1990s.

See also: **automated teller machine**; **debit card**; **smart card**.

cash economy (010, 310)
Part of a national economy which uses cash to make all payments. This may occur either because of a shortage of banking facilities or because of a desire to evade tax. In modern economies, much of the **black** or **informal economy** is of this nature.

cash flow (520)
1 The net amount of money received by a firm over a given period.

2 Retained profits and funds set aside for depreciation. This flow permits a firm to finance its own investment.

cash flow accounting (540)
Accounting based on transactions which are recorded when payment is actually made. Contrast with **accrual accounting**.

cashless society (310)
A modern economy which uses **credit cards** and direct debiting of bank accounts to make payments, instead of notes and coins.

See also: **debit card**.

cash limit (320)
A method of controlling government spending in the UK which replaced a constant-prices system. From 1974 to 1976, cash limits were used for several public sector building programmes and from 1976 for about 60 per cent of central government expenditures. Originally, the government calculated the real value of current programmes and then added an amount to compensate for some or all of inflationary increases. From 1981, the system was simplified by expressing public expenditure targets entirely in cash terms.

cash management account (310)
A bank deposit of US commercial banks which is a **checking account** that pays a return linked to investments. Originally designed by Merrill Lynch (with the processing done by Bank One, Columbus, Ohio) in 1977 to evade the strictures of **Regulation Q**.

See also: **NOW account**.

cash price–earnings ratio (310)
A modified version of a **price–earnings ratio**, with earnings measured as post-tax earnings + non-cash provisions (e.g. depreciation). This ratio removes some of the effects of conservative accounting, making international comparisons more meaningful. But as depreciation reflects the capital intensity of an industry, the cash price–earnings ratio will undervalue service industry shares.

cash ratio (310)
See: **cash–deposits ratio**.

cash transfer (320, 910)
A unilateral payment by a government to a person or a firm. Many welfare benefits are of this kind.

Cassel, Karl Gustav, 1866–1945 (030)
After studying mathematics at Uppsala University, Sweden, he became professor of economics at Stockholm University in 1902. He was a founder of modern Swedish economics, especially noted for his *Theory of Social Economy* (originally published 1918) and his monetary writings. He rejected both labour and **marginal utility** theories of value in favour of price theory which he also applied to his study of the **rate of interest**. He relied on the **quantity theory of money** in his monetary economics and was anti-Keynesian. His pupils included **Ohlin** and **Myrdal**.

Mitchell, W.C. (1969) *Types of Economic Theory*, vol. 2, ch. 16, New York: A.M. Kelley.

casualization (810)
The process of changing employment from regular and permanent to occasional and part-time forms. This is done to increase the flexibility of a labour force.

catallactics (010)
The study of all market phenomena, i.e. of actions conducted on the basis of monetary calculation.

von Mises, L. (1949) *Human Action*, 3rd edn, New Haven, CT: Yale University Press.

catalytic policy mix (310, 320)
A mixture of major and subsidiary policies: the latter are used as a catalyst to avert the undesired effects of a major policy.

catastrophe theory (210)
The applied mathematical study of discontinuities which states how many stable equilibria exist given a choice of control variables but does not indicate which of them will be in a particular system. A 'catastrophe' occurs when transition from one equilibrium to another produces instability in the system.

Poston, T. and Stewart, I. (1978) *Catastrophe Theory and its Applications*, London and San Francisco, CA: Pitman.

Saunders, P.T. (1980) *An Introduction to Catastrophe Theory*, Cambridge: Cambridge University Press.

catching-up hypothesis (050)
1 The idea that in the post-1945 period the countries which had lost a great deal of their capital stock in the Second World War and had to renew it experienced higher growth and productivity through having modern plant and machinery.

2 More generally, the raising of the national income of any low productivity country. Thus, gross investment (including replacement investment) has been regarded as a more important determinant of economic growth than net investment.

Abramovitz, M. (1986) 'Catching up, forging ahead, and falling behind', *Journal of Economic History* 46: 385–406.

categorical grant (320)
A grant from central/federal government to a lower level of government to be spent on only a particular category of expenditure. Such grants can be based on a formula (e.g. reflecting the size and age distribution of the population) or on a project (e.g. introducing a new educational curriculum). They usually require matching funds by state or local government.

CATS (310)
See: **Computer-Assisted Trading System**.

CBD (930)
Central business district (of a city).

CBI (610)
See: **Caribbean Basin Initiative**; **Confederation of British Industry**.

CBO (320)
Congressional Budget Office (USA).

CBOE (310)
See: **Chicago Board Options Exchange**.

CBS Tendency index (310)
The price index of the leading shares traded on the Amsterdam stock exchange.

CCC (310)
See: **Commodity Credit Corporation**; **Competition and Credit Control**.

CCT (320)
See: **compensating common tariff**; **compulsory competitive tendering**.

CD (310)
See: **certificate of deposit**.

CDB (310)
See: **Caribbean Development Bank**.

CEA (140, 310, 320)
See: **Council of Economic Advisers**.

CEAO (420)
See: **Communaut Economique de L'Afrique de l'Ouest**.

CEC (420)
Commission of the European Communities.

Cedal (430)
An international agency for clearing bank cheques.

See also: **Euroclear**.

ceiling (140)
A peak in economic activity; the maximum level of production in a **business cycle** or **trade cycle** after which there is a downturn in output, employment and prices. The peak is often associated with full employment of the factors of production: shortages of skilled

labour and **bottlenecks** in production bring about a decline from peak activity.

See also: **floor**.

ceiling price (520)
Maximum price set under a system of price control. If, as is often the case, this price (OC in the figure) is less than the market equilibrium price OE, there will be excess demand MN and some need for rationing to allocate goods.

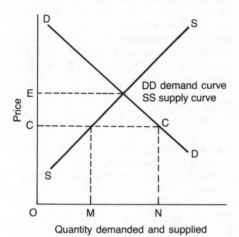

DD demand curve
SS supply curve

Quantity demanded and supplied

Celler–Kefauver Antimerger Act 1950 (610)
This US Federal Act, amending the **Sherman** and **Clayton** Acts, limited the expansion of firms by merger by making it illegal for major firms to acquire their competitors' assets or stock if the effect is a substantial reduction in competition or a contribution to the creation of a monopoly.

CENIS (420)
See: **Centre for International Studies**.

Census of Manufactures (220)
A regularly published statistical account of the economic activities of the firms of the manufacturing sector of a national economy. In the USA, this census was first conducted in 1809 and has been published quinquennially since 1967.

Census of Retail Trade (220)
A survey of the economic activities of re-tailing **establishments** and **firms**. In the USA, it was first published in 1929; since 1967 there has been a census every five years.

Central Arbitration Committee (830)
UK body established in 1975 with the concerns of **sexual discrimination**, **collective bargaining** agreements and pay structures, as well as making awards if employers refuse to disclose information for collective bargaining purposes.

central bank (310)
The bank of any country which ultimately guarantees the **liquidity** of the banking system as a whole and usually owned by the government (in the USA, the Federal Reserve System is owned by the member banks). By setting interest rates for discounting the short-term **bills** of the banking system and by **open market operations**, a central bank is able to exert a powerful influence over the size of the **money supply**. Other methods of control over the banking and financial systems include the prescribing of reserve assets ratios, the issuing of directives and the examination of the accounts of banks and other financial institutions.

Although the oldest central bank is Sweden's Riksbank (founded in 1668), the Bank of England was the first central bank to specialize as a central bank, i.e. largely to abandon its private functions and to concentrate on issuing banknotes, acting as the government's bank in managing the national debt and controlling the money supply and the exchange value of the pound sterling. In the nineteenth century, Britain's example influenced France, the Netherlands, Austria, Norway, Denmark, Belgium, Spain, Germany and Japan to set up their own national banks. The USA's Federal Reserve System of twelve district banks was set up in 1913.

See also: **Bank of England**; **Bundesbank**; **Federal Reserve System**.

centrally planned economy (070, 120)
1 An **economy** whose investment and production is coordinated by a central governmental body.

2 A **command economy**. Inspired by the celebrated Soviet five-year plans of the 1930s, many countries in Eastern Europe and in the Third World used this alternative to the **market economy** but found it impossibly inefficient with the result that in the late 1980s it was in many senses abandoned. In this type of economy information is regularly collected to form the basis of a forecast of economic activity and to construct proposals for the future development of production. There is an annual issue of targets for subordinate **state enterprises**. Some economies of this type have tried to reform their planning mechanism, e.g. Hungary with its major economic reform of 1 January 1968.

Dembinski, P. (1990) *The Logic of the Planned Economy. The Seeds of the Collapse*, trans. by K. Cook, Oxford: Clarendon Press.
Goodhart, C.A.E. (1987) 'Why do banks need a central bank?', *Oxford Economic Papers* 39: 75–89.

See also: **indicative planning; market socialism**.

central occupation (810)
The main occupation which characterizes an industry and is essential to its working, e.g. doctors and nurses in medical services, farmworkers in agriculture.

central place theory (930)
An explanation of how a continuous hierarchy of economic activities determines the optimal locations of cities. It takes into account **threshold population** size and the **ideal limit** of consumers' travel to trading enterprises. The central place is the settlement, in a region which complements it, offering goods and producing services for consumers at dispersed points. The central place is often located at the geographical periphery: its location is determined by the laws of marketing, traffic etc.

Christaller, W. (1966) *The Central Places of Southern Germany*, Englewood Cliffs, NJ: Prentice Hall.
Losch, A. (1954) *The Economics of Location*, New Haven, CT: Yale University Press.

Centre for International Studies (420)
Founded in 1951 at the Massachusetts Institute of Technology.

Centre for Policy Studies (010)
An independent London-based economics research institute founded in 1975 with the aims of research and education in economic and social affairs. It is noted for being oriented towards market solutions in much of its work.

centre–periphery system (420)
A system of international economic relations consisting of industrial centres of the world which are active and the periphery which is passive. The periphery produces and exports raw materials to the centre; the centre receives a disproportionate share of income and is slow to transmit technical knowledge to the periphery – if it does, it is mainly in the exporting industries.

CEO (510)
See: **chief executive officer**.

CEPAL (420)
Commissión Economica para América Latina, i.e. the United Nations Economic Commission for Latin America.

CEPGL (420)
Communité économique des Pays des Grands Lacs, i.e. the **Economic Community of the Countries of the Great Lakes**.

certificate of deposit (310)
A marketable bank deposit receipt which has the advantage of allowing the holder to gain the higher rate of interest associated with fixed or long-term deposits. Certificates of deposit (CDs) were introduced in the USA in 1961 and grew in volume after 1973 when **Regulation Q** no longer insisted that there had to be a ceiling to the rate of interest which could be earned. Dollar CDs have had to be registered securities from 1983 onwards. The Eurodollar CD was introduced in London in 1966 and the sterling CD in 1968. Companies, and even banks, depositing surplus funds short term and obtaining CDs both increase their investment income and maintain their liquidity.

Certification Officer (830)
UK official whose post was established in 1975 with the particular remit of certifying

that trade unions are independent; also concerned with the political funds of trade unions.

CES production function (210)
See: **constant elasticity of substitution production function**.

CET (420)
See: **common external tariff**.

CETA (810)
See: **Comprehensive Employment and Training Act (USA)**.

ceteris paribus (010)
Latin expression meaning 'other things being equal'. A term used from the mid-nineteenth century, especially in **partial equilibrium analysis** when the relationship between two variables is investigated, all other variables which might be influential being assumed to have unchanging values. This is a useful concept in demand analysis as a demand curve shows the relationship between price and quantity demanded with income, tastes and the prices of other goods held constant.

CFA franc (430)
Communauté Financière Africaine franc: this has a fixed parity with the French franc.

See also: **zone franc**.

CFF (430)
See: **compensatory financial facility**.

CFTC (310)
See: **Commodity Futures Trading Commission**.

CGT (320)
See: **capital gains tax**.

chaebol (510)
Korean group of giant companies controlled by a family-owned holding company.

See also: **zaibatsu**.

chain bank (310)
A bank linked to others through common stockholding. Banks of this kind were present in Chicago as early as 1893.

chain index method (210)
A measure proposed by Champernowne to enable a conventional production function to be built which is compatible with marginal productivity theory. All alternative production techniques are arranged in a 'chain' for some predetermined rates of profit.

Champernowne, D.G. (1953) 'The production function and the theory of capital: a comment', *Review of Economic Studies* 21, 112–35.

chain migration (840)
A sequential process of migration with one phase of migration linked to subsequent phases of migration. A major example is when the first cohort of migrants induces subsequent flows of migrants consisting of their relatives and friends who have been persuaded to move because of the information sent back by the 'pioneers'.

Chamberlin, Edward Hastings, 1899–1967 (030)
Educated at the universities of Iowa, Michigan and Harvard where his PhD, supervised by Allyn **Young**, formulated the theory of **monopolistic competition**, his principal achievement. Although Joan **Robinson** produced a theory of **imperfect competition** in the same period, Chamberlin was always keen to differentiate his theory from hers.

Chamberlin, E.H. (1933) *Theory of Monopolistic Competition*, Cambridge, MA: Harvard University Press.
Kuenne, R.E. (ed.) (1967) *Monopolistic Competition Theory: Studies in Impact: Essays in Honor of Edward H. Chamberlin*, New York: Wiley.
Robinson, R. (1971) *Edward H. Chamberlin*, New York: Columbia University Press.

Chancellor of the Exchequer (320)
UK finance minister who is the ministerial head of the Treasury. He is responsible for proposing changes in public expenditure and taxation, the conduct of monetary policy nationally and internationally and all currency matters.

change in demand or supply (010)
An increase or decrease which causes a shift in the demand or supply curve. A shift in the

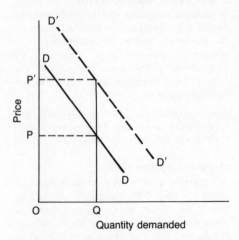

Quantity demanded

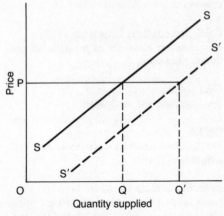

Quantity supplied

demand curve from DD to D'D' raises prices for each quantity, e.g. from OP to OP' at OQ. An increase in supply from SS to S'S' leads to more being supplied at each price level, e.g. from OQ to OQ' at OP. This is not caused by a price change, which would result in a movement along the particular curve, but by a change in the *ceteris paribus* conditions.

chaos theory (210, 310, 430)
An analysis of random movements applied to the price data of stock and currency markets, as well as to meteorology. Chaotic behaviour appears random in that changes in prices or other economic variables show no regular periodicity and are not part of a structure detectable by statistical tests. However, more sophisticated tests offer a chance of identifying underlying non-linear mathematical structures.

Baumol, W.J. and Benhabib, J. (1989) 'Chaos: significance, mechanism and economic applications', *Journal of Economic Perspectives* 3: 77–105.

Gleick, J. (1988) *Chaos Making a New Science*, London: Heinemann.

Grauwe, P. de and Vansauten, K. (1990) 'Deterministic chaos in the foreign exchange market', Paper 370, London: Centre for Economic Policy Research.

Savit, R. (1988) 'When random is not random: an introduction to chaos in market prices', *Journal of Futures Markets* 8: 271.

See also: **butterfly effect**.

CHAPS (310)
Clearing House Automatic Payment System (UK).

characteristics theory of consumer demand (020, 530)
Consumer theory based on the assertion that consumers demand the characteristics of goods rather than the goods themselves. For example, instead of there being a demand for housing, there is a demand to live in a house with certain amenities located in a pleasant area. Kelvin Lancaster proposed this alternative to traditional utility-based consumer theory.

Lancaster, K. (1971) *Consumer Demand: A New Approach*, New York: Columbia University Press.

charge (010)
1 The price of a service.

2 A right over property given to a creditor in return for a loan.

See also: **bank charges**; **binomial charge**; **capacity charge**; **emission charge**; **user charge**.

charge card (310)
A plastic card issued by a financial institution, such as a bank or a retailer, which allows the holder to charge the sum due for the purchase of goods or services to an account. This reduces the need to hold cash for transactions purposes and provides the

holder with credit until the account is payable. Major examples of such cards include those issued by American Express and the Diners' Club.

See also: **credit card**; **debit card**.

chartered company (510)

A British company established by a Royal Charter. Several, in particular the East India Company and the Hudson's Bay Company, were set up in Elizabethan England around the beginning of the seventeenth century.

chartism (040, 210, 310)

1 A technique of market analysis which predicts prices by extrapolating future price movements from a chart of previous price fluctuations. This has been applied to stock market and foreign exchange market price movements. It is argued that prices represent all influences on demand and supply, including information. Recurrent patterns, e.g. a 'head and shoulders' shape, are used to predict changes in trends.

2 A political movement in England and Scotland of the 1830s and 1840s for the reform of the franchise, named after a charter presented to parliament.

Edwards, R.D. and Magee, J. (1966) *Technical Analysis of Stock Trends*, 5th edn, Boston, MA: John Magee.

chart point (310, 430)

A significant point on a graph of price movements, e.g. of the value of a currency, which usually prompts intervention in that market.

cheap money (310)

A policy of keeping interest rates low to encourage capital accumulation and economic development. In the UK, this policy was launched by the War Loan Conversion of June 1932 and continued until 1951: under it, the **bank rate** was only 2 per cent. During the Second World War and afterwards until 1951, interest rates were pegged at a low level in the USA, easing the cost of servicing the national debt. Subsequently it was followed as a monetary policy in some Latin American countries. A policy of this kind has its problems. Real interest rates can become negative, generating an excess demand for credit, with the consequence that finance has to be rationed rather than allocated by interest rates.

check (310)

See: **cheque**.

checking account (310)

A US commercial bank deposit which is available for immediate use by the writing of a check. These deposits are part of the **M1** money supply. Until 1980 they did not bear interest. In the UK, they are known as '**current accounts**'.

See also: **Depository Institutions Deregulation and Monetary Control Act 1980**; **NOW account**.

check-off provision (830)

A clause in an employment contract by which an employer promises to deduct **trade union** subscriptions from workers' pay. A provision of this kind lowers the cost of trade union administration and stabilizes trade union membership as many persons will remain in the union through inertia.

Chenery, Hollis Burnley, 1918– (030)

A prominent US development economist. A graduate in mathematics, engineering and economics from Arizona, Oklahoma, Virginia and Harvard, where he was professor from 1965 to 1970. Subsequently, he was economic adviser to the president of the **World Bank** from 1970 to 1972 and then the Bank's Vice-President in charge of development policies. His quantitative approach to development economics views self-sustaining economic growth as a function of industrialization, which is itself associated with a switch from agricultural to industrial products in the commodity structure of a country's exports. In 1959, he published a widely used **input–output** text. He collaborated with **Arrow** and others in 1961 to produce the **constant elasticity of substitution production function** which substantially replaced the universally used **Cobb–Douglas production function**.

Arrow, K.J., Chenery, H.B., Minhas, B.S. and Solow, R.M. (1961) 'Capital–labour substitution and economic efficiency', *Review of Economics and Statistics* 43: 225–50.

Chenery, H.B. and Clark, P. (1959) *Interindustry Economics*, New York: Wiley.

cheque (310)

A written instruction for transferring a bank deposit from one person to another. In the nineteenth century, the cheque gradually replaced banknotes and bills of exchange as a means of settling claims. Today, **cheque cards** have made the cheque even more acceptable. The extent to which it is used for monetary transactions varies from country to country: the heaviest use of the cheque for transactions purposes is in France where in 1985 cheques were used for more than 80 per cent of non-cash transactions, compared with 65 per cent in the UK.

See also: **debit card**; **eftpos**.

cheque card (310)

A plastic card issued by a bank which guarantees a cheque up to a specified amount.

See also: **credit card**; **debit card**; **smart card**.

Chicago Board Options Exchange (310)

The world's largest **options** market, trading over half of the US options contracts which are subject to **Securities and Exchange Commission** regulations. It was created by the Chicago Board of Trade in 1973. Originally it dealt in call options; put options were introduced in 1977. The majority of options traded are based on the **Standard & Poor 100** stock index.

Chicago School (030)

A group of liberal US economists which first acquired its identity in the 1930s under the leadership of Frank **Knight**, Jacob **Viner** and Henry C. **Simons**; prominent since 1950 have been Milton **Friedman**, George **Stigler**, Ronald **Coase**, James **Buchanan** and Gary **Becker**, who share an all-embracing belief in the power of market forces to solve most economic problems and the desirability of minimizing the role of the state. They also believe that man is a rational agent with the constant aim of maximizing his advantages. Recent crusades of the School have included their advocacy of monetary policy and of unrestricted capitalism.

Friedman, M. and Friedman, R.D. (1962) *Capitalism and Freedom*, Chicago, IL: University of Chicago Press.

Patinkin, D. (1981) *Essay on and in the Chicago Tradition*, Durham, NC: Duke University Press.

Reder, M.W. (1982) 'Chicago economics: permanence and change', *Journal of Economic Literature* 20: 1–38.

Simon, H.C. (1948) *Economic Policy for a Free Society*, Chicago, IL: Chicago University Press.

Stigler, G.J. (ed.) (1988) *Chicago Studies in Political Economy*, Chicago, IL: University of Chicago Press.

chief executive officer (510)

The person appointed by the board of directors of a company, corporation or other organization to ensure that its decisions are implemented so that the organization follows the principles laid down by the board in its day-to-day operations. The chief executive officer (CEO) is sometimes also a director or president or chairman. The different functions of the organization are coordinated by the CEO.

Child, Sir Francis, 1642–1713 (030)

London banker who was the first banker to abandon the **goldsmith banking system** in favour of issuing banknotes. From 1698 till his death he sat as Member of Parliament for various constituencies.

Chinese modernization drive (120, 130)

The successor to the **Cultural Revolution**. From 1978 it has attempted to achieve rapid growth of production by means of a ten-year plan with ambitious targets, e.g. the doubling of coal and steel output.

Riskin, C. (1987) *China's Political Economy*, Oxford: Oxford University Press.

'Chinese Wall' (310)

The separation of the corporate finance department from the investment and trading departments of an investment bank (USA) or merchant bank (UK).

CHIPS (310)

See: **Clearing House Interbank Payments System (New York).**

chi-squared distribution (210)

The distribution of chi-squared statistics

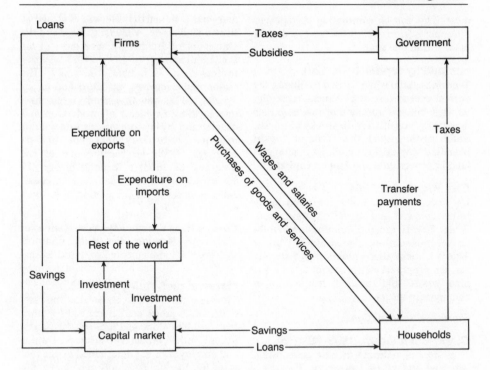

where chi is the sum of the squares of the deviations of observations from their sample mean divided by the square of the standard deviation of the population from which the sample is taken. There are different chi-squared distributions corresponding to different **degrees of freedom**.

choice variable (210)
An independent variable in an **objective function** which an economic agent attempts to maximize or minimize. Also known as a decision variable, policy variable.

Churitsuroren (830)
National Federation of Independent Unions: this Japanese national federation of trade unions was merged with Domei in 1987 to form **Rengo**.

churning (530, 630)
1 Cancelling an existing insurance policy and purchasing a new one as a replacement.

2 Frequent changes in a portfolio of securities. Commission-hungry life-insurance

agents and stockbrokers often propose a rapid turnover of this kind.

CIF (220, 430)
See: **cost, insurance and freight**.

circuit breaker mechanism (310)
A price limit or trading halt used in major US stock markets. If the market drives the **Standard & Poor 500** index twenty points in either direction, the trading session will be terminated. This intervention in price determination prevents fluctuations from creating excessively high prices or a price collapse such as happened in the market crash of October 1987.

See also: **Brady Commission**.

circular flow (010)
The circulation of expenditures and incomes throughout an economy, describing the relationship between households, firms, the government, the capital market and the rest of the world. (See the figure above.)

circular migration (840)
Temporary or repetitive population move-

ment. This can be **commuting** or repeated movements from one's residence to a distant place within one year.

circulating capital (010, 520)
Working capital which is used to finance the current expenditure of a business, especially its wage bill and purchase of raw materials and energy, together with stocks of goods. **Smith** distinguished this form of capital from fixed capital, i.e. buildings, machinery, land improvements and **human capital**.

Civil Rights Act 1964 (820)
US Federal statute which outlawed many forms of racial and sexual discrimination. Under Title II, racial discrimination in public accommodation was forbidden; under Title VI, racial discrimination in federally assisted programs was proscribed; Title VII made sexual and racial discrimination in employment illegal.

See also: **discrimination**.

Clark, Colin Grant, 1905–89 (030)
A pioneer of **national income** accounting, educated at Oxford University. He was a lecturer at Cambridge University from 1931 to 1937 before emigrating to Australia where in the period 1938–52 he played a leading role in Queensland, including being Under-Secretary of State for Labour and Industry. From 1953 to 1969 he was Director of the Institute for Research in Agricultural Economics of Oxford University before retiring to the University of Queensland, Australia. His pioneering work on national income accounting included the major advance of making one of the first calculations of the **multiplier**. In 1940, he broadened his interests to consider the nature of economic development. He was also well known for his writings on population and land use.

Clark, C. (1932) *The National Income, 1924–31*, London: Macmillan.
—— (1940) *Conditions of Economic Progress*, London: Macmillan.
—— (1962) *Growthmanship: a Study in the Methodology of Investment*, 2nd edn, London: Institute of Economic Affairs.
—— (1977) *Population, Growth and Land Use*, rev. edn, London: Macmillan.

Clark, John Bates, 1847–1938 (030)
US economist famous for the theory of **marginal productivity**. He was educated at Brown University, Amherst College and the University of Heidelberg. For most of his academic career, from 1895 to 1923, he was a professor at Columbia University. His major achievement, in *Distribution of Wealth* (1899), was to extend **marginalism** into tackling problems of production and distribution by his use of the principle of marginal productivity. In *Capital and its Earnings* (1888) he became one of the founders of modern capital theory. In *Philosophy of Wealth* (1885) he used **classical economics** as the foundation of his own economic theory.

Clark, A.H. and Clark, J.M. (1938) *John Bates Clark: A Memorial*, New York: Columbia University Press.

classical dichotomy (010, 030)
The view attributed to **classical economists** that real variables are determined by other real variables alone and monetary variables by only other monetary variables. Output and employment are determined by the real wage but the money supply can change the general price level without affecting relative prices. **Patinkin** used this term to describe this theoretical stance. **Keynes** was much concerned when advancing from his *Treatise on Money* to his *General Theory* to demolish this dualism. But with the advent of the **New Classical** School there has been a revival of this view.

classical economics (030)
The dominant school of British economics from 1752 to 1870. David **Hume**, in his attack on **mercantilism**, anticipated a new approach to economics but it was Adam **Smith** in *The Wealth of Nations* (1776) who is credited as being the virtual founder: all subsequent writers of the School used Smith as a starting point. The School was grand in its aims, providing theories of value, growth, distribution, international trade, public finance and money. All the major figures – **Smith**, **Ricardo**, **Malthus** and John Stuart **Mill** – wrote comprehensive texts, in most cases entitled 'Principles'. Their economic liberalism was manifest in their limited view of the role of the state and in their attack on the **Corn Laws**, which were incompatible

with free trade, economic growth and international specialization. **Ricardo** inspired **Marx**; more recently Smith has been regarded as an apostle of the **New Right**.

Coats, A.W. (ed.) (1971) *The Classical Economists and Economic Policy*, London: Methuen.
Hollander, S. (1987) *Classical Economics*, Oxford: Basil Blackwell.
O'Brien, D.P. (1975) *The Classical Economists*, Oxford: Clarendon Press.

classical model (210)

A formal macroeconomic model of the economy which assumes that factor and product prices are completely flexible so that there are no rigidities which prevent market clearing. Such an economy will have full employment of its resources when it is in equilibrium. **Keynes** associated this view of the economy particularly with the French economist Jean Baptiste **Say**, although it is possible to find other classical economists who use similar assumptions.

classical savings theory (020, 030)

See: **class savings theory**.

class savings theory (020, 030, 110)

The supposition that in a two-class society consisting of capitalists and workers only capitalists save and workers consume all of their incomes. This is an integral part of Cambridge growth theories.

Kaldor, N. (1956) 'Alternative theories of distribution', *Review of Economic Studies* 23: 83–100.

Clayton Act 1914 (610)

The important amendment to the US **Sherman Act 1890** which extended federal **antitrust** law. It forbad **price discrimination**, tying arrangements and exclusive dealing which lessened competition, and the acquisition of another corporation's stock if it was likely to reduce competition or lead to the creation of a monopoly; it also allowed triple damages to those suffering breaches of the antitrust law. It exempted labor unions and agricultural associations from antitrust actions.

See also: **Celler–Kefauver Antimerger Act**; **Robinson–Patman Act**.

Clean Air Act Amendments 1970 (720)

US federal statute which required the **Environmental Protection Agency** (EPA) to set air quality standards for specified pollutants and to issue control technology guidelines for stationary emission sources. The EPA, which attempts to control all sources of pollution, sought a 90 per cent reduction in hydrocarbon and carbon monoxide emissions by 1975.

clean float (430)

An **exchange rate** regime in which market forces freely determine the value of currencies as there is no intervention by governments and central banks.

See also: **dirty float**; **fixed exchange rate**; **floating exchange rate**.

clear income (320)

Taxable income which is above the amount of personal and other allowances permitted by a government's revenue service.

clearing (010, 310)

1 The matching of demand and supply in a particular market.

2 The exchange between banks of the cheques drawn upon them.

clearing bank (310)

A British **commercial bank** which accepts deposits from the public and gets its name from being a member of the Clearing House which 'clears' cheques by settling interbank indebtedness. There are separate sets of clearing banks for England and Wales, Scotland and Northern Ireland. The Scottish and Northern Irish banks also have the right to issue banknotes. A bank of this kind is distinguished from other financial intermediaries in that its reserves are the monetary liabilities of the government sector, i.e. bills, bonds and deposits with the central bank.

clearing house (310)

The financial institution which settles the mutual indebtedness of commercial banks by clearing cheques. A bank with a net debt after the clearing to another bank will settle by drawing a cheque on its deposit with the central bank.

Clearing House Interbank Payments System (310)

New York automated clearing facility for transferring dollars between major American banks, branches of foreign banks and some subsidiaries of out-of-state banks. CHIPS, for short.

clearing market (010)

A free market with flexible prices which quickly establishes an equilibrium between demand and supply, eliminating any excess demand or supply. Financial markets provide excellent examples.

See also: **disequilibrium economics**; **equilibrium**.

cliometrics (219)

The quantitative study of history which originally was carried out in the USA with the profitability of slavery and the role of railroads as its principal subjects for research. Elaborate econometric analysis has been applied to the study of economic growth.

McCloskey, D.N. (1978) 'The achievements of the cliometric school', *Journal of Economic History* 38: 13–28.

clipping (310)

Debasing a coinage made of precious metals by cutting off part of the edge. This problem for monetary authorities was solved first by milling the edges and later by the introduction of **token money** and **banknotes** which had no intrinsic value to be removed.

See also: **Gresham's law**.

closed economy (070, 420)

An **economy** which does not engage in international trade. There are no economies of this type in the world today but in the past there were, e.g. Japan which for centuries was closed to foreigners. The concept is important theoretically as it makes possible simple macroeconomic models, uncomplicated by international trade.

See also: **autarky**; **open economy**.

closed population (840)

A population with no migration between it and other areas. The size of this population will depend entirely on birth and death rates.

closed shop (830)

An arrangement between a **trade (labor) union** and a management to restrict employment in a particular place of work or occupation to members of that union. A pre-entry closed shop has the rule that only trade union members can apply for work; in a post-entry closed shop a worker must become a member before or on joining the firm. The Trade Union and Labour Relations Act 1974 (UK) passed during the period of office of a Labour government made possible universal enforcement of the closed shop. The subsequent aim of British Conservative governments was to remove the pre-entry closed shop (Industrial Relations Act 1971 and Employment Act 1980); the European Court in 1981 ordered the British practice to end the rail closed shop. The strongest argument in its favour is the equitable view that as all employees benefit from a union's bargaining all should pay union dues. Some employers have argued that a closed shop promotes harmonious industrial relations. In the USA, the post-entry closed shop is called a **'union shop'**. Even in countries such as France where the closed shop is illegal, shops of this kind still exist, e.g. in the docks and in printing.

club good (010)

A good which is available to a group of individuals and hence is a mixture of **private** and **public goods**. Non-members can be excluded but a member's consumption is not diminished by another member's. Examples of club goods include many forms of entertainment, e.g. the cinema and sporting facilities.

Club of Rome (110)

A group of leading economists and scientists who studied the effects of economic growth from 1968 onwards. Their study of poverty, environmental issues, urbanization, unemployment, inflation and the nature of growth led them to set out the conditions for a global equilibrium in their famous *Limits to Growth* report.

Meadows, D.H., Meadow, D.L., Randers, J. and Behrens, W.W. III (1972) *The Limits to Growth: a Report for the Club of Rome's Project on the Predicament of Mankind*, London: Earth Island.

CMEA (430)

See: **Council for Mutual Economic Aid**.

CMO (310)

See: **collateralized mortgage obligation**.

CMSA (220, 840)

See: **Consolidated Metropolitan Statistical Area**.

CO (830)

See: **Certification Officer**.

Coase, Ronald Harry, 1910– (030)

US economist who was born in Middlesex, England, and graduated in commerce from the London School of Economics. He taught there and at Dundee before emigrating to the USA in 1951, holding academic appointments at Buffalo, Virginia and Chicago (from 1964 to 1979). His principal contributions to economic theory have been his analyses of the nature of the **firm** and of **social cost**. He argues that the main point in establishing a firm is to reduce the costs which result from using the price mechanism. Beginning with **Pigou**'s discussion of social cost, Coase says that it is wrong to consider how to restrain A if A harms B as we should look at the reciprocal nature of their relationship, taking into account both the marginal and the total effects of, for example, factory pollution which kills fish but if stopped would reduce industrial output. The legal liability, where possible, should be apportioned through the market; the taxation of polluters does not help the injured party as he/she does not receive the tax revenue. Pollution regulators should secure the optimum amount of pollution which will maximize the value of production, a value which depends on property rights. His many applied studies include an examination of broadcasting, monopoly pricing and antitrust enforcement.

Coase, R.H. (1988) *The Firm, the Market and the Law*, Chicago and London: University of Chicago Press.

Coase theorem (020, 720)

The proposition that the value and composition of the national income is unaffected by the precise pattern of liability for pollution which the perpetrators and victims have determined. Thus **externalities** do not lead to a misallocation of resources provided that there are no **transaction costs** and **property rights** are clearly defined. Private and social costs will be equal under perfection.

Coase, R.H. (1960) 'The problem of social cost', *Journal of Law and Economics* 3: 1–44.

COB (310)

Commission des Opérations de Bourse: the Stock Exchange Commission of France.

Cobb–Douglas production function (020, 110, 210)

An equation which shows physical output as the product of labour and capital inputs. This function predicted rewards to labour and capital that were close to the observed shares of manufacturing income in national income. The Cobb–Douglas approach was dominant in the analysis of economic growth from 1945 to 1961.

cobweb (010, 210, 710)

A dynamic model of the relationship between demand and supply in a particular market. Central to the model is the assumption that there is a time lag between planning, and completing, production. A familiar application, not surprisingly, is agricultural production (particularly hog/pig production) which often has a twelve-month production period. It is assumed that (1) supply depends solely on the expected price for the product, (2) actual market price adjusts to demand so as to eliminate excess demand instantaneously, (3) expected price is equal to the previous equilibrium price, with the length of delay determined by the production lag, (4) there are no inventories and (5) neither buyers nor sellers have an incentive to speculate. Whether there is movement to equilibrium in the model or not depends on the relative **elasticities** of the demand and supply curves. If the elasticity of demand exceeds that of supply, there will be a movement to the original equilibrium price and output; if elasticity of supply is

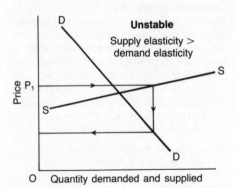

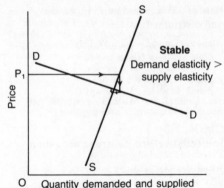

greater then there will be continuing disequilibrium until the elasticities change (see figures above).

Nerlove, M. (1958) 'Adaptive expectations and cobweb phenomena', *Quarterly Journal of Economics* 72: 227–40.

Cocom (420)

Coordinating Committee for Multilateral Export controls: the regulator of exporting high technology products from Western countries to the East. Products scrutinized include computers, telecommunications and machine tools.

coefficient of correlation (210)

Referred to as *r* by statisticians and used as a measure of the interrelatedness of two variables. This coefficient is measured by the formula

$$\frac{\Sigma(x\,y)}{\sqrt{(\Sigma x^2\, \Sigma y^2)}}$$

A perfect negative relationship has the value –1; a perfect positive relationship is +1. Values in between these extremes will depend on how strong the relationship between *x* and *y* is.

coefficient of determination (210)

A ratio of the explained variation to the total variation of values from a regression line, usually referred to as r^2. It is measured by the formula

$$\frac{\Sigma\{[Y\,(\text{estimated}) - Y(\text{mean})]^2\}}{\Sigma\{[Y(\text{actual}) - Y(\text{mean})]^2\}}$$

This ratio can range from 0 to 1, being 0 if all the variation is unexplained and 1 if all the variation is explained.

See also: **linear correlation**.

coefficient of multiple correlation (210)

A statistic which measures the extent to which changes in a dependent variable are explained by the joint variation in the independent variables chosen to explain it. It is the square root of the **coefficient of multiple determination**.

coefficient of multiple determination (210)

For two independent variables this coefficient, $R_{1.23}$, is equal to $1 - s_{1.23}^2/s_1^2$, where $s_{1.23}$ is the standard error of an estimate of variable X_1, on independent variables X_2 and X_3, and s_1 is the standard deviation of X_1.

coefficient of variation (210)

The ratio of a **standard deviation** to an **arithmetic mean** of a set of values, usually expressed as a percentage. This is a better measure of the dispersion of a set of values than the standard deviation as it can be used for different measures with different magnitudes and can cope with two measures expressed in different units, e.g. monetary and physical.

cognitive consonance (010)

The state of a cognitive system which has ideas and beliefs in a state of harmony.

cognitive dissonance (010)

The coexistence of cognitions which do not fit with each other. As a consequence of this dissonance, persons will avoid situations and information likely to increase such discomfort. This theory of Festinger's has been applied by economists to the explanation of work behaviour, home ownership and discrimination.

Akerlof, G. and Dickens, W.T. (1982) 'The economic consequences of cognitive dissonance', *American Economic Review* 72: 307–19.

Festinger, L. (1957) *A Theory of Cognitive Dissonance*, Evanston, IL: Row, Peterson.

See also: **economics and psychology**.

coinage (310)

Pieces of metal of a standard size and weight which are stamped by a sovereign power to give them the status of money. Coins were first used as money by the Lydians (Greek inhabitants of what is now West Turkey) in the seventh century BC. The first coins were made of electrum, a natural alloy of gold and silver. Silver, bronze and copper were later used in ancient Greece and the Roman Empire. Copper coins, used for small transactions, were issued with a monetary value in excess of the value of metal used, establishing the principle of token money which is the nature of coinage today. The first problem of coinage, clipping and forgery, was solved by a change in production method from hammering to milling to ensure a standard size; the second problem, the inconvenience of transporting it to carry out large financial transactions, was remedied by the use of banknotes.

coincident indicators (140, 220)

Measures of economic activity used by economic forecasters to track cyclical movements in the economy. The main ones used are employment in non-agricultural enterprises, personal income less transfer payments, and indices of total industrial production and manufacturing and trade sales.

See also: **economic indicators**.

COLA (820)

Cost of living adjustment: a provision in a US labor contract which provides for automatic wage increases according to increases in the **consumer price index**.

Colbertism (040, 610)

Government intervention in industry, named after the French **mercantilist** Jean Baptiste Colbert (1619–83) who successfully reformed the French economy after 1649. In France, the home of Colbertism, the government's ability to subsidize industry and follow protectionist polices has been limited since entry to the **European Economic Community** in 1958.

See also: **dirigisme**.

collar (310)

A combination of a **cap** and a **floor** which gives an interest rate a fixed range.

collateralized mortgage obligation (310)

A **mortgage** with different interest rates to different classes of bondholders.

collecting bank (310)

Any bank, other than the payer bank, handling a bank item, e.g. a **cheque**, for collection.

collective bargaining (830)

Negotiations between a **trade (labor) union** and a single employer or employers' association over pay, working conditions and other employment matters. It can only be genuine if the parties are free to initiate discussions and reach a settlement: under **incomes policies** and in countries where trade unions have little independence from the state, this is not possible. It is usually bilateral, but sometimes other interested parties are at the bargaining table, e.g. in teachers' negotiations in parts of the USA where parents are represented. It can take place at different levels – national, industrial, the firm or workplace. The level at which the major decisions are made distinguishes one country's system sharply from another. In Japan, the enterprise level is very important; in Germany, the industrial level. In the USA, the bargainers produce a legally enforceable contract; in the UK, a framework for individual employment contracts.

Collective bargaining makes possible the collective provision of workplace 'public goods', e.g. safety, conditions, lighting, heating, speed of the production line, grievance procedures, pension plans. It permits the individual to express his/her own preferences without the danger of being sacked. Also it helps to change the social relations of the workplace, bridging the gap between labour and capital, by making possible the enforcement of labour contracts.

Bean, R. (1985) *Comparative Industrial Relations: an Introduction to Cross-national Perspectives*, London: Croom Helm.

Clegg, H.A. (1976) *Trade Unionism under Collective Bargaining. A Theory Based on Comparisons of Six Countries*, Oxford: Basil Blackwell.

Coddington, A. (1968) *Theories of the Bargaining Process*, London: Allen & Unwin.

Kochan, T.A. (1980) *Collective Bargaining and Industrial Relations*, Homewood, IL: Irwin.

—— (1986) *The Transformation of American Industrial Relations*, New York: Basic Books.

Sisson, K. (1987) *The Management of Collective Bargaining. An International Comparison*, Oxford: Basil Blackwell.

See also: **exit-voice**.

collective good (010, 320)

A **public good** allocated by political decisions, not by the market.

collectivization of agriculture (120, 710)

The reorganization of a country's agriculture into state farms thereby depriving peasants of land ownership and management. Collectivization in the USSR was introduced in 1929 but was not implemented in a major and systematic way until the 1930s: it was accompanied by much resistance and a famine which killed millions. Subsequently, other countries following the principles of Marxist-Leninism have attempted draconian changes of this kind, e.g. Mao's China and Ethiopia.

collusion (610)

Joint action, usually by **oligopolists**, to control prices and market shares. It is illegal in most capitalist countries, e.g. in the USA under **antitrust** legislation. As Adam **Smith**, the apostle of competition, observed in his *Wealth of Nations* (Book I, ch. X, pt II), 'People of the same trade seldom meet together, even for merriment and diversion, but the conversation ends in a conspiracy against the public, or in some contrivance to raise prices.'

colon (430)

The currency of Costa Rica and El Salvador.

Combination Acts (040, 830)

British legislation of 1799 and 1800 which, like the common law, outlawed **trade union** membership and activities amounting to conspiracy. The repeal of these Acts in 1824 began the organization of labour in England.

Comecon (420)

See: **Council for Mutual Economic Aid**.

COMET (140, 210)

An econometric model of European economies whose name is abbreviated from 'COmmon market MEdium Term model'. It was created in 1970 and based on eight national models for West Germany, France, Italy, the Netherlands, Belgium, the UK, Ireland and Denmark. It is dynamic, giving predictions over time paths of five to ten years. It models the real sector of these economies: monetary and financial elements, represented by interest rates, are exogenous. The interdependence of the economies are chiefly described by trade flows. One of the applications of the model has been to develop the methodology of **European Community** economic policy.

Barten, A.P., d'Alcantara, G. and Carrin, G.J. (1976) 'COMET: a medium-term macroeconomic model for the European Economic Community', *European Economic Review* 7: 63–115.

See also: **linkage model**.

Comex (310)

See: **Commodity Exchange of New York**.

Comit index (310)

The price index of the leading shares traded on the Milan stock exchange.

command and control regulation (720)

Administrative and statutory rules which require selected pollution sources to use specific control devices; also, the application of emissions standards to sources of pollution which have been narrowly defined. Critics of this approach to **pollution control** point out that it ignores both the extent of pollution damage and the costs of regulation.

command economy (070, 120)

An **economy** in which the orders of a

central planning authority to lower level economic organizations have the force of law. Lower level organizations are instructed to follow particular practices and to use stated prices, inputs and output targets. The first modern economy of this type was devised by Lenin who was inspired by the German military organization of the First World War. Until the mid-1980s, the planning mechanism of the Soviet-type economy still had many of these characteristics.

See also: **perestroika**.

commanding heights (610)

1 The basic industries of an economy, usually including energy, transport and telecommunications. It is argued that, as a high proportion of their output consists of **intermediate goods**, governmental control of these industries is an effective form of government intervention in the economy as a whole.

2 Education and training which are basic to the performance and growth of industry.

See also: **nationalized industry**.

commercial bank (310)

A bank which provides a wide range of banking services, including receiving deposits from the public and the making of loans. Increasingly, with more competition in the financial sector, these banks have extended their activities to include insurance, mortgage finance and a wide range of business finance, previously the concern of investment/merchant banks alone.

Ballarin, E. (1987) *Commercial Banks amid the Financial Revolution: Developing a Competitive Strategy*, London: Harper & Row; Cambridge, MA: Ballinger.

See also: **clearing bank**; **retail bank**; **wholesale bank**.

commercial bill (310)

A short-term **bill of exchange** by which the person who draws it promises to pay the drawee the sum specified on a particular future date, one, two, three or six months hence. This method of finance was extensively used in Britain in the early nineteenth century before banks were prepared to make short-term advances in the

form of overdrafts to their customers and is still a popular form of short-term finance. When a bill of this kind is accepted by an **accepting house**, becoming a bank bill, it is possible for the drawee to obtain immediate payment at a discount (fixed according to the ruling short-term money market interest rate).

See also: **treasury bill**.

commercial paper (310, 520)

A form of short-term company borrowing, usually for thirty days. These unsecured IOUs permit companies to borrow directly from investors, bypassing banks and bond markets. Banks, however, are used as agents to place the paper; sometimes investment banks underwrite the IOUs investing themselves. This type of financing, long used in the USA, was introduced into the UK in 1986 and is now also used in many other countries, including France, Australia, Hong Kong and Singapore.

See also: **IOU money**.

commercial policy (420)

The international trading policy of a government with respect to import duties/quotas and export subsidies. These policies have been a central issue in economics since the **mercantilists** first debated the merits of **tariffs**.

See also: **General Agreement on Tariffs and Trade**.

Committee of Twenty (430)

A committee of twenty leading members of the **International Monetary Fund**, officially known as the 'Committee on the Reform of the International Monetary System' which had the task of considering the possibility of reviving a **Bretton Woods** type of **pegged exchange rate** regime and the supply of international reserve assets. The floating of several exchange rates prevented it from reaching its central objective. Its final report was in June 1974.

commodification (310)

The transformation of money into a **commodity**. This has occurred because **commercial banks** now resemble industrial conglomerates with a range of financial products. Marx had previously stated that the nature of exchange under capitalism is to change money into a unique commodity exchangeable with all commodities.

commodity (010)

1 Something, usually physical, which can be bought and sold and is directly measurable. The concept is used extensively in both **Marxian economics** and **general equilibrium** analysis since **Hicks**. **Marx** argued that through the exchange process goods lose their use value, becoming 'citizens of the world' and merely the vehicle for merchants to earn **surplus value**. **Sraffa** regarded a commodity as a good or service produced by a unique combination of factor inputs.

2 A raw material or primary product.

commodity agreement (420)

An international agreement between producing and consuming countries to stabilize prices and organize quotas for major metals and foodstuffs.

The **United Nations Conference on Trade and Development** recommended eighteen agreements in 1977 but only achieved them for sugar, cocoa, tin, rubber and coffee.

Commodity Credit Corporation (710)

US federal body set up by the **Agricultural Adjustment Act 1933** to provide a price support system for US farmers. With funds supplied by the US Federal Treasury, it lends to farmers who pledge their crops as collateral. Farmers can deliver their crops to the CCC in lieu of repaying the loan and any accumulated interest. These crops can be resold by the CCC if their market price is greater than the 'loan rate', i.e. the price on which the loan was based.

Commodity Exchange of New York (310)

The major US metals exchange in 1870. Most of its trading is in **futures**.

commodity fetishism (010)

Marxian term for a fantastic attitude towards production, i.e. regarding a social relationship between men as a relation between things which are not considered according to their **use value**.

See also: **commodity**.

Commodity Futures Trading Commission (310)

US federal commission set up in 1974 and operational since 1975 which regulates the eleven US futures exchanges, its members and brokerage houses. It aims to ensure fair trading and financial integrity, e.g. by requiring customer funds to be kept in separate bank accounts. It covers a wide range of futures trading, including trading in agricultural commodities, currencies, metals and securities.

commodity reserve currency (430)

A **currency** whose value is based on that of a 'basket' of commodities representative of average consumption. This currency tends to maintain its value over time, as happened under the **gold standard**, and can take a variety of forms reflecting the technical characteristics of commodities at a particular time and the desired level of stability. However, it has been argued that few commodities are suitable for inclusion in the 'basket', e.g. on account of storage difficulties, but using commodity futures could eliminate many of these problems.

Friedman, M. (1953) *Essays in Positive Economics*, pp. 204–50, Chicago, IL: University of Chicago Press.

commodity stabilization schemes (430)

International agreements to introduce order into the international markets for primary commodities, usually with the aim of helping less developed countries. These schemes usually attempt to stabilize prices in order to prevent the agricultural incomes of these countries falling below their present levels.

See also: **buffer stock; commodity agreement; price stabilization; primary commodity prices**.

commodity tax (320)

A tax on a good, usually taking the form of a **sales tax** or an **excise duty**.

commodity terms of trade (420)

See: **net barter terms of trade**.

commodity trade structure (420)

The composition of a country's imports and

exports classified by major product groups. The structure is some indication of the stage of economic development of the country, e.g. Third World countries tend to have a higher proportion of **primary products** amongst their exports. The commodity structure is used to test certain hypotheses about international trade, e.g. the **Heckscher–Ohlin trade theorem**.

common access resources (710)

Jointly owned natural resources, e.g. a piece of agricultural land open to all adjoining a town. The major departure from the principle of common access occurred in Britain from the thirteenth century onwards when common land was enclosed into private holdings.

Common Agricultural Policy (420, 710)

The major economic policy of the **European Community** costing over two-thirds of the Community's budget. The principles of the policy were formulated at the Stresa Conference of 1958 and embodied in Articles 38 to 47 of the **Treaty of Rome**. It was more protectionist in nature than several of the national agricultural policies that it replaced. The policy started in the first Mansholt Plan of 1960 and it intended to control the 'agriculture' of the member countries in the widest sense of farming and all related industries, including fertilizer producers, machinery and food processing. Implementation of the policy was slow, e.g. the target price for cereals, the central agricultural commodity of the Community, was not agreed until December 1964. The European Agricultural Guidance and Guarantee Fund was set up to finance refunds on exports to third countries, intervention measures to stabilize markets and common measures, including structural modifications.

It has used a 'single price system' of target prices throughout the Community for fixing intervention prices and frontier crossing point **cost, insurance and freight** prices. These prices are expressed in Council regulations. Price support has been intended both to support farmers' incomes and to make the Community self-sufficient in agricultural produce. But it has been very costly as over-production has led to at least

60 per cent of the agricultural budget being spent on disposing of surpluses. Temporary bans on production and the giving of surpluses to charities are used from time to time. Mansholt in 1968 in his *Agriculture 1980* set out a ten-year plan for restructuring European agriculture, including the retiring of farmers and the concentration of agricultural production into larger and more efficient units. The Plan achieved little as it met with national resistance and was seen as an attack on the principle of small family farms. This policy has reduced European Community imports from the rest of the world and insulated Community domestic prices for agricultural produce from world price fluctuations, destabilizing the prices and incomes of the farmers of other countries. Within the European Community, the policy has redistributed income from consumers and taxpayers to producers and discriminated against industry. In countries such as the UK, higher food costs have met with much criticism; in developing countries, many farmers have gone out of business through being excluded by so large a market as the European Community. The **Uruguay Round** of the General Agreement on Tariffs and Trade negotiations has attempted to reduce the protectionism of the CAP.

common cost (010)

The cost of an input which is simultaneously used in the production of several goods and services of a firm.

See also: **joint cost**.

common currency (430)

A currency which can be used by several countries who still retain their own currencies; not a **single currency**. It has been suggested that the **ecu** may take on this role.

See also: **hard ecu**.

common external tariff (420)

The tariff protecting a free-trade area, e.g. the **European Community**. Some countries outside the area may be permitted to have privileged access, e.g. those Third World countries allowed by the **Lomé Convention** to export to Community countries preferentially.

See also: **customs union**.

common market (420)

A **customs union** within which there is free movement of labour and capital, no tariffs between the countries which are part of the union and a **common external tariff** to exclude other countries from the market. The **European Community** is a successful modern example. A common market can in many respects behave like a national economy as all firms of the same industry are in competition across national boundaries and can draw upon the same pool of labour and financial capital. The absence of tariffs within this market enables production to be allocated according to the principle of **comparative advantage**.

See also: **single market**.

common ownership (010, 610)

1 Rights over property conferred upon a group, e.g. the use of land by residents of a village.

2 Ownership by the state or one of its agencies, e.g. a **nationalized industry**.

Commons, John Roger, 1862–1945 (030)

US labor economist who was a founder of **institutional economics**. Born in Hollandsburg, Ohio, and educated as a graduate student at Johns Hopkins University: he was never able to finish a college or university degree course. He held academic posts at Wesleyan University and Syracuse University. Much of his life was spent in empirical work in Wisconsin, constructing an index of wholesale prices, investigating labor unions and discovering the economic concepts used by the courts. He took as the foundation of economics volitional theories of value and cost, rather than **utility** or a **commodity**. He saw in the cases of the US Supreme Court the working rules which guide and restrain individuals in transactions, which are the basic economic units. 'Value' and 'economy' were treated as the transactions of millions of people who are engaged in valuing and economizing. His consideration of legal cases also led him to analyse the nature of bargaining power.

Commons, J.R. (1893) *The Distribution of Wealth*, New York: Macmillan.
—— (1905) *Trade Unions and Labor Problems*, Boston, MA: Ginn.
—— (1924) *The Legal Foundations of Capitalism*, New York: Macmillan.
—— (1934) *Institutional Economics; Its Place in Political Economy*, New York: Macmillan.
—— (1934) *Myself*, New York: Macmillan.
Harter, L.G. (1962) *John R. Commons: His Assault on Laissez-Faire*, Corvallis, OR: Oregon State University Press.
Rutherford, M.H. (1983) 'J.R. Commons' institutional economics', *Journal of Economic Issues* 17: 721–44.

See also: **Ayres**; **Galbraith**; **Veblen**.

common stock (310)

The **equity** capital of a US corporation. The owner of common stock is entitled to vote in general meetings, to receive declared dividends and to obtain a share in the net assets of the corporation on its dissolution. This stock does not usually have a **par value**.

Commonwealth Grants Commission (320)

An independent Australian statutory body founded in 1933 with the original aim of dealing with states needing special assistance. Now it makes special grants to the states to enable services to conform to minimum standards. Most of these grants are unconditional, i.e. not **earmarked**.

See also: **federal finance**; **unconditional grant**.

communal economy (070)

An **economy** consisting of communes which are the basic units of production in which, usually, income is equally distributed and there is no outside ownership of capital. Most of the production of the communes is for their own consumption as they tend to aim for self-sufficiency; modern technology is often deplored and strict rules govern the conduct of the commune members. Many examples of these idealistic communities exist, including Robert Owen's experiment at New Lanark, Scotland, in the nineteenth century, the Israeli kibbutz and, in the USA, the Shakers and the Hutterites.

See also: **autarky**.

Communauté Economique de L'Afrique de l'Ouest (420)

A **customs union** with joint sectoral policies set up in 1974 with the Ivory Coast, Mali, Mauritania, Niger, Senegal and Upper Volta as members.

commune (610)

An association of persons jointly owning a productive enterprise and managing it themselves. The most famous examples are the Paris Commune of 1871, the Israeli kibbutz and Robert Owen's commune in the early nineteenth century.

See also: **common ownership**.

communism (060)

A society with common ownership of capital and a distribution of incomes according to need. Under Marxist-Leninism it is strictly defined as the final stage of socialism when the state has withered away, everyone is equal (as members of a universal proletariat) and there is no division of labour. Marx's vision was exceedingly vague as his concern was to analyse contemporary capitalism rather than future socialism. The nearest to communism has been in small idealistic communities; larger societies are unlikely to consent to such levelling. The term was often applied loosely to the centrally planned state capitalist countries of the **Comecon** and China.

Daniels, R.V. (ed.) (1965) *Marxism and Communism: Essential Readings*, Syracuse, NY: Singer.

See also: **command economy**; **socialism**.

community charge (320)

A local British tax, often called the 'poll tax', levied on all adults over 18 years old. It was introduced in Scotland in 1989 and in England and Wales gradually from 1990. It replaced the existing **rates** system and was combined with a standard business rate throughout the country. A principal aim of this type of local government finance was to encourage the adult population to bring pressure upon their local governments to be more moderate in their expenditure: former non-ratepayers would have had no reason to oppose local government overspending. Critics opposed its high collection cost and regressive nature (only giving rebates to the very poor), and it was stated that a community charge should only be used to finance **public goods**. Inevitably with any change in a taxation system there are gainers and losers. In 1991, it was decided to replace it with a modified property tax, to be known as the **council tax**.

HMSO (1986) *Paying for Local Government*, Cmnd 9714.

Mason, D. (1985) *Revising the Rating System*, London: Adam Smith Institute.

community programme (810)

UK employment measure to help the long-term unemployed by providing them with jobs of benefit to the community, e.g. rehabilitating wasteland. These are offered on a temporary basis and are often disliked for being low paid.

See also: **workfare**.

commuting (930)

Daily journeys of workers between their homes and places of work. When a transport and road network makes places distant from a centre of production more accessible, then house-building occurs in outlying areas, causing land and property prices to rise. Other effects of commuting include increased traffic congestion and the difficulty of financing city services used by, but not paid for, commuting workers.

See also: **circular migration**; **fiscal mobility**.

company (510)

A legal entity or corporate body brought into existence by registration under the Companies Acts (1844 and subsequently in the UK). A company is owned by shareholders whose legal personalities are distinct from the corporate body, and it has a range of activities defined under its Articles of Association. For the past hundred years this has been a dominant form of business organization in capitalist economies. The existence of companies is compatible with **socialism**, provided that the state sets the economic and social aims of each company.

See also: **corporation**; **firm**.

company town (930)

A town run by one firm, e.g. a place run by a mining company which provides all jobs, services and housing. Such towns have been criticized for permitting unscrupulous firms to perpetrate many forms of exploitation, including the monopoly sale of poor quality goods at inflated prices.

company union (830)

A **trade (labor) union** dependent on the company which approves it. Only the employees of that company are permitted to be members. In the nineteenth and twentieth centuries, especially in the USA, organized labour objected to these fake unions.

See also: **enterprise union; sweetheart contract; truck**.

comparable worth (820)

Equal productivity; the basis for paying workers the same. A principle adopted in Australia in 1972 and introduced in three uniform steps by June 1975 to counter **sexual discrimination**.

McGavin, P.A. (1983) 'Equal pay for women: a reassessment of the Australian experience', *Australian Economic Papers* 22: 48–59.

See also: **Equal Pay Acts 1963 and 1970**.

comparative advantage (010, 410)

The principle justifying individuals or nations specializing in those economic activities which they perform relatively better than others. From its first enunciation in 1815 by **Torrens**, this principle has been used to explain the pattern of international trade and specialization in terms of a country's relative efficiency in producing goods. It advances Smith's doctrine of **absolute advantage** which was a simple extension of his **division of labour** principle. Torrens and **Ricardo** argued that, even if one country was more productive in every agricultural and industrial activity, trade would still take place if the internal production cost ratios were different from country to country. Although this theory advanced international trade theory, it was later criticized for assuming constant costs, ignoring transport costs and for not explaining at what ratio exchange would take place. John Stuart Mill, with his **law of reciprocal demand**, completed the theory by solving the problem of what actual exchange rate would result from trade.

Ricardo's example of trade in cloth and wine between England and Portugal is that to produce a given amount of each commodity the following amounts of labour are required in each country:

	England	Portugal
Cloth	100 men	90 men
Wine	120 men	80 men

Thus, England can produce cloth relatively more cheaply than wine and Portugal can produce wine more cheaply than cloth. The countries will both gain by increased specialization in the production of the good for which they have a comparative advantage, even though Portugal has an absolute advantage in the production of both commodities.

comparative costs (410)

See: **comparative advantage**.

comparative statics (010, 030)

A technique of economic analysis which consists of comparing one equilibrium position with a later one which has come about through changes in the values of **parameters** and **exogenous variables**. **Keynes** used this method; **Robertson** and **Harrod** preferred dynamic methods which, unlike comparative statics, have the advantage of showing how an earlier equilibrium is transformed into a later one.

compensated demand curve (010, 210)

A demand curve constructed so that a

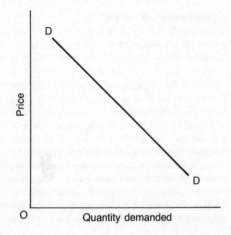

consumer's initial level of **utility** is constant because his money income has been adjusted. This curve eliminates the **income and substitution effect** of price changes so that only the **substitution effect** is in force.

compensating common tariff (420)
A **tariff** which keeps the rest of the world as well off after the formation of a **customs union** as it was previously.

compensating wage differential (820)
A differential in wages or salaries which is created to compensate for a poor attribute of a job, e.g. a health hazard or variable earnings. The major reason for such compensation is that unless firms pay their employees more on account of these undesirable characteristics they will find it difficult to retain their staff or find new recruits.

compensation principle (020)
The rule that redistribution leads to an improvement in economic welfare if those who gain an increase in real income and welfare are able to compensate the losers and still be better off. This major principle of modern **welfare economics** was devised by **Kaldor** and **Hicks** to deal with the problem of making interpersonal comparisons of **utility**; it has often been applied in **cost–benefit analysis**.

Mishan, E.J. (1981) *Introduction to Normative Economics*, New York: Oxford University Press.

compensatory finance (320)
Expenditures by a government to offset **leakages** from the **circular flow** of income. Thus, the impact of taxes, savings and imports which reduce the value of the **multiplier** for a national economy can be reduced by a government increasing its public expenditure and boosting exports through subsidizing export industries.

compensatory financial facility (430)
An **International Monetary Fund** arrangement since 1963 to help with fluctuations in commodity prices which cause a shortfall in the value of exports. Repayments are made to the International Monetary Fund over a three- to five-year period.

See also: **additional facilities**.

competition (010)
The state of a market in which several suppliers of goods or services struggle with each other to acquire the custom of buyers. The principal types of competition are **perfect**, duopolistic, **monopolistic** and oligopolistic. Adam **Smith** and **Marshall** analysed perfect competition; **Cournot** presented a model of **duopoly**; **Chamberlin** propounded a theory of monopolistic competition. The analysis of **oligopoly** is not so closely associated with one theorist. Competition has often been criticized by socialists and other idealists for bringing about an unfair distribution of incomes and discouraging cooperation.

Competition and Credit Control (310)
UK discussion paper proposing new techniques of monetary policy which would combine effective control over credit conditions with competition and innovation. Its proposals included (1) the requirement that all banks hold not less than 12½ per cent of their sterling deposit liabilities in specified reserve assets, which included cash at the Bank of England, money at call, treasury and local authority bills and British government securities with less than one year to run, (2) the placing of **special deposits**, variable in amount, by the banks with the Bank of England and (3) the withdrawal of Bank of England support for the **UK gilts market**. These proposals were implemented in the 1970s.

'Competition and Credit Control', *Bank of England Quarterly Bulletin* 11, 189–93, 1971.

competition policy (610)
The set of statutory measures of a country, or of the **European Community**, which attempts to control dominant monopolies, **restrictive practices** and **anticompetitive practices**, to monitor **mergers** and to protect consumers.

In the UK, a series of measures from 1948 increasingly widened the scope of this policy. The Monopolies and Restrictive Practices (Inquiry and Control) Act 1948 permitted the Board of Trade to refer to the newly constituted Monopolies and Restrictive Practices Commission monopoly situations where one-third of the supply of goods was supplied by one firm, or two or more interconnected firms, in order to ascertain whether that situation was against the 'public interest', which was regarded as the promotion of efficiency, the suitable pricing of goods for domestic and foreign markets and technical progress. The Commission's report on 'Collective discrimination' recommended the separate and judicial investigation of restrictive practices. The Restrictive Trade Practices Act 1956 set up a register of permitted restrictive agreements and a Restrictive Practices Court to ascertain whether it was right to regard an agreement as against the public interest. The legislation was also extended in 1964 by the Resale Prices Act to cover individual enforcement of **resale price maintenance**. References to the renamed Monopolies and Mergers Commission were possible under the Monopolies and Mergers Act 1965 where a monopoly situation was strengthened or the value of assets taken over was in excess of £5 million. The investigation of firms supplying services was another concern of the 1965 Act. Further legislation on restrictive practices in the 1968 Restrictive Trade Practices Act brought **information agreements** within the ambit of the Restrictive Practices Court. The Fair Trading Act 1973 set up the office of Director-General of Fair Trading with wide powers to investigate and refer to the Monopolies and Mergers Commission; the monopoly situations which could be investigated included those with only a quarter of the market, not only nationally, but also in local areas; the concept of 'public interest' was clarified by relating it to 'competition'. The Competition Act 1980 transferred investigation of prices to the Director-General of Fair Trading and gave him the task of investigating **anticompetitive practices**; under the Act, various public bodies, e.g. bus and water authorities, could be referred to the Monopolies and Mergers Commission for a consideration of their efficiency and costs, the service provided and possible abuse of a monopoly situation. The 1984 Act consolidated the legislation.

The **European Economic Community** from its inception regarded the promotion of competition as a major policy goal. The **Treaty of Rome** in Articles 3, 7, 37 and 85–94 deals with many aspects of the promotion of competition. State monopolies, restrictive agreements, abuses of dominant positions in markets, the control of public enterprises by national governments and state aid to industries by national governments are all covered by the policy.

In the USA since 1890 the federal government has pursued an active competition policy known as **antitrust**.

George, K.P. and Joll, C. (eds) (1975) *Competition Policy in the UK and the EEC*, Cambridge: Cambridge University Press.
Steiner, J. (1990) *Textbook on EEC Law*, 2nd edn, Pt 2, Section B, London: Blackstone Press.

See also: **antitrust**; **Competition Acts**.

Competitive Equality Banking Act 1987 (310)

US federal statute which provides for transactions between member banks of the **Federal Reserve** and their subsidiaries and holding company affiliates to be on the same terms as those offered to unaffiliated companies. A bank was broadly defined to include institutions receiving deposits, having deposit insurance and being engaged in commercial lending.

competitive fringe (610)

The smaller firms which coexist with a few large firms in an oligopolistic industry: these firms have no influence over the market, especially in the setting of prices.

competitive process (610)

A process consisting of two opposing tendencies: the transfer mechanism which reallocates the market shares of the less efficient firms to the more efficient and the **innovation** mechanism which enables firms lagging behind their competitors to introduce new products or processes to reassert their position in a market.

Downie, J. (1958) *The Competitive Process*, London: Duckworth.

competitive tendering (320)

See: **compulsory competitive tendering**.

competitive trading (010)
The traditional method of exchange in a market consisting of buyers and sellers using their relative market strengths to reach an agreed single market price.

See also: **barter; countertrade**.

complement (010)
A good which is consumed in conjunction with another, e.g. petroleum with a car. Whether two goods are complements of each other can be discovered by measuring the **cross price elasticity of demand** between them. If the cross-elasticity is negative, then the good is a complement.

See also: **substitute**.

compliance cost (010, 320)
The cost of complying with a government regulation, including taxation. Such costs are incurred by the private sector and by governmental organizations below the level of central/federal government. The costs of compliance include accountants' fees and the **opportunity cost** of the time spent in filling up forms.

composite commodity (010)
A collection of goods representing purchasing power in general, or money as it is a medium of exchange. This composite is only possible if the prices of other goods remain constant. **Hicks** introduced the concept.

Hicks, J.R. (1939) *Value and Capital*, ch. 2, Oxford: Oxford University Press.

See also: *ceteris paribus*.

composite index (310)
1 The price index of the leading shares traded in Manila and Kuala Lumpur.

2 Toronto's stock market index.

composite insurance company (630)
An insurance company transacting a wide range of life and non-life insurance business.

composite rate tax (320)
UK tax on the income derived from bank and building society interest on deposits which was abolished in 1991.

compound interest (310)
Cumulative interest which is paid on both the original amount lent and subsequent interest which is added to the **principal**. If the total accumulation period is long, the total sum becomes immense compared with the original sum. Not surprisingly, **Keynes** asserted that 'there is no more powerful force than compound interest'.

Comprehensive Employment and Training Act 1973 (USA) (810)
US federal Act which consolidated previous training programs, chiefly designed to train youth. The Act's central aim was to give every youth and adult an opportunity to work. CETA decentralized planning procedures and implementation, which included on-the-job training. The Job Corps set up under Title IV was a residential program to provide remedial work and skills training for severely disadvantaged youths.

Comptroller of the Currency (310)
US office set up under the **National Banking Act** 1863 originally to deal with currency and monetary matters but the task of chartering and monitoring national banks given to it under the National Bank Act 1864 has become its principal concern.

compulsory competitive tendering (320)
The requirement by UK central government departments that local authorities put out major services, e.g. street cleaning, to **tender**. In many cases, the contract is awarded to the original local authority service.

compulsory savings (010)
See: **forced saving**.

Computer-Assisted Trading System (310)
Toronto-based securities trading system, the first of its type to receive orders from abroad electronically and to direct them immediately to its trading floor.

See also: **Stock Exchange Automated Quotation System**.

concentration (610)
The extent to which an industry is domi-

nated by a few firms. This can be measured by examining the proportion of production, sales, value added or employment attributable to the largest firm or firms. **Monopoly**, **duopoly** and **oligopoly** are the most concentrated of market forms; **perfect competition** is the least. British industry is more concentrated than that of the USA or other West European countries, partly because of its smaller domestic markets, which necessitate few firms per industry if **economies of scale** are to be achieved, and partly because of the weakness of the British policy on mergers.

See also: **aggregate concentration; concentration ratio; Gini coefficient; Herfindahl–Hirschman index; Lerner index; Lorenz curve; relative concentration**.

concentration economy (010, 930)
An **economy of scale** arising from the concentration of industry in a particular area.

See also: **agglomeration economy**.

concentration ratio (610)
1 An absolute ratio (sometimes called a leading firms ratio) which shows the percentage of sales, output, assets, value added or employment which can be ascribed to the largest firms of the industry, usually the top four or five. These ratios are more accurate if they are adjusted for imports and exports.

2 A relative ratio which is based on a size distribution of firms showing, for example, what proportion of firms has what proportion of output; **Lorenz curves** and **Gini coefficients** are used for this purpose.

See also: **aggregate concentration; Herfindahl–Hirschman index; Lerner index; N-firm concentration ratio**.

concrete labour (810)
The labour required to produce a particular product, e.g. a piece of furniture. Labour in this qualitative sense creates use values.

See also: **abstract labour**.

conditionality (310)
Lending to a debtor on condition that the loan is used for a specific purpose so that there is less risk of default in servicing the loan. It is argued that the **International Monetary Fund** and **World Bank** in making this stipulation make 'conditionality' a **public good**.

Condorcet criterion (010, 320)
A voting procedure by which the candidate is chosen on the basis of defeating all the others by obtaining the majority of the votes in pairwise elections.

Confederation of British Industry (610)
The major representative body for British industry, including both private and public sector firms. It makes known the view of industry on such bodies as the **National Economic Development Committee**. The CBI was created in 1965 as a result of the merging together of the Federation of British Industries (founded in 1916), the British Employers' Federation and the National Association of British Manufacturers.

confidence interval (210)
The range within which, to a certain percentage, one is confident that a sample statistic lies. Thus, with a 95 per cent confidence interval, if we sample 1,000 voters to ascertain their current opinion of the government we can be confident that only fifty are unrepresentative of the population as a whole. Confidence intervals are stated for **means**, **standard deviations**, proportions and differences.

See also: **confidence level**.

confidence level (210)
A confidence limit, or **critical value** expressed as a percentage.

confluence analysis (210)
A general statistical method used in econometrics, especially by **Frisch** and others from the 1930s onwards. It attempts to discover the different linear relationships between several observable variables, taking into account measurement errors.

Frisch, R. (1934) *Statistical Confluence Analysis by Means of Complete Regression Systems*, Oslo: Universitetets økonomiske institutt.

conglomerate (510)
A large firm, particularly in the USA, with

many subsidiary firms producing unrelated goods and services so as to reduce risk. Famous US conglomerates include ITT, LTV, Litton, Textro and Gulf and Western. Their recent growth has been hampered by the opposition of the US Department of Justice and periods of falling stock market prices. Their past growth was based on a simple mathematical truth that if a company with a high **price–earnings ratio** takes over one with a lower price–earnings ratio, the acquiring company's earnings per share will automatically rise, helping to finance further acquisitions.

conglomerate merger (520, 610)

A **merger** between two firms with different products and activities. These mergers are motivated by the desire to use under-utilized resources, particularly management and marketing. Although it is hoped that the merger will create a financially strong firm, rather than a firm with an increased market share, experience has shown that many mergers of this kind have not been financially successful.

Congressional Budget and Impoundment Control Act 1974 (320)

Major US federal statute which reformed the budget process by changing the fiscal year from 1 July to 1 October to give Congress more time to consider the Budget, created new budget committees, introduced a first budget resolution to establish ceilings on expenditure, revenue and debt and made anti-impoundment provisions to stop the President from seizing money voted to particular programmes: previously the President could refuse to spend monies for purposes which had been the subject of appropriation bills despite Congressional approval.

See also: **Gramm–Rudman–Hollings Act**.

consideration (310)

The value of a stock exchange transaction expressed in a particular currency. Also, it refers in the law of contract of common law jurisdictions (i.e. England, the USA and some Commonwealth countries) to the advantage or detriment which establishes a particular contract.

CONSOB (310)

Commissione nazionale per le società e la borsa: the Stock Exchange Commission of Italy, founded in 1974.

consol (310)

A consolidated fund stock ('Consolidated Annuity') of the British government issued as an unredeemable fixed-interest security. When first issued in 1751, they were introduced as a means of replacing a variety of government bonds of different maturities and interest rates with a single government stock. The yield on consols has often been used as a measure of the long-term rate of interest. The consols which are still traded in the UK are the 2 per cent issue of 1888 which was vaguely described as being redeemable on or after 1923.

Consolidated Fund (320)

The fund of the British central government into which all direct and indirect tax revenues and other receipts are paid. Prior to its establishment in 1787, separate funds existed for each type of government revenue.

See also: **funding**.

Consolidated Fund standing services (320)

An item of the British budget covering expenditures which do not require annual approval by parliament, e.g. interest on the national debt and the salaries of judges.

Consolidated Metropolitan Statistical Area (220, 840)

A large metropolitan complex of the USA of which a **Primary Metropolitan Statistical Area** is a component.

consolidation loan (310)

A loan offered by a financial institution to replace the several outstanding loans of a debtor. The replacement loan will be less costly to service each month and will be over a longer period. Persons with burdensome credit card debts can use loans of this kind, which are often secured on residential property.

consortium bank (310)

A bank jointly owned by a number of other banks for the purposes of giving small banks representation in a financial centre. These consortia deal with specific types of financing which require substantial resources, particularly major loans.

conspicuous consumption (010)
Expenditure on expensive goods to impress others with one's wealth and status rather than to satisfy basic needs. **Veblen** was the first to analyse ostentation of this nature.

constant capital (010)
The **Marxian** term for raw materials and machinery. This form of capital transfers only its own value, originally created by labour, to the finished product.

See also: **organic composition of capital**; **variable capital**.

constant elasticity of substitution production function (210)
A production function in which the elasticity of input substitution is constant at 1 or some other value. This production function succeeded the **Cobb–Douglas production function**.

Arrow, K.J., Chenery, H.B., Minhas, B.S. and Solow, R.M. (1961) 'Capital–labour substitution and economic efficiency', *Review of Economics and Statistics* 43: 225–50.

constant prices (220)
A measure of an economic variable deflated to allow for price changes, e.g. the national income at constant prices would show national income for a number of years at the prices of one year.

constant returns to scale (010)
See: **returns to scale**.

constrained market pricing (010, 610)
A concept used by US regulatory agencies, such as the **Interstate Commerce Commission**, for the regulation of prices such that prices constrained by competition are deregulated and other prices have to be set in the range between a floor price equal to marginal cost and a ceiling price which is equal to the **stand-alone cost**.

consumer credit (310, 920)
Credit granted by banks, finance houses and other financial institutions usually to purchase consumer durables and other goods and services except houses. The volume of this credit can be controlled by altering its price, i.e. by changing interest rates or the minimum size of initial deposits.

Consumer Credit Act 1974 (920)
UK statute which set up a system of consumer protection administered by the Director-General of Fair Trading. Agreements for credit under £5000 were regulated, businesses conducting consumer credit or consumer hire were licensed, credit advertisements were controlled and consumers were allowed a cooling-off period in which agreements could be cancelled.

consumer durable (010, 920)
A consumer **good** which is not immediately consumed but renders a stream of services, usually over a period of years. Vehicles, electrical goods and other durable household articles are major examples. Unlike the services of houses, there is no inclusion of the continuing benefits of consumer durable ownership in national income accounts and no allowance for their depreciation. Thus, although consumer durables resemble the fixed capital used by firms, they are classified as part of consumption. However, as their purchase often requires **consumer credit**, like fixed capital, the demand for them can be affected by monetary policy.

See also: **brown good**; **white good**.

consumer equilibrium (020)
That choice of expenditures, using a given income, which will maximize a consumer's **utility**. Formally it is expressed in the statement that each ratio of marginal utility from a particular good relative to its price is equal to every other such ratio throughout the consumer's purchases (if it is not it will be possible to redistribute one's expenditures to increase total utility). This equilibrium is based on the **law of diminishing marginal utility**.

$$\frac{\text{marginal utility of good A}}{\text{price of A}} = \frac{\text{marginal utility of good B}}{\text{price of B}}$$

$$= \ldots$$

$$= \frac{\text{marginal utility of good n}}{\text{price of n}}$$

Consumer Expenditure Survey (220)

US survey of the current expenditure of US residents which began in 1979. It is used to revise the **consumer price index** and is conducted by the Bureau of the Census for the Bureau of Labor Statistics. Information is collected from a panel which is interviewed five times every three months and from records kept by participating households over a specified fortnight.

consumerism (920)

Concerted action to make firms pursue the interests of consumers, even at the cost of shareholders' incomes. Action can take the form of lobbying parliaments for legislation, protest marches and legal suits. In response to these campaigns, many Western countries since the 1960s have introduced elaborate consumer protection legislation to ensure that consumers get a fair deal before, during and after buying a good or service. In the USA, for example, the **Federal Trade Commission** supervises advertising, the Fair Packaging and Labeling Act 1965 prevents inadequate product information on packages and labels, the Consumer Credit Protecting Act 1968 requires a simple statement of the details of loans, the Fair Credit Reporting Act 1970 allows consumers access to their credit reports and a variety of safety acts protect the users of cars, toys and other products. In the UK, the **Consumer Credit Act 1974** provides protection for British consumers.

However, there are still opponents of consumer protection who argue that regulation is an expensive and bureaucratic procedure which unduly restricts the behaviour of firms. Also, some consumers may be prepared to endure lower quality to make some purchases fall within their budgets.

Evans, J. (1980) *Consumerism in the United States*, New York: Praeger.

Swann, D. (1979) *Competition and Consumer Protection*, Harmondsworth: Penguin.

See also: **consumer sovereignty**.

consumer price index (220)

US price index which shows the average change in the prices of a representative basket of goods and services purchased for daily living by US households. Data are collected on the prices of food, clothing, housing, fuels and services etc. from eighty-five areas. Market prices, including indirect taxes, are used and each item is weighted according to its importance in consumers' budgets. The Bureau of Labor Statistics began the compilation of this index in 1919. Two versions of it are published: the **CPI-U** and the **CPI-W**.

See also: **Consumer Expenditure Survey**; **retail price index**.

consumer protection legislation (920)

Measures to enforce minimum standards in the provision of goods and services, to provide advisory services for consumers and, in the case of public corporations (UK), to establish users' councils to handle complaints. The principal measures which protect the British consumer are the Sale of Goods Act 1979, the Trade Descriptions Acts 1968 and 1972 and the Consumer Credit Act 1974. In the USA, the Food and Drug Administration and the Consumer Product Safety Council energetically protect the consumer.

See also: **consumerism**.

consumer society (070, 920)

A society which devotes a high proportion of its income to luxury goods and undertakes little saving. Only **market economies** have been prosperous enough to choose this lifestyle.

See also: **conspicuous consumption**.

consumer sovereignty (010, 530)

The decisive power of consumers to determine the amount and pattern of production by freely choosing goods and services in accordance with their preferences. Adam **Smith** in his rejection of **mercantilism** turned the goal of economic activity to satisfying the consumer rather than producers. **Neoclassical economics** built many of its theories on the notion of **consumer equilibrium**. Given the growth of large corporations with huge advertising budgets, **Galbraith** and others have challenged this view of the influence of consumers. Also, the increase in the role of government and the importance of **merit goods** has reduced the power of individual consumers in modern economies.

See also: **countervailing power**.

consumer's surplus (010)

The area, shaded in the figure, under an individual consumer's demand curve which shows the difference between what a consumer is willing to pay and what actually is paid. It will be greater for richer consumers as they have a higher demand; hence, when the price structure is designed to reflect consumer incomes, higher income groups pay more for a good service, e.g. employed persons are charged more than unemployed. This major concept, introduced into economics by **Dupuit** and refined by **Marshall** and **Hicks**, has become a major tool of **cost-benefit analysis**.

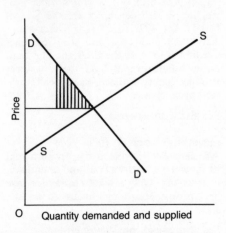

O   Quantity demanded and supplied

Bergson, A. (1975) 'A note on consumer's surplus', *Journal of Economic Literature* 13: 38–44.
Deaton, A. and Muellbauer, J. (1980) *Economics and Consumer Behavior*, New York and Cambridge: Cambridge University Press.

See also: **producer's surplus**.

consumption externality (010)

The effects of one person's consumption on the production and consumption of others, e.g. the effects of cigarette smoking on the health of non-smokers who are forced to be 'passive smokers' and are compelled to pay for the consequences of smoking on the health of smokers through higher medical insurance premia or higher taxes.

See also: **externality**.

consumption function (010, 210)

The relationship which shows aggregate consumption as a function of income (measured absolutely, relatively or permanently at current or constant prices) and possibly also wealth or the rate of interest. As consumption is the major part of national expenditure, the consumption function is central to models of income determination. **Keynes** in his *General Theory* inspired much of later work, which has included the **absolute income**, **relative income**, **permanent income** and **life-cycle** approaches.

consumption tax (320)

A tax levied on actual expenditures with the hope that it will encourage saving. In wartime when it has been necessary to curb consumption, taxes of this kind have been levied as an alternative to rationing.

See also: **expenditure tax**.

contango (310)

A charge made by a stockbroker for carrying over a sale or purchase of a security to the next accounting period. Also, in commodity markets it refers to spot prices being lower than futures prices.

See also: **backwardation**.

contemporaneous externality (010)

An economic activity which affects another type of production in the same time period, e.g. beekeeping which helps fruit farming.

See also: **sequential externality**.

contestable markets thesis (020)

Baumol's view that competition can be maintained by the state ensuring that an industry's barriers to entry are kept low. Under such circumstances, free entry and exit will maintain the market in a competitive state. This thesis is compatible with recent British **competition policy**.

Baumol, W.J., Panzar, J.C. and Willig, R.D. (1982) *Contestable Markets and the Theory of Industry Structure*, New York: Harcourt Brace Jovanovich.

contingency claims contracting (820)
See: **employment contract**.

contingency table (210)
A table in which the columns and rows are observed frequencies so that the expected frequency of a particular hypothesis can be investigated. These tables can be extended to more than two dimensions.

contingent fee (010)
A fee paid only on the successful outcome of an activity, e.g. a fee for a lawyer's services which is a percentage of the damages awarded to a plaintiff. It has been argued that this fee system encourages vexatious litigation in the USA.

contingent market (010, 630)
A market, particularly an insurance market, which transfers **risk** from those facing it to those who are prepared to undertake it. An example of this is when a shipowner faced with the risk of the loss of a ship can transfer the risk to **Lloyd's** insurers. If the insurance market is in equilibrium, the insurance premium should settle at the rate which equates the marginal cost of insurance to the marginal benefit of losing an undesired risk.

contingent valuation (720)
Valuation of commodities not traded in markets, e.g. clean air, landscapes and wildlife. The valuation is based upon the responses of individuals to questions about what their actions would be if a particular hypothetical situation were to occur. When the average of responses has been calculated, with weighting if necessary, the valuation of the population for a **public good** is ascertained. A proxy measure which has been used is the travel cost a person will incur to benefit from that environment.

Brookshire, D., Ives, B. and Schulze, W. (1976) 'The valuation of aesthetic preferences', *Journal of Environmental Economics and Management* 3: 325–46.

continuity thesis (030)
The view that there is a continuum between the allocation theory of **classical** and **neoclassical economists** with the consequence that there was no marginal revolution in the 1870s. Thus it is asserted that **Marshall** was not overturning classical economics but using the sharper tools of mathematics to clarify Ricardian economics as stated by John Stuart Mill.

Shove, G.F. (1942) 'The place of Marshall's *Principles* in the development of economic theory', *Economic Journal* 52: 294–329.

See also: **marginalists**.

continuous variable (210)
A variable, expressed in symbolic form, e.g. x or y, which can assume any value between two given values.

See also: **discrete variable**.

contract compliance (320, 820)
Obeying the terms and conditions of governmental contracts awarded to private sector firms. This approach has often been used, especially in the USA, as a means of advancing employment policies, e.g. the employment of women, blacks and disabled persons.

See also: **Fair Wages Resolution**.

contract curve (010)
1 A curve connecting the points of tangency of two individuals' respective **indifference curves** such that the **marginal rate of substitution** for them is the same.

2 An **isoquant** showing where the marginal rate of technical substitution is the same for the production of two different goods.

See also: **Edgeworth box**.

contracting (010, 530, 820)
Forming an agreement to supply a factor of production or a product.

See also: **employment contract**; **tendering**.

contractionary national income gap (010)
See: **deflationary gap**.

contractual savings (010, 910)
Savings which are made under a contract

which specifies regular payments into a fund over a minimum time period. The advantage to pension funds and life assurance companies of savings of this type is that they make possible long-term institutional investments, e.g. in real estate.

contracyclical policy (140)
See: **countercyclical policy**.

contribution standard (160)
A principle of income distribution which asserts that the productivity of different kinds of resources should determine income distribution. This principle is derived from the **marginal productivity theory** of distribution and is criticized on the grounds that it is very difficult to apply as a factor of production's own productivity is often inseparable from others.

See also: **equality standard**.

controlled market (010)
A market regulated by a central or local government. There can be control over price-setting, in the quantities which can be sold or in the range of people who are allowed to buy and sell. Many European countries in the past gave the police the power to regulate markets; today the principal organizations regulating prices have been set up under national price or agricultural policies. In practice, it is difficult to have complete control over a market as the prices set are unlikely to be permanently in equilibrium, thus giving buyers and sellers an incentive to evade the controls.

See also: **black market**; **prices policy**.

convergence hypothesis (070)
The supposition that different types of economy are becoming similar. This view was popular from the 1960s because **Soviet-type economies** modified their planning methods by making more use of the price system and market economies became more corporate and sympathetic towards public enterprise. It was argued that all economies were becoming **mixed economies**. Although economic reforms using prices have become increasingly popular in Eastern Europe, privatization has caused **market economies**

to revert more to their original form which was more capitalist than mixed.

conversion (310)
Replacing one kind of stock market security with another. Major types of conversion occur when an equity replaces a debenture, or a dated government bond is replaced by an undated one.

convertible currency (430)
A **currency** which can be exchanged for gold or a major currency. After the Second World War, the British pound did not return to full convertibility until 1958; in the late twentieth century, East European currencies have been the last major currencies to remain inconvertible.

See also: **Bullionist controversy**.

cooperative (510, 610)
A group of producers or consumers who join together to share the rewards of production including profits from retailing. The oldest consumers' cooperative was founded in Rochdale, Lancashire, in 1844; many producer cooperatives were founded in the USA and the UK in the last quarter of the nineteenth century. Unfair business competition, especially the withholding of supplies, destroyed many of the US cooperatives but some of the British cooperatives founded then still survive in printing, clothing and footwear manufacture. Self-management of Yugoslav enterprises and the large workers' cooperatives at Mondragon (in the Basque region of Spain) have attracted much attention in the past thirty years. All these enterprises have had to face the problems of under-investment (as producer-members often prefer present wages to future profits), low **productivity** and a lack of managerial experience. But poor performance has not been universal, as Mondragon shows.

Ireland, N.J. and Law, P.J. (1982) *The Economics of Labour-Managed Enterprises*, London: Croom Helm.
Vanek, J. (1970) *The General Theory of Labour-Managed Market Economies*, Ithaca, NY: Cornell University Press.

See also: **industrial democracy**; **workers' participation**.

cooperative federalism (320)
A federal state with much intergovern-

mental cooperation between federal and state governments. In particular, the different layers of government jointly participate in many programmes.

See also: **dual federalism; fiscal federalism.**

core (020, 210)

A set of possible equilibrium prices. As originally devised by **Edgeworth** in *Mathematical Psychics* (1881), it corresponds to all **Pareto-efficient** positions in a two-person, two-good economy which show improvement after trade. This concept has been applied to the study of cooperative games and is shown by the contract curve in the **Edgeworth box** diagram. The core coincides with a set of price equilibria under **perfect competition**, i.e. **general equilibrium.**

See also: **headline rate.**

core economy (010, 420)

A major economy, usually a **market economy**, which plays a major role in world trade.

core firm (510, 610)

A giant corporation which dominates a market.

core inflation rate (150)

The underlying trend in **inflation** which depends solely on past labour and capital costs and firms' **expectations** of changes in such costs. This rate changes only if expectations based on extrapolating from past costs change. To bring the core inflation rate of a major economy, such as the USA's, down to zero could require a steady fall in national output for several years. This rate is usually estimated by excluding volatile food and energy prices from the **consumer price index**.

Eckstein, O. (1981) *Core Inflation*, Englewood Cliffs, NJ, and London: Prentice Hall.

core region (730, 940)

A dominant or leading region of a country which often includes the capital city. The accumulation of physical and **human capital** is encouraged there by the **agglomeration** and **concentration economies** possible in such a large population.

corner solution (210)

An answer to an **optimization problem** in which one of the variables in a **trade-off** is zero at an optimum.

Corn Laws (040)

The series of English laws from the reign of Edward IV which protected English agriculture by imposing tariffs on the import of corn to maintain its price; also export bounties (subsidies) were granted to farmers. **Classical economists** such as **Smith** objected to this interference with **free trade**; **Ricardo** viewed it as an encouragement to production which would expand agriculture, a form of production subject to the **law of diminishing returns**, and bring about a decline in the rate of profit and a **stationary state** in the economy. The growing manufacturing interest also opposed **protection** which kept up food prices and wages. The Laws were repealed by the government led by Sir Robert Peel in 1846.

corn model (020, 030)

Ricardo's simple model of an economy with one commodity, corn, which is both the single input and single output of that country. Corn provides subsistence for workers who produce an annual output of corn. Thus a single commodity is both the intermediate and final product.

See also: **Sraffa.**

cornucopia (010)

An abundance of consumer goods possible only in a high income capitalist country, e.g. the USA.

corporate finance (310, 520)

Specialist financial services to corporations and other large organizations. Advice is given on raising new capital and on acquisitions.

corporate income tax (320)

A separate tax on firms which has the advantage of being easier to collect than an income tax applied to both persons and firms. As it is a tax on a special kind of factor income, pure corporate profits, it does not affect output in the short or long run.

corporate morality (610)

The maintenance of high ethical standards by businesses. This requires honesty in the accounting and other statements of corporate activity, high quality safe products, participation in community programmes, care for the environment, an awareness of the long-term interests of the economy in its investment policy and prompt payment of taxation in order to contribute sufficiently to public expenditure.

corporate state (070)

A state considerably influenced by relatively few large firms and trade unions which jointly, with the collaboration of the government, make the major economic decisions on which the running of an economy is based. Italian fascism of the interwar period took this form; UK governments of the 1960s and 1970s, according to their critics, adopted such a political philosophy. As the proportion of output produced by a few major companies increases in the USA and other Western countries, **corporatism** becomes a more important issue.

See also: **minimal state; state monopoly capitalism**.

corporate veil (310)

The disguises of firms to prevent government and shareholders knowing all of their activities, including the extent of their income. Shareholders' ignorance of a company's actual behaviour leads them to underestimate the true value of a company, e.g. they ignore the effect of current corporate saving on prospective **price–earnings ratios** and hence the stock market valuation of the company. Governments collect less in corporate taxation because of their ignorance of firms' total earnings.

corporation (510, 610)

A privately or publicly owned firm whose powers and activities are defined in the statute or articles which set it up. It is the major way of organizing a large firm in many countries and hence is responsible for most industrial and commercial output of several national economies. As most large corporations, whether in the public or private sectors, are to a large extent controlled by their managers, many have asked to whom they are ultimately responsible.

See also: **managerial models of the firm; multinational corporation; public enterprise; transnational corporation**.

corporation income tax (320)

A major tax used for raising revenue for the US federal government. To avoid its constitutionality being challenged in the courts, it was levied as an excise on the privilege of doing business as a corporation. Until 1941, it raised more revenue than the **individual income tax**. The tax is paid in two instalments in the first six months of the year following the tax year in which a corporation's income arises.

corporation tax (320)

A direct tax on the profits, after interest and depreciation, of companies. Separate income taxation for individuals and companies enables different rates to be charged. The yield from the corporation tax varies from country to country as a consequence of different tax rates and differences in corporate profitability.

corporatism (070)

Control of an economy by giving major economic decision-making to corporations, industrial ministries and, in some economies, leading **trade (labor) unions**. This was said to be the character of the UK economy in the 1960s and 1970s and has long been true of France.

See also: **corporate state; indicative planning**.

corrective subsidy (320)

A **subsidy** given to a firm as an incentive for internalizing an **externality**; a payment to cover the **social costs** borne by a firm.

See also: **Pigovian subsidy**.

corrective tax (320)

An **indirect tax** used to counter **externalities** thereby bringing about a **Pareto** equilibrium.

See also: **effluent fee**.

correlation (210)
The extent to which two variables are inter-dependent. Unlike **regression**, this calculation is not used to predict the value of one variable from the other.

See also: **autocorrelation; coefficient of correlation; Durbin–Watson statistic; multiple correlation; non-linear correlation; rank correlation; Spearman's rank correlation formula**.

correspondent bank (310)
A bank which accepts deposits from another bank located in another area to provide local services for it. Many banks internationally have this arrangement to be able to make payments in different currencies. In the USA, the **unit banking** system necessitated correspondent banking as a means of transferring funds between different localities.

corridor (010)
A range above and below the equilibrium path of an economy. Within the corridor, normal market forces bring the economy back to the equilibrium path.

'corset' (310)
The method of Bank of England control over commercial banks' liabilities in force from December 1973 to June 1980. A limit was placed on the amount of banks' sterling deposits and foreign currency deposits lent in sterling: if the limit was exceeded, a special deposit, bearing no interest, had to be lodged at the Bank of England. Banks objected to the way in which it encouraged companies to lend directly to each other rather than using banks as intermediaries. The removal of the corset led to an upsurge in the money supply.

See also: **disintermediation**.

cost–benefit analysis (130, 210)
The evaluation of an investment project with a long-term perspective from the viewpoint of the economy as a whole (although it is sometimes used in the private sector) by comparing the effects of undertaking the project with not doing so. This form of analysis was designed to provide a means for evaluating public works and development projects in cases where the value of them could be measured empirically. It can be traced back to **Dupuit**'s *De la mesure de l'utilité des travaux publics* (1844) but it was first applied as a technique for assessing projects under the US Flood Control Act 1936. The theoretical justification for many cost–benefit procedures was slight until **Hicks** published an article in 1943 on **consumers' surpluses**. A calculation of the **net present value** of expected costs and expected benefits makes it possible to use the decision rule that a project will only be undertaken if the benefits exceed the costs. The maximization of net social benefits came to be regarded as the appropriate criterion for selecting a project. The benefits and costs can be real (tangible or intangible) or pecuniary. Tangible benefits can often be equated with increased output, intangible benefits with prestige and the creation of something beautiful and pecuniary benefits with a change in the relative remuneration of an industry or an occupation.

Hicks, J.R. (1943) 'The four consumers' surpluses', *Review of Economic Studies* 11: 31–41.
Pearce, D.W. (1983) *Cost–Benefit Analysis*, 2nd edn, London: Macmillan.

See also: **compensation principle**.

cost-effectiveness analysis (210, 320)
An analysis of the costs of alternative programmes designed to meet a single objective. The programme which costs least will be the most cost effective. This form of analysis was first developed when Robert McNamara was Secretary of Defense (USA) in the 1960s.

See also: **planning programming; budgeting**.

costing margin (520)
An addition to average direct costs to cover indirect costs and provide a normal level of net profit under **full-cost pricing**. This rule is most likely to be used in a mature oligopolistic industry which is not faced with potential competition.

Andrews, P.W.S. (1949) *Manufacturing Business*, London: Macmillan.

cost, insurance and freight (220, 430)
The full-cost valuation of imports paid by purchasers. International trade statistics

usually measure imports 'CIF' so that all the charges of international trade are included in balance of payments accounts.

cost leader (610)

The lowest cost producer of an industry. This leadership is usually established by **economies of scale**, exclusive rights over new technology or preferential access to raw materials. A cost advantage has often been the basis of monopoly power.

cost of living adjustment (820)

See: **COLA**.

cost of living index (220)

Now termed in the UK the **retail price index**. It shows changes in the cost of purchasing a bundle of goods and services representative of the average consumer. The Ministry of Labour and its successor the Department of Employment have had the task of maintaining the index as it is of crucial importance to wage bargaining.

See also: **consumer price index**.

cost-push inflation (150)

Inflation caused by an autonomous increase in costs in the absence of an increase in demand. The principal cost increases are wage increases forced by powerful trade unions, imported raw material costs pushed up by international producers' cartels and the profit **mark-ups** of oligopolistic firms.

cost ratio (540)

The ratio to sales of factory costs, administrative costs, research and development costs, capital expenditure, selling costs or distribution costs.

cottage industry (040, 610)

An industry whose production takes place in workers' homes. Handloom weaving before the Industrial Revolution was organized in this way; now, **networking** and **telecommuting** are home-based.

See also: **domestic system; home production; homework; networking economy; proto-industrialization**.

Council for Mutual Economic Aid (420)

The intergovernmental council (abbreviated Comecon) established in 1949 between the USSR, Bulgaria, Czechoslovakia, Hungary, Poland and Romania, which has promoted mutual international trade and the coordination of national economic plans. (Albania joined in 1949, East Germany in 1950, Mongolia in 1962 and Vietnam in 1978; Romania weakened its ties in 1973 by making separate agreements with the European Community; Yugoslavia became an associate member in 1964; China and North Korea have enjoyed observer status since 1964.) It was established by Stalin to provide a socialist 'market' to oppose the worldwide capitalist market – hence Comecon was called 'the Russian Marshall Plan'. To Comecon were added the **International Bank for Economic Cooperation** and the **International Investment Bank** as alternatives to the **International Monetary Fund**.

Initially, Comecon agreed on general goals for trade and technical assistance which led to the joint organization of scientific research, technical assistance in the building of industrial plants and the development of mineral resources. In 1954, a step was made towards economic integration by the coordination of five-year plans and in 1955 production priorities for member states were established. Multilateral trade agreements were recommended, as was the coordination of energy policies. Although in 1961 'Basic Principles' for the long-term plans of member countries were drawn up, Soviet proposals the following year for a single plan and a single planning authority were rejected as being an encroachment on national sovereignty. The International Bank of Economic Cooperation was chartered in 1963 to arrange multilateral payments and short-term credits and the International Investment Bank was created in 1970 to finance specific projects which were part of coordinated five-year plans. In 1970, medium- and long-term cooperation up to 1980 was agreed; to implement this, central economic planning machinery was set up in Moscow. In 1987, direct links within Comecon between productive enterprises and research institutes of the USSR and Eastern Europe in the form of joint ventures were set up. To avoid currency negotiations, dividends could be paid in goods. The political convulsions of 1989 in Eastern Europe provoked some members of Comecon to call for a more market-oriented approach to their economic decision-making. Comecon was dissolved in June 1991.

Schiavone, G. (1981) *The Institutions of Comecon*, London: Macmillan.

council housing (930)
UK housing owned by local government. Less of the UK housing stock is now publicly owned as a result of the Conservative government policy in the 1980s of allowing council house tenants to purchase the houses which they had for a long time rented at less than market rates. Economists have been concerned that much of this housing has been let at less than market rents and by the impact on geographical labour mobility of access to housing being dependent on continued residence in the same locality.

Council of Economic Advisers (140, 310, 320)
The team of three in the USA which advises the President on the state of the economy. This Council was set up under the Employment Act 1946. A principal task of the Council is to assist the President in preparing his annual Economic Report to the Congress, a report which formulates broad guidelines for stabilization policy and other aspects of the government's economic programme. The academics chosen as members of the Council will usually have political views close to those of the Administration.

council tax (320)
UK local property tax proposed by the government in 1991 as a replacement of the **community charge**. Poorest households would be exempt from it; other households would be assessed on the assumption that two adults live in the household (a single person would have a rebate of 25 per cent). The value of each property would be placed within one of seven bands, which would be defined differently for England, Scotland and Wales.

countercyclical policy (140)
Government policy to reduce fluctuations in national economic activity by stabilizing prices, investment or **aggregate demand**. To be successful as a policy, the timing of

government spending has to be such as to restore the economy to an equilibrium path, the trend line through cyclical fluctuations. Since 1933 Sweden has been the best-known user of such policies but in the 1950s, when **demand management** was believed to be a possible art, many Western economies used monetary, fiscal and other policies to reduce fluctuations in the gross domestic product and in employment. In less developed countries it is more difficult to have successful countercyclical measures because fluctuations in climate and in export demand (which are of central importance to primary producers) cannot be controlled by governments, because poverty itself is more a product of long-run factor shortages than deficiency in home demand and because taxation and expenditure affect a smaller percentage of the population.

Baumol, W.J. (1961) 'Pitfalls in contracyclical policy: some tools and results', *Review of Economics and Statistics* 43: 21-6.

See also: **investment reserve system**; **Swedish budget**.

counterparty capital (310)
The capital required by a securities house to cover the risk that a party being dealt with in the settlement system has little or no credit to meet a payment due.

counterpurchase (420)
Countertrade which is not entirely barter as the exporter requires part payment in cash.

countertrade (420)
Barter or parallel sales and purchases; a method of trade between East and West which has been used to minimize the need for East European countries to use hard currencies.

Hammond, G.T. (1990) *Countertrade, Offsets and Barter in International Political Economy*, London: Pinter.
Korth, C.M. (ed.) (1987) *International Countertrade*, New York: Quorum.

countervailing power (010, 140, 610, 830)
The power of an opposing group, e.g. of a trade union facing a large firm, or of a major consumer facing a monopolist/oligopolist. The best examples of it occur under **bilateral monopoly**. **Galbraith** regarded such power

as a means of stabilizing and rendering more fair the capitalist system.

Galbraith, J.K. (1952) *American Capitalism: The Concept of Countervailing Power*, London: Hamish Hamilton; Boston, MA: Houghton Mifflin.

See also: **consumer sovereignty**.

country fund (310)

A fund of stocks and shares invested in the securities of only one country. These funds provide a means of investing in countries whose stock exchanges allow only limited access by foreigners. As such funds are less liquid than **open-ended funds** which can invest globally, they often sell at a discount to their net asset value.

coupon (310)

1 Originally the warrant which had to be presented to obtain interest on a bond.

2 The nominal rate of interest, e.g. £5 per £100 of nominal stock. It is to be distinguished from the bond's **yield** which will be higher than the coupon if the market price of the bond is lower than its nominal price, and vice versa.

Cournot, Antoine Augustin, 1801–77 (030)

French mathematician and philosopher who was a major founder of mathematical economics. His important work, which was to inspire **Marshall** considerably, formulated the law of demand (with demand curves constructed for the first time in economics), rigorously expounded theories of **duopoly**, **bilateral monopoly** and **oligopoly**, and examined the incidence of **indirect taxes** and costs. As a French civil servant and academic he also wrote on probability and epistemology. His principal work on economics was *Recherches sur les Principes Mathématiques de la Théorie des Richesses* (1838), republished in English as *Researches into the Mathematical Principles of the Theory of Wealth* (New York, 1960).

Theocharis, R.D. (1983) *Early Developments in Mathematical Economics*, 2nd edn, ch. 9, London: Macmillan.

Cournot's duopoly model (020)

A market model of two springs and two proprietors, each of whom independently seeks to maximize his income. As proprietor A has no direct influence on the sales of water from proprietor B's spring, A can only adjust his price but B is forced to accept A's price. If A's sales are D_1 and B's sales are D_2, the final and stable equilibrium occurs where

$$f(D_1 + D_2) + D_1 f'(D_1 + D_2) = 0$$
$$f(D_1 + D_2) + D_2 f'(D_1 + D_2) = 0$$

Cournot, A. (1897) *Researches into the Mathematical Principles of the Theory of Wealth*, trans. by N.T. Bacon, ch. 7, New York: Macmillan.

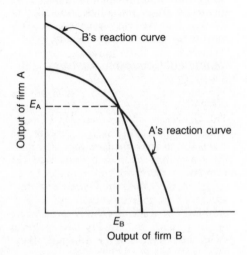

B's reaction curve

Output of firm A

E_A

A's reaction curve

E_B

Output of firm B

See also: **duopoly**.

cover (310)

Earnings available to shareholders divided by the total amount of dividend paid. Thus, if cover is 3.2, the dividend is covered more than three times so that it is unlikely that dividend will have to be cut in the next year and the company has sufficient retained earnings to be able to expand. However, a company with a high cover for a number of years appears to be unadventurous and neglecting growth opportunities.

cowboy (510)

A small-scale business, often in the construction industry, which dishonestly performs a contract and then rides away before non-performance of the contract is discovered.

cowboy economy (070, 720)

An **economy**, like the US economy, which behaves as if natural resources are infinite in supply and that nature can absorb any amount of refuse. **Boulding** coined this term to describe the 'Wild West' philosophy still prevalent in modern USA.

See also: **spaceman economy**.

Cowles Commission (210)

US econometric research centre which was founded in Colorado Springs in 1932 and subsequently moved to Chicago University in 1939 to avoid the Colorado state income tax which affected its publisher benefactor. It was noted in its early days for the distinctive econometric methodology of **Haavelmo** and his followers which concentrated on the problems of simultaneity, identification and estimation.

Haavelmo, T. (1944) 'The probability approach in econometrics', *Econometrica (Supplement)* 12: 1–115.

Hildreth, C. (1986) *The Cowles Commission in Chicago, 1935–55*, Berlin: Springer Verlag.

See also: **econometrics**.

CPE (070)

See: **centrally planned economy**.

CPI (220)

See: **consumer price index**.

CPI-U (220)

A version of the US **consumer price index** for all urban consumers which covers about 80 per cent of the US population.

CPI-W (220)

A version of the US **consumer price index** for all urban wage earners and clerical workers which covers about 32 per cent of the US population.

CPP (540)

See: **current purchasing power**.

CPS (320)

See: **Centre for Policy Studies**; **current population survey**.

craft union (830)

A **trade (labor) union** which draws all of its membership from a 'trade', i.e. a few closely related occupations, e.g. in engineering or printing. Many of the first unions in the UK and the USA were of this nature. Craft unionism has been blamed for much **demarcation** which, as it restricts the use of labour to fewer tasks, raises labour costs. Unskilled workers, before forming general unions, resented the craft unions for maintaining a labour elite.

See also: **general union**; **industrial union**.

crawling peg (430)

An exchange rate adjustment method which gradually changes the par value of an exchange rate by small amounts. This is less disruptive than **devaluation** or revaluation which can encourage speculation.

creative accounting (540)

The manipulation of the accounts of a firm, or other enterprise, to produce a more favourable picture of its financial state. Profits are made to appear higher to induce a rise in the company's share price; costs are inflated to justify product price increases. A variety of methods can be used, e.g. changing the method of allocating expenses, changing the valuation of assets and using more convenient exchange rates than those ruling at the time of the transaction. Some of these practices are within the rules of company law; others are so questionable as to amount to deception. British local authorities in the 1980s used many devices to increase their spending, including selling their principal buildings and leasing them back, barter (e.g. exchanging council land for a new building), rescheduling debts and capitalizing current expenditure (e.g. including house repairs in its capital programme).

Griffiths, I. (1986) *Creative Accounting: How to Make Your Profits What You Want Them to Be*, London: Sedgeworth & Jackson.

creative destruction (620)

Schumpeter's description of the evolutionary process inherent in **capitalism** as entrepreneurs employ new products and new processes to supplant the old.

Schumpeter, J.A. (1976) *Capitalism, Socialism*

and Democracy, 5th edn, New York: Harper; London: Allen & Unwin.

creative federalism (320)

A cooperative partnership between the federal, state and local governments of the USA which led to many new programmes. President Lyndon B. Johnson used this term to describe US federalism in the 1960s.

See also: **cooperative federalism**; **dual federalism**; **fiscal federalism**.

credit (310, 520)

A loan, or an agreement to lend money, which will be repaid at a later date. It refers in macroeconomics to bank lending as credit is chiefly analysed in the context of discussions of the money supply; in microeconomics it has a broader meaning, encompassing all the sources of finance available to firms (including **trade credit**) and to households.

In the past two decades there has been a great increase in the amount of credit given to households on the basis either of collateral (a house in the case of a building society mortgage) or of **credit scoring** for hire purchase expenditure on consumer durables. The creation of new credit instruments, e.g. the **credit card**, has resulted in an expansion in the total volume of credit.

Beckman, T.N. and Foster, R.S. (1969) *Credits and Collections: Management and Theory*, 8th edn, New York: McGraw Hill.

credit card (310)

A means of purchasing consumer goods and services by presenting a card issued by a bank, financial institution or retailer permitting the buyer to settle in part or in full the amount payable. Major examples of these include Visa and Mastercard. Such cards, in use in the USA since 1950 and in Britain since 1966, have contributed to the large increase in consumer debt. As the banks financing these cards advance the amount due to retailers and collect from the cardholders later, they bring about a short-term increase in the money supply. Like the development of other modern financial arrangements, credit cards have made it more difficult for central banks to control the money supply.

See also: **charge card**; **debit card**; **smart card**.

credit crunch (310)

A shortage of bank loans and other forms of **credit** which brings about the curtailment of a business's activities or even its collapse. Credit can be limited by its price, by the type of borrower or by the state of the lender's balance sheet relative to the criteria used by a regulatory body (this often happened in the USA under **Regulation Q**); in the last case the crunch comes because the lender cannot use his funds.

Wojnilower, A.M. (1980) 'The central role of credit crunches as recent financial history', *Brookings Papers on Economic Activity* 2: 277–326.

credit money (310)

Banknotes and bank deposits. This **medium of exchange** has gradually displaced coinage made of precious metals.

credit multiplier (310)

See: **money multiplier**.

credit rating (430)

Measuring the creditworthiness of a government or corporation. For a government, a scale from the lowest (0) to the best (100) using the information supplied by leading international banks is used; for corporations, the most famous rating is conducted by **Standard & Poor**.

credit rationing (310)

Control by a central bank of the total volume of **bank deposits** by restricting the total amount which can be borrowed or by excluding types of borrower. The aim of this rationing is to reduce the risk of borrowers defaulting or to prevent increases in interest rates. In the UK this was traditionally done by the **bank rate** which provided the basis for all other interest rates. However, in the UK as elsewhere a greater variety of controls has been employed. The recent growth of a variety of money markets, where interest rates are largely determined within each market, has weakened the power of central banks to exercise complete control.

See also: **'corset'**; **special deposit**.

credit reserves (430)

Gold and foreign currency reserves of

central banks which are used to settle inter-country indebtedness. Increasingly, major currencies, such as those of the USA, Germany, Japan, Switzerland and the UK, have been held in preference to gold.

credit scoring (310)
Assessments of applicants for credit using a points system. A score is awarded for each of the applicant's characteristics, e.g. home ownership, employment and payment record for previous credit. Credit is granted if the total score is above the acceptance level.

Credit Suisse index (310)
An index of the prices of leading Swiss securities.

credit tranche facility (430)
An **International Monetary Fund** lending facility to help a member country to deal with a short-term balance of payments problem. The loan has to be repaid over a three-to five-year period. It is similar to a **compensatory financial facility**.

credit union (310)
A friendly society whose members save to provide small loans at an interest rate lower than the market rate to other members in need of financial assistance. The group forming a credit union usually resides in the same area, works for the same employer or belongs to another association, e.g. a church. In the depressed areas of Britain in the 1980s they have become popular alternatives to the main financial institutions. By 1990, 310 were formed in the UK with over 40,000 members; the USA has more than 60 million persons in credit unions. Credit unions appeared in Germany as early as the 1860s.

crisis (140)
In Marxian economics, a phase of the **trade cycle** which is the upper turning point when an economy turns down from a **boom** to a **recession**. **Marx** believed that such crises were inevitable under **capitalism** and would occur every ten years. It is asserted that a crisis occurs for two reasons. The preceding increase in employment has pushed up wages and reduced the rate of profit below the normal level, cutting back capital accumulation; also, producers who are slow to innovate have higher costs and may go bankrupt, spreading a collapse of firms throughout the economy. Crises, according to Marxists, are inevitable under capitalism because of continual capital accumulation without the coordination of investment decision-making which planning would achieve.

Sweezy, P.M. (1942) *The Theory of Capitalist Development: Principles of Marxian Political Economy*, chs 8–10, New York: Oxford University Press; London: D. Dobson.

crisis management (510)
Working out strategies to deal with possible disasters, e.g. floods, interference with the quality of a product or an act of war. Not only do the emergency services of police, fire brigades and ambulances have to consider worst case scenarios but firms have to make allowance for possible crises: they may do this by maintaining **excess capacity** and keeping large inventories, e.g. to guard against a disruption in the supply of crucial components.

critical value (210)
The lower or upper value of a **confidence interval**.

cross price elasticity of demand (010)
The responsiveness of the quantity demanded of one good to a change in the price of another good. It can be measured, for example, as the ratio of the percentage change in quantity demanded of good A to the percentage change in the price of good B. If A and B are substitutes the cross price elasticity is positive; it is negative if A and B are complements. The concept has been used extensively by analysts of market concentration and **antitrust** lawyers as it indicates whether the dissimilar output from different firms is supplied to one or several markets.

See also: **elasticity**.

cross-section data (220)
Data referring to different groups at the same point in time, e.g. wages of workers in different countries at a particular date. Economic analysis based on **time series** data faces the problem of the effects of the

passage of time on **exogenous variables**; cross-sectional analysis eliminates this difficulty.

cross-subsidization (520)

The financing of an unprofitable part of an enterprise by a more profitable part. Thus a public enterprise, for example, instead of following the rule of attributing costs properly to each division to make each part of that enterprise individually financially accountable, will allow the profitable divisions to finance loss-making divisions. In the private sector, cross-subsidization occurs within firms which allow some of their products to be sold at less than incremental cost. To ensure maximum efficiency, firms should avoid this practice as far as possible.

cross-trading (010)

A method of disposing of all the goods a seller offers in a market by selling the same good at different prices throughout a trading day, with prices falling towards the end of the day.

crowding hypothesis (820)

The view that **discrimination** occurs because some workers are crowded into the few occupations without barriers to entry. Women's wages, for example, have been depressed by an excess supply to the few jobs traditionally available for women. Both John Stuart **Mill** and **Edgeworth** clearly used this model of discrimination.

See also: **occupational segregation**.

crowding out (310, 320)

An alleged effect on private sector demand of an increase in public expenditure. It is argued (especially by **monetarists**) that **Keynesian-style** budget deficits will raise borrowing with the effect of increasing interest rates which will lead to a reduction in private sector investment and expenditure on consumer durables. The stimulative effect of increased government expenditure will be cancelled out by expenditure reductions in the private sector. The reduction in business investment, in the long term, will further reduce the ability of the private sector to spend. The size of this effect depends strongly on the **elasticity** of **IS–LM curves**. In the figure, although an increase in

government expenditure raises the IS curve from IS_1 to IS_2, because of the inelasticity of the LM curve the rate of interest rises from r_1 to r_2 without an increase in national income. Crowding out may also occur because increased government spending changes private sector **expectations** about the future of the economy, thereby reducing the amount of investment carried out.

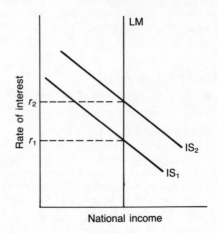

Carlson, K.M. and Spencer, R.W. (1975) 'Crowding out and its critics', *Federal Reserve Bank of St Louis Review* 57, 2–17.
Friedman, B.M. (1978) 'Crowding out or crowding in? Economic consequences of financing government deficits', *Brookings Papers on Economic Activity* 9, 593–641.

crude population rate (840)

The ratio of births or deaths, or other demographic events, to the average total population of a country at the midpoint of a specified period, usually a year. These rates are called 'crude' because the population used in the denominator is not adjusted to give the measure theoretical significance, e.g. a crude birth rate per total population is less useful in a demographic model than a birth rate per women of child-bearing age.

CS (220)

See: **cross-section data**.

CSO (220)

Central Statistical Office (UK) which is responsible for the regular publication of leading economic statistics.

CTD (310, 320)
Certificate of tax deposit.

CTN (630)
Confectioner, tobacconist and newsagent: a British firm which combines these types of retailing.

CTT (320)
See: **capital transfer tax**.

Cultural Revolution (040, 060)

A change in the organization of the Chinese society and economy in the late 1960s and 1970s. This revolution challenged the division of labour previously practised, especially by breaking down the division between the town and countryside. Revolutionary factory committees were set up to implement changes which included using five-year plans only as general guidelines, requiring administrators to work two or three days per week in manual work and the setting up of work teams involved in matters as diverse as production planning, assigning production tasks, establishing safety regulations and managing welfare funds. Mass action was used to unify the working class.

Bettelheim, C. (1974) *Cultural Revolution and Industrial Organization in China. Changes in Management and the Division of Labour*, trans. by A. Ehrenfeld, New York and London: Monthly Review Press.

cum dividend (310)

A stock exchange security with the entitlement to receive an imminent dividend.

cumulative multistage cascade system (320)

A sales tax on the gross value of a commodity at each stage of production which does not allow a rebate of taxes paid at earlier stages of production. This tax was in force in West Germany until the end of 1967, in Luxemburg until the end of 1969 and in the Netherlands until the end of 1968.

cumulative preference share (310)
See: **preference share**.

cumulative security (310)

A stock exchange security which accumulates unpaid interest or preference dividends so that the holder does not suffer from a year of poor profitability. In return for this greater security of income, many cumulative **preference shares** are without voting rights.

currency (430)

The official money currently circulating in a country and available for immediate use as a medium of exchange. It can take the form of coins, **banknotes** and, in a broader sense, **bank deposits**. Currencies are called by various names, the most popular being dollar, franc and kroner. The value of a currency is regarded as an overall indicator of world opinion about that country's economy. Apart from the use of prudent fiscal and monetary policies to boost confidence in a currency, there are other ways of making a currency attractive. A central bank can produce beautiful banknotes, offer **convertibility** into another currency or raise its interest rates to encourage foreign holdings of that currency. A few small countries – Luxemburg, Panama and Liechtenstein – do not have their own currencies.

See also: **coinage**.

currency appreciation (430)

A rise in the international value of a currency. If, for example, more French francs are exchanged than previously for the same amount of US dollars, the dollar has appreciated.

currency basket (430)

A combination of currencies to produce a common unit, e.g. the **ecu**. The values of these currencies are weighted, e.g. by shares in world trade or the gross national products of the countries participating.

currency depreciation (430)

A fall in the international value of a currency as less of another currency is exchanged for one unit of one's own. Residents of one country using the currency in other countries will have their purchasing power per unit of the currency reduced. Depreciation can occur very rapidly in foreign exchange markets in reaction to bad news about the state of the economy issuing the currency.

currency devaluation (430)

A fall in a **fixed exchange rate** which reduces

the value of a currency in terms of other currencies. The pound, for example, was devalued in 1949 from US$4.03 to US$2.80 and in 1967 from US$2.80 to US$2.40. The aim of devaluation is to improve the balance of payments current account, as the change in the exchange rate by raising import prices and lowering export prices will reduce imports and increase exports, provided that there is a price-elastic demand for both and the possibility of diverting production to exports and substitutes for imports by reducing domestic expenditure.

See also: **J-curve; Marshall–Lerner condition**.

currency market (430)
See: **foreign exchange market**.

currency reform (430)
Replacing an existing currency which has lost its value with a new currency. Germany after the First and Second World Wars provides good examples of this. On an appointed day, holdings of the old currency are replaced by the new at a particular exchange rate. The intention of such reform is to restore confidence in the money used by a state. In some extreme cases where a currency has been severely devalued, it has changed its name, e.g. in Peru the sol de oro became the inti.

currency revaluation (430)
A deliberate increase in the price of a currency which has a fixed exchange rate. This is undertaken to reduce a balance of payments surplus. Revaluation is often prompted by the requests of countries in deficit who hope to compete more easily in international markets. As a consequence of a revaluation, a central bank suffers losses from the fall in value of its foreign exchange holdings: taxpayers ultimately bear these losses as central banks are usually owned by governments.

Currency School (030, 310)
A group of British economists who, following **Ricardo**, believed that the note issue should be convertible and strictly determined by the amount of gold possessed by the Bank of England. The leaders of the School, Robert **Torrens** and Samuel **Loyd** (later Lord Overstone) convinced the British Prime Minister Sir Robert Peel of their theory – hence the **Bank Charter Act of 1844** which was to provide the framework for many of the operations of British banking until 1980.

Felter, F.W. (1965) *Development of British Monetary Orthodoxy, 1719–1875*, Cambridge, MA: Harvard University Press.

currency stabilization scheme (430)
An international arrangement by which a group of states agrees to link the exchange rate values of their currencies to gold, a leading currency (e.g. the US dollar) or an **artificial currency**. The first scheme in the post-1945 period was **Bretton Woods**; the major one in force at the present time is the **European Monetary System**.

currency swap (430)
A capital market exchange of a loan in one currency for a loan in another, e.g. a fixed interest dollar loan for a floating interest loan in Swiss francs.

current account (310, 430)
1 A bank account of a British clearing bank which is immediately available for settling payments. In the past, bank accounts of this type never earned interest; some now do. In the USA they are known as **checking accounts** or **sight deposits**.

2 A subaccount of a nation's **balance of payments** accounts consisting of visible and invisible trade plus private and official current transfers; capital flows are in the separate capital account.

See also: **NOW account.**

current assets (520)
The assets of a firm convertible into cash within a period of twelve months. They consist of stock-in-trade, work-in-progress, debts owed to the firm, readily realizable investments, bills receivable, prepayments, cash at the bank and in hand.

See also: **current liabilities**.

current cost accounting (540)
A form of accounting which includes adjustments for the effects of inflation. Britain's

Statement of Standard Accounting Practice 1980 required adjustments to be made to **depreciation** for fixed assets which had risen in price, to sales figures for the higher cost of replacing stocks and to monetary working capital.

See also: **inflation accounting; Sandilands Report**.

current deposit (310)
A bank deposit of a UK bank which is payable on demand, now termed a **sight deposit**.

See also: **demand deposit; time deposit**.

current liabilities (520)
The debts of a firm payable within the current accounting period, usually twelve months, which include sums owed by creditors and bills payable. These are liquid if payable within a month; otherwise, 'deferred'.

See also: **current assets**.

current operating profit (520)
The current value of output sold over a period, less the current cost of related inputs.

current population survey (840)
A survey of US households which is undertaken by the US Census Bureau. Its monthly surveys are used to provide data on employment, unemployment, wages and hours statistics. Also it provides annual figures on school enrolments, living arrangements, annual incomes, poverty status and other important socio-economic variables.

current prices (220)
A measurement of an income variable at the prices of the period for which data were collected, e.g. consumption at current prices would show for years X, Y and Z the actual cost of purchasing such goods and services at the prices ruling in years X, Y and Z respectively.

current purchasing power (540)
The historic value of an asset adjusted by changes in a retail price index.

See also: **inflation accounting**.

current ratio (540)
The ratio of **current assets** to **current liabilities** of a firm. Also known as a working capital ratio or 2:1 ratio following the rule of thumb that assets should be twice liabilities, unless the seasonal or speculative nature of the firm requires more working capital. This is the principal measure of the **liquidity** of a firm.

customize (530)
To modify the standard design of a **consumer durable** by minor changes in its appearance or functions to allow its owner to express his or her personality, e.g. replacing small car/automobile wheels by larger ones.

customs union (420)
A group of countries with a **common external tariff** but with free trade amongst themselves and free movement of labour and capital. The **European Community** is a major example of such an arrangement. Many theories about customs unions are based not only on how free trade based on **comparative advantage** is beneficial but also on **location theory** to understand the changes within the customs union, e.g. the movement of capital and population towards **growth poles** creating a dynamic effect of a union.

C'vr (310)
See: **cover**.

CW (820)
See: **comparable worth**.

cyclical trade (420)
A type of **intra-industry trade**, particularly in agricultural products which are traded north to south between the two hemispheres in one harvest and south to north in the other part of the year.

cyclical unemployment (140, 810)
Recurrent unemployment which occurs at particular phases of the **business cycle**, starting with the downturn from a boom. This unemployment is caused by a deficiency of **aggregate demand** and is associated with a fall in the number of job vacancies.

cyclical variations (210)

Movements in a **time series** brought about by the **business** or **trade cycle**. These components of changes in the values of a variable can be removed from raw data by first removing seasonal variations by making a **seasonal adjustment** and then dividing the adjusted data by corresponding trend values.

D

D (310)
A security regarded as of questionable value by the rating agency **Standard & Poor**.

See also: **AAA**; **BBB**; **BB**; **C**; **DDD**.

DAC (430)
Development Aid Committee of the Organization for Economic Cooperation and Development. It publishes annual reports on the size of aid flows to developing countries.

daisy-chain scheme (320)
A commercial scheme for passing a commodity through a chain of company subsidiaries to avoid taxation.

data (220)
Measured observations obtained from official or privately collected statistics: the raw material of empirical economics.

data-mining (210)
Persistent and repeated attempts to find significant relationships between variables. However, the excessive zeal of the researcher may produce a false relationship. This misuse of **econometrics** gives undue prominence to insignificant economic relationships.

David Hume Institute (610)
An economic research institute founded in 1985 and now based in Edinburgh, Scotland, with Sir Alan Peacock as its first executive director. It has examined the economics of regulation, broadcasting, small firms and banking.

Davignon Plan (630)
The plan, named after the **European Communities'** Industry Commissioner Viscount Etienne Davignon, of the European Coal and Steel Community in 1980 to restructure the European steel industry. State aid was offered (mainly for environmental improvements or research and development) pro-

vided that there was a cut in steel-making capacity. Minimum prices were set together with production quotas to cover 85 per cent of the Community's output. The Plan has succeeded to the point of scrapping production quotas by the end of 1987 and using market forces to complete the adjustment process.

dawn raid (310)
A method of acquiring the shares of a company which was popular in London in the early 1980s. A company was taken over by rapid purchase of shares at the beginning of the working day. Since shares were acquired at different prices, the International Stock Exchange Council has now regulated this technique.

DAX (310)
The leading share index of the stock exchanges of Germany.

days of grace (310)
The extra days after a debt, e.g. an insurance premium, is due in which the debtor is allowed to pay.

DC (220)
Developed country. Many of these are members of the **Organization for Economic Cooperation and Development**.

DCE (310, 430)
See: **domestic credit expansion**.

DCF (520, 540)
See: **discounted cash flow**.

DDD (310)
Standard & Poor's credit rating of a security which reflects that servicing of it is in default or in arrears.

See also: **AAA**; **BBB**; **BB**; **C**; **D**.

deadweight loss (010)
A loss of **consumer's surplus** by buyers not matched by a corresponding **producer's sur-**

plus. This concept is crucial to much of **welfare economics**, e.g. the analysis of the effects of a monopoly, of taxes and of tariffs. The size of the deadweight loss depends on the elasticity of demand or supply.

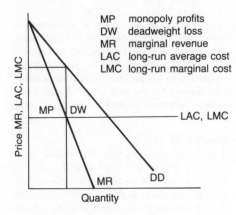

MP	monopoly profits
DW	deadweight loss
MR	marginal revenue
LAC	long-run average cost
LMC	long-run marginal cost

Deane, Phyllis Mary, 1918– (030)
Educated at Glasgow University. Research officer at the National Institute for Economic and Social Research from 1941 to 1945, at the Colonial Office from 1946 to 1949 and at the Department of Applied Economics, Cambridge, from 1950 to 1951. Fellow of Newnham College, Cambridge, from 1961 to 1983 and professor of economic history from 1981 to 1982. She has produced several works on colonial national income accounting and the celebrated *The First Industry Revolution* (Cambridge: Cambridge University Press, 1965) and *The Evolution of Economic Ideas* (Cambridge: Cambridge University Press, 1978), one of the finest introductions to the history of economic thought.

debasing a currency (310)
An action taken by a monetary authority which reduces the value of the money it issues, e.g. by reducing the intrinsic value of the currency or by over-issuing banknotes. This is usually done to finance government expenditure and to extract a high level of **seignorage**.

debenture (310)
A company or corporation security, usually taking the form of a fixed interest loan, which is secured on the assets of a company.

debit card (310)
A card which makes possible the immediate debiting of a bank account at the time of purchasing goods or services; an 'electronic cheque book'. In the late 1980s major British clearing banks, for example, made arrangements with retailers to introduce this system which makes possible transactions without the use of **cash**, **cheques** or **credit cards**. Credit is only given to debit cardholders with permission to overdraw.

Debreu, Gerard, 1921– (030)
A French émigré to America in 1948, who was educated in mathematics in Paris and subsequently became professor at Chicago, Yale and Berkeley (since 1960). With Arrow in 1954, he used topological methods to prove the existence of **general equilibrium**. His *Theory of Value, an Axiomatic Analysis* (1959, 1971) produced a more sophisticated exposition of competitive price theory, using set theory and topology. In 1983 he was awarded the **Nobel Prize for Economics**. His work is characterized by a purely theoretical rather than empirical approach.

Debreu, G. (1983) *Mathematical Economics: Twenty Papers of Gerard Debreu*, Cambridge: Cambridge University Press.

debt (310, 320, 520)
The liabilities of a firm, a government or a household. A company's debt often takes the form of fixed interest **debentures**, cumulative non-voting preference shares and short-term bank loans. A government has **bills** as short-term debt and long-term debt is issued as **bonds**. Households' debts include bank loans and liabilities incurred to purchase property and consumer durables.

debt contract (310)
An agreement to lend money.

debt–equity swap (310, 430)
The exchange of a fixed interest debt for an equity shareholding. Countries with large debts to Western banks have been offered this solution to their indebtedness. Previously, swaps took the form of banks giving loans to companies wanting to make an

investment in a debtor country. Fixed interest debt has also grown in Third World countries because of the lack of developed stock markets in them.

See also: **securitization**.

debt-led growth (110, 430)
Economic development financed by borrowing, usually from foreign countries. This turned out to be a disastrous policy in the 1970s as it led to the **Third World debt problem**.

debt neutrality (320)
Non-responsiveness of a portfolio to changes in the mixture of taxes and borrowing used by a government to finance the public sector's real spending programme on goods and services.

debt policy (310, 320)
The course of action taken to manage a country's **national debt**. The official approach often adopted is to maintain market conditions so as to maximize the present and future demand for government debt, but such a policy stance may be in conflict with credit/interest rate policy.

debt ratio (310)
See: **gearing**.

debt restructuring (310, 520)
Changing the **maturities** of the debts of a government or a firm so that it is easier to service them. Restructuring usually takes the form of lengthening the maturity of debt and is allowed by creditors who would otherwise have little prospect of receiving any interest and repayment of the **principal**.

debt service indicators (310, 430)
A measure of the ability of a borrower to meet capital and interest payments on a debt. The principal approaches are first the debt–service ratio (interest and capital repayments due divided by export earnings), second the cash flow ratio ((current account surplus minus interest payments) divided by export earnings) and third the solvency ratio (the percentage of a country's export earnings which it would have to devote to debt servicing to keep its total debt–export ratio

on a declining trend). The great increase in the foreign indebtedness of Third World countries after 1970 prompted the use of other measures of a country's ability to at least service its debts.

debt trap (310)
The consequence for a government, or an individual, of borrowing at a rate of interest greater than the rate of growth of its income causing its current expenditure on items other than debt servicing has to be increasingly reduced.

decelerator (320)
A fiscal change, e.g. a cut in public expenditure or an increase in taxation, which counteracts the expansionary effects of the investment accelerator.

See also: **accelerator principle**.

decentralized market economy (070)
An **economy** in which major investment, pricing and production decisions are taken by economic agents below the level of central government; allocation is according to market conditions rather than planning targets.

See also: **centrally planned economy**; **economic devolution**.

decile (210)
The value obtained from a set of data arranged in order of magnitude by dividing it into ten equal parts. The first, or lowest, decile is sometimes used as a benchmark for calculating **low pay**.

See also: **lower quartile**; **median**; **percentile**; **upper quartile**.

decimalization (310)
A change in the currency of a country so that the basic unit is divisible into one hundred parts. The French franc and US dollar have been divided into a hundred cents since the eighteenth century and the Australian dollar since 1966. In the UK in 1971 the pound, previously divisible into twenty shillings or 240 pence, was made equivalent to 100 new pence. It is feared that this type of currency change leads to consumers losing their **price perception** and unwittingly accepting price

increases. However, the quotation of prices in old and new forms reduces this disguised inflation.

decision cycle (010, 320)
The recurrent round of the economic decisions made by national governments and other economic agents. Exchange rate decisions have to be made several times a day; many commodity prices and interest rates are changed weekly; tax changes, wages and product prices annually; and major investment decisions infrequently.

decision variable (210)
See: **choice variable**.

decreasing returns (010)
See: **returns to scale**.

dedicated budget (320)
A budget which can only be spent on the types of public expenditure prescribed by particular legislation. As much of US federal budgeting has this inflexibility, it is more difficult for the Executive to change public spending without Congressional agreement.

See also: **earmarking**; **ringfencing**.

deemed tax (320)
US corporate tax concession which is equal to the amount of total income tax already paid abroad. If a US corporation has a pre-tax income of $2 million on which it has paid $1 million and it remits $500,000 in dividends to the USA, then its deemed tax will be $1 million x 0.5, the proportion it remits in dividends.

deep discount bond (310)
A bond carrying little or no interest which is sold below its redemption value. Investors will thus make a capital gain by holding it to the date of redemption and, in many cases, reduce their total tax burden as income taxation is often more punitive than capital gains taxation.

de facto population (840)
A counting of the population according to where they were on census night. This is a popular form of census, especially in developing countries.

See also: *de jure* **population**.

deficiency payment (710)
A form of governmental subsidy to farmers equal to the difference between the market price of an agricultural commodity and the price set under an agricultural policy to achieve a desired level of farmers' incomes.

See also: **intervention price**.

deficit financing (320)
1 Government spending which is not fully financed by its revenue and is usually undertaken to reduce unemployment and to stimulate the growth of output. This type of financing, also known as 'pump priming', has often taken the form of **public works**. **Keynes** recommended that the government's current expenditure budget should be in balance but that its capital budget could go into deficit in times when aggregate demand needed to be stimulated.

2 The financing of a balance of payments deficit.

See also: **functional financing**.

deflation (010, 210)
1 A reduction in **aggregate demand**. A deflationary policy is chosen by governments to correct balance of payments deficits and lower the price level: extra taxation and lower public expenditure are the principal methods used.

2 A fall in the average price level.

3 The elimination of price increases from an index of production or consumption. Economic statisticians are frequently engaged in 'deflating' time series to separate real from nominal changes.

deflationary gap (010)
The excess of aggregate supply over aggregate demand of a national economy. This overall situation of an economy at less than full employment has often encouraged, since **Keynes**, policies of deficit spending.

degrees of freedom (210)
The number of observations in a sample minus the number of population **parameters** to be estimated by the sample.

de-industrialization (610)
The decline of a country's manufacturing

industry absolutely or relatively. This fall in manufacturing activity is most noticeable in employment but a slower rate of growth, or even a fall, in output and a fall in the world share of trade in manufactures also measure this change. Most **Organization for Economic Cooperation and Development** countries have experienced de-industrialization in the past twenty years as economic activity has switched from manufacturing to service industries. Marxist economists are much concerned with this because of their view that what is productive is the creation of goods, not of services.

Blackaby, F. (1979) *De-Industrialisation*, London: Heinemann Educational.
Bluestone, B. and Harrison, B. (1982) *The De-industrialization of America: Plant Closings, Community Abandonment, and the Dismantling of Basic Industry*, New York: Basic Books.
Rodwin, L. and Sazanami, H. (eds) (1989) *De-industrialization and Regional Economic Transformation: The Experience of the United States*, Boston, MA, and London: Unwin Hyman.

de jure population (840)
The population permanently resident in a particular area.

See also: *de facto* population.

delinking (420)
The breaking off of trading and other relationships between Third World countries and Western countries. It is argued that the benefits of such a course of action include an increased freedom to shape the development of that country, as well as less chance of economic exploitation by foreign investors.

See also: **dependency theory**.

Delors Plan (420)
The plan of the European Community Committee for the Study of Economic and Monetary Union of 1989 chaired by Jacques Delors, the President of the **European Community**. The European Community set up the Committee to propose a progression from the Single European Act 1985 to a **single currency** and a common monetary policy throughout the European Community. It was proposed that there should be three stages in the movement to the Committee's goals. The first stage would be the

greater convergence of economic performance through coordination of budgetary and monetary policies, possibly with a European Reserve Fund with reserves drawn from each participating central bank. The second stage would provide a medium-term framework for key economic objectives so that stable economic growth could be achieved. Precise rules of a non-binding nature would be created for annual budgets and the finance of government activity, and a European System of Central Banks for the formulation of a common monetary policy would be set up.

Committee for the Study of Economic and Monetary Union (1989) *Report on Economic and Monetary Union in the European Community*, Luxemburg: Office for Official Publications of the European Communities.

See also: **Eurofed; European Monetary System; European Monetary Union; Werner Report**.

Delphi method (520)
A method of business forecasting used by many large US corporations which consists of panels of experts expressing their opinions of the future and then revising them in the light of their colleagues' views so that bias and extreme opinions can be eliminated.

delta stock (310)
The least traded stocks and shares which are not quoted on the **Stock Exchange Automated Quotation System**.

See also: **alpha stock; beta stock; gamma stock**.

demand (010)
1 The amount of factors of production or their products desired at a particular price.

2 Total expenditure on a good or service. This is shown graphically in a **demand curve**.

demand curve (010)
A schedule relating the quantity demanded of a good, service or factor of production to different prices of it. Although John Stuart **Mill** first had the idea of such schedules, it was **Cournot** and the **marginalists** who introduced them to economics. As the curve shows the relationship between only two

variables, the *ceteris paribus* assumption has to be made. Much controversy has arisen about the nature of the Marshallian demand curve, particularly the circumstances under which there can be a movement along the demand curve without affecting the assumption that real income is constant. The normal demand curve is assumed to be downward sloping because of the psychological belief underlying the **law of diminishing marginal utility**.

Quantity demanded

See also: **Giffen paradox**; **price–consumption curve**.

demand deposit (310)
Funds held at a bank with a notice period of less than seven days. They can take many forms, including **checking accounts**, certified cashier's and officer's cheques, travellers' cheques, letters of credit sold for cash, withheld taxes, withheld insurance and **time deposits** whose notice of withdrawal has expired.

See also: **NOW account**.

demand for money (310)
The demand for cash or a bank deposit rather than for an asset such as a stock certificate or bond. Keynes, by distinguishing the **transactions**, **precautionary** and **speculative demands for money**, revolutionized monetary theory. It is a broader theory about the motivation for holding money than the **quantity theory** assertion that money is held solely for transactions pur-

poses. The demand for money by a representative individual can be considered, in terms of **marginal utility**, as being the result of balancing the imputed yield from holding it (the convenience and security of a cash-holding) against the cost in terms of interest income forgone. Discussions of **monetarists'** views have led to many econometric studies of demand for money functions which have shown them to be less stable than originally asserted.

Fisher, D. (1989) *Money Demand and Monetary Policy*, Hemel Hempstead: Harvester Wheatsheaf.

demand management (310, 320)
Discretionary changes in national **monetary** and **fiscal policies** which attempt to change the level of **aggregate demand**. Under the influence of **Keynesianism** such policies were very popular in the 1950s and 1960s. However, some critics of demand management have asserted that frequent changes destabilized the economy.

See also: **fine-tuning**.

demand-pull inflation (150)
Inflation which has its origin in **excess demand**. **Keynes** introduced this approach to inflation in his *How to Pay for the War* (1940). The notion of an 'inflationary gap', i.e. an excess of aggregate demand over aggregate supply at full employment, was used to explain this phenomenon instead of the view inherent in the **quantity theory of money** that inflation was caused by an increase in the money supply. The fullest form of demand-pull inflation is when there is excess demand in both factor and product markets.

See also: **demand-shift inflation**.

demand-shift inflation (150)
Inflation brought about by a structural change in an economy which permanently raises demand as a consequence of increases in wages and in the prices of capital goods in expanding sectors being communicated to other sectors. It is a mixed form of inflation as changes in both demand and cost bring about the ultimate increase in product prices.

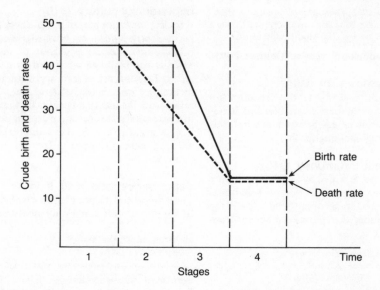

demarcation (810, 830)

The separation of the tasks of a particular occupation from others. Thus, for example, in an engineering plant where there is demarcation, tasks will be assigned separately to mechanical, electrical and electronics engineers. **Craft unions**, anxious to protect the work available for their members, have been keen to follow this practice, especially in the UK. The inflexibility in the use of labour brought about by this practice has lowered productivity and increased labour costs.

See also: **job control unionism**.

dematerialization (310)

Paperless settlement of stock exchange transactions. In the case of London, this is scheduled to begin in 1992.

See also: **paperless entry; Taurus**.

demerger (610)
See: **unbundling**.

demerit good (010)
See: **merit bad**.

demographic accounting (840)

The tabulation of the population according to its characteristics and its states (at birth, death and place) at various dates.

Stone, R. (1971) *Demographic Accounting and Model-building*, Paris: OECD.

demographic transition (840)

A model showing a society's population changes through four stages (see the above figure): stage 1 is the traditional society with little population growth, a stable population with a high birth rate counteracted by an equally high death rate; stage 2 shows rapid population growth because improved health care has pushed down the death rate but the birth rate is still high; in stage 3 there is a population decline caused by couples desiring fewer children; stage 4 is a mature society with a stable population, brought about by higher incomes and better education, where couples have about two children each. Many Third World countries are still in the second stage; most of the **Organization for Economic Cooperation and Development** countries are in stage 4.

Caldwell, J.C. (1976) 'Toward a restatement of demographic transition theory', *Population and Development Review* 2: 321–66.
Notestein, F.W. (1945) 'Population: the long view', in T.W. Schultz (ed.) *Food for the World*, Chicago, IL: University of Chicago Press.

demography (840)

The study of the size and composition of human populations, particularly births, deaths and migration. Both historical recording and projections of future populations are calculated to provide the basis for economic and social planning.

Pressat, R. (1972) *Demographic Analysis: Methods, Results, Applications*, London: Edward Arnold; Chicago, IL: Aldine Atherton.

See also: **population census**; **Malthus**; **Petty**.

demometrics (210, 840)
The measurement of the relationship between socioeconomic variables and demographic variables, e.g. between income levels and interregional migration.

denationalized money (310)
Money which is issued by a variety of private and foreign banks and not by a national government. Money of this kind is less likely to be debased; also, banks can benefit from **seignorage**.

Hayek, F.A. (1990) *Denationalisation of Money – the Argument Refined*, 3rd edn, London: Institute of Economic Affairs.

See also: **debasing a currency**; **free banking**.

Denison residual (110)
Advances in knowledge and associated explanations of economic growth. Denison discovered the important growth determinant in his study of the USA and eight West European countries for the period 1950–62.

Denison, E.F. (1967) *Why Growth Rates Differ*, ch. 20, Washington, DC: Brookings Institution.

Dennison's law (010)
This states that the private sector saving of companies and households is a constant proportion of national income. This relationship held for twenty-five years but it is now being disputed.

department (610)
1 Part of an economy or economic organization.

2 A branch of capitalist production, according to **Marx**, who divided the economy into three departments: Department I, the means of production, i.e. energy, machines and tools, raw materials and buildings; Department II, consumer goods which reconstitute both the labour force and capitalists, contributing to their well-being; Department III, luxury goods, weapons, which renew neither constant nor variable capital.

dependency culture (910)
A society, or major part of it, which becomes permanently dependent on **transfer incomes** because the extensive provision of welfare benefits has inhibited work and individual effort. This concern of several governments, including those of the USA and the UK, arises from the fear that benefits fix the poor in a perpetual state of relative deprivation. It is also argued that excessive international **aid** can have the same effect on whole countries.

dependency ratio (840, 910)
The proportion of a population which has to be supported. It is commonly measured as

$$\frac{\text{children under the age of 15} + \text{adults over 64}}{\text{number of adults in the labour force}} \times 100 \text{ per cent.}$$

The value of this ratio is large when high birth rates for several years have increased the proportion of children in a population or much international emigration has left an old population.

See also: **grey society**.

dependency theory (020, 130)
Exploitation theory applied to small countries. It has been observed that a small country which exports agricultural commodities finds that the control of its economy (its trade, shipping, insurance, banking and port facilities) passes to foreigners, who are often associated with a local wealthy elite. The economy suffers from the repatriation of profits and imports, both of which are detrimental to domestic industries. The deterioration in local industry reduces industrial employment and pushes indigenous workers into the subsistence sector. In order to counteract the losses created by dependency, this approach to the study of development recommends fast independent growth and the granting of priority to basic needs. Criticisms of the theory include the view that it was mainly applicable to some tropical colonies from 1900 to 1950, that it exaggerates the extent of profit repatriation and that it fails to provide a single optimal set of prices and allocation.

Frank, A.G. (1978) *Dependent Accumulation and Underdevelopment*, London: Macmillan.

dependent economy (420)
An economy closely linked with another, either through economic treaties (see **Comecon**) or through dependence on a narrow range of exported goods. Many Third World countries are dependent on a single export, e.g. Mauritius on sugar and Zaire on copper.

See also: **branch economy**.

depletable externality (720)
An **externality** which by affecting one person affects others less, e.g. horse manure used in gardening.

See also: **pollution control**.

deposit account (310)
An interest-bearing bank account (UK) which cannot be withdrawn without due notice (in most cases, at least seven days). In the USA, such accounts are known as savings accounts or time deposits.

deposit base (310)
Narrow money.

See also: **M0; M1**.

deposit insurance (310)
Insurance issued to protect the deposits held in banks and other financial institutions. In the USA, the major scheme is that of the **Federal Deposit Insurance Corporation** which, since 1933, has insured the deposits of the member banks of the Federal Reserve System and of non-member banks which choose to join.

Recent instability in the banking system of the USA has put deposit insurance under a great strain. Critics of it assert that insurance makes banks more reckless in their lending policies, bringing about the financial difficulties which insurance seeks to avoid.

See also: **Banking Act 1979**.

Depository Institutions Deregulation and Monetary Control Act 1980 (310)
US federal statute which increased fair competition in US banking by imposing universal reserve requirements of 3 per cent of the first $25 million of deposits and 12 per cent for deposits in excess of this amongst commercial banks, mutual savings banks, savings banks, savings and loan associations and credit unions, gave the **Federal Reserve** power to ask for supplemental reserves of 4 per cent of deposits for up to ninety days, authorized the Federal Reserve to charge for its services, legalized **NOW** accounts and phased out many interest rate ceilings.

See also: **Hunt Commission**.

deposit-taking business (310)
A commercial bank, or other financial institution, licensed to conduct financial business according to the rules of a central bank, e.g. the Bank of England.

See also: **Banking Act 1979**.

depreciation (210, 430, 520)
1 The decline in value of an asset. Asset depreciation is measured by accountants using different rule of thumb methods. Under the straight-line method, the annual amount of depreciation is equal to a fraction of the capital expenditure (the value of an asset divided by its life). Other methods include the 'declining balance' approach, which makes depreciation equal to a fraction of the written-down value of the asset, and the 'sum of the digits' approach by which a fraction of the capital expenditure declines linearly over time. True economic depreciation, the replacement cost of physical wear and tear, is difficult to calculate as capital markets are often imperfect.

2 The fall in value of a currency under a **floating exchange rate** regime.

See also: **currency appreciation**.

depression (140)
A fall in national output which continues for a few years. Over the past 200 years, there have been several depressions, especially in the nineteenth century, in the economies of Western countries. The term is often more loosely used to refer to a period of extensive unemployment and business failures. The early 1930s is usually cited as the major recent example of a depression in the strict sense of a long-period fall in output.

See also: **Great Depression; recession.**

depression pole (010, 310)
See: **liquidity trap.**

deprival value (540)
A measure of the value of an asset to its owner; the lower of the replacement cost or **economic value**.

See also: **Sandilands Report.**

deregulation (310, 610)
Abolition of governmental regulations, especially for prices and the operations of publicly owned organizations, with the aims of lowering prices, through more competition, and of stimulating the growth of small businesses. Examples of deregulation to date include the securities markets of New York and London, US airlines and British buses. Deregulation of stock markets occurred in the USA in 1975, in the UK in 1986 and in Japan gradually in the mid-1980s: such large-scale changes have hence been called '**Big Bang**'. In banking the USA amended its regulatory bank legislation in the **Depository Institutions Deregulation and Monetary Control Act of 1980** and the **Garn–St Germain Depository Institutions Act of 1982**, ceilings on interest rates have been removed and **thrifts** have been allowed to diversify their financial activities, e.g. credit cards and commercial and industrial loans.

Critics of deregulation argue that safety suffers, the industry is destabilized and there is less provision for underused services thought desirable for social reasons. Some large bank failures in the 1980s have, in part, been attributed to the removal of regulatory safeguards.

Kahn, A.E. (1988) *The Economics of Regulation*, Cambridge, MA: MIT Press.

Majone, G. (1990) *Deregulation or Re-regulation? Regulatory Reform in Europe and the United States*, London: Pinter.

See also: **economic devolution.**

derivative (210, 310)
1 A sophisticated financial product, e.g. **swap**, **warrant**, **option** and **future** available in **security**, commodity and currency markets. The product is derived from a simple transaction in a **spot market**.

2 A function $f'(x)$ of x which shows the slope of a graph of the function x. For the function x to be at a maximum or a minimum, it is necessary that this derivative be zero. Major derivatives in economics include **marginal cost**, **marginal revenue**, the **marginal propensity to consume**, the **marginal propensity to import** and the **marginal product of labour**.

derived demand (010)
The demand for a factor of production derived from its **marginal productivity**, e.g. there is a demand for labour in the construction industry because of a demand for houses. Derived demand will change by the same amount as final demand if the ratio between factor input and consequent output is constant, which is unlikely in a period of technological change.

deserving poor (910)
Those with low incomes through no fault of their own, e.g. the victims of a trade depression. The distinction between the deserving and undeserving poor has been used to deprive the latter of welfare benefits.

See also: **Poor Laws; poverty.**

destructive competition (010)
Fierce competition, often in the form of price wars, which drives many firms out of an industry and weakens those who remain.

devalorization (010)
The process which reduces the value of **capital** through a fall in the price of intermediate or final goods, or as a result of bankruptcy.

devaluation (430)
See: **currency devaluation.**

development (110)
1 The movement of an economy from agricultural activities using simple technology to the production of industrial products and a range of services using modern technology. (Even three centuries ago **Petty** regarded development as the growth of service industries.)

2 The cumulative growth of per capita income, accompanied by structural and institutional changes (although per capita income is a crude measure unless problems of measuring the **gross domestic product** and its distribution are taken into account). Post-1945 development policies have often failed to help the poorest 40 per cent of the world's population because of the urban bias of many aid programmes but, nevertheless, these policies have achieved lower rates of infant mortality, more hospital beds, an increased supply of piped water and the building of many all-season roads.

Kitching, G. (1989) *Development and Underdevelopment in Historical Perspective. Populism, Nationalism and Industrialization*, rev. edn, London: Routledge.
Lipton, M. (1977) *Why Poor People Stay Poor*, London: Temple Smith.
Little, I.M.D. (1982) *Economic Development: Theory, Policy and International Relations*, New York: Basic Books; New York: McGraw-Hill.
Myrdal, G. (1956) *Development and Underdevelopment*, Cairo: National Bank of Egypt.

See also: **industrialization**.

development bank (310)
A bank which specializes in the provision of finance for development projects in developing countries and depressed regions. The major international development banks use both capital subscribed by donor countries and capital borrowed from international capital markets to support particular projects and programmes, often over the medium term. The principal international development banks are the **International Bank for Reconstruction and Development**, the **International Finance Corporation**, the **Inter-American Development Bank**, the **Asian Development Bank**, the **African Development Bank**, the **Caribbean Development Bank**, the **European Investment Bank**, the **European Bank for Reconstruction and Development** and the **International Investment Bank**.

development economics (110, 130)
Growth theory applied to the economic problems of developing countries. In a sense, it started with **Smith's** *The Wealth of Nations* which was concerned with an analysis of the causes of economic growth but it boomed as a subject in the period of de-colonialization in the 1950s. When development economists began devising growth policies for less developed countries, they were inspired by Soviet economic management of the 1930s, wartime economic management and the **Marshall Plan** for recovery in Western Europe. Criticism of the industrialization bias of early development plans, and their consequent environmental effects, made **intermediate technology** increasingly popular as a development strategy.

Hirschman, A.O. (1981) 'The rise and decline of development economics', in his *Essays in Trespassing*, New York: Cambridge University Press.
Meier, G.M. (1989) *Leading Issues in Economic Development*, 5th edn, New York and Oxford: Oxford University Press.
Myint, H. (1980) *The Economics of Developing Countries*, London: Hutchinson.

development planning (060, 130)
The use of **central planning** in Third World countries as a route to economic development. The earliest plans were carried out before and after the Second World War in British, French, Belgian and Portuguese colonies. These plans were characterized by a crash investment programme, especially in the public sector, and a commitment to rapid industrialization.

development policy (110)
See: **aid; development**.

DIDMCA (310)
See: **Depository Institutions Deregulation and Monetary Control Act 1980**.

difference equation (210)
An equation which relates a variable measured at one time to variables measured at previous times. This mathematical device is much used in dynamic economics, e.g. in the case of a **cobweb** the quantity supplied in year $t + 1$ is a function of the price in year t. Difference equations can be linear or non-linear, homogeneous or non-homogeneous, of first or second order.

Goldberg, S. (1958) *Introduction to Difference Equations*, New York: Wiley.

differential tax incidence (320)
The burden of one tax compared with another.

See also: **tax incidence**.

differential theory of rent (010, 710)

The theory of **Anderson**, **Ricardo** and others which asserted that the rent on land subject to **diminishing returns** arose from differences in fertility or location with no rent being paid on the least fertile or most distant land. As the margin of cultivation is extended, the total amount of rent paid increases.

differentiated good (010, 530)

A good which is made to appear different from its market rivals by being sold under a brand name and packaged differently. Recognition of this marketing device made a great contribution to the formation of the theory of **monopolistic competition**.

See also: **branding**; **brand loyalty**; **product differentiation**.

differentiated marketing (530)

A marketing strategy with separate marketing programmes for each product of a firm.

differentiated product (010, 530)

See: **product differentiation**.

differentiation (210, 530)

1 A major business strategy to acquire some monopoly power by the differentiation of products, or of their marketing and distribution to the consumer.

2 A mathematical method of calculating the derivative of a function; this is much used in **neoclassical economics**.

See also: **branding**; **monopolistic competition**; **product differentiation**.

diffusion index (140, 210)

A measure used to identify **business cycles**. The standard diffusion index is calculated by giving a value to each component series so that the value is 0 per cent for a decrease, 50 per cent if there is no change in the overall number rising or falling, or 100 per cent if there is an increase over a given time period. In the USA, *Business Cycle Indicators*, published from 1961, has measured diffusion for twenty-one economic indicators.

diffusion rate (620)

The proportion of output of an industry which uses a particular technique by a stated date, e.g. the percentage of the steel industry using technique X by 1990. This is a major measure of technical progress and of **innovation**. High rates of diffusion are encouraged by the possibility of cost reduction and by energetic advisory and information services.

Dillon Round (420)

The fifth round of tariff reductions, organized by the **General Agreement on Tariffs and Trade**, which took place in 1960–1. Under it, the USA agreed to a 20 per cent reduction in tariffs on 20 per cent of its dutiable imports. As the concessions were concentrated on manufactures, the Round had little effect on the exports of less developed countries whose industrialization was at a low level. It was of far more importance for bilateral deals between the USA and industrialized countries.

diminishing marginal rate of substitution (010)

The smaller amount of a good (service) which is acquired by sacrificing one unit of another. This is applied as a rule of consumer behaviour which states that at the same level of utility a consumer will sacrifice decreasing amounts of good Y to obtain extra units of good X. This is usually expressed as an **indifference curve**.

Hicks, J.R. (1939) *Value and Capital*, ch. 1, Oxford: Clarendon Press.

diminishing marginal utility law (010)

This states that the amount of satisfaction derived from the consumption of successive units of the same good (service) will decline. The law is used to explain the downward-sloping nature of the normal **demand curve**, to resolve the so-called **water and diamonds paradox** and to justify redistribution from the rich to the poor. Although **Bentham**, **Senior** and **Jevons** are noted for their clear exposition of this law, hints of it appeared earlier in economic writings.

diminishing returns law (010, 710)

The decline in output which occurs as successive units of a variable factor of production are applied to a fixed factor. The most used example of this law was the application of increasing amounts of labour to a fixed amount of land with the consequence that the **marginal product** of labour declined. This view of agricultural production was central to much of **classical economics**, including **Ricardo**'s model of the economy. The US economist Henry Charles Carey (1793–1879) was one of the few economic writers of the nineteenth century to argue that in a developing economy there are increasing returns to land as cultivation proceeds from the least to the most fertile land.

Carey, H.C. (1848) *The Past, The Present and The Future*, Philadelphia, PA: Carey & Hart.

See also: **returns to scale**.

dinar (430)
The currency of Algeria, Bahrain, Iraq, Jordan, Kuwait, Libya, South Yemen, Tunisia and Yugoslavia.

Dinks (840)
Double-income, no kids: US professional couple with a high joint income and no dependants.

direct and indirect taxation (320)
Two broad categories of taxation differentiated according to administrative arrangements, incidence or the characteristics of taxpayers. Income taxes, for example, can be paid directly to revenue authorities, can directly reduce taxpayers' real incomes and can be directly related to taxpayers' characteristics. On the other hand sales taxes, for example, are indirectly paid by an individual through purchasing goods and services, are not directly related to the personal circumstances of a taxpayer and can have their incidence shifted to the producer. Direct taxation is regarded as more equitable but it is more difficult and expensive to collect.

See also: **tax incidence**.

direct cost (010)
1 A production cost directly attributable to the cost of producing one unit of a particular output.

2 Variable cost.

See also: **indirect cost**.

direct foreign investment (430)
1 Investment in productive facilities by a foreign company, e.g. the purchase or building of factories.

2 The purchase of stocks and shares which give a foreign company control over existing real assets.

See also: **multinational corporation**; **portfolio investment**.

direct–indirect taxes ratio (320)
A measure of the **tax structure**; the yields from the various types of tax are compared to see their relative importance as sources of revenue.

direct labour organization (320, 510)
A department of a British local authority carrying out building, street cleansing or other activities itself rather than contracting them out to private sector firms. The low productivity of some of these direct labour organizations has led to them being criticized. In the 1980s, the UK government began the replacement of direct labour organizations by private firms through **competitive tendering** in an attempt to reduce the cost of local government services.

directly unproductive profit-seeking activities (010, 420)
Activities which yield pecuniary returns but do not produce goods or services. A major example of these is the evasion of **tariffs**.

Buchanan, J.M., Tellison, R.D. and Tullock G. (eds) (1980) *Toward a Theory of the Rent-Seeking Society*, College Station, TX: Texas A & M University Press.

direct product profitability (520)
A measure of a retailer's net profit after all labour, equipment and storage costs attributable to that product have been deducted. This is a more precise cost accounting technique than the previously popular method of calculating gross profit margins and then deducting from them the average costs of handling and storage for each product. The knowledge gained from

applying the direct product profitability method enables a retailer to have a more optimal product mix and a better use of shop space.

direct sale (530)
A sale to a customer without the use of an agent and the payment of agent's commission. This is a cheaper way of selling, especially for services such as insurance.

direct tax (320)
See: **direct and indirect taxation**.

dirham (430)
The currency of Morocco and the United Arab Emirates.

dirigisme (610)
State intervention in society and direction of the economy as practised in France from the seventeenth century.

See also: **Colbertism; mercantilism**.

dirty float (430)
An exchange rate regime which, for the most part, is dominated by market forces but occasionally has interference by governments and central banks to prevent an excessive fluctuation in the value of a currency.

See also: **floating exchange rate**.

discomfort index (210)
Okun defined this as the sum of the unemployment rate plus the rate of inflation.

discounted cash flow (520, 540)
A method of investment appraisal which discounts the future benefits and costs of an investment to discover its present value. The method can be used to evaluate whether an investment project is worthwhile either by following the rule that the present value of benefits must exceed the present value of costs, or by considering whether the **internal rate of return** is acceptable compared with that on other investment projects.

discounted share price (310)
A share price which takes into account expectations of future changes in earnings per share. As stock markets are constantly responding to information about particular companies' prospects, the announcement of a fall or rise in company profits can often have little impact on a share price.

discount house (310)
A financial institution, peculiar to the City of London, which borrows **money at call** from the banks and other institutions and invests it in **treasury bills**, high quality **commercial bills** and **certificates of deposit**. The twelve discount houses, forming the money market, act as a buffer between the commercial banks and the Bank of England. Banks short of cash will recall money lent to the money market which then has to discount bills to balance their banks. The Bank of England as lender of last resort is always prepared to lend to discount houses, by discounting bills, in order to preserve the liquidity of the banking system as a whole.

Curiously, many of these discount houses are now owned by clearing banks who could easily abolish them by abandoning an agreement not to compete in the money market which has existed since the 1930s: the banks prefer this unusual buffer between themselves and the Bank.

discounting (210)
A method used to value at the same date economic flows and stocks which have originated at different dates. A typical use of discounting is to convert the expected future incomes from an asset to present values using a **discount rate**.

See also: **discounted cash flow**.

discount market (010)
The money market which specializes in transactions in short-term financial assets.

See also: **short-term money market**.

discount market loans (310)
See: **overnight money**.

discount rate (010, 310)
1 The rate of interest charged by a **central bank** to lower level financial institutions (usually **commercial banks**) for discounting their bills, i.e. lending them money, often when acting as the **lender of last resort**.

2 The rate used for discounting future values to the present. In **cost–benefit**

analysis there is a distinction between a private and a social rate of discount. A private rate of discount reflects the time preference of private consumers; a social rate is based on the government's view, which can be more long-sighted as it attempts, in most cases, to take into account the welfare of future generations.

discount window (310)

US term for lending to depository institutions by each of the twelve district **Federal Reserve Banks**. Originally, from 1913 to 1916, this was the only lending a Federal Reserve Bank could make. It can take the form of adjustment credit to meet a temporary need for funds or extended credit to help banks whose business is seasonal in character and to cope with special circumstances, e.g. the effects of a change in the financial system. Other lending is by the discounting of eligible paper, e.g. a commercial or agricultural loan made by the bank to a customer. Before 1980, such lending was only possible for Federal Reserve Banks; now, under the **Depository Institutions Deregulation and Monetary Control Act 1980**, it is open to all depository institutions except bankers' banks which maintain transaction accounts or non-personal time deposits. Discount window loans are usually only a small proportion of bank reserves, e.g. less than 3 per cent in 1985. Such lending can be used in **monetary policy** instead of **open market operations**.

Mengle, D.L. (1986) 'The discount window', *Federal Reserve Bank of Richmond Economic Review* 72, 3: 2–10.

discouraged workers hypothesis (810)

The view that workers give up **job search** activity because high unemployment rates and a lack of hiring by businesses make it unlikely that they will succeed in gaining employment. Lack of search means that these workers cease to have the status of being unemployed and so drop out of the **labour force**.

See also: **additional worker hypothesis**.

discrete variable (210)

A variable which can take only some of the values between two given values, e.g. the number of countries in the world can be 50, 100 or 200 but not 1.8.

See also: **continuous variable**.

discriminating monopoly (010)

See: **price discrimination**.

discrimination (820)

Unfair and unfavourable treatment of a group of workers or other persons; setting different wages for workers with the same productivity but different personal characteristics, i.e. sex, age or race, or refusing to hire them. Different schools of economics have chosen different approaches to the issue, **neoclassical** economists such as **Becker** examining how a taste for discrimination affects the demand for each group while others have placed discrimination in the context of wider concerns such as class conflict.

Becker, G.S. (1971) *The Economics of Discrimination*, Chicago, IL: University of Chicago Press.
Marshall, R. (1974) 'The economics of racial discrimination: a survey', *Journal of Economic Literature* 12: 849–71.
Reich, M. (1981) *Racial Inequality*, Princeton, NJ: Princeton University Press.

See also: **ageism; horizontal discrimination; racial discrimination; sexual discrimination; vertical discrimination**.

diseconomy of scale (010)

A rise in **average costs** as a consequence of an increase in output which is shown in the positively sloped part of an average cost curve. Early writers on the subject attributed such diseconomies to the managerial problems of coordinating the activities of large enterprises; later writers noted other sources of diseconomies, including material fatigue, increases in the marginal cost of attracting more customers and rising factor prices – how many of these 'causes' are valid depends on how strict a definition of these diseconomies is used.

See also: **economy of scale**.

disembodied technical progress (620)

An increase in productivity brought about by, for example, organizational changes or learning-by-doing, without the installation of new capital goods.

See also: **embodied technical progress**.

disequilibrium (010)

1 An economic system in a state of **excess demand** or **excess supply**.

2 The state of an economic system whose key variables continue to fluctuate around **equilibrium** or around the equilibrium growth path. This can happen because of the **expectations** of the economic agents or because of **lags** in the system.

See also: **equilibrium**.

disequilibrium economics (020)

The analysis of markets which do not clear or of national economies with less than full employment. In macroeconomics, the **dynamic multiplier** shows how disequilibrium occurs in the economy as a whole and in the **multiplier–accelerator model** changes in the national income are studied. **Keynesian** economics is believed to be essentially a theory of disequilibrium rather than a theory of **general equilibrium** as **Neo-Keynesians** would assert.

Barro, R.J., Howitt, P.W. and Grossman, H.I. (1979) 'Macroeconomics: an appraisal of the non-market clearing paradigm', *American Economic Review* 69: 54–69.

Hey, J.D. (1981) *Economics in Disequilibrium*, Oxford: Basil Blackwell.

Muellbauer, J. and Portes, R. (1979) 'Macroeconomics when markets do not clear', in W. Branson (ed.) *Macroeconomic Theory and Policy*, ch. 16, New York: Harper & Row.

Samuelson, P. (1939) 'Interactions between multiplier analysis and the principle of acceleration', *Review of Economic Statistics* 21 (May): 75–8.

disequilibrium money (310)

The mismatch between the demand for and supply of money brought about by lags which prevent **supply-side shocks** from affecting the demand for money. These shocks in money and credit markets lead to asset prices overshooting their equilibrium level.

disequilibrium price (010)

A price which does not equate demand with supply. In the figure, P_e is the equilibrium price. Above P_e prices will be determined by the demand curve; below it, by the supply curve.

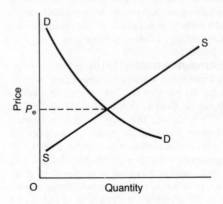

disguised unemployment (810)

That part of the **labour force** which consists of employed workers with a low productivity. This often occurs because of the low level of investment per worker or because labour is reluctant to move to more productive and higher paid work in the more modern sectors of an economy. In output terms, they make little contribution to the gross domestic product. Countries or regions with large agricultural sectors, e.g. less developed countries and southern regions of the **European Community**, often have a great deal of this sort of unemployment.

disincentive effect (320)

The discouraging effect of a tax on the supply of effort or the number of persons available for work. The best example of this effect is an income tax with a high marginal rate. This can result in a **backward-bending labour supply curve**.

See also: **incentive effect**.

disinflation (310, 320)

The reduction of inflation to a very low level. A major way of attempting to reach this goal is to lower **aggregate demand** by the use of **monetary** and **fiscal policies**.

disintermediation (310)

Bypassing the banking system by direct

borrowing and lending between companies/ corporations or other users and suppliers of finance. When the Bank of England introduced the **'corset'** as a means of reducing bank lending, disintermediation enabled companies to continue to borrow short term when refused credit by their bankers.

disposable income (320)
1 **Personal income** plus **transfer income** net of all taxes levied on incomes.

2 The amounts of money a person can spend or save in a given time period.

See also: **final income**.

dissaving (310)
1 The spending of accumulated savings.

2 A net increase in borrowing.

distortion (010)
The failure to reach a welfare optimum because the social marginal cost of producing goods is less or more than the social marginal benefit of consuming that good. **Welfare economics** is much concerned with distortions when analysing taxation and monopoly.

distortionary tax (320)
A biased tax which causes inefficiencies. Many specific taxes, e.g. those levied on the products of one industry but not on those of another, have this character of changing the post-tax allocation of demand.

distribution (010)
1 The division of the national product among the factors of production in the form of wages, profits, interest and rent. The first economic writer to examine the distribution of income as a separate issue was **Turgot** in his *Réflexions sur la formation et la distribution des richesses* (1766). Despite John Stuart **Mill**'s attempt to separate the laws of production from the laws of distribution, there has always been an intimate relationship between distribution and other economic theories. Socialist economists have made the study of distribution a major concern.

2 The distribution of one type of income between persons or between groups.

3 The last stage of production in which goods or services reach final consumers.

See also: **labour's share of national income**; **post-Keynesians**.

distributional/social weights (160, 210)
The increased weighting of one social or income group in **cost-benefit analysis** to give that group more importance, e.g. if the lower quartile of an income distribution is given a **weight** of 4 but the upper quartile is given only 1 then costs and benefits affecting the lowest income group will be regarded as four times as important as those of the top group.

disturbance term (210)
A variable, positive or negative in value, or error term which indicates the extent to which the dependent variables of a regression equation fall short of the central value of the independent variables. In the equation $I = a(Y - Y_1) + u$, I is net investment, Y is this year's income, Y_1 is last year's income and u is the disturbance term showing the extent to which I is more or less than the central value of $a(Y - Y_1)$. This term reflects the random element in economic relationships.

disutility (010)
A negative satisfaction, e.g. pain, tiredness, unhappiness. It is argued that study and work create disutility justifying higher earnings to better educated and more productive workers as a form of compensation. Consumption of a good or service, according to the law of **diminishing marginal utility**, can continue to the point that **utility** turns into disutility, e.g. a few glasses of claret can give a person utility, a few litres severe disutility. A **bad** produces disutility.

See also: **labour disutility theory**.

divergence indicator (430)
The margin by which a currency in the **Exchange Rate Mechanism** can diverge from its central or **par value**. This is ±2.25 per cent except for the later entrants to the mechanism, e.g. Italy and the UK, which can diverge by 6 per cent in either direction to make adjustment to a fixed exchange rate easier.

divergence threshold (430)

The crucial value of the **divergence indicator** for a currency of the **Exchange Rate Mechanism**. At this value, either a change in the domestic economic policies of the country concerned or a change in the **par value** of its currency is required.

diversification (010)

1 The production of a range of products by a firm.

2 The establishment of several industries in a region or a country.

3 The spreading of investments over a range of assets with different degrees of risk in a portfolio. Ultimately diversification is always concerned with minimizing the risk of a loss of income.

See also: **conglomerate**.

divestment (520, 610)

The disposal of part of the assets of a firm; the opposite of a **merger**. An appraisal of the activities of a diversified firm often results in divestment as a means of rationalizing its interests.

dividend (310)

The variable return to **equity** shares, decided by the board of directors of a company/corporation according to its policy on distributing its profits, after taxes and all charges have been paid. For preference shares, the dividend is at a fixed rate determined when they are first issued to the public, unless there is a right to participate in residual profits.

dividend net (310)

The rate of dividend paid in the last year, less income tax paid at the standard rate.

dividend yield (310)

The yearly return on each £100 or $100 invested:

$$\text{yield } (\%) = \frac{\text{nominal value of a share} \times \text{dividend } (\%)}{\text{market price} \times 100} \times 100$$

when the dividend is quoted in percentage terms.

Divisia money index (220, 310)

A combination of different measures of money weighted by the amount of interest paid on each, as the higher the interest rate, the less the monetary instrument is 'money' in the narrow sense of being cash. The growth of interest-bearing current accounts has made the index less useful.

Divisia, F. (1925–6): 'L'indice monétaire et la théorie de la monnaie', *Revue d'Economie Politique* 39: 842–64, 980–1008.

See also: **money supply**.

division of labour (010, 620)

Specialization of productive activity either by persons in different occupational groups undertaking particular tasks or by dividing a task into its component operations. Although earlier writers had mentioned the principle, Adam **Smith**, with his famous example of pin-making, made it a central explanation of the growth process. He noted that such specialization would save time as there would not have to be frequent changes from one activity to another, that workers would become more dextrous and that the analysis of jobs would make possible the introduction of machinery. However, he was aware that workers would become dull through repetitive tasks – a Smithian point often misinterpreted by **Marxists**: division of labour in itself can produce **alienation** amongst workers, whether or not they own the capital they use.

division of thought (010, 620)

Specialization in the processing of information and acting upon that information. Specialists of this kind will be engaged either in strategic planning or on daily executive tasks.

Arrow, K.J. (1979) 'The division of labour in the economy, the polity and society', in G.P. O'Driscoll (ed.) *Adam Smith and Modern Political Economy: Bicentennial Essays on The Wealth of Nations*, Ames, IA: Iowa State University Press.

div net (310)

See: **dividend net**.

DLO (320, 510)

See: **direct labour organization**.

DME (070)
See: **decentralized market economy**.

do-able (110)
A development strategy which emphasizes projects and methods which local populations want as there is much more chance of them being maintained in the long term.

Dobb, Maurice Herbert, 1900–76 (030)
British Marxist economist, educated at Cambridge and the London School of Economics, and a fellow of Trinity College, Cambridge, from 1924 to 1967 and Reader in Economics from 1959. Throughout his academic career his ideological stance as a Communist Party member informed his views and his writings. As a defender of Soviet-style economic planning, he participated in major debates with von **Mises** and von **Hayek**. His analysis of **capitalism** defended the Marxian interpretation of economic history, provoking a long-running controversy amongst Marxists. He was a close and sympathetic collaborator with **Sraffa** in the editing of **Ricardo**'s works and the provider of an alternative view of the growth of economic theory, seeing it descending from **Quesnay** through **Ricardo** and **Marx** to **Leontief** and Sraffa. Current policy issues also concerned him: he was able to make use of a Ricardo–Marx two-sector model to make policy recommendations for less developed economies.

Dobb, M.H. (1946) *Studies in the Development of Capitalism*, London: Routledge.
—— (1966) *Soviet Economic Development since 1917*, London: Routledge.
—— (1978) 'Maurice Dobb Memorial Issue', *Cambridge Journal of Economics* 2, 2.

dole bludger (910)
An Australian unemployed person who does not seek work but enjoys a life of leisure financed by social security benefits. Abolition of unemployment benefit was intended to force such persons into retraining or job search.

dollar (430)
The name of the USA's currency since 1785. Other countries, including Hong Kong, Canada and Australia, have followed the American lead. The term is derived from the Bohemian thaler introduced in 1517. 'Yen' (Japanese) and 'yuan' (Chinese) both mean dollar.

dollarization (310)
The use of a foreign currency for domestic monetary transactions because one's own currency is depreciating rapidly through high inflation. The dollar has been used more in this way than other currencies in the post-1945 period.

See also: **dual exchange rate**.

dollar overhang (430)
US dollars held outside the USA in the 1960s which were in excess of the gold backing for them.

See also: **monetary overhang**.

dollar standard (430)
The basis of value for **International Monetary Fund** currencies, the US dollar, under the **Bretton Woods** system (1968–73), a successor to the **gold standard**. Unlike the linkage of currencies to gold, this standard did not require the holding of dollars within countries as the basis of domestic currencies, thus making it a less potent system of international money.

domain (210)
The set of values which a variable can take.

See also: **continuous variable**; **discrete variable**.

Domar, Evsey David, 1914– (030)
A founder of modern economic growth theory. Educated in the universities of California (Los Angeles), Michigan and Harvard. Early in his career he was an economist with the **Federal Reserve** Board of Governors and then at the **Cowles Commission** before serving as a professor at the Massachusetts Institute of Technology from 1958 to 1972. He is best known for founding, with **Harrod**, economic growth theory in the **Harrod–Domar model**; his other works include studies of taxation and comparative economic systems.

Domar, E.V. (1957) *Essays in the Theory of*

Economic Growth, New York: Oxford University Press.

Domei (830)

Japan Federation of Labour: this labour union national federation was merged with Churitsuroren to form **Rengo** in 1987. In 1987, Domei had 2.09 million members.

domestic absorption (010)

The total use made of a nation's goods and services in consumption, investment and government expenditure.

domestic banking system (310)

The banking institutions of a particular country. These receive deposits from the public, lend at home and abroad and effect the transfer of funds. As the ultimate guarantor of the **liquidity** of a banking system, a national **central bank** operates and, to a large extent, attempts to control all **wholesale** and **retail banks**.

The greater sophistication attributed to the banking systems of Western countries is a product of the long period and relative freedom they have had to develop a variety of financial instruments, unlike the **monobanks** of Soviet-type economies whose role was limited through subservience to a system of central planning.

The Second World War created an excessive volume of public sector debt which made possible a post-war expansion in bank advances to meet the demands of private sector borrowers. Other changes have been a widening of the range and activities of commercial banks, including new techniques and financial products, particularly in the UK and the USA. In the USA in the 1960s, for example, there was a switch from asset management to liability management; later there was a shift from fixed rates to variable rates for lending. In assessing a domestic banking system one of the most commonly used indicators is the trend in the prices of the stocks and shares of issued bank securities as these reflect investors' confidence.

Lewis, M.K. and Davis, K.T. (1981) *Domestic and International Banking*, Cambridge, MA: MIT Press; Hemel Hempstead: Philip Alan.

See also: **banking; derivative**.

domestic credit expansion (310, 430)

Growth of the money supply, adjusted by the deficit/surplus on the **balance of payments** current and capital accounts. It was first used in Britain in 1968 and was a popular monetary target then with the **International Monetary Fund**.

It asserts that a balance of payments deficit leads to a reduction in the expansion of the domestic money stock as there is excess spending overseas. Conversely, a money supply expands with a balance of payments surplus, increasing foreign currency reserves. This measure was introduced to produce a more useful monetary aggregate for open economies.

See also: **monetarism; money supply**.

domestic resource cost (410)

The **opportunity cost** of using a factor of production to produce one unit of output, divided by the international value added by producing that unit. This is used as an alternative measure to the **effective rate of protection**.

domestic system (040, 630)

A primitive form of production in which **merchant capitalists** advance capital to self-employed craftsmen and artisans who, using their own simple tools, make a product. Before the Industrial Revolution, the textile industry was organized in this way in Britain.

See also: **advanced organic economy; Asiatic mode of production; cottage industry; homework**.

dominant firm (610)

A firm with most of the sales of a market which can act as a price-leader. Under **oligopoly**, the presence of dominant firms is common.

See also: **competitive fringe**.

dong (430)

The currency of Vietnam.

Donovan Commission (UK) (830)

The Royal Commission on Trade Unions and Employers' Associations of 1965–8 which was chaired by Lord Donovan. This group of experts on industrial relations concluded that Britain had two systems of industrial relations: a formal system characterized by industry-wide collective agreements on pay, hours of work and other employment conditions; and an informal system at the factory level which set earnings supplements to national wage rates, causing 'wage drift' and using unofficial strikes to enforce workers' demands. The creation of this dual system was partly attributed to the full-employment conditions of the 1950s and 1960s in the UK. To remedy the faults of the industrial relations system of that period, the Commission recommended the limitation of industry-wide agreements to those matters which could be effectively regulated at the industry level and the introduction of factory agreements to replace informal understandings.

Royal Commission on Trade Unions and Employers' Associations 1965–8 (1968) *Report*, London: HMSO, Cmnd 3623.

See also: **industrial relations; shop steward**.

double counting (220, 540)
Recording something twice with the result that in the process of aggregating individual items into a total the total is incorrectly too large. In **national income** accounting, double counting is a crucial problem to be avoided, e.g. it is essential to ensure that **transfer incomes** are not added to **factor incomes** when estimating the national income as transfer incomes are derived from factor incomes.

double factorial terms of trade (420)
Net **barter terms of trade** multiplied by the ratio of the productivity change index for one's export industries and the productivity change index for a foreign country's export industries. This measure of the **terms of trade** indicates the exchange rate between domestic and foreign factor services.

See also: **single factorial terms of trade**.

double switching (010)
See: **reswitching**.

double taxation of savings (320)
A feature of income taxation which taxes both the income out of which savings are made and the income from the savings when they are invested.

double-taxation relief (320)
A tax credit allowed against the tax payable by a resident of a country on account of income already having been taxed abroad, e.g. if a US citizen has already been taxed in France, then that will be taken into account when calculating that person's liability for paying US taxation.

This relief is only possible if there is a tax treaty between the two countries concerned or between states in a country, such as the USA, with a federal constitution. In the USA where the rate of individual income tax can vary from state to state, a person who resides in one state and works in another can gain relief by being given tax credits by one state.

See also: **deemed tax**.

Douglas, Paul Howard, 1892–1976 (030)
A US economist who was taught, and much influenced by, John Bates **Clark** at Columbia University. For most of his academic career, i.e. from 1920 to 1924 and from 1927 to 1948, he was a professor at Chicago, before being US Senator for Illinois in the period 1948–66. As senator, he fought for family allowances, old age pensions and pro-union legislation.

In 1928, he used **marginal productivity theory** as the foundations of the **Cobb-Douglas production function**, the leading approach on the subject until 1961. His early work on wages included a seminal study of **labour force participation** which related wages to participation within major US cities and an attempt to vindicate **marginal productivity theory**.

Douglas, P.H. (1934) *Theory of Wages*, New York: Macmillan.
Douglas, P.H. and Cobb, C.W. (1928) 'A theory of production', *American Economic Review (Supplement)* 18: 139–65.

Douglas Amendment 1965 (310)
An amendment to the Bank Holding Company Act 1956, of the USA, which prohibited bank holding companies from acquiring banks in other states.

Dow Jones Industrial Average (310)
The leading US index of stock market prices, which is an unweighted arithmetic average of the thirty industrial shares most widely quoted in the USA. Averages are also

published every trading day for transportation and utilities stocks, as well as a composite index combining the movements in the three indices.

See also: **Standard & Poor 500**.

downsizing (810)
Reducing the size of a labour force by making workers redundant. A term particularly applied to the staff reductions made by securities houses after 1987.

See also: **Big Bang**.

DPP (520)
See: **direct product profitability**.

DRC (410)
See: **domestic resource cost**.

drug economy (310)
The part of a national **economy** which uses the proceeds from the sale of illegal drugs. It is so large in some economies, including the USA, that it is sufficient to keep consumer spending buoyant whatever macroeconomic policy is being followed. In the USA, examination of large and suspicious cash deposits at banks, possible evidence of drug-dealing, are required under the Money Laundering Act 1986 and the Anti-Drug Abuse Act 1988. In the UK, a court can order the confiscation of the assets of drug traffickers.

See also: **laundering money**.

DRY (010)
Disposable real income.

DTB (310)
Deutsche Terminboerse: Germany's futures and options market founded in 1990.

DTP (630)
Desktop publishing.

DTR (320)
See: **double-taxation relief**.

dual-decision hypothesis (020)
Clower's re-interpretation of **Keynes**'s unemployment equilibrium by distinguishing 'notional' demand (the demand of households at prices which reflect a full-employment equilibrium) from 'effective' demand (the demand of households whose actual incomes have fallen through unemployment). Adjustment to unemployment equilibrium takes place through incomes and not through relative prices. This hypothesis recognizes that, in a market system, a household cannot buy and sell what it pleases if there is excess supply in the economy, and attempts to reconcile **Walras's law** with **Keynes**'s *General Theory*.

Clower, R.W. (ed.) (1969) *Monetary Theory*, Harmondsworth: Penguin, ch. 19.

dual economy (070, 130)
A national **economy** with a rich modern sector and a poor traditional sector. Originally this term was used to describe many colonial economies after the Second World War.

Boeke, J.H. (1953) *Economics and Economic Policy of Dual Societies, as Exemplified by Indonesia*, New York: Institute of Pacific Relations.

dual exchange rate (430)
The two values of a currency determined separately for different sets of monetary transactions, e.g. a fixed exchange rate can be used for normal commercial transactions and a floating rate for capital account transactions. Mexico is one country which has followed this system.

See also: **multiple exchange rate**.

dual federalism (320)
The constitutional arrangement of federal and state governments acting separately but in parallel. This traditional view of the US constitution implied that federal government was mainly concerned with interstate commerce and production was the concern of the states.

See also: **cooperative federalism; fiscal federalism**.

dual labour market (820)
The division of the labour market into a primary sector which has the better jobs and a secondary sector which has inferior jobs. The primary sector consists of large firms offering training and high remuneration but the secondary sector is characterized by many small marginal firms offering small rewards and prospects to their workers. The primary sector firms use **internal labour markets** but in the secondary sector there is

heavy reliance on the **external labour market**. Students of sexual and racial **discrimination** frequently use this concept, pointing out that women and blacks are often trapped in the secondary market.

dummy variable (210)

A variable in an econometric equation which can only take the values 0 or 1 and is used to refer to being in one state or another, e.g. married or not married, living in one century or another. A shift dummy reflects an **exogenous** shift; a slope dummy reflects a change in the slope of a function.

dumping (010, 420)

The sale of goods by a firm or government at a price which is below their cost of production with the aim of increasing a market share or avoiding the costs of storage of unsold goods. Although in some countries the practice is encouraged, and made possible, by means of government subsidization, there is much opposition to dumping, e.g. the **General Agreement on Tariffs and Trade** has an International Dumping Code and the USA passed the Anti-Dumping Act in 1921. In some cases, dumping can only be prevented by retaliatory acts such as the imposition of duties or the severing of trading relationships.

Jackson, J.H. and Vermulst, E.A. (eds) (1990) *Antidumping Law and Practice. A Comparative Study*, Hemel Hempstead: Harvester Wheatsheaf.

Dunlop, John Thomas, 1914– (030)

A leading US expositor of labour economics who was educated at the University of California at Berkeley. Apart from governmental posts, including being US Secretary of Labor 1975–6, he has held a succession of academic posts at Harvard University from 1936. Throughout his distinguished career, he has pursued his interests in wage determination and labour–management relations in the context of many national economies, including those of the USA, Eastern Europe and the Third World. His detailed work on the relationship between **market structures** and wage-setting has contributed to the analytical linking of industrial organization and labour economics.

Dunlop, J.T. (1944) *Wage Determination under Trade Unions*, New York: Macmillan.
—— (1957) *The Theory of Wage Determination*, New York: Macmillan.
Dunlop, J.T., Kerr, C., Harbison, F.H. and Myers, C.A. (1960) *Industrialism and Industrial Man*, Cambridge, MA: Harvard University Press.

duopoly (010)

An industry with two firms. Each duopolist's output and prices will depend on the market actions of the other. **Cournot's** analysis of 1838 considered two firms making an identical product, each aiming to maximize its profits on the assumption that the other firm kept its output constant. He proved that equilibrium would be reached with equal division of the market and the charging of the same price, a price lower than a monopolist's price but higher than under **perfect competition**.

See also: **Bertrand duopoly model**; **Cournot duopoly model**; **spatial duopoly model**; **Stackelberg duopoly model**.

DUP (010)

See: **directly unproductive profit-seeking activities**.

Du Pont formula (540)

An analysis of the determinants of the difference between an actual rate of return on investment and the budgeted return. Return on investment = return on sales x asset turnover.

Dupuit, Arsène Jules Etienne Juvénal, 1804–66 (030)

French engineer educated at l'Ecole Polytechnique des Ponts et Chaussées. In his work on public utilities, especially the construction of bridges and public works, he pioneered the use of **cost–benefit analysis**. He was one of the earliest **marginalists**, introducing a demand curve related to marginal utility and suggesting the notion of **consumer's surplus**. His contributions to economics are chiefly contained in two articles, 'De la mesure de l'utilité des travaux publics' (1884) and 'De l'influence des péages sur l'utilité des voies de communication' (1849) in the *Annales des ponts et chaussées*. **Jevons** and **Marshall** recognized him as their forerunner.

Ekelund, R.B. Jr (1968) 'Jules Dupuit and the early theory of marginal cost pricing', *Journal of Political Economy* 76: 462–71.

Durbin-Watson statistic (210)

A test for the presence of autocorrelated disturbances. This statistic (DW) is calculated as the ratio of the sum of the squares of the differences between regression residuals in the present period and in the previous time period to the sum of the squares of the residuals in the present period. These disturbances are usually absent if the DW statistic has a value of about 2.

See also: **autocorrelation; disturbance term**.

Dutch auction (530)

A method of selling which consists of an auctioneer inviting a bid much higher than what is regarded as likely to be acceptable to the buyers. The starting price is gradually reduced until a buyer shouts 'mine' and accepts the item at that price. In Holland, an automated method is used for such auctions: the buyers face a 'clock' with prices on its face and a pointer moves gradually counter-clockwise from the higher to the lower prices.

See also: **auction**.

Dutch disease (610)

The harmful consequences for a national economy of discovering natural resources, especially the decline in traditional industries brought about by the rapid growth and prosperity of a new industry, as happened in the Netherlands as a result of the discovery of North Sea gas. There are many economies which have experienced this phenomenon in the past, e.g. Jamaica with its bauxite industry, Venezuela with its petroleum industry. New dominant industries can afford to pay wages far in excess of other industries, and so the latter raise their wage levels and cause unemployment. The successful new industry has high exports, creating a foreign exchange surplus and raising the country's exchange rate with the consequence that other industries of the economy become internationally uncompetitive. In the case of the Netherlands, rising prosperity brought about higher levels of welfare benefits which have persisted after the downturn in the economy, causing immense difficulties for the financing of public expenditure.

Corden, W.M. and Neary, J.P. (1982) 'Booming sector and de-industrialization in a small open economy', *Economic Journal* 92: 825–48.
Wijnbergen, S. van (1984) 'The Dutch disease: a disease after all?', *Economic Journal* 94: 41–55.

DW statistic (210)

See: **Durbin–Watson statistic**.

dynamically inconsistent policy (310, 320)

A policy which makes decisions which later cease to be optimal.

dynamic economics (020)

The study of the movement of an economy from a particular state at a particular date to another state later, usually using **lagged variables**. Although **classical** economists such as Adam **Smith** and John Stuart **Mill** were concerned to study the nature of economic progress, it was particularly **Robertson, Harrod, Hicks** and the **Stockholm School** in the 1930s who began the creation of formal dynamic models of **economic growth** and change. The inclusion of time in the study distinguishes this approach from static models of economic systems. In dynamic models, at least one variable is measured at a different time from the others; subscripts are attached to each variable to indicate the date(s) to which they refer.

See also: **comparative statics; static model**.

E

early retirement scheme (910)
A modern proposal to reduce unemployment, or make space in a firm for younger workers, by lowering, or making more flexible, the statutory retiring age. The principal aim of such schemes to redistribute jobs from older to younger workers can be frustrated if the rising productivity of the firm's labour force reduces its total demand for labour.

earmarked gold (310)
Gold held at US Federal Reserve Banks for foreign and international accounts; it is not part of the US gold stock.

earmarking (320)
The allocation of public revenue exclusively to the carrying out of a particular function of government, e.g. using the proceeds of television licences in the UK to finance the British Broadcasting Corporation. Some governments have rejected the earmarking approach because of the inflexibility it introduces into public finances, arguing that different types of public expenditure grow at different rates from various tax revenues. Nevertheless, this principle is often followed in the case of social expenditure and is seen as another method of controlling it.

See also: **dedicated budget**; **ringfencing**; **trust fund**.

earnings (520, 820)
1 Total pre-tax pay of employees, consisting of basic wages/salaries and all other premium and bonus elements.

2 The income of a business available for distribution to shareholders.

3 The share of the proceeds of production going to a factor of production.

See also: **income**.

earnings per share (310)
Pre-tax earnings divided by the number of shares entitled to a variable dividend. This ratio, when used as an indicator of the long-term growth potential of a company, should be compared with other indicators of a firm's performance, including its market share and its research and development expenditure.

earnings ratio (540)
Net profit (excluding preference dividends) divided by equity capital.

earnings yield (310)
This equals earnings (per cent) x par value/market price; e.g. for a company with a dividend of 25 per cent earned on a share with a **par value** of £1 with a market price of 125p, the earnings yield is 25 x 100/125 = 20 per cent.

easy money policy (310)
A relaxed monetary policy which permits high rates of growth of the money supply to keep interest rates low. This has been advocated as a means of keeping aggregate demand high and unemployment low. Britain and the USA used the policy in the years immediately following the Second World War.

easy rider (320, 830)
See: **free rider**.

EAT (830)
See: **Employment Appeal Tribunal**.

EBRD (430)
See: **European Bank for Reconstruction and Development**.

ECA (130, 430)
Economic Commission for Africa.

See also: **European Cooperation Administration**.

Eclectic Keynesians (030)
See: **New Keynesian**.

econometrics (210)

The measurement of economic relationships using statistical techniques, and the testing of economic theories. Econometrics has become the basis for **economic forecasting**.

It was inseparable from mathematics and statistics as an academic discipline until the foundation of the Econometrics Society in 1931. Although this quantitative approach to economics goes back to **Petty**, in the twentieth century it owes its origins to Henry Moore's attempt in 1911 to provide statistical evidence for **marginal productivity** theory. Gradually it changed its emphasis from searching for constant economic laws to probabilistic models.

The major techniques most frequently used are **multiple regression**, **two-stage least squares** and a multitude of tests to prevent problems such as **autocorrelation**. After 1945, the growth of macroeconomics and the more sophisticated study of consumer behaviour have inspired a great volume of econometric work. The data used are either time series provided by official governmental statistical organizations or cross-section data collated through surveys.

Griliches, Z. (1983) *Handbook of Econometrics*, Amsterdam: North-Holland.

Haavelmo, T. (1944) 'The probability approach in econometrics', *Econometrica (Supplement)* 12: 1–115.

Pagan, A. (1987) 'Three econometric methodologies: a critical appraisal', *Journal of Economic Surveys* 1: 3–24.

Pagan, A.R. and Wickens, M.R. (1989) 'A survey of some recent econometric methods', *Economic Journal* 99: 962–1025.

Marchi, N. de and Gilbert, C. (eds) (1989) *History and Methodology of Econometrics*, Oxford: Clarendon Press.

Walters, A.A. (1968) *An Introduction to Econometrics*, London: Macmillan.

See also: **Cowles Commission**.

economic agent (010)

A person or firm with the power to make decisions about output, investment, prices, etc.

Economic and Social Council (430)

United Nations council elected by the General Assembly of the UN which coordinates its economic and social work. Its commission's remit includes population, human rights, the status of women, drugs and regional problems. It has fifty four members.

economic base multiplier (940)

See: **regional multiplier**.

economic climate (140)

The persisting state of an economy apparent in its general trends over a specific time period.

See also: **economic weather**.

Economic Community of the countries of the Great Lakes (420)

An economic association of Zaire, Rwanda and Burundi set up in 1979 to establish trade agreements.

Economic Community of West African States (420)

An economic association with free movement of labour and a proposed **common external tariff** set up in 1975. The member countries are Benin, Gambia, Ghana, Guinea, Guinea-Bissau, Ivory Coast, Liberia, Mali, Mauritania, Niger, Nigeria, Senegal, Sierra Leone, Togo and Upper Volta.

economic cost (010)

See: **opportunity cost**.

economic crime (910)

A crime which is undertaken for financial gain. Its specific nature depends on the rules of a particular economic system. In the Soviet Union, where frequent use has been made of this concept, it covers both the theft of state property and the illicit making of profits; in the UK, it refers to fraud and **insider dealing**.

See also: **economics of crime**.

economic development (110)

See: **development**.

economic devolution (010)

1 The transfer of all economic decision-making to individual households and businesses.

2 The principal characteristic of a **minimal state**.

economic forecasting (140)

Predictions of the values of particular economic variables, often on the basis of extrapolation of past trends, modified by other information and using the techniques of **econometrics**. National economic forecasting is an essential element of **demand management**, as well as a first stage in national and corporate planning. The forecasts drawn up by private institutes and newspapers provide different views of the future from those published by the government.

Fildes, R. (ed) (1988) *World Index of Economic Forecasts*, 3rd edn, Aldershot: Gower Press.

See also: **linkage models**; **Treasury model**.

economic geography (730)

Economic analysis of the location of economic activity, together with the study of land use and urban areas. Although von Thunen was, in a sense, the father of locational analysis, it was not until the 1950s that much detailed work was done in this branch of geography.

Lloyd, P.E. and Dicken, P. (1977) *Location in Space: A Theoretical Approach to Economic Geography*, New York: Harper & Row.

See also: **land economy**.

economic good (010)

A scarce good, yielding **utility**, which must be allocated either by rationing or the price mechanism; not a **free good**.

economic growth (110)

The growth in the total, or per capita, output of an economy, often measured by an increase in real **gross national product**, and caused by an increase in the supply of **factors of production** or their **productivity**.

This approach was central to **Smith's** *Wealth of Nations* and to much of **classical economics**. **Harrod** and **Domar** in 1948 were major founders of modern growth theory. Growth theorists have wedded their work to **development economics** and to a study of **economic planning**. Ecologists and others concerned about the scarcity of natural resources have advocated zero economic growth rates as appropriate for the late twentieth century but a writer as early as John Stuart **Mill** (in his *Principles of Political Economy*, Book IV, ch. 6) extolled the benefits of an economy in a stationary state.

Mishan, E.J. (1977) *The Economic Growth Debate. An Assessment*, London: Allen & Unwin.

Rostow, W.W. (1990) *Theorists of Economic Growth from David Hume to the Present*, New York: Oxford University Press.

economic incidence (320)

See: **tax incidence**.

economic indicators (140, 220)

Statistics which are used in economic forecasting to analyse the state of an economy. Overall indicators of economic activity include indices of industrial production, manufacturing output, engineering orders, retail sales volume, registered unemployment and unfilled vacancies. Indicators of output show the growth of production of principal industries; indicators of external trade include indices of export and import volume, the visible and current balances and the terms of trade plus the size of the official reserves; financial indicators include changes in various measures of the **money supply**. Inflation indicators include those for retail prices, basic materials and wholesale prices of manufactured products.

See also: **coincident indicators**.

economic institution (070)

1 An organization which is a component of an **economy**.

2 A system of **property rights**.

3 A norm of economic behaviour.

4 A decision-making unit.

5 A type of contract, e.g. a form of insurance to cover a particular sort of risk.

Wiles, P.J.D. (1977) *Economic Institutions Compared*, Oxford: Basil Blackwell.

economic integration (420)

The joining together of economic activities, especially the trade of several countries. This can take different forms, including **free trade**

areas, customs unions, common markets and federations of national economies. Different forms of integration can be distinguished by the extent to which individual national governments retain independence in decision-making.

See also: **European Monetary System**.

economic journals (010)

The learned periodicals, mostly published quarterly, containing articles and book reviews, which, by presenting the research findings of the economics profession, give the clearest indication of the present state of the subject. Some of them, e.g. the *American Economic Review*, attempt to cover all branches of economics but increasingly journals specializing in a particular branch of the discipline have been started. Many economists only publish articles and avoid publishing books because of the status of the journals as the principal means of communication in the economics profession. The latest development in many of these periodicals has been to include reviews of computer software as well as of books. The leading academic journals of economics include *American Economic Review, Bank of England Quarterly Review, Economica, Economic Journal, Journal of Industrial Economics, Journal of Political Economy, Manchester School of Economic and Social Studies, National Institute Economic Review, Oxford Economic Papers, Quarterly Journal of Economics, Review of Economic Studies, Review of Economics and Statistics.*

See also: **financial journalism**.

economic life (210, 520)

The period during which an asset is expected to yield a rate of return. For the purposes of calculating **depreciation**, assets are assumed to have a standard life. Houses are given a notional life of 80 years, coalmines 100 years and machines 8, 16 or 25 years.

economic man (010)

A person, motivated by self-interest, who attempts in consumption, work and leisure to maximize his total utility. Much of **classical** and **neoclassical** economics makes this assumption about human nature. To behave as an economic man, it is necessary to engage in many mathematical calculations.

See also: *homo economicus*; *homo sovieticus*.

economic methodology (030)

The different approaches to the task of formulating economic theories and models. Economists have inevitably been influenced by parallel debates in science, especially Popper's assertion of the falsification principle, Kuhn's emphasis on paradigms and the Lakatos stress on scientific research programmes. Nevertheless, at different stages of the development of economics particular works on economic methodology have been prominent. In the classical period, **Ricardo** demonstrated the power of simple economic model-building when setting out the effects of protectionism on wages, profits, rent and economic growth, John Stuart **Mill** that of the *a priori* abstract approach to formulating economic theories, and Senior that of the crucial difference between normative and positive issues. In the 1930s, **Robbins** clearly set economics apart from other social science disciplines by making the study of 'ends and means which have alternative uses' central to the subject. With the growth of mathematical economics and econometrics in the twentieth century, it was inevitable that the empirical testing of theories became the major way in which economists went about their work: writers such as **Samuelson** guided economics in this direction. However, the empirical thrust of much of present day economics is balanced by the wrestlings of welfare economists who have sought to put value judgements on a sounder basis.

Blaug, M. (1980) *The Methodology of Economics, or How Economists Explain*, Cambridge and New York: Cambridge University Press.

Keynes, J.N. (1891) *The Scope and Method of Political Economy*, London: Macmillan.

Kuhn, T.S. (1970) *The Structure of Scientific Revolutions*, Chicago, IL: University of Chicago Press.

Popper, K. (1959) *The Logic of Scientific Discovery*, New York: Harper Torch Books.

Robbins, L. (1949) *An Essay on the Nature and Significance of Economic Science*, London: Macmillan.

Samuelson, P.A. (1947) *Foundations of Economic Analysis*, Cambridge, MA: Harvard University Press.

See also: **economics as rhetoric**.

economic methods (120)

The use of the market or the price mechanism as part of **perestroika**.

Aganbegyan, A. (1988) *The Challenge to Economics of Perestroika*, London: Hutchinson.

economic model (210)

A simplified picture of economic reality showing the interrelationships between a few economic variables. **Cantillon**, **Quesnay** and **Ricardo** were the first economists to formalize their economic theories in this way. With the increasing use of mathematics and **econometrics** by economists, economic models have become more complex.

economic paradigm (030)

A major principle which is central to a school of economics as it provides a fundamental analytical tool of economic theorizing. **Marginalism** and **neoclassical economics**, for example, have been able to demonstrate the powerful applications of the marginal concept backed up by calculus. In periods when there has been great dissatisfaction with the state of economics, a cry for a new paradigm is often heard: in the 1930s the concepts of Keynes in his *General Theory* provided one for a generation of macroeconomists.

Latsis, S.J. (ed.) (1976) *Method and Appraisal in Economics*, Cambridge and New York: Cambridge University Press.

See also: **economic methodology**.

economic planning (120)

The allocation of economic resources and the determination of production on the basis of a plan; the alternative to allocation by markets. The Soviet plans of the 1930s were the first major attempts to organize entire national economies according to this method. In the post-war period, French **indicative planning** has also attracted much attention. Governments also use planning for aspects of their economies, particularly in the cases of regional development and major investment. Since planning essentially commits a government to a future course of action, it can lead to many inflexibilities, including slow reaction to change, especially in the foreign trade sector. As planners rely greatly on **economic forecasting** the difficulties of modelling complex economies can make the quality of the plans suffer. Also planning necessitates much bureaucracy which is both costly and often opposed to enterprising behaviour. Increasingly planning, e.g. in the USSR and Hungary, has allowed the re-introduction of market mechanisms for small-scale production. In the 1990s, it is unlikely that many economies will make extensive use of this system of allocation.

Cave, M. and Hare, P.G. (1981) *Alternative Approaches to Economic Planning*, London: Macmillan.

See also: **centrally planned economy**; **development**.

economic profit (010)

The surplus of revenue over all costs, including the opportunity costs of employing all inputs.

See also: **accounting profit**.

economic programming (510)

The coordination of the independent production decisions of independent companies in late capitalist economies.

economic rent (010, 930)

1 Part of the earnings of a scarce factor of production in excess of its **transfer earnings** arising from its scarcity (See the figure overleaf).

2 A factor's earnings over its **opportunity cost**, according to **Pareto**.

3 The full market rate for housing services. As land was regarded in **classical economics** as the only fixed factor of production, it alone earned rent. However, as any factor of production can be fixed in supply, 'rent' can be earned by any factor of production. Popular examples of factors with an **inelasticity** of supply abound; labour can earn economic rent as persons with rare talents (e.g. opera singers and top sports players) have high earnings largely consisting of economic rent.

See also: **council housing**; **rent**.

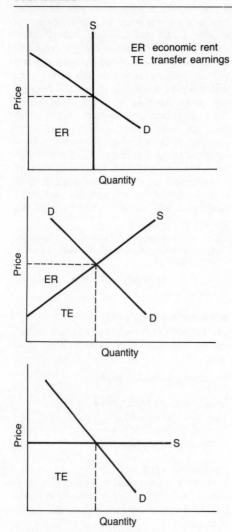

ER economic rent
TE transfer earnings

Price

Quantity

Price

Quantity

Price

Quantity

economics (010, 030)

'The study of the general methods by which men co-operate to meet their material needs' (Sir William Beveridge); 'the study of mankind in the ordinary business of life' (Marshall); 'a science which studies human behaviour as a relationship between ends and scarce means which have alternative uses' (L. Robbins); 'Economics investigates the arrangements between agents each tending to his own maximum utility' (Edgeworth); 'Wants, Efforts, Satisfaction – this is the circle of Political Economy' (Frederic Bastiat); 'Not a gay science...what we might call...the dismal science' (Thomas Carlyle).

First discussed by the Ancient Greeks, and the subject of general textbooks since the eighteenth century, economics has changed its focus as the concerns and techniques of its practitioners have developed. Originally the word meant 'household management' as the household was the basic economic unit of the time, including both farming and manufacturing activities. But the Greeks also, to their credit, raised the basic issues of value, the nature of money and the division of labour.

The word 'économistes' was first used by the French **Physiocrats** in the 1760s and in that century **Cantillon** and Adam **Smith** produced the first comprehensive treatises on the subject. Smith, and his classical disciples, produced theories of growth, value, distribution and taxation. **Cantillon**, the **Physiocrats** and **Ricardo** introduced into economics the activity of model-building. Although methodological debates were present in the subject as early as John Stuart **Mill** and Nassau **Senior** (particularly the tedious debate about deductive and inductive approaches), it was **Dupuit**, the **marginalists** and **Edgeworth** who first encouraged a mathematical treatment of economic theory.

The hints of earlier writers have provided the foundations for twentieth-century economists: issues of welfare, raised by **Marshall** and his follower **Pigou**, have led to a formal study of welfare economics; the concern for measurement, first proposed by **Petty**, has inspired the econometric testing of economic theories; the wider discussion of economics as **'political economy'** has linked economics to ideological positions in current policy debates; the later Keynes produced a general theory of the economy which determined the post-war agenda for macroeconomic theory. The increased size of the economics profession (in Britain there were only sixteen professional economists in 1908!) has inevitably led to subdivision of the subject, especially in more empirical areas.

There are many excellent general introductory texts, justly popular in many universities. The reader would gain much from those of Samuelson and Nordhaus, Begg, Fischer and Dornbusch or Lipsey and Steiner.

economic sanctions (420, 430)

Trade and financial penalties and barriers to trade imposed upon a country in order to induce it to change its basic political system or policies. Occasions when this strategy has been used include the 1930s when Italy invaded Abyssinia, the 1960s when Southern Rhodesia (now Zimbabwe) refused to adopt a system of majority rule, the 1980s to force South Africa to treat all racial groups equally and 1990–1 to end Iraq's occupation of Kuwait.

The use of sanctions has long been available as an ultimate economic weapon (e.g. the Continental System of Napoleon at the beginning of the nineteenth century), but it has always been difficult to enforce sanctions universally. In the form of a trade embargo, sanctions stimulate domestic industry to produce import substitutes; this movement of an economy to **autarky** causes losses in economic welfare as production cannot be concentrated in the most efficient industries. Article 41 of the Charter of the United Nations mentions sanctions as a permissable form of international action.

Carter, B.E. (1989) *International Economic Sanctions*, Cambridge: Cambridge University Press.
Curtin, T. and Murray, D. (1965) *Economic Sanctions and Rhodesia*. London: Institute of Economic Affairs.
Hufbauer, G. and Schott, J. (1985) *Economic Sanctions Reconsidered*, Washington, DC: Institute for International Economics.

economics and psychology (020)

Psychological theory has been used in economics to improve the modelling of the motivation of economic agents, to understand how human beings behave when faced with uncertainty and to learn about the formulation of preferences. Psychology has contributed to many areas of economics, including the examination of entrepreneurship, unemployment, poverty, taxation and marketing.

Earl, P.E. (1988) *Psychological Economics: Development, Tensions, Prospects*, Boston, MA: Kluwer.
—— (1990) 'Economics and psychology: a survey', *Economic Journal* 100: 718–55.
MacFadyen, A.J. and MacFadyen, H.W. (eds) (1986) *Economic Psychology: Intersections in Theory and Application*, Amsterdam: North-Holland.

See also: **bounded rationality; cognitive consonance; cognitive dissonance**.

economics as rhetoric (030)

A disciplined form of conversation that rejects modernist quantitative economics, which has prediction as its goal, in favour of a literary approach which examines the nature of economists' various arguments, recognizing the metaphors used and questioning the objectivity of the subject.

Klamer, A., McCloskey, D.N. and Solow, R.M. (eds) (1989) *The Consequences of Economic Rhetoric*, Cambridge: Cambridge University Press.
McCloskey, D.N. (1983) 'The rhetoric of economics', *Journal of Economic Literature* 21 (June): 481–517.
—— (1986) *The Rhetoric of Economics*, Brighton: Wheatsheaf.

See also: **economic methodology**.

economics of crime (910)

1 A branch of **neoclassical** economics which analyses the decision-making of criminals in terms of a comparison of the marginal benefit of succeeding and the **marginal cost** of being detected and sentenced. This celebrated analysis of **Becker**'s is mainly applicable to the study of property offences.

2 A study of the effects of allocating resources to law enforcement and crime prevention. The poor quality of crime statistics, partly caused by varying rates of reporting of offences, makes empirical work difficult.

Anderson, R.W. (1976) *The Economics of Crime*, London and Basingstoke: Macmillan.
Andreano, R. and Siegfried, J.J. (1980) *The Economics of Crime*, Cambridge, MA: Schenkman.
Becker, G.S. (1968) 'Crime and punishment: an economic approach', *Journal of Political Economy* 76: 169–217.

economics of law (020, 610)

1 The economic analysis of legal issues, especially property rights, negligence, contract and crime, as well as the more obviously related areas of regulation, competition and monopoly.

2 The application of price theory and statistical methods to the study of legislation, legal decisions and courts of law. **Commons** was one of the first economists to use legal materials to further economic analysis. **Coase** pioneered the rigorous application of economics to a legal problem – in his case the law of nuisance. **Stigler** and others brought the illumination of economics into dark areas of **regulation**. Posner demonstrated that most branches of the law can benefit by the use of economic concepts. The valuation of costs and benefits and the application of the notion of **opportunity cost** to many legal problems are the principal ways in which economists have shown themselves to be invaluable colleagues of lawyers.

Such is the importance of this modern branch of economics that several journals specialize in blending economic and legal analysis, notably *Journal of Law and Economics*, *Journal of Legal Studies*, *International Review of Law and Economics* and *Journal of Law, Economics and Organization*.

Ogus, A.I. and Veljanovski, C.G. (eds) (1984) *Readings in the Economics of Law and Regulation*, Oxford: Clarendon Press.

Polinsky, A. (1989) *An Introduction to Law and Economics*, Boston, MA: Little, Brown.

Posner, R.A. (1986) *Economic Analysis of Law*, 3rd edn, Boston, MA: Little, Brown.

'Symposium on law and economics', *Columbia Law Review* 85: 899–1116, 1985.

Veljanovski, C. (1990) *The Economics of Law. An Introductory Text*, London: Institute of Economic Affairs.

See also: **economics of crime**.

economic summits (430)

Meetings of the **Group of Seven** which attempt to coordinate the economic policies of the major world economies. These have taken place annually since the oil-price shock of 1973–4.

- Rambouillet (November 1975) approved of intervention to maintain the orderliness of financial markets (Canada was absent)
- Puerto Rico (June 1976) made the reduction of unemployment and inflation central goals
- London (May 1977) announced growth targets for the Group of Three
- Bonn (July 1978) extended growth targets to all of Group of Seven, using West Germany as the initiator of growth

- Tokyo (June 1979) fixed ceilings for oil imports
- Venice (June 1980) changed the emphasis of economic policy to the lowering of inflation rates
- Ottawa (July 1981) announced the goals of cutting public sector debt and reducing the rate of growth in the money supply
- Versailles (June 1982) ordered a study of intervention to stabilize exchange rates
- Williamsburg (May 1983) ordered a study of the international monetary system
- London (June 1984) tackled the world debt problem by announcing arrangements for debt rescheduling
- Bonn (May 1985) continued to support strict fiscal and monetary policies
- Tokyo (May 1986) agreed on more economic cooperation and ordered a study of appropriate economic indicators
- Venice (June 1987) announced continued support for the **Louvre Accord**; also Japan agreed to reflate its economy
- Toronto (1988) provided a framework for the rescheduling of Third World debt
- Paris (1989) was principally concerned with the global environment and international traffic in drugs
- Houston (1990) discussed the aftermath of the collapse of communism in Eastern Europe, set up a study of appropriate methods to revive the Soviet economy and agreed to phase out subsidies to farmers.

economic system (010, 070)

The system of ownership, institutions and allocation mechanisms of an economy. Ownership is the principal criterion for distinguishing various forms of **socialism** from **capitalism**. Institutions indicate the degree of freedom from central control, particularly the nature of trade unions, productive enterprises and banks. Methods of allocation contrast planned with market economies. University and college courses on comparative or alternative systems contrast different types of economy.

See also: **economic institution; economy**.

economic union (420)

This uniting of national economies consists of four elements. A **single market**, **competition policy**, common policies on structural change and regional development, and macroeconomic policy coordination by the imposition of binding rules for budgetary policies, especially by stating upper limits for budget deficits and by defining an overall **fiscal stance**. A union of this kind has been proposed for the **European Community**.

See also: **Delors Plan**.

economic value (540)
See: **replacement cost**.

economic weather (140)
The short-term conditions under which an economy operates over periods as short as a week, a month or a quarter of a year.

See also: **economic climate**.

economic welfare (010)
The total satisfaction which the residents of a country receive from the consumption of goods and services available to it. Increasingly there have been attempts to move beyond **national income** measures as a proxy estimate of economic welfare to the use of a wider range of social and economic indicators so that **externalities** and the subtleties of human tastes can be taken into account. It is recognized that the total welfare conferred by the production of goods and services must be viewed alongside welfare losses, e.g. more income is judged within the context of the amount of leisure enjoyed by workers. A high welfare country usually has a high proportion of the population owning the major types of consumer durable, e.g. washing machines and television sets; a low welfare country has poor housing, much pollution and long working hours.

Dissatisfaction with an economy has several indirect indicators, including the incidence of alcoholism, the rate of suicide, infant mortality rates, life expectancy, disease and disability rates.

See also: **measure of economic welfare**; **social welfare**.

economism (010)
A taste for material success. To Marxists, economism amounts to pursuing intermediate economic goals instead of ultimate political goals. In modern economies, workers with low economism often end up in the **secondary labour market** where there is little training and small chance of economic advancement.

economy (010, 070)
1 The market order.

2 A set of exchanges; the entirety of the economic activities of one nation using the same currency. Economies have been described in various ways.

See also: **advanced organic economy; auto-economy; barter economy; black economy; blue economy; bootblack economy; branch economy; cash economy; centrally planned economy; closed economy; command economy; core economy; communal economy; cowboy economy; decentralized market economy; dependent economy; drug economy; dual economy; enclave economy; estate economy; financial economy; first best economy; formal economy; hansom cab economy; informal economy; market economy; mature economy; mesoeconomy; mineral-based economy; mixed economy; modern economy; moonlight economy; networking economy; one-crop economy; open economy; parallel market economy; permanent arms economy; pink economy; primitive economy; protean economy; psychological economy; pure credit economy; revenue economy; second economy; self-sufficient economy; shadow economy; share economy; shortage economy; socialist economy; Soviet-type economy; spaceman economy; steady state economy; underground economy; villa economy; warehouse economy**.

economy of scale (010)
A reduction in long-run **average cost** as a result of an expansion in output which leads to increasing **returns to scale**. To measure a purely scale effect, it is necessary to make some strict assumptions: that, as output changes, there is no change in techniques used, factor prices are constant and the same degree of vertical integration holds as output changes. Scale economies may arise in many aspects of a firm's operations – its financing, marketing and production. An excellent example of a scale economy is the spreading of a fixed cost over a larger output, e.g. typesetting costs spread over an increased

print run. In the figure, there are economies of scale up to output OP but diseconomies at higher outputs.

Gold, B. (March 1981) 'Changing perspectives on size, scale and returns: an interpretive survey', *Journal of Economic Literature* 19: 5–33.

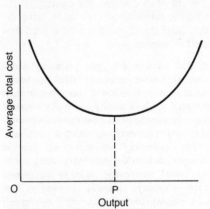

See also: **diseconomy of scale**; **economy of scope**.

economy of scope (010)

A reduction in average cost brought about by the joint production of two or more goods (or services) by a single firm, rather than by several firms. The similarities of the products permit the use of the same factor inputs for the different products, e.g. marketing, basic research. A good example of an economy of scope is in the transport industry which uses the same fixed capital for passenger and freight transport.

Panzar, J.C. and Willig, R.D. (1981) 'Economies of scope', *American Economic Review* 71 (May): 268–72.

See also: **economy of scale**.

economy of size (010)

A reduction in average cost resulting from the growth in size of a firm, e.g. the managerial economies arising from the multiplant nature of a large firm or from its superior type of marketing organization.

ECOWAS (420)

See: **Economic Community of West African States**.

ecu (430)

The European Currency Unit, a composite basket of currencies consisting of the currencies of **European Community** countries. In 1990, the Deutschmark comprised about 30 per cent, the French franc about 19 per cent, sterling about 12 per cent and the Italian lire about 10 per cent of this basket.

It is increasingly used in commercial banking transactions because its greater stability makes it more suitable for fixing contractual terms than a national currency. Employees of the European Commission are paid in ecus and even Bank of England treasury bills are denominated in them. It is equal in value to the **European Unit of Account**.

See also: **hard ecu**.

Edge Act corporation (310)

A type of US financial corporation in existence since 1919 which can receive deposits from foreign governments and other non-US residents and of US citizens whose deposits are transmitted abroad. It can also hold foreign securities and engage in foreign exchange activities. These corporations can either be banking corporations mainly concerned with accepting deposits or corporations principally involved in investing in foreign non-banking firms. The advantages of being a corporation of this kind are that they can operate across state boundaries, in the case of international transactions, and that their investments can be wider than those of Federal Reserve member banks, e.g. in foreign finance.

See also: **McFadden Branch Banking Act**.

Edgeworth, Francis Ysidro, 1845–1926 (030)

Irish-born economist and statistician who received a classical education at Trinity College, Dublin, and Oxford. He was appointed to a lectureship in logic and afterwards the Tooke Chair of Political Economy at King's College, London, in 1890. From 1891 to 1922 he was Drummond Professor of Political Economy at Oxford. A natural mathematical ability enabled him to write the very influential *Mathematical Psychics* in 1881, much admired by **Marshall**: in it he applied mathematics to **utilitarianism**, analysed the nature of contract in a free market and invented **indifference curves** and **contract curves**, still much used in international and labour economics. In many articles he made major contributions to the theories of **index** numbers and probability theory. Also, he was the first editor of the *Economic Journal*, from 1891 to 1926.

Creedy, J. (1986) *Edgeworth and the Development of Neoclassical Economics*, Oxford: Basil Blackwell.
Edgeworth, F.W. *Collected Papers*.
O'Brien, D.P. and Presley, J.R. (eds) (1981) *Pioneers of Modern Economics in Britain*, ch. 3, London: Macmillan.

Edgeworth box (410)

This depicts the trading relationships between two persons or two countries using **indifference curves** and a **contract curve** which joins the points of tangency where each indifference curve of X touches an indifference curve of Y. In the figure, I_{X1}–I_{X7} and I_{Y1}–I_{Y7} are the indifference curves of consumer X and consumer Y respectively. CC is the contract curve. The **marginal rates of substitution** are equalized for each consumer.

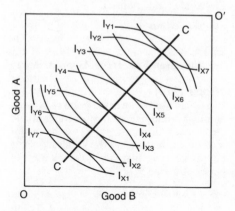

EEA (430)

See: **exchange equalization account**.

EEC (420)

See: **European Economic Community**.

EFA (310)

See: **expedited funds availability**.

EFF (430)

See: **extended fund facility**.

effective demand (010)

The value of **aggregate demand** which is equal to **aggregate supply**. Keynes introduced this concept in his *General Theory*.

Amadeo, E.J. (1989) *Keynes's Principle of Effective Demand*, Aldershot: Edward Elgar.
Keynes, J.M. (1936) *The General Theory of Employment, Interest and Money*, Book I, ch. 3, London: Macmillan.

See also: **effectual demand**.

effective exchange rate (430)

An index of a currency's international value in terms of a basket of currencies, weighted by the relative importance of each foreign country in the trade of the currency concerned, e.g. for sterling, the basket of currencies would include the US dollar, the Japanese yen and the Deutschmark and the weights would reflect Britain's trade with the USA, Japan and Germany.

effective rate of assistance (420)

Value added to a country's production as a result of **protection** as a proportion of the value added by producers under free trade. This is calculated by the formula $(A-B)/B$, where A is the domestic price of a good, including a tariff minus the subsidized cost of inputs per unit of output and B is the world price of a good minus the unsubsidized cost of inputs per unit of output.

effective rate of protection (420)

This measures the extra value added, as a result of **tariffs**, as a proportion of the free-trade value added. The most commonly used formula is $t_e = t_1 - kt_2/(1 - k)$, where t_e is the effective rate of tariff protection, t_1 is the tariff rate on output, t_2 is the tariff rate on input and k is the proportion of total price accounted for by inputs.

effective tax rate (320)

The average rate of tax levied on gross personal income. In the case of a company, it can refer to taxation as a proportion of value added.

effectual demand (010)

The notion stated by **Malthus** in his *Principles of Political Economy* of a level of demand in a national economy such as to bring about full employment of land and labour. He used this idea to challenge the complacent view of **Say** that there could not be a general **glut**. Effectual demand, Malthus asserted, could be increased by landlords employing menial servants, more distribution of wealth to the middle classes and **public works** employment for the poor. **Keynes** saw Malthus as one of his precursors in the formulation of macroeconomic ideas.

Eltis, W.A. (1980) 'Malthus's theory of effective demand and growth', *Oxford Economic Papers* 32: 19–56.

Rutherford, R.P. (1987) 'Malthus and Keynes', *Oxford Economic Papers* 39: 175–89.

See also: **effective demand**.

efficiency ratio (540)

Standard hours for actual output divided by actual hours for actual output multiplied by 100.

efficiency real wages (820)

Real wages relative to **productivity**.

efficiency wage (820)

A wage measured with reference to the 'exertion of ability and efficiency required of the worker' (Marshall). He asserted that there would be a tendency towards efficiency wages or earnings in the same district. Many firms attempt to base their wage structure on this principle.

Marshall, A. (1920) *Principle of Economics*, 8th edn, Book VI, ch. 3, London: Macmillan.

See also: **local labour market**.

efficient estimator (210)

The statistic of two sampling distributions with the same mean but the smaller **variance**.

efficient job mobility (820)

Movement of workers to different jobs in response to a changing pattern of demand which results in the elimination of labour shortages.

See also: **labour mobility**.

efficient market (010)

A market characterized by prices which reflect all available information. A semi-strong version of such a market is one with prices which fully reflect all publicly avail-able information; a weak version is one whose prices reflect past prices. In a market of this kind, profits cannot be made by studying historical price data as the traders have already used them. This concept is crucial to the macroeconomic theory of the **Rational Expectations** School. The efficient market hypothesis applied to the stock market is the **random walk** hypothesis.

effluent fee (720)

A charge to a polluter which gives the right to discharge into the air or a water course a noxious emission. Although this approach to pollution control has been criticized as a 'licence to pollute', it does encourage firms to minimize the discharge of pollutants. Ideally, the fee should be fixed such that the revenue from it is equal to the marginal costs of pollution. An early example of the use of these fees has been in Germany's Ruhr Valley; there are also cases of its use in the USA, France and the Netherlands.

See also: **pollution control; pollution tax**.

EFT (310)

Electronic funds transfer.

See also: **eftpos**.

EFTA (420)

See: **European Free Trade Association**.

eftpos (310)

Electronic funds transfer at point of sale, i.e. automatic debiting of customers' bank or credit card accounts. This is the major method of introducing the **cashless society** but unlikely to replace the present variety of payment methods.

See also: **debit card**.

egalitarianism (010, 160)

1 Advocating universal suffrage.

2 Equality of opportunity because there are no barriers to entering any occupation with or without the financial means being offered to facilitate entry.

3 An absence of income differentials.

See also: **Bentham**.

EIB (430, 940)

See: **European Investment Bank**.

eigenprices (010, 210)

The economically rational prices of an economy derived from the actual state of an economy, as shown in an **input–output** table. Each eigenprice is a full-cost price, reflecting the input–output coefficients for the production of that good. Eigenprices make output and factor prices consistent, taking into account the final yield of an economy and the principle of full-cost pricing. Actual prices are irrational if they diverge from eigenprices. Eigenprices are 'ideal' because factors of production are rewarded according to their marginal revenue products.

Seton, F. (1985) *Cost, Use and Value. The Evaluation of Performance, Structure and Prices across Time, Space and Economic Systems*, Oxford: Clarendon Press.

elasticity (010)

The responsiveness of the value of one economic variable to a change in the value of another which is related to it. The most common use of the concept is **price elasticity of demand** which shows the responsiveness of quantity demanded to change in price or income. This concept, one of the most durable tools of the economist, is used extensively in price theory, international economics and industrial economics.

See also: **cross price elasticity of demand; elasticity of supply; income elasticity of demand**.

elasticity of demand (010)

See: **cross price elasticity of demand; income elasticity of demand; price elasticity of demand**.

elasticity of expectations (010)

Hicks defined this as the ratio of the proportional change in the expected future values of X to the proportional change in its current value. If this is equal to unity, expected values and current values change in the same direction and by the same proportion, e.g. if present prices double then it is expected that future prices will double also.

elasticity of substitution (010)

The ease with which one factor of production can be substituted for another. If the elasticity of substitution is greater than unity for a factor of production, then an increase in its supply will increase its relative share of the national income. **Hicks** introduced this concept in his *Theory of Wages* (1926) to show the effect of a change in the supply of one factor, assuming two factors only and constant returns to scale, on the marginal productivity of the other. The concept has been extensively used in the study of **production functions** and the analysis of the effects of **inventions**.

Bronfenbrenner, M. (1960) 'A note on relative shares and the elasticity of substitution', *Journal of Political Economy* 68: 284–7.

elasticity of supply (010)

The responsiveness of the quantity supplied to a change in the price of that factor, good or service. In the short term, supply can be increased only by using existing factors of

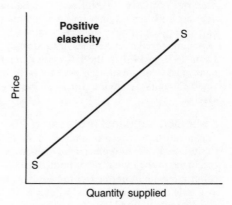

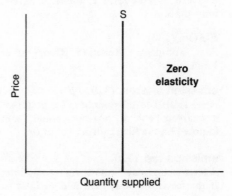

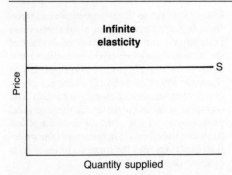

Price

Infinite
elasticity

S

Quantity supplied

production more intensively (e.g. by over-time working); in the long term supply can be increased by increasing factor supply (e.g. recruiting and training more workers, increasing the capital stock). Supply elasticities increase as the time period lengthens, as demonstrated (in the figures above) by the changing slope of the supply curves (S).

eligible liability (310)
Sterling deposit liabilities (excluding deposits with an original maturity of over two years) + sterling resources obtained by switching foreign currencies into sterling. From 1971 to 1981 in the UK, commercial banks had to maintain 12½ per cent of their eligible liabilities in the form of **reserve assets**.

embodied technical progress (620)
Technical improvements embodied in the capital stock. Net or replacement investment can increase the extent of embodied technical progress as in both cases the equipment available and chosen for purchase will usually embody the latest technology.

See also: **disembodied technical progress**; **innovation**.

EMCF (430)
See: **European Monetary Cooperation Fund**.

emission charge (320, 720)
A fee related to the quantity of a pollutant discharged, e.g. a noxious liquid, and imposed on the firm causing pollution.

emission fee (720)
A fee which gives a firm the right to pollute. If the fee is too low, then it does little to

prevent pollution levels from rising; if too high, it may require expensive monitoring and prevent the production of any output at all.

emission reductions banking (720)
An environmental control policy which allows an emissions source which reduces its emissions more than legally required to 'bank' the right to pollute more in the future so that over a time period the flow of emissions is on average at the legal limit.

empirics (210)
Empirical findings acquired through observation and experiment.

employee ratios (520)
Measures of a **labour force** which include (1) capital employed per employee, a **capital-labour ratio**, (2) sales per employee, a measure of the **productivity** of sales staff, (3) profit per employee, a measure of labour utilization, (4) average wage per employee, a measure of labour costs.

Employee Stock Ownership Plan (830)
An arrangement for a company to set up an employee trust to allow employees to acquire the shares of the company. These schemes have flourished in the USA and the UK. In the USA, the National Center for Employee Ownership (NCEO) estimated in 1986 that 8,000 US firms had such schemes by then, covering 10 million to 11 million workers, i.e. 8 per cent of the total national workforce. The company makes regular tax-deductible contributions to the Employee Stock Ownership Plan. Ownership exercises a strong psychological effect on workers: someone earning £18,000 per annum would accumulate £32,000 in ten years' time. It is mainly a scheme for the more successful firms. In the UK, the Companies Act of 1989 helped to accelerate the growth of these schemes by allowing companies more freedom to purchase their own shares. In developing countries, there is scope for such schemes as a means of redistributing wealth from rich elites to the poor. The usefulness of the schemes is judged by the extent to which employees become more profit conscious, management–worker communica-

tions are improved and the recruitment and retention of staff are facilitated.

See also: **industrial democracy**; **workers' participation**.

employers' association (830)
A federation of firms of one industry which jointly engage in **collective bargaining** with the **trade unions** representing their workers. As employers usually apply negotiated wages to all of their workers, irrespective of their union membership, collective bargaining covers a larger part of the labour force than that part which is unionized. These associations often represent their industries on other matters, e.g. proposed legislation.

employment (010, 810)
The engagement of a factor of production in a productive activity with the result that it receives a factor income. Employment gives people wages or salaries and rewards capital with interest or profits. Increased labour force participation makes more persons available for employment; economic growth makes possible actual employment growth. Even in advanced economies with an employed labour force static in size, technological change effects many sectoral shifts in the composition of employment.

Employment Act 1946 (010, 810)
Federal statute of the USA which set out major economic goals for the USA, including the **full employment** of labour and other resources. Under the Act, the **Council of Economic Advisers** was established. The Act sought to promote 'maximum employment' rather than **full employment**; it did not guarantee a high level of employment by pledging the use of federal resources to job creation programmes.

Employment Act 1980 (830)
UK statute which provided for the financing of secret ballots on trade union matters such as strike action, the election of union officials and the amendment of trade union rules. The protection of trade union members was increased by making it unlawful unreasonably to refuse trade union membership or to terminate it and to require trade unions to make compensation if a member's complaint was well-founded. The

Act also narrowed **secondary action** which was exempt from actions in tort to those actions relating to the breaking of a contract of employment.

Employment Act 1982 (830)
This UK statute extended industrial relations legislation by declaring contracts for the supply of goods and services void if only members of a specified trade union can carry out the work or if a trade union has to be recognized. Also, there was a requirement that only union officials could authorize trade union acts. Damages could be recovered from trade unions, employers' associations, their trustees, members and officials, except for protected property, e.g. a political fund. The limit for damages was set at £250,000 for the largest unions with 100,000 or more members.

Employment Act 1988 (830)
This UK statute amended labour legislation by stating various rights of union members, including a right to a ballot before industrial action, a right of access to the courts, a right to inspect a union's accounting records and a right to require an employer to stop deductions of union subscriptions. Also, the Act stated that trade union funds cannot be used to pay fines imposed by a court and that industrial action to enforce membership of a **closed shop** is a tort.

Employment Appeal Tribunal (830)
UK body established in 1975 to hear appeals from industrial tribunals, particularly concerning discrimination and unfair dismissal.

employment contract (820)
The terms on which a person is hired by a firm. Williamson distinguishes four types: recurrent spot contracting (by which an employee is hired from day to day); contingency claims contracting (being hired depends upon the occurrence of an event, e.g. ball-boys are needed at Wimbledon on a fine day); authoritative contracting (a master–slave contract, a modern example might be military conscription) and **internal labour market** contracting (a flexible form of hiring to the senior posts of an organization determined by managerial rules).

Williamson, O.E., Wachter, M.L. and Harris, J.E. (1975) 'Understanding the employment relation: the analysis of idiosyncratic exchange', *Bell Journal of Economics* 6: 250–78.

See also: **implicit contract theory; invisible handshake**.

employment function (020)
The desired level of employment as a function of the demand for output.

Ball, R.J. and St Cyr, E.B.A. (1966) 'Short term employment functions in British manufacturing industry', *Review of Economic Studies* 33: 179–207.

Employment Institute (810)
London-based institute founded in 1985 and originally headed by Richard Layard and Sir Richard O'Brien. It has enjoyed widespread political support for its **neo-Keynesian** approach to the problems of British unemployment. It has advocated some general reflation, special measures for the long-term unemployed and infrastructure investment.

employment multiplier (010, 820)
The first version of a formal **multiplier** which was suggested by **Kahn** in 1930. It shows the ratio of secondary to primary employment. Primary employment consists of the jobs in an industry where the investment occurs and in associated industries, e.g. those producing and transporting raw materials; secondary employment is the consequential employment in the production of consumption goods to meet the increased expenditure of the recipients of wages and profits in the primary industries. When examining the employment effects of government expenditure, it is important to realize that the employment multiplier varies with the type of expenditure, whether consumption, capital or personnel spending. Expenditure directly on personnel obviously has the greatest multiplier effect.

Kahn, R.F. (1931) 'The relation of home investment to unemployment', *Economic Journal* 41: 173–98.

empty nester (840)
A married person in late middle age whose children have moved elsewhere leaving an 'empty nest'.

See also: **Third Age**.

EMS (430)
See: **European Monetary System**.

EMU (420, 430)
See: **European Monetary Union**.

enclave economy (070, 130)
1 An isolated **economy** without forward and backward economic linkages within it, e.g. an agrarian economy which imports its tractors and fertilizers and exports its products. In such economies, an economic activity does not have any spin-offs in terms of services and processing and so there is an absence of the dynamic effects of intersectoral growth.

2 A subeconomy of an advanced economy, e.g. in the USA ethnic groups have formed distinct subeconomies with, for example, Cubans or Mexicans comprising both the owners and workers.

endogenizing the exogenous (210)
The inclusion in an economic model of something which previously was regarded as given. Classical economists, for example, regarded full employment as given whereas **Keynes** included it as a variable in his model of the national economy. **Expectations** were often regarded as given but now many economic models include them.

See also: **endogenous variable; exogenous variable**.

endogenous variable (210)
An economic variable whose values are determined by the other(s) of an economic model.

See also: **exogenous variable**.

endowment effect (310)
Increase in a bank's profitability as a result of a rise in interest rates.

Engel, Ernst, 1821–96 (030)
German statistician who, after a training in mining in Germany and Paris, directed Bureaux of Statistics in Saxony and Prussia. In 1857 he propounded '**Engel's law**', one of the first major empirical findings in economics which is still respected today.

Engel coefficient (010, 220)

Expenditure on food, beverages and tobacco as a proportion of final private consumption expenditure.

Engels, Friedrich, 1820–95 (030)

The principal intellectual collaborator of **Marx** from 1844. Although coming from a family which owned textile mills in the Rhineland and Manchester, he was a social critic from the age of 18. He never attended university but came under the influence of the Young Hegelians in Berlin. His practical knowledge of business was to temper Marxian theory. His interest in economics began with an essay *Outlines of a Critique of Political Economy* (1844). His analysis of industrialization and his prophecy of a proletarian revolution impressed Marx. They jointly wrote *Die Heilige Familie* (*The Holy Family*) (1845), *Die Deutsche Ideologie* (*The German Ideology*) (1845–6) and *Manifest der Kommunistischen Partei* (*The Communist Manifesto*) (1848). Engels is also noted for his *Umrisse zu einer Kritik der Nationalökonomie* (*Outlines of a Critique of Political Economy*) (1844) and *Die Lage der arbeitenden Klasse in England* (*The Condition of the Working Class in England*) (1945), as well as his posthumous editing of the second and third volumes of Marx's *Das Kapital*. His frequent financial help to the Marx family maintained his great friend in his chosen career. Living in retirement for twenty-six years, he was able to prepare the remainder of Marx's *Das Kapital* from mounds of notes.

Carver, T. (1983) *Marx and Engels: The Intellectual Relationship*, Brighton: Wheatsheaf.

Henderson, W.O. (1976) *The Life of Friedrich Engels*, 2 vols, London and Portland, OR: Frank Cass.

Engel's law (020)

The assertion that, as income rises, the proportion spent on food falls. Formally, this can be stated as the **income elasticity of demand** for food is less than unity.

engine of growth (110)

1 The mechanism, often said to be international trade, which starts an economy's expansion. This view has been contrasted with the view that trade is a 'handmaiden'. The concept has been attributed to **Robertson**.

2 A major economy of the world, e.g. the USA, which is so large that its expansion generates a demand for imports which stimulates many other national economies.

English auction (530)

A method of selling an item which begins with the first bid being requested by the auctioneer and ends when the bids reach an uncontested peak. The item is sold to the highest bidder, provided that the bid is not less than the seller's reserve price. The earliest auctions in the Roman Empire were probably of this kind since 'auction' is derived from the Latin word 'auctus' meaning 'increase'.

See also: **auction**.

English disease (050)

The consequences of poor industrial relations and industrial organization manifest in strikes, low productivity and low growth.

enterpriser (510)

See: **entrepreneur**.

enterprise union (830)

A Japanese **trade union** covering all the workers below supervisor level within an enterprise or within an establishment of that enterprise. The union has its headquarters on company premises and is often run by company employees on secondment from their usual employment. This is the most important level of unionism in Japan as most of workers' contributions are spent at this level and vital wage bargaining is done. Often an enterprise union is given the task of allocating between types of worker the gross addition to the enterprise's wage bill. Although there were 72,605 unions by 1989, this does not imply a weak union movement as there is joint action through their national federations, the major ones having been **Rengo**, **Sohyo**, **Domei**, **Shinsanbetsu** and **Churitsuroren**. Since 1948, statistics on Japanese unions have been produced by the Basic Survey on Trade Unions.

See also: **company union; local union**.

enterprise zone (930)

A local British or US area, often a decaying inner city, selected for special government help in the form of exemption from rates and from many governmental regulations. The purpose of these zones is to encourage the location of new industries and new jobs by reducing the factor cost of doing so. The creation of such zones leads to conflict between local authorities and businesses within and without these areas as the latter can suffer a loss of industry.

See also: **regional policy**.

entrepreneur (010, 510)

The fourth factor of production, after land, labour and capital, which organizes production and undertakes the risk of an enterprise. In **joint stock companies**, the risk-bearing is undertaken by the shareholders; in small businesses, usually by the manager-proprietor. The idea of entrepreneurship was introduced into economics by **Cantillon**, literally to mean the 'undertaker', i.e. a person who buys at a fixed price and sells at an uncertain price. Subsequently different economists debated alternative definitions which include risk-bearer, organizer of production, innovator and decision-maker in circumstances which give people unequal access to information. New entrepreneurs are often well-educated persons with managerial experience having small firms in areas with wealthy local markets.

Casson, M.C. (1982) *The Entrepreneur: An Economic Theory*, Oxford: Robertson.
Gilder, G. (1984) *The Spirit of Enterprise*, New York: Simon & Schuster; Harmondsworth: Viking Books, Penguin Books.
Knight, F.H. (1921) *Risk, Uncertainty and Profit*, Chicago, IL: Chicago University Press.
Schumpeter, J.A. (1934) *The Theory of Economic Development*, Cambridge, MA: Harvard University Press; London: H. Milford.

envelope curve (010)

A curve which encloses a whole family of curves, each of which contributes at least one point to the envelope. The main use of envelope curves is in relating long-run to short-run cost curves. In the figure $SATC_1$ – $SATC_4$ are short-run average total cost curves; LRAC is the long-run average total cost curve.

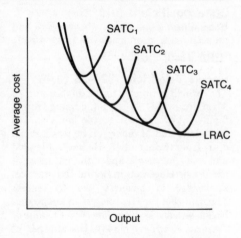

environmental determinism (010, 720)

The doctrine that economic and social activities are determined by the physical environment, particularly the climate. Development economists have used this concept to account for some areas of the world being less developed than others and to account for the international division of labour.

environmental issues (720)

World population growth, the demand for exhaustible resources, the loss of topsoils and forests, and pollution are the principal matters discussed.

Environmental Protection Agency (720)

Washington-based US federal agency established in 1970 for research into the environment and the control of pollution. It reinforces the efforts of other federal agencies and coordinates the anti-pollution work of state and local governments. It is concerned with air, water, radiation, solid waste, pesticides and toxic substances.

environmental tax (320, 720)

A tax on a polluter related to the external costs of private production.

See also: **effluent fee**.

EOC (830)

See: **Equal Opportunities Commission**.

EP (420)
See: **export promotion**.

EPA (140, 210)
1 A world econometric model of the Japanese Economic Planning Agency which includes nine country models (of the seven major **Organization for Economic Cooperation and Development** countries, Australia and South Korea) and six trading regions.

2 Environmental Protection Agency.

Amano, A., Maruyama, A. and Yoshitomi, M. (eds) (1982) *EPA World Economic Model*, vols 1 and 2, Tokyo: Economic Planning Agency.

See also: **linkage models**.

eps (310)
Earnings per share: these are usually larger than the dividend per share as few companies distribute all their earnings to their shareholders.

Equal Employment Opportunity Commission (810)
US federal commission in operation since 1965 which was created by Title VII of the Civil Rights Act 1964. It is concerned with **discrimination** on the basis of the leading personal characteristics of age, sex, race, colour, religion and national origin in employment matters of wages, hiring, firing, promotion and training.

See also: **Equal Opportunities Commission**.

equality (010, 160)
The achievement of the same amount of **economic welfare** per head or the same economic opportunities for each individual. As the creed of **egalitarianism**, it denies differences in innate abilities and argues that superior abilities are merely the product of training.

See also: **human capital**.

equality standard (160)
An idealistic approach to income distribution which gives equal shares to all by equalizing per capita incomes. Critics of this approach assert that human nature is not so altruistic as to tolerate a system of reward which ignores differences in individual persons' contributions to output and that a fall in labour productivity is a likely consequence of using this policy.

See also: **altruism**; **contribution standard**; **egalitarianism**; **needs standard**.

equalizing wage differential (820)
A wage differential which compensates a worker for a non-pecuniary aspect of a job, e.g. the degree of risk or the dirtiness of working conditions. These differentials discourage labour mobility to more pleasant occupations. **Cantillon** and **Smith** were both aware of this reason for wage differentials.

Equal Opportunities Commission (830)
UK body set up in 1976 to deal with complaints about **sexual discrimination**. Initially the bulk of complaints concerned job adverts specifying applicants of a particular sex; subsequently the issues covered have included a wider range of grievances. It publishes annual statistics on sexual wage differentials.

Equal Pay Act 1963 (USA) (820)
US federal statute which sought to equalize male and female pay for workers in interstate commerce. Employment discrimination against women and ethnic minorities was dealt with under Title VII of the Civil Rights Act 1964.

Equal Pay Act 1970 (UK) (820)
UK legislation which enforced the principle of equal pay for equal work: this was to apply to all collectively bargained agreements and **statutory minimum wage rates** by 1975. Despite the Act, there is still a divergence between male and female earnings, reflecting **occupational segregation** of women, differences in hours worked and promotion policies of firms.

Equal Pay Directive (820)
A directive issued by the European Commission in 1975 to counter discrimination in pay, especially on the grounds of sex.

equal product curve (010)
See: **isoquant**.

equilibrium (010)

A state of balance such that a set of selected interrelated variables has no inherent tendency to change. In economics, a major example is the balance of the forces which equate demand and supply. **Smith** in his discussion of prices used the idea of market prices fluctuating around the natural price which can be considered a central price towards which market prices tend. The **subsistence theory of wages** regarded expansions and contractions of a population as equilibrating forces which make the subsistence wage rate the long-run equilibrium wage. An equilibrium can exist for an economy as a whole, for a sector of it, for a particular market or for an institution, such as a firm. Although the term is applied principally to static models, there can be an equilibrium in dynamic models when variables proceed along an equilibrium-type path. Equilibria can be stable or unstable, temporary or permanent: some of them do not exist. The Marshallian and Keynesian cross-diagrams are the most famous diagrammatical representations of equilibrium (E, equilibrium).

Fisher, F.M. (1983) *Disequilibrium Foundations of Equilibrium Economics*, Cambridge: Cambridge University Press.
Samuelson, P.A. (1965) *Foundations of Economic Analysis*, 2nd edn, New York: Athenaeum.

See also: **general equilibrium**; **temporary equilibrium**.

equilibrium GNP (010)

The level of real national income at which **aggregate demand** equals **aggregate supply**, i.e. desired expenditure equals the quantity of goods and services supplied in that economy.

equilibrium price (010)

The price which equates demand and supply in a market in a particular time period.

equipment trust bond (520)

A financial arrangement for leasing equipment. The holder of the bond owns the equipment and then leases it to the firm which has issued the bond via a trustee. The trustee pays the interest and principal to the bondholder, receiving rental payments from the issuer of the bond.

equity (310)

1 **Ordinary shares**.

2 **Common stock**.

3 The portion of a company's capital which does not earn a fixed rate of interest. Equity-holders usually receive dividends which vary with the profitability of the company/corporation and its profit distribution policy. The issue of equity shares enables a company to expand its capital and to spread business risk.

4 Fairness.

See also: **horizontal equity**; **Rawlsian justice**; **vertical equity**.

equity joint venture (310, 610)

A business jointly owned and run by a private firm and a governmental organiza-

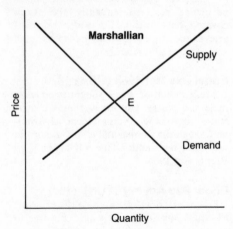

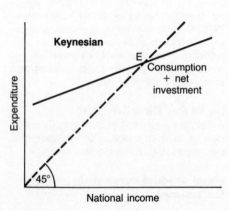

tion which is financed partly by equity capital so that the return to the private investor is a variable dividend. This arrangement made possible investment by capitalist firms in **centrally planned economies**. To the participating government there is the advantage of not having to pay fixed interest charges. China, for example, has invited foreign investors, mostly from Hong Kong, to participate in new business ventures of this kind. Also, many East European countries turned to this organizational form after 1989 as a means of reconstructing their economies.

See also: **European Bank for Reconstruction and Development; joint venture**.

equity-linked mortgage (310)

A method of purchasing commercial or residential property. The lender offers to pay, for example, half the current interest rate on the mortgage in return for acquiring half the equity in the property (or another proportion). This device makes it possible for borrowers to obtain finance for large property purchases and for lenders to benefit from the capital appreciation of properties.

equity taxation (320)

Taxation based on the fairness principle that each person should suffer an equal sacrifice. 'Sacrifice' is an ambiguous term as it can refer to equality in absolute terms or at the margin.

See also: **ability to pay**.

equity warrant (310)

An option to buy an **ordinary share** or **common stock** at a fixed price in the future which is issued in the form of a bond with a low **coupon**. In the case of **Eurobonds**, the warrant is issued attached to a bond denominated in a particular currency. However, the warrant is often detached and traded separately. The popularity of this cheap method of stock market speculation is reflected in the rapid increase in warrant prices.

ERA (010, 420, 810)

See: **effective rate of assistance; exchange rate agreement**.

ERDF (940)

See: **European Regional Development Fund**.

ergonomics (810)

The scientific study of the physical methods of work with the aim of minimizing effort and maximizing output. Inspired by the study of the practical problems of using military equipment in the Second World War, it became a recognized discipline in 1949. Much work has been done on the appropriate ways of displaying information, on the study of machine controls and on the relationship between a worker and the physical environment.

Singleton, W.T. (ed.) (1982) *The Body at Work*, Cambridge: Cambridge University Press.

ERM (430)

See: **Exchange Rate Mechanism**.

ERP (430)

European Recovery Program.

See also: **Marshall Plan**.

error (210)

The difference between observed and true values brought about by chance rather than systematically.

See also: **probable error; standard error of estimate; Type I error; Type II error**.

ESA (220)

See: **European System of Accounts**.

escalator clause (520, 820)

A clause in a contract which revises payments due under that contract in line with changes in a specified price index. In times of considerable inflation, these clauses are popular in labour and building contracts, as well as in tax schedules and social security benefits.

See also: **COLA**.

ESOP (830)

See: **Employee Stock Ownership Plan**.

establishment (220, 610)

A place of business, a factory or a plant which is part or the whole of a **firm**.

estate economy (130)

An underdeveloped economy with much of its agriculture organized into large estates, usually foreign owned. Malaysia with its rubber plantations, Ceylon with its tea plantations and Argentina with its cattle ranches had this character. Although wages of the estate workers were low by international standards, they were high enough to induce the movement of workers from subsistence agriculture. These estates were the basis of development for several ex-colonial countries.

ETAS (220)

Economic Trends Annual Survey (UK).

ethical unit trust (310)

British equivalent of a **social conscience fund**.

EUA (430)

See: **European Unit of Account**.

Euler's theorem (210)

The rule that, if factors of production are paid according to their **marginal products**, the total product will be distributed completely if and only if there are constant **returns to scale**. The theorem is of importance when considering the application of the **marginal productivity of wages** since if there are diminishing returns and workers are paid according to their marginal products, the total wage bill will be less than the total product. Conversely, if there are increasing returns to scale and workers' wages equal their marginal products, the total wage bill will be more than the value of their output.

See also: **returns to scale**.

Eurobank (310)

A bank which is able to receive **time deposits** and make loans in currencies other than that of the country in which it is located.

Eurobond (310)

A long-term bond marketed internationally by an international syndicate of banks in countries other than that which has the currency in which the bond is denominated, e.g. a bond in French francs can be marketed anywhere outside France. The advantage of this type of financial instrument is that it escapes national financial regulations.

Eurobond market (430)

An international market, founded in the early 1960s, as a **primary** and **secondary market** in bearer bonds issued outside the country of that particular currency. The anonymity of this market has attracted investors who wish to remain discreet about their holdings. Previously able to avoid any regulation, it is now under the **Association of International Bond Dealers** in the UK. It has become a leading world securities market; in its **primary market** role, Credit Suisse First Boston has been the major issuing firm.

Eurocheque (310)

A **cheque** which can be written in any one of a number of **currencies**.

Euroclear (430)

An international agency for clearing bank **cheques**.

See also: **Cedal**.

Eurocurrency market (430)

The international market dealing in bank deposits in the major currencies, including the US dollar, yen, Deutschmark, Swiss franc, French franc, guilder and **ecu** which has been in existence since the 1950s. Its early growth was stimulated by **Regulation Q** which encourages the expatriation of US dollars in search of higher interest rates.

Eurodollar (310, 430)

Dollars on deposit with banks outside the USA, some of them the European branches of US banks. Originally, the attraction of such deposits was that they could evade the **reserve requirements** needed for domestic deposits and any restrictions on maximum interest rates (**Regulation Q**). As a consequence of US balance of payments deficits, dollars are supplied for the reserves of the central banks other than the **Federal Reserve System**. Increases in Eurodollar deposits are encouraged by the investment facilities and interest rates of the Eurobanks. There is also a small creation of Eurodollars by the Eurobanks themselves.

Eurodollar market (310, 430)

A wholesale money market dealing in expatriate US dollars, outside the control of national banking authorities. However, increasingly the **Bank of England**, the **Bundesbank** and the US **Federal Reserve Banks** have introduced controls on the foreign banks within their jurisdiction. Despite these controls, the banks operating in this market are more competitive than other commercial banks because their operating costs are lower as a consequence of the insistence on minimum deposits of at least £50,000.

Euroequity (310)
An **equity** of one country which is placed in another, e.g. the sale of Fiat shares in Germany.

Eurofed (430)
A proposed **central bank** for the **European Monetary System**, resembling the **Federal Reserve System** of the USA in that the different central banks of the separate European countries will contribute to the formulation and execution of policy at federal level.

de Cecco, M. and Giovanni, A. (eds) (1990) *A European Central Bank?*, Cambridge: Cambridge University Press.

Eurofranc (310, 430)
A franc deposit in a non-French bank in Europe but outside France.

Euromarket (310)
A financial market which trades in financial instruments that are denominated in currencies other than that of the country where that market is located, e.g. trading in London in bonds denominated in French francs.

Euromoney deposit (310, 430)
A bank deposit in another currency, e.g. US dollars, French francs, Swiss francs and yen.

European Bank for Reconstruction and Development (430)
The development bank founded in 1991 and based in London which lends to the East European countries in order to ease their transition from centrally planned to market economies. Its capital was raised from **European Community** institutions and forty-one countries. Its lending policy is to make

40 per cent of its loans for infrastructure investment and 60 per cent for private sector commercial investment.

European Communities (420)
The three organizations consisting of the European Coal and Steel Community, established in 1952, the **European Economic Community**, established in 1958, and the European Atomic Energy Community, also established in 1958. The original member states of each of the three Communities were France, West Germany, Italy, Belgium, the Netherlands and Luxemburg. In 1967 the original institutional structures of the three Communities were merged to create the common executive, judicial and legislative institutions of the **European Community**.

European Community (420)
The name given to the **European Communities** since 1967. The original six member states (France, West Germany, Italy, Belgium, the Netherlands and Luxemburg) were joined, in 1973, by the UK, Ireland and Denmark, followed by Greece in 1982, and Spain and Portugal in 1986. The signatory countries of the European Community hoped to promote a greater equality of incomes between nations and regions, to raise the rate of economic growth, to help Third World countries and to establish a major economic power, rivalling the USA and the USSR. By 1987, the European Community had a population of 323 million inhabitants, making it the largest market in the industrialized world (USA, 244 million; Japan, 122 million), but Japanese per capita income was then 48 per cent higher and US per capita income 40 per cent higher than in the European Community. The industrial strength of the European Community lies especially in its chemical, transport equipment and industrial machinery industries.

El-Agraa, A.M. (1990) *The Economics of the European Community*, 3rd edn, New York and London: Philip Allan.

See also: **European Economic Community**.

European Cooperation Administration (430)
The US agency which administered **Marshall Aid** to Europe, 1948–52.

European Currency Unit (430)
See: **ecu**.

European Economic Community (420)

A **customs union** of Western Europe, also known as the Common Market. It was founded by the Treaty of Rome in 1958 when France, West Germany, Italy, Belgium, the Netherlands and Luxemburg agreed to enter into a customs union with a common external tariff, mobility of labour and capital between the nation states and a common agricultural policy. In 1967 its institutional structures were merged with those of the European Coal and Steel Community and the European Atomic Energy Community to form the common institutions of the **European Community**.

European Free Trade Association (420)

Founded in 1959 as the alternative European trade organization to the **European Economic Community** with Austria, Denmark, Norway, Portugal, Sweden, Switzerland and the UK. Its members are now Austria, Finland, Iceland, Liechtenstein, Norway and Sweden (Denmark, Portugal and the UK left on joining the European Economic Community). At its inception, EFTA aimed to expand economic activity, full employment and productivity in its area, to trade on the basis of fair competition and to remove tariffs between members by 1 January 1970. Although it reduced **tariffs** in 1961 and quotas among members during 1961–6, it was not originally intended to be a **customs union**, i.e. with a **common external tariff** in the Association. After 1973, a series of agreements between EFTA and the European Economic Community reduced tariffs between the member countries: by 1977 duties on most industrial goods between EFTA and the European Economic Community had been abolished.

European Investment Bank (430, 940)

The major lending institution of the **European Community** which was founded in 1958 to provide loans to assist 'the balanced and smooth development of the Common Market' with an initial capital of $1000 million. It provides loans for three types of project: the modernization of less developed regions, the conversion of undertakings to new types of production and employment, and the financing of projects of interest to several member countries. In its first fifteen years, 60 per cent of its lending went to Italy, in particular to assist the development of the Italian South.

European monetary cooperation (430)

A series of plans and agreements which led to the launching of the **European Monetary System** in 1979. It began with the Barre Plan and the Hague Summit of 1969 and was followed in 1971 by the **Werner Report** and the European Council of Ministers' resolution. These initiatives resulted in an agreement between **European Community** central banks in 1970 to provide a short-term monetary support system, a central banks' medium-term financial assistance scheme in 1972, the 'snake in the tunnel' short-term financing facility in European Community currencies of April 1972 to February 1973, the joint floating of European currencies, and the 'snake outside the tunnel', March 1973 to March 1979. Prior to 1979, there were unsuccessful attempts towards European monetary union in the Tindemans Report of 1976 and the Jenkins initiative of 1977.

European Monetary Cooperation Fund (430)

Part of the **European Monetary System** which finances imbalances in payments between the countries participating.

European Monetary System (430)

The West European system for aligning exchange rates and bringing about a convergence in monetary policies. It came into being when West Germany, France, Denmark, the Netherlands, Italy, Belgium and Ireland decided in 1979 to change their exchange rates only within a joint consultation procedure. The principal components of the system are the **ecu**, the **Exchange Rate Mechanism** and credit mechanisms. Major currency alignments have taken place in September and November 1979, March and September 1981, February and June 1982,

March 1983, July 1985, April 1986 and January 1987. The size of realignments has tended to increase over time: by the 1980s they were as great as 10 per cent per realignment. Under the system, Ireland and Italy, the highest-inflation countries, have suffered deteriorating competitiveness and other countries, particularly Belgium and Denmark, have improved. The system is a hybrid of a fixed rate system and a managed float.

It has so far achieved a zone of exchange rate stability in Europe, brought about a convergence in the economic policies of the members, cut inflation rates drastically and created very close cooperation amongst the central banks concerned. Progressively, capital controls between the members have disappeared. However, the European Monetary System still suffers from the fact that national monetary authorities regard their own country's interests as paramount.

Coffey, P. (1984) *The European Monetary System – Past, Present and Future*, Amsterdam, Dordrecht and Lancaster: Nijhoff.

de Grauwe, P. and Papadenos, L. (1990) *The European Monetary System in the 1990s*, Harlow: Longman.

See also: **European monetary cooperation**.

European Monetary Union (420, 430)

The proposal to have the **ecu** as the **single currency** of the **European Community** by 1997. To achieve this goal requires a step-by-step use of the ecu for all monetary transactions. Gradually all deposits with banks and other financial institutions would be denominated in ecus; company financing and the payment of taxes would also be in ecus. After a transitional period in which nationally issued banknotes would state the ecu equivalent, a full change to a single currency would occur. To achieve this union, monetary policies throughout the European Community would have to converge and **collective bargaining** would have to reflect a Europe-wide inflation rate.

See also: **Delors Plan**; **hard ecu**.

European Recovery Program (430)

See: **Marshall Plan**.

European Regional Development Fund (940)

A **European Community** fund which offers regional assistance, particularly for infrastructure projects, in member countries.

European Social Charter (820, 830, 910)

The social policy proposed in the preamble to the **Single European Act** which would improve employment and social conditions throughout the **European Community** by introducing minimum wages, standards of health and safety at work and welfare benefit entitlements. Critics have objected to an increase in labour costs which would make the poorer **European Community** countries less competitive.

European system of accounts (220)

This classifies household expenditures by categories of use. It is a coherent framework for the presentation of the national income accounts of the member countries of the **European Community**. The principal accounts are:

1 Domestic accounts
   Goods and services account
   Production account
   Generation of income account
   Distribution of income account
   Use of income account
   Capital account
   Financial account
2 Rest of the world accounts
   Current transactions account
   Capital account
   Financial account.

(1980) *European System of Integrated Economic Accounts ESA*, 2nd edn, Luxemburg: Statistical Office of the European Communities, 1980.

European Unit of Account (430)

A basket of the currencies of the member countries of the **European Economic Community**. Each currency is weighted according to its standing and amount in circulation.

evolutionary theory of the firm (020, 510)

A study of the determinants of the 'destiny' of firms which rejects the view that firms are maximizers and asserts that firms' actions have evolved from their own traditions. Innovatory change is only accepted in a crisis; it is not part of a long-term growth plan. **Marshall**, with his biological analogies for the growth of the firm, was a founder of this theoretical approach. The viable firm, according to **Alchian**, has profits greater than are needed to maintain current activities; under conditions of **uncertainty**, managers cannot predict the outcome of their decisions so that luck is quite important.

Alchian, A. (1950) 'Uncertainty, evolution and economic theory', *Journal of Political Economy* 58: 211–21.
Nelson, R.R. and Winter, S.G. (1982) *An Evolutionary Theory of Economic Change*, Cambridge, MA: Beltrap Press of Harvard University Press.

See also: **Penrose**.

ex ante, ex post (010, 310, 320)
A widely used distinction in macroeconomics, coined by **Myrdal**, to distinguish what is planned (i.e. *ex ante*) from what actually happens (i.e. *ex post*). These alternative concepts are often used in discussions of investment and welfare. If, for example, *ex post* investment is less than what was planned, then the expectations of the investor have not been realized.

Myrdal, G. (1939) *Monetary Equilibrium*, London: William Hodge.

ex ante variables (010)
Measures of what is planned or intended, e.g. intended investment. These have been used since the **Stockholm School** and **Keynesians** started modern macroeconomics; increasingly *ex ante* measures have been used to estimate **expectations**. In practice, surveys of business enterprises are used to ascertain intended levels of production, investment and employment.

See also: *ex post* **variables**.

excess burden of a tax (320)
The **deadweight loss** from a tax which can be considered to be either the deadweight loss suffered by taxpayers in excess of what the government collects or the amount in excess of taxes being collected that the consumer

would give up in exchange for the removal of all taxes.

See also: **tax incidence**.

excess capacity (010, 640)
1 In competitive theory, a level of output below that level of output which minimizes average total cost.

2 More generally, any output level less than the maximum amount technically possible.

See also: **X-efficiency**.

excess capacity theorem (020)
The theoretical outcome of **monopolistic competition** which holds that profit-maximizing firms choose a level of production that is lower and with higher average costs than under **perfect competition**. In the figure ATC is average total cost, MC is marginal cost, D is demand, AR is average revenue, MR is marginal revenue, OP is X the profit-maximizing price, OQ_2 is the profit-maximizing output and Q_1Q_2 is the excess capacity.

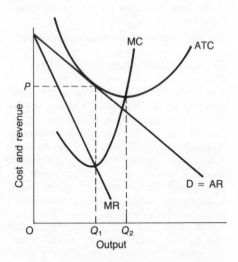

See also: **profit maximization**.

excess demand (010)
The amount by which demand exceeds supply at a given price. As excess demand can be positive or negative, it is a useful way of stating the relationship between demand

and supply: when a market is in equilibrium, excess demand is zero. The rate of excess demand can be measured as (demand – supply)/supply. Markets subject to maximum price control are usually characterized by long-term positive excess demand which necessitates rationing and encourages the growth of **black markets**: East European countries have provided many examples of this.

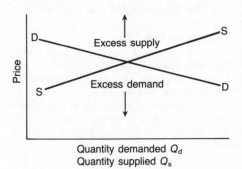

Quantity demanded Q_d
Quantity supplied Q_s

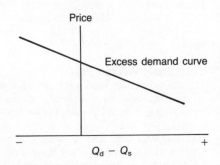

excess supply (010)
Supply, less demand, at a given price. It can be regarded as negative excess demand.

exchange controls (430)
Various means of supporting a currency by controlling overseas investment and expenditures, first advocated by **Plato**. These usually take the form of restrictions on the purchases of foreign currency and on the export of capital. Britain had such controls from 1939 until 1979 when, helped by North Sea oil revenues, sterling needed no such support. France used exchange controls in 1981 to defend the franc; the Italian lira long needed such help. When exchange controls are in force, **black markets** in currency are

tolerated by most governments as a means of delaying the formal announcement of change in the official rate.

See also: **dual exchange rate**.

exchange cross rate (430)
The value of one of the world's leading currencies against each of the nine others. The ten currencies concerned are US dollar, sterling, Deutschmark, yen, French franc, Swiss franc, Belgian franc, Dutch guilder, Italian lira and Canadian dollar. These are published daily in leading financial newspapers. This can be regarded as the exchange rate between currencies B and C when the exchange rates between A and B and A and C are known already: this cross-rate should be consistent with the other exchange rates.

exchange efficiency (010)
1 An exchange of goods which makes at least one person better off, without anyone being worse off.

2 A **Pareto** improvement.

Exchange Equalization Account (430)
The account of the **Bank of England** which holds British foreign exchange reserves. After Britain abandoned the **gold standard**, from 1932, the establishment of the Account was necessary to provide a mechanism for supporting sterling through the sale and purchase of gold and foreign currencies: the Account sells foreign currency to buy pounds when there is a desire to stabilize or improve the sterling exchange rate.

exchange rate (430)
The price of a **currency** in terms of another, e.g. how many US dollars can be bought for one pound sterling. Such rates vary because of changes in the relative demand for different countries' goods and services and because national **monetary** and **fiscal policies** are inconsistent with each other. Differences in tax rates and in interest rates cause capital flows which affect a country's balance of payments and, consequently, its exchange rate. An overvalued exchange rate leads to a **current account** balance of payments deficit and bearish speculative capital

movements; an undervalued exchange rate creates a current account surplus and an influx of capital. Volatile exchange rates and volatile interest rates coincide.

Isard, P. (1978) *Exchange Rate Determination: A Survey of Popular Views and Recent Models*, Princeton, NJ: International Finance Section, Department of Economics, Princeton University.
Witteveen, H.J. (1982) *The Problem of Exchange Rates*, New York: Group of Thirty.

exchange rate agreement (430)

A foreign exchange **hedging** technique which requires only the net amount owed at the end of a banking day to be paid. Previously, purchases and sales of a foreign currency at different dates required several transactions; this kind of agreement requires only one.

Exchange Rate Mechanism (430)

A crucial element of the **European Monetary System** which links the values of participating European currencies and limits the extent of their fluctuations to 2.25 per cent against the rest in the system, unless a wider band has been specially negotiated, e.g. Spain's and the UK's 6 per cent. Also it produces indicators of currency divergence against the **ecu**, makes available short-term credit to support intervention in foreign exchange markets on behalf of currencies which diverge too far and, in extreme cases, realigns currencies at new **exchange cross rates**. The ERM reduces speculative gains from changes in exchange rate movements and concentrates the minds of investors on the interest rate offered for deposits in a particular currency, unless there are frequent realignments.

Giavazzi, F. and Spaventa, L. (1990) *The 'New' EMS*, Paper no. 369, London: Centre for Economic Policy Research.

exchange rate regime (430)

The system chosen by national governments for the mutual determination of their exchange rates. The main choice is concerned with the extent to which there are fixed parities between different currencies, e.g. under the **Bretton Woods** system and under the **European Monetary System** or **floating exchange rates**.

exchange rate target zone (430)

A softer version of a fixed exchange rate regime which permits wide bands for each currency participating provided that the countries concerned take corrective action when the values of their currencies come close to their limits.

Williamson, J. (1985) *The Exchange Rate System*, Washington, DC: Institute for International Economics.

See also: **European Monetary System**.

exchange risk (430)

The risk of an exchange rate changing with the consequence that the value of one's holding of another currency is lowered. A **multinational corporation**, for example, constantly faces the risk when doing business in another country that the foreign currency it acquires there will fall in value.

Exchequer (310)

The British government's account held at the Bank of England. Holding this account is one of the activities of the Bank as a **central bank**.

Exchequer White (310)

The daily internal Bank of England statement which shows its cash needs by detailing flows into and out of the Bank, chiefly as a consequence of the Government's receipt of tax payments and disbursements of governmental expenditures. If the Bank is short, it will buy bills; if there is excess cash in the banking system, it will sell them.

excise duty (320)

An indirect tax levied on a specific good, especially petrol, alcohol or tobacco. Duties of this kind have been an important source of government revenue in some countries, e.g. the USA, for longer than **income taxes**. Given the **inelasticity** of demand for these goods, they provide a reliable source of revenue. Also, the duties have been imposed as **tariffs** to protect domestic industries from the competition of imports.

See also: **direct and indirect taxation**.

excise tax (320)

See: **excise duty**.

exclusion principle (010)

A major characteristic of a **private good**: one person's consumption excludes others' consumption, e.g. my consumption of a piece of fruit excludes your consumption of it. **Public goods** are non-exclusive, e.g. my consumption of the benefits of the nation's armed services does not reduce your consumption.

ex dividend (310)

An **ordinary share** which does not bear the entitlement to receive the dividend recently announced and payable at that time.

executive leasing (510)

The offering of management services by experienced mid-career managers for short periods, usually for less than a year. Leasing is attractive to companies when a particular type of skill is needed either to cope with an unusual task, e.g. organizing a merger, or during an interregnum until a permanent executive is appointed.

Exim (310)

See: **Export Import Bank**.

exit-voice (010, 830)

A distinction used by Hirschman to classify the physical or verbal methods individuals use to reveal their preferences. 'Voice' can take the form of voting (as in democratic politics) or complaints (as under grievance procedures); 'exit' is movement away from a less desired situation, e.g. a particular employment, region or country. 'Exit-voice' can be applied to collective or individual choice.

Hirschman, A.O. (1970) *Exit, Voice and Loyalty: Responses to Decline in Firms, Organizations and States*, Cambridge, MA: Harvard University Press.

See also: **Tiebout hypothesis**.

exogenous expectations (010)

Expectations which are given and are thus excluded from an economic model or theory. Few economists would now take this view of expectations.

exogenous variable (210)

An economic variable whose values are not determined by the other variables of an economic model.

See also: **endogenous variable**.

expectations (010, 140)

The views of households or firms or governments about the future. They are based either on a simple view that the future will be like the past or on a more sophisticated view that the future will be partly like the past and partly different because of responses to previous forecasting errors. This is now the dominant theme of much of macroeconomics. The study of expectations has become much more elaborate than it was in the hands of **Myrdal** and **Keynes**.

See also: **adaptive expectations**; **ex ante variables**; **exogenous expectations**; extrapolative expectations; **Keynes expectations**; **rational expectations**; **regressive expectations**.

expedited funds availability (310)

The prompt availability of check deposits by US commercial banks.

expenditure function (020)

An equation which is used to describe the consumption possibilities for a consumer at a given set of prices.

expenditure tax (320)

A tax based on the amount actually spent by a consumer. It is argued that such a tax may be easier to collect than capital or income taxes and that the growth of personal savings (which would escape the tax) is encouraged. There have been many supporters of this type of taxation, including John Stuart **Mill**, **Marshall**, Irving **Fisher**, **Kaldor** and the **Meade** Committee.

Kaldor, N. (1955) *An Expenditure Tax*, London: Allen & Unwin.

See also: **double taxation of savings**.

expense preference (510)

A manager's weighted preference for a particular type of cost. As managers often prefer an expansion of staff (as a means of being in charge of a larger establishment), they will prefer extra expenditure on staff to other forms of expenditure.

expense ratio (540)
See: **cost ratio**.

expensive easy money (310)
Okun regarded this as **credit** which is extensively available (easy) but at high interest rates (expensive).

experience good (010)
A **good** which is usually purchased frequently by a consumer who acquires information about it through repeat purchases.

See also: **search good**.

expert system (630)
Computer software which reproduces the expertise of a specialist by providing a set of rules and a knowledge base so that a user is asked a set of questions before the computer program gives advice. The many applications
of these systems include controlling production plants and insurance underwriting.

explicit contract (010, 830)
An agreement whose terms are stated clearly by the parties. This is usually in writing and legally enforceable.

See also: **implicit contract theory**.

explicit cost (010)
Actual money expenditure incurred to obtain a factor of production or a good or service.

See also: **implicit cost**.

exploitation (720, 830)
1 Using or misusing a natural resource. Extraction of minerals constitutes use; misuse X arises from causing long-term damage to the environment.

2 Treating labour unjustly by either paying it less than its **marginal product** or extracting **surplus value** from it.

export (420)
The sale to a resident of another country of a good or service which is domestically produced. Exports net of imports are included in the **gross domestic product**. Unless an economy is self-sufficient, it will be necessary for it to export in order to be able to pay

for the imports demanded by its residents. The volume of a country's exports has many determinants, including the exchange rate, marketing methods, delivery times, product design and the extent of government subsidization, especially the guarantee of export finance so that firms will not be discouraged from exporting by the risk of buyers' defaulting.

See also: **import**.

Export Import Bank (310)
Washington bank set up in 1934 as an agency of the US federal government to facilitate and finance exports, e.g. by issuing guarantees, direct loans and insurance programmes to minimize buyers' default.

export promotion (420)
A set of measures, usually taken by a national government, to subsidize the marketing overseas of domestically produced goods and to guarantee foreign payment for them.

export subsidy (320, 420)
A reduction in the cost of exports brought about by a government grant. There can be reductions in the costs of labour, of capital or of export financing, as well as more favourable tax treatment. Adam **Smith** referred to such subsidies as 'bounties'.

ex post variables (010, 210)
Variables which show actual economic outcomes, e.g. the amount of fixed investment which has taken place. In the 1930s there was much discussion in macroeconomics of how *ex ante* savings and investment that were different in amount became equal *ex post*.

See also: *ex ante* **variables**.

extended fund facility (430)
A type of **International Monetary Fund** loan introduced in 1974 which is granted to a country which agrees to an economic adjustment programme over a three-year period. Repayment begins four and a half years after the loan is granted and is extended over a six-year period. A facility which was used to the extent of about $100 million annually in the 1970s, and by the mid-1980s had risen to

over \$2 billion per year. It can be used in conjunction with a **supplementary financing facility**.

external account (430)

1 The **balance of payments** accounts of a nation.

2 A bank account of a person who is not a resident of the country.

external balance (430)

The state of a country's **balance of payments** such that it is neither in deficit nor in surplus. In accounting terms, the balance of payments always balances because of the principles of double-entry bookkeeping. However, in economic terms, for a country to have an external balance there must be an equality between the flows of payments and receipts between that country and the rest of the world in a given time period.

Meade, J.E. (1951) *The Theory of International Economic Policy*, vol. I *The Balance of Payments*, ch. 10, London and New York: Oxford University Press.

Swan, T.W. (1963) 'Longer run problems of the balance of payments', in H.W. Arndt and W.M. Corden (eds) *The Australian Economy*, Melbourne: F.W. Cheshire.

See also: **internal balance**.

external debt (320, 430)

The debt a country owes to foreign banks and governments which accumulates through its persistent **balance of payments** deficits. An attempt to achieve economic growth in a short time period is often the cause of such indebtedness. In extreme cases of foreign indebtedness, national governments will attempt to reschedule their debts and, in a crisis, apply to the **International Monetary Fund** for loans.

See also: **internal debt**.

external economy of scale (010, 610)

A reduction in the average costs of a firm as a result of the expansion of the whole industry of which it is part. A major example of these economies occurs in the case of the training of labour: the general expansion of an industry requires more skilled labour so that the large firms undertaking training will provide a pool of suitable labour for other firms.

See also: **internal economy of scale**.

externality (010)

The benefit or cost to society or another person of a private action (e.g. production or consumption); a third-party effect. Since **Pigou**'s discussion of the distinction between **social** and **private cost**, it has been a central concept of **welfare economics**. 'Internalizingan externality', in the case of an external cost, can be achieved by a government levying taxes equal to the difference between a private cost and a social cost.

external labour market (820)

A market consisting of competing employers and competing workers. Workers can and will enter firms at different pay and status levels but often with lower remuneration than in oligopolistic firms with **internal labour markets**. Much of the external labour market is coterminous with the **secondary labour market**.

external shock (420, 430)

A large unanticipated change in world economic conditions, especially a shift in the **terms of trade**, a slowdown in the growth of world export demand or increases in the interest rates set by world financial markets. However, the major shocks of the 1970s, particularly the increase in the price of oil, had an uneven impact on the prosperity of particular nations with producing countries welcoming the shocks and consumers having to make major adjustments.

See also: **structural adjustment policy; supply-side shocks**.

extrapolative expectations (010)

Expectations which are based on the past level of an economic variable and whether that variable is increasing or decreasing in value.

Metzler, L.A. (1941) 'The nature and stability of inventory cycles', *Review of Economics and Statistics* 23: 113–29.

extremum (210)

An extreme value, i.e. a maximum or a minimum.

See also: **optimization problem**.

F

factor-augmenting technical progress (110, 620)
Technical progress arising from an increase in factor **productivity**, in the absence of an increase in the stock of capital or the size of the labour force.

factor cost (010, 220)
The cost of employing a factor of production; a valuation of output equal to the incomes actually received by factors. The **national income** measured at factor cost excludes indirect taxes, net of subsidies.

factor endowment (010, 410, 720, 850)
1 Quantities of land, labour, capital and entrepreneurs owned by a particular country. This uses a stock approach to consider the total wealth of a country. The crudest measures of the size of a country would be in terms of its land area, population and labour force; more elaborate estimates of its wealth would include a calculation of the amount of **human capital** it has and the replacement cost value of its physical capital.

2 The ratio of one factor to another. This indicates the extent to which the country's production is predominantly **capital intensive** or **labour intensive**. Attention has been paid to factor endowment by international trade theorists, particularly **Heckscher** and **Ohlin** who have attempted to examine the extent to which a country's trade is a reflection of the scarcity or abundance of particular factors of production.

See also: **stock and flow concepts**.

factorial terms of trade (420)
The **net barter terms of trade** multiplied by the **productivity** change in a country's export industries (single factorial terms) or by the ratio of the index of productivity change of the country's export industries to the corresponding index for the foreign export industries producing its imports (double factorial terms). This modification of the net barter terms of trade is made to show the welfare effects of the terms of trade, because an increase in productivity, for example, which worsens a country's terms of trade indicates that it is sharing its productivity gain with another country.

See also: **terms of trade**.

factor income (160)
Part of the national product distributed to a particular factor of production. The factor labour receives wages and salaries, the factor land receives rent, and capital earns interest and profits.

factoring (520)
The sale, at a discount, of debts due to a firm. The factor purchasing these rights is entitled to collect the amount due. Factoring can be used to increase the short-term funds available to a business enterprise or to finance exporting.

See also: **bill of exchange**.

factor market (010)
A market for a **factor of production**. The most prominent of these markets are the labour market and the capital market. In such markets the buyers are firms and the sellers are households – a reversal of the roles of firms and households in product markets. The principal task of such markets is to arrive at a **market clearing price**. Factor markets are linked to product markets because the demand for a factor of production is derived from the demand for its product.

factor of production (010)
An input which produces a good or service. Before the eighteenth century it was common to classify all factors as either **land** and **labour**; later, **capital** and entrepreneurship were considered as separate factors of production. In many modern economics models, only labour and capital are included as factors of production.

See also: **entrepreneur**.

factor price equalization theorem (410)

This asserts that free trade in **final goods** brings about the equalization of factor prices, especially of labour and capital, throughout the world.

Lerner, A.P. (1952) 'Factor prices and international trade', *Economica* 19: 1–15.

factor productivity (010)

Output per unit of a factor input, e.g. output per person employed. To measure the **productivity** of one factor of production requires holding other factors' inputs constant – a difficult task, especially in the case of capital.

factor tax (320)

A tax levied on a particular income-earning **factor of production**. Taxes on capital, taxes on residential and commercial property and taxes on employment are examples of this type of tax.

fad (010)

1 A speculative **bubble**.

2 A demand which causes the price of a good or service to be temporarily much higher than its intrinsic value.

fair trading (420)

Genuine **free trade** in which there are no attempts to have hidden subsidies to export industries and protection of domestic industries to prevent imports, e.g. by imposing rigorous quality controls; selling under a system of free competition. Until there is fair trading in Europe, the **Single Market** will be impossible.

See also: **dumping**.

Fair Wages Resolution (820)

A resolution of the British House of Commons, first passed in 1891 (and followed by many local authorities), which stipulated that government contractors should not employ workers under terms and conditions less favourable than those negotiated under collective bargaining for that trade or industry. In recent years many of the cases which led to the raising of wages concerned cleaning firms. The Conservative government, consistent with its belief that

the setting of minimum wages under wages councils contributed to unemployment, repealed the Resolution, with the consent of Parliament, in 1983.

Family Expenditure Survey (220)

UK sample survey of the characteristics of households, including earnings, education, unemployment and consumption. This survey, published annually by the UK Department of Employment, reports on

- Household characteristics
- Expenditure
- Income
- Regional characteristics
- Regional expenditure
- Regional income.

FAO (130, 420, 710)

See: **Food and Agricultural Organization**.

Farm Credit System (310, 710)

US federation of thirty-seven banks consisting of 387 lending associations owned by the farmers who borrow from them. There are three banks in each of the twelve districts of the **Federal Reserve System** and another bank which specializes in the sale of bonds to Wall Street institutions. It was established by Congress between 1916 and 1933.

The purpose of the system is to provide credit to farmers and ranchers during their 'growing season'. Before the establishment of the Farm Credit System, it was hard for farmers to borrow because money was very scarce in most rural areas. Federal government guarantee of the farm credit system's bonds gives the banks of the farm credit system 'agency status' on Wall Street. The excessive borrowing by farmers when farm land values were high in the early 1970s and 1980s led to the creation of large farm debts.

Gifford Hoag, W. (1976) *The Farm Credit System*, Danville, IL: Interstate Printers and Publishers.

FAS (420)

See: **free alongside**.

FCO (610)

See: **Federal Cartel Office**.

FDI (430)

See: **foreign direct investment**.

FDIC (310)
See: **Federal Deposit Insurance Corporation**.

featherbedding (820)
Work practices which attempt to maintain employment by low labour productivity methods. These practices include payment for time when no work is performed.

See also: **demarcation**.

Fed (310)
See: **Federal Reserve System**.

Federal Cartel Office (610)
The United States agency which monitors mergers, thus making a major contribution to the running of US **antitrust** policy.

Federal Deposit Insurance Corporation (310)
US regulatory body founded in 1933 to insure depositors against bank failures and to take on the role of chartering national commercial banks. It is largely financed by assessments on the deposits held by insured national and state banks. When an insured bank fails, each depositor can claim up to $100,000 from the FDIC. To protect depositors, the FDIC can also facilitate bank mergers through loans and the purchase of assets from insured banks. Its three directors include the **Comptroller of the Currency**. Critics of the principle of deposit insurance assert that it encourages banks to have imprudent lending policies.

federal finance (320)
Public finance arrangements between central and state governments in a country with a federal constitution, e.g. the USA, Germany, Canada, Australia and Switzerland. There can be **revenue-sharing** of money raised from taxation or different types of taxation at each level of government. Federal finance systems vary in (1) the degree of fiscal autonomy of lower levels of government, (2) the extent to which a federal government imposes limits on the power of lower levels of government to borrow and (3) the degree of independence of a federal budget from those of sub-federal governments.

Hughes, G.A. (1987) 'Fiscal federalism in the UK', *Oxford Review of Economic Policy* 3: 1–23.
Pechman, J.A. (1977) *Federal Tax Policy*, 3rd edn, Washington, DC: Brookings Institution.

See also: **US federal finance**.

federal funds (310)
The reserve deposits of banks and other financial institutions of the USA which are held in a **Federal Reserve** Bank. Since these deposits earn no interest, banks want to minimize the size of their holdings and increase their investment in assets, e.g. loans, which will increase their profitability.

federal funds market (310)
The US money market in which commercial banks sell short-term financial assets.

federal funds rate (310)
The rate at which the member banks of the **Federal Reserve System** trade reserves with each other. Banks with more reserves than required lend their surplus to other banks with a deficiency. Although this rate is determined by the demand for and supply of excess reserves in the banking system, the Federal Reserve can influence it.

See also: **prime rate of interest**.

Federal Home Loan Board (310)
US independent federal agency established in 1932 to provide a credit reserve for member savings institutions specializing in home mortgage lending, i.e. savings and loan associations, cooperative banks, homestead associations and insurance companies.

See also: **Federal Savings and Loan Insurance Corporation**.

Federal Open Market Committee (310)
A committee of the US **Federal Reserve System** which sets the policy for the use of the principal instrument of US monetary policy, **open market operations**. It is the New York Federal Reserve Bank which executes the policy. The Committee consists of seven of the Board's governors plus five of the presidents of the regional Federal Reserve Banks, one of whom is always the President of the Federal Reserve Bank of New York. It was given its statutory auth-

ority under the Banking Act 1933 but it had existed as an informal investment committee of the Federal Reserve Banks from 1922. During and after the Second World War until 1952, the federal open market committee had a policy of maintaining interest rates at low levels, whilst in the 1970s, a policy of attempting to achieve target rates of growth for monetary aggregates.

Federal Reserve Bank (310)
See: **Federal Reserve System**.

Federal Reserve Note (310)
US financial instrument issued by the **Federal Reserve Banks** which is legal tender and used to be backed by gold or silver. It is the major form of US currency.

Federal Reserve System (310)
The US system established in 1913 which carries out the functions of a **central bank** for the USA. The original aims of the System were to give the country an elastic currency, to provide facilities for **discounting** commercial paper and to improve the supervision of banking. Heading the System is a Board of Governors in control of twelve district reserve banks with banking responsibility for a region of the USA (e.g. District 1 is the Federal Reserve Bank of Boston, District 2 is the Federal Reserve Bank of New York and District 12 the Federal Reserve Bank of San Francisco) and member banks below the Reserve Banks in a pyramid of authority. There is also a **Federal Open Market Committee** and a Federal Advisory Council. The seven Governors are appointed by the US President, with Senate approval, and serve for fourteen years: they appoint the directors of the twelve district banks, fix **reserve** and **margin** requirements and determine **discount rates** and major banking regulations. The principal tasks of the district banks are to supervise member banks in their respective regions, to provide cheque collection services, to supply coin and currency, to lend to member banks at the discount rate and to act as the fiscal agent of the US Treasury, collecting taxes, marketing and redeeming Treasury securities and paying interest on them. Fewer than 60 per cent of US commercial banks have membership of the Federal Reserve: if they do, they have the advantages of cheaper

banking services but the disadvantage of losing profits through having to meet tougher **reserve** requirements.

The changing monetary policies of the Federal Reserve reflect the dominant economic policy thinking of the decades of its history. The Roosevelt and Truman Administrations of the 1930s and 1940s gave it the task of maintaining **full employment** and pegging interest rates at a low level. The Reagan Administration of the 1980s asked it to use monetary aggregates as its principal targets.

Beckhart, B.H. (1972) *Federal Reserve System*, New York: American Institute of Banking.
Moore, C.H. (1990) *The Federal Reserve System: A History of the First 75 Years*, Jefferson, NC: McFarland.

Federal Savings and Loan Insurance Corporation (310)
Founded in 1934 to insure shareholders in federal savings and loan associations (**thrifts**). Its overseer is the **Federal Home Loan Bank Board**. It insures savings up to $100,000 in amount and is financed by the premiums paid by insured financial institutions and by interest received on its own investments. It is also authorized to borrow from the US Treasury. By 1987 it had run out of funds to reimburse depositors and needed to be recapitalized by the savings bank industry. The higher deposit insurance premiums charged by the Federal Saving and Loan Insurance Corporation caused many thrifts to change to the **Federal Deposit Insurance Corporation** scheme.

See also: **Resolution Trust Corporation**.

Federal Trade Commission (610)
US federal commission established in 1914 to maintain competitive enterprise in the USA and formulate competition policy. It seeks to prevent general trade restraints and price discrimination and to ensure accurate credit cost disclosure. The federal trade commission enforces its judgements through voluntary cooperation with the offending parties or through litigation.

See also: **antitrust**.

Federal Trade Commission Act 1914 (610)
This federal statute of the USA both established the **Federal Trade Commission**

as an independent agency and gave it authority to investigate and declare illegal 'unfair' and 'predatory' competitive practices.

Fed funds (310)
See: **federal funds**.

Feldstein, Martin, 1939– (030)
US economist who has made specialist studies of welfare policies. He was educated at Harvard and Oxford universities, returning to the former to be professor of economics from 1967. His work has concentrated on macroeconomics, fiscal policy, including its effects on employment and investment, and health insurance. He became president of the influential **National Bureau for Economic Research** in 1977.

felicific calculus (010)
Bentham's method of judging the worth of an action by calculating the likely pleasure or pain which would result.

See also: **utilitarianism**.

female economists (030)
In the period of **classical economics** Jane **Marcet**, author of *Conversations on Political Economy* (1816), Harriet **Martineau**, author of the bestselling *Illustrations of Political Economy* (issued monthly from 1832 to 1834), and Harriet Taylor, later to be the wife of John Stuart **Mill**, were well known. University courses were opened to women in the late nineteenth century and Mary Paley, who married Alfred **Marshall**, was one of the first to teach economics at Cambridge. In the twentieth century, the important works of Rosa **Luxemburg**, Joan **Robinson**, Barbara **Wootton**, Anna **Schwartz**, Edith **Penrose**, Phyllis **Deane** and Anne O. **Krueger** have killed the myth that economics is an exclusively male subject.

FES (220)
See: **Family Expenditure Survey**.

feudalism (040)
The hierarchical medieval system of power and production in European countries with the monarch at the top and serfs tied to the land at the bottom. More recently the term has been loosely used to describe private

agricultural estates in Latin America and Japanese industrial companies with varying degrees of justification.

Strayer, J.R. (1965) *Feudalism*, New York: Van Nostrand Reinhold.

FF curve (410)
A curve showing the combinations of national income and the rate of interest for which the trade balance is zero. It is usually positively sloped but with full international capital mobility it becomes horizontal.

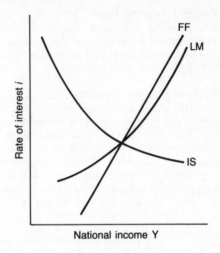

See also: **Mundell–Fleming model**.

fiat money (310)
Anything which is declared to be acceptable as **money** by a **central bank** or finance ministry in charge of the currency. It is this declaration, rather than the intrinsic value of the money as a good (as is the case with gold and silver coinage), which gives it value. Fiat money mostly takes the form of banknotes.

See also: **token money**.

FIBS (540)
Financial information and budgeting systems.

fiduciary issue (310)
An inconvertible issue of banknotes not backed by gold: as the name suggests, these notes are issued in faith. In the nineteenth century when banknotes constituted a larger proportion of the **money supply** than now,

controlling the size of the fiduciary issue was important: this is no longer so.

See also: **Bank Charter Act 1844**; **fiat money**.

FIFO (210, 540)

First in, first out; a method of valuing physical stocks which, by assuming the oldest stocks will be used first, values at historic cost. The method has largely been abandoned in favour of the **LIFO** principle. The FIFO method has the effect of including in profits the effects of stock appreciation, thus giving an unrealistic picture of a firm's financial state.

filière concept (120, 610)

A French term for vertical lines of production intimately linked together. When applied to industrial planning, it means that planning for a particular sector extends to planning both for the industry concerned and for the industries linked to it.

See also: **linkage**.

filtering (930)

The downgrading of residential property, either by its being split into smaller units affordable by lower income groups or by the movement of more prosperous residents to outer suburbs. Urban economists use this to explain the creation of inner city slums. Chicago is a major example of this process.

Fimbra (310)

Financial Intermediaries, Managers and Brokers Regulatory Association (London).

See also: **self-regulatory organization**.

FIML (210)

Full-information maximum likelihood: an estimation method for simultaneous equation econometric models.

See also: **LIML**.

final demand (010)

The demand for goods and services by the ultimate consumers, domestic and foreign households.

final good (010)

A good directly used by its ultimate con-sumer, unlike an **intermediate good**. The distinction between final and intermediate goods is crucial to the construction of an **input–output** table.

final income (320)

The amount of disposable income available to a household for expenditure and saving. It is measured as gross earnings minus taxation and social security contributions plus housing benefits and transfers.

final offer arbitration (830)

See: **pendulum arbitration**.

financial accounting (540)

The recording of the business transactions of a firm in a manner ordered by the legislation of the country of domicile of that firm. The main elements of it are the construction of a balance sheet to measure the assets and liabilities of a firm on a particular day and the construction of a profit and loss account which shows revenue, expenditure and profit over a period of time, usually three, six or twelve months.

See also: **accounting**; **management accounting**.

financial asset (310)

A piece of paper which entitles its holder to interest or dividends. In the past the major types of financial asset were stocks and shares of governments and companies. Recent innovations in financial markets have produced more sophisticated versions of these, including a variety of types of **equity**.

financial capital (310, 520)

The money invested in a business to establish and extend it. In the case of a company/corporation it can take various forms, including fixed interest **debentures**, **preference shares** and **ordinary shares**.

financial conglomerate (310)

A bank or other depository institution which offers a wide range of lending and credit facilities. British **building societies** and US **thrifts** have increasingly followed the practice of commercial banks by diversifying into new areas of financial services, aiming to offer customers a wide range of financial products and services. By becoming conglomerates they have become exposed to risks of a kind they have not been used to, and this, together with the increased number of participants in so many financial markets, has threatened profit margins.

Benston, G. (ed.) (1983) *Financial Services*, Englewood Cliffs, NJ: Prentice Hall.

financial crisis (310)

The simultaneous collapse of related financial institutions brought about by the attempts of investors, speculators, lenders and depositors to liquidate their assets. This liquidation occurs because of a change from optimistic to pessimistic **expectations**. An exogenous event such as a major war or a natural disaster can destabilize markets and create a crisis. A speculative investment boom with the promotion of many dubious schemes and **overtrading** are also common causes of crises. These crises can occur within one economy or in several which are interlinked as happened in 1929. The role of a central bank in restoring liquidity and general business confidence is crucial.

Altman, E.I. and Sametz, A.W. (eds) (1977) *Financial Crises: Institutions and Markets in a Fragile Environment*, New York: Wiley.
Bordo, M. (1991) *Financial Crises*, Aldershot: Edward Elgar.
Galbraith, J.K. (1955) *The Great Crash*, Boston, MA: Houghton Mifflin.
Kindleberger, C.P. (1978) *Manias, Panics and Crashes*, London: Macmillan; New York: Basic Books.
Kindleberger, C.P. and Laffargue, J.P. (eds) (1982) *Financial Crises: Theory, History and Policy*, Cambridge: Cambridge University Press.

See also: **bubble**.

financial economy (070)

An **economy** which uses a variety of financial assets and services, other than money, for the purposes of exchange and storing value; a 'post-money' economy.

Podolski, T.M. (1986) *Financial Innovation and the Money Supply*, Oxford: Basil Blackwell.

'financial engineering' (310, 520)

The making of major deals, as opposed to daily trading, by investment bankers on Wall Street, New York. Mergers and major underwriting are examples of this.

financial intermediary (310)

An institution which collects deposits and makes loans. Apart from the prominent example of banks, there are many financial intermediaries today including building societies (savings and loans institutions), insurance companies and hire-purchase finance houses. The creation of many new types of institution has made the task of monetary control more difficult for central banks and finance ministries.

financial investment (310)

The purchase of financial assets, e.g. stocks and shares. As most of the financial assets traded represent claims to past investment in fixed capital and inventories, financial investment is different from '**investment**'.

financial journalism (010, 310)

The specialized reporting of financial and economic news. It had its origins in the reporting of prices in Antwerp and Venice in the sixteenth century and in *Lloyd's List*, founded 1734. Newspaper articles on financial matters appear to have been pioneered in Britain, as London was the first major financial centre. Thomas Massa Alsager became the first financial editor of *The Times* in 1817, although the *Weekly Register* of Baltimore was a pioneer of US business journalism from 1811. Early reports concentrated on stock movements and banking liquidity but, with the participation of major economic writers in journalism, the financial press broadened its interests to an examination of home and foreign economies. *The Economist* was founded in 1843 by James Wilson (a former Financial Secretary to the Treasury), *The Statist* in 1873 by Sir Robert Giffen, *Financial News* in 1884 and the *Financial Times* in 1888 (the last two merging in 1945).

Many leading economists, including **Keynes**, **Samuelson** and **Galbraith** have regularly contributed to the press. This is one of the most demanding forms of journalism as a great deal of technical expertise is required, as well as personal integrity to resist the demands of many businesses and interest groups wanting favourable coverage.

Parsons, W. (1989) *The Power of the Press*, Aldershot: Edward Elgar.

financial leverage ratio (520)

Total debt as a proportion of total assets; also known as **gearing**. This is an indication of the extent to which a firm has to meet interest payments. If a firm which suffers a downturn in its gross profits has high leverage, it could face insolvency.

See also: **leverage; leveraged management buyout**.

financial panic (310)

A lack of confidence in a banking system which causes depositors to reclaim their deposits, thereby bringing about the collapse they fear. In a centralized banking system, a collapse in part of the system can be overcome by a central bank helping to restore liquidity.

See also: **bubble; financial crisis; run on a bank**.

financial policy (520)

For a firm, this will include its attitude towards raising capital, distributing dividends, structuring its debt and investing its surplus funds.

Financial Reporting Council (540)

UK council set up in 1990 to replace the Accounting Standards Committee. With its subsidiaries, the Accounting Standards Board and Review Panel, it can make regulations on the form of company accounts to standardize the treatment of, for example, **goodwill** and **off-balance-sheet finance**.

Financial Services Act 1986 (310)

This UK statute set out the regulation of investment business in the UK and also regulated the business of insurance companies and friendly societies. (**The Bank of England, Lloyd's** and **clearing houses** are exempt from its provisions.) It made provision for the Secretary of State to recognize 'self-regulating organizations' to regulate the carrying on of investment business by enforcing rules on their members and to recognize 'professional bodies' to regulate professions. The Act regulates the promotion and advertising of investment schemes and can ban persons as unfit to conduct investment business.

Anderson, R.W. (1986) 'Regulation of futures trading in the United States and United Kingdom', *Oxford Review of Economic Policy* 2: 41–57.

Financial Statement and Budget Report (320)

An annual report of the UK Treasury on Britain's recent economic performance and forecasts for the next year. The major sections of the Report detail output and expenditure aggregates, movements in the retail price index, the growth of money gross domestic product at market prices, the current account balance of payments and the public sector borrowing requirement. This Report is colloquially referred to as the 'Red Book'.

financial supermarket (310)

See: **financial conglomerate**.

financial system (310)

A set of interrelated institutions which collect savings and distribute them to borrowers, making possible the separation of the ownership of wealth from the control of physical capital. The more developed an economy is, the greater its range of financial instruments, e.g. since 1960 the US and British financial systems have produced a large range of new instruments, e.g. **derivatives**, in order to meet the different needs of savers and borrowers. New financial facilities contribute to economic growth.

Drake, P.J. (1980) *Money, Finance and Development*, Oxford: Robertson.

Financial Times Actuaries All-Share Index (310)

A London stock market price index designed by actuaries and compiled by the *Financial Times* which began in 1962. The purpose of this index is to indicate the level of the whole UK equity market by including over 700 shares, more than 80 per cent of market capitalization.

Financial Times Industrial Ordinary Share Index (310)

A price index of thirty leading industrial shares traded on the **International Stock Exchange** of London which was first published in 1935. This valuation of stock market shares is made at the beginning of each trading day, hourly throughout and at the end of the day.

Financial Times Stock Exchange 100 Share Index (310)

A price index of the shares of the 100 largest companies traded on the **International Stock Exchange** of London. It was introduced in 1984 as a means of basing futures contracts on the UK equity market. Popularly known as 'Footsie'.

fine-tuning (310, 320)

The frequent use of monetary and fiscal policies to avoid prolonged recessions and inflation and to keep a national economy steadily on course. The over-ambitious attempts of the US Administration to achieve precise goals led Walter Heller to describe such a policy as 'fine-tuning'. As a policy it ran into difficulties partly because those using it believed that disturbances were caused by **aggregate demand** and not by **supply shocks**. The problems of ignoring supply shocks became vividly clear after the oil-price increases of 1974.

firm (010, 510)

1   The basic unit for organizing production which performs the crucial role of linking product, factor and money markets.

2   An administrative organization utilizing a pool of resources.

3   A business organization under a single management with one or more **establishments**.

A firm can be classified according to the number of persons owning it or according to the extent of the liability of its owners for the firm's debts. A sole trader is the single owner with unlimited liability; a partnership has joint ownership but unlimited liability; companies/corporations are owned by many shareholders with limited liability.

Putterman, L. (ed.) (1987) *The Economic Nature of the Firm, A Reader*, Cambridge: Cambridge University Press.

firm consumption (010, 610)

The proportion of a firm's production which it consumes itself, e.g. the electricity which a power station consumes to run its own operations.

See also: **intermediate good**.

first best economy (010, 210)

An abstract model of a real economy in which resources are allocated according to the rules of **Pareto optimality**.

first degree price discrimination (010, 530)

Selling different units of output at different prices so that each price is the maximum amount of money a consumer will pay.

See also: **price discrimination**.

First Development Decade (110)

The 1960s; the declared aim of President John F. Kennedy for that period when he launched the USA's Peace Corps.

first economy (060)

A socialist economy following the dictates of the national plan. It consists of governmental agencies, state-owned firms, cooperatives and other officially registered institutions.

See also: **second economy**.

first price auction (310, 530)

A method of selling whereby the buyers submit sealed written bids with the item going to the highest bidder. This method is used weekly by the US Treasury when it issues its short-term securities, and also by Scottish solicitors for the sale of houses.

See also: **auction**.

First World (070, 730)

Developed free-market **economies** which were early to industrialize and, until the emergence of large oil revenues in developing countries, had the highest per capita incomes.

See also: **Second World**; **Third World**.

fiscal approximation (320)

Bringing the tax rates of different countries into line, e.g. the different rates of **value-**

added tax in the European Community as a preparation for the Single Market of 1992.

See also: tax harmonization.

fiscal crisis (320)

A shortage of tax revenues to finance a desired level of public expenditure. Marxists and others have asserted that there is a built-in tendency for modern fiscal systems to head for crisis as there are increasing demands for egalitarianism and more public services not matched by a desire to pay more taxation. When there is a concern with the disincentive and allocative effects of higher rates of tax, it is difficult to raise extra tax revenue, making a fiscal crisis incurable.

fiscal dividend (320)

Tax reductions and/or increases in government expenditures.

See also: fiscal drag.

fiscal drag (320)

The reduction in personal disposable income which results from tax rates not being adjusted for inflation; the increase of tax revenue at a faster rate than public expenditure. The spending power of taxpayers is 'dragged' down by an increase in average tax rates, e.g. if pre-tax incomes rise by 10 per cent and personal allowances are not increased then many taxpayers will be pushed into higher tax-bands. The Rooker–Wise Amendment of 1975 has attempted to reduce much of fiscal drag in the UK; in the USA, the Tax Reform Act of 1980 indexed the US individual income tax for the same reason. Fiscal drag can be remedied by a fiscal dividend.

Council of Economic Advisers (1962) 'Automatic stabilizers and fiscal drag', in *Annual Report of the Council of Economic Advisers*, Washington, DC: US Government Printing Office.

fiscal federalism (320)

The system of sharing tax revenues and public expenditure commitments between a central government and state governments. By making grants to lower levels of government, a national government can determine the standard of provision of public services, especially education. Different levels of government can be financed by different types of tax, e.g. an income tax for the national level but sales and property taxes for the state and local levels, or by the different governments of a country sharing in the revenues from the same range of taxes.

Barnett, R.R. and Meadows, J. (1989) *The Political Economy of Fiscal Federalism*, Aldershot: Edward Elgar.
Oates, W.E. (1972) *Fiscal Federalism*, New York: Harcourt Brace Jovanovich.

See also: federal finance.

fiscal illusion (320)

An unawareness of actual fiscal policy because of the poor definitions used of 'taxes', 'spending' and 'deficits'. By not making explicit the financing of every government programme, the size of a fiscal stimulus cannot be properly measured. Illusion can only be cured by identifying for each fiscal instrument its direct effect on the economy and its indirect effects through the changing of household budget constraints.

fiscal incidence (320)

See: budget incidence.

fiscal indicators (320)

Measures of the fiscal effects of a government which include national and regional expenditures and net lending.

fiscalist (320)

An economic policy-maker who prefers fiscal to monetary policies. Many Keynesians tend to favour a fiscal approach on the grounds that it can be used to pursue a greater range of policy aims than monetary policy.

fiscal mobility (320)

The geographical movement of taxpayers from high tax to low tax areas. The extent to which this is possible depends on several factors including the availability of housing and employment and the non-tax attractions of different places.

See also: Tiebout hypothesis.

fiscal neutrality (320)

The characteristics of a government's public finance policy which does not favour one group of persons, type of consumption or behaviour over another. The extent of neutrality is apparent from a study of a country's tax and benefit structure. As a policy, neutrality is recommended because its non-interventionist character gives greater freedom to individuals. A way of implementing it is by abolishing most tax allowances.

See also: **neutral budget**; **tax structure**.

fiscal policy (320)
The taxation and expenditure policy of a government. Prior to **Keynes**, economists were chiefly interested in **tax incidence**; subsequently, they accorded fiscal policy a more active role, making it a major part of **stabilization policy** in the 1950s and 1960s. The extent to which fiscal policy can be employed depends on what a government can observe of economic behaviour (thus it cannot tax the **black economy**), on behavioural responses to fiscal changes and on time **lags**.

See also: **fine-tuning**; **fiscal neutrality**.

fiscal rectitude (320)
A strict fiscal policy of cutting public expenditure and reducing the amount of government borrowing, usually with the aim of keeping a national budget in balance or surplus for several years. This policy has often been recommended by the **International Monetary Fund** to correct balance of payments deficits.

fiscal stance (320)
The combination of taxation and expenditure chosen by a government; the effect of the public sector on the level of **aggregate demand**. The most popular approach to measuring this, the size of a government's deficit, is only valid if there has been no change in economic conditions.

See also: **public finance**.

Fisher, Irving, 1867–1947 (030)
The celebrated US economist who made major contributions to capital, interest and monetary theory. During his long career as student and professor at Yale University (1892–1935), he published many influential works. His doctoral thesis, *Mathematical Investigations in the Theory of Value and Price* (1892) advanced general equilibrium theory; his *The Nature of Capital and Income* (1906) and *The Rate of Interest* (1907) introduced the important distinctions between real and nominal interest rates and between stocks and flows. Many works on monetary economics, including *The Purchasing Power of Money* (1911) and *Booms and Depressions* (1932) showed a progression from an exposition of the **quantity theory of money** to a concern with stabilization policies. His contribution to economic statistics in *The Making of Index Numbers* (1927) is well known. His other writings on nutrition, prohibition and pacifism made him known to a wider public.

Schumpeter, J.A. (1948) *Ten Great Economists from Marx to Keynes*, Oxford: Oxford University Press.

Fisher effect (310)
An effect of monetary policy which causes nominal interest rates to rise to a level which will reflect price changes.

Fisher theorem (150, 310)
This states that if expected inflation rises by 1 per cent the nominal expected rate of return on real capital assets and the yields on bills and bonds will rise by the same amount. Thus anticipated inflation has a neutral effect on portfolio and capital markets.

Fisher, I. (1896) 'Appreciation and interest', *Publications of the American Economic Association* 3, 11: 331–42.

five-year plan (120)
A medium-term national economic plan, first used in the USSR in 1928 and subsequently followed by many developing countries including India and China. These plans set targets for the economy as a whole and for particular sectors. Early plans used principally physical output targets but subsequent plans have set more goals, sometimes in conflict with each other. The broad framework of the five-year plan is supplemented by an annual operational plan which sets detailed goals for individual enterprises.

See also: **central planning**; **development**.

fix (310)
Twice daily fixing of the price of gold by the London Gold Market.

fixed capital (520)
Investment in buildings and equipment. Demand for fixed capital is determined within the framework of a firm's plan, including its sale projections and the cost of finance.

See also: **gross domestic fixed capital formation.**

fixed cost (010, 520)
A cost to an enterprise which is incurred even when that enterprise's output is zero. These costs occur in the short run: the principal examples of them are equipment costs and the costs of factors of production which a firm has contracted to pay for a minimum period of time, e.g. managerial staff. In the long term, all costs become variable as fixed capital can be changed and contracts revised.

See also: **average total cost; quasi-fixed factor; variable cost.**

fixed exchange rate (430)
An exchange rate whose value is tied to gold or a major currency or basket of currencies. The **gold standard** was not used after the Second World War, being replaced by a **dollar standard** under **Bretton Woods** until 1971. Later in Europe a fixed exchange rate regime tied several currencies to other European currencies under the **Exchange Rate Mechanism** of the **European Monetary System**. Currencies with a fixed parity are permitted to vary only within a narrow range above and below par value. Fixed exchange rates promote stability in international trade but carry the cost of holding greater reserves of foreign currencies and other reserve assets. A revaluation or devaluation of a fixed exchange rate creates considerable problems of adjustment in the national economy concerned.

fixprice (010)
A price which is determined exogenously outside the model of a market. **Keynesian economics** with its assumptions of a floor to the rate of interest and to money wages employs this method. In an economy with much oligopolistic industry, firms fix their prices independently of market forces and can be in a state of **disequilibrium** for a considerable time by increasing or decreas-

ing their stocks. Some would argue that there was a fixprice economy as early as 1890.

Hicks, J.R. (1965) *Capital and Growth*, ch. 7, Oxford: Clarendon Press.

See also: **flexprice.**

flat grant (320)
See: **grant in aid.**

flat rate tax (320)
An **income tax** which is at the same rate for every level of income. The justification for a tax of this kind is its simplicity and lack of disincentive effects inherent in some forms of tax progression. However, a flat rate tax is likely to be an unfair burden on low income groups if the rate at which it is levied is high.

See also: **progressive tax.**

flat tax (320)
See: **flat rate tax.**

flexible exchange rate (430)
See: **floating exchange rate.**

flexible firm (510)
A firm with a core of permanent employees and a periphery of temporary workers whose labour force fluctuates in size according to the demand for its products. In Japan, many industries have this type of organization through the extensive use of subcontractors who themselves have the flexibility which comes from employing temporary workers.

flexprice (010)
A price which freely fluctuates in order to equate demand with supply, e.g. a price determined at an **auction**. Such a view of prices is central to **Marshallian** economics.

Hicks, J.R. (1965) *Capital and Growth*, ch. 7, Oxford: Clarendon Press.

See also: **fixprice.**

flight from money (310)
A reduction in the **demand for money** because of an expectation of rising prices or a fall in nominal interest rates.

flip-flop arbitration (830)
See: **pendulum arbitration.**

floating exchange rate (430)

A market-determined exchange rate which can change continuously as it is not pegged to another currency or to gold by a central bank. Canada, after the Korean War, floated the Canadian dollar from 1950 to 1962 and again in 1970 after the Vietnam War; Lebanon from 1950 and Japan and some West European currencies from August to December 1971 also floated their currencies. In practice, an exchange rate can be stabilized by speculation or central bank intervention, the latter being 'a dirty float'. Although lower reserves of gold and hard currencies are needed under a floating exchange rate regime, this regime has disadvantages, including a greater amount of uncertainty amongst exporters.

MacDonald, R. (1988) *Floating Exchange Rates: Theories and Evidence*, London: Unwin Hyman.

floating rate note (310)

A long-term security whose rate of interest is linked to short-term interest rates. Some of these notes are perpetuals with no maturity date. Changes in the US and UK rules concerning the definition of primary bank capital has substantially reduced the demand for these notes, although their yields, which are higher than those for commercial paper and certificates of deposit, will continue to make them attractive to many money market investors.

See also: **primary capital**.

floor (140, 310)

1 The trough of a **business cycle** or **trade cycle** after which production, employment and prices rise.

2 The minimum rate of interest which an issuer of a floating rate security is required to pay.

See also: **cap**; **ceiling**; **collar**.

flooring (310)

See: **floor planning**.

floor planning (310)

Inventory financing by US commercial banks, e.g. to contribute to the purchase by dealers in **consumer durables** of the goods they have on display.

floor price (010, 710, 820)

A minimum controlled price, e.g. minimum wages or agricultural product prices. **Minimum wage** laws are enforced by inspectorates; agricultural prices are prevented from falling below pre-set minima by government purchases of excess production. If P_1 is the floor price and P_e is the equilibrium price the government can satisfy both producers and consumers by purchasing quantity AB.

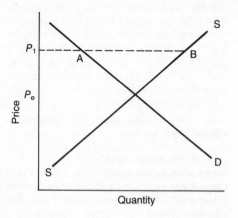

flotation (310)

The market debut of a company when its shares are offered to the public for the first time. The motives for a flotation include the desire of the original owners to reduce their financial stake in that company as well as the wish to obtain more finance.

flow (210, 220)

See: **stock and flow concepts**.

flow of funds account (210, 220)

A component of a system of **national income** accounts which shows financial transactions between the major sectors of the economy. The transactions analysed are purchases and sales, and transfers such as taxes and dividends. The sectors used are different types of business, non-profit organizations, central and local government, banks, savings institutions, insurance, other finance and the rest of the world.

Bain, A.D. (1973) 'Flow of funds analysis: a survey', *Economic Journal* 83: 1055–93.

National Bureau of Economic Research (1962) *The Flow of Funds Approach to Social Accounting: Appraisal, Analysis and Applications. Studies in Income and Wealth*, vol. 26, Princeton, NJ: Princeton University Press.

flypaper effect (320)

The effects of giving grants, particularly under a system of federal finance, to governments and not individuals: the grants 'stick' to their use for expenditure purposes and are not used to reduce the level of taxation as might be the case if individuals received those grants directly.

See also: **dedicated budget; earmarking; ringfencing**.

FOB (420)

See: **free on board**.

FOMC (310)

See: **Federal Open Market Committee**.

Food and Agriculture Organization (130, 420, 710)

Rome-based United Nations agency, founded in 1945. It aims (1) to raise nutrition levels, (2) to improve the efficiency of the production and distribution of all agricultural products and (3) to improve the condition of rural populations. The FAO provides an information service, technical assistance and the promotion of national and international action, including international **commodity agreements**.

food chain (710)

The linked stages of production of food from the original farmer to the ultimate consumer.

football pool (310)

A method of gambling on the outcome of a number of football matches on the same day. The fixed stakes of the punters are accumulated in a fund out of which dividends are paid to those who have successfully predicted the outcome of matches, with most points going to a prediction of teams which score the same number of goals as each other. The balance of the weekly fund is acquired by the pools promoter.

footloose industry (630)

An **industry** which can be located anywhere without incurring extra locational costs. Heavy industries, e.g. steel and shipbuilding, are not footloose; new industries using microchip technology can locate in many places without increasing their costs, although proximity to large markets or the availability of regional subsidies will guide them to particular locations.

See also: **locked-in industry**.

footloose knowledge (620)

Technical knowledge which is not specific to any production process and is interchangeable between industries.

See also: **locked-in knowledge**.

Footsie (310)

Slang for **Financial Times Stock Exchange 100 Share Index**.

forced labour (320)

Taxation of employment earnings which means that a person has to work longer hours than is necessary to obtain a given income. **Nozick** advances this argument in his discussion of redistribution.

Nozick, R. (1974) *Anarchy, State and Utopia*, ch. 7, Oxford: Basil Blackwell; New York: Basic Books.

forced saving (010)

1 Involuntary saving which arises in an economy when it is at full employment and has an excess supply of loans. That excess supply pushes down the market rate of interest and stimulates an increased demand for investment finance which brings about general inflation. As a consequence of a rise in prices, those with fixed incomes can consume less and so savings are 'forced' out of them: this extra saving finances the extra investment. This view was widely held by members of the Classical School, including **Bentham, Thornton, Malthus** and John Stuart **Mill**; in the twentieth century, **Robertson** and **Pigou** were also adherents of this doctrine. Part of **Keynes's** transition in thinking which resulted in his *General Theory of Employment, Interest and Money* was to reject this doctrine.

2 Compulsory saving as part of a tough fiscal policy was recommended by **Keynes** as a method of financing the Second World War. He argued that it was necessary to take a proportion from current incomes to prevent current consumption from exceeding domestic production and imports and creating inflation. This 'deferred pay' would accumulate at compound interest in friendly societies and the Post Office Savings Bank. The scheme was adopted and the forced savings were gradually repaid in the form of post-war credits after 1945 as the economy recovered.

Corry, B.A. (1962) *Money, Saving and Investment in English Economics, 1800–1850*, ch. 3, London: Macmillan; New York: St Martin's Press.

Hayek, F. von (1932) 'A note on the development of the doctrine of forced saving', *Quarterly Journal of Economics* 47: 123–33.

Keynes, J.M. (1940) *How to Pay for the War* (reprinted in his *Collected Works*, vol. 9, pp. 367–439, London: Macmillan).

Machlup, F. (1943) 'Forced or induced saving: an exploration into synonyms and homonyms', *Review of Economics and Statistics* 25: 26–39.

Fordism (510)

A late, and successful, stage of capitalism characterized by large-scale production, semi-skilled labour, easy credit and mass consumption. This concept is based upon the production methods of the Ford Motor Company, particularly its use of assembly lines for automobile production.

foreign aid (430)

Grants, loans on favourable terms or the supply of services by governments or charitable bodies to less developed countries. In its favour, it has been argued that aid creates the notion of an international human community, reduces political tension within countries by encouraging balanced development and increases the priority of development within less developed countries. A shortage of domestic savings and balance of payments problems in the early stage of expansion, when imports exceed exports, will retain the need for aid. As it is difficult to decide the basis for selecting aid recipients, it has been suggested that poverty, a good record in economic and social policies or a good performance in raising the share of savings and taxes in the national income should be used as alternative criteria.

Aid is given for many purposes including relief (often consumer goods are sent to alleviate a short-term supply deficiency, e.g. famine relief to Ethiopia), reconstruction (as in the rebuilding of an economy after a war, e.g. the **Marshall Plan**), stabilization (especially short-term help with a country's balance of payments until adjustments are made to its economy) and long-term development to raise the level of per capita incomes permanently. Critics of aid programmes point out that aid can have the defects of creating economic or political dependence, introducing inappropriate technology or spending disproportionately on urban populations.

Casson, R. (1986) *Does Aid Work?*, Oxford: Oxford University Press.

Mosley, P. (1986) *Overseas Aid: Its Defence and Reform*, Hemel Hempstead: Harvester Wheatsheaf.

See also: **bilateral aid**; **multilateral aid**; **tied aid**.

foreign direct investment (430)

Investment in the businesses of another country which often takes the form of the setting up of local production facilities or the purchase of existing businesses. It is to be contrasted with **portfolio investment** which is the acquisition of securities. FDI has been much criticized, in the case of **multinational corporations**, as a form of neo-colonialism, but in its favour it can be said that it increases the level of investment in countries which otherwise would be under-capitalized and, as dividends vary with the prosperity of an industry (and a high proportion is re-invested in the local economy), it can be less burdensome than the servicing of fixed interest borrowing. For political reasons in the past, a disproportionate amount of direct investment in Third World countries has gone to Brazil, Mexico and South Africa, as well as to the **European Community** to escape the **common external tariff**. Some advanced economies fear the takeover of their industries by stronger, foreign economies, e.g. the USA is anxious about Japanese investment in many parts of the US economy.

foreign exchange (430)

The **currencies** or short term monetary claims of foreign countries.

Douch, N. (1989) *The Economics of Foreign Exchange*, Cambridge: Woodhead Faulkner.

foreign exchange market (430)
A market in which currencies are exchanged for each other. Both spot and forward trading are used. In 1991, the top banking centres measured as a percentage share of Reuters currency quotations were: London 17%, New York 15%, Singapore 11%, Hong Kong 11%, Zurich 7%, Tokyo 6%, Paris 5% and Frankfurt 4%. As the most important influence on these markets is company cash flows, this in a sense makes **multinational corporations** mini-banks through their **corporate finance** activities. Central banks intervene to achieve a desired exchange rate for their own currencies. If they force their exchange rates down, speculators will leave the market. A stable exchange rate at the desired level usually requires active use of **monetary** and **fiscal policies**.

See also: **forward market**; **spot market**.

foreign trade multiplier (010, 430)
The ratio of a change in income to the change in exports and domestic investment which have generated that extra income. It is measured for an **open economy** without taxation as $1/(1 - MPC + MPM)$, where MPC is the **marginal propensity to consume** and MPM is the **marginal propensity to import**. The multiplier is crucial to explanations of the path to **balance of payments** equilibrium and to the transmission of cyclical fluctuations throughout the world.

See also: **multiplier**.

foreign trade organization (420)
A state agency of a **Comecon** country which exports and imports on behalf of state enterprises of a particular sector of a national economy. From the 1920s, it was a major organization of the Soviet economy. However, with Hungary as an example, enterprises in Comecon countries have increasingly been allowed the choice between trading directly or through foreign trade organizations.

See also: **state trading organization**.

foreign trade zone (420)
A tariff-free area, often around a port or an airport, which, by allowing the duty-free import and export of goods, can permit flourishing manufactures.

forex (430)
Foreign exchange, or forward foreign exchange.

forex trading (430)
Foreign exchange trading which is a major determinant of exchange rates. This volatile trading, sensitive to political events and movements in **economic indicators**, is conducted at several locations throughout the world. **Hedging** is continuously practised to reduce currency fluctuations. The growth of **multinational corporations** has greatly increased the volume of business in foreign exchange markets.

forfaiting (310)
A method of financing exporting. The exporter's bank assumes the risk of the buyer not paying by advancing the value of the exports to the exporter and discounting a **bill of exchange** or **promissory note** in a secondary financial market where the market rate of interest is charged for the period until the buyer has paid in full. This originated as a method of financing West German exports to Eastern Europe but now is used to finance both exports and specific capital projects; only a minuscule amount of world trade is financed in this way.

See also: **export promotion**.

forfait system (320)
A system of taxation which uses indirect indicators of income, e.g. a sole proprietor's life-style or average profit margins, to assess a person for payment of a lump-sum tax. This system is used in France to assess taxes on the incomes of farmers, unincorporated businesses and the professions. It has many applications in less developed countries.

forint (430)
The currency of Hungary.

formal economy (010)
1 Economic activities which are officially recorded.

2 That part of an **economy** in which

labour is predominantly supplied by employees of firms and public enterprises.

See also: **blue economy**; **underground economy**.

formal indexation (320)
Automatic adjustments to income tax allowances in line with rises in retail prices at regular intervals. The nature of this mechanism for protection against inflation is decided by legislative enactments.

See also: **bracket creep**; **Rooker–Wise Amendment**.

forward integration (510, 610)
The expansion through merger of the productive activities of manufacturers into wholesaling and distribution. This was made possible by advances in transport and information systems and resulted in greater production **economies of scale** as manufacturers' markets expanded.

See also: **vertical integration**.

forward linkage (110, 940)
See: **linkage**.

forward market (430)
A market in currencies, commodities or securities which fixes prices for future delivery. The forward rates determined are linked to **spot rates** by **speculation** and **hedging**.

fountain pen money (310)
Money created by a banker who uses a pen to approve a loan. This increases the bank deposit of the borrower and adds to total bank credit.

Fourth World (070, 730)
The poorest least developed countries of the world, about twenty-five in all.

See also: **First World**; **Second World**; **Third World**.

fractional reserve banking (310)
A banking system which uses **high-powered money** as only a fraction of its total assets rather than **100 per cent reserve banking**. According to the country and phase of banking evolution, cash, and assets which can be quickly converted into cash without

capital loss, can be as little as a third or a quarter of the total volume of commercial banks' deposits. This system has made possible a major increase in credit in many countries in the past hundred years.

franchise (530)
A legal privilege allowing a firm under licence to sell another firm's products and use its trade name. In return for the use of a famous name and much free marketing promotion, an initial payment and often a royalty of 5–10 per cent of gross sales are requested. As it is a condition of some franchises that supplies be obtained from the franchising company, competition law in the USA and Western Europe has tried to prevent such agreements. The arrangement is widespread in the fast food trade.

franchise financing (520)
The financing of public works such as bridges, airports and power stations by foreign private investment. Examples include the Anglo-French Channel Tunnel and various public works in Turkey, Malaysia and Jordan. A typical implementation of the method would be the creation of a **joint equity venture company** owned by the contractor, the operator and the customer utility. Borrowing from banks and credit agencies for the financing of construction is on the security of revenue from the project. When the loan is repaid, the host government owns the new public work.

franchise gap (430)
A band around the value of a currency in which it can be bought and sold.

See also: **Common Agricultural Policy**.

fraud (310, 520)
1 Deceitful accounting.

2 Misappropriation of funds.

See also: **creative accounting**; **long fraud**.

free alongside (430)
A type of exporter's price quotation, including delivery to a designated vehicle of the importer who then pays for subsequent transportation.

free banking (310)

A *laissez-faire* monetary system in which banks compete freely without state control and have the power to issue their own banknotes. However, even the most ardent supporters of this freedom would admit that some restrictions are necessary to guarantee the liquidity of the banking system and price stability. In the USA, free banking laws were passed in the early nineteenth century, beginning with Michigan in 1837 and New York and Georgia in 1838. Anyone could set up banks subject to minimum capital requirements prescribed by each state, and their note issues had to be backed by bonds deposited with a state auditor and redeemable on demand. There was free banking in Scotland from 1810 to 1845.

Dowd, K. (1989) *The State and the Monetary System*, Hemel Hempstead: Philip Allan.

Glasner, D. (1989) *Free Banking and Monetary Reform*, Cambridge: Cambridge University Press.

Rockoff, H. (1975) *The Free Banking Era: A Reconsideration*, New York: Arno Press.

Free Banking School (030)

A group of early nineteenth-century English writers on monetary matters who argued that England should follow the Scottish principle of having several banks with note-issuing power, thus ending the monopoly of the Bank of England.

White, L.H. (1984) *Free Banking in Britain: Theory, Experience and Debate, 1800–45*, Cambridge: Cambridge University Press.

See also: **Banking School**.

free depreciation (320, 520)

The amount of depreciation of an asset permitted by a taxation authority before actual wear and tear has taken place. All, or part, of the value of an asset is written off at the beginning of its life as a means of giving an investment grant to a firm. In general, depreciation allowances are generous if the notional life of the asset for tax purposes is longer than its true life.

free good (010)

A good with a zero price. This is possible because its supply is either abundant or rationed. A free good is the opposite of an **economic good**.

free market (010)

A market in which buyers and sellers are free to contract on whatever terms they wish, without governmental interference.

free on board (420)

A measure of the value of trade which excludes insurance and transport costs. Exports are usually valued this way as it is assumed that importers will pay such costs.

freeport (420, 730)

An enclave in which imported goods are processed and then re-exported. This production arrangement has been a great success in many places, including Hamburg, South Korea and the Caribbean, but less so in the UK in which six freeport schemes were launched in 1984. They were popular as far back as the Middle Ages, when they were known as 'staples'.

See also: **in-bond manufacturing**.

free rider (320, 830)

An individual who does not pay for the goods or services he/she consumes. Free riders include non-residents using the public services of a city and non-unionized workers who gain wage increases achieved under **collective bargaining**, without paying dues to a union to represent them. In the case of public goods the free-rider problem has resulted in the finance of such goods by general taxation; under trade unionism, the existence of free riders has led to demands for a **union** or **closed shop**.

free trade (420)

International trade, unhindered by **tariffs**, other restrictions on imports and export subsidies. This freedom was strongly recommended by the **classical economists** on the basis of **absolute advantage**, in the case of **Smith**, or **comparative advantage** in the cases of **Ricardo** and **Torrens**. Today, it is recommended as a means of achieving international specialization of production and maximization of world economic welfare. In practice, completely free trade is rare. There are always particular interest groups and industries within a country demanding **protection**, with varying degrees of success. Even within a **customs union** there can be disguised protection, e.g. within the **Euro-**

pean **Community** through the imposition of quality and other controls. In the post-1945 period, the **General Agreement on Tariffs and Trade** has attempted to prevent a return to the extensive protectionism characteristic of the 1930s. In the 1980s there was some support for protectionism, especially in the USA and in **newly industrialized countries**. Free trade has always been most strenuously advocated by major countries with trade surpluses, e.g. the UK in the nineteenth century and the USA in the 1950s and 1960s.

Bhagwati, J. (1988) *Protectionism*, Cambridge, MA: MIT Press.
Corden, W.M. (1974) *Trade Policy and Economic Welfare*, Oxford: Clarendon Press.

See also: **Corn Laws**; **protection**; **Smoot–Hawley Tariff Act 1930**.

free-trade area (420, 730)

A group of independent nations with free trade among them, but not necessarily with a joint trading policy for the rest of the world.

See also: **European Free Trade Association**.

frequency curve (210)

A curve constructed from a **frequency distribution** which can be obtained from a **frequency polygon**. The different shapes of these curves include **symmetrical**, **skewed**, **J-shaped**, **reverse J-shaped**, **U-shaped**, **bimodal** and **multimodal**.

frequency distribution (210)

An arrangement of **raw data** into classes which are then tabulated, e.g. the prices of houses can be classified as $100,000–$149,999, $150,000–$199,999 etc. and presented in two columns of house prices and the number of houses in each price range.

frequency polygon (210)

A graph of the frequency of classes of a distribution often constructed by joining the midpoints of the tops of the rectangles in a **histogram**.

See also: **frequency curve**.

frequency table (210)

See: **frequency distribution**.

frictional unemployment (810)

Short-period unemployment brought about by workers changing jobs. This minimum level of unemployment, which coexists with job vacancies, occurs even when an economy is at **full employment** and is a feature of all types of national **economy**. Frictional unemployment is often measured by the number of persons unemployed for less than a short period, e.g. eight weeks. Labour market policies can reduce this type of unemployment by making job information more available and accurate and by subsidizing search costs.

Friedman, Milton, 1912– (030)

US economic prophet of **capitalism** and **monetarism** and leading libertarian economist. After an education at Rutgers, Chicago and Columbia universities, he was professor at Chicago from 1948 to 1979. His pronounced **libertarian economics** led to his appointments as adviser to Barry Goldwater (unsuccessful US presidential candidate in 1964) and President Richard Nixon. He was awarded the **Nobel Prize for Economics** in 1976.

Friedman's long advocacy of monetarism has consisted of a powerful revival of the **quantity theory of money**, reasserting that changes in the **money supply** explain changes in the levels of prices and economic activity. He is also noted for his contributions to economic methodology (1953), his **permanent income** approach to the **consumption function** and his explanation of **stagflation** (1968) which modified the **Phillips curve** (by the inclusion of **expectations**) and introduced the concept of the **natural rate of unemployment**.

Although much of Friedman's economics is anti-Keynesian in character, like **Keynes** he ignores many micro-issues in favour of a heavy reliance on economic aggregative analysis. His distinctive approach to **economic methodology** is to argue that the fruitfulness of an economic theory must be judged by predictions which are empirically corroborated. Using **Fisher**'s theory of capital, Friedman was able in his study of the **consumption function** to use the concept of permanent income, allowing expectations of future income to be a determinant of current expenditure. He re-instated the quantity theory of money by turning it into a theory of the demand for money as the k of the Cambridge equation $M_d = kPY$ with k, according to Friedman, a variable, *not* a constant. He was able to extend the Keynesian liquidity preference theory into a more modern portfolio approach. The Great Depression, in his monetary history with Schwartz, he attributed to the **Federal Reserve System**'s reducing the US money stock in the period 1929–33 by one-third. In the stock market crashes of October 1987, many monetary authorities were anxious to avoid the same mistake.

De Marchi, N. and Hirsch, A. (1988) *Milton Friedman*, Brighton: Harvester Wheatsheaf.
Friedman, M. (1953) *Essays in Positive Economics*, Chicago, IL: Phoenix Books.
—— (1956) *Studies in the Quantity Theory of Money*, Chicago, IL: University of Chicago Press.
—— (1957) *A Theory of the Consumption Function, A Study by the National Bureau of Economic Research, New York*, Princeton, NJ: Princeton University Press.
—— (1982) *Capitalism and Freedom*, Chicago and London: University of Chicago Press.
Friedman, M. and Schwartz, A.J. (1963) *Monetary History of the United States, 1867–1960*, Princeton, NJ: Princeton University Press.
—— and —— (1982) *Monetary Trends in the United States and the United Kingdom: Their Relation to Income, Prices and Interest Rates, 1867–1975*, Chicago, IL: University of Chicago Press.
Thygessen, N. (1975) 'The scientific contributions of Milton Friedman', *Scandinavian Journal of Economics* 79: 56–98.

fringe banking crisis (310)
See: **secondary banking crisis**.

fringe benefits (820)
Benefits in kind which constitute part of the remuneration of many employees, especially in managerial jobs. These additions to wages and salaries can either be provided collectively, e.g. sports and leisure facilities, or individually – a company car, a low interest mortgage, free health insurance etc. In the USA they amounted to 17 per cent of the compensation of blue-collar workers in 1951 and 30 per cent (in some large corporations, 50 per cent) in 1981. Their incidence is higher for unionized than for non-unionized workers and are usually worth more to higher income groups because many fringe benefits are not subject to taxation.

See also: **labour cost**.

Frisch, Ragnar Anton Kittil, 1895–1973 (030)
A Norwegian economist who did much to establish **econometrics** as a separate academic subject. After training, under his father, as a goldsmith and an education in Oslo and France, he was professor of economics, Oslo, from 1931 to 1965. He founded the Econometric Society in 1930 and was awarded the first **Nobel Prize for Economics** (with **Tinbergen**) in 1969. His advice to the Norwegian Labour Party in the 1930s and 1950s – to adopt central planning for key industries – applied his econometric ideas; his fiscal advice was similar to **Keynes**'s. After early work on demand theory which rigorously derived a consistent theory from basic axioms, he devoted much attention to the creation of a logical national accounting system, to economic planning and to the application of decision modelling to economic policy-making. He was a pioneer in the development of dynamic economic theory.

Arrow, K.J. (1960) 'The work of Ragnar Frisch, econometrician', *Econometrica* 28: 175–92.

FRN (310)
See: **floating rate note**.

front-end loading (310, 520)
A type of scheme for repaying a loan with lower initial instalments. Initially, only interest is paid; capital is repaid in the later instalments. This is an attractive form of borrowing for low income households and firms.

fronting loan (310)
A loan from a parent corporation to a local foreign subsidiary which uses the 'front' of an international bank to channel the loan. There is more chance of repayment to an international bank in times of political turmoil as many countries are reluctant to upset major financial institutions.

frostbelt (730)
See: **snowbelt**.

FSA (310)
See: **Financial Services Act**.

FSBR (320)
See: **Financial Statement and Budget Report**.

FSLIC (310)
See: **Federal Savings and Loan Insurance Corporation**.

FTC (610)
Federal Trade Commission.

See also: **Federal Trade Commission Act 1914**.

F test (210)
The ratio of the **variances** of two independent samples of the variance of one population which has a **normal distribution**. This **significance test** is used to test joint hypotheses with two or more regression parameters.

FTO (420)
See: **foreign trade organization**.

FT-SE 100 (310)
See: **Financial Times Stock Exchange 100 Share Index**.

FTZ (420, 730)
Free-trade zone.

See also: **free-trade area**.

full-cost pricing (020)
A theory of pricing first advanced in Oxford studies in 1938 by Hall and Hitch as a challenge to **marginalism**. Prices, according to their observation of businessmen's behaviour, were calculated on the basis of average variable cost plus a gross profit margin (which would finance fixed costs) or average total cost with a net profit margin. Many questioned the view that such a rigid pricing policy would be followed if there were great changes in demand either making possible higher prices and greater profits or necessitating price cuts so that at least variable costs would be covered. Out of the theory came the assertion that oligopolists have a **kinked demand curve**.

Hall, R.L. and Hitch, C.J. (1939) 'Price theory and business behaviour', *Oxford Economic Papers* 2: 12–45.

full employment (010, 810)
The maximum use of a **factor of production**, especially labour. In the labour market, full employment occurs when unemployment has fallen to an irreducible minimum which is approximately the level of frictional unemployment. In the USA, the **Employment Act** 1946 made government responsible for economic stability and growth; in the UK, Beveridge's *Full Employment in a Free Society* (1944) introduced the same goal explicitly. It can be argued, however, that many governments have only paid lip-service to it as a goal; control of inflation has often taken precedence. Many would argue that it is a dangerous goal, unsettling the labour market and bringing about lower productivity as a strong desire to maintain employment can overheat an economy.

Ginsburg, H. (1983) *Full Employment and Public Policy: The United States and Sweden*, Lexington, MA: Lexington Books; Toronto: D.C. Heath.

See also: **natural rate of unemployment**.

full employment budget (320)
The budget of a central government adjusted by deducting expenditure relating to unemployment and by adding the extra tax revenues the unemployed would contribute if in employment. This permits the calculation of the underlying **fiscal stance**. Such budget balances are regularly published in the USA.

See also: **structural deficit**.

functional financing (320)
A framework for public finance policies proposed by **Lerner** which would require the government to use every policy instrument available to contribute to the prevention of inflation and deflation and the promotion of the general interest, rather than following traditional goals of governments such as balancing the budget.

Lerner, A.P. (1943) 'Functional finance and the Federal debt', *Social Research* 10 (February): 38–51.

functional income distribution (160)
The distribution of the **national income**

between the factors of production, usually land, labour and capital. Statistics on this indicate, for example, the proportion of the national income going to wages and salaries.

See also: **labour's share of national income**.

fundamental contradiction of capitalism (110)

The conflict in industrial development between the need for national planning and the fragmentary nature of the individual plans of each capitalist. **Marx** asserted that this contradiction leads to **crises**.

fundamental equilibrium (430)

For a **balance of payments** this occurs when the current and capital accounts are jointly in balance and the economy is internally balanced at a full employment level. A departure from equilibrium can result in an under-use of resources, inflation and inefficiency.

See also: **internal balance; external balance**.

funding (310)

Conversion of short-term debt to long-term debt. Before governments had control over **central banks**, funding was seen as a means of protecting a treasury against a short-term collapse of confidence in government securities leading to heavy sales of **treasury bills** and **government bonds**. Funding can also be practised by a firm, e.g. it can raise cash to pay off short-term liabilities such as bank loans by issuing shares, thereby lengthening its debt.

funding gap (320)

A shortage of revenue to meet the expenditure demands on a fund. This problem is often encountered in the public sector since a variety of forces, e.g. demographic changes, can lead to expanding programmes; also, for ideological and other reasons there may be a reluctance to increase taxes. Economies in recession often have a gap of this kind as a fall in incomes reduces tax revenues and a rise in unemployment increases welfare expenditures.

See also: **budgetary policy; Gramm–Rudman–Hollings Act**.

fungible asset (310)

An **asset** which loses its identity when used. **Working capital**, unlike **fixed capital**, has this character.

future goods (010)

The product of **investment**. By the sacrifice of present consumption, it is possible to devote resources to capital goods which by a **roundabout method of production** creates a greater volume of future goods than the present goods not available for consumption today.

See also: **Böhm-Bawerk**.

futures (010)

An agreed contract for the sale or purchase of an asset, currency or commodity at a future date.

See also: **option; spot price**.

futures market (310, 430)

A currency, commodity or security market which permits present dealing for future delivery. In the 1980s there was a considerable increase in futures markets for financial assets. Centres for futures trading include Chicago, London, New York, Paris and Toronto. The 'products' include commodities, currencies and **stock market price indices**. Trading is done 'on the margin', i.e. only a small percentage of the value of the contract has to be paid by the buyer or seller, but further margin calls are made if there is an adverse market movement against the contracting party. Falls in the value of futures contracts in the autumn of 1987 prompted further calls to be made.

FY (320)

Fiscal year (USA): the twelve-month period chosen by government or a business organization for accounting purposes. In 1974, the starting date for the US government's fiscal year was changed from 1 July to 1 October, partly to enable Congressional appropriations to be made by the start of the fiscal year.

G

GAB (430)
See: **General Agreement to Borrow**.

gains from trade (410)
The increase in output or welfare received by a country, or the world as a whole, through international trade making possible the specialization of production. The theory of **comparative advantage** demonstrates how this is possible.

See also: **absolute advantage**.

Galbraith, John Kenneth, 1908– (030)
A Canadian American liberal economist who has achieved astounding publishing success in his books on capitalism, the Great Depression, the affluent society and the industrial state. With a training in agriculture in Ontario and in agricultural economics at Berkeley, California, he has taught at Harvard University since 1949. His early work on industrial price rigidities and on price controls made use of his wartime experience as head of the Price Section of the US Office of Price Administration. In 1952, *American Capitalism* launched his career as a bestselling economic guru. His works contain strikingly novel analyses, e.g. of consumers' **countervailing power** to large oligopolists, of the contrast between private affluence and public squalor and of the managerial nature of modern capitalism. Outside the university, he was a leading adviser to President John F. Kennedy and his ambassador to India. Much of his writing has the broad sweep of an eighteenth-century economist who has espoused the mixed economy: this approach is not without its critics as modern economists are often irritated by his avoidance of the empirical testing of his theories. But it is greatly to his credit that one of his most thorough books is his late survey of economic thought in 1987.

Galbraith, J.K. (1938) *Modern Competition and Business Policy*, Boston, MA: Houghton Mifflin; London: Hamish Hamilton.
—— (1952) *A Theory of Price Control*, Cambridge, MA: Harvard University Press.
—— (1952) *American Capitalism: the Concept of Countervailing Power*, London: Hamish Hamilton.
—— (1954) *The Great Crash 1929*, Boston, MA: Houghton Mifflin; London: Hamish Hamilton.
—— (1958) *The Affluent Society*, London: Hamish Hamilton.
—— (1967) *The New Industrial State*, Boston, MA: Houghton Mifflin; London: Hamish Hamilton.
—— (1973) *Economics and the Public Purpose*, Boston, MA: Houghton Mifflin; London: Hamish Hamilton.
—— (1987) *A History of Economics: The Past as Present*, London: Hamish Hamilton.
Reisman, D.A. (1980) *Galbraith and Market Capitalism*, New York: New York University Press.

galloping inflation (150)
See: **hyperinflation**.

game theory (020, 210)
The study of the 'behaviour of independent decision makers whose fortunes are linked in an interplay of collusion, conflict and compromise' (Shubik). The theory is central to much formulation and testing of models in economics as it studies multilateral decision-making. The earliest exponents of the art were **Cournot**, **Edgeworth**, **Böhm-Bawerk** and **Zeuthen**. Much of the theory recognizes uncertainty; recently it has taken into account ignorance of rules, incomplete information and indefinite time horizons. Important solution concepts utilized are the **Nash** equilibrium, the **core**, the **von Neumann–Morgenstern stable set** and the **Shapley** value. Major applications include **bilateral monopoly**, **duopoly**, planning processes, **welfare economics** and the study of markets and monetary institutions.

Neumann, J. von and Morgenstern, O. (1983) *Theory of Games and Economic Behaviour*, Princeton, NJ: Princeton University Press.
Schotter, A. and Schwodiauer, G. (1980) 'Econ-

omics and the theory of games. A survey', *Journal of Economic Literature* 18: 479–527.

Shubik, M. (1983) *Game Theory in the Social Sciences: Concepts and Solutions*, Cambridge, MA, and London: MIT Press.

gamma stock (310)
The least active stock or share quoted on the **Stock Exchange Automated Quotation System.**

See also: **alpha stock; beta stock; delta stock.**

Gang of Four (050)
The Republic of Korea, Taiwan, Hong Kong and Singapore.

See also: **newly industrialized country.**

GAO (320)
See: **General Accounting Office.**

gap analysis (310)
Banking analysis of the relationship between the interest rates and maturities of assets and liabilities. The 'gap' is the amount of assets with variable rates financed by fixed rate liabilities.

Garn St Germain Depository Institutions Act 1982 (310)
The sequel to the **Depository Institutions Deregulation and Monetary Control Act** 1980 which continued the deregulation of the US banking industry, particularly through the removal of interest rate ceilings.

GATT (420)
See: **General Agreement on Tariffs and Trade.**

gazumping (930)
Breaking an agreement to sell a house because another prospective buyer has offered a higher price in the period between an oral promise to sell and the exchange of contracts. A sharp practice prevalent in England in the 1970s and 1980s.

GDP (220)
See: **gross domestic product.**

GDP deflator (150)
The ratio of the **gross domestic product** at current prices to gross domestic product at constant prices multiplied by 100. It is the weighted average of the detailed price indices used to deflate the gross domestic product: the weights used reflect the importance of each category of output in the gross domestic product.

GE (020)
See: **general equilibrium.**

gearing (310, 520)
The ratio of a bank or other company's total borrowings of a fixed term or perpetual nature to its shareholders' funds and minority interests.

gender discrimination (010, 810, 820)
See: **sexual discrimination.**

General Accounting Office (320)
An independent US agency, outside the Executive Office, directly responsible to the US Congress for seeing that the funds voted by Congress are spent as enacted in legislation.

General Agreement on Tariffs and Trade (420)
A multilateral trade agreement signed in 1947 which covers all major trading countries with the exceptions of the USSR and China. It was originally intended to be part of the International Trade Organization, a body which would have policed international transactions and, together with the **International Monetary Fund** and the **World Bank**, constituted a new international economic system. As the **International Trade Organization** was never established, the General Agreement on Tariffs and Trade remains as a treaty. Under Article 1, each contracting party to the agreement pledged to offer most favoured nation treatment to the others; Article 3 challenged trade discrimination by requiring contracting parties to charge only domestic taxation on imports from treaty partners; Articles 11 to 15 stated that quantitative restrictions on imports were permitted, after consultation, for balance of payments reasons. Trade has gradually been liberalized in a number of rounds of negotiations.

Most disputes between members have been solved, with the exception of the problem of the subsidization of agricultural products. But it can be argued that the continued existence of **voluntary export restraints** and deals such as market-sharing have retained **protection** in a modern guise. To make the Agreement more effective, it has been suggested that there should be regular meetings of the trade ministers of member countries and that the General Agreement on Tariffs and Trade secretariat should be given powers to police the terms agreed. Its current membership consists of 107 members and 28 associate countries.

Oxley, A. (1990) *The Challenge of Free Trade*, Hemel Hempstead: Harvester Wheatsheaf.

See also: **Dillon Round**; **Kennedy Round**; **Tokyo Round**; **Uruguay Round**.

General Agreement to Borrow (430)

The credit line set up by the **Group of Ten** for the **International Monetary Fund** in 1962 to provide loans to the Group's members. The facility was enlarged in January 1983 when other International Monetary Fund members were permitted to contribute to it and make use of it in emergencies.

general equilibrium (010, 020)

The state of an economy in which all its markets for consumer goods, capital goods, labour services, financial assets and money are in equilibrium and the economy is in overall balance. The leading **marginalist Walras** was the first economist to set out the conditions for general equilibrium. Today, the basic questions about such an equilibrium always include whether the solution proposed exists, whether it is unique and whether it is stable. General equilibrium analysis has the advantage of being flexible enough to be able to incorporate many goals and resources in a model. It is contrasted with **Marshall's partial equilibrium analysis** and is a half-way house between microeconomics and macroeconomics.

Allingham, M. (1975) *General Equilibrium*, New York: Wiley; London: Macmillan.

Kornai, J. (1971) *Anti-Equilibrium and the Tasks of Research*, Amsterdam: North-Holland.

Weintraub, E.R. (1974) *General Equilibrium Theory*, London and Basingstoke: Macmillan.

See also: **Arrow–Debreu model**.

general fund (320, 520)

Part of a budget which provides finance for a variety of purposes.

See also: **dedicated budget**.

general government net worth (310)

The fixed capital stock of central or local government less its net financial liabilities. This **balance sheet** approach to the study of government finance has been suggested as a framework for assessing a government's ability to sustain its economic policies. It also has the useful function of making governments distinguish productive investments from debt servicing.

General Household Survey (220)

A sample survey used in the UK to collect data on the labour force and on household expenditure.

generalized least squares (210)

An improved method of estimating relationships between economic variables. Each observation is weighted by the reciprocal of the **standard deviation** of the disturbance concerned before applying the **least squares method**.

generalized medium (010, 310)

Something which is generally acceptable for many transactional purposes: **money** performs this in modern economies as it can be used to effect exchanges in numerous markets and measure the value of millions of different types of goods and services.

See also: **medium of account**; **medium of exchange**; **money**.

generalized system of preferences (420)

A proposal made at the 1964 meeting of **United Nations Conference on Trade and Development**, and accepted in 1968, that developed countries grant preferential tariff treatment for imports of manufactures and semi-manufactured products from developing countries. Those granting preferential treatment include the USA, the **European Community**, Canada, Australia and Japan.

See also: **most favoured nation**.

general market equilibrium (210)

The **equilibrium** of a market with several

interdependent commodities traded with, for each commodity, the quantity demanded being equal to the quantity supplied.

Dorfman, R., Samuelson, P.A. and Solow, R.M. (1958) *Linear Programming and Economic Analysis*, ch. 13, New York: McGraw-Hill.

See also: **isolated market equilibrium**.

general sales tax (320)
An **indirect tax** levied on the sales of most consumer goods and services, usually expressed as a percentage of the value of the purchases.

See also: **expenditure tax**.

general strike (830)
Simultaneous **strikes** in most major industries of a country: famous examples include the UK's in 1926 and several in Poland and Sweden in the 1980s. These strikes often start in a major sector and become general through sympathetic action.

General Theory (030)
See: **Keynes's General Theory**.

general training (810, 850)
Training of members of a labour force in skills which are of use to many employers, e.g. word processing. There is a case for education of this kind to be provided by an educational institution, or financed by an industry as a whole, to avoid an employer gaining no return to the investment made in a worker's training because the worker moves to another job.

See also: **human capital; specific training**.

general union (830)
A **trade (labor) union** which organizes workers from different occupations and industries, e.g. the Teamsters (USA), the Transport and General Workers' Union (UK). General unions are often so large as to dominate a national trade union movement.

See also: **craft union; industrial union**.

generative city (930)
A city whose existence and growth is a major cause of the growth of a region. The best example in most countries is the capital city.

See also: **parasitic city**.

gentrification (930)
Improvement of older working class inner city housing by rich professionals, e.g. in San Francisco and South London.

See also: **yuppie**.

geographical trade structure (420, 730)
Analysis of a nation's international trade showing the countries of origin of its imports and the countries of destination of its exports. This structure reflects international trading agreements and the extent of economic interdependence among countries. In the UK, for example, membership of the **European Community** from 1972 has brought about a switch from trade with the Commonwealth to trade with major European economies, especially Germany.

See also: **commodity trade structure**.

geometric mean (210)
The square root of a set of numbers which have been multiplied together, e.g. the square root of 27 is the geometric mean of 3 and 9.

See also: **arithmetic mean; harmonic mean**.

geometric progression (210)
A series of numbers which increases by a constant, or common, ratio, e.g. 2, 4, 8, 16 where 2 is the common ratio. **Malthus** asserted that population grows according to this progression.

See also: **arithmetic progression**.

George, Henry, 1839-97 (030)
US economist and politician famous for advocating that all taxation should be raised from a single tax on land, an idea which had its origins in the writings of the **Physiocrats** and the classical theory of **differential theory of rent**. He regarded increases in land values in the nineteenth century as a major cause of inequality and injustice in society. His famous work, *Progress and Poverty* (1879), which was very popular in the USA in the 1880s and 1890s, is still closely studied in the many Henry George Schools of Economics which provide expositions of the master's ideas throughout the world. The Henry George Foundation of America, founded in 1926 and based at Columbia, MD, still

researches into land value taxation and site value taxation.

German economic institutes (140)

Kiel, Hamburg, Essen, Munich and Berlin. All of these are engaged in regular economic forecasting and policy analysis.

German Historical School (030)

Successive generations of German economists in the nineteenth and early twentieth centuries who took a holistic approach to economics, attempting to examine all economic phenomena, using material from social history. Their researches included fiscal policy, administration, industrial organization, cities, bank credit, government and private enterprise. The earliest writers of this school were Bruno Hildebrand, Wilhelm Roscher and Karl Knies, the leader was Gustav von Schmoller (1838–1917) and the later writers were Arthur Spiethoff, Werner Sombart (1863–1941) and Max Weber (1864–1920).

Weber, M. (1958) *The Protestant Ethic and the Spirit of Capitalism*, trans. by T. Parsons, New York: Scribner.

Gerschenkron effect (110, 210)

The effect of the choice of a particular base year on an index of industrial output. In a largely agrarian society, the base year chosen will determine the rate of growth exhibited by that index. This was originally applied to the Soviet economy by the Austro-American economic historian Alexander Gerschenkron (1904–78).

Gerschenkron, A. (1947) 'The Soviet indices of industrial production', *Review of Economics and Statistics* 29: 217–26.

gestation period (010, 640)

The time it takes for production or a capital project to be completed. Classical economists, e.g. **Ricardo**, asserted that the average period was twelve months, as in agriculture where there is only one harvest per year.

GHS (220)

See: **General Household Survey**.

Giffen, Sir Robert, 1837–1910 (030)

Born in Strathaven, Scotland. After careers in law and journalism (he was assistant editor of *The Economist* from 1868 to 1876 and city editor of the *Daily News* from 1873 to 1876), he became a civil servant working at the Board of Trade as chief of the statistical department and then Assistant Secretary until his retirement in 1897. A founder of the Royal Economic Society and famous for the **Giffen paradox**.

Giffen, R. (1904) *Economic Inquiries and Studies*, London: G. Bell.
Mason, R.S. (1989) *Robert Giffen and the Giffen Paradox*, Hemel Hempstead: Philip Allan.

Giffen good (010, 520)

A good which is increasingly demanded as its price rises. **Giffen** noted this exception to the normal demand curve inverse relationship between price and quantity demanded of a good in the case of an essential foodstuff.

Giffen paradox (030)

An exception to the normal inverse relationship between price and quantity demanded made famous by **Giffen**. Giffen noticed in the case of bread consumption that the quantity demanded rose when the price did, an exception to the general law of demand. If a poor family spends its income on bread and meat, a rise in the price of bread would make it impossible for it to afford a discrete amount of meat, with the consequence that there would be an excess of income after maintaining the same level of bread consumption which would be used to purchase more bread – hence an increased consumption of bread despite a rise in its price. **Income and substitution effects** analysis is used to explain this paradox: the income effect outweighs the substitution effect and there is a change in the sign of the income effect from positive to negative.

In the figure, I_1 and I_2 are the indifference curves of a particular consumer faced with the choice between goods F and G. There is a fall in the price of good G (more of it can be obtained for a fixed amount of F) expressed by a shift in the budget line from AC to AD but there is also a fall in the quantity demanded of it from Or to Oq as the income effect yz is more than the substitution effect xz.

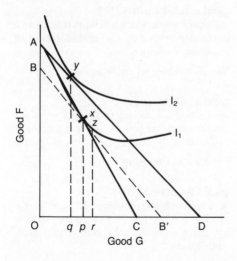

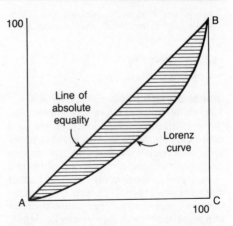

Boland, L.A. (1977) 'Giffen goods, market prices and testability', *Australian Economic Papers* 16: 72–85.

Stigler, G.J. (1947) 'Notes on the history of the Giffen paradox', *Journal of Political Economy* 55: 152–6.

gifts tax (320)

A tax on the transfer of personal capital to someone else (often a close relative) which usually exempts smaller gifts of any one year. The tax is imposed to prevent persons from avoiding inheritance taxes by transferring ownership before death.

gilt-edged security (310)

See: **gilts**.

gilts (310)

UK government **securities** with the government guarantee that interest will be paid and capital repaid on its redemption day (if any). The term arose because of the high value of these bonds.

Gini coefficient (210, 610)

A measure of income distribution, devised by the Italian demographer and statistician Corrado Gini (1884–1965). It is the ratio of the area between a **Lorenz** curve and the line of absolute equality (shaded in the figure) to the area of the entire triangle below that line (ABC). It has also been applied to the measurement of **industrial concentration**.

Ginny Mae (310)

See: **Government National Mortgage Association**.

giro (310)

A system for transferring bank deposits long used in most European countries and offered as a service by the British Post Office from 1968 and by British clearing banks shortly afterwards. Instead of a transfer being effected by a cheque, the holder of a giro account instructs the bank concerned to make a change in its ledgers to pay another giro account-holder a particular amount of money.

GLAM (840)

Grey, leisured, affluent, married: the key socioeconomic group of the late twentieth century, aged between 45 and 59 years.

Glass–Steagall Act (310)

Banking Act 1933 (USA) which separated **investment banking** from deposit-taking banking with the aim of discouraging speculation and conflicts of interest, e.g. between underwriting new share issues and normal **commercial bank** lending. It banned the payment of interest on demand deposits and allowed the **Federal Reserve System** to set **reserve requirements**. Since 1980, there have been US calls for the repeal of the Act so that US banks can have as wide a range of financial products as European banks. Japan's version of Glass–Steagall (Article 65 of its Securities and Exchange Law) was also much criticized.

Benston, G.J. (1990) *The Separation of Com-*

mercial and Investment Banking. The Glass-Steagall Act Revisited and Reconsidered, London: Macmillan.

gliding rate (430)
See: **sliding parity**.

global deregulation (310, 320, 430)
The abolition of exchange controls, tax barriers, fixed dealing commissions and limitations on overseas investment together with the creation of new financial instruments which foreigners can use. More and more countries are heading down the path of deregulation. Since 1979, the UK, Japan, Germany and many other countries have abolished their exchange controls. Japan, long reluctant to allow foreigners to invest in their country, has allowed more foreign access to their financial markets. Also, the New York and London Stock Exchanges have undertaken massive deregulation.

See also: **Big Bang**; **Mayday**.

global monetarism (430)
A proposed regime of **fixed exchange rates** with a collective monetary policy for participant countries. The aim of this form of **monetarism** is to stabilize the average price of traded goods.

GLS (210)
See: **generalized least squares**.

glut (010)
Excess supply of all or most goods and services. Classical economists regarded a glut as a general economic depression, characterized by falling output, employment and prices – it was only temporary as price changes were expected to restore the economy to a full employment equilibrium.

See also: **effectual demand**; **Malthus**; **Mill, John Stuart**; **Say's law**.

GmbH (510)
Gesellschaft mit beschränkter Haftung: a German or Swiss private company.

GNMA (310)
See: **Government National Mortgage Association**.

GNP (220)
See: **gross national product**.

goal equilibrium (210)
An **equilibrium** which attempts to achieve a particular aim, e.g. the maximization of consumers' utility.

See also: **non-goal equilibrium**.

goal system (320)
A method of raising tax revenue which requires each tax office to achieve a quota of tax revenue.

See also: **tax farming**.

goal variable (210)
A policy objective which is part of the objective utility function of a policy-maker, e.g. price stability, a balance of payments equilibrium.

See also: **instrument variable**; **target variable**.

going concern (510)
A commercial organization, usually a firm, which is expected to continue to operate for the foreseeable future.

going rate (820)
A wage rate which is regarded as the acceptable pay at a particular time for an occupational group. Often it is the pay set by a major employer or bargaining group.

See also: **key rate**; **wage round**.

goldbug (430)
Someone in favour of a return to the **gold standard**.

gold bullion standard (430)
A **fixed exchange** rate system which existed in its purest form from 1880 to 1914. National currencies were valued in terms of weight units of gold, and exchange rates were fixed through the medium of gold. If international transactions were not in balance then internal adjustment was needed in the debtor country. Currencies on the gold standard were convertible into each other merely with the cost of shipping gold from one country to another. The key player of the system was the **central bank** of each country as it had the tasks of contracting the internal money supply – in the case of a

balance of payments deficit to produce a credit contraction, and the reverse in the case of a balance of payments surplus. Both domestically and internationally, gold was ideal because of its unique qualities as a standard of value and as a medium of exchange. It applied the **one-price law** throughout the world, permitting gold to flow according to the price **specie-flow mechanism**. But too little cooperation between the central banks (many of whom were reluctant to follow the harsh rules of the system) weakened the automatic effects of the gold standard. The gold standard was in force in the UK from 1717 to 1931 (apart from the Napoleonic Wars and the First World War). Before the First World War the **Bank of England**, as the creditor country of the world, operated according to the rules, but the USA did not do so when it had a similar task after 1918: when it had a great inflow of gold, it did not allow domestic prices to rise. When debtor countries introduced **exchange controls** and entered into trade wars, the gold standard was at an end.

Bordo, M.D. and Schwartz, A.J. (eds) (1984) *A Retrospective on the Classical Gold Standard 1821–1931*, Chicago, IL: University of Chicago Press.

See also: **commodity reserve currency**; **dollar standard**; **gold exchange standard**.

gold demonetization (430)
Ceasing to use gold as the basis for valuing a currency. The major example of this was when the US dollar replaced gold after the collapse of the **Bretton Woods** system as the peg for many currencies.

See also: **dollar standard**.

golden age (110)
A period of steady growth with continuous full employment. In this age, the **warranted rate of growth** is equal to the **natural rate of growth**.

Robinson, J. (1962) *Essays in the Theory of Economic Growth*, London: Macmillan.

golden handcuffs (820)
A gratuity or deferred benefit given to an employee to discourage him/her from moving to another employer.

golden handshake (820)
A gratuity given to an employee on retiring from a firm.

golden hello (820)
A gratuity of a substantial amount offered to a potential employee to induce him/her to join a firm.

golden parachute (310, 510, 820)
A financial arrangement made by a company director to secure future income, e.g. a consultancy in the event of a company takeover.

golden rate (820)
An excessive rate of pay for overtime which is several times the normal rate for working contracted hours.

golden rule (110)
Equating the rate of profit with the rate of growth. In the theory of **economic growth**, it is the optimal growth path for an economy such that the maximum level of consumption per head of a population is sustained.

Phelps, E.S. (1961) 'The golden rule of accumulation: a fable for growthmen', *American Economic Review* 51: 638–43.

golden share (310)
A voting share in a company, especially one which has been privatized, which can prevent the company from being taken over and gives the holder the power to insist that the company be run in a prescribed way. The UK government retained such shares when it privatized **nationalized industries**.

See also: **privatization**.

Golden Triangle (730)
1 Thailand, Laos and Burma: the most important opium-producing region in the world.

2 The megalopolis of NW Europe.

3 The business centre of Pittsburgh, Pennsylvania.

gold exchange standard (430)
The linking of a currency to a currency which is on the gold standard so that it acquires a stability which makes it useful as a

reserve currency. This substitute for the gold standard was in force in the 1920s (in the UK from 1925 to 1932) and in effect in the 1960s.

See also: **dollar standard**; **gold bullion standard**.

gold franc (430)

An **artificial currency** used by the International Telecommunications Union (Geneva) to express telecommunications charges of different countries in the same 'currency'. In 1865, the Telegraph Convention adopted the French franc as the monetary unit to be used in calculating international tariffs as it was a major hard currency. In 1928, to avoid the problem of fluctuations in the value of the franc, a standardized 'gold franc' equal to 10/31 of a gramme of gold was the basic unit chosen. In 1947, many countries were dissatisfied with the system but the proposal to devalue the gold franc was rejected as it meant a reduction in international telegraph and telephone rates. Lacking an alternative, the system continued. However, the gold franc was never a reserve currency (accounts are settled in national currencies) but merely a unit of account: thus it only has one of the functions of money. Since the floating of currencies in 1971, the conversion of gold francs into national currencies has produced divergent results. Also, gold francs of different values are used for different types of transactions, e.g. the value for shipping tolls is different from that for telegrams. In 1987, the value of the gold franc was fixed with 3.0061 gold francs equal to 1 special drawing right.

gold market (310, 430)

The market with official and private dealings in gold coin and bullion. In March 1968, US monetary authorities persuaded European authorities to separate private and monetary gold markets, creating a two-tier market. The USA wanted South Africa to sell all its gold to the private market so that the price would come down to $30 or $32 to shake central banks' confidence in gold. However, world inflation made gold a popular private holding and so its price approached $70 by mid-1972. The London Gold Market has been run by five firms since 1919, i.e. N.M. Rothschild, Samuel Montagu, Mocatta and Goldsmid, Sharps,

Pixley and Westpac (formerly Johnson Matthey Bankers). Internationalization of financial markets brought about proposals to admit foreign traders.

gold reserves (310, 430)

Gold holdings of a **central bank** which are used only for transactions with other central banks. The amount of gold reserves in the world at any time is equal to the amount produced less the private demand for jewellery, dentistry and hoarding, together with past accumulations.

See also: **gold bullion standard**.

gold shortage (430)

The world shortage of gold from 1900 to 1972. In this period, US wholesale prices rose 300 per cent, a much greater rise than in the monetary gold price (up only 75 per cent). The shortage was brought about to a large extent by the small margin between the production cost and the selling price of gold, a disincentive to producers. An increase in the price of gold pushed up US Treasury holdings from $7 billion in 1934 to $20 billion in 1939 but the shortage continued, exacerbated by the Second World War and the post-war demand for gold.

goldsmith banking system (310)

The seventeenth-century beginnings of modern commercial banking in the City of London. Goldsmiths who accepted personal and business gold-holdings also lent out such deposits until they discovered that only a certain proportion of deposits would be reclaimed in a particular period and so it was possible to lend by granting loans in the form of deposit receipts. This was, in effect, the beginning of the **fractional reserve banking** system.

gold standard (430)

A basis for the value of a national currency which can take the form of a **gold bullion standard** or a **gold exchange standard**.

Gold Standard Commission (1982) *Report to Congress of the Commission on the Role of Gold in the Domestic and International Monetary System*, Washington, DC: US Government Printing Office.

good (010)

1 A tangible output rather than a **service**.

2 Output which bestows **utility** on the person possessing it.

See also: **bad; brown good; consumer durable; illth; wealth; white good**.

Goodhart's law (310)

This states that any measure of the **money supply** behaves differently when it becomes an official target by the very act of targeting it. Named after Charles Goodhart, formerly chief monetary adviser at the Bank of England, who reached this conclusion after studying the monetary events of the period 1971–3 in the UK.

goodwill (520)

An intangible asset of a firm which adds to its worth. A major example is 'a good reputation' resulting from a firm having established markets and good relations with customers or suppliers. Goodwill causes the market value of a firm to be in excess of its **book value**.

Gosplan (060, 120)

The Soviet central planning organization which had the task of collecting economic data from all the republics of the USSR and their subordinate organizations to draw up medium five-year plans and annual operational plans. Its well-known five-year plans began with a plan for industry covering the years 1923–4 to 1927–8. It also had to audit enterprises to check that plans had been followed. It had the important task of material balancing, i.e. matching expected demand with expected supply.

Gossen, Hermann Heinrich, 1810–58 (030)

An early **marginalist** who was educated in law and government in the universities of Bonn and Berlin. After a spell as an indolent civil servant from 1834 to 1847, he worked in the insurance industry. His short work of 1854 expounded the law of **diminishing marginal utility**, analysed market exchange, examined the nature of rent and provided the basis for a theory of **labour supply**. His contribution to economics was acknowledged by both **Jevons** and **Marshall**.

Gossnab (060, 120)

The central supplies committee of the USSR which had the task of allocating materials to enterprises. In the 1990s, its role is to change to being a wholesaler of capital goods.

government bond (310)

A long-term stock market security issued by a central, state or local government which is either irredeemable or to be repaid after a stated number of years.

See also: **gilts**.

government broker (310)

The stockbroker who deals in markets on behalf of a government. In London, the senior partner of Mullens & Co. has the task of dealing in **gilts** for the Bank of England.

government intervention (320)

A series of measures undertaken by a government to achieve goals not guaranteed by a market system, i.e. fairer income and wealth distribution, **public goods**, **merit goods**, improved **social welfare**, appropriate infrastructure investment and a full equilibrium for the economy. Intervention can avoid chaos by establishing **property rights**, controlling access to economic activities and regulating monetary operations. But intervention has its shortcomings: the use of price controls and the limiting of competition frequently distorts markets.

See also: **fine-tuning; fiscal policy; monetary policy; prices policy**.

Government National Mortgage Association (310)

US association responsible for issuing guarantees of the securities backed by a pool of Federal Housing Administration and Veterans Administration mortgage loans. Known as 'Ginny Mae'.

government role (320)

The economic functions carried out by governmental organizations, together with the range of policies which affect the economic behaviour of firms and households. Under **laissez-faire** principles, a government's role will be minimal – not much more than defence and law and order – so that market forces will not be curbed. The earliest lists of the functions of government in the works of **Petty**, **Smith** and John Stuart **Mill** were slightly longer – Petty approved of state financing for clergy and doctors, Smith of the building of bridges and the provision of schools, Mill of some government participation in the running of industry. In the nineteenth and twentieth centuries, the growth of trade unions and socialist parties together with the theory of **economic planning** have persuaded many governments to extend their functions and to influence the pattern of production and the distribution of incomes. Only in the **Soviet economy** before the 1960s was there an attempt to give governments so large a role as to leave little decision-making power in the hands of other economic agents.

government security (310)

A **bill** or **bond** issued by a local, regional or central government. Lower levels of government tend to borrow for shorter periods than central governments. The ultimate guarantor of the payment of interest and the repayment of the sum borrowed is usually the central government.

grace (310)

See: **days of grace**.

gradualist monetarism (030, 310)

A form of **monetarism** which accepts that the association between money supply increases and price increases is a long-term phenomenon. Thus, in the short run, there is a limited role for the stimulation of **aggregate demand** through the use of **fiscal** and **monetary policies**. However, monetarists of this kind would prefer there to be no **demand management** because of their belief that, as an economy is basically self-adjusting, manipulation of aggregate demand would cause fluctuations. **Friedman** (USA) and Laidler (UK) adhere to this view; the **New Classical Economics** writers are instant monetarists.

See also: **instant monetarism**.

graduated income tax (320)

A tax on income with a different rate for different bands of income.

See also: **bracket creep**; **progressive tax**.

graduate tax (320)

A tax on the earnings of graduates imposed to recover the public expenditure incurred in financing a person's college or university education. The tax is related to future earnings and there can be a 'tax holiday' covering the first few years of employment or until a threshold level of income has been reached. Proponents of the tax argue that it makes possible a greater expansion in the number of students; opponents assert that this increase in taxation will discourage participation in higher education.

Gramm–Rudman–Hollings Act (320)

The Balanced Budget and Emergency Deficit Control Act 1985 (US federal statute). This set a legal target for the federal budget deficit of $171.9 billion in 1986, with the contradictory requirement that automatic spending cuts should be limited to $11.7 billion, making the deficit target unattainable without an increase in tax revenues. After 1986, the deficit target was $144 billion in 1987, falling to zero in 1991. But at the beginning of 1991, a projected deficit of $318 billion was announced. This draconian measure has given questionable powers to the **Office of Management and Budget** and **Congressional Budget Office** as well as necessitating unpopular spending cuts in successive years. In 1986, the US Supreme Court ruled the automatic **sequestration** provision of the Act unconstitutional.

grant in aid (320)

US federal grant to state or local governments which can be a flat grant (equal to the sum raised by a state government), a proportionate grant (proportional to the contribution of the recipient government) or a percentage grant (percentage of the cost to the recipient government for maintaining a particular programme). The purpose of these grants is to ensure that a desired level of public service is reached in all the states whatever the ability or willingness of individual states to finance it.

grants economics (020)

A type of economics which studies both two-way transfers (exchanges) and one-way transfers (grants). To understand grants is to be able to comprehend the nature of much of fiscal policy, as it is concerned with providing **transfer incomes** for persons who exchange nothing for them, and of expenditure programmes which create social goods. This type of economics is also useful in the analysis of international **aid**.

Boulding, K.E. (1973) *The Economy of Love and Fear: A Preface to Grants Economics*, Belmont, CA: Praeger.

gravity model (730, 840)

A method of predicting the amount of interaction between two places. It asserts that interaction is directly related to the product of the two populations and inversely to the distance between the places concerned. A familiar version of these models takes the form $M_{ij} = P_i P_j / d_{ij}^2$ where M_{ij} is the amount of movement between i and j, P_i is the population of place i, P_j is the population of place j and d_{ij} is the distance between places i and j. The interaction M_{ij} can be the number of migrants, the volume of goods transported, the number of letters and telephone calls etc. Distance can be measured in various ways, including route miles and transport cost. More sophisticated models take into account the characteristics of the populations, weighting them accordingly.

Carrothers, G.A.P. (1956) 'An historical review of the gravity and potential concepts of human interaction', *Journal of the American Institute of Planners* 22: 94–102.

Great Depression (040)

1 The period 1873–96 in the English economy when agriculture was especially depressed.

2 The period 1929–36 when world trade, partly through **protection**, and the cautious fiscal policies of national economies, suppressed the level of economic activity.

Friedman, M. and Schwartz, A.J. (1966) *The Great Contraction*, Princeton, NJ: Princeton University Press.
Kindleberger, C.P. (1986) *The World in Depression, 1929–39*, London: Allen Lane. (reprinted 1987, Harmondsworth: Penguin).
Saul, S.B. (1969) *The Myth of the Great Depression*, London and Basingstoke: Macmillan.

Temin, P. (1976) *Did Monetary Forces Cause the Great Depression?*, New York: W.W. Norton.

See also: **beggar-my-neighbour policy**; **depression**; **recession**; **slump**.

Great Leap Forward (060)

China's attempt in its Second Five-Year Plan of 1958–62 to replace Soviet-type planning with its own over-ambitious development schemes. A system of large-scale rural communes in the agricultural sector and the use of labour-intensive methods and decentralization of productive activities were introduced. A symbol of this change was the installation of a small steel furnace in each village. Continued economic failure, natural disasters and the withdrawal of Soviet technical assistance brought the experiment to an end in 1960.

Bernstein, M.A. (1988) *The Great Depression*, New York and Cambridge: Cambridge University Press.

Great Society (910)

The visionary programme of President Lyndon B. Johnson announced in 1964 to move beyond the goals of a rising **gross national product** and **full employment** to a more moral and spiritual society. In practice, it meant a set of complex federal programmes, in many respects similar to the **New Deal**, which included action on poverty, education, housing, Medicare and equal opportunities. President Nixon announced its demise in 1973.

green conditionality (720)

The rule that lending and expenditure is subject to the condition that the environment is not harmed.

green currency (430)

The exchange rate for converting the agricultural prices of the **European Community** into the domestic prices of a particular member country, originally expressed in **European unit of accounts**.

greenmail (520)

A method of preventing the takeover of one's company by the purchase of holdings made by possible predators and **arbitrage**.

green pound (430)
The **green currency** used by the UK.

green revolution (710)
The transformation of agriculture in Third World countries since 1945 by irrigation, the use of fertilizers and better seeds. It was hoped that substantial increases in the yields of wheat and rice would reduce many world food shortages as well as hunger in the less developed countries. Radical critics of the green revolution assert that the technology used is often monopolized by large commercial farmers who come to dominate agriculture and create a landless proletariat.

Cleaver, H.M. (1972) 'The contradictions of the Green Revolution', *American Economic Review* 62: 176–86.

Poleman, T.T. and Freebairn, D.K. (eds) (1973) *Food, Population, and Employment: The Impact of the Green Revolution*, New York: Praeger.

green stripe price (310)
A stock market price on a visual display unit of the **Stock Exchange Automated Quotation System** which shows the best price quoted by any market-maker for small transactions in a particular stock.

Gresham's law (310)
'Bad money drives out good.' A maxim of Sir Thomas Gresham (1519–79), the founder of the Royal Exchange, London, who asserted it in 1560 with reference to base silver coin. The contemporary experience of coinage being debased through **clipping** prompted this observation. The law operates because of the public's propensity to hoard more valuable currency, thereby withdrawing it from circulation.

grey belt (730, 840)
An area with a high proportion of retired people in its population. In many countries, the grey belt is situated on the coastline with the best climate.

See also: **ageing population**.

grey market (310)
Unofficial market in newly issued shares prior to official dealings in them. It exists in European financial centres but not in the USA. Only the orders of large institutions are handled.

grey Monday (310)
16 October 1989 when the Financial Times Stock Exchange 100 share index dropped by 70.5 points on the London market. This was less drastic than **Black Monday**'s fall of 500.

grey society (840)
A society whose population has a high proportion of elderly persons. The decline in the birth rate and increased life expectancy experienced by many industrialized countries have produced increasingly ageing populations. The principal economic problems for an economy arising from this change in the age distribution are the financing of pensions and the reduction in the size of its labour force with the consequence of a declining or stationary **national income**.

See also: **ageism**.

gross dividend yield (310)
The return to a stock market investment before the deduction of any tax.

See also: **dividend net**.

gross domestic fixed capital formation (220)
National expenditure in a given time period on physical productive assets, e.g. buildings, civil engineering works, machinery, equipment and vehicles. It consists of both **net investment** and **replacement investment** to maintain the capital stock intact. This form of investment is to be distinguished from investment in inventories and in financial assets.

gross domestic product (220)
The total output of goods and services produced within a given country in a particular time period. It is equal to the sum of the **value added** by each industry, net of all inputs, including imported **intermediate goods**: this is equal to the **factor incomes** of all persons engaged in domestic production. Gross domestic product together with net property income from abroad, constitutes gross national product.

See also: **national income**.

gross federal debt (310)
The broadest definition of the US federal

debt which includes the borrowings of the US Treasury and of various federal agencies.

See also: **total public debt**.

gross national product (220)

The total value of the economic activity of a country in a given time period, including replacement investment, valued at **factor cost** or **market prices**. It is used as a crude measure of **economic welfare**. Its growth can be divided into real growth and growth due to inflation.

See also: **national income**.

gross social product (220)

Gross national product of a centrally planned socialist economy.

gross state product (220)

The **gross domestic product** of the labour and property located in a particular state of the USA.

Group of Five (430)

The finance ministers of the USA, UK, France, Germany and Japan who meet informally to discuss international monetary problems and to set the agenda for the **Group of Ten**.

Group of Seven (430)

A grouping of finance ministers and **central bank** governors of the leading Western economies – Canada, Italy, USA, UK, France, Germany and Japan. They signed the **Louvre Accord** and in December 1987 continued with their search for international monetary stability by recommending the elimination of large international payments deficits through a clarification of national economic objectives, especially for fiscal policy. Since November 1975 they have held annual **economic summits** attended by heads of government and finance ministers.

Group of Ten (430)

A group of leading capitalist countries founded informally as the 'Paris Club' in 1956 and formally established in 1982. It consists of the USA, the UK, West Germany, France, Belgium, the Netherlands, Italy, Sweden, Canada and Japan, together with Switzerland in an honorary capacity. It agreed in 1962 to lend its

currencies to the **International Monetary Fund** under the **General Agreement to Borrow**. The Group also discusses international monetary arrangements, usually at the **Bank for International Settlements**.

Group of Twenty-four (420)

The inner circle of the **Group of 77** which conducts many negotiations on behalf of less developed countries at the United Nations.

Group of Thirty (430)

The Consultative Group on International Economic and Monetary Affairs Incorporated set up in 1978 with the aim of studying in depth the international dimensions of economics and finance. The Group's distinguished individual members, first chaired by Mr Johannes Witteveen, a former **International Monetary Fund** managing director, are joined in six monthly meetings by invited outsiders. It was originally financed by the Rockefeller Foundation, now by banks and corporations.

Group of Seventy-seven (420)

The group of **less developed countries** at the United Nations: all of these countries attended the first meeting of **United Nations Conference on Trade and Development** in 1964.

growth (110)

See: **economic growth**.

growth accounting (110, 210)

The analysis of **national income** figures to ascertain the relative contribution to growth made by increased quantities of factor inputs, increased **productivity** and **technical progress**.

Denison, E. (1967) *Why Growth Rates Differ*, Washington, DC: Brookings Institution.

growth pole (940)

The massing of a population in a great urban concentration of 10 million or more to achieve external **economies of scale**, with the object of reviving a depressed region; the establishment of a group of industries which cluster around an expanding industry. Although this was a new aspect of many regional policies in Western Europe in the 1960s, it can be traced back to Sir William

Petty who wanted the English economy to reach the levels of Dutch productivity by the relocation of population into a confined area of England.

growth theory of the firm (510)

A hypothesis which states that a firm attempts to maximize its growth, subject to a takeover restraint. Marris and **Penrose** advanced this theory as a plausible explanation of managerial behaviour. Penrose argues that there is an internal process of development in firms which leads to cumulative movements of growth or decline: this argument is then expanded to take into account mergers and acquisitions. It is essentially an optimistic account which regards large **diseconomies of scale** as unlikely.

Marris, R. (1964) *The Economic Theory of Managerial Capitalism*, London: Macmillan.
Penrose, E.T. (1959) *The Theory of the Growth of the Firm*, Oxford: Basil Blackwell.

See also: **managerial models of the firm**.

GSP (220, 420)

See: **generalized system of preferences; gross social product; gross state product**.

guilder (430)

The currency of Holland, Netherlands Antilles and Surinam.

guild socialism (120, 610)

A British movement of the interwar period which emphasized **workers' participation**. It was proposed that each industry should be run by its own national guild and that these guilds should be coordinated by a supreme council. S.G. Hobson in *The National Guilds – An Inquiry into the Wage System and the Way Out* (1914) was a leading thinker of the movement, as were G.D.H. Cole and other early members of the Fabian Society. Guild socialists rejected market systems of allocation in favour of **economic planning**. However, the movement's lack of policy towards the depression of the 1930s contributed to its demise.

Cole, G.D.H. (1972) *Self Government in Industry*, London: Hutchinson.
Glass, S.T. (1966) *The Responsible Society: The Ideas of the English Guild Socialist*, London: Longman.

Gulf Plus (720)

The price of crude or refined oil secretly agreed in 1928 between the major oil companies. Wherever oil was exported from, it would be priced as if it had travelled from the Gulf of Mexico. This anticompetitive price was intended to equalize the prices of all oil available to a particular consumer.

See also: **basing-point pricing; posted price**.

H

Haavelmo, Trygve, 1911– (030)

A major founder of **econometrics** who was awarded the **Nobel Prize for Economics** in 1989. He was educated at the University of Oslo where he was professor of economics from 1948 to 1979. In 1946–7 he was at the **Cowles Commission**. His important contributions to quantitative economics include the formulation of economic theories in probabilistic terms and the study of interdependence problems.

Haberler, Gottfried, 1900– (030)

An Austro-American economist, educated at the University of Vienna and lecturer and later professor of economics and statistics there from 1928 to 1936, working at the Finance Division of the League of Nations from 1934 to 1936 and crowning his career as Professor of International Trade at Harvard from 1936 to 1971. His books of the mid-1930s are his principal monument. In one, he brilliantly restated the classical doctrine of **comparative advantage** in terms of **general equilibrium** theory; in the other, he synthesized **business cycle** theories, providing a basis for the empirical testing of hypotheses about economic fluctuations. Later in his career he made many proposals for the reform of the **international monetary system**, discussing the conditions under which a **devaluation** of a currency in a **pegged exchange rate** regime improves a country's balance of payments.

Bhagwati, J.N. and Chipman, J.S. (1980) 'Salute to Gottfried Haberler on the occasion of his 80th birthday', *Journal of International Economics* 10: 313–18.
Haberler, G. (1936) *Theory of International Trade, with its Application to Commercial Policy*, London: William Hodge.
—— (1937) *Prosperity and Depression*, 5th edn, London: Allen & Unwin.

Hahn, Frank Horace, 1925– (030)

Born in Berlin, the son of a celebrated German philosopher and mathematician, he came to Britain as a teenager and graduated from the London School of Economics. Subsequently, he taught at Birmingham from 1948 to 1960 and Cambridge from 1960 to 1967 before holding chairs at the London School of Economics from 1967 to 1972 and at Cambridge from 1972 and Harvard in 1973–4. The leading theme of his works has been **mathematical economics**, particularly in its applications to **general equilibrium** theory. His first interest was in income distribution; then his concerns were to build on the foundations of Hicks's *Value and Capital* and to study stability. Also, his joint work with **Arrow**, *General Competitive Analysis* (1971), is a landmark in modern economics. In his works, Hahn has rigorously set out the conditions for order in a competitive market, a line of inquiry justified in his Cambridge Inaugural Lecture, 'On the Notion of Equilibrium in Economics' (1972).

Hahn, F. (1985) *Money, Growth and Stability*, Cambridge: Cambridge University Press.

Haig–Simons definition of income (010)

Personal income regarded as the sum of the market values of rights expressed in consumption and the change in the value of assets in a given time period.

Simons, H.C. (1938) *Personal Income Taxation: the Definition of Income as a Problem of Fiscal Policy*, Chicago, IL: University of Chicago Press.

Hang Seng Index (310)

The index of stock market securities traded on the Hong Kong Stock Exchange.

Hansen, Alvin Harvey, 1887–1975 (030)

US economist, educated at Yankton College, Dakota, and the University of Wisconsin who was professor at Harvard University from 1937 to 1962; previously, from 1933 to 1934, he was Director of

Research for President Roosevelt's Committee of Inquiry on National Policy in International Relations. For forty years he was a leading US exponent of **Keynesian** theory and of **fiscal policy**. His frequent use of **IS–LM curves**, a synthesis of classical and Keynesian economics, led to the diagram being named after both him and **Hicks**. Although he originally had a negative reaction to **Keynes's** *General Theory*, by the age of 52 he had become an avid Keynesian.

Barber, W.J. (1987) 'The career of Alvin H. Hansen in the 1920s and 1930s: a study in intellectual transformation', *History of Political Economy* 19: 191–205.

hansom cab economy (070, 610)
An **economy** which strives to keep its traditional industries in production, regardless of market demand.

hard commodity (720)
A mineral such as copper or iron ore.

hard currency (430)
A currency which retains a high value against others for long periods of time, usually because of a favourable balance of payments year after year. Such currencies are very popular as **reserve currencies**. Major hard currencies of the world have included the yen, the Deutschmark and the Swiss franc.

See also: **soft currency**.

hard ecu (430)
A version of the **ecu** proposed by the UK as initially a **common currency** which could be used in the **European Community** for all monetary transactions alongside existing national currencies. Eventually the hard ecu could become a **single currency**.

harmonic mean (210)
This is calculated for a set of values by taking the ratio of the number of values to the sum of the reciprocals of each value. The harmonic mean of 5, 12 and 16 is 3 divided by $1/5 + 1/12 + 1/16$.

See also: **arithmetic mean**; **geometric mean**.

Harrod, Sir Roy Forbes, 1900–78 (030)
Oxford economist from 1922 to 1967, as well as philosopher, biographer and prolific economic journalist. In his training at Oxford he was greatly influenced by **Edgeworth** but subsequently he learned much from **Keynes**, becoming a leading disciple and expositor, as well as his official biographer.

As an economist, he was best known for his contributions to the debates which led to Keynes's *General Theory*, for his works on the **trade cycle** which introduced the novelty of combining the multiplier with the accelerator, for his path-breaking growth theory in his London School of Economics lectures of 1948 and for his work on international economics for which he was awarded a readership at Oxford. He participated in most of the major price theory debates of his time, both at Cambridge on **imperfect competition** and at Oxford on **full-cost pricing**. He was a close adviser to Churchill in the Second World War.

Harrod, R.F. (1936) *The Trade Cycle*, Oxford: Clarendon Press (reprinted New York: Augustus M. Kelly, 1965).
—— (1948) *Towards a Dynamic Economics: Recent Developments of Economic Theory and their Application to Policy*, London: Macmillan.
Phelps-Brown, E.H. (1980) 'Sir Roy Harrod: a biographical memoir', *Economic Journal* 90: 1–33.

Harrod–Domar model (110)
A major model of economic growth which was independently asserted by both **Harrod** and Domar in 1948. It uses the concepts of the **natural rate of growth** and the **warranted rate of growth**.

Domar, E.D. (1957) *Essays in the Theory of Economic Growth*, pp. 70–82, New York: Oxford University Press.

Havana Charter (420)
The written agreement which set up the **International Trade Organization** in 1947–8. It sought to promote balanced growth by the abolition of **exchange controls**, trade barriers (with the exception of protection for **infant industries**) and discrimination. It advocated **full employment** throughout the world. It was signed by most Western countries; Czechoslovakia was the only East European country to do so. All signatories had to grant **most favoured nation** treatment to the others. The Havana Charter is doctri-

nally connected with the **International Monetary Fund** in its opposition to trade restrictions and to monopoly.

See also: **General Agreement on Tariffs and Trade**.

Hawtrey, Sir Ralph, 1879–1971 (030)

British civil servant and monetary theorist. After graduating in mathematics from Trinity College, Cambridge, he worked in the Treasury from 1904 to 1945, after which he held his first academic post as professor of international economics at Chatham House, London, from 1947 to 1952.

As a leading monetary theorist of his time, he used an income approach to monetary theory, thereby integrating monetary theory with general economics. His theory of the **trade cycle** attributed fluctuations to the instability of bank credit: he argued that short-term, not long-term, interest rates should be used to regulate credit. He was a late convert to the view that the provision of **public works** can be used to revive a depressed economy. In his generation he was unusual in that he learned his economics from his Treasury superiors, not from **Marshall** as did his Cambridge contemporaries. His most important works were *Currency and Credit* (1919), *Capital and Employment* (1937) and *The Art of Central Banking* (1930).

Davis, E.G. (1981) 'R.G. Hawtrey', in D.P. O'Brien and J.R. Presley (eds) *Pioneers of Modern Economics in Britain*, London: Macmillan.

Hayek, Friedrich A. von, 1899– (030)

Libertarian moral philosopher and economist who was born and educated in Vienna, where he graduated with doctorates in jurisprudence and economics. His long academic career, which culminated in sharing a **Nobel Prize for Economics** with **Myrdal** in 1974, began as Director of the Austrian Institute for Business Cycle Research in 1927 and privatdozent at the University of Vienna in 1929. His guest lectures at the London School of Economics, published as *Prices and Production* in 1931, took the unpopular view of the **trade cycle** that high levels of consumption would cause falling investment and depression. As professor at the London School of Economics from 1932 to 1950, he wrote on capital theory in *Profits, Interest and Investment* (1939) and in *The Pure Theory of Capital* (1941); his respect for John Stuart **Mill** is evident in *John Stuart Mill and Harriet Taylor* (1951). Subsequently, he became a professor at Chicago from 1950 to 1962 and at Freiburg from 1962 to 1965.

Parallel to his economics writing has been a series of works on psychology and libertarian political philosophy. A central theme of his attack on **socialism** is his exposition of the role of information in economic decision-making: information can always be used more efficiently in a decentralized economy than in a centralized planning system. This stance is based on his observation that the competitive market system generates information on demand and supply by changes in product prices and consequently factor prices, providing incentives for factors to move to the best uses. In his macro-theory Hayek goes beyond a simple **quantity theory of money** in aggregate terms to considering the effects on relative prices of monetary disturbances. Combining that approach with the Austrian theory of the trade cycle he demonstrates that credit affects prices and production. He has long opposed Keynesian-style macroeconomic management as it relies on economic omniscience: a free market can generate better information.

Barry, N.P. (1979) *Hayek's Social and Economic Philosophy*, London: Macmillan.
Butler, E. (1983) *Hayek: His Contribution to Political and Economic Thought*, London: Temple Smith.
Hayek, F.A. (1944) *The Road to Serfdom*, London: Routledge.
—— (1963) *The Sensory Order: An Inquiry into the Foundations of Theoretical Psychology*, Chicago, IL: University of Chicago Press.
—— (1976) *The Constitution of Liberty*, London: Routledge & Kegan Paul.
—— (1982) *Law, Legislation and Liberty: A New Station of Liberal Principles*, London: Routledge & Kegan Paul.
Wood, J.C. and Woods, R. (1991) *Friedrich A. Hayek. Critical Assessments*, London: Routledge.

headline rate of inflation (220)

The rate of UK price inflation as stated by the **retail price index** which includes mortgage interest, value-added tax, local taxation and excise duties. It is the most publicized inflation rate.

See also: **underlying inflation rate**.

head tax (320)
See: **poll tax**.

health economics (910)
Evaluation of the effectiveness of health care, particularly by examining the social **opportunity costs** of alternative forms of treatment. The peculiar nature of the market for health care – that doctors have a major influence on both demand and supply – has attracted attention, as has the study of the options available for financing such services.

Drummond, M.F. (1980) *Principles of Economic Appraisal in Health Care*, Oxford: Oxford University Press.
McGuire, A., Henderson, J. and Mooney, G. (1987) *The Economics of Health Care*, London: Routledge.
Smith, G.T. (1987) *Health Economics: Prospects for the Future*, London: Croom Helm.

See also: **quality-adjusted life years**.

heavy industry (610)
An industry using raw materials heavy in weight, and a great amount of fixed capital, e.g. shipbuilding. The decline of such industries in the twentieth century has produced **de-industrialization** in many Western countries.

See also: **light industry**.

heavy share (310)
UK company share whose market value is high relative to the average for similar companies. As a consequence, companies may issue bonus shares to their shareholders to reduce the share price.

See also: **penny share**.

Heckscher, Eli Filip, 1879–1952 (030)
Swedish economist and economic historian who was professor at the Stockholm Business School from 1909 to 1929. His monumental historical works on **mercantilism** and population are as famous as his contribution to international trade theory, now known as the **Heckscher–Ohlin trade theorem**.

Heckscher–Ohlin trade theorem (410)
An explanation of international trade in terms of the relative **factor endowments** of different countries: thus, for example, a country with an abundance of labour would export goods produced by labour-intensive methods more than capital-intensive goods. In the absence of transport costs and specialization, trade would eventually bring about factor price equalization. Empirical examination of this theory has not awarded it very high marks – hence the **Leontief paradox**.

Heckscher, E. (1949) 'The effect of foreign trade on the distribution of income', in H.S. Ellis and L.A. Metzler (eds) *Readings in the Theory of International Trade*, Philadelphia: Blakiston.
Ohlin, B. (1967) *Interregional and International Trade*, Cambridge, MA: Harvard University Press.

hedging (140, 430)
Dealings in **futures markets** to cover spot positions to reduce the risk of price movements, especially in commodity and currency markets. Hedging permits producers to stabilize their incomes because selling futures protects a producer against a price fall.

See also: **spot market**.

hedonic output (010)
Output measured in terms of both quantity and quality.

Spady, R. and Friedlaender, A.F. (1978) 'Hedonic cost functions for the regulated trucking industry', *Bell Journal of Economics* 9 (Spring): 159–79.

hedonic price (010)
The shadow price of the characteristic of a commodity, e.g. the value of a good view from a house. The concept is much used in **cost–benefit analysis** and in environmental economics, e.g. for valuing the level of amenities such as good air quality.

Rosen, S. (1974) 'Hedonic prices and implicit markets: product differentiation in pure competition', *Journal of Political Economy* 82: 34–55.

hedonic wages (820)
The factor payment offered by an employer

for a bundle of job characteristics, including status, training opportunities and working conditions. This wage is determined by the interaction between the demand of and supply for both worker characteristics and job characteristics.

Lucas, R.E.B. (1977) 'Hedonic wage equations and psychic wages in the returns to schooling', *American Economic Review* 67: 549–58.

helicopter money (310)
An unanticipated increase in the nominal stock of money which leads to an increase in demand for goods and a rise in the general price level of an economy.

Herfindahl–Hirschman index (210, 610)
A measure of market **concentration**. In an industry with i firms, the index is calculated as follows:

$$H = \sum_i s_i^2$$

where s_i is the market share of the ith firm. The index reflects both the number of firms and their relative size. The value of the index will be 1 if there is only one firm in the industry and tend towards unity if there are only a few firms or some firms of much greater size than others.

heteroscedasticity (210)
The property of a **linear regression** model with a changing **variance** of its disturbances.

See: **homoscedasticity**.

H-form (510)
A type of enterprise organized as a holding company: each of its divisions will be affiliated with the parent company as a subsidiary company. Corporate staff of a holding company are principally concerned with financial evaluation, using similar criteria to those employed by stock market analysts.

See also: **M-form**; **U-form**; **X-form**.

Hicks, Sir John Richard, 1904–89 (030)
The greatest Oxford economist of the twentieth century. His Oxford education in mathematics and philosophy, politics and economics led to a lectureship at the London School of Economics from 1926 to 1946 where he was able to be influenced by an alternative to the **Marshallian** economics of Cambridge, particularly **Wicksell**'s ideas, although his interest in Keynesian ideas drove him to Cambridge for a year at the summit of the *General Theory* debate. Much of the rest of his life, as a professor at Manchester from 1935 to 1946, as a fellow of Nuffield College, Oxford, from 1946 to 1952 and in the senior Oxford chair as Drummond Professor of Political Economy from 1952 to 1965, he was to be a major extender and clarifier of Keynesian ideas.

The breadth of Hicks's gigantic contribution to economics, much of which is the bread and butter of economics teaching in the West, is evident in his long series of books and articles since 1932, which was recognized in the award of a **Nobel Prize for Economics**, shared with **Arrow**, in 1972 for his early work on **welfare economics**. His first work, *A Theory of Wages* (1932), went beyond traditional labour economics to consider the **elasticity of substitution** and the relative income shares of labour and capital. His *Value and Capital* (1939) expounded consumer theory by using **indifference curves**. His careful reaction to Keynes's *General Theory* was in his celebrated article of 1937 in *Econometrica* – 'Mr Keynes and the Classics' (one of the most re-published articles in economics) – which introduced **IS–LM** analysis into macroeconomics, clarifying the contrast between goods and money markets and between what was old and new in Keynesian theory. Subsequently, Hicks, seeing the over-use of the apparatus, regarded it as an albatross. His *Social Framework* (1942), unusually for an introductory economics textbook, used **national income** accounting as a starting point. In the post-war period, his range was considerable: economic dynamics in *A Contribution to the Trade Cycle* (1950), a development of **revealed preference** theory in *A Revision of Demand Theory* (1956), growth theory in *Capital and Growth* (1965) and in *Capital and Time: a Neo-Austrian Theory* (1973) and historical development in *A Theory of Economic History* (1969). With his wife Ursula, he was co-author of works on **public finance**. Throughout his long academic career his many applications of **general equilibrium** theory enabled him to provide a powerful synthesis of microeconomics and macroeconomics.

Baumol, W.J. (1972) 'John R. Hicks' contribution to economics', *Swedish Journal of Economics* 74: 503–27.

Hahn, F. (1990) 'John Hicks the theorist', *Economic Journal* 100: 539–49.

Helm, D. (1984) *The Economics of John Hicks*, Oxford: Basil Blackwell.

Hicks, J.R. (1979) 'The formation of an economist', *Banca Nazionale del Lavoro Quarterly Review* 130: 195–204.

Hicks, J., Sir (1991) *The Status of Economics*, Oxford: Basil Blackwell.

Hicks charts (010)
See: **IS–LM curves**.

Hicksian income measure (010)
'The maximum value which [a man] can consume during a week, and still expect to be as well off at the end of the week as he was at the beginning.' This measure suggested in Hicks's *Value and Capital* (1939, ch. 14) relies on the concept of **expectations**. It can be contrasted with the approach of **Meade** and **Stone** who defined money income as the sum of the money value of consumption plus the increase in the money value of one's capital assets.

hidden reserves (310)
Bank reserves allowed by law to be kept off a bank's published balance sheet to increase its perceived strength. All British **clearing banks** used to be permitted to make such provisions before 1968 but now only **merchant banks** in the UK have this privilege.

hidden unemployment (810)
1 Underemployed labour. The extent to which employed labour is working below its capacity is evident by comparing **productivity** or wage levels of different sectors of an economy. **Soviet-type economies** were noted for their low wages and low productivity as the state's full employment policy and willingness to pay the wage bill gave managers no incentive to economize in the use of labour. Although the labour force enjoys easy secure employment, the economy suffers from chronic labour shortages and low quality products from unmotivated workers. It was one of the aims of **perestroika** to reduce this problem. Many European economies still have considerable labour reserves in their agricultural sectors.

2 That part of a population which is arguably part of the labour force but is excluded from a measure of unemployment because of the definition of unemployment used.

hiding hand (010)
An economic mechanism which allows underestimated difficulties to be offset by the unestimated creative response to them.

hierarchical decomposition principle (510)
An analysis of an organization into a vertical slice of operating activities and a horizontal slice of strategic planning which correspond to the lower and higher parts of the hierarchy.

Simon, H.A. (1962) 'The architecture of complexity', *Proceedings of the American Philosophical Society* 106 (December): 467–82.

—— (1973) 'Applying information technology to organization design', *Public Adminstration Review* 33 (May–June): 268–78.

high employment surplus (320)
An estimate of the excess of tax revenues over government expenditures at a **full employment** level of national income. This is used as a yardstick of a government's **fiscal stance**.

See also: **structural deficit**.

high-leveraged takeover (310, 610)
A takeover mainly financed by fixed interest finance, e.g. borrowing from banks.

high-powered money (310)
Currency, bankers' balances at a **central bank** and other eligible reserve assets of deposit banks. An increase in the supply of this money permits a multiple expansion of bank deposits because of the operation of the **money multiplier**, e.g. a central bank in an open market operation buys bonds from the public thereby increasing the amount of cash available to banks.

See also: **fractional reserve banking**.

high technology industry (610, 620)
An **industry**, usually **capital intensive**, requiring a high level of **research and development** to maintain its international standing. Leading examples are the aerospace and computer industries.

high-yield financing (310)
A type of financing taking the form of **junk bonds**.

hire purchase (310)
The hiring of a good, especially a **consumer durable**, by a customer who, on the completion of paying instalments equal to the full price of the good plus interest, owns it.

Hirschman, Albert Otto, 1915– (030)
A leading development economist. Born in Berlin and educated at the Sorbonne, the London School of Economics and Trieste, he emigrated to the USA in 1941. He was financial adviser at Columbia from 1952 to 1956, and has held a succession of chairs at American universities – Yale, Columbia, Harvard and Princeton, where he has been since 1974. His work as a development economist has taken the unusual path of advocating unbalanced economic development, based on key industries producing intermediate products. His **exit-voice** analysis has provided a new method of examining the organizational response to a decline of firms, suggesting that a firm changes rather than goes out of business.

Hirschman, A.O. (1958) *The Strategy of Economic Development*, New Haven, CT: Yale University Press.
—— (1970) *Exit, Voice and Loyalty: Responses to Decline in Firms, Organizations and States*, Cambridge, MA: Harvard University Press.
—— (1981) *Essays in Trespassing: Economics to Politics and Beyond*, Cambridge: Cambridge University Press.

histogram (210)
A method of presenting a **frequency distribution** graphically in a number of rectangles varying in size according to the number of observations in each class.

Historical School (030)
See: **German Historical School**.

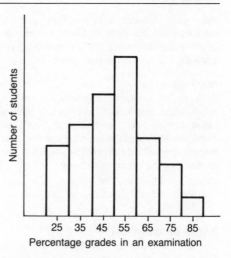

Percentage grades in an examination

historic cost (540)
The original valuation of an asset. This measure is respected by accountants because of its objectivity and verifiability. However, in periods of **inflation**, this value must be adjusted to take into account specific price changes for the asset if an accurate current valuation is to be obtained.

See also: **inflation accounting**; **replacement cost**.

HLT (310, 520)
See: **high-leveraged takeover**.

HOBS (310)
Home and office banking systems, which allow access to banking facilities away from banking premises.

hog cycle (140)
An alternation between excess demand and excess supply in the pig market in the USA; the cycle inspired the **cobweb** theorem.

holding company (510)
A company consisting of a number of subsidiary companies substantially owned by the parent.

See also: **bank holding company**; **H-form**; **pyramiding**.

holding gain (520)
The gain to a business arising from the current market value of its assets being more

than their historical cost. This gain is realized when the asset is sold or, in the case of raw materials, when the raw materials are embodied in a sold finished good.

hold-up (010)

A form of economic opportunism which arises when assets and investments have a value specific to an exchange, e.g. an employee with **specific training** can use that **human capital** investment as the basis for demanding higher remuneration.

Goldberg, V.P. (1976) 'Regulation and administered contracts', *Bell Journal of Economics* 7: 426–48.

home banking (310)

The use of banking facilities at home by means of a computer terminal linked to the main computer of a particular bank. Each home, in a sense, is a personalized branch of the single bank. Home banking was first offered by the Nottingham Building Society (UK) in November 1983, and then by Australia's Commonwealth Banking Corporation. By September 1984, seventy-one US banks and other financial institutions offered such a facility. In France, fifty banks offer the limited service of transmission of bank statements to home television sets. This service is attractive to banks for it is a cheaper method of expansion for a geographically concentrated bank than the opening of new branches.

homeless (930)

The condition of being without any housing. This occurs because of insufficient income to pay the market rates for purchasing or renting a home or because there is an insufficient housing supply. Rent controls (by reducing the supply of private sector housing) and insufficient repairs to the national housing stock magnify this problem. Geographical mobility from poorer to richer parts of a country, especially a capital city, produces hordes of homeless people who often in desperation have to use discarded cardboard boxes as shelter.

home production (010, 810)

Non-market production of goods and services in households. Much of this work is carried out by married women not participating in the labour force and it often involves as many weekly hours as average employment in the labour market; it is a common form of production in less developed countries. Allocation of time by home producers will depend on the relative values placed on each good or service produced.

Gronau, R. (1980) 'Home production – a forgotten industry', *Review of Economic Statistics* 62: 408–16.
Havrylyshyn, O. (1976) 'The value of household services: a survey of empirical estimates', *Review of Income and Wealth* 22: 101–31.

homework (810)

Working as a subcontractor at home doing **labour-intensive** work, e.g. addressing envelopes or tailoring. Work of this type has represented the most famous example of exploitation in industrialized societies: **trade unions** have found it difficult to alleviate as it is difficult to organize and protect so dispersed a labour force. British **wages councils** investigated this type of work but found there was little they could do to solve the problem. Now that it is possible through computerization for many workers to undertake tasks which were previously carried out in offices, 'homework' can be a more lucrative occupation.

See also: **networking economy**.

homo economicus (010)

'Economic man' – the self-interested economic agent. In **classical** and **neoclassical economics** the **utility-maximizing** objectives of individual economic agents were taken to be the basis of economic activity.

See also: **altruism**.

homogeneous good (010)

A good of which each unit is regarded by consumers as identical with the others. Thus consumers may be indifferent as to whether to buy one bag of potatoes rather than another. Although there may be differences which are analysable by chemists and others, consumers regard the differing aspects of different units as irrelevant to their purchasing decisions. Under **perfect competition**, it is essential that goods are homogeneous so that individual firms have no monopoly power.

See also: **branding; product differentiation**.

homoscedasticity (210)
The property of a linear regression model which has disturbances with constant **variance**.

See also: **heteroscedasticity**.

homo sovieticus (010)
An altruistic economic agent who does not need economic incentives to produce. He is prepared to work for the sake of the common good, including overall production. In the late twentieth century this type of person is more mythical than real; *homo economicus* is a more common species.

See also: **economic man; Soviet-type economy**.

horizontal discrimination (820)
The unfair treatment of persons in the same category, e.g. in the labour market men and women in the same occupational group who have unequal pay, despite doing the same work. A great deal of legislation in the 1960s and 1970s, e.g. the **UK's Equal Pay Act** and US civil rights legislation, attempted to remove discrimination of this kind.

See also: **discrimination; vertical discrimination**.

horizontal equity (160, 320)
The identical treatment of individuals (or groups) with the same amount of a relevant characteristic, for example, income. Following this principle, families, e.g. of the same size with the same income pay the same amount in taxes.

See also: **vertical equity**.

horizontal integration (610)
The **merger** of firms in the same industry, usually to reduce competition and to obtain **economies of scale**. Mergers of this kind are viewed with great suspicion in **competition policy**.

See also: **vertical integration**.

hot money (430)
Short-term international capital flows induced by differences in interest rates and the relative appreciation and depreciation of national currencies. These flows add to the volatility of a balance of payments.

See also: **capital flight**.

household behaviour (010)
The behaviour of members of a household, individually or collectively, in product and factor markets. An examination of their motivations and aims explains consumer behaviour, as well as **labour supply** and the supply of savings. A comprehensive analysis of such behaviour includes an examination of personal spending patterns and of all factor markets.

household decision-making (010, 810)
Choices, reflecting individual tastes and influenced by taxation, which determine behaviour in product and factor markets. The major decisions made are the choices between work and leisure and between saving and spending as well as about gifts and the composition of assets. Such analysis is crucial to an understanding of labour force participation and the **consumption function**, as well as being the basis of much of neoclassical theorizing.

See also: **labour force participation rate; neoclassical economics**.

human capital (850, 910)
The education and training embodied in a human person which gives rise to increased income in the future. Human capital measures should include an estimate of formal and informal training, as well as income forgone during the period of training: in practice, the measurement of human capital is often restricted to measuring the cost of formal training only. Human capital can be 'general', i.e. useful in many occupations such as reading and writing, or 'specific', i.e. useful only to employment in a particular firm or job, such as a knowledge of the internal accounting procedures of a **transnational corporation**. Although estimates of human capital were attempted by Sir William **Petty**, for example, and the concept was clearly explained by Adam **Smith**, it was not until the 1960s, through Gary **Becker** and Theodore **Schultz**, that the concept was extensively applied in economics.

Critics of this approach have argued that

calculations of the rate of return to human capital investments ignore social returns and that it is difficult to separate human capital investment from personal consumption; in a sense, all personal expenditure has a possible effect on future earnings, including expenditure on health, clothing and socializing. However, there have been useful applications of the theory to the study of **job search** in labour markets, **wage** differentials and **migration**.

Becker, G.S. (1964) *Human Capital: A Theoretical and Empirical Analysis, with Special Reference to Education*, New York: Columbia University Press.
—— (1981) *A Treatise on the Family*, New Haven, CT: Harvard University Press.
Blaug, M. (1975) 'The empirical status of human capital theory', *Journal of Economic Literature* 14: 827–55.
Mincer, J. (1974) *Schooling, Experience and Earnings*, New York: National Bureau of Economic Research.
Psacharopoulos, G. (1981) 'Returns to education: an updated international comparison', *Comparative Education* 17: 321–41.

human scale economics (030)

An economic philosophy based on need and not money. As there is a concentration on simple food and housing needs, it is possible to use **barter** as the means of exchange.

Hume, David, 1711–76 (030)

Scottish philosopher, historian and economist who, within the scope of only nine essays of his *Political Discourses* (first published 1752), provided an important rejection of **mercantilist** ideas, heralding the new dawn in economics of which Adam **Smith** was to be principal luminary. His account of the price **specie-flow mechanism** refuted much of previous **mercantilist** thought; his praise of manufacturing exposed the narrowness of **Physiocracy**; his discussion of taxation showed an early awareness of incidence problems. Although his *History of England* was immensely successful in his day, his philosophical and economic ideas now command more attention.

Rotwein, E. (ed.) (1955) *David Hume: Writings on Economics*, London: Nelson.

See also: **David Hume Institute**.

Humphrey–Hawkins Act 1978 (310, 320)

US federal statute, formally known as the Full Employment and Balanced Growth Act, which extended the **Employment Act** 1946 by emphasizing economic priorities as the basis of the economic goals set for the US President. It also established procedures to improve the coordination between the President, Congress and the Federal Reserve System with the hope of improving the formulation of economic policy.

Hunt Commission (310)

The body which investigated the US securities industry recommending more freedom for financial firms to respond to new technology and the emergence of new types of financial firms.

Report of the President's Commission on Financial Structure and Regulation, Washington, DC: US Government Printing Office, 1971.

See also: **Mayday**.

hurdle rate of return (520)

The minimum rate of return to an investment project which justifies its being undertaken.

hybrid auction (310)

A method of selling government bonds used in Japan. Most of an issue is allocated conventionally through a syndicate but the remainder is auctioned. Bidders make a quantity bid, rather than a price bid, committing themselves to taking a certain amount of an issue. The price will be fixed by the subsequent price negotiated by the syndicate.

See also: **auction**.

hybrid income tax (320)

A combination of a comprehensive income tax and an expenditure tax. It is 'hybrid' because it departs from the comprehensive nature of an income tax. It was gradually introduced in Japan to encourage savings, e.g. in the form of tax-exempt savings and flat rate capital gains tax.

See also: **double taxation of savings**.

hyperinflation (150)

An inflation rate of more than 50 per cent on

a monthly basis. In extreme cases, prices can double in one day. The best known examples have been Germany in 1923, Hungary in 1946 and some Latin American countries in the 1980s. Germany's inflation rose from a mark valued in the summer of 1914 at 4.2 to the US dollar to 4,200,000,000,000 on 15 November 1923. This type of inflation forces people to abandon the use of money in favour of **barter** and **indexation**. **Saving** is discouraged and fixed income groups with little bargaining power, including the **rentier** class, suffer a massive fall in income. Governments, finding it difficult to collect taxes, often resort to increasing the money supply as a source of income in such circumstances.

Siklos, P.K. (1990) *War Finance, Hyperinflation and Stabilization in Hungary, 1938–48*, London and New York: Macmillan and St Martin's Press.

hypothecation (320)
1 Pledging a security without delivering it.
2 Relating a particular tax revenue to a particular public expenditure.

See also: **dedicated budget**; **earmarking**; **mortgage**; **ringfencing**.

hysteresis (810)
The hypothesis, applied to the study of **unemployment**, which states that a level of unemployment does not have a tendency to return to an equilibrium rate and certainly not the **natural rate of unemployment**. (Originally a term used by James Ewing in the 1880s to describe the properties of ferric metals.) In the UK, hysteresis has been used as an explanation of persisting unemployment throughout the 1980s. It has been noted that, when an economy expands, the increased demand leads to higher wages for workers at present employed rather than to employment for the jobless. Also, a long duration of unemployment de-skills workers, making it less likely that they will be re-employed.

Cross, R. (1988) *Unemployment, Hysteresis and the Natural Rate Hypothesis*, Oxford: Basil Blackwell.

I

i (010)
Rate of interest.

I (010)
Net investment.

IATA (630)
See: **International Air Travel Association**.

IBEC (430)
See: **International Bank for Economic Cooperation**.

IBELs (310)
See: **interest-bearing eligible liabilities**.

IBF (310, 430)
International Banking Facility.

IBRD (310)
See: **International Bank for Reconstruction and Development**.

ICC (010, 610)
See: **income–consumption curve**; **Interstate Commerce Commission**.

ICCH (430)
International Commodities Clearing House.

ICFC (310)
Industrial and Commercial Finance Corporation.

ICOR (110)
See: **incremental capital–output ratio**.

ICU (430)
See: **International Clearing Union**.

IDA (430)
See: **International Development Association**.

IDB (310)
See: **Inter-American Development Bank**; **inter-dealer broker**.

ideal limit (930)
The maximum distance a consumer will travel to purchase goods.

See also: **central place theory**.

identification problem (210)
The **econometric** problem of discovering from data which equation is being estimated. A major example of this is the problem of separating demand from supply curves when attempting to construct a demand curve from raw data. If, over a period of time, there are shifts in a demand curve, different observations A, B, C and D will be on different demand curves X_1X_1–X_4X_4 and so a supply curve (line YY) rather than a demand curve has been identified. As this problem arises because the *ceteris paribus* conditions do not hold, only by collecting data on such background variables is it possible to identify a demand curve.

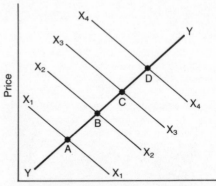

Quantity demanded and supplied

IEA (010, 720)
See: **Institute of Economic Affairs**; **International Energy Agency**.

IET (320)
See: **interest equalization tax**.

IFC (310)
See: **International Finance Corporation**.

IFS (320)
See: **Institute of Fiscal Studies**.

IIB (430)
See: **International Investment Bank**.

IIF (430)
See: **Institute for International Finance**.

illth (010)
Goods and services which give negative satisfaction; the opposite of wealth. Many goods can be regarded as both wealth and illth, e.g. tobacco. A term coined by John Ruskin in the nineteenth century.

Ruskin, J. (1985) *Unto this Last*, essay 4, London: Penguin; New York: Viking Penguin.

See also: **bad**; **wealth**.

ILO (830)
See: **International Labour Office**.

IMF (430)
See: **International Monetary Fund**.

IMM (310)
See: **International Monetary Market**.

immigration (840)
The permanent settling of persons from other countries. Immigrants take up a new residence to escape the poverty or persecution of their original countries, to increase their personal and **economic welfare** in a new country or to join relatives who have already migrated. The effects of immigration on a country include, at the macro-level, impacts on inflation, technical progress and public expenditure and, at the micro-level, a change in the pattern of demand for goods and services and extra labour supply to particular labour markets. Immigrants are absorbed into an economy in different ways: as **entrepreneurs**, as members of the **secondary labour market** or into enclaves.

Piore, M.J. (1979) *Birds of Passage: Migrant Labor and Industrial Societies*, New York: Cambridge University Press.

See also: **enclave economy**; **migration**.

immiseration (910)
The increasing poverty of the working class under **capitalism**. **Marx** did not equate this simply with a fall in real wages as immiseration has also psychological and spiritual dimensions.

Plamenatz, J. (1975) *Karl Marx's Philosophy of Man*, Oxford: Clarendon Press.

See also: **alienation**; **division of labour**.

immiserizing growth (110)
A decline in the **economic welfare** of a country, despite an expansion of its production and exports, brought about by a deterioration in its **terms of trade**.

Bhagwati, J.N. (1958) 'Immiserizing growth: a geometrical note', *Review of Economic Studies* 25: 201–5.
Johnson, H.G. (1967) 'The possibility of income losses from increased efficiency or factor accumulation in the presence of tariffs', *Economic Journal* 77: 151–4.

IMO (830)
See: **International Miners' Organization**.

impact multiplier (020, 210)
The impact on a national economy in a given year of the exogenous variables for that year and the endogenous variables for prior years.

Goldberger, A.S. (1959) *Impact Multipliers and the Dynamic Properties of the Klein-Goldberger Model*, Amsterdam: North-Holland.

imperfect competition (610)
A market, similar to **monopolistic competition**, first identified by Joan **Robinson**. The term is also used in the broad sense to refer to all markets without all the characteristics of **perfect competition**.

Robinson, J. (1933) *The Economics of Imperfect Competition*, London: Macmillan.

imperialism (070)
See: **capitalist imperialism**.

implementation lag (310, 320)
The time it takes to institute a discretionary change in policy. These lags are usually shorter for **monetary policy** than for **fiscal policy** as in the former case a sudden announcement of a change in interest rates can be made whereas fiscal changes often need legislation.

See also: **recognition lag**.

implicit contract theory (020, 830)

A labour market theory which asserts that labour contracts can be successfully based on expectations, e.g. of promotion or stable employment, instead of on legally binding terms. The theory recognizes that in many employment relationships there is a deficiency of information. Typically, an employment contract is incomplete because it omits reference to work effort and so an employer has to monitor the contract to achieve the exchange of a 'fair day's pay' for a 'fair day's work'. However, it has been argued that some contracts are more explicit than originally thought, as evidenced by union resistance to unfavourable revisions of them. Nordhaus applied the theory to unemployment: implicit contracting, he asserts, explains short-term, but not persistent, unemployment. The theory assumes that wages are sticky and that employees will accept such contracts because of their aversion to risk.

Okun, A.M. (1981) *Prices and Quantities*, Washington, DC: Brookings Institution.
Rosen, S. (1985) 'Implicit contracts: a survey', *Journal of Economic Literature* 23: 1144–75.

implicit cost (520)

A cost of production which is not included in the accounts of a business but nevertheless is incurred. This often happens when firms are owned by sole proprietors who underestimate the cost of their labour.

See also: **explicit cost**.

implicit marginal income (010, 320, 910)

The amount by which a subsidy goes down when income rises. This is usually caused because welfare benefits are stopped when other income reaches a particular level.

See also: **poverty trap**.

implicit price deflator (220)

The ratio of the gross national product at current prices to the gross national product at constant prices x 100. This deflator is produced as a by-product of **national income** accounting.

implied price index (210)

See: **implicit price deflator**.

import (420)

The purchase of a good or a service which has been produced by another country. Exports net of imports are included in calculating a country's **gross domestic product**. An economy at the beginning of an expansionary phase will often increase its imports of raw materials and semi-finished goods. An **open economy** will have a high volume of imports: the smaller or more specialized an economy is, the more it will have to import to satisfy consumers' demand for a wide range of goods and services.

See also: **export; inter-industry trade; intra-industry trade; marginal propensity to import**.

import penetration ratio (420)

The ratio of imports to domestic consumption for a class of goods of a particular country. This measure reflects non-tariff trade restrictions at a particular time but does not separate these effects from other reasons for importation (e.g. a lack of domestic product substitutes) and is not adjusted for overvaluation or undervaluation of a currency.

import substitution (130, 420)

A development policy which encourages domestic production. This is achieved in various ways including the imposition of **tariffs** to keep out foreign-produced goods and the reduction in the prices of home-produced goods through subsidization or a change in their quality.

See also: **infant industry**.

impossibility theorem (020)

Arrow's assertion that under democracy majority choice produces a stalemate, as an unambiguous social choice cannot be achieved if there are more than two options facing voters. Assume individuals A, B and C and options x, y and z. A prefers x to y and y to z; B prefers y to z and z to x; C prefers z to x and x to y. Each option is thus ranked first by one of the three individuals, second by another. Since there is no overall favourite, there is a stalemate.

Arrow, K.J. (1966) *Social Choice and Individual Values*, 2nd edn, New York: Wiley.

impure public good (320)
See: **mixed good**.

imputed income (010, 320)
The benefit received from a service which is not measured in a monetary transaction. Some forms of such incomes are estimated to obtain a fuller measure of the **gross national product**: this happens in US national income accounting because the food grown and consumed by farmers is included. Also, to raise more revenue from an income tax the imputed income from owner-occupied houses can be added to income actually received by taxpayers.

IMRO (310)
Investment Managers Regulatory Organization (London).

See also: **self-regulatory organization**.

in-bond manufacturing (420, 630)
The manufacturing of duty-free imported raw materials which are processed and assembled for re-export. In some cases, the **value-added tax** of the country ultimately purchasing them is levied. This arrangement between Mexico and the USA has flourished since the 1960s.

incentive compatible (010)
A state of affairs under which an individual has no incentive to change, e.g. under **perfect competition** when a buyer or seller accepts market determination of prices and cannot benefit by attempting to influence them.

incentive contract (320, 520)
A type of contract often made between governmental bodies and private firms which consists of a fixed part (which is a function of the expected cost) and another part (which is proportional to the difference between the expected cost and the actual *ex post* cost). A private contractor has the greatest incentive to keep costs down if he expects to lose most of the difference between the *ex ante* and *ex post* costs.

See also: *ex ante*, *ex post*.

incentive effect (320)
The effect of a tax on the supply of an activity, especially work. A progressive income tax can have incentive effects if individuals want to achieve a target post-tax income and can only do this by working harder in the face of steep tax progression.

See also: **disincentive effect**; **impact multiplier**; **progressive tax**.

incentive pay scheme (820)
A wage or salary system which relates all or part of employment earnings to the output of a worker. Manual (blue-collar) workers have often had the opportunity to participate in **productivity** schemes, including being paid by the number of 'pieces' produced rather than by the amount of time supplied; sales staff often have a high proportion of their pay in the form of commission; managerial staff in many organizations are given an opportunity to participate in a profit-sharing scheme. Workers are most likely to increase their productivity when a new scheme is introduced – hence the suggestion that incentive schemes should be periodically replaced.

incidence (320)
See: **tax incidence**.

income (010)
The flow of value, expressed in money or in goods and services, accruing to a government, a firm or an individual over a specified time period.

Parker, R.H., Harcourt, G.C. and Whittington, G. (eds) (1986) *Readings in the Concept and Measurement of Income*, 2nd edn, Oxford: Philip Allan.

See also: **Haig–Simons definition of income**; **Hicksian income measure**; **money income**; **psychic income**; **real income**; **stock and flow concepts**; **wealth**.

income and substitution effects (020)
The effects of a price change. The income effect occurs because a fall in price raises real

income (or lowers it if the price rises); the substitution effect encourages more consumption of the good which has become relatively cheaper (the opposite if the price has increased). Thus, in the figure, when the price of good B falls, this consumer moves from combination x to combination y and chooses OQ of B instead of combination OP. An extra **budget line** is inserted to separate the price effect into income and substitution effects and another combination z is discovered. The price effect is the movement x to y (PQ on the horizontal axis); the income effect is the movement from z to y (RQ on the horizontal axis). The substitution effect is the movement from x to z (PR on the horizontal axis).

These effects are analysed in the study of consumer behaviour to determine the effect of a price change on quantity demanded, in the study of **tax incidence** as prices are affected and in the study of **labour supply** to discover the particular **trade-off** between work and leisure chosen by a worker.

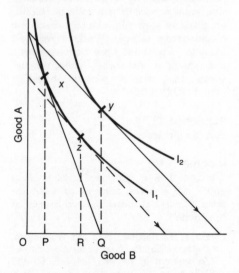

See also: **Slutsky effect**; **Slutsky equation**.

income–consumption curve (010)

A graphical representation of the relationship between changing amounts of consumption of alternative goods as real income changes, using **indifference curves** and **budget lines**. The parallel budget lines show real income increasing as there is movement

away from the origin. The income–consumption curve joins together the points of tangency between indifference curves I_1, I_2, I_3 and I_4 and budget lines representing different income levels. The curve can be used to demonstrate which of two goods is the **inferior good**.

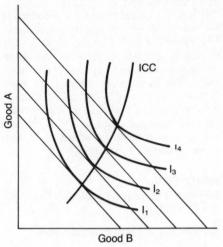

See also: **Engel's law**; **price–consumption curve**.

income differential (160)

The ratio of the average income of one group of persons to another. (Persons can be grouped according to occupation, location, industry or type of income.) The most studied differentials are in the labour market, i.e. occupational, industrial and regional wage differentials; in capitalist societies, differences between employment and investment incomes are also of concern to researchers. In idealistic societies, there is an aversion to large differentials as **egalitarianism** is often a major goal, e.g. **Plato** believed that the richest member of society should not be more than four times better off than the poorest member of society.

See also: **wage differentials**.

income elasticity of demand (010, 210)

The ratio of the percentage increase in demand for a good or service to an increase in income. Thus, if an increase in income of 4 per cent is associated with an increase in demand for food of 2 per cent, the income elasticity will be 0.5. Income elasticities for foodstuffs and agricultural raw materials are often less than 1 with the consequence that the divergence in economic prosperity between primary producing countries and industrialized countries increases in periods of world economic growth. Income elasticities are positive for normal goods and negative for inferior goods. In the figure, A is a luxury good as more of it is demanded at higher incomes, B is a normal good and C is an inferior good as less of it is demanded at higher incomes.

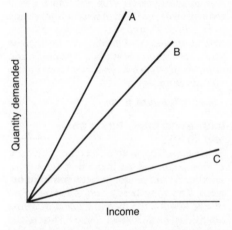

See also: **Engel's law**; **price elasticity of demand**.

income splitting system (320)

A method of taxing the income of married couples. The aggregated income of the couple is halved and then the income tax is levied on each half. The couple pays double the amount on the notional equal incomes. There are several variants of this system.

incomes policy (820)

A macroeconomic policy which directly controls factor incomes. It has been pursued by many Western countries since 1945 as an alternative to **fiscal** and **monetary policies** with the hope that by controlling wage-fixing in the labour market the rate of increase of product prices would be reduced. The most extreme form is a wages freeze, e.g. the UK's in 1966. Milder forms include setting a norm for wage increases in line with

the rise in **productivity**, allowing for exceptional increases (e.g. to help low paid workers, to alleviate a manpower shortage or to preserve comparable pay for different occupational groups), or an exhortation to pay smaller increases (**moral suasion**).

Many countries, including the UK and the USA, have only used incomes policies intermittently, but the Netherlands is exceptional in achieving the implementation of a long-term policy from 1948 to the 1960s. Some incomes policies have included restrictions on increases in company dividends in order to restrain all types of personal incomes: however, this approach has produced distortions in capital markets.

There were many US experiments in incomes policies in the period 1962–71, some of which inspired the form of British incomes policies. In January 1962 the US **Council of Economic Advisers** published *Guideposts for Noninflationary Wage and Price Behavior* in which the trend in productivity was used as the general guidepost for non-inflationary wage settlements. Specific guideposts were abandoned in 1967 but in 1970 a National Commission on Productivity was set up; inflation alerts were published when there were significant wage and price increases. In 1971 there was a ninety-day wage–price freeze: its sequel was the setting up of a tripartite Pay Board and a Price Commission. The effectiveness of this policy has long been debated: it is difficult to establish that the guideposts reduced wage inflation.

The UK has had statutory incomes policies from 1966 to 1970 and from 1972 to 1974, compulsory policies from 1975 to 1977 and voluntary policies from 1948 to 1950, 1961 to 1962 and 1977 to 1979. There was a tendency to impose an incomes policy in a crisis in the most severe form – a wage freeze for up to one year – and then to relax the policy by permitting exceptions to the principle that wage increases should be in line with general productivity increases. An innovation of the 1970s was to choose as a wage norm a flat rate cash increase; this helped the lower paid but reduced wage differentials, opening the door to a flood of subsequent wage claims.

Some observers of incomes policies are more sympathetic towards them. **Rostow**, for example, has noted that in 1984 Japan,

West Germany and Switzerland were able by means of incomes policies to have lower prime interest rates, lower unemployment, lower inflation and large balance of payments surpluses. In sum, to be successful an incomes policy should provide more helpful economic and financial information and education in its use to wage bargainers, as well as an element of real wage increases.

Claudon, M.P. and Cornwall, R.R. *An Incomes Policy for the United States: New Approaches*, Boston, MA: Nijhoff.

Holden, K., Peel, D.A. and Tompson, J.L. (1987) *The Economics of Wage Control* , Basingstoke: Macmillan.

Urquidi, V.L. (ed.) (1989) *Incomes Policies*, Basingstoke: Macmillan.

See also: **collective bargaining**.

income statement (540)
See: **profit and loss account**.

income support (320, 910)
A welfare payment in the form of a cash sum. This alternative to in-kind benefits gives welfare recipients more freedom in their spending.

income tax (320)
A tax levied on taxable income. It is a complex tax because of different rates for different types of income, exemption of some types of income (particularly fringe benefits) and allowances/deductions for various categories of expenditure (e.g. expenses related to employment, charitable covenants). It was first used in England in 1435, 1450 and from 1798 to 1805 to finance the Napoleonic Wars; from 1842, it has been a permanent feature of the UK tax system. In the USA it was used to finance the Civil War from 1861 to 1872 but an attempt to reintroduce it in 1894 failed as it was declared unconstitutional, making necessary the 16th Amendment to the US Constitution in 1913 to authorize the taxation of incomes. The principal theoretical justification advanced for the tax is the **sacrifice theory**.

In all countries, income tax is invariably paid on employment income, dividends, net business income, income from immovable property and the income of farmers and small traders. Sometimes it is paid on some types of fringe benefit, **imputed income** from home ownership, pensions, unemployment benefit and sickness benefits.

See also: **direct and indirect taxation; tax evasion**.

income terms of trade (420)
A measure of the purchasing power of exports in terms of imports. The formula used for calculating it is

$$I = \frac{P_x}{P_m} \times Q_x$$

where Q_x is the volume of exports (I is income, P is price, Q is quantity, x is exports and m is imports). This is a more useful indication of the effect of international trade on a country's national economy than the **net barter terms of trade** because income terms take into account both the prices and volumes of trade but net barter terms ignore volume changes.

See also: **terms of trade**.

increasing opportunity costs law (010)
The **trade-off** between an increasing amount of one good and an increasing amount of another in an economy with **full employment**. The opportunity cost of having more of one good is the increasing cost of losing quantities of the other good. This is the principle underlying a **production possibility frontier**.

increasing returns to scale (010)
An increase in output at a faster rate than factor inputs. From Adam **Smith** onwards, theorists of **economic growth** have been interested in investigating the circumstances in which there can be increasing returns to particular industries or a national economy as a whole. Classical economists asserted that agriculture was subject to diminishing returns and increasing returns were only possible in manufacturing.

Young, A. (1928) 'Increasing returns and economic progress', *Economic Journal* 38: 527–42.

See also: **Kaldor's laws; returns to scale; Verdoorn's law**.

incremental capital–output ratio (110)
The extra amount of capital needed to

produce one more unit of output. In the simplest of accelerator models, the accelerator coefficient is equivalent to the incremental capital–output ratio. Changes in efficiency, rather than in technology, can change the ratio. It is always difficult to measure because of the problems of measuring capital.

See also: **accelerator principle**.

incremental cost (010)
See: **marginal cost**.

indecomposability (010)
The interrelatedness of an economic system such that the product of each industry is used as an **intermediate good** of at least one more industry. If every industry, including itself, uses it as an intermediate product, then there is perfect indecomposability.

See also: **input–output analysis**.

indexation (150, 210)
An adjustment clause in contracts to maintain the real value of the items central to the contract. Clauses of this kind are much used in building contracts, labour contracts (often used in the USA and Israel) and for government bonds (e.g. in France and the UK in the 1980s to attract savers). As indexation accepts and institutionalizes inflation, it has attracted much criticism.

Dornbusch, R., Simonsen, M.H. and Vargas, F.G. (1983) *Inflation, Debt and Indexation*, Cambridge, MA: MIT Press.

See also: **COLA; escalator clause**.

index-linked gilt (310)
A government bond with a link between a price index and the bond's capital value and yield. These gilts, popular in times of inflation, are attractive to unadventurous investors desirous of a low risk portfolio and steady real income. Finland introduced these gilts in 1947, France in the 1950s and the UK in 1975.

index number (210)
A device for measuring changes in an economic variable, especially **national income** or prices over a period of time. The value of the variable in the initial year (the 'base' year) is set equal to 100 and the value for each subsequent year is calculated as a percentage of it. To calculate quantity changes, e.g. in the **gross domestic product**, the components of the gross domestic product are weighted by the prices of each item; to calculate price changes, quantity weights reflecting the relative amounts consumed or produced are used. The best known indices are those of **Laspeyres** and **Paasche**. Before **Jevons** and others constructed index numbers in the 1860s, there was little accurate knowledge of the precise degree of inflation in industrialized economies, and there was often a confusion between the causes and amount of **inflation**.

Allen, R.G.D. (1975) *Index Numbers in Theory and Practice*, London: Macmillan.
Stuvel, G. (1989) *The Index-Number Problem and its Solution*, London: Macmillan.

index-tracking fund (310)
An investment fund which invests in the specific securities which are included in a major **stock market price index**. Although the value of units of the fund rise and fall with the index, the upward trend in these indices gives investors long-term growth.

indicative planning (120)
Central economic planning which is based on influential forecasts which indicate the direction in which an economy is expected to go. Fiscal inducements, rather than governmental direction as in the traditional **Soviet-type economy**, are used to encourage private sector firms to carry out sufficient investment. Although **Robertson**, as early as 1915, was one of the earliest propounders of the view that business fluctuations could be reduced by the joint forecasting of business investment, the major implementation of it has been in France since 1946 under the original Monnet Plan and its many successors. In the UK, the **National Plan** attempted to introduce this type of planning for nine months from 1965 to 1966.

indicators (140, 220)
See: **coincident indicators; economic indicators**.

indicator variable (210)
An economic statistic which describes the current state of an economy and guides a

policy-maker in his/her actions, particularly whether to deflate or reflate the economy.

See also: **coincident indicators**; **economic indicators**.

indifference curve (010)

A curve representing many combinations of two goods, all of which give the consumer the same level of **utility**. As each combination renders the same utility, the consumer is 'indifferent' as to which bundle of goods to choose. The curves further from the origin represent higher levels of utility. Indifference curves must not intersect for otherwise two different levels of utility are represented at the point of intersection (X in the figure). Also there is inconsistency as combination C is preferred to combination A and combination B to combination D.

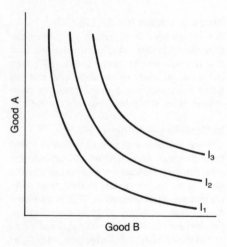

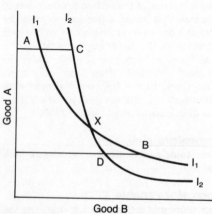

indirect cost (010)

Overhead and other costs not directly attributable to the cost of producing one unit of output; a **fixed cost**.

See: **direct cost**.

indirect tax (320)

See: **direct and indirect taxation**.

individual income tax (320)

US **income tax** introduced in 1913 and now the major source of federal government revenue. It is a progressive tax with a countercyclical impact.

indivisibility (010)

The nature of a **factor of production** or commodity which is only supplied in discrete amounts, not increasing or decreasing in quantity continuously. Energy or liquid raw materials, for example, are divisible but a piece of capital equipment or a skilled employee will be available only in minimum-sized quantities. Indivisibilities are responsible for many fixed costs in the short run and give rise to production **economies of scale** at high levels of output.

induced technical progress (620)

The effect on productivity of changes in relative factor prices.

inducement good (010)

A consumer good which will stimulate producers to make other goods in exchange for it. Such goods are of great importance in developing countries. David **Hume** advanced this argument in support of manufacturing.

inducement mechanism (110, 620)

The means of effecting economic change, especially a shock to an economy which brings about technical progress. **Inventions** and their application to production have been induced by major wars as well as by more minor events such as industrial strikes. Development economists have often referred to this mechanism.

industrial action (830)

1 **Strikes**, go-slows, working-to-rule.

2 Seizing control of a factory, according to the principles of **syndicalism**.

3 The donation of a day's work, in the USSR, to celebrate Lenin's birthday.

Industrial and Commercial Finance Corporation (310, 520)

A British financial organization founded in 1945 jointly by the **Bank of England** and the London and Scottish **clearing banks** to provide long-term capital for small and medium-sized businesses. The Corporation was thought to be necessary because of the so-called '**Macmillan gap**'.

industrial capitalism (040)

The phase of **capitalism** after the Industrial Revolution; the stage of economic development following **merchant capitalism**. The economy was dominated by privately owned industries during this period.

industrial concentration (610)

See: **concentration**.

industrial democracy (510, 830)

Participation by employees in the management and/or ownership of their firms. Varied schemes range from the distribution of shares (popular in Britain in the 1950s and 1980s to prevent re-nationalization), works councils which disseminate management proposals and producer **cooperatives**. Recently, there has been much debate about the form of workers' representation on company boards and the scope for workers' cooperatives. Germany's two-tier company structure since 1950 (the upper tier with 50 per cent worker representatives but the lower with executive directors alone) partially inspired the **Bullock Committee's** recommendations of 1977. The short-lived experiments of British Steel and the Post Office have been the major UK attempts at worker democracy to date. Some of the cooperatives in older UK small-scale industries such as clothing and footwear have had a continuous history in the English Midlands since the 1890s. More ambitious, larger unit cooperatives have flourished at Mondragon, Spain.

Thimm, A. (1980) *The False Promise of Co-determination: The Changing Nature of Europe in Workers' Participation*, Lexington, MA: Lexington Books.
Thomas, H. and Logan, C. (1982) *Mondragon*, London: Unwin Hyman.
Vanek, J. (1970) *The General Theory of Labor Managed Economies*, Ithaca, NY: Cornell University Press.
Witte, J.F. (1980) *Democracy, Authority and Alienation in Work. Workers' Participation in an American Corporation*, Chicago, IL: University of Chicago Press.

See also: **workers' participation**.

industrial dispute (830)

1 A breakdown in labour–management relations usually resulting in the partial or total withdrawal of labour on the instructions of a **trade union**.

2 Strike.

industrialization (110)

A stage in **development** which consists of shifting resources from agriculture into manufacturing. It is variously measured by manufacturing's percentage share of **gross domestic product**, gross industrial output per capita, energy consumption per capita or industrial exports as a percentage of total exports. To finance industrialization, extra real resources are necessary; these can be found by obtaining foreign exchange through increasing agricultural and manufactured exports or by increasing the domestic rate of savings. Although this is still an issue in Third World countries, the countries of the **Organization for Economic Cooperation and Development** are more concerned with **de-industrialization** and the switch of resources into the service sector.

industrial muscle (830)

The ability of a group of workers to press a demand for increased wages or improved working conditions because they are in an industry producing essential goods or services. Workers in energy and transport industries have usually been more powerful in **collective bargaining** because the withdrawal of their labour creates a crisis in a national economy.

See also: **strike**.

industrial organization (610)

Also known as industrial economics, this applied branch of microeconomics was to some extent founded to provide theoretical support for the analysis of **antitrust** but now includes the examination of all the functions of management. A major aspect of the subject is the study of market structures and an examination of the implications of those structures for pricing, investment and company performance. In a sense, this subject was started by **Marshall** in his *Economics of Industry* and *Principles of Economics* (Book IV).

Mason, E.S. (1957) *Economic Concentration and the Monopoly Problem*, Cambridge, MA: Harvard University Press.

Stigler, G.J. (1968) *The Organization of Industry*, Homewood, IL: Richard D. Irwin.

See also: **structure–conduct–performance model**; **theory of the firm**.

industrial policy (610)

Measures which attempt to speed the process of resource allocation among or within industrial sectors with the aim of correcting market distortions. Much of industrial policy is concerned to prevent a complete international specialization of labour and is often **protectionist** in character, unless the policy is part of an international agreement. As an alternative to chauvinistic industrial policies, it has been suggested that the **Organization for Economic Cooperation and Development** might produce an overall industrial policy for a number of countries: the specific national industry marked out for expansion would then be able to develop with the help, and not the competition, of other advanced countries. The **mercantilists** were among the first to advocate industrial policies.

In Japan, industrial policy attempts to anticipate and accelerate response to market signals. Subsidization of research and development and guidance is offered to growth sectors. The **Ministry of International Trade and Industry** offers differential help to sectors and firms, including tax incentives, export–import measures and technology subsidies. In France, industrial policy measures are part of the national and sectoral plans. France's largest bank, the Caisse des Dépôts et des Désignations, finances the largest industrial projects. In Germany, the three major banks, themselves with substantial industrial investments, collaborate with the **Bundesbank** in implementing industrial policy. The German Ministry of Economy supports research and development and training. The industrial policies of the **newly industrialized countries** include attempts to save expenditure on imports and the pursuit of regional and industrial balance. In USA industrial policy is conducted at the level of states: popular policies have been the encouragement of 'silicon valleys' and other concentrations of high technology industries. The establishment of the **European Community**'s **single market** threatens the existence of West European national industrial policies.

Adams, R.G. and Klein, L.R. (eds) (1983) *Industrial Policies for Growth and Competitiveness*, Lexington, MA: D.C. Heath.

Behrman, J.N. (1984) *Industrial Policies: International Restructuring and Transnationals*, Lexington, MA: D.C. Heath.

industrial relations (830)

1 A study of the rules governing the relationships between employers and **trade (labor) unions** at national, industry or firm level.

2 An examination of the procedures for fixing wages, cooperating in production and deciding workplace discipline.

Industrial relations systems are examined with respect to the 'actors' participating in the system, i.e. employers, unions and governments, to the levels at which relations take place, i.e. national, industrial or company, and to the legislative framework within which the actors are allowed to perform. These systems are usually classified according to the degree of their centralization and the extent to which they are cooperative (as when there is **worker's participation** in management) or adversarial (in the sense that employers and unions oppose each other until a compromise settlement can be reached).

Clegg, H.A. (1976) *The System of Industrial Relations in Great Britain*, 3rd edn, Oxford: Basil Blackwell.

See also: **industrial democracy**; **strike**.

Industrial Reorganization Corporation (610)

The British state-financed financial institution in existence from 1967 to 1971 which attempted to restructure British industry. It provided finance to bring about desirable **mergers** between **firms** so as to make them more internationally competitive, British Leyland being one of its more famous cases. Also, it invested directly in several high technology firms. The subsequent Conservative government abolished it because of its belief that government-financed bodies should not be engaged in risky investment activities.

Hague, D.C. and Wilkinson, G.C.G. (1983) *The IRC – An Experiment in Industrial Intervention: a History of the Industrial Reorganization Corporation*, London: Allen & Unwin.

See also: **National Enterprise Board**.

industrial revolution (040, 620)

A discontinuity in the growth of an economy, taking the form of a rapid rate of technical progress which leads to a sustained increase in per capita real incomes, usually accompanied by a change in the occupational structure as there is a change from handicraft to factory production, and urbanization of the population. **Rostow** mentions four industrial revolutions. The first industrial revolution was in the 1780s associated with the textile industry, the second the railway boom of the 1830s and 1840s, the third based on steel, machine tools and motor vehicles which came to an end in the 1970s and the fourth, which is now taking place, based on electronics and biology. A disruptive feature of the fourth is the use of robots to replace workers in manufacturing, creating unpredictable and undesired employment effects.

Deane, P. (1979) *The First Industrial Revolution*, 2nd edn, Cambridge: Cambridge University Press.

See also: **take-off**.

industrial share (310)

An **equity** in an industrial company/corporation.

industrial society (610)

A term developed by **Marxists** in Europe and the USA in the 1950s to describe a society with large-scale industrial production. A capitalist or a non-capitalist society can take this form. The advent of **Keynesianism** and improved techniques of industrial management, it was hoped, would produce a stability in society, particularly in the relationship between capital and labour.

Kerr, C. (1962) *Industrialism and Industrial Man: The Problems of Labor and Management*, London: Heinemann.

industrial training grant (810)

A payment made by central government or by a fund financed by the firms of an industry to pay for vocational training. Without such grants it would be difficult for many small firms to finance adequate training and there would be a tendency for firms undertaking little training to attempt to acquire trained workers by paying above-market wage rates. In a period of great technological change, industrial training has become central to the survival and successful future of many firms.

See also: **general training**.

industrial union (830)

A **trade (labor) union** which is the sole organizer of labour in a particular industry. Germany has sixteen industrial unions to organize its labour force. Many have suggested a similar structure for British unions (who had recommended industrial unionism to the Federal Republic of West Germany) but have stumbled on the major obstacle to such change – the dismemberment of powerful **general unions**.

See also: **craft union; enterprise union**.

industry (010, 610)

A group of **firms** producing the same principal product. In a broad classification of industries, all industrial activity of an economy can be divided into only ten or a hundred industries but narrower classifications make possible a division into as many as a 1,000 or more. Types of industry are contrasted as **heavy** or **light**, mature or high tech, smokestack or **sunrise**.

See also: **Standard Industrial Classification; two-digit industry; three-digit industry**.

inelasticity (010)

The unresponsiveness of one economic variable to another; demand or supply elasticity less than unity in value. In product markets, demand is inelastic for essential goods and services, including goods that produce addiction. In labour markets, the short-term supply of labour is usually inelastic for most occupations as training takes time.

See also: **elasticity**.

inequality (010, 160)

The character of a particular **income** or **wealth** distribution such that there are different rather than equal shares for members of a population. In developed countries, inequality arises from **wage differentials**, the regional distribution of economic activity and accumulations of income-earning assets. Inequality is more severe in less developed countries because **unemployment** is much greater, unemployment benefits are rare and much labour is more immobile.

The effects of inequality have long been debated. Some argue that it leads to inefficiency as many in a population, seeing little chance of economic advancement, are unwilling to sacrifice present consumption to make possible economic development and are likely to underinvest in their children's education; others point to the devastating effects on productivity and economic growth of the lack of incentives in an **egalitarian** society.

Atkinson, A.B. (1982) *The Economics of Inequality*, 2nd edn, Oxford: Clarendon Press.
Townsend, P. (1979) *Poverty in the United Kingdom*, Harmondsworth: Penguin.

See also: **Gini coefficient; Lorenz curve**.

inertial effect (320, 820)

A government's passive acceptance of an economic condition inherited from a previous government, e.g. acceptance of wage increases previously negotiated.

inertial inflation (150)

The expected rate of **inflation** which is built into an economy. This rate is based on historical experience and assumed in contracts.

infant industry (610)

A new industry with a low output and high average cost. As it is usually uncompetitive relative to producers in other countries, it often attracts assistance under an **industrial policy** or through **protection**.

See also: **tariff**.

infant industry argument (420)

The case for tariff **protection** for a new **industry** with high unit costs (often because its labour force is untrained, its fixed capital is expensive or it lacks production experience) to enable it to increase its output and reduce its unit costs until it is internationally competitive. This has often been regarded as the most justifiable of reasons for a tariff as the social benefits of setting up a new industry outweigh the private cost of being denied lower priced imports. However, experience has shown that many of these 'infants' have not reached adulthood.

Baldwin, R.E. (1969) 'The case against infant-industry tariff protection', *Journal of Political Economy* 77: 295–305.

inferior good (010)

1   A good which is demanded less as consumers' incomes rise.

2   A good with a negative **income elasticity of demand**. Some foodstuffs, e.g. potatoes, rice and margarine, are in this category. An inferior good can be distinguished from a **normal good** in an income–demand curve.

See also: **Giffen paradox; income elasticity of demand**.

infession (150)

World inflation caused by a breakdown in the world monetary system which leads to world recession. This concept was introduced to provide a better explanation of the **stagflation** of the 1970s.

inflation (150)

A general sustained rise in the price level which reduces the purchasing power of that country's currency. It has been ascribed to increases in the money supply, excess demand, rises in public expenditure (particularly in times of war), the behaviour of the labour market and changes in costs – in the case of the 1970s, oil price increases.

Brown, A.J. (1985) *World Inflation since 1950*, Cambridge: Cambridge University Press.
Fleming, J.S. (1976) *Inflation*, Oxford: Oxford University Press.

See also: **core inflation rate; cost-push inflation; hyperinflation; inertial inflation; inflation accounting; menu-costs of inflation; pure inflation; shock inflation;**

shoe leather costs of inflation; **structural inflation**; **wage-push inflation**.

inflation accounting (540)

Accounts which measure costs, revenue, profit and loss at constant prices. Major professional bodies of accountants have produced conventions to deal with the effects of inflation so that a true and accurate description of the financial state of an enterprise is achieved. The current cost approach is used in the UK, Australia, Canada and New Zealand. In the USA, the **Securities and Exchange Commission** requires large corporations to use the replacement cost approach, stating both specific price changes and movements in the general price index.

Tweedie, D.P. and Whittington, G. (1984) *The Debate on Inflation Accounting*, Cambridge: Cambridge University Press.

See also: **current cost accounting**; **Sandilands Report**.

inflation-adjusted deficit (320)

That part of a government's fiscal deficit which has been deflated by a price index.

inflationary gap (010)

The excess of **aggregate demand** over **aggregate supply**. This difference is the cause of **demand-pull inflation** and is usually illustrated as in the figure.

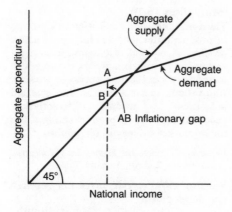

inflation illusion (150)

See also: **money illusion**.

inflationist (150)

A person who advocates inflation as a means of stimulating an economy. This is recommended on the grounds that gross profit margins increase in a period of inflation, making possible increased net investment and employment.

inflation tax (150, 320)

A tax which fines employers and/or workers who permit wages to rise above a rate of growth of wages desired by a government. Its aim is to make labour more competitive through bringing about a reduction in unemployment. More generally, it has been regarded as a reduction in the resources of households and firms because a government has sanctioned an increase in the money supply and caused inflation.

See also: **forced saving**; **marginal employment subsidy**; **seignorage**; **tax-based incomes policy**.

informal economy (070)

Part of an **economy** consisting of unrecorded and often illegal economic activities. In developing economies the informal sector is the subsistence agricultural sector, in developed economies subcontracting activities such as tailoring. The dynamic of this sector, springing from the avoidance of governmental regulation, produces well-known consequences – long hours, a disregard for safety, do-it-yourself activities and **barter**. Also known as the unofficial economy.

Alessandrini, S. and Dallago, B. (eds) (1987) *The Unofficial Economy: Consequences and Perspectives in Different Economic Systems*, Aldershot: Gower.

Thomas, J.J. (1989) *Informal Economic Activity*, Hemel Hempstead: Philip Allan; Cambridge, MA: MIT Press.

See also: **black economy**; **time budget survey**.

information agreement (610)

A **restrictive practice** consisting of the circulation of prices and/or costs to members of a business association with a view to encouraging them to restrict competition by setting similar product prices. In the UK such agreements, some of which have existed throughout the twentieth century, have been within the scope of restrictive trade practices legislation since 1968.

See also: **competition policy**.

information cost (010, 510)

The cost to an organization of obtaining knowledge of the environment in which it operates.

information technology (620)

Methods of generating, processing and communicating information, especially using computer hardware and software. **Expert systems**, data networks and electronic mail have revolutionized many functions of management and made possible the globalization of financial markets. In modern economies it has become central to the working of most firms and could be responsible for the beginning of a new **long wave**.

Zorkoczy, P. (1982) *Information Technology. An Introduction*, London and Marshfield, MA: Pitman.

information theory (210)

The principles underlying the criteria used to select summary statistics which describe empirical distributions. Information is used to revise previous probabilities.

Kullback, S. (1959) *Information Theory and Statistics*, New York: Wiley.

infrastructure (730)

The basic services or **social capital** of a country, or part of it, which make economic and social activities possible by providing transportation, public health and education services and buildings in which community activities can take place. Railways, airports, hospitals, schools, roads, sewerage systems and reservoirs constitute the major types of social capital. Although in the nineteenth century many of these were financed privately (e.g. the railways), after 1945 in many countries most infrastructure investment has been the responsibility of the public sector. Countries with the poorest infrastructures are either those with low per capita incomes, i.e. the less developed countries, or those with governments practising *laissez-faire* policies which seek to minimize the role of the state.

inheritance tax (160, 320)

A tax on **wealth** transferred after the decease of an individual. This tax aims to raise revenue and bring about an intergenerational shift in wealth distribution. Inheritance taxes have long had their advocates, e.g. John Stuart **Mill**, as a major method of reducing **inequality** in society.

in-home banking (310)

See: **home banking**.

injection (010)

A stimulus to **aggregate demand**, e.g. net investment or exports, which raises the level of the **national income** by causing a **multiplier** expansion of incomes. Injections are exogenous in character.

See also: **exogenous variable**; **leakage**; **withdrawal**.

in-kind transfer (320)

Provision of a good or service by a government, often freely or at less than market prices, to low income individuals and families. The aim of these 'gifts' is to increase the welfare of persons with low incomes and few resources to obtain food, housing and medical care. The transfers can take various forms including food stamps, housing vouchers and free access to medical services or subsidized medical insurance.

See also: **transfer income**.

innovation (620)

The application of an **invention** to a process of production or the introduction of a new product. A method of measuring an innovation is by estimating the extent to which an industry uses the new process or product. Innovations occur more in concentrated industries as **product differentiation**, necessitating frequent product changes, is a major market strategy of **oligopolies**.

Freeman, C. (1982) *The Economics of Industrial Innovation*, 2nd edn, London: Pinter.

See also: **diffusion rate**; **invention**; **research and development**.

innovation possibility frontier (620)

A line showing the trade-off between *labour-augmenting* and *capital-augmenting* technical progress. It is assumed that firms seek to maximize the instantaneous rate of unit cost reduction.

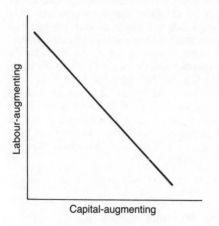

Capital-augmenting

input-output analysis (210)

A tabular summary of the flows of goods and services between industries and the final demand of an economy with the output of each sector being the inputs of other sectors

(see typical table below). The technology of the economy determines the ratios (or coefficients) of each input to the output it helps to produce, in the case of inter-industry trade; institutional factors, including custom, will determine the input–output ratios for the household sector. The static version of input–output analysis can be solved by ordinary linear equations; the dynamic version (which includes, as well as flows, stocks of goods and fixed capital) uses linear difference equations for its solution. The pioneer of the technique, **Leontief**, first produced an input–output table for the US economy in 1936, although **Quesnay** produced a flow table for the French economy in 1758.

In its static form, this analysis shows how much the n industries of an economy have to produce to satisfy the total demand for each particular product. It is assumed that in each industry there are constant returns to scale, a fixed input–output ratio and a homogeneous product. The model is 'open' if there are both n industries and a sector, e.g. households, which exogenously determines final demand; it is closed if the model shows relationships only between the n industries.

| | | | | Purchases | | | | | | | |
Sales	Ind. 1	Ind. 2	Ind. 3	etc.	A	B	C	D	E	F
Industry 1										
Industry 2										
Industry 3										
etc.										
Imports										
Total goods and services										

A total intermediate output of industries
B final buyers – current expenditure
C final buyers – gross domestic capital formation
D final buyers – exports
E total final output B + C + D
F total output A + E

Simultaneous equations are used to determine the inputs required for final demand to be satisfied. Dynamic versions of input–output analysis can take into account time lags in production, the adjustment of output to excess demand and the accumulation of inventories and fixed capital.

Leontief, W.W. (1951) *The Structure of the American Economy*, 2nd edn, New York: Oxford University Press.
—— (1986) *Input–Output Economics*, 2nd edn, New York: Oxford University Press.

INSEE (220)

Institut National de la Statistique et des Etudes Economiques. The French governmental body which collects and assembles French economic statistics.

inside lag (010, 310, 320)

A time lag which occurs either because it takes time to recognize the state of an **economy** or because it takes time to take action to remedy an undesired state of affairs. A lag of this kind is either a **recognition lag** or an **implementation lag**. Such lags can be reduced by **automatic stabilizers** which, by their nature, operate without any decision-making response to a change in an economy.

See also: **outside lag**.

inside money (310)

A type of **money** which arises from private sector debt. The principal example of this in modern economies is the commercial bank deposit which is matched by a loan to another person in the private sector.

Gurley, J.G. and Shaw, E.S. (1960) *Money in a Theory of Finance*, Washington, DC: Brookings Institution.
Johnson, H.G. (1969) 'Inside money, outside money, income, wealth and welfare in contemporary monetary theory', *Journal of Money, Credit and Banking* 1 (February): 30–45.

See also: **outside money**.

insider trading (310)

Stock market trading based on financial information gained improperly from inside a firm. A typical situation is that of an employee of the mergers and acquisitions department of a **merchant/investment bank** trading in the stock of the company involved by using the veil of a **nominee account** or even a company set up for such transactions in a country noted for its secrecy, e.g. Liechtenstein. A large stockholding is built up by carefully timed transactions of a magnitude not to attract attention and then sold well before a bid is announced. Insider trading is investigated in the USA by the **Securities and Exchange Commission** and in the UK by the Department of Trade and Industry, with a view to the prosecution of offenders. In the UK, it was made an offence subject to criminal proceedings under the Companies Act 1980 and subsequently under the Company Securities (Insider Dealing) Act 1985.

Rider, B.A.K. (1983) *Insider Trading*, Bristol: Jordan.

insider wage setting (820)

Wage determination within a firm which results in increased productivity being passed on as increased wages for the existing labour force. If the 'insiders' were concerned with the labour force as a whole they would be willing to accept a lower rate of pay which their employers would be able to offer also to persons outside the firm, thereby expanding employment.

Lindbeck, A. and Snower, D.J. (1989) *The Insider-Outsider Theory of Employment and Unemployment*, Cambridge, MA, and London: MIT Press.
Solow, R.M. (1985) 'Insiders and outsiders in wage determination', *Scandinavian Journal of Economics* 87: 411–28.

See also: **outsider wage setting**.

insolvency (520)

The condition of a legal person with liabilities in excess of assets. This inability to meet the demands of creditors usually leads to **bankruptcy**.

instant monetarism (030, 310)

The school of thought, usually identified as **New Classical**, which believes that wage and price adjustment are almost instantaneous as the wages and prices set are expected to be at the equilibrium level.

See also: **gradualist monetarism**.

Institute for International Economics (420)
Founded in 1981 and based at Washington, DC. It studies international economics in the widest sense to include trade policies, exchange rates, Japan's role in the world and the Third World debt.

Institute for International Finance (430)
Founded in 1984 and based in Washington. **Commercial banks** set it up to collect information on developing countries and their debts. Although the Institute's main role is still data collection, it has coordinated debt rescheduling.

Institute of Economic Affairs (010)
An independent educational trust founded in 1957 and situated in London. Academic economists, as well as major politicians, have produced hundreds of pamphlets, and some books, on policy issues, especially in its Hobart Papers series. It has consistently advocated the application of market principles to the major economic problems of the day. It was founded by Anthony Fisher and Ralph Harris; Arthur Seldon was its most famous director.

See also: **Adam Smith Institute**; **David Hume Institute**.

Institute of Fiscal Studies (320)
An independent, privately financed London-based institute founded in 1971 which prepares regular assessments of British fiscal policy and also undertakes many detailed studies of particular aspects of public finance.

institution (070)
See: **economic institution**.

institutional economics (030)
A succession of US economists, beginning with **Veblen**, who have used a variety of social science disciplines to analyse the structure of economies, the process of economic change and the nature of economic decision-making. Prominent contributors to this approach include John **Commons** and **Ayres**. **Galbraith** is the last major figure of the school.

Samuels, W.J. (1988) *Institutional Economics*, 3 vols, Aldershot: Edward Elgar.

institutional investor (310)
A pension fund, insurance company, bank or other institution with a large portfolio of securities. After 1950, these investors diversified their portfolios by increasingly purchasing **equities**.

instrument variable (210)
An economic variable which can be directly controlled by a governmental authority responsible for an economic policy. These variables include bank reserve ratios and short-term interest rates.

Tinbergen, J. (1970) *On the Theory of Economic Policy*, Amsterdam: North-Holland.

See also: **goal variable**; **target variable**.

insurance (010)
A method of sharing **risks**. Originally it was chiefly concerned with insuring shipping, the riskiest of business ventures in earlier centuries, but the principle was extended to cover all types of risk, including damage to property, personal injury and death. The fairest type of insurance is where the cost to the insured of premiums and the cost to insurers of administration does not exceed the total payout on risks which have occurred. However, the monopoly power of many insurers permits them to make excessive profits. The government insures some risks in the public sector and should, it is argued, underwrite personal injury compensation in the private sector. Insurance against risk is not universal. Its absence can be explained on the grounds of **moral hazard** as insurance induces recklessness and of **adverse selection** as only the worst risks apply for insurance.

Borch, K. (1988) *Economics of Insurance*, Amsterdam: North-Holland.

insurance market (310)
A market which arranges the sharing of a large **risk** amongst many individuals. The best example is **Lloyd's** of London, noted for marine and aviation insurance but prepared to consider any risks except standard life cover.

Insurance Ombudsman Bureau (630)

A regulatory body for the British insurance industry which covers the insurance groups and companies which have volunteered to come under its jurisdiction.

See also: **self-regulatory organization**.

intangible wealth (010, 540)

An **asset** which generates income because of the legal rights or trading reputation of its owner. The major examples are **patents**, trademarks, copyrights, **franchises** and **goodwill**.

See also: **tangible wealth**.

integrated pollution control (720)

A system of pollution licences covering a wide range of industries to control the overall levels of air and water pollution in a particular area.

See also: **Environmental Protection Agency**; **pollution control**.

intellectual property (620)

Intangible property resulting from inventive activity, e.g. patents, trademarks and copyrights.

Rushing, F.W. and Brown, C.G. (eds) (1990) *Intellectual Property. Rights in Science, Technology and Economic Performance*, Boulder, CO: Westview Press.

Inter-American Development Bank (430)

Founded in 1960 by the USA and nineteen Latin American countries to provide finance for development projects in those countries, largely from private sources. Originally only the countries of the Organization of American States were members. In 1983, it established the Intermediate Financing Facility to defray up to 5 per cent per annum of interest charges paid by borrowers on certain loans from the Bank.

See also: **development bank**.

inter-dealer broker (310)

A London broker who enables gilt-edged **market-makers** to record anonymously on an electronic noticeboard their requests to buy or sell blocks of government stocks.

interdependent economy (070, 420)

An **economy** with close trading links with another economy.

See also: **open economy**.

interest (010)

The income which is paid to the owner of capital for its use.

See also: **rate of interest**.

interest-bearing eligible liabilities (310)

Customer's interest-bearing deposits with British **clearing banks**.

See also: **eligible liability**.

interest elasticity of savings (010, 310)

The responsiveness of **savings** to a change in the **rate of interest**. In many empirical studies, savings appear to be interest **inelastic** and so other savings theories have been advanced, especially the **life-cycle** approach.

interest equalization tax (320)

US federal tax introduced in July 1963 which increased the cost of foreign portfolio borrowing on the US market by 1 per cent. This fiscal measure was designed to reduce the capital outflow from the USA.

interest rate cartel (310)

An agreement between London **clearing banks** to set the same interest rates for borrowers and depositors; abolished in 1971.

interest rate swap (310)

An exchange of a fixed interest rate arrangement for variable interest rate repayments. Despite the high risk of these swaps, in practice the return on the deal can be as low as one-twentieth of 1 per cent. This form of rescheduling debts was used in the 1980s by British local authorities and led to great losses when interest rates rose.

interest risk (010, 310)

A risk which arises from unexpected changes in the rate of interest. A business, for example, which is financed by bank loans rather than **equity** will face greater financial charges when interest rates suddenly rise.

See also: **exchange risk**.

intergenerational distribution of income (160)

1 The relationship between the incomes of persons alive today and their descendants. One way of effecting an intergenerational transfer is for a generation to increase the income of its successors through abstaining from consumption now and undertaking long-term investments. If individuals are reluctant to make such sacrifices, governments can raise taxation to effect long-term improvements in economic welfare; this is often cited as a major justification for state educational expenditure.

2 The relationship between the incomes of workers currently in the labour force and those retired from it.

See also: **overlapping generations model**.

intergenerational equity (160, 320)

Fairness, particularly in public finance, between this and future generations. According to the **benefit approach to taxation** each generation should pay its own expenses, but in practice capital projects are often financed, as are wars, by public debt which is a burden to future generations.

Ferguson, J.M. (ed.) (1964) *Public Debt and Future Generations*, Chapel Hill, NC: University of North Carolina Press.

inter-industry trade (420, 610)

Trade in different goods and services between different industries, e.g. the exchange of agricultural products for machines. Trade of this kind occurs most often between economies at different stages of development, especially between countries of the First and Third Worlds. Increasingly trade between developed countries, e.g. within the **Organization for Economic Cooperation and Development**, has become **intra-industry trade**. Within a national economy, inter-industry trade flows are shown in an **input–output analysis**.

INTERLINK (140, 210)

An economic forecasting model of the twenty-three **Organization for Economic Cooperation and Development** countries plus eight regions with 7,000 equations based on a **Keynesian** expenditure approach, providing short- and medium-term forecasts for the world economy. It enables policy-makers to examine the relationship between national **monetary** and **fiscal** policies by considering international feedback effects. Only broad macroeconomic factors are taken into account.

OECD (1982) *OECD Interlink System: Structure and Operation*, vol. 1, Paris: OECD.

See also: **linkage models**.

interlinked transaction (010)

The tying of a purchase in one market with one in another, e.g. the purchase of equipment and raw materials or the servicing of it. In developing countries, it is common to find the provision of credit tied to a tenancy or to the provision of agricultural labour. Interlinking reduces **transactions costs** but has long been a method of monopoly exploitation.

Bardhan, D.K. and Rudra, A. (1978) 'Interlinkage of land, labour and credit relations: an analysis of village survey data in East India', *Economic and Political Weekly* 13: 367–84.

interlocking directorship (310)

A directorship of a person who is also on the board of other companies or corporations. The holding of the financial stock of several firms by one person makes possible collusive behaviour. Sections 7 and 8 of the **Clayton Act** forbid such directorships if competition is lessened substantially or another **antitrust** provision is violated as a consequence.

Intermarket Trading System (310)

The US electronic stock market which links US regional stock exchanges with the two New York exchanges and the **National Association of Securities Dealers Automated Quotation System**. The Intermarket Trading System's display terminals state the current prices of that trader's market, together with the best price available elsewhere. Despite the convenience of the system, it is not a threat to the New York Stock Exchange.

intermediate good (010)

A good used in the production of another,

e.g. steel used in electrical goods industries. Intermediate goods can be identified by an **input–output** table.

See also: **final good**.

intermediate target (210)
A guide to the policy strategy needed to reach an ultimate policy goal, e.g. a rate of growth of the money supply which will achieve inflationless economic growth.

intermediate technology (620)
Production methods which use simple tools and **labour-intensive** techniques. This approach was a reaction to large-scale development schemes which attempted to convert traditional societies rapidly into modern industrialized societies, with all the consequential unemployment and environmental problems.

See also: **appropriate technology**; **Schumacher**.

intermediation (310)
The bringing together of lenders and borrowers (savers and investors) by a bank or other financial institution. This activity attempts to reduce market imperfections which have arisen from uneven amounts of information in the market and **economies of scale**, provides insurance against risk and responds to the different preferences of lenders and savers for holding a financial asset.

See also: **disintermediation**.

internal balance (010)
The **full employment** level of **aggregate demand** for a country, assuming that there is complete mobility of labour and constant money wage rates. This is contrasted with **external balance**. It is the task of macroeconomic policy-makers to achieve internal and external balances simultaneously. (See figure below.)

Meade, J.E. (1951) *The Theory of International Economic Policy*, vol. I, *The Balance of Payments*, ch. 10, Oxford: Oxford University Press.

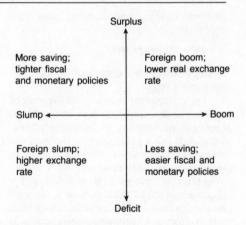

internal debt (320)
The debt a government owes to the firms and households of the country it rules. This is the result of not raising sufficient taxes to meet expenditure.

See also: **external debt**.

internal economy of scale (010)
An **economy of scale** which occurs within a firm or other organization and benefits it alone. An example is the fall in unit costs brought about by spreading the initial tooling costs for a production line. In a **Soviet-type economy**, most economies are internal as all enterprises, agencies and industrial ministries are linked together into a monolithic organization.

See: **external economy of scale**.

internalizing an externality (010)
See: **externality**.

internal labour market (820)
A labour market existing within a large firm. In such markets, most recruitment is of young workers as most senior positions are filled through the internal promotion of employees trained by the firm. There is a proliferation of job grades and a salary system based on seniority to encourage workers to remain within the firm. Most examples of these markets are within monopolistic and oligopolistic firms. The phenomenon was first noted by Clark Kerr when he discussed the 'balkanization' of labour markets.

Kerr, C. (1959) 'The balkanization of labor

markets', in E.W. Bakke (ed.) *Labor Mobility and Economic Opportunity*, Boston, MA: MIT Press; New York: Wiley.

—— (1969) *Marshall, Marx and Modern Times: The Multidimensional Society*, London: Cambridge University Press.

See also: **external labour market**.

internal labour market contracting (820)
See: **employment contract**.

internal market (420)
1   The market to be created in the **European Community** from 1992 with no barriers to trade or economic mobility. Some would like this increased degree of integration to lead to the creation of a single European bank, issuing a single currency for all member countries.

2   The trading relationships between the parts of a large firm. **Multinational corporations** are noted for such markets.

See also: **Delors Plan**; **Eurofed**; **single market**.

internal rate of return (520)
The **discount rate** which makes the net present value of an investment project equal to zero. This is a widely used method of investment appraisal as it takes into account the timing of cash flows. In **cost–benefit analysis** it is measured by the formula

$$\sum_{j=0}^{n} \frac{B_j - C_j}{(1 + i)^j}$$

i is the internal rate of return.

Internal Revenue Service (320)
The principal office for collecting US taxes, established in 1862. It has sixty-two district offices and 60,000 tax agents. It enforces all internal revenue laws except for alcohol, tobacco, firearms and explosives. Its cost-effectiveness is high as its costs are only 1 per cent of the total tax revenue it raises.

internal search (820)
The job search by an employer limited to his own labour force. This method of recruitment operates either by inducing existing workers to switch from their present to different jobs or by getting their present employees to pass on to friends and relatives notice of internal vacancies. This approach to hiring has become more common through the growth of **internal labour markets**.

International Air Travel Association (630)
Founded in 1945 in Havana, covering most scheduled airlines, with aims which include promoting safe, regular and economical air transport. In practice, it has been a major example of an international **cartel** which has kept fares high on many international routes by licensing few operators. Licences were awarded for operating lucrative routes, e.g. across the Atlantic, if the same airline undertook to fly on loss-making routes. State-owned airlines have been avid to maintain such protection. However, such a restriction on competition is increasingly challenged in the case of flights between the countries of the **European Community**.

International Bank for Economic Cooperation (430)
A **Comecon** organization founded in 1964 to help the non-capitalist world in a way similar to the **World Bank**'s financing of the development of other countries.

International Bank for Reconstruction and Development (430)
See: **World Bank**.

International Banking Act 1978 (310)
US federal statute, the first after the Second World War to deal with the overseas activities of banks. It gave **Edge Act corporations** authority to engage in a wider range of activities. The Federal Reserve was allowed to authorize the creation of international banking facilities in the form of loan accounts for non-US purposes to be used by US overseas affiliates or foreign parties. Parity of treatment was given to foreign and domestic banks, especially in interstate operations: thus the same rules on bank branching applied. Under the Act, foreign banks are required to have federal deposit insurance on deposits over $100,000.

International Clearing Union (430)
A set of international institutions proposed by **Keynes** at **Bretton Woods**. The ICU was

to be the world's banker by setting up a World Bank which would be able to make adjustments of **exchange rates**, as well as providing a Board for International Investment, a scheme of commodity controls and an International Economic Board. Keynes hoped that this new set of institutions would combat the evils of the **trade cycle**. Exchange rate stabilization was to be achieved by fixing each exchange rate in terms of a new international bank money, **bancor**, which would itself be fixed in terms of gold. **Central banks** would keep their accounts with the ICU to settle outstanding balances at the par value of their currencies expressed in bancor. Bancor credit balances, with the approval of central banks in credit, would be used to finance debtor countries. Overdraft facilities would give countries time for adjustment. Each country would have a 'quota', i.e. a maximum debit balance, equal to the sum of the country's exports and imports on the average of the three pre-war years. If the quota was exceeded by more than one-quarter, then the country would be entitled to devalue up to 5 per cent without the consent of the ICU. If the quota was exceeded by more than one-half, then the ICU would require a stated devaluation, control of outward capital transactions and the surrender of a suitable percentage of gold or other liquid reserve assets. If the quota was exceeded by more than three-quarters, then a country could be declared in default and no longer entitled to draw on its account without the approval of the governing body of the ICU. Thus, this proposal was a step towards a world central bank operating in an international currency.

See also: **International Monetary Fund**; **World Bank**.

International Commodities Clearing House (430)
The centre of London's **futures** and **option** markets, as well as Australian and New Zealand exchanges. It is owned by six British **clearing banks**.

international comparisons (070, 220)
Assessment of the relative performance of different national **economies**. Since 1945 the advent of **national income** accounting has led to **gross domestic product** and **gross**

national product measures being frequently used for this purpose. Microeconomic institutions are also compared with a view to remodelling them in the light of foreign experience. Before the systematic and regular collection of economic statistics, international comparisons in the form of travellers' accounts of foreign countries were often used by economists, e.g. **Petty**, **Smith** and **Malthus**.

international comparisons of the cost of living (070, 220)
The cost of purchasing the same representative bundle of goods and services in different countries of the world. Regular surveys are carried out to ascertain the proper levels of remuneration for executives employed by international firms and organizations. Japan is relatively expensive and the UK quite inexpensive.

international competitiveness (220)
A comparison of the prices of goods of different countries, or of unit labour costs, expressed in the same currency. To avoid the problems of translating one currency into another, sometimes the comparison is made in terms of the amount of labour time needed to produce a particular good, e.g. a car with a 2-litre engine.

International Development Association (430)
Formed in 1960 as an affiliate of the International Bank for Reconstruction and Development (**World Bank**) to provide **soft loans** to developing countries who are unable to borrow because of their low credit standing.

International Energy Agency (720)
Vienna-based organization of the **Organization for Economic Cooperation and Development** countries (with the exception of Finland, France and Ireland) founded in 1974 to develop policies for the conservation of energy and the production of energy alternatives to oil.

International Finance Corporation (430)
Affiliate of the **World Bank** founded in 1956 and based in Washington, DC. It seeks to further the economic growth of less

developed countries by supplementing the investment of private capital in private enterprises.

International Investment Bank (310)

A bank set up by **Comecon** in 1971 to finance long-term capital projects.

See also: **development bank**.

International Labour Organization (830)

Founded in 1919 with its constitution derived from Part XIII of the Versailles Peace Treaty after demands from an international meeting of trade unions at Berne. Its General Conference works on the principle of tripartite representation from each country – of two government delegates, one workers' delegate and one employers' delegate. The worker and employer representatives on the governing body are elected internationally. It collects statistics on working conditions, passes conventions and receives annual reports on whether they have been implemented. Member states have a duty to enact domestic legislation to make effective a convention or recommendation within twelve months of its enactment. The ILO's constitution was rewritten by the Philadelphia Charter of 1946 to take into account its twenty-five years of experience and to make it part of the United Nations Organization. Its basic principles were stated as follows:

1 labour is not a commodity;
2 freedom of expression and association for all;
3 redistribution of international income to poorer countries;
4 war against want within countries by the promotion of common welfare;
5 lasting peace in the world through justice.

Member states play a lesser role in the ILO than in many other international organizations because of workers' and employers' representatives. National Ministries of Labour have been accorded an enhanced and international importance through the existence of the ILO. The Nobel Peace Prize was awarded to it in 1969 in recognition of its efforts. By 1988, it had 150 members.

International Labour Conventions and Recommendations 1919–81, with supplements, Geneva.

international liquidity (430)

Internationally acceptable means of paying for the goods and services supplied by any country in the world. Under the **gold bullion standard**, gold was used for the purposes of international settlement. Now, in addition to gold, the major currencies of the world, particularly the US dollar, the Deutschmark, the yen and the pound sterling, are used as well as **special drawing rights** of the **International Monetary Fund**. The growth of **Eurocurrency markets** has also increased liquidity.

Williamson, J. (1973) 'Surveys in applied economics: international liquidity', *Economic Journal* 83: 685–746.

International Miners' Organization (830)

Paris-based federation of national miners' trade unions.

International Monetary Fund (430)

International agency founded at Bretton Woods in 1945 and now located in Washington, DC, with 151 member countries providing a pool of currencies, gold and **special drawing rights** to stabilize **currencies**. The only major countries outside it are the USSR and Switzerland. It was set up to end the **beggar-my-neighbour** policies of the 1930s by establishing an exchange rate regime. **Keynes** had wanted an **International Clearing Union** providing automatic credit to countries in difficulties but the US view that it should be a small tightly controlled fund, obeying the rules of US capitalism, prevailed. Originally under Article 1 of its Charter, the IMF's broad objectives included facilitating the balanced growth of free international trade according to the principle of **comparative advantage**. In practice, it has been principally concerned with broad macroeconomic policies designed to reduce the **balance of payments** deficits and currency difficulties of member countries. Criticisms of its policies include the view that it forces adjustment on the countries in difficulty, rather than on those who have caused balance of payments deficits, e.g. by contributing to a change in the **terms of trade**. The departments of the IMF cover the major areas of the world, stabilization programmes, research on international monetary economics and the provision of advice on public finance and central banking.

See also: **additional facilities**.

International Monetary Market (310)

A Chicago-based market established in 1982 for dealing in money futures.

international monetary system (430)

The financial arrangements between sovereign states in force at a particular time. These consist largely of agreements for the fixing of exchange rates and the settlement of debts, particularly balance of payments deficits. Countries have a choice between market mechanisms under **floating exchange rates** or an order managed by an international body. The most famous international monetary systems have been the **gold standard**, **Bretton Woods** and the **European Monetary System**.

Solmon, R. (1977) *The International Monetary System, 1945–76: An Insider's View*, New York and London: Harper & Row.

Tew, B. (1982) *The Evolution of the International Monetary System, 1945 to 1981*, London: Hutchinson.

International Securities Regulatory Organization (310)

The partner with the **International Stock Exchange** since 1986 in regulating the market activities of British stock exchanges.

International Standard Classification of Occupations (810)

The **International Labour Office**'s standardized description of occupations based on the type of work performed, the degree of specialization and the skills required to perform particular jobs. This is a hierarchical classification with four layers. It has inspired a number of national occupational classifications.

International Labour Office (1990), *ISCO-88: International Standard Classification of Occupations*, Geneva: ILO.

International Stock Exchange (310)

The federation of UK and Irish stock exchanges created in 1973. The principal exchange is London with subsidiary floors in Dublin, Liverpool, Birmingham and Glasgow. London now has no trading floor, unlike New York and Tokyo. It is governed by the Council of the Stock Exchange.

International Trade Organization (420)

An international organization recommended by the **Havana Charter** but never established. **United Nations Conference on Trade and Development**, founded in 1964, achieved what was intended to be the role of the International Trade Organization.

See also: **General Agreement on Tariffs and Trade**.

international trade theory (410)

A succession of attempts to explain why nations trade particular goods with each other. The best known early theories are of **absolute advantage** and **comparative advantage**; later theories include the **Heckscher–Ohlin** factor endowment theory. Many of these theories assume that commodities are mobile but factors of production are not.

Jones, R.W. and Kenen, P.B. (1984) *Handbook of International Economics*, vol. 1, Amsterdam: North-Holland.

international union (830)

An association of US **local unions** and their affiliates abroad. The largest is the famous Teamsters union, which organizes a considerable range of occupations from truck drivers to nurses. The majority of internationals are affiliated to the **AFL–CIO** (102 of 168 in 1980).

international union federation (830)

An association of national **trade (labor) unions** concerned with all the issues affecting the labour of one industry. Statistics on wages, bargaining and work conditions are collected and, occasionally, industrial action is undertaken to help the bargaining of trade unions, especially in their dealings with **multinational corporations**. The industries with these federations include coal, chemicals, motor manufacturing and printing.

international wage levels (070, 820)

Comparisons of the average earnings of workers of the major industrial countries. These are used in conjunction with productivity figures to calculate unit labour costs as a guide to the international competitiveness of national economies.

inter-nation equity (070, 320)

1 Fairness in the worldwide distribution of tax revenues by attempting to ensure that each national treasury receives the tax yield it deserves. A crude method of achieving this is by international treaties which reciprocally agree that all income is taxed at source. The considerable growth of **transnational corporations** has made this a major policy issue.

2 The equal economic treatment of different nations, e.g. by **free trade**.

See also: **transfer pricing**.

interpersonal utility comparisons (010)

Comparisons of the amount of **utility** (or 'satisfaction') acquired by different persons. The consequence of the difficulty of making such comparisons is that schemes of redistribution which are proposed as a means to increasing economic welfare can in many cases be justified only on political grounds. In the twentieth century **welfare economics** has attempted to validate comparisons of this kind.

Interstate Commerce Commission (610)

US federal commission set up in 1887 by the Interstate Commerce Act to regulate rail traffic across state boundaries. This was one of the earliest US attempts to control monopoly and achieve fair prices, together with an adequate standard of service across the nation. This Washington-based commission today also regulates trucks, buses, oil pipelines and inland water transportation.

interval estimate (210)

An estimate in a range between two numbers of a population **parameter**.

See also: **point estimate**.

intervention price (710)

The price of an agricultural commodity at which a governmental agency begins to purchase that commodity in order to maintain its price at that level and to stabilize farmers' incomes. In the **European Community**, under the **Common Agricultural Policy**, intervention prices are guaranteed minimum prices which attempt to stabilize individual commodity markets.

See also: **Common Agricultural Policy**.

intra-industry trade (420)

International trade between countries in the same type of good with both countries being exporters and importers. This has happened increasingly in the **European Community**, e.g. in the car industry. The growth of **transnational corporations** and the consequent increased international specialization of production has made this type of trade flourish. The greatest degree of intra-industry trade is when there is an equal amount of exports and imports in that good; the lowest is when a country predominantly imports primary products and exports manufactures. The formula used to measure this type of trade is

$$B_i = (X_i + M_i) - \frac{|X_i - M_i|}{X_i - M_i}$$

It shows the extent to which the absolute amount of the commodity exports (X) in a particular industry or a commodity grouping is offset by imports (M) in the same grouping.

Greenaway, D. and Milner, C. (1986) *Economics of Intra-Industry Trade*, Oxford: Basil Blackwell.

See also: **border trade**; **cyclical trade**.

intrapreneur (510)

A company employee who is financed by his/her employer to set up an independent company and become a subcontractor. This financial arrangement gives talented persons a greater independence than regular work in a large organization would provide.

Lessen, R. (1987) *Intrapreneurship: How to be an Enterprising Individual in a Successful Business*, Aldershot: Wildwood House.

intrinsic value (010)

See: **value in use**.

invention (620)

A discovery of a new product or process of production which is often crudely measured by **patent** statistics. Economists have analysed the rate of invention as a function of the **business cycle**, the type of market or the organization of scientific research.

See also: **innovation; research and development**.

inventory (520)

The stocks of goods held by a firm for the purposes of production or final sale. An increase (or decrease) in an inventory will be a form of investment (disinvestment). Because of fluctuations in final demand, unintended investment (or disinvestment) often occurs and is frequently the most volatile component of national output.

See also: **Kitchin cycle**.

inventory cycle (140)

Fluctuations in the stocks of raw materials, semi-finished goods and goods available for sale within an economy. Changes in inventories occur more frequently than fluctuations in fixed investment. Anticipated and unanticipated changes in final demand, changes in the cost of financing stockholdings and errors in the planning of production all generate inventory cycles.

See also: **Kitchin cycle**.

inverse elasticity rule (010)

This states that the **price elasticity of demand** for a good is inversely proportional to price minus marginal cost divided by price (if all **cross price elasticities of demand** are ignored). Thus the margin between price and cost is large when elasticity is small: under **monopoly**, there will be a very **inelastic** demand and the ability to make **supernormal profits**.

See also: **Lerner index**.

investment (010)

1 An addition to the stock of capital goods in the public or private sector over a given time period. Gross investment includes both this net investment and replacement investment to keep the stock intact. Theories of the determination of the volume of investment include the **accelerator principle** and **marginal efficiency of capital** approaches.

2 The purchase of a **financial** asset.

Junanker, P.N. (1972) *Investment: Theories and Evidence*, London: Macmillan.

See also: **capital theory; financial investment; human capital**.

investment appraisal (520)

The calculation of the prospective return to an investment project with a view to ascertaining whether it is worthwhile. The different methods used by firms include calculating the **rate of return**, the **discounted cash flow** and the **net present value**. Large-scale investments in the public sector often make use of **cost–benefit analysis**.

Lumby, S. (1982) *Investment Appraisal and Related Decisions*, Wokingham: Van Nostrand Reinhold.

Merrett, A.J. and Sykes, A. (1986) *Capital Budgeting and Company Finance*, London and Harlow: Longman.

investment banking (310)

A specialist type of US banking which is concerned with **corporate finance**, **arbitrage** in secondary markets and the underwriting of and dealing in **securities** and consists of either executing the orders of other investors or proprietary trading when a bank deals on its own account. The **Glass–Steagall Act** ordered the separation of investment from deposit-taking banking, thereby preventing the growth of **financial conglomerates** to the extent which has subsequently become possible in the UK. In the USA the top **'bulge-bracket' firms** are virtually an oligopoly, having 80 per cent of the business in debt and other securities markets.

See also: **merchant bank**.

investment climate (520)

The mood or level of business confidence which will affect the rate of investment in an economy.

See also: **animal spirits; economic climate**.

investment dollar pool system (430)

A method of exchange control. Persons of a non-dollar country wishing to purchase US securities are only allowed to acquire them by purchasing them from another local resident or by borrowing them. A tougher version of this system used in the UK prior to 1979 required 25 per cent of foreign currency proceeds from the sale of assets to be sold in the official market; also dividends on dollar investments had to be repatriated through the official exchange market.

investment reserve system (140)

A method of encouraging countercyclical private sector investment. In prosperous times, tax incentives encourage firms to accumulate reserves which are in later years spent on capital projects when the economy is heading for recession.

Since 1938 in Sweden there has been a policy of influencing the timing of capital expenditures by fiscal incentives to reduce fluctuations in the national economy. Companies can set aside up to 50 per cent of pretax profits in non-interest bearing Bank of Sweden accounts in return for tax reductions: after five years, 30 per cent of a deposit can be used at the request of the company tax-free and at other times, in recessions, the government can authorize the release of these funds tax-free to stimulate the economy. In addition, since the mid-1960s, these funds can be used to help depressed regions whatever the state of the national economy.

See also: **countercyclical policy**.

investment trust (310)

An investment trust whose assets consist of stocks and shares. It offers the investor the opportunity of benefiting from a spread of different investments. This type of trust was invented by Foreign and Colonial in 1886 (still a market leader). Compared with **unit trusts**, they have the advantages of **gearing** in that loan capital can be used for the benefit of shareholders, of lower costs and of being able to retain their underlying shares during a stock market panic.

invisible foot (160, 320)

A reduction in redistribution caused by political competition. Invisibility comes about because of the difficulties of observation, quantification and measurement. An example of an invisible foot would be the movement of people between locations to obtain a better mix of taxes and public expenditure, thereby invisibly creating an efficient resource allocation.

See also: **fiscal mobility**; **Tiebout hypothesis**.

invisible hand (010, 030)

The underlying mechanism of a market economy which causes self-interested economic agents through exchange to promote the general good of society. The idea originated in the discussion of natural law by the English philosopher John Locke but is usually associated with Adam **Smith** who, in his *Theory of Moral Sentiments* and less so in his *Wealth of Nations*, developed this **Physiocratic** notion. Smith's use of the principle was less sensational than **Mandeville**'s which described how private vices promote public virtue. Ahmad has identified four functions of the 'invisible hand': to limit the size of the landlord's stomach, to curb the residual selfishness of a landlord, to optimize production and to preserve the natural order.

Ahmad, S. (1990) 'Adam Smith's four invisible hands', *History of Political Economy* 22: 137–43.

invisible handshake (820)

An informal understanding between an employer and workers or between a firm and its customers whose terms are not legally binding because of their implicit nature. Employers make such tacit agreements as part of their pursuit of long-term profitability. This concept was inspired by **Okun**'s study of **stagflation** in the 1970s.

See also: **implicit contract theory**.

invisible trade (420)

International trade in services, particularly banking, insurance, shipping, tourism and professional advice. This is the principal economic activity of the City of London and other leading financial centres.

See also: **balance of payments**.

involuntary employment (810)

Not wanting to work at a given wage but still doing so.

involuntary unemployment (810)

1 Lack of jobs.

2 Being unable to obtain employment at a given wage rate.

3 A case of **disequilibrium** in the labour market. **Keynes** is particularly associated with identifying this type of **unemployment**, partly because he prescribed an increase in **aggregate demand** to eliminate it.

See also: **voluntary unemployment**.

IO (610)
See: **industrial organization**.

IOB (630)
See: **Insurance Ombudsman Bureau**.

IOU money (310)
Money in the form of a promise to pay based on the debt of a firm or an individual. Much of this money is in the form of bank deposits.

See also: **bill of exchange**; **commercial paper**.

IPC (720)
See: **integrated pollution control**.

IPE (720)
International Petroleum Exchange.

IPMA (310)
International Primary Markets Association.

IPR (620)
Intellectual property rights.

See also: **property rights**.

IRA (910)
Individual retirement account (USA).

IRC (610)
See: **Industrial Reorganization Corporation**.

iron law of wages (820)
The **subsistence** theory of wages used by many **classical economists**. It was argued that if workers are paid more than subsistence there will be an increase in population which, with a short time lag given that child labour was used, will increase the labour force, in turn pushing wages back to the subsistence level. Conversely, wages below the subsistence rate will reduce the population, cause excess demand for labour and push wage rates back up to subsistence. The law, in essence, described a long-run equilibrium wage rate. Adam **Smith** challenged the law on the empirical grounds that food prices and wages often

move in different directions. Growing real wages in the nineteenth century also refuted the law.

IRR (520)
See: **internal rate of return**.

IRS (320)
See: **Internal Revenue Service**.

IS (010)
1 The equilibrium of investment and savings, usually expressed as one of the curves in the **IS-LM** diagram. An increase in government expenditure, with its multiplier effects, will cause the IS curve to shift outwards from the origin.

2 **Import substitution**.

Isard, Walter, 1919– (030)
US authority on regional science, of German descent, who was educated at Temple and Harvard universities and taught at Harvard, Philadelphia (1956–79) and Cornell universities. His revival of **location theory** led to his founding regional science which placed location theory in the wider economic context of **general equilibrium** theory by using **input–output analysis** and **regional multipliers** and linked it to other social sciences.

Isard, W. (1956) *Location and Space Economy*, Cambridge, MA: MIT Press and Wiley.
Isard, W. and Bramhall, D.F. (1960) *Methods of Regional Analysis*, Cambridge, MA: MIT Press and Wiley.
Isard, W. and Langford, T.W. (1971) *Regional Input–Output Study: Recollections, Reflections and Diverse Notes on the Philadelphia Experience*, Cambridge, MA: MIT Press.

See also: **regional economics**.

ISCO-88 (810)
See: **International Standard Classification of Occupations**.

ISE (310)
See: **International Stock Exchange**.

Islamic banking (310)
A distinctive type of banking which attempts to avoid the Koranic prohibitions concerning riba (**usury**). Usury was objected to both for exploiting the poor who needed to

borrow and for giving a reward unrelated to productive effort. Later medieval Islamic thinkers devised intricate hiyal (stratagems) to circumvent this problem. Today, Islamic banks impose service charges, instead of interest, on bank loans; these charges, based on a percentage of the value of the loan, resemble interest. Also, money lenders often lend in kind, e.g. purchasing a piece of equipment and then leasing it to the borrower who pays instalments which, in total, are in excess of the original purchase price.

There have been Arab-owned banks since the 1920s, the period in which the Banque Misr of Egypt and the Arab Bank of Palestine were founded. After the oil price rise of 1973–4, new banks operating according to strict Islamic principles have been established. The largest are in Saudi Arabia: the Islamic Development Bank founded in 1975 as a specialist development assistance agency not dealing with the general public, the Al-Baraka Group founded in 1982 and the Al-Rajhi Company founded in 1985. To allow riba-free participation in Western markets, Dar al-Maal al-Islami, the House of Islamic Funds, was founded in Geneva in 1981: although it has some short-term funds in cash and commodities, it invests chiefly in property and equities.

The expansion of Islamic banks into competition with traditional banking is difficult as they cannot be accepted as commercial banks in Western countries until they have Western government securities as part of their assets; their lack of official status prevents them from soliciting for deposits from the public. Although Islamic banks are often regarded as a new development in banking, Islamic authors argue that many banking principles, including the use of bank deposits and cheques, have been practised from the early days of Islam.

Abdeen, A.M. and Shook, D.N. (1984) *The Saudi Financial System in the Context of Western and Islamic Finance*, Chichester: Wiley.

Rodinson, M. (1974) *Islam and Capitalism*, London: Allen Lane.

Saleh, N.A. (1986) *Unlawful Gain and Legitimate Profit in Islamic Law: Riba, Gharar and Islamic Bartering*, Cambridge: Cambridge University Press.

Wilson, R. (1983) *Banking and Finance in the Arab Middle East*, London: Macmillan.

Islamic fiscal policy (320)

The application of the principles of the Koran, particularly the avoidance of **usury**, to the financing of a government's expenditure. Islamic governments aim to balance their budgets to avoid borrowing; if borrowing is needed, government securities can be issued at less than their redemption value as a means of disguising an interest payment. Also, there are severe problems in raising revenue as purchase tax exploits the needy and incomes are too low to have a broad-based income tax. Even the special tax under Islamic law, the 'zakat', which is an annual wealth tax, can only be used to finance social purposes, mainly at the local level.

island (810)

A location of jobs or employers such that at a point in time firms cannot move but workers can. On each island, the competitive labour market there sets wages equal to the **marginal product of labour** on that island; as productivity differs from island to island, so do wage offers. Workers engage in job search to find islands with better wages.

Lucas, R.E., Jr and Prescott, E.C. (1974) 'Equilibrium search and unemployment', *Journal of Economic Theory* 7: 188–209.

See also: **job search**.

IS-LM curves (010, 310, 320)

Investment–savings and liquidity–money curves. An apparatus invented by **Hicks** (who originally called them IS and LL curves) and **Hansen** to synthesize the Keynesian macroeconomic system; Hicks was to regret its excessive use by other economists. The IS curve, plotting the rate of interest i against national income Y, joins together all combinations of i and Y for which $I = S$, shows equilibrium in the goods market; the LM curve, plotted on the same axes, shows equilibrium in the money market as at each point on the curve the demand for money is equal to its supply. **Keynesians** believe that the IS curve is steep, with the consequence that fiscal policy is more powerful than **monetary policy**; **monetarists** suggest a steep LM curve with **crowding-out** the consequence of fiscal expansion (i increases; Y is unchanged). Changes in government expenditure shift

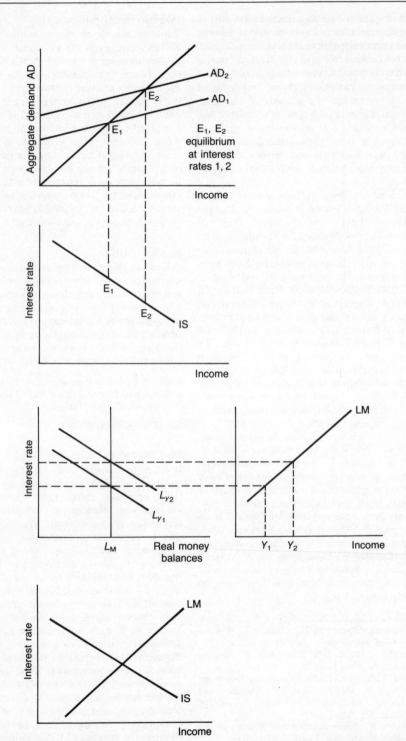

the IS curve and raise or lower national income and the interest rate; an expansion of the money supply effects a shift in the LM curve (from LM_1 to LM_2 say) and reduces interest rates but increases income.

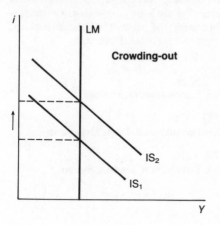

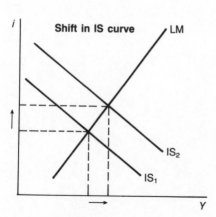

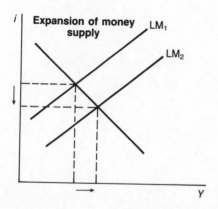

Hicks, J.R. (1937) 'Mr Keynes and the "Classics": a suggested interpretation', *Econometrica* 5: 147–59.

Young, W. (1987) *Interpreting Mr Keynes*, Cambridge: Polity Press.

isocost (010)

A straight line which shows different combinations of two factors of production for the same cost. The slope of the line will alter if the relative prices of the factors change.

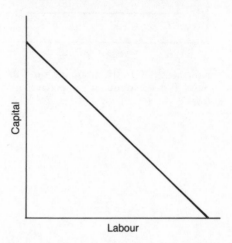

isolated market equilibrium (210)

A market for one good or one service in which the quantity demanded equals the quantity supplied.

See also: **general market equilibrium**.

isolated state (940)

Von **Thünen's** model of a **closed economy** which showed optimum locations for agricultural activities.

See also: **location theory**.

isoproduct (010)

See: **isoquant**.

isoquant (010)

A curve showing different minimum combinations of two factors of production producing the same level of output; also known as an isoproduct curve. In the figure each isoquant shows the output which results from different combinations of two inputs, capital and labour: C is the isoquant for

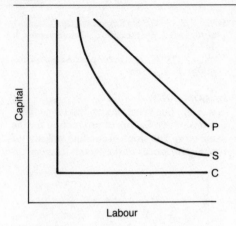

complements; S is the isoquant for substitutes; P is the isoquant for perfect substitutes.

ISRO (310)
See: **International Securities Regulatory Organization**.

issuing house (310)
A financial institution concerned with arranging the issue of new **shares** in accordance with the current regulations of the International Stock Exchange.

See also: **underwriter**.

IT (620)
See: **information technology**.

ITO (420)
See: **International Trade Organization**.

ITS (310)
See: **Intermarket Trading System**.

J

Jackson Amendment (420)

An amendment to US trade law proposed in 1975 by Senator Jackson: it denies **most favoured nation** status to countries which do not permit free emigration.

Jamaica Agreement (430)

An agreement made by members of the **International Monetary Fund** in 1974 whereby the Fund sold one-third of its gold stock, making the profits of the sale the basis of a special trust fund which provides balance of payments assistance on soft terms to the poorest countries.

See also: **soft loan**.

Japanese tax system (320)

A tax system after 1945 with many of the characteristics of the US tax system, i.e. the use of **income tax** as a major source of revenue, no **value-added taxes** and with most collection of taxes by central government with local government reliant on central government grants. Japan's income tax was first introduced in 1887, assuming its modern form in 1940. The present system was to a large extent designed by the **Shoup Mission**.

Ishi, H. (1989) *The Japanese Tax System*, Oxford: Clarendon Press.
Tax Advisory Commission (1960 onwards), *Proposals* (in Japanese).

jawbone (310, 820)

Attempting to achieve voluntarily by persuasion the goals of **monetary** or **incomes policies** as an alternative to statutory controls. Also known as **moral suasion**.

J-curve (430)

A curve showing the effects of the **devaluation** of a currency with a **fixed exchange rate** on the **balance of payments** current account. It is based on the observation that initially after devaluation, before there can be responses to the changed import and export prices, the total cost of imports will be higher and the total value of exports lower. An appreciation of a currency, conversely, will produce an inverted J-curve. The curve plots the balance of payments current account balance against time (in the figure, t_d is the date at which devaluation occurs).

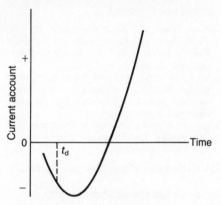

Jevons, William Stanley, 1835–82 (030)

A leader of the **marginalist** school who was educated at the Mechanics Institute High School, Liverpool, and University College, London. His university studies began with chemistry and mathematics and were interrupted by four years in Australia as assayer to the Sydney Mint before he returned to study political economy and logic. In Australia, his first researches were into climate and the effects of railways on land values and rent; also there he acquired the habit of 'pricking off curves' on squared paper to study fluctuations in economic time series. He held academic posts at Owen's College, Manchester, and Queen's College, Liverpool, before becoming professor of political economy from 1876 to 1881 at University College, London. He drowned in 1882.

His principal works were *A Serious Fall in the Value of Gold Ascertained and its Social Effects Set Forth* (1863) which introduced a new method of measuring price changes,

The Coal Question: An Inquiry Concerning the Progress of the Nation and the Probable Exhaustion of the Coalmines which caused a national scare and his *Theory of Political Economy* which was regarded by **Keynes** as 'the first modern book on economics'. Jevons's theory of exchange was the focal point of his *Theory*: by switching from cost to subjective **utility** as the basis of **value** he was able to begin the precise theorizing which constitutes **neoclassical** microeconomics. His theory of the **rate of interest** made a contribution to the development of marginal productivity theory. His influence on the development of economics in England was profound.

Collison Black, R.D. and Konekamp, R. (eds) (1972) *Papers and Correspondence of William Stanley Jevons*, vols 1–7, London and Basingstoke: Macmillan.

Schabas, M. (1990) *A World Ruled by Number: William Stanley Jevons and the Rise of Mathematical Economics*, Princeton, NJ: Princeton University Press.

Stigler, G.J. (1946) *Theories of Production and Distribution: The Formative Period*, ch. 11, New York: Macmillan.

See also: **marginalism**; **Menger**; **Walras**.

job acceptance schedule (820)

The relationship between a real wage rate and the number of persons prepared to accept jobs. Changes in the ratio of real wages to unemployment benefit can cause shifts in this schedule.

See also: **voluntary unemployment**.

jobber (310)

A specialized dealer on British stock exchanges who, from 1908 until 1986, bought and sold stocks and shares from stockbrokers, but not from the general investing public. This system of separating functions was peculiar to Britain and was supported on the grounds that it separated the risk of unsold stock (jobber's risk) from the risk of unpaid accounts (broker's risk). This distinctive arrangement of the London market was replaced by a system of **market-makers**.

See also: **Big Bang**.

job centre (820)

UK centres provided by the government to assist in job search by providing information on vacancies. Originally they were intended to separate the two principal functions of the former employment exchanges, the payment of unemployment benefit and the placement of the unemployed with employers notifying vacancies. It was hoped that an improved public employment service would make it more attractive to employers and would reduce the amount of frictional unemployment in the economy. Re-merger of them with benefit offices occurred in 1987.

job cluster (820)

The occupations of an **internal labour market** which are subject to the same wage determination process because of custom, technology or an administrative process. For each cluster, there is a **key rate**.

job control unionism (830)

A form of **trade (labor) unionism** which insists on strict **demarcation** for each job and a particular wage rate being linked to a highly defined job. There are examples of this in both the US and British labour markets.

See also: **featherbedding**.

job hopping (820)

Movement from job to job to acquire employment information, e.g. about the characteristics of employers, of other workers, of working conditions. This is a common practice of young workers in times of low unemployment.

See also: **search unemployment**.

job search (820)

See: **search cost**; **search unemployment**.

job security (810)

Guaranteed tenure of a job. This **trade (labor) union** goal is realizable in only certain types of employment, particularly public sector white-collar jobs and employment in major oligopolistic firms. The Japanese system of **permanent employment** is a leading case, although even that is less prevalent than imagined by foreign observers.

See also: **white-collar worker**.

job sharing (810)

The splitting of full-time jobs so that each job is performed by two persons. This type of scheme is primarily proposed as a means of reducing unemployment by converting full-time jobs into part-time jobs. The occupations for which this has been tried include teaching and social work. Although it is always feared that job-sharing will lead to an increase in total labour costs, especially social security contributions, recruitment and training costs, it can be argued in favour of sharing that shorter hours raise productivity as the division of jobs reduces the boredom which comes from long hours spent on the same task.

Johnson, Harry Gordon, 1923–77 (030)

A prolific Canadian economist, who in his bustling life wrote forty-one books and pamphlets and 526 learned articles and edited five leading journals, covering the whole range of economics. He was educated at the universities of Toronto, Cambridge and Harvard. In his industrious career, he was a fellow of King's College, Cambridge, from 1949 to 1956, professor of economics at Manchester from 1956 to 1959, and professor at Chicago from 1959 to 1977, combining that chair with other academic posts, particularly one at the London School of Economics from 1966 to 1974 which he relinquished, in a blaze of publicity, because of UK taxation. A central interest of his career was international economics, to which he often returned, as well as monetary theory, development economics and the major economic policy issues of the day. His much-used pen attacked vulgar applications of Keynesianism and collectivism.

Johnson, H.G. (1958) *International Trade and Economic Growth: Studies in Pure Theory*, London: Allen & Unwin.
—— (1967) *Economic Policies towards Less Developed Countries*, London: Allen & Unwin.
—— (1969) *Essays in Monetary Economics*, 2nd edn, London: Allen & Unwin.
—— (1971) *Aspects of the Theory of Tariffs*, London: Gray-Mills Publishing.
—— (1972) *Macroeconomics and Monetary Theory*, London: Allen & Unwin.

joint cost (010)

The cost of producing two or more goods or services which arise from the same inputs. Joint costs are not divisible into the separate costs for each good or service. Many managerial and research costs are of this nature. John Stuart **Mill** in his *Principles of Political Economy* Book III, ch. 16, laid down the rule that the sum of the prices of joint products must equal their joint cost. Today, joint costs are often arbitrarily allocated between products using an indirect measure, e.g. an analysis of the time of a manager.

See also: **indivisibility**.

joint demand (010)

The demand for **complements**, e.g. for computers and software, which is such that an increase in the demand for one leads to an increase in the demand for the dependent complement. There is often an inverse relationship between the price of one good and the demand for its complement, e.g. cheaper cameras encourage an increase in the demand for photographic supplies, because consumers allocate so much of their incomes to a particular activity which requires several related goods to pursue it.

See also: **cross price elasticity of demand**.

joint equity venture company (610)

A firm which is jointly owned by a public authority or government and a private company. This is a popular way for foreign companies to invest in countries with substantial public sectors or state planning. Sometimes the company only exists as long as it takes to undertake a major project, e.g. the building of a bridge.

See also: **venture capital**.

joint products (010)

Products which are the inseparable consequence of a single production process, e.g. cattle farming yields milk, meat and hides, coalmining produces coal, coke, gas and a variety of chemicals. In many cases, the rate of production for each of the products is the same.

joint stock company (510)

A firm permitted under company legislation to be a distinct legal personality with its members subscribing shares of the capital and having limited liability. By the mid-nineteenth century in the UK the need for large amounts of capital led to such companies gradually replacing partnerships in many industries.

joint venture (610)

The creation of a new firm by at least two private or public enterprises for the purpose of carrying out a particular project. This type of organization made possible the gradual introduction of private capital into communist countries, e.g. Yugoslavia and China.

Morris, R.M. (1987) *Joint Ventures: an Accounting Tax and Administrative Guide*, New York: Wiley.

See also: **joint equity venture company**.

J-shaped frequency curve (210)

A **frequency curve** with a positive slope.

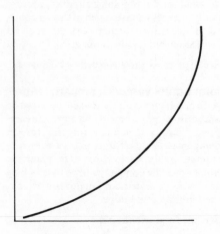

Juglar cycle (140)

A cycle in economic activity lasting seven to eleven years. It was first identified by Clement Juglar (1819–1905) in 1862. He noticed such cycles in prices, interest rates and central bank balances.

Juglar, C. (1862) *Les Crises Commerciales et leur Retour Périodique en France, en Angleterre et aux Etats Unis*, English trans. by W. Thom from the 3rd edn, 1916; reprinted 1968, Farnborough: Gregg Press.

See also: **Kitchin cycle**; **Kondratieff cycle**; **Kuznets cycle**.

junior debt (310)

A loan which is of lower rank than **senior debt** in the event of a company defaulting.

junk bond (310)

High yielding, high risk bonds which are rated below the investment grades assigned by the top US bond **credit rating** agencies Standard & Poor and Moody's. Although the risk of default is great, their high yield has made them very popular. Also, they have provided a vehicle for entrepreneurs to take over slumbering corporations. Junk bonds first made their appearance in the USA in the 1920s; by 1990 over $200 billion in 1,000 issues of these securities were outstanding. Such bonds have enabled non-blue-chip US corporations to raise very large sums of money, originally through the principal broker Drexel Burnham Lambert, which handled half of such new issues until its collapse in 1990. Investors willing to buy them included specialized **mutual funds**, the US government, insurance companies and **savings** and **loans associations**. An effect of the junk bond has been to draw to the attention of **commercial banks** the need for more finance for small firms.

Rubin, S.M. (1990) *Junk Bonds: After the Crises*, London: Euromoney.
Yago, G. (1991) *Junk Bonds: How High Securities Restructured Corporate Finance*, New York: Oxford University Press.

See also: **blue chip**.

Jurgensen Report (430)

A report to the world economic summit in Williamsburg, Virginia in 1983 on central bank intervention in currency markets.

just-in-time production (510)

A method of reducing stocks by producing goods only when they are wanted. This approach to the scheduling of production reduces the costs of holding inventories/stocks and increases the pace of production. It is extensively used in Japan and is increasingly being followed by UK manufacturers.

just price (010, 030, 820)

The price which gives labourers a just

recompense and in the estimation of buyers and sellers, or of magistrates with price-fixing powers, is fair. This approach to price theory was central to the economic thinking of **Aquinas** and his contemporaries. It contains elements of both the **labour theory of value** and the concept of **utility**.

Demant, V.A. (ed.) (1930) *The Just Price. An Outline of the Mediaeval Doctrine and an Examination of its Possible Equivalent Today*, London: Student Christian Movement.

Hollander, S. (1965) 'On the interpretation of the just price', *Kyklos* 18: 615–34.

just wage (820)

The wage which reflects a worker's contribution to society. **Aquinas** and his scholastic contemporaries expounded this ethical view of wages. Today, Islamic scholars argue that the just wage is unrelated to time spent as time is valueless. Also, modern writers on **wage differentials** and **incomes policies** have implicitly used concepts of fairness and justice.

Fogarty, M. (1961) *The Just Wage*, London: G. Chapman.

K

K (010, 220)
1 The capital stock.
2 A thousand.

Kahn, Richard Ferdinand, 1905-89 (030)

Famous in the development of **Keynesian economics** for his influential article on the employment **multiplier**. Educated at King's College, Cambridge, where he remained a fellow from 1929 to his death; professor of economics from 1951 to 1972. His *Making of Keynes' General Theory* (1984) illuminated the development of **Keynes**'s thought from 1923 to 1936. He was opposed to modern **neoclassical economics** in the USA and **monetarism**.

Kaldor, Nicholas (Lord), 1908-86 (030)

A Hungarian economist, at school in Budapest and at university in Berlin and at the London School of Economics where he was subsequently on the academic staff, from 1932 to 1937. He served as Director of the Research and Planning Division of the UN Economic Commission for Europe from 1947 to 1949, after which he was a fellow of King's College, Cambridge, rising to a chair of economics which he held from 1966 to 1975. He was awarded a peerage in 1974.

His prolific writings on taxation, growth and distribution are available in his collected papers. He was a precocious Keynesian who turned to growth theory and the study of increasing returns, emphasizing the importance of the manufacturing sector as the impetus to the expansion of the economy. His long career as a tax adviser to UK, Indian and various Third World governments produced a range of tax proposals, including the **selective employment tax** which was in force in the UK from 1966 to 1970: it taxed employment in the service sector to encourage manufacturing. His clear disapproval of the policies of **Thatcher-**

ism was evident in his *The Scourge of Monetarism* (1982).

Kaldor, N. (1978-80) *Collected Economic Essays*, London: Duckworth.
Thirlwall, A.P. (1987) *Nicholas Kaldor*, Brighton: Wheatsheaf.

Kaldor-Hicks compensation principle (010)

A compensation test of **welfare economics** stating that there will be a net gain in **social welfare** if those who have welfare gains can both compensate losers and still have a net gain for themselves.

Hicks, J.R. (1939) 'Foundations of welfare economics', *Economic Journal* 49: 696-712.
Kaldor, N. (1939) 'Welfare propositions of economics and interpersonal comparisons of utility', *Economic Journal* 49: 549-52.

Kaldor's laws (110)

The laws relating to economic growth set out by **Kaldor** in his Cambridge inaugural lecture in 1966. These three laws state that there is a strong relationship between the growth of manufacturing output and the growth of total output, that the growth of manufacturing output is a powerful cause of the growth of the productivity of manufacturing industry and that a faster rate of growth of manufacturing output is positively related to the rate of industrial labour mobility from non-manufacturing to manufacturing industry.

Thirlwall, A.P. (1987) *Nicholas Kaldor*, ch. 7, Brighton: Wheatsheaf.

See also: **Verdoorn's law**.

Kalecki, Michal, 1899-1970 (030)

A Polish economist who independently discovered many of the key concepts of the Keynesian system. After studying engineering at the polytechnics of Warsaw and Gdansk, he became a freelance economic journalist and analyst at the Polish Research Institute for Business Cycles and Prices, from 1929 to 1937. At the Oxford Institute of Statistics, from 1940 to 1955, he worked on wartime rationing schemes and refined his study of economic dynamics and cycles. From 1955 to 1970 he was economic adviser to the Polish government and then Polish representative at the United Nations. His major contribution to macroeconomics was late in being acknowledged (the translation from Polish was delayed) despite Joan **Robinson**'s frequent praise. With **Marx** as his starting-point, he developed a long-run model of equilibrium growth integrating it with his **business cycle** theory. He believed that **full employment** was a short-lived phenomenon. He has been a great inspiration for the **post-Keynesians**. He provided an account of the microfoundations for macroeconomics in his theory of **mark-up** pricing (the mark-up reflecting the relative power of an oligopolistic firm in an industry). This pricing theory is then applied to both the distribution and level of the national income as the prices of oligopolists will have a crucial effect on cyclical movements of national output. His model of the economy combines Marx's scheme of **reproduction** and the **multiplier**.

Feiwel, G.R. (1975) *The Intellectual Capital of Michal Kalecki*, Knoxville, TN: University of Tennessee Press.

Kalecki, M. (1954) *Theory of Economic Dynamics: an Essay on Cyclical and Long-run Changes in the Capitalist Economy*, London: Allen & Unwin.

—— (1969) *Introduction to the Theory of Growth in a Socialist Economy*, trans. from 2nd Polish edn by Z. Sadowski, Oxford: Basil Blackwell.

—— (1987) *Selected Essays on Economic Planning*, Cambridge: Cambridge University Press.

Osiatinsky, J. (1990 onwards) *The Collected Works of M. Kalecki*, Oxford: Oxford University Press.

Sawyer, M.C. (1985) *The Economics of Michal Kalecki*, Basingstoke: Macmillan.

Kantorovich, Leonid Vitalievich, 1912– (030)

Russian mathematician and economist, the principal originator of **linear programming**. After graduating in mathematics from Leningrad University in 1930, he taught in Leningrad before becoming professor at the University of Leningrad in 1934. From 1939 he concerned himself with major applications of mathematics to economics. His many achievements merited the Lenin Prize in 1965 and, with Tjalling **Koopmans**, the Nobel Prize for Economics in 1975. Much of his work was concerned with improving socialist **economic planning**, recommending decentralization and the use of **shadow pricing**; he has lived to see many of his recommendations incorporated into Soviet planning reforms.

Kantorovich, L.V. (1960) 'Mathematical methods of organizing and planning production', *Management Science* 6: 363–422.

—— (1965) *The Best Use of Economic Resources*, trans. by P.F. Knightsfield, Oxford and New York: Pergamon.

Ward, B. (1960) 'Kantorovich on economic calculation', *Journal of Political Economy* 68: 545–56.

Katona effect (150)

The effect of creeping inflation on saving. Katona argued that in such inflationary times there would still be expectations of rising real incomes so individuals would continue to invest in fixed interest securities: the rate of inflation would be sufficiently low for money still to be regarded as 'safe'. In times of runaway inflation, there would be scare buying and hoarding of goods.

Katona, G. (1960) *The Powerful Consumer: Psychological Studies of the American Economy*, ch. 12, New York: McGraw-Hill.

Keidanven (510)

Federation of Economic Organizations (Japan).

keiretsu (510)

A confederation of loosely related Japanese companies based on having a common banker or supply network.

See also: **zaibatsu**.

Kennedy Round (420)

A set of tariff reductions arranged under the auspices of the **General Agreement on Tariffs and Trade** which took place from 1964 to 1967. This sixth round of multilateral trade negotiations reduced tariff rates by up to 50 per cent across the board, except for items such as steel, textiles, clothing and footwear where there were considerable employment implications. President J.F. Kennedy was authorized to make this reduction under the US **Trade Expansion Act** of 1962.

See also: **Dillon Round**; **Tokyo Round**; **Uruguay Round**.

key currency (430)

A major international medium of exchange. A country whose currency is in great demand because of being a key currency has the advantage of being able to finance its balance of payments deficits easily, as the USA has found since 1951.

See also: **sterling area**.

Keynes, John Maynard (Lord), 1883–1946 (030)

The most influential Western economist of the twentieth century. With the benefit of an academic background (his father John Neville Keynes wrote an important book on economic methodology before becoming a university administrator), a brilliant degree in mathematics and tuition from **Marshall** in economics, he passed second in the civil service examinations. He worked in the India Office, 1906–8, before returning to lecture in economics at Cambridge (1908–20) and was a fellow of King's College, Cambridge, until his death. Despite his major economic writing and editorship of the *Economic Journal* (1911–45), the leading UK economics journal, he had time to advise the Treasury in two world wars, serve on the Royal Commission on Indian Finance and Currency (1913–14), the Macmillan Committee on Finance and Industry (1929–31) and the Economic Advisory Council (1930–9), chair an insurance company, be a patron of the arts, be a leading bibliophile and write extensively and entertainingly on many aspects of public affairs.

His early works were largely not concerned with economic theory, apart from a monograph on Indian currency. His attack on the Versailles Peace Treaty in *The Economic Consequences of the Peace* (1919) showed great skill for attacking the core of bad policy; his *A Treatise on Probability* (1921) indicated that, like his Bloomsbury Group friends, he was capable of tackling a tough philosophical issue.

In a series of three books, he groped towards a theory which was to dominate Western macroeconomics for over thirty years. His trilogy *A Tract on Monetary Reform* (1923), *Treatise on Money* (1930) and supremely *The General Theory of Employment, Interest and Money* (1936) contain the major Keynesian contribution to economics. Connected together are theories of the **consumption function**, **aggregate demand**, the **multiplier**, the **marginal efficiency of capital**, **liquidity preference** and **expectations**. Keynes had, he believed, dealt a mortal blow to the complacent depression-inducing economics of **classical economics**. Soon after his 1936 triumph his health deteriorated; but he was able to advise on the financing of the war and the setting up of a new international economic order (**Bretton Woods**) to succeed the crises of the interwar period. Although he was a member of the Liberal Party and described by Lenin as 'a bourgeois of the first water', he recommended the extinction of the **rentier** class and the socialization of investment. His parents attended his funeral.

Harrod, R.F. (1951) *The Life of John Maynard Keynes*, London: Macmillan.
Johnson, E. and Moggridge, D. (eds) (1971–87) *The Collected Writings of John Maynard Keynes*, 30 vols, London and New York: Macmillan.
Keynes, M. (ed.) (1975) *Essays on John Maynard Keynes*, London and New York: Cambridge University Press.
Lawson, T. and Pesaran, H. (eds) (1985) *Keynes' Economics: Methodological Issues*, London: Croom Helm.
Skidelsky, R. (1983, 1990) *John Maynard Keynes: A Biography*, London: Macmillan.
Wood, J.C. (1963) *Critical Assessments of John Maynard Keynes*, London: Croom Helm.

See also: **Cambridge Circus**.

Keynes effect (010)

The indirect effect on the demand for commodities resulting from a change in the general price level. This price level will affect the price of bonds and hence interest rates, the level of net investment and so the demand for commodities. A shift in the **LM curve** shows that this effect is in operation.

Ackley, G. (1951) 'The wealth–saving relationship', *Journal of Political Economy* 59: 154–61.

Keynes expectations (020)

Expectations in the short term about the price a producer expects to get for his product and in the long term about the returns to extra capital expenditure. The latter, crucial to his concept of the **marginal efficiency of capital**, was regarded by **Keynes** as a central innovation of his *General Theory*. Unlike other theories of expectations, the concept is not used as a central element in a theory of inflation.

Keynesian cross diagram (010, 210)

A simple macroeconomic model of the national economy derived from Keynes's *General Theory* which can be used to expound the theory of **aggregate demand** and demonstrate the effects of fiscal policy and the **multiplier**. Planned expenditure is plotted against national output to indicate various levels of national output for which the economy can be in equilibrium or disequilibrium. It cannot cope with the problems of inflation and monetary policy, unlike **IS–LM curves**.

See also: **equilibrium**.

Keynesian economics (030)

A distillation of the ideas in **Keynes's** *General Theory* into a macroeconomic theory and policy consisting principally of a model of aggregate income and expenditure using **IS–LM curves**, an emphasis on the importance of the investment **multiplier**, an assertion that the **liquidity preference** schedule is stable in the long run and unaffected by the actions of central banks and an insistence on the major importance of **fiscal policy** so that money and the rate of interest are of little importance to the management of the economy. Keynesian policy is most popularly regarded as the use of national budget deficits to maintain full employment. Although it was frequently praised in the 1950s and 1960s, it is doubtful whether many Western governments have pursued such policies for sustained periods of time. Heller cites the 1964 US tax cut of the Johnson Administration which he claims created 7 million jobs, doubled profits and increased gross domestic product by one-third. Other popular examples, e.g. the **New Deal**, have subsequently been challenged as only ephemeral exercises in applied Keynesianism. Just as **Marx** is reputed to have said 'je ne suis pas une marxiste' Keynes would have found it difficult to have accepted uncritically membership of the Keynesian School.

Coddington, A. (1976) 'Keynesian economics: the search for first principles', *Journal of Economic Literature* 14: 1258–73.

Hall, P.A. (ed.) (1989) *The Political Power of Economic Ideas: Keynesianism across Nations*, Princeton, NJ: Princeton University Press.

Hamond, O.F. and Smithin, J.N. (eds) (1988) *Keynes and Public Policy After Fifty Years*, Aldershot: Edward Elgar; New York: New York University Press.

Hicks, J. (1974) *The Crisis in Keynesian Economics*, Oxford: Basil Blackwell.

Hutton, W. (1986) *The Revolution that Never Was: An Assessment of Keynesian Economics*, London: Longman.

Leijonhufvud, A. (1968) *On Keynesian Economics and the Economics of Keynes*, New York: Oxford University Press.

Patinkin, D. and Clarke Leith, J. (1977) *Keynes, Cambridge and the General Theory*, London: Macmillan.

Wattel, H.L. (ed.) (1986) *The Policy Consequences of John Maynard Keynes*, Basingstoke and London: Macmillan.

Keynesian equilibrium (010)

A short-term equilibrium in a static model of an economy which is not necessarily a **full employment** equilibrium.

Keynes Plan (430)

See: **International Clearing Union**.

Keynes's *General Theory* (030)

The General Theory of Employment, Interest and Money, first published in 1936, is perhaps the most influential economics book to have been written in the twentieth century. It begins with an attack on the postulates of classical economics and an assertion of the principle of **effective demand**, lists definitions and ideas then discusses the propensity to consume, the inducement to invest, money wages and prices before an epilogue relating the *General Theory* to the **trade cycle**, **mercantilism** and future social philosophy. Keynes accepted the summary of the *General Theory* made by **Harrod** in a letter of 30 August 1935: 'Your view, as I understand it is broadly this: – Volume of investment determined by marginal efficiency of capital schedule and the rate of interest. Rate of interest determined by the liquidity preference schedule and the quantity of money. Volume of employment determined by the volume of investment and the multiplier. Value of the multiplier determined by the propensity to save.'

Admirers of Keynes have seen a development of the theory of the rate of interest and the crucial use of expectations in this grand theory but critics, including **Lucas**, have disliked the tone of the book and the decision of Keynes to work in units of money and labour alone to discuss economic aggregates; also, it has often been stated that the theory is not as 'general' as Keynes declared, that it is crippled by the use of the **comparative statics** method and that it needed later growth theory to complement it.

Clarke, P. (1988) *The Keynesian Revolution in the Making, 1924-36*, Oxford: Clarendon Press.

Keynes, J.M. (1936) *The General Theory of Employment, Interest and Money*, London: Macmillan.

Vicarelli, F. (ed.) (1985) *Keynes's Relevance Today*, London: Macmillan.

key rate (820)

A wage rate set by an **internal labour market** which links it to the **external labour market**. A key rate is associated with each **job cluster** of a particular firm's internal market.

kickback (010, 520)

See: **sweetener**.

kinked demand curve (010)

A curve shaped like half of a mansard roof which describes the behaviour of non-collusive **oligopolists**. It is based on the idea that these oligopolists will follow each other in cases of price decreases but not when one of them raises prices. Thus a demand curve results which consists of the joining together of two demand curves – the demand curve of the firm which raises its prices and the market demand curve. The theory, although suspect empirically, has been used to account for price rigidity in oligopolistic markets. In the figure the demand curve D up to output OK is elastic and so, if a firm raises its price, total revenue will fall; beyond output OK the demand curve of the firm, which is also the industry's demand curve, is inelastic and so a decrease in price will lower total revenue also (AR is average revenue, MR is marginal revenue and MC is marginal cost).

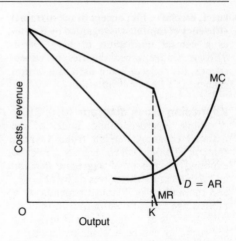

Hall, R.L. and Hitch, C.J. (1939) 'Price theory and business behaviour', *Oxford Economic Papers* 2: 12–45.

Reid, G.C. (1975) *The Kinked Demand Curve Analysis of Oligopoly: Theory and Evidence*, Edinburgh: Edinburgh University Press.

Sweezy, P.M. (1939) 'Demand under conditions of oligopoly', *Journal of Political Economy* 47: 568–73.

Kitchin cycle (140)

A cycle in general economic activity of three to five years' duration, mostly caused by changes in inventories (stocks). Kitchin first identified this type of fluctuation in 1923. When economists refer to the 'business cycle' they often mean this cycle.

Kitchin, J. (1923) 'Cycles and trends in economic factors', *Review of Economics and Statistics* 5: 10–16.

See also: **Juglar cycle**; **Kondratieff cycle**; **Kuznets cycle**.

Klein, Lawrence R., 1920– (030)

A celebrated US econometrician noted for his leadership of research groups which produced influential large-scale econometric models of the UK and US economies in the period 1955–75. He is also well known as an interpreter of **Keynes**. After a university education at Berkeley, California, and the Massachusetts Institute of Technology, he spent most of his academic career as a professor at the University of Pennsylvania. He was awarded the **Nobel Prize for Economics** in 1980.

Klein, L.R. (1968) *The Keynesian Revolution*, 2nd edn, London: Macmillan.
—— (1983) *The Economics of Supply and Demand*, Oxford: Basil Blackwell.

Knight, Frank Hyneman, 1885-1973 (030)

A founder of the **Chicago School**, being professor at Chicago from 1927 to 1955 after an education at Tennessee and Cornell universities. His doctoral thesis, published as *Risk, Uncertainty and Profit* (1921) is a classic of twentieth-century economics; it stated that profit 'arises out of the inherent, absolute unpredictability of things, out of the sheer brute fact that the results of human activity cannot be anticipated...'. His social philosophy is expounded in *The Ethics of Competition* (1935). His other contributions include an onslaught on the Austrian measurement of capital in terms of a period of production, **Pigou**'s notion of **social cost** and post-war social engineering.

Kondratieff cycle (140)

A long wave in economic activity identified in 1926 from index numbers of commodity prices by N.D. Kondratieff, who was born in 1892 and died sometime after his arrest in 1930. This cycle lasts forty-five to sixty years and is associated with cycles in investment in basic capital goods, e.g. transportation systems. Commodity prices rise in the upswing and fall in the downswing. For England, he noted troughs in 1789, 1849 and 1896 and peaks for 1814, 1873 and 1920; for France, peaks in 1873 and 1920 with a trough in 1896; for the USA, peaks in 1814, 1866 and 1920 with troughs in 1849 and 1896. (Each cycle is measured from peak to peak or trough to trough.) It is difficult to justify the use of price data in the manner of Kondratieff for more recent years of the twentieth century as the ending of the **gold standard**, the growth of **oligopoly**, major changes in **aggregate demand** and **indexation** of wage contracts have changed the relationship between prices and general economic activity.

Kondratieff, N.D. (1935) 'The long waves in economic life', *Review of Economics and Statistics* 17: 105-15.
Mager, N.H. (1986) *The Kondratieff Waves*, New York and London: Praeger.
Solomou, S. (1987) *Phases of Economic Growth,*

1850-1973: Kondratieff Waves and Kuznets Swings, Cambridge: Cambridge University Press.

Koopmans, Tjalling C., 1910- (030)

Dutch econometrician and economist who shared the **Nobel Prize for Economics** with **Kantorovich** in 1975 for his work on **linear programming**. Although educated in mathematics and physics at the universities of Utrecht and Leiden, he turned to econometrics and economics when he worked at the League of Nations in Geneva from 1936 to 1940. Subsequently, he was at the **Cowles Commission**, University of Chicago, from 1944 to 1955 and a professor at Yale from 1955 to 1981. His major contributions to activity analysis (operations research) were used to solve transport problems in the Second World War and during the 1948 Berlin airlift.

Koopmans, T.C. (1937) *Linear Regression of Economic Time Series*, Haarlem: De Aerren F. Bohn.
—— (1957) *Three Essays on the State of Economic Science*, New York: McGraw-Hill.

Kornai, Janos, 1928- (030)

Hungarian mathematical economist, educated in science at the Hungarian Academy of Science and in economics at the Karl Marx University of Economics, Budapest. He has been professor of economics at the Hungarian Academy from 1967 and at Harvard from 1986. Apart from his mathematical modelling of the planning process, he is famous for his attack on Walrasian **general equilibrium** theory and for his demonstration of how quantity, not price, balances supply and demand. Recently he has studied the similarities between communist and capitalist economies. His ideas have had considerable influence in the West.

Kornai, J. (1959) *Overcentralization in Economic Administration: a Critical Analysis Based on Experience in Hungarian Light Industry*, London: Oxford University Press.
—— (1967) *Mathematical Planning of Structural Decisions*, Amsterdam: North-Holland.
—— (1971) *Anti-Equilibrium on Economic Systems Theory and the Tastes of Research*, Amsterdam: North-Holland.
—— (1980) *The Economics of Shortage*, Amsterdam: North-Holland.
—— (1982) *Growth, Shortage and Efficiency: A*

Microdynamic Model of the Socialist Economy, Oxford: Basil Blackwell.

koruna (430)
The currency of Czechoslovakia.

krone (430)
The currency of Denmark, Iceland, Norway and Sweden.

Krueger, Anne Osborn, 1934– (030)
Educated at Oberlin College and the University of Wisconsin. After teaching economics in the universities of Wisconsin and Minnesota from 1955 to 1982, she became Vice President, Economic Research, of the **World Bank**. Her contributions to international trade theory include an examination of the relationship between income differentials and factor endowments and applications of **rent-seeking**. Her applied work includes trade studies of Turkey, India and Korea.

kursmakler (310)
See: **specialist**.

kurtosis (210)
The extent to which a distribution is peaked relative to a **normal distribution**. A highly peaked distribution is leptokurtic, a flat-topped distribution platykurtic and a low peaked distribution mesokurtic (see figures).

Kuznets, Simon S., 1901–85 (030)
US economist and statistician of Russian origin. After emigration to the USA in 1922, he was educated at Columbia University and began his distinguished career in a project with Wesley **Mitchell** on national income at the US **National Bureau of Economic Research**. He was professor at the universities of Pennsylvania (1930–54), Johns Hopkins (1954–60) and Harvard (1960–71). His work on statistical data earned him the **Nobel Prize for Economics** in 1971.

His major contributions to economics have consisted of reconstructing US national income accounts from 1869, discovering cycles of fifteen to twenty years in the economy which he set out in *Secular Movements in Production and Prices* (1930) and investigating the relationship between growth and income distribution. In his long 929-page book, *National Income and its*

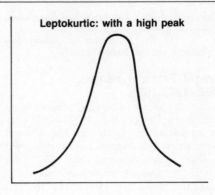

Leptokurtic: with a high peak

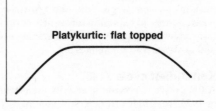

Platykurtic: flat topped

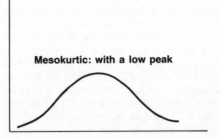

Mesokurtic: with a low peak

Composition, 1919–38 (1940) he showed his great care in the use of accounting concepts and the refining of raw data.

His approach to the study of economic growth led him to examine productivity and social costs and to formulate the thesis that the dominating factor in economic growth is the proportion of labour and capital of a country devoted to its growth industries. He noted that income inequality increased with economic growth in poor countries and the reverse in rich countries. Although regarded as the father of **national income** analysis, he has been the most wary critic of its use as an indicator of **economic welfare**.

Lundberg, E. (1971) 'Simon Kuznets' contribution to economics', *Scandinavian Journal of Economics* 73: 444–61.

Kuznets curve (110)

This shows the relationship between economic growth and income distribution, plotting income per capita against percentile or decile shares of different income groups. The share of top income groups is constant but income inequality falls for other income groups as per capita income rises.

Kuznets, S.S. (1955) 'Economic growth and income inequality', *American Economic Review* 45: 1–28.

Kuznets cycle (140)

A cycle in economic activity lasting fifteen to twenty-five years which was first identified by **Kuznets** in 1930. Changes in residential and other types of construction, particularly brought about by large-scale immigration, create these cycles. Each cycle consists of three phases: (1) the rebound from depression, taking three to six years; (2) steady growth at full employment, lasting seven to eleven years; (3) depression or stagnation of four to seven years' duration with high unemployment in most years. Phase (2) was stimulated by large-scale immigration in the case of the USA. The cycle has been less pronounced since 1945.

Kuznets, S.S. (1967) *Secular Movements in Production and Prices: Their Nature and Their Bearing on Cyclical Fluctuations*, Boston, MA, and New York: A.M. Kelly.

See also: **Juglar cycle**; **Kitchin cycle**; **Kondratieff cycle**.

kwanza (430)

The currency of Angola.

L

L (310)
A measure of the US money supply which consists of **M3** + nonbank public holdings of US savings bonds + short-term Treasury securities + commercial paper + bankers acceptances (net of + money mutual market fund holdings of these assets).

Labor Management Relations Act 1947 (830)
See: **Taft–Hartley Act**.

Labor Management Reporting and Disclosure Act 1959 (830)
See: **Landrum–Griffin Act 1959**.

labor union (830)
See: **trade union**; **US labor union**.

labour (010, 810)
A **factor of production** which consists of the effort and time of human beings engaged in the production of goods or services. The notions of **human capital** and **economic rent** blur the distinction between this factor and **capital** and **land**.

See also: **forced labour**; **labour supply**.

labour-augmenting technical progress (620)
Technical progress which raises output with the same number of manhours as at full employment.

See also: **capital-augmenting technical progress**.

labour cost (820)
All the costs of employing a person. In addition to wages or salaries, there are often **fringe benefits** and group facilities to be financed by an employer. In countries such as the USA where **collective bargaining** covers a wide range of issues, total labour costs can be considerably greater than the total wage and salary bill.

labour disutility theory (020)
One of Adam **Smith**'s labour theories of value which asserts that **value** is proportional to the 'toil and trouble', or **disutility**, of producing it.

See also: **labour theory of value**.

labour force (810)
All the persons of a country who are employed for a minimum number of hours per week, e.g. twelve, or are self-employed or are unemployed. The most difficult problems of labour force measurement arise from counting the unemployed and those engaged in economic activity within households. Some countries, including the USA, use **job search** as an indicator of an unemployed person's attachment to the labour force. The size of a national labour force will be determined by permanent international **immigration** and a combination of natural increase and **labour force participation rates**.

See also: **homework**; **unemployment**.

labour force participation rate (810)
The proportion of the population or a section of the population which is in the labour force. Thus if a country has 20 million women aged 25 to 44 years of whom 15 million are in the labour force, the labour force participation rate for women is 75 per cent. In many advanced countries, most of labour force growth is attributable to changes in labour force participation rates.

Labour force participation has been studied as a product of the decision-making of a household and regarded as being determined by wages, unemployment, education and attitudes to work. In the twentieth century, the most noticeable change in labour force participation in industrialized countries has been the increasing participation by married women. This has occurred because a reduction in **sexual discrimination** has opened higher education and most occupations to women, and the reduction in the birth rate, changing attitudes to women's abilities and the rise in real wages have increased the **opportunity cost** of not working. There has been a slight decline in male labour force participation. In the UK, labour force participation rates are usually referred to as 'activity rates'.

Bowen, W.G. and Finegan, T.A. (1969) *The Economics of Labor Force Participation*, Princeton, NJ: Princeton University Press.

See also: **additional worker hypothesis**; **discouraged worker hypothesis**.

labour intensive (610)

A method of production which uses a greater amount of labour relative to capital than other methods. Typically, only simple machines are used so that most production costs are labour costs. In countries short of capital, especially in the Third World, such methods are widespread in many sectors. But in advanced countries goods made by craftsmen and personal services, e.g. hairdressing, are always labour intensive.

See also: **appropriate technology**; **capital intensive**.

labour-managed firm (510, 830)

See: **industrial democracy**.

labour market (820)

A factor market consisting of firms as buyers and workers as sellers which exists to match job vacancies with job applicants and to set wages. It is linked to the product market because the demand for labour is derived from the demand for goods and services. Much of the notion of the demand for labour is derived from **marginal productivity theory**; the determinants of **labour supply** have attracted much more attention. It is often difficult to analyse labour markets because it is not clear who is participating in a particular market, especially one international in scope, e.g. a market for financial dealers.

Addison, J.T. and Siebert, W.S. (1979) *The Market for Labor: An Analytical Treatment*, Santa Monica, CA: Goodyear.

See also: **dual market**; **external market**; **internal labour market**; **local labour market**; **search cost**.

labour market policy (820)

Attempts to improve the **clearing** of labour markets. Central to the policy is the role of governmental agencies in reducing the **search costs** of employers and workers by providing free information. Many countries, e.g. Sweden and the UK, offer the services of employment agencies freely. However, the roles of private agencies and press advertising have always been important. A successful labour market policy will remove the coexistence of unemployment and unfilled vacancies (i.e. **disequilibrium**) as well as contributing to the reduction of wage inflation.

See also: **job centre**.

labour market rigidities (820)

Barriers to the free fixing of wages by each firm and region of a country and to the free movement of workers between occupations, regions and industries. Rigidities are particularly caused by national wage-fixing, **apprenticeship** schemes and housing policies which make it very costly to change residence. Divergent regional unemployment rates and high wage inflation are symptoms of such rigidities.

See also: **mobility trap**.

labour mobility (810)

See: **mobility of labour**.

labour power (010, 810)

1 The capacity of a worker to work for a given period of time.

2 Potential labour services, according to **Marx**, which are regarded by capitalists as commodities with both use and exchange values.

See also: **human capital**.

labour process theory (020, 830)

Marxist theory which shows the changing forms of the submission of labour to capital by analysing social relationships between workers and capitalists to show how **surplus value** is created and values are transformed into prices.

labour's share of national income (220)

The ratio of total wages and salaries of an

economy to national income. In the twentieth century, there have been increases in some Western countries in labour's share, possibly because of the growth in the **human capital** stock and **prices** and **income policies** which have squeezed profits.

Phelps Brown, E.H. and Browne, M.H. (1968) *A Century of Pay. The Course of Pay and Production in France, Germany, Sweden, the United Kingdom and the United States of America 1860-1960*, ch. 4, London: Macmillan; New York: St Martin's Press.

See also: **functional income distribution**.

labour standard (310, 820)
The value of money in terms of labour. **Hicks** asserted that after the abandonment of the **gold standard** in 1931 which made the determination of wages take place within a given monetary framework, **monetary policy** adjusts the equilibrium level of wages to the actual level. Thus the value of money is the consequence of the behaviour of the wage-fixing institutions of a state. The labour standard is a national standard, unlike the international **gold standard**. Hicks's long interest in labour economics ensured that he took into account both economic and social determinants of wages.

Hicks, J.R. (1955) 'The economic foundations of wage policy', *Economic Journal* 65: 389–404.

See also: **commodity reserve currency**.

labour supply (810)
The supply of persons, hours or effort for the production of goods and services. The labour supply includes both those employed and those not employed but desirous of being so. More persons are supplied through increases in the population (**natural increase** or by **immigration**) and through increases in **labour force participation rates**; more hours are typically supplied through overtime working; more effort is encouraged by productivity-based bonus schemes.

See also: **labour force**.

labour theory of value (020)
One of the oldest **value** theories, suggested even by **Aristotle**, but not clearly expounded until the **classical economists** made it a central feature of their theorizing. Both

Adam **Smith** and **Ricardo** attempted to relate long-term equilibrium value to the labour input of production but **Marx** is best known as an adherent of this view. Labour theories have a variety of forms, e.g. Adam Smith's three versions of labour quantity (the value of a good is proportional to the amount of labour needed to make it), labour command (the value of a good is proportional to the amount of labour of others obtained in exchange) and labour disutility (value is proportional to the toil and trouble incurred in production). **Neoclassical** economists firmly dismissed such theories in favour of a **marginal utility** approach. **Jevons** stated that once labour is expended in production it no longer enters into value but is lost and gone forever.

Meek, R. (1973) *Studies in the Labour Theory of Value*, London: Allen & Unwin.

See also: **value**.

lacking (010)
Robertson's term for **saving**.

Laffer curve (320)
A graphical representation of the relationship between **average tax rates** and total tax revenues which asserts that above a certain average rate of tax total tax revenue will decline. The curve is named after Professor Arthur Laffer, a prominent economic adviser to US President Reagan in the 1980s and a popular leader of the **supply-side** school of economics. Although Laffer's supporters are eager to specify more clearly

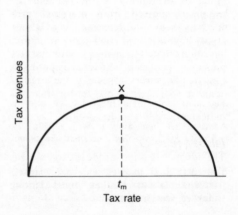

the shape of the curve, it still has the curious feature of associating each tax revenue with two tax rates, one high and the other low, except at point X where government revenue is at a maximum (t_m is the tax rate which maximizes tax revenues). The curve implies that, as there is a ceiling to the amount a government can raise, there is a limit to the level of public goods which can be provided. **Dupuit** in 1844 stated the same principle.

LAFTA (420)
See: **Latin American Free Trade Association.**

lag (010, 320)
The period of time which elapses between the change in value of an economic variable and the appearances of the effects of that change, e.g. the time lag between an income tax cut and an increase in consumer spending. These lags can be technological, psychological or institutional. They are a common feature of most economic relationships but are noticeably prevalent in matters of **fiscal policy** because a lapse of time is necessary before legislation and institutional behaviour can be adjusted: it takes time to change tax law, to pay out incomes and to spend money.

See also: **administration lag; implementation lag; inside lag; Lundberg lag; outside lag; Robertsonian lag.**

lagged variable (210)
A dependent variable in an equation which refers to a period previous to the time referred to by the independent variable.

lagging indicator (140, 220)
A series of economic statistics which changes after the turning points of a **reference cycle**. The principal indicators of this kind are consumer income and spending and interest rates.

See also: **coincident indicators; economic indicators; leading indicators.**

laissez-faire (320)
The doctrine, first propounded by the **Physiocrats**, that economic activities should follow their natural course, being subjected to few, if any, governmental regulations in order to encourage production and give consumers complete freedom. Thomas Carlyle described it as 'anarchy plus the constable'. As new roles for the state have been acknowledged, there are few adherents of the doctrine in its purest form.

Viner, J. (1960) 'The intellectual history of *laissez-faire*', *Journal of Law and Economics* 3: 45–69.

See also: **minimal state.**

land (710)
The fixed factor of production described by **Ricardo** as 'the original and indestructible powers of soil'; now used to refer to all natural resources. **Petty** and **Cantillon** both regarded it as the basis, with labour, of value, the latter asserting a par between land and labour as a particular quantity of land is necessary to provide subsistence to a worker, e.g. 1 worker = X acres. In practice it is difficult conceptually to separate land from other factors of production: its return is merged with that of the return to the capital expended upon it and other factors of production can be as fixed in supply for long periods of time.

Barlowe, R. (1978) *Land Resource Economics and the Economics of Real Estate*, Englewood Cliffs, NJ: Prentice Hall.

See also: **economic rent; differential theory of rent; rent.**

land economy (710, 930)
The study of property valuation and the economic factors determining the capital costs of land and buildings within an economy. This study comprehends the examination of the development of bare land to meet the market demands of the economy for accommodation, supply and property investments, ranging from those of agricultural land through to the optimal development of urban properties, e.g. offices and retail developments. Land economy matches demand for accommodation with the needs of the property investor and the restrictions of planners.

land ownership (710)
The distribution of the land of a country, a product of its land tenure system, much of which is based on custom enshrined in a country's property laws. Countries which

have undergone a socialist revolution often have transferred much land to the state or to small peasant proprietors. The pattern of land ownership is a crucial determinant of agricultural efficiency: too much division of land into small farming units affects the productivity for most types of agricultural production.

Landrum–Griffin Act 1959 (830)

US federal labor statute which responded to cases of corruption in several labor unions by giving union members a Bill of Rights which guaranteed participation in the determination of dues and initiation fees, protection of freedom of speech and information on the financial status of their union. Rules for the filing of union constitutions and union committee decisions and election of union officials and the exclusion of Communist Party members were also features of the Act.

See also: **Norris–La Guardia Act 1932**; **Taft–Hartley Act 1947**; **Wagner Act 1935**.

large-scale models (140, 210)

An econometric model of a national economy which uses hundreds of equations to estimate the relationship between economic variables. These try to simulate different government policies and are the basis of major economic forecasts.

See also: **linkage models**.

laser banking (310)

Banking which specializes in the financial needs of a particular region or type of customer or has a narrow range of functions.

See also: **niche bank**.

Laspeyres index (210)

A price or output index which uses the weights of the original year. The price index will be

$$\frac{\Sigma p_1 q_0}{\Sigma p_0 q_0}$$

where p_1 are the prices of the later year, p_0 are the prices of the base year and q_0 are the 'weights' of the base year. The output index will be

$$\frac{\Sigma p_0 q_1}{\Sigma p_0 q_0}$$

where q_1 are the quantities produced in the later year, q_0 are the quantities produced in the base year and p_0 are the prices of the base year being used throughout to value quantities.

last in, first out (540, 810)

1 A principle for the rotation of inventories/physical stocks. In UK **national income** accounting conventions it enables all items to be valued at current prices; a firm using this principle is able to finance the replacement of stocks in inflationary periods.

2 The employment policy of firms which lay off first the workers who have been recruited most recently.

late capitalism (040)

The **long boom** in Western capitalist economies after the Second World War which was regarded by Mandel and other Marxist writers not as a new epoch in capitalist development but as a further development of **monopoly capitalism** which could be analysed according to the laws of capitalist development set out by **Marx** in *Das Kapital*.

Mandel, E. (1972) *Late Capitalism*, trans. by Joris De Bres, rev. edn 1975, London: Verso; New York: Routledge, Chapman & Hall.

Latin American Free Trade Association (420)

An association of Argentina, Brazil, Chile, Mexico, Paraguay, Peru and Uruguay created by the Montevideo Treaty in 1960 (Colombia, Bolivia and Venezuela subsequently joined) with the aim of creating completely free trade between these countries by 1980. Failing to achieve its objective, LAFTA was superseded by the Latin American Integration Association in 1980.

Lauderdale (James Maitland), Eighth Earl of, 1759–1830 (030)

British political economist and politician who was educated at Edinburgh and Oxford universities. He was Member of Parliament for Newport from 1780 until he succeeded to his father's peerage in 1789. He is noted for being one of the first economic writers to consider macroeconomic issues. In his important work, *Inquiry into the Nature and Origin of Public Wealth and into the*

Means and Causes of its Increase (1804), he praised extra spending as a means of increasing public wealth and attacked both saving and sinking funds as ways of diminishing it. He also provided the first integrated theory of **profit** and **capital** and proposed **utility** in place of labour as the basis of value.

Paglin, M. (1961) *Malthus and Lauderdale: The Anti-Ricardian Tradition*, New York: Augustus Kelly.

laundering money (310, 430)
The transfer of cash or bank deposits through several banks in order to disguise the ownership of it and its place of origin. This technique, long used by criminals to disguise ill-gotten gains, is extensively used by the world's drug barons today.

See also: **drug economy**.

Lausanne School (030)
A group of economists of the **marginalist** school who worked in Switzerland in the late nineteenth century. With **Walras** and **Pareto** as its leaders it developed **general equilibrium** analysis and set out the criteria for welfare optima. There are many prominent descendants of this School, including **Hicks**, **Samuelson**, **Arrow** and **Hahn**.

Lautro (310)
Life Assurance and Unit Trusts Regulatory Organization, a London-based **self-regulatory organization**. One of its earliest policies, in 1987, was to recommend the cutting of independent intermediaries' commission on the sale of life bonds from 5.2 per cent to 3 per cent over a four-year period, harmonizing the commission with the rate for the sale of **unit trusts**.

See also: **Financial Services Act 1986**.

law and economics (020, 610)
See: **economics of law**.

law of diminishing marginal utility (010)
See: **diminishing marginal utility law**.

law of diminishing returns (110, 710)
See: **diminishing returns law**.

law of one price (010)
See: **one-price law**.

law of reciprocal demand (410)
John Stuart **Mill**'s explanation of the **terms of trade** which emerge from two nations exchanging their goods according to **comparative advantage**.

See also: **reciprocal demand law**.

law of reflux (310)
A banking 'law' expounded by Adam **Smith** and later by the **Banking School** that there could not be a permanent over-issue of notes as any excess would return to the issuing bank, being of no use.

See also: **real bills doctrine**.

law of satiable wants (010)
The general tendency for persons to derive **utility** from only a limited quantity of a good or service.

See also: **diminishing marginal utility law**.

law of value (010)
The mechanism in a **capitalist** society for distributing total labour power between branches of production via the prices of products. A consequence of the law is that the pattern of investment is determined according to the deviation of specific rates of profit from the average rate of profit.

law of variable proportions (010)
The **diminishing returns law**.

See also: **returns to scale**.

LBO (310, 520)
Leveraged buyout.

See also: **leveraged management buyout**.

lc (430)
Local currency.

LCH (020)
See: **life-cycle hypothesis**.

LDC (730)
See: **less developed country**.

LDMA (310)
See: **London Discount Market Association**.

LEA (610)
See: **Local Enterprise Agency**.

leading firms ratio (610)
See: *N***-firm concentration ratio**.

leading indicators (140, 220)
A series of economic statistics which changes prior to a change in **reference cycles** of an economy. The principal leading indicators are the index for the construction industry, the index for industrial materials prices, new orders for industrial durable goods, profits, business failures and common stock prices.

See also: **economic indicators**; **lagging indicator**.

leads and lags (430)
The advancing (leading) of payments and the delaying (lagging) of receipts, particularly in international trade. If the view is taken that a country's currency is about to depreciate, or be devalued, then traders of that country, in order to protect themselves against losses, will pay earlier for imports and will delay converting export receipts into the depreciating currency. It has been argued that in the past **devaluations** of currencies were precipitated by the leading and lagging payments, e.g. the devaluation of the pound sterling in 1967.

leakage (010)
A withdrawal from the **circular flow** of national income, especially savings, imports or taxation. The **multiplier** effect of leakages is to reduce the level of the national income.

See also: **injection**.

leaky bucket (320)
The partial failure to redistribute the entire yield from taxes on the rich through **transfer incomes** to the poor. These leakages include administrative and **compliance costs**, and distortions in working, investing and saving behaviour. Anti-poverty programmes are often leaky in these ways. The term was invented by **Okun**.

learning-by-doing (620)
The increase in productivity which results from repeated performance of a particular activity. Adam **Smith** recognized this in his discussion of the **division of labour** principle. Modern theorists of growth and international trade have considered this form of learning as an explanation of technical progress independent of the scale of production.

Arrow, K.J. (1962) 'The economic implications of learning by doing', *Review of Economic Studies* 29: 155–73.

learning curve (010, 620)
A graphical representation of the relationship between cumulative productivity and cumulative output. The relationship, which has been observed in several manufacturing industries, states that productivity increases through the experience of production.

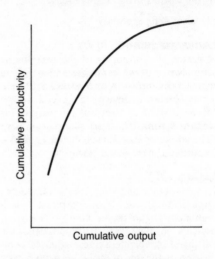

Cumulative output

See also: **Kaldor's laws**; **Verdoorn's law**.

least squares method (210)
A method of obtaining the best-fitting line to a set of observations by minimizing the squares of the deviations of the values plotted from a line going through the values. The line can be described by the equation $Y = a + bX$ where a and b are constants, Y is the dependent variable and X is the independent variable and is the regression curve of Y on X.

See also: **scatter diagram**.

legal tender (310)
Money decreed by a central bank or a currency commission as being acceptable for

the discharge of any financial obligation in that country. This makes **token money** acceptable.

Leibenstein, Harvey, 1922– (030)

US economist who was educated at North-western and Princeton universities. In his career he was professor at Berkeley from 1960 to 1967 after which he was Professor of the Economics of Population at Harvard. His studies of business decision-making inspired him to invent the concept of **X-efficiency** in 1966.

Leibenstein, H. (1966) 'Allocative efficiency versus X-efficiency', *American Economic Review* 56: 392–415.

lek (430)

The currency of Albania.

lemonade stand capitalism (070, 610)

An ideal type of **capitalism** consisting of small one-person businesses operating under **perfect competition**.

lemons market (010)

The market for used cars of less than average quality: the famous example used by **Akerlof** to illustrate **asymmetric information**. As sellers have more information than buyers, quality uncertainty about the cars will have the effect, in the manner of **Gresham's law**, that good cars leave the market so that only lemons are traded. This principle is applicable to insurance, the employment of minorities, the costs of dishonesty and credit markets in underdeveloped countries. Guarantees, brand names and the licensing of professionals can be used to protect against such uncertainty.

Akerlof, G. (1970) 'The market for lemons: quality uncertainty and the market mechanism', *Quarterly Journal of Economics* 84: 488–500.

lender of last resort (310)

The chief function of a **central bank** – to guarantee the **liquidity** of a banking system by always being the ultimate source of credit. Thus in the UK, the **Bank of England** is always prepared to lend to the money market by discounting the bills held by the **discount houses**; in the USA, the twelve

Federal Reserve Banks will discount the bills of member banks.

lending rate (310)

The rate of interest on bank loans which varies according to the type of customer. In the UK, major quoted companies are charged base rate plus 1 per cent, small companies base rate plus 2 per cent and personal borrowers base rate plus 5 per cent.

Leontief, Wassily W., 1906– (030)

The pioneer of **input–output analysis**. He was born in St Petersburg, Russia, where his father was a professor of labour economics at the city's university from which he himself graduated before further study in Berlin. After a period as economic adviser to the government of China, he emigrated to the USA, spending from 1931 to 1932 at the National Bureau of Economic Research, Wash-ington, before beginning his long tenure of a Harvard professorship. He was awarded a **Nobel Prize for Economics** in 1973.

His work on input–output analysis started with a paper on the subject in 1925 and the publication of the first input–output table for the US economy in 1925. Later he developed his model by incorporating the effects of excess capacity, price changes and technical progress. In 1973, he ambitiously began the modelling of the world economy using input–output methods. His input–output studies led him to advocate five-year planning for the USA as a means of reducing the costs of labour and capital being unemployed in phases of the **business** cycle. Another celebrated study in applied economics was his attack on the **Heckscher–Ohlin** theorem of international trade in 1954. Leontief has objected to many aspects of **Keynesian economics**, particularly its methodology which, because it relies so much on the definitions used, produces inevitable conclusions and policy prescriptions.

Leontief, W.W. (1951) *The Structure of the American Economy, 1919–39*, 2nd edn, New York: Oxford University Press.
—— (1966) *Input–Output Economics*, New York: Oxford University Press.
—— (1966, 1977) *Essays in Economics: Theories, Facts and Policies*, Oxford: Basil Blackwell.

Leontief paradox (410)

An empirical contradiction of **Heckscher–**

Ohlin international trade theory that international trade is based on the relative factor endowments of different countries. It was found that US exports are **labour intensive** and her imports **capital intensive**, despite the capital abundance of the US economy.

Leontief, W.W. (1956) 'Factor proportions and the structure of American trade: further theoretical and empirical analysis', *Review of Economics and Statistics* 38: 386–407.

leptokurtic (210)
See: **kurtosis**.

Lerner, Abba Ptachya, 1903–82 (030)
An Anglo-American economist, born in Bessarabia (USSR), who emigrated as a child to Britain. After working as a businessman, he studied and taught at the London School of Economics from 1929 to 1939. In 1939 he emigrated to the USA, where he was to teach in nine universities, including Berkeley from which he retired in 1979. His measure of monopoly power published in 1934 helped to found the **marginal cost pricing** rule of applied **welfare economics**. His London School of Economics doctoral thesis was published as *The Economics of Control* in 1944: it sets out the basic principles to be followed by an economic policy-maker, including **Pareto optimality**, equal distribution of income and budgeting with reference to employment and price effects. He was an early convert to **Keynesianism** which he enhanced by his work after 1945 on the problem of controlling inflation, including the construction of his anti-inflation plan.

Colander, D.C. (ed.) (1983) *Selected Economic Writings of Abba P. Lerner*, New York: New York University Press.
Scitovsky, T. (1984) 'Lerner's contribution to economics', *Journal of Economic Literature* 22: 1547–71.

See also: **market anti-inflation plan**.

Lerner effect (010, 320)
An upward shift in the **consumption function** caused by an increase in the level of money or public debt claims, leading to a **full employment** equilibrium level of public debt.

Lerner, A.P. (1948) 'The burden of the national debt', in *Income, Employment and Public Policy – Essays in Honour of Alvin H. Hansen*, New York: W.W. Norton.

Lerner index (610)
The measure of the degree of **monopoly** which uses the formula: price–marginal cost divided by price. This measure follows directly from the standard treatment of monopoly with an **inelastic** demand curve showing a divergence between **price** and **marginal cost** at the profit-maximizing level of output. Under **perfect competition**, this index will be zero for firms in a state of long-run equilibrium.

See also: **concentration**; **Herfindahl–Hirschman index**.

less developed country (130)
A country with a low per capita income, a large agricultural sector and often with little industrialization, high population growth, low life expectancy and able to export only a few products. Previously called 'an underdeveloped country'.

See also: **economic development**; **poverty**.

letter of credit (310)
A document issued by a bank which guarantees payment of sums due under **bills of exchange** and **cheques**. In most cases, these letters are requested by importers who are thus made sufficiently creditworthy to be able to order goods from foreign exporters.

level of significance (210)
The maximum probability at which a **Type I** error is risked. Usually the levels chosen are 0.01 (1 per cent) or 0.05 (5 per cent).

leverage (310, 320, 520)
1 The ratio between a company's long-term debt and the total capital it employs.

2 **Gearing**.

3 The difference between the actual level of **gross domestic product** and the hypothetical level which would result in the absence of receipts and expenditures of the public sector. The Musgraves measured it as

$$L = \frac{1}{1 - c + m} \times [(1 - g)P - (c - m)(R - \mathrm{Tr})]$$

where P is government purchases, R is its

receipts, Tr are transfers, g is the government's propensity to consume, c is the private propensity to consume and m is the private propensity to consume imports.

Musgrave, R.A. and Musgrave, P.B. (1968) 'Fiscal policy', in R.E. Caves and associates (eds) *Britain's Economic Prospects*, ch. 1, Washington, DC: Brookings Institution; London: Allen & Unwin.

leveraged management buyout (310, 520)
The purchase of a company by its management using fixed interest loans, which increases the **leverage** of the newly constituted company. The need to service the loans often makes managers more cost-conscious, thereby increasing the profitability of the company.

See also: **management buyout**.

Lewis, William Arthur (Sir Arthur), 1915–91 (030)
A West Indian economist who was educated at the London School of Economics and Manchester University where he was professor of economics from 1948 to 1958 before becoming principal and vice-chancellor of the University of the West Indies from 1958 to 1963, president of the Caribbean Development Bank from 1970 to 1973, and professor at Princeton University from 1963 to 1970 and from 1973. With **Schultz**, he was awarded the **Nobel Prize for Economics** in 1979 for his work in **development economics**. His early work was on price theory and **public utilities** but his fame was established by a celebrated article, published in the *Manchester School* in May 1954 which gave birth to much study of developing countries as **dual economies**.

Datta, A. (1986) *Growth and Equity: A Critique of the Lewis–Kuznets Tradition with Special Reference to India*, Calcutta and New York: Oxford University Press.
Lewis, W.A. (1955) *Theory of Economic Growth*, London: Allen & Unwin.
—— (1966) *Development Planning: The Essentials of Economic Planning*, London: Allen & Unwin.
—— (1978) *Growth and Fluctuations, 1870–1913*, London: Allen & Unwin.
—— (1978) *The Evolution of the International Economic Order*, Princeton, NJ: Princeton University Press.

Lewis–Fei–Ranis model (110)
A model of economic development for a two-sector **closed economy** in which the growth of the industrial sector increases demand for the agricultural sector's produce and attracts labour from the low productivity agricultural sector thus raising overall output and productivity of the economy as a whole. As there are few developing economies which are isolated from the effects of international trade, the application of the model is limited.

Fei, J.C.H. and Ranis, G. (1965) *Development of the Labor Surplus Economy*, Homewood, IL: Richard D. Irwin.
Lewis, W.A. (1954) 'Economic development with unlimited supplies of labour', *Manchester School* 22: 139–91.

LFPR (810)
See: **labour force participation rate**.

LGS (310)
See: **liquid assets and government securities**.

liberal collectivism (070)
See: **social liberalism**.

Liberman, Yevsei, 1912– (030)
Soviet economist and professor at the Institute of Engineering and Economics, Kharkov University, whose proposals for reforming the planning system, published as *Plan, Profit and Premium* in 1962, led to major changes in the running of Soviet enterprises, set out in the Enterprise Statute of 1965. He criticized the use of gross output as the key performance target and suggested that some notion of 'profit' acceptable to socialist theory should be employed. It was hoped that this change would lead to more efficient use of factor inputs and would make possible the setting up of incentive funds in each enterprise to reward more productive managers and workers.

libertarian economics (030)
A school of economics which emphasizes the importance of markets and the limited role of governments. Although the **Physiocrats** and some of the classical economists preached this *laissez-faire* approach, it is particularly associated with the **Austrian, Chicago**

and **Neoclassical Schools**, making Friedrich von **Hayek** and Milton **Friedman** its gurus.

LIBOR (310)
See: **London Inter-Bank Offered Rate**; **SIBOR**.

lifeboat operation (310)
The rescue of British **secondary banks** in 1973–4 by the **Bank of England**, assisted by London and Scottish **clearing banks**. Imprudent lending by non-clearing banks during the property boom caused many of these minor banks to have an increased number of bad debts. The nature of the Bank's help was compared with a rescue of the shipwrecked.

life-cycle hypothesis (020)
Ando and Modigliani's theory of **saving** and the **consumption function** which recognizes that for each age group there is an associated **average propensity to consume** and so a change in a country's age distribution will affect aggregate saving and consumption. This hypothesis has been applied to the financing of pensions as during a person's working life saving is accumulated which is spent in retirement. A reverse life-cycle hypothesis asserts that at the beginning of one's working life there is dissaving to finance education, house purchase or consumer durables: expenditure precedes saving in these cases.

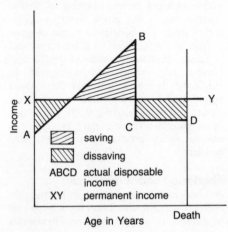

Ando, A. and Modigliani, F. (1963) 'The life cycle hypothesis of saving: aggregate implications

and tests', *American Economic Review* 53: 55–84.

lifetime averaging (320)
See: **long-term averaging**.

LIFFE (430)
See: **London International Financial Futures Exchange**.

LIFO (540, 810)
Last in, first out.

See also: **FIFO**.

light industry (610)
An industry using raw materials and components light in weight and noted for a great amount of **value added**, e.g. the computer assembly industry.

See also: **heavy industry**; **industry**.

limited company (510)
A firm owned by shareholders whose liability is limited to the amount of capital subscribed. Since the mid-nineteenth century this has been a powerful means of financing large firms. The extent to which this form of organization is used varies from country to country. In Germany, for example, as it is viewed with suspicion, very few companies are limited liability and public. The development of **secondary markets** in unlisted securities has encouraged the movement to limited liability.

See also: **GmbH**; **joint stock company**; **plc**; **Unlisted Securities Market**.

limit price (010)
The highest common price set by a group of sellers colluding together which they believe they can charge without new firms seeking to enter that industry in search of high profits.

LIML (210)
Limited-information maximum likelihood: an estimation method for simultaneous equation econometric models.

See also: **FIML**.

Lindahl equilibrium (210, 320)
A set of 'Lindahl prices' such that at those prices everyone demands the same level of each **public good**. These prices are

individuals' shares of the tax burden. This equilibrium is the equivalent of a competitive equilibrium for an economy with public goods. All markets for private goods are perfectly competitive and the government provides public goods. Pareto optimality is achieved by an appropriate redistribution of income.

Milleron, J.C. (1972) 'Theory of value with public goods: a survey article', *Journal of Economic Theory* 5: 419–77.

Lindahl price (320)
The share of total tax revenue paid by an individual which is the basis for his/her 'demanding' **public goods**. This price is equal to the **marginal utility** from a public good. The sum of Lindahl prices for an economy is equal to the cost of supplying public goods.

linear correlation (210)
See: **linear regression**.

linear programming (210)
An optimization technique originally applied to two problems: the transportation problem of determining the cheapest pattern of routes to supply a number of markets from a number of sources and the diet problem of determining the cheapest diet which will provide a minimum nutritional intake. Since the first use of this technique in the 1940s, it has come to be used extensively in the public and private sectors.

Baumol, W.J. (1958) 'Activity analysis in one lesson', *American Economic Review* 48: 837–73.
Dorfman, R., Samuelson, P.A. and Solow, R.M. (1958) *Linear Programming and Economic Analysis*, New York: McGraw-Hill.
Gass, S.I. (1969) *Linear Programming Methods and Applications*, 3rd edn, New York: McGraw-Hill.
Luenberger, D.E. (1984) *Introduction to Linear and Non-Linear Programming*, 2nd edn, Wokingham and Reading, MA: Addison-Wesley.

linear regression (210)
The relationship between two variables which approximates graphically to a straight line.

See also: **least squares method**.

line item veto (320)
The power to veto part of a budget whilst approving the rest. In the USA, forty-three governors can veto parts of State Budgets but the US President has no such power over the Federal Budget.

linkage (010, 110)
The forward or backward connection between industries at different stages of production. An application of the concept is in the measurement of the increases in employment and value added brought about by the expansion of one part of an economy. Most aspects of an economy – prices, taxes, public expenditure, technology and information – are considered. Some enthusiasts, who have emphasized linkages as the key to economic growth, have ignored the existence of resource constraints.

See also: **backward linkage**; **forward linkage**.

linkage models (140, 210)
Large-scale econometric models which link together national macroeconomic models to show the relationships between major national economies, especially trade and monetary flows and **exchange** rates. See **EPA**, **MCM**, **INTERLINK** and **COMET**.

Lipsey, Richard G., 1928– (030)
A Canadian economist educated at the University of British Columbia, Toronto, and the London School of Economics, where he was later lecturer and professor from 1958 to 1964. He was professor at Essex from 1964 to 1969 and subsequently at Queen's University in Kingston, Ontario.

He is famous to hundreds of thousands of students in the Western world for his textbooks: *An Introduction to Positive Economics*, first published in 1963, which is, as its name suggests, strongly empirical in tone and hence has been frequently revised; and *Economics*, which was first published in 1966 in the USA. He first made his mark as an economist with his joint article with Lancaster, 'The general theory of the second best' (*Review of Economic Studies*, June 1956), which made a major contribution to welfare economics. Subsequently, in a series of articles on inflation, he provided the microeconomic explanations for the **Phillips curve**. His numerous other works include articles on **customs unions**, **location theory** and monetary theory.

Lipsey, R.G. (1991) *The Collected Essays of Richard G. Lipsey*, 3 vols, Aldershot: Edward Elgar.

liquid assets (520)
Cash plus short-term assets (loans and bills of exchange soon to mature) which can be quickly converted into cash without a capital loss to the asset holder.

liquid assets and government securities (310)
The **required reserve ratios** of Australian trading banks which must be equal to 18 per cent of their total deposits.

liquid assets ratio (310)
A reserve assets ratio which takes into account both **cash** and monetary assets soon to mature and hence convertible into cash with small risk of capital loss. At various times from 1971 the UK banks, for example, were asked to have different liquidity ratios, the required percentage changing with the re-definition of liquid assets.

liquidity (310)
The characteristic of **assets** which are immediately available for the discharge of financial obligations: the most liquid of assets is **cash**. For there to be pure liquidity, it is necessary that the asset market is perfect with the consequence that the sale of an asset does not affect its price and that the asset is riskless because its price is constant. Securities are only liquid if there is an organized market for them.

liquidity preference (310)
Reasons for holding money classified by **Keynes** according to motive. He identified the **transactions, precautionary** and **speculative demand for money**.

See also: **IS–LM curves**.

liquidity trap (310)
The minimum floor to the rate of interest. **Keynes** expounded the view that the **speculative demand for money** would introduce this factor price rigidity because security prices would rise to a level that investors consider a maximum and consequently interest rates would reach a minimum. This 'trap' challenges the classical view that complete flexibility in factor prices brings about a full employment equilibrium.

lira (430)
The currency of Italy, Malta and Turkey.

List, Friedrich, 1789–1846 (030)
German economist and leading defender of **protectionism** who was professor of economics at the University of Tubingen from 1817 to 1819, a journalist in the USA from 1825 to 1832 and subsequently US consul at Leipzig and then Baden. He campaigned vigorously for the creation of a German railway system and Zollverein, or **customs union**. He committed suicide. His most celebrated work was *The National System of Political Economy*, originally published in 1841. In it he is very critical of Adam **Smith**'s 'cosmopolitan', or **free trade**, economics for assuming that there was the universal peace which free trade requires and for ignoring the fact that Britain had grown strong through protectionism. List argued that **free trade** was to the benefit of merchants rather than to the advantage of a nation as a whole for the basis of national economic power is the encouragement of 'productive powers', especially manufacturing, through protection.

See also: **mercantilism**.

listed bank (310)
See: **clearing bank; commercial bank**.

listed company (310)
A company whose securities are quoted in the list of a stock exchange's traded stocks. This listing increases the marketability of a company.

listed security (310)
A stock or share whose price is published on the official list of a stock exchange. The **International Stock Exchange** insists that for a company's securities to be listed it must agree to publish regularly many types of financial information, in addition to what is required under company legislation.

little dragons (730)
South Korea, Taiwan, Hong Kong, Singapore.

See also: **newly industrialized country**.

Lloyd's (310)
London insurance market founded in the coffee house of Edward Lloyd in 1688. It consists of underwriting members with unlimited liability for the risks they have underwritten and non-underwriting members. Syndicates of underwriters are responsible for most of the risk. Originally, Lloyd's was concerned with marine insurance but it has diversified its interests to fire, accident, motor and aviation insurance. Lloyd's Agents throughout the world and the Lloyd's List provide crucial information for the insurance industry. Although based in the UK, Lloyd's has long done most of its business with US insurance companies.

Hodgson, G. (1984) *Lloyd's of London. A Reputation at Risk*, London: Allen Lane Viking Press.

LMBO (310, 520)
See: **leveraged management buyout**.

LM curve (010, 310)
See: **IS–LM curves**.

loanable funds theory (310)
A popular theory of the determination of the **rate of interest** which was dominant before **Keynes**'s *General Theory*. Under the theory, the investment demand for funds and the supply of loanable funds through savings would in equilibrium bring about a unique rate of interest.

loanshark (310)
A person lending money at exorbitant rates of interest usually to borrowers with no collateral and no access to conventional lenders such as banks. This form of lending has long been a major activity of organized crime.

loan stock (310)
A stock exchange security with a fixed rate of interest and, usually, prior entitlement to payment out of any available earnings.

See also: **debenture**.

Local Enterprise Agency (610)
An agency in the UK financed by private sector firms to help potential entrepreneurs to set up in business. The principal form of aid offered is the free provision of specialist services.

local government finance (320)
The financing of the government of a region, city or district by local taxation and charges, and grants from central government. At the local level property taxes, local sales taxes and local income taxes are the principal forms of taxation used. In order to maintain the same standards of service throughout a country, a national government often provides grants to cover part of local costs, e.g. educational expenditures. Major problems arise if the local revenue is too small to meet local needs, e.g. if there is a large non-resident population, as in New York City, using facilities without paying full local taxes. Also, if there is not a clear separation of powers between the levels of government, a local government might pursue macroeconomic policies, e.g. employment policies, which are too expensive for it to finance, as has happened in the UK. Although property taxes are often a major source of local revenue and provide an additional tax base, they have been criticized for their regressive nature over some ranges of incomes.

See also: **community charge**; **federal finance**; **fiscal mobility**; **rates**.

local labour market (820)
A geographical market which brings together buyers and sellers within a given area, often defined as a journey-to-work area in which employers and workers are in close contact with each other. **Classical economists**, following Adam **Smith**'s celebrated discussion of **wage differentials**, believed that the free movement of workers in response to wage differentials would bring about an equalization of the net advantages of employment. Labour economists believe that there are fewer market imperfections, especially of an informational kind, in these local markets than in other labour markets. However, the conflict between **internal** and **external labour markets** has made it more difficult to see local markets of this kind functioning in a classical manner. Also, the

271

concept applies mostly to markets for less skilled workers. Managerial and professional workers consider themselves participants in the wider national and international labour markets.

Robinson, D. (ed.) (1970) *Local Labour Markets and Wage Structures*, London: Gower.
Smith, A. (1776) *The Wealth of Nations*, ed. by R.H. Campbell and A.S. Skinner, Book I, ch. 10, Oxford: Clarendon Press, 1976.

See also: **labour market**; **labour mobility**.

local monopoly (730)
See: **spatial monopoly**.

local public good (320)
A **public good** locally provided for the benefit of a local community and financed largely out of local taxation; a spatially limited public good.

See also: **Tiebout hypothesis**.

local union (830)
US **labor union** which organizes workers in one establishment, company or craft and hence is the smallest part of a labor union. In 1982, the average local union had only 200 members. Locals play a significant role in collective bargaining, especially in the negotiation of labor contracts between labor and management, and are combined into federations known as **international unions**. A labor union member has direct contact with the local, and not the international, union.

See also: **company union**; **enterprise union**.

location theory (730)
A study of the determinants of the geographical distribution of agriculture, industry and other economic activities. An early influential model was von **Thünen**'s which viewed the location of activities in terms of concentric rings around a central urban market with land uses and land values being reduced the further they were from the centre. Later theorists, including Lösch, sought to explain how industrial activity would be located at the point of minimum transport cost and maximum profitability, given the dispersion of raw material sources and consumers. As the theory of the firm was expanded to consider aims other than **profit maximization**, location theory took into account the possibility that a location could be chosen to satisfice rather than maximize the benefit to a firm and that sales rather than profits were of dominant concern. Much of location theory is now incorporated into urban economics and regional economics as location theorists have increasingly studied urban settlements.

Beckman, M. (1968) *Location Theory*, New York: Random House.
Hall, P. (ed.) (1966) *Von Thünen's Isolated State* (1826), Oxford and New York: Pergamon Press.
Isard, W. (1956) *Location and the Space Economy*, Cambridge, MA: MIT Press.
Losch, A. (1954) *The Economics of Location*, New Haven, CT: Yale University Press.

locked-in effect (310)
1 The effect of rising interest rates on the holding of government bonds. Holders of long-term government securities in times of rising interest rates (and hence falling bond prices) are reluctant to sell because of the consequent capital losses.

2 The effect of capital gains taxes being greater than inheritance taxes so that shareholders can benefit from refraining from selling stocks that have appreciated in value and passing them untaxed to their heirs.

locked-in industry (630)
An industry which cannot easily move because some locations are more expensive than others.

See also: **footloose industry**.

locked-in knowledge (620)
Technical knowledge which is specific to a particular production process and is not transferable to other processes; also known as 'tacit' knowledge.

See also: **footloose knowledge**.

lockout (830)
Industrial action by an employer to prevent employees from working until they agree to the terms and conditions of employment proposed by him/her.

See also: **strike**.

logistic cycle (040, 140)
A cycle in economic activity of 150–300

years' duration which when plotted as a graph (of industrial production against time) approximates to the statistical logistic curve of an expansion phase followed by a stagnation phase. The first cycle was from 1100 to 1450, the second from 1450 to 1750 and the third has not been completed.

Cameron, R. (1973) 'The logistics of European economic growth: a note on historical periodization', *Journal of European Economic History* 2: 145–58.

See also: **Kondratieff cycle**; **long wave**.

logrolling (320)
The political practice, extensively practised in the USA, of legislators trading votes. A vote is given for a particular proposal in return for voting for another proposal. Thus, projects with only minority support can be approved because their proposers have given their votes on other issues. The concept is essential to understanding how US federal public expenditure is sanctioned.

Lombard rate (310)
The rate of interest usually ½ per cent above the **discount rate** charged by the **Bundesbank** when acting in its capacity as **lender of last resort**. Banks can borrow for up to three months against the collateral of certain high quality securities, which include Treasury bills and federal bonds.

Lomé Convention (130, 420)
An agreement, originally signed in 1975 and subsequently extended in 1980 and 1985, which is unique in north–south relations. It is between the members of the **European Community** and forty-six developing countries of Africa, the Caribbean and the Pacific which exempts these less developed countries from all industrial and 96 per cent of agricultural tariffs of the European Community and is established through European Development Fund technical and financial assistance. Although another seventeen less developed countries have become beneficiaries, Asian countries are still excluded. The granting of aid under this scheme is now subject to human rights being respected in the recipient country. The amount of aid per capita provided is only a few US dollars per head.

Alting von Geusau, F.A.M. (ed.) (1977) *The Lomé Convention and a New International Economic Order*, Leyden: Sijthoff.

London Discount Market Association (310)
London's nine **discount** houses which constitute Britain's short-term money market.

London Inter-Bank Offered Rate (310)
The interest rate on dollar deposits lent between first class banks in London. Its principal use is as the base interest rate on which the prices of **Eurodollar** and other **Eurocurrency** loans are calculated. The **International Monetary Fund** uses it as a benchmark for calculating the interest rate on most of its lending. These loans specify an agreed spread above a LIBOR three- or six-month rate, usually of ½–2 per cent. There is no set procedure or set time for changing LIBOR. Other financial centres, including Paris, Singapore and Tokyo, have offered rates.

See also: **PIBOR**; **SIBOR**; **TIBOR**.

London International Financial Futures Exchange (430)
A market founded in 1982 which deals in a wide range of **futures** in financial securities, including gilts, US treasury bonds and Eurodollars; founded in 1982. It is smaller than the leading Chicago market, founded in 1972. New York, Canada and Australia have similar markets.

London Traded Options Market (310)
A market associated with the **International Stock Exchange**, founded in 1978. In 1990, it agreed to merge with the **London International Financial Futures Exchange**.

long (430)
A foreign exchange surplus. A foreign exchange dealer is 'in long' when his bank has a surplus of a particular currency.

See also: **short**.

Long Boom (040, 110)
The period from the 1940s to 1960s (or 1990 some state) which was characterized by historically high economic growth rates, low

unemployment and fairly stable prices. Cheap oil prices helped to sustain the boom.

long fraud (520)

A method of luring a supplier into advancing **trade credit** through acquiring a reputation for settling accounts. The fraudster reliably pays all debts when due and, after establishing such trustworthiness, incurs a large debt, e.g. on a major order, and then disappears.

longitudinal data (210)

Statistical information on changes to a cohort through time, e.g. the career of persons.

See also: **time series**.

long period (010)

1 The period in which all adjustments have been made to a price change.

2 The period in which supply is very elastic as a great expansion in the quantities of factors of production is possible.

See also: **elasticity of supply**; **Marshallian long period**.

long-term credit bank (310)

A bank which makes long-term loans to finance industry and arranges the issue of securities. Major examples of these banks are three state-owned Japanese banks, the Industrial Bank of Japan, the Long-Term Credit Bank of Japan and Nippon Credit Bank. Exposure to domestic declining industries in which they have long invested and increasing competition from other banks have forced them to diversify into new markets, including the international syndicated loan market.

long-term income averaging (320)

A method of calculating **income** to produce fairer progressive taxation of persons with fluctuating incomes. Without averaging, a person with only occasional years of high income would be taxed much more heavily in those years than is fair when the years of low income are taken into consideration. The principal method suggested is to tax cumulative average income in order to avoid long-term taxation unduly reflecting the few years of high income. However, there are critics of this system as the stabilization effects of progressive taxation are reduced. Australia has repeatedly attempted to deal with this problem. In the USA, the **Tax Reform Act of 1986** eliminated income averaging but reduced tax burdens by cutting top marginal tax rates.

Musgrave, R.A. and Shoup, C.S. (eds) (1959) *Readings in the Economics of Taxation*, pp. 77–92, London: Macmillan.

long wave (140)

A cycle in economic activity of about fifty years' duration, usually referred to as the **Kondratieff cycle**. This cycle in time series data was noted as early as 1847 by Hyde Clarke. A variety of explanations has been suggested for these waves, including a cluster of major **innovations**, wars, major changes in transportation systems and major changes in primary product markets.

Reijnders, J. (1990) *Long Waves in Economic Development*, Aldershot: Edward Elgar.
van Duijn, J.J. (1983) *The Long Wave in Economic Life*, London: Allen & Unwin.

See also: **logistic cycle**.

Lorenz curve (160, 210, 610)

A graphical representation of **inequality** first proposed in 1905 by US-born statistician Max Otto Lorenz. On the vertical and horizontal axes are measured accumulated percentage distributions, e.g. of firms and their sales. This is used in the study of **income** distribution and of industrial **concentration**.

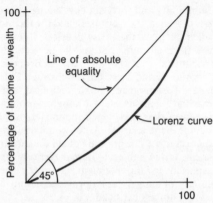

Percentile groups of individuals

loss function (210)

This shows the deviation of a data point from a least squares fitted line through a scatter of points measured on the vertical axis as a function of the deviation measured on the horizontal axis.

See also: **least squares method**.

loss leader (530)

A good or service which is sold at less than the cost of producing it as an inducement to consumers to use a particular retail outlet. Supermarkets have made much use of this marketing device.

Lotharingian axis (730)

See: **Rhinelands hourglass**.

Louvre Accord (430)

An agreement of February 1987 between the leading industrialized nations of the **Organization for Economic Cooperation and Development** to stabilize **exchange rates** between major currencies by maintaining the value of the US dollar in a period with a large US balance of payments deficit. The USA promised to use fiscal measures to reduce demand for imports and Japan and West Germany promised to employ monetary and fiscal means to expand their economies, with the hope the demand for US exports would increase. In order to keep the dollar's value high, higher US interest rates and a fall in stock market values were inevitable. The Accord provides a useful forum for the discussion of the economic policies of leading economies and their international implications.

lower quartile (210)

The value of a set of numbers such that three-quarters of the numbers are greater in value; the seventy-fifth **percentile**. This value is often calculated as a benchmark to measure **low pay**.

See also: **median; upper quartile**.

low pay (160, 820)

The pay of workers in the bottom part of the earnings structure. Various measures of low pay include being paid less than the lower quartile of earnings (bottom 25 per cent), less than the level of social security benefit or less than is paid to comparable workers. Increasingly low pay rather than less than **subsistence** wages, is regarded as relative deprivation – even Adam **Smith** and David **Ricardo** recognized that the notion of subsistence varies with time and place, being not only sufficient for food, housing and clothing but enough to participate fully in a particular society. The low pay problem is narrower than the poverty problem as it concerns only employed persons who either regard it as a problem because they are paid less than their marginal products or regard it as unjust to receive little for working normal hours. Suggestions for removing this labour market problem include **minimum wage** legislation, a narrowing of **wage differentials** and **incomes policies** biased towards the low paid.

loyalty bonus (310)

The extra shares awarded to the original shareholders of a company for retaining their investment for a stipulated period. Bonuses of this kind have been a feature of British **privatization** issues.

Loyd, Samuel Jones, 1796–1883 (030)

English banker and leading monetary theorist of the **Currency School**. Educated at Cambridge University; Baron Overstone from 1850. As a Member of Parliament and subsequently adviser to the **Bank of England**, he opposed many of the banking innovations of his day, including joint-stock banking. His recommendations formed the basis for the **Bank Charter Act 1844**.

McCulloch, J.R. (ed.) (1858) *Tracts and Other Publications on Metallic and Paper Currency*, London: Longman.

O'Brien, D.P. (ed.) (1971) *The Correspondence of Lord Overstone*, 3 vols, Cambridge: Cambridge University Press.

Ltd (520)

Private limited company (UK). Before the Companies Act 1980 the term also referred to public limited companies.

See also: **plc**.

LTOM (310)

See: **London Traded Options Market**.

LTU (810)
Long-term unemployed.

Lucas, Robert E., Jr, 1937– (030)

US economist, originally trained as a historian at Chicago University, where he has been John Dewey Distinguished Service Professor of Economics since 1980. As a vigorous advocate of the theory of **rational expectations**, he has become a leader of the **new classical economics** school.

Lucas, R.E. (1981) *Studies in Business-Cycle Theory*, Oxford: Basil Blackwell.
Lucas, R.E. and Sargent, T.E. (1981) *Rational Expectations and Econometric Practice*, London: Allen & Unwin.

Lucas supply function (020)

This states that output is the function of growth in technological progress and population, output in the previous period and errors in expectations of the price level:

$$y_t = k_t + \gamma (p_t - p_t^*) + \lambda Y_{t-1}$$

in which y is real output, p_t is the price level, p_t^* is the expected price level, γ and λ are parameters and k_t is the growth term. This function introduced a different notion of expectations from **adaptive expectations**.

Luddite (040, 620)

1 A member of a gang of English craft workers led by Ned Ludd in the period 1811–13 who showed opposition to the introduction of textile machines in Nottingham, England, and surrounding places and the consequent loss of employment by smashing the machines at night.

2 A person who takes **industrial action** in an attempt to prevent the implementation of technical change.

lump of labour fallacy (820)

The view that in at least the short run there is a fixed demand for labour. Employment can only be increased by job sharing and the creation of jobs by reducing the hours worked by the existing labour force. This opinion suggests that macroeconomic policy is limited in its ability to stimulate an economy.

lump-sum tax (320)

A tax of the same amount whatever the activity or circumstances of the taxpayer, e.g. a **poll tax**. A lump-sum tax on a firm increases its fixed costs but leaves **marginal cost** the same, and thus the output and price of a profit-maximizing firm is unaffected in the short run. In the long run, however, when all costs are variable, a high lump-sum tax could cause some firms to shut down.

Lundberg, Erik Filip, 1907– (030)

Leading Swedish specialist on the theory and policy of the **trade cycle**. He was educated at Stockholm University and subsequently was professor of economics there from 1946 to 1965. From 1937 to 1955 he was Director of the Economic Research Institute. His exposition of trade cycle analysis has been applied to Swedish stabilization policy.

Lundberg, E. (1937) *Studies in the Theory of Economic Expansion*, London: P.S. King.

Lundberg lag (010)

The slow adjustment of production to changes in income which causes investment or disinvestment in stocks as sales respond more rapidly than output. When incomes are rising, sales are more than output and so stocks are run down, causing unintended disinvestment; when incomes are falling, there is an unintended investment in stocks.

Luxemburg, Rosa, 1870–1919 (030)

Prominent socialist writer who was born in Zamosc, Poland, the daughter of a Jewish businessman. Educated at the Russian Second Gymnasium for Girls, Warsaw, and Zurich University where she graduated with a doctorate in law and political science in 1897 (her thesis on *The Industrial Development of Poland* was an original work of economic history arguing against the formation of a nation-state of all Polish nationals). She spent much of her life as a political journalist in Germany and as organizer of the Social Democratic Parties of Germany and Poland. As early as 1904, despite following many of Marx's ideas, she criticized Lenin for his autocratic centralist views. Many aspects of the Bolshevik Revolution of 1917 in Russia upset her, including the methods used and the signing of the Treaty of Brest–Litovsk with Germany. In her greatest work, *The Accumulation of Capital*

(1913), she developed the Marxian idea of capital accumulation, predicting that, as further capital accumulation is impossible in a closed economy, imperialist expansion into foreign markets and less developed countries would occur so that capitalists would be able to obtain further **surplus value**. Like her other economic writings, it was notable for its powerful historical illustrations. She was assassinated by a soldier outside a hotel in Berlin and her body was thrown into the River Spree, later to be recovered and buried.

Luxemburg, R. (1951) *The Accumulation of Capital*, London: Routledge & Kegan Paul.
Nettl, J.P. (1966) *Rosa Luxemburg*, London: Oxford University Press.

Luxemburg effect (430)

The causal relationship between the flow of money capital and the flow of capital goods from a metropolis to colonies or other satellites. Rosa **Luxemburg** asserted that this could assume different forms including loans between states, **portfolio investment** in foreign-owned enterprises and direct investment in overseas subsidiaries. The metropolis benefits from this in that the money flows generate a demand for its capital goods and the repayment of loans by satellites force them into economic dependence.

luxury (010)

A superior good or service which can be, and increasingly is, demanded at higher income levels. The poor cannot afford luxuries; the rich, having been able to satisfy basic needs, have a choice between purchasing luxuries or saving. The concept of **income elasticity of demand** is used to identify luxuries: if that elasticity is greater than 1, then the good or service is a luxury. Luxuries are often purchased to show the high ranking status of a person.

See also: **Giffen paradox**; **inferior good**; **income and substitution effects**; **Veblen good**.

M

M (010, 310, 420)
1 The money supply.

2 Imports.

M0 (220, 310)
The narrowest definition of the money supply consisting only of notes and coin in circulation plus bankers' deposits with the Banking Department of the **Bank of England**. This measure was introduced into the UK in October 1983 and given increasing prominence in Treasury statements from October 1985. So many payments are made by the transfer of bank deposits that M0 is only a partial picture of economic activity in a modern economy. Also changes in the method of wage payment from cash to cheque change the extent to which M0 is representative. However, it has recently been regarded as a useful guide to the size of the **black economy** which is dominated by cash transactions. Changes in M0 can lead or lag **nominal gross domestic product**.

M1 (220, 310)
Non-interest-bearing components of the **wide monetary base** plus private sector non-interest-bearing sterling sight bank deposits (UK). Currency outside the Treasury, Federal Reserve Banks and vaults of depository institutions plus travellers' checks of nonbank issuers plus demand deposits of all commercial banks plus **other checkable deposits** (USA).

M2 (220, 310)
A measure of the money supply created in 1982 in the USA to provide a good transactions measure of money. In the USA, it consists of **M1** plus overnight and continuing contract repurchase agreements and overnight Eurodollars issued to US residents plus **money market deposit accounts** plus savings and time deposits of less than £100,000 plus balances in general purpose and broker–dealer **money market mutual funds**. In the UK, it consists of **M1** plus private sector interest-bearing sterling bank deposits plus private sector holdings of retail building society shares and deposits and national savings bank ordinary deposits.

M3 (310)
In the USA this is defined as **M2** plus large denomination time deposits and term repurchase liabilities plus term Eurodollars held by US residents at foreign branches of US banks and the banks of the UK and Canada plus institution-only **money market mutual funds**.

M3c (220, 310)
Sterling M3 plus private sector holdings of foreign currency bank deposits ('c' refers to the currency assets included).

M4 (220, 310)
Sterling M3 plus private sector holdings of **building society** shares and deposits and sterling certificates of deposit minus building society holdings of bank deposits and bank certificates of deposit, and notes and coin.

M5 (220, 310)
M4 plus holdings by the private sector, other than building societies, of money market instruments (bank bills, treasury bills, local authority deposits), certificates of tax deposit and national savings instruments (excluding savings certificates, **SAYE** and other long-term deposits).

MABP (430)
See: **monetarist approach to the balance of payments**.

machinery question (620)
The effect on unemployment of the introduction of machinery. **Classical** economists, especially **Ricardo**, took the view that an increase in **fixed capital** would reduce the size of the **wages fund** and be injurious to workers, whereas John Stuart Mill

presented a more subtle analysis of the variety of effects of increasing **capital-labour ratios**. This issue of technological unemployment is still pertinent to many discussions in development economics.

Berg, M. (1980) *The Machinery Question and the Making of Political Economy 1815–48*, Cambridge: Cambridge University Press.

Mill, J.S. (1848) *Principles of Political Economy: With Some of their Applications to Social Philosophy*, Book I, ch. 6, ed. by J.M. Robson, Toronto: University of Toronto Press, 1965, Vol. I.

Nicholson, J.S. (1892) *The Effects of Machinery on Wages*, rev. edn, London: Sonnenschien.

Ricardo, D. (1817) *Principles of Political Economy and Taxation*, ch. 31, ed. by R.M. Hartwell, Harmondsworth: Penguin, 1971.

Machlup, Fritz, 1928–83 (030)

An Austro-American economist who was born near Vienna and educated at the University of Vienna, where he was taught by Ludwig von **Mises**, the supervisor of his doctoral thesis on the gold standard. In 1933 he emigrated to the USA and held chairs at the universities of Buffalo from 1933 to 1947, Johns Hopkins from 1947 to 1960, Princeton from 1960 to 1971 and New York for the remainder of his life. He was a leading authority on international monetary cooperation which is evident in his seventeen books and almost one hundred articles (e.g. *Remaking the International Monetary System* (1968) on that subject). His other interests in economics included the **theory of the firm**, the **patent** system and **economic methodology**.

Dreyer, J.S. (1978) *Breadth and Depth in Economics: Fritz Machlup: The Man and His Ideas*, Lexington, MA: Lexington Books.

Macmillan Gap (310, 520)

An institutional gap in the range of financial institutions which was observed by the Macmillan Committee on Finance and Industry (UK) of 1931. Small and medium-sized firms found it difficult to raise finance as they were too small to issue shares but reluctant to use expensive bank advances. It was thought that the performance of many companies, especially in export markets, was adversely affected by their shortage of capital. Since 1931, many new financial institutions, including the **Industrial and Commercial Finance Corporation**, have been set up to deal with this problem. Also, the availability of **venture capital** and the growth of the **Unlisted Securities Market** have provided more finance for such firms.

macroeconomic demand schedule (010)

The schedule showing different combinations of the price level and real income such that planned spending is equal to actual output, assuming that interest rates maintain the money market in equilibrium.

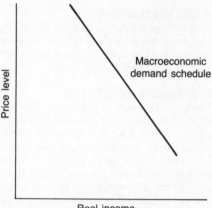

macroeconomic policy (310, 320)

Measures used by governments to influence major economic aggregates, especially **gross national product, unemployment, inflation** and the **money supply**. Macro-policies have been possible since 1945 with the growth of **national income** accounting, other increases in economic data collection and the theoretical framework provided by **Keynes**, his successors and rivals. Increasingly it has been difficult to separate macro-policies from micro-policies, particularly in the labour market.

See also: **Employment Act 1946; full employment**.

macroeconomics (020)

The study of the relationship between economic aggregates, particularly national income, total consumption, investment and the money supply. Although **Robertson** in his *A Study of the Trade Cycle* in 1915 was perhaps the first economist to emphasize the importance of considering output in aggregate terms, the **Keynesian** revolution made this new approach a concern of economics; the associated advent of **national income** accounting provided data to measure the relationships. Since macroeconomics is used to analyse governments' economic policies, it is inevitably surrounded by controversy.

Blanchard, O.J. and Fischer, S. (1989) *Lectures on Macroeconomics*, Cambridge, MA, and London: MIT Press.
Phelps, E.S. (1990) *Seven Schools of Macroeconomic Thought*, Oxford: Clarendon Press.

magic quadrilateral (010)

Joan **Robinson**'s description of an economy which simultaneously has full employment, fast economic growth, stable prices and a balance of payments equilibrium.

Mahalanobis model (120)

The basis of the second Indian five-year plan of the 1950s which propounded the view that a shift to investing in machines to make capital goods, i.e. heavy industry, instead of investment in light industry would eventually produce a higher level and faster growth rate of consumption. In some senses this was a repetition of the philosophy of the early Soviet five-year plans. The model has been criticized for neglecting supply constraints, other than a shortage of capital, and for ignoring the fact that many industries supply both intermediate and final goods. The model is named after Prasanta Mahalanobis (1893–1972) who was a world-renowned authority on statistical sampling and a member of the Indian Planning Commission 1955–67.

Malinvaud, Edmond, 1923– (030)

Leading Western econometrician and economic theorist who has had much influence on the construction of economic models. He was born in Limoges, France, and was educated in law at the Ecole Polytechnique, Paris, before turning to statistics. He was Professor-Director at the Ecole National de la Statistique et de l'Administration Economique from 1957 to 1966 and Director General of **INSEE**. His researches have included the normative theory of optimal resource allocation and the proper rules for the definitions fundamental to economics statistics.

Malinvaud, E. (1972) *Lectures on Microeconomic Theory*, trans. by A. Silvey, Amsterdam: North-Holland.
—— (1980) *Statistical Methods of Econometrics*, 3rd edn, Amsterdam: North-Holland.
—— (1980) *Profitability and Unemployment*, Cambridge: Cambridge University Press.
—— (1985) *The Theory of Unemployment Reconsidered*, 2nd edn, Oxford: Basil Blackwell.

malleable capital (010, 110)

Physical capital which can instantly and costlessly be changed into another form. A term much used in neoclassical growth theory to dispense with the problem of expectations.

Malthus, Thomas Robert, 1766–1834 (030, 840)

A leading classical economist who played a major part in founding modern **demography**. After Cambridge, where he was a student and fellow of Jesus College from 1784 to 1805, for the rest of his career he was professor of modern history and political economy at Haileybury College, Hertfordshire, training clerks for the East India Company.

The optimism of William Godwin's *Enquiry Concerning Political Justice* (1793) prompted him to write *An Essay on the Principle of Population* (1798) which asserted that population grows in a **geometrical progression** but that the means of subsistence increases in only an **arithmetic progression**. Unless population growth is subject to a preventive check (e.g. abortion) or a positive check (war, famine, pestilence) there will be misery and vice. In subsequent editions he included more analysis of population statistics and another check ('moral restraint'). Despite contemporary criticism, it became a pillar of the **Ricardian** system. Later, socialists and other critics attacked such pessimistic predictions for ignoring the beneficial effects of technical progress. Nevertheless Malthus's *Essay* was a major theoretical inspiration to Charles Darwin when he was formulating the theory of evolution. Malthus's *Principles of Political Economy* (1820) provided a fuller analysis of value and price theory than **Ricardo** and discussed the problem of a deficiency in '**effectual demand**' ('a general glut'), causing

Keynes to rank Malthus as one of his major predecessors as a macroeconomic theorist.

Cunningham Wood, J. (1986) *Thomas Robert Malthus: Critical Assessments*, London: Croom Helm.
James, P. (1979) *Population Malthus, His Life and Times*, London: Routledge & Kegan Paul.
Wrigley, E.A. and Souden, D. (eds) (1986) *The Works of Thomas Robert Malthus*, 8 vols, London: Pickering & Chatto.

managed currency fund (310)

An investment fund with its assets in several currencies which creates profits for investors by buying and selling foreign currencies in anticipation of fluctuations in their value and from earnings arising from deposit-holdings and interest on short-term bonds.

managed floating system (430)

The post **Bretton Woods** exchange rate regime in which the extent to which exchange rates could freely move to establish their market values was limited by the intervention of **central banks**.

See also: **dirty float**.

management accounting (540)

The financial appraisal of the past, present and future activities of a firm. It includes **cash budgeting** (a prediction of future cash inflows and outflows which indicates what further finance is required), **capital budgeting** (appraisal of investment plans) and **transfer pricing**. Management accountants are also concerned to monitor the design of present accounting systems to prevent fraud and to meet the growing needs of management for information. It developed from cost accounting in response to the increasing complexity of large firms.

See also: **accounting**; **financial accounting**.

management buyout (310, 520)

A management's purchase of a company from its shareholders. Buyouts have become increasingly popular in the UK and the USA since the 1960s as many managers fear the dismemberment of their company by a receiver. Often managers finance the acquisition by fixed interest borrowing using the collateral of the company's assets in a **leveraged buyout**.

See also: **asset stripping**.

management by objectives (510)

The setting of specific targets for subordinate managers relating to each of their tasks so that the individual efficiency of each unit of an organization can be monitored regularly.

managerial models of the firm (020, 510)

Explanations of the behaviour of a **firm** according to its dominant aims. The various aims assumed include sales maximization, **profit maximization**, **managerial utility function maximization** and maximization of the rate of growth of the firm. It has been argued that the passing of the control of firms from shareholders to managers has been responsible for a change of aims. However, some Marxists argue that the aims of firms essentially remain the same as shareholders and managers have similar socioeconomic backgrounds.

Marris, R. (1964) *The Economic Theory of Managerial Capitalism*, London: Macmillan.

managerial revolution (070, 510)

James Burnham's theory that after 1914 there was a transition from a capitalist to a managerial society with the class of managers dominant, operating most effectively where the state owns the means of production. Because managers became the ruling class, they exploited workers just as individual capitalists had done before, ensuring that there would be an unequal distribution of income. As managers without capital will not be guided by a profit motive, the economy they run will be less subject to cyclical fluctuations and crises and can be successfully planned; this planning will take a long-term view which will encourage invention and innovation. Much of Burnham's argument is couched in Marxist terms as in his career as professor of philosophy at New York University (1932–54) his dominant concern was a socialist critique of contemporary society. **Galbraith** and others have viewed this revolution more loosely as a recognition of the transfer of power in corporations from shareholders to hired managers.

Burnham, J. (1945) *The Managerial Revolution*, Harmondsworth: Penguin.

managerial utility function maximization (510)

Maximization of the satisfaction of the managers of a **firm**. The utility of managers will be increased if their status improves by an enlargement of staff expenditures, as this shows ability to manage, or if managerial salaries and profits are higher than an acceptable minimum level.

Williamson, O.E. (1964) *The Economics of Discretionary Behavior: Managerial Objectives in a Theory of the Firm*, Englewood Cliffs, NJ: Prentice Hall.

Manchester School (030, 040)

Disraeli's term for the nineteenth-century Lancashire cotton manufacturers and politicians who strenuously advocated **free trade**. The original centre of the School was the Anti-Corn Law League (founded in 1838 by Richard Cobden and John Bright) but it expanded its *laissez-faire* principles over other policy issues. It was more of an action group than a school of economics; contemporary German **protectionists** contemptuously called it 'Manchestertum'.

Grampp, W.D. (1960) *The Manchester School*, Stanford, CT: Stanford University Press.

See also: **Corn Laws**.

Mandeville, Bernard, 1670–1733 (030)

Dutch born doctor of medicine and essayist who, after his education at the University of Leiden, settled in London. In a series of poems and essays compiled as *The Fable of the Bees* (1714 and 1724) he demonstrated that private vices such as vanity, fraud and theft promote the public good by providing much employment. In a sense he anticipated the **invisible hand** principle of **Smith** and the *'laissez-faire'* views of some **classical economists**.

Hayek, F.A. (1966) 'Mandeville', *Proceedings of the British Academy* 52: 125–41.
Mandeville, B. (1970) *The Fable of the Bees*, ed. by P. Harth, Harmondsworth: Penguin.

manpower forecasting (140, 810)

Estimating the future demand of and supply for labour. These forecasts can be made for a nation, a region or a firm. They consist of deriving a demand for labour forecast from an output forecast and fixed labour–output coefficients (sometimes revised by informed management opinion) and a supply of labour forecast based on population projections, **labour force participation rates** and estimations of labour migration.

manpower policy (810)

Various measures to train the **labour force**, increase **labour force participation rates**, improve the allocation of the existing labour force and bring about a close match between labour demand and supply in the future. The first step in the operation of this policy is to prepare a manpower forecast, often by applying fixed labour–output coefficients to output forecasts. From these forecasts it is possible to see which instruments of manpower policy should be chosen, e.g. training measures to eliminate an expected shortage of skilled workers. Although many countries had active manpower policies during the Second World War as the demands of the armed forces for personnel created labour shortages elsewhere in most economies, it was not until the 1950s and 1960s that the UK and the USA pursued active policies.

See also: **labour market policy**.

MAP (150)
See: **market anti-inflation plan**.

Marcet, Jane, 1769–1858 (030)

Wife of a distinguished physician and daughter of a Swiss merchant but one of the best known writers on economics in the nineteenth century. Her *Conversations on Political Economy, in which the Elements of that Science are Familiarly Explained* (1816), published ten years after her successful *Conversations on Chemistry*, anticipated some of **Ricardo**'s ideas and was praised by both him and **Say**. Her stern summary of classical economics takes the form of conversations between Mrs B and Caroline on twenty-one topics, including property, division of labour, capital, wages, population, the condition of the poor, revenue from factors of production, value, money, foreign trade and expenditure. Caroline is encouraged to study economics as 'you will seldom hear a conversation amongst liberal-minded people without some reference to it'.

See also: **female economists**.

marginal cost (010)

The cost of producing another unit of output. Whether marginal cost falls, rises or is constant depends on whether there are increasing, decreasing or constant **returns to scale**.

See also: **average incremental cost**.

marginal cost of abatement (010, 720)

The cost of removing the last unit of a nuisance, e.g. a noise or some form of physical pollution. This measure can be used to see whether it is worthwhile to reduce the external costs of an activity, e.g. to calculate the expense of reducing a noise by a decibel at a time until an acceptable level has been reached.

marginal cost pricing (020, 520)

Setting a price so that it is equal to the **marginal cost** of producing that good or service. It is justified on the grounds of maximizing social efficiency. In practice, there are difficulties in following this rule. Deficits can arise for a firm with declining **average total costs**, and consequently falling marginal costs, as prices, if set equal to marginal costs, would fail to cover fixed costs. However, these can be covered separately – by government subsidy or by a **two-part tariff**, part of which would be 'the price of entry' to the market, e.g. a telephone rental can cover fixed costs and the charge for calls marginal costs. Computational experience in applying this principle has increasingly dealt with the problems of fixed costs, complex production and distribution systems and changes in demand and technology. Critics of this type of pricing remain concerned about its **monopoly** and income distribution effects.

Rees, R. (1984) *Public Enterprise Economics*, ch. 5, London: Weidenfeld & Nicolson.

marginal efficiency of capital (010, 520)

The rate of discount which will make the present value of a stream of annual incomes from an investment in fixed capital equal to the current supply price of that asset. The concept can be expressed in a diagram: net investment I will expand until it reaches I_1 where the marginal efficiency of capital MEC is equal to the rate of interest i.

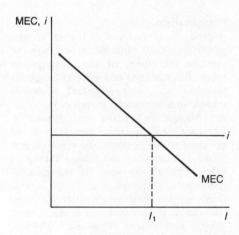

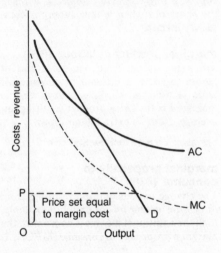

Keynes, J.M. (1936) *The General Theory of Employment, Interest and Money*, Book IV, ch. 2, London: Macmillan; New York: St Martin's Press.

marginal efficiency of investment (010, 520)

The **internal rate of return** on capital, net of the rate of interest.

marginal employment subsidy (820)

A government subsidy given to firms for the creation of every additional job above a stated reference level of employment. This scheme can be more effective than a general employment subsidy as it targets pockets of severe unemployment.

marginal firm (610)

An established firm of an industry which is only earning **normal profits** and would leave that industry if its net earnings were less. This concept is crucial to **perfect competition**.

marginalism (010)

An economic method, central to **neoclassical economics**, much used since 1870 in economics. In most cases, it compares an incremental change in one variable with such a change in another, e.g. a change in total costs compared with a change in total revenue. It assumes automatic movement to **equilibrium** and ignores institutional impediments.

marginalists (030)

A group of economists of the 1870s who powerfully used differential calculus to examine the effects of small changes in economic quantities and were amongst the founders of the **neoclassical economic** school. Simultaneously, **Jevons** in Manchester, **Menger** in Vienna and **Walras** in Lausanne emphasized the notion of **marginal utility** as central to value theory, thereby abandoning the **labour theory of value** popular with many of the **classical economists**. Although many have viewed their work as a revolution in economics, they had many predecessors who share their glory, particularly **Cournot**, **Thünen**, **Dupuit** and **Gossen**.

Black, R.D., Coats, A.W. and Goodwin, C.D.W. (1973) *The Marginal Revolution in Economics*, Durham, NC: Duke University Press.

See also: **continuity thesis**.

marginal physical product (010)

The extra amount of output from employing another unit of a factor of production, e.g. labour or capital.

See also: **marginal revenue product; returns to scale**.

marginal principle of allocation (010)

Allocation based on paying attention to the distribution of the last unit of resources so that the most efficient allocation of resources results. This principle, introduced by the **neoclassical economic** school, is at the heart of much decision-making – especially at the level of the firm.

marginal private cost (010)

The cost to a household or firm of producing an extra unit of output.

See also: **marginal social cost**.

marginal private damage (520, 720)

The cost to a firm of producing another unit of a good or service which generates externalities, e.g. a chemical works will have to bear the costs of corroded pipes.

See also: **marginal social damage**.

marginal productivity theory (020, 820)

A theory of the demand for a **factor of production** by a profit-maximizing firm. It is asserted that labour or capital will be demanded until the **marginal revenue** from employing it is equal to its **marginal cost**. The theory, first expounded by John Bates **Clark**, has been used to explain wage determination but, as it says nothing about supply, is only useful in explaining wages in the short run when labour supply is completely **inelastic**.

marginal product of labour (010)

The extra output from one more unit of labour input. It is difficult to measure for large sectors and so, as a proxy, what is measured is the extra product resulting, on average, from an extra labour input.

See also: **average incremental cost**.

marginal propensity to consume (010)

The change in consumption resulting from increasing income by one unit. For example, if all the additional income is consumed, the marginal propensity to consume (MPC) is 1;

if only one-half, the MPC is 0.5. This measure is essential in **consumption function** and **multiplier** analysis. Consumer research shows that MPCs are usually lower for higher income groups.

marginal propensity to import (010, 420)

The change in the value of imports brought about by income increasing by one unit. If all extra income is spent on imports, the marginal propensity to import (MPM) is 1; if only 10 per cent is spent on imports, the MPM is 0.1. Calculation of the MPM is essential to a measurement of the **foreign trade multiplier**.

marginal propensity to save (010)

The change in saving resulting from income increasing by one unit. In a simple economy described by the equation national income = consumption + saving, the **marginal propensity to consume** plus the marginal propensity to save is equal to unity. An economy with a high marginal propensity to save will have little scope for **multiplier** expansion of its national income as saving is a withdrawal from the **circular flow** of income.

marginal rate of substitution (010)

1 The amount of one good which a consumer receives as compensation for giving up one unit of another good.

2 The ratio of the **marginal utilities** of two goods.

3 The slope of an **indifference curve**.

Hicks, J.R. (1939) *Value and Capital*, ch. 1, Oxford: Oxford University Press.

marginal rate of transformation (010)

The reduction in the amount of output of good X as a consequence of an additional unit of a related good Y being produced; the slope of the **production possibility frontier**. This marginal rate is equal to the marginal cost of Y divided by the marginal cost of X.

marginal revenue (010)

The increase in total revenue resulting from output increasing by one unit. Under **perfect competition**, a firm's marginal revenue will equal the price of its product as its demand curve is horizontal. For a firm to maximize its profits, it must choose the output level where its marginal revenue is equal to marginal cost.

marginal revenue product (010)

A **marginal physical product** (MPP) multiplied by the **marginal revenue** obtained from that unit. Under **perfect competition**, as price is equal to **marginal revenue**, the marginal revenue product (MRP) is equal to the product of the MPP and price. The MRP shows the addition to the **total revenue** of a firm of producing another unit.

marginal social cost (010)

The extra cost to society of one unit of output.

See also: **externality**; **marginal private cost**.

marginal social damage (010, 720)

The total private and non-private cost to society of producing another unit of a good or service which injures persons and the environment, e.g. a chemical works with pollutant by-products will increase the private costs of its owner and also any member of society coming into contact with the pollution. There is no incentive to abate pollution if the marginal cost of abatement is greater than the marginal social damage.

See also: **marginal cost of abatement**; **marginal private damage**.

marginal tax rate (320)

The amount of tax paid on an extra unit of money income. In the study of labour supply, marginal tax rates are often calculated to see whether high marginal rates have an incentive or disincentive effect on labour supply. An incentive effect occurs if a taxpayer has a target post-tax income which can only be achieved by working more after a rise in the marginal rate of tax; a disincentive effect occurs if a higher marginal tax rate makes the taxpayer opt for leisure instead of work.

See also: **average tax rate**.

marginal utility (010)

The amount of satisfaction obtained from consumption of the last unit of a good or service. Although there were hints of such an analytical tool in economics before 1870, particularly in **Bentham**'s writings, it was the **marginalists** who were first to make extensive use of the concept, employing differential calculus. The **law of diminishing marginal utility** was enunciated simultaneously.

See also: **cardinal utility; util; utility**.

margin call (310)

A broker's demand for additional cash. This request insures a broker against a price fall as an investor deposits an amount of cash with his broker proportionate to the value of share purchases.

margin of safety (540)

Total sales revenue minus breakeven point sales revenue.

See also: **breakeven level of income**.

margin requirements (310)

The banking rule imposed by the **Federal Reserve System** on its member banks which determines the minimum amount which has to be paid in advance for the purchase of stock market securities.

margins (820)

Additions to the Australian **basic wage** to reward different skills and create **occupational wage differentials**.

margin trading (310)

Purchases of securities which only require payment for a portion of the transaction, with interest being charged on the debit balance. If the margin were 20 per cent only $20,000 of a purchase costing $100,000 would be requested by a broker. In the USA, the practice has long been common, contributing to the financial panic of 1929 as then small investors with few resources used loans to purchase stock; when the loans were recalled, the demand for and prices of stocks collapsed.

See also: **margin requirements**.

mark (430)

The currency of Germany which was created out of separate West and East German currencies in 1990; the dominant currency of Europe.

market (010)

A medium for exchanges between buyers and sellers. Some markets are physically located in one place; others connect buyers and sellers by telephone, fax and telex, especially in the case of financial markets. Markets for goods and services are termed 'product' markets; for labour and capital, 'factor markets'. There is a linkage between factor and product markets in that the demand for a factor is derived from the demand for its product. Dealers in a market seek to create an **equilibrium** between demand and supply at a particular price. However, the existence of many market imperfections, e.g. **monopoly** and **asymmetric information**, distort markets. A full set of markets must include markets for **futures** and for risk-taking. Markets have also been classified according to whether they are **fixprice** or **flexprice**.

See also: **black market; bond market; buyer's market; capital market; clearing market; common market; contingent market; controlled market; currency market; discount market; dual labour market; efficient market; Eurobond market; Eurodollar market; external labour market; factor market; federal funds market; forward market; free market; futures market; gold market; grey market; insurance market; internal labour market; internal market; International Monetary Market; labour market; lemons market; local labour market; London Traded Options Market; missing market; over-the-counter market; primary market; primary labour market; second market; secondary market; secondary labour market; securities market; seller's market; shallow market; short-term money market; spot market; swap market; third market; UK gilts market; Unlisted Securities Market; US treasury bond market; white market; wholesale money market**.

marketable discharge permit (720)

A permit to discharge air and water pollutants up to a standard level of environmental quality which can be sold to another firm. This is a modified pollution offset system.

Krupnick, A., Oates, W. and Van De Verg, E. (1983) 'On marketable air pollution permits: the case for a system of pollution offsets', *Journal of Environmental Economics and Management* 10: 233–47.

McGartland, A.M. and Oates, W.E. (1985) 'Marketable permits for the prevention of environmental deterioration', *Journal of Environmental Economics and Management* 12: 207–28.

See also: **transferable discharge permit**.

market adjustment (010)

The changes in prices and quantities which occur when demand and supply change in a market.

market anti-inflation plan (150)

A proposal to keep the general price level stable but individual prices flexible by a system created by legislation which would issue sales rights to firms. These rights would equal current net sales at pre-existing prices, corrected for changes in a firm's capital and labour inputs and the average growth in national productivity. Relative prices could change by a firm buying sales rights unused by other firms.

Lerner, A.P. and Colander, D.C. (1980) *MAP: A Market Anti-inflation Plan*, New York: Harcourt Brace Jovanovich.

See also: **incomes policy**; **Lerner**; **prices policy**.

market balance of payments (430)

The balance of demand for and supply of a country's currency in the exchange market at a given exchange rate.

See also: **balance of payments**.

market clearing (010)

Adjusting demand and supply to each other until an **equilibrium** is established.

market clearing price (010)

The ruling price in a particular period for which there is sufficient demand to equal the amount supplied, even if there are simultaneous shocks to the economy. Some markets rarely appear to be without clearing prices as they are in disequilibrium for long periods of time, e.g. the labour market where involuntary unemployment and vacancies coexist for long periods of time.

market concentration (530, 610)

The concentration of sales of an industry or a market accounted for by the largest firms, e.g. the proportion of electrical goods sales sold by the largest four firms.

See also: **aggregate concentration**.

market demand (010)

The demand for a good or service by a consumer who pays for it.

See also: **sponsor demand**.

market discrimination coefficient (010, 820)

Becker's measure of pure discrimination which is a residual after differentials due to variations in education, skills and job experience have been removed. It is measured by the formula

$$MDC = \frac{Y(W)}{Y(N)} - \frac{Y_0(W)}{Y_0(N)}$$

where $Y(W)$ and $Y(N)$ are the actual incomes of the dominant group W and the oppressed group N respectively and the incomes Y_0 are those in the absence of discrimination.

See also: **discrimination**.

market distortion (010)

A market allocation which fails to reach a social optimum. Sometimes this occurs because of government intervention.

market economy (010, 070)

An **economy** with extensive private ownership of capital and allocation of goods and services by the price mechanism in the absence of government intervention. The **Physiocrats** and the **classical economists** praised this form of economy; **neoclassical economists** have analysed it in detail, e.g. by showing how a system of **competitive trading** is used for the exchange of all commodities. For a market economy to flourish, goods must be available in competitive markets at prices which reflect their long-run scarcities and businesses must be motivated by profit.

market equilibrium (010)

A state of rest for a market when the quantity of a good traded is constant and prices do not move up or down, with the consequence that there is no incentive for buyers or sellers to modify their behaviour. In the simplest case of a market relationship, only the relationship between price and quantity is analysed. If anything else which could affect the quantities demanded and supplied changes, the **equilibrium** is disturbed, e.g. if consumers' incomes or tastes change, the weather is poor, there is a change of government or a war.

See also: **disequilibrium; equilibrium**.

market failure (010)

1 The malfunctioning of a market because of imperfections in it.

2 **Externalities** because a market is producing social costs.

3 The lack of a market for a particular good or service, as in the case of **public goods**.

The most familiar of failures are **unemployment**, persistent shortages of particular skills, balance of payments disequilibria, the production of **private goods** at considerable external cost, regional problems and unanticipated inflation.

See also: **market distortion; missing market**.

market forces (010)

1 Demand for and supply of **factors of production** and the goods and services produced by them.

2 The determinants of prices, investment and output in competitive markets.

3 The system of allocation which is the alternative to **economic planning**.

market form (610)
See: **market structure**.

market-maker (310)

A stockbroker who both carries out clients' orders to buy or sell and trades on his/her own account. By being prepared to buy and sell at all times, he/she creates a market in stocks and shares. The **International Stock Exchange** copied this system from the **National Association of Securities Dealers Automated Quotation** system when the jobbing system peculiar to Britain was abandoned in 1986. But London did not follow the narrow New York rule of having a single market-maker per stock. In 1987, there were

forty in London, a much larger number than thought necessary.

See also: **jobber; primary dealer**.

market power (010, 610)

A buyer's or seller's ability to influence a market price. For a seller, this power, the consequence of the **inelasticity** of the demand curve facing it, often results in high profits.

See also: **concentration**.

market prices (220)

A valuation of the national income which includes indirect taxes net of subsidies.

See also: **factor cost; gross national product**.

market rate of interest (310)

The **rate of interest** set by a particular financial market.

See also: **natural rate of interest; Wicksell**.

market share (530, 610)

The proportion of the sales of an industry sold by a particular firm or group of firms. This share is the basis of the concept of an **aggregate concentration** ratio and is often used as a major managerial goal.

market socialism (120)

1 A planned economy which attempts to improve allocation by using markets. This type of economy has met with increasing problems, e.g. Yugoslavia has experienced high inflation, low growth and rising unemployment with a consequential call for more rigid policies.

2 Various forms of workers' control and self-management.

Devine, P.J. (1988) *Democracy and Economic Planning*, Cambridge: Polity Press.
Prout, C. (1985) *Market Socialism in Yugoslavia*, Oxford: Clarendon Press.

See also: **industrial democracy; workers' participation**.

market structure (610)

1 The organizational form of a market.

2 The number of firms, buyers and products related to each other. The principal structures are competitive, oligopolistic and

monopolistic. The structure has a major effect on the freedom of a firm to make economic decisions and also affects the level of product prices. Such structures form a continuum differing from each other by the degree of **concentration** in that market.

See also: **duopoly; monopolistic competition; oligopoly; perfect competition.**

marking (310)

1 The valuation of assets or income.

2 A recorded sale or purchase of securities.

See also: **historic cost.**

markka (430)

The currency of Finland.

Markov chain model (210, 840)

Probabilistic analysis showing how each state in an evolutionary process produces the next state in a finite chain. This has been applied to the study of reproduction and migration, e.g. migration between two countries depends on past movements of population.

Bartholomew, D.J. (1982) *Stochastic Models for Social Processes*, 3rd edn, New York and Chichester: Wiley.

Markovitz, Harry Max, 1927– (030)

Educated at the University of Chicago and professor at Rutgers University since 1980. He has been principally concerned in his works with the theory of rational behaviour under uncertainty and portfolio theory. He has contributed to production theory and the creation of software to aid business decision-making. In 1990, he shared the **Nobel Prize for Economics** with **Sharpe** and **Miller** for his contribution to portfolio theory.

mark-up pricing (520)

The formation of a product price by adding a percentage for profit to unit average cost. A gross mark-up includes a contribution to **overhead costs**; a net mark-up does not, as the unit cost includes a contribution to overheads, assuming a particular output. The theory was designed as a realistic alternative to using marginal measures to calculate prices. It has been asserted that this pricing method is a major cause of **cost-push inflation**.

See also: **Kalecki.**

marriage allowance (320)

The additional tax relief given to married people to enable a spouse to be more easily supported; also known as marriage deduction.

See also: **income splitting system.**

Marshall, Alfred, 1842–1924 (030)

The Cambridge economist who dominated economics in Britain from the late nineteenth century to the 1930s. After graduating in mathematics at Cambridge in 1865 and becoming a fellow of St John's College, Cambridge, he turned to the study of ethics and psychology. It was his passionate interest in social questions which led him to economics, beginning with a translation of **classical economics** into mathematics and some papers on international trade theory. In 1877 he married a pupil, Mary Paley (with whom he wrote his first book, *The Economics of Industry* (1879)), and was appointed Principal and Professor of Political Economy at the new University College, Bristol. From 1885 to 1908 he was professor of political economy at Cambridge, retiring early to concentrate on his writing.

It was the publication of his *Principles of Economics* in 1890 which established his leadership of the economics profession. This beautifully written book, which relegates difficult points to footnotes and appendices, was intended to build on the theories of the classical and **marginalist** schools an integrated analytical framework for the subject. His vast knowledge of economic history and the industrial and labour conditions of his day is evident throughout. He achieved an exposition of price theory which is still basic to modern **microeconomics**. **Elasticity of demand**, the distinction between short and long periods, the concept of **economic rent**, **consumers' surplus** and internal and external **economies of scale** are all carefully explained. Some innovations, e.g. the **representative firm**, were less successful. His sympathy for much of classical economics and his reading of psychology gave him an organic view of the development of firms.

He intended to publish a second volume to cover industrial fluctuations, money and international trade but it was not until 1923 that he was able to do so in his *Money, Credit and Commerce*, when it was too late for him to write with the force he had achieved in his *Principles* or to refine his analysis. By achieving the separation of the teaching of economics from the other 'moral sciences' he soon made Cambridge the centre of British economics. His star pupils **Pigou** and **Keynes** used many of his analytical tools and continued the veneration of him and his works.

Guillebaud, C.W. (ed.) (1965) *Marshall's Principles of Economics*, Variorum Edition, London: Macmillan.

O'Brien, D.P. and Presley, J.R. (eds) (1965) *Pioneers of Modern Economics in Britain*, ch. 2, London: Macmillan.

Pigou, A.C. (ed.) (1925) *Memorials of Alfred Marshall*, London: Macmillan.

See also: **continuity thesis**.

Marshallian demand curve (010)

Marshall's graphical representation of a demand schedule showing the relationship between two variables, price and quantity demanded, assuming that any other determinants of demand remain the same as prices change. **Friedman** and others have discussed the implications of the *ceteris paribus* assumptions, especially the difficulty of keeping real income constant as prices change.

Friedman, M. (1953) *Essays in Positive Economics*, pp. 47–99, Chicago, IL, and London: University of Chicago Press.

Marshall, A. (1920) *Principles of Economics*, 8th edn, Book 3, ch. 3 and Mathematical Appendix.

Marshallian long period (010)

A period of several years in which normal prices are established, the **factors of production** are adjusted to demand and the supply of these factors is changed – a stationary state similar to that assumed in **Ricardo**'s theory of value. **Marshall** distinguished it from the period of secular change in which there is a 'gradual growth of knowledge, of population, and of capital, and the changing conditions of demand and supply from one generation to another'.

Marshall, A. (1920) *Principles of Economics. An Introductory Volume*, 8th edn, Book V, ch. V, London: Macmillan.

Marshallian methodology (030)

The **partial equilibrium analysis** central to **neoclassical economics**. Marshall, fond of the motto *natura non facit saltum* (nature does not make a jump), was concerned to demonstrate the continuous nature of economic change, examining economic phenomena 'a bit at a time' so that the forces which bring about **equilibrium** could be adequately examined. He forged new tools to achieve his analytical goals: these included substitution, the **elasticity** coefficient, the **representative firm**, **consumers' surplus**, **quasi-rent**, internal and external **economies of scale**, **prime** and **supplementary cost**, the short run and the long run.

Marshallian short period (010)

The period of time when output can only be increased by using existing factor supplies more intensively.

Marshallian stability (010)

Market stability brought about by the adjustment of quantity to differences between demand price and supply price. A new **equilibrium** is not achieved if price or quantity moves in the wrong direction or if there is over-adjustment of price or quantity.

See also: **cobweb**.

Marshall–Lerner condition (430)

The values of **price elasticities of demand** for imports and exports required for a **devaluation** of a currency to succeed in improving a country's **balance of payments**. The condition states that the sum of the price elasticities of demand for imports and exports, measured in the same currency, must be more than unity and **elasticities of supply** must be high. Thus if the demand for imports is not elastic enough to discourage consumption of them when import prices have risen consequent on devaluation, the demand for exports can be so elastic that the increased value of imports induced by devaluation will compensate. This is a **partial equilibrium** approach as only import and export markets are considered.

See also: **J-curve**.

Marshall Plan (430)

US **aid** to sixteen countries of Western Europe proposed by General George Marshall, US Secretary of State, which, in the form of economic and military grants and loans, amounted to $16.4 billion in the period 1948–52. Western Europe's loss of overseas investments, the ending of much of its trade with Eastern Europe and the decline in its **terms of trade** necessitated outside help. In 1946, large European balance of payments deficits required immediate US assistance which consisted of shipments of goods and finance for reconstruction. It was given to these countries, members of the **Organization for Economic Cooperation and Development**, as part of the European Recovery Programme and was administered by the European Cooperation Administration.

The recipient countries were expected to follow orthodox economic policies to control inflation, get their exchange rates at the right level and adjust their domestic policies to achieve an external balance. It was hoped that Marshall Aid would avoid a major world depression after the Second World War by giving US dollars to Europe to enable them to finance imports from the USA, but the dollar gap was slow to disappear and the amount of Marshall Plan assistance far from generous: more was given after the Plan than during the period of its operation. The Plan hoped to create a new international order by linking Europe, North America and the Third World. The USA would purchase raw materials from less developed countries which would then be able to buy exports from Western Europe. The economic plight of East European countries after 1989 has prompted demands for a similar major aid initiative.

Hogan, M.J. (1987) *The Marshall Plan. America, Britain and the Reconstruction of Western Europe, 1947–52*, Cambridge and New York: Cambridge University Press.

Wexler, I. (1983) *The Marshall Plan Revisited: The European Recovery Program in Economic Perspective*, Westport, CO: Greenwood.

See also: **European Bank for Reconstruction and Development**.

Martineau, Harriet, 1802–76 (030)

Leading popularizer of economics in England in the mid-nineteenth century. Born in Norwich, the daughter of a Unitarian cloth manufacturer, she studied **Smith**, **Ricardo** and **Malthus** from the age of 14 and was inspired to write on political economy by Jane **Marcet**'s popular work. Severe deafness forced her to adopt a literary career, which she successfully did with her twenty-four part *Illustrations of Political Economy, Fables with Morals*, beginning with an account of life in the wilds of South Africa. This work followed the typical classical division of the subject into production, distribution, exchange and consumption, and gained her a˜reputation as a female Malthusian. She said that the research materials she used were 'the standard works on the subject of what I then took to be a science'.

Fox, C. (1883) *Harriet Martineau's Autobiography*, 2 vols, London: Virago Press.

Martineau, H. (1859) *Illustrations of Political Economy*, 9 vols, London: Routledge, Warner & Routledge.

See also: **female economists**; **Malthus**.

martingale (210)

Originally a French betting system in which the stakes are doubled after each loss to assure a favourable outcome with a high probability of success. This mathematical model of a fair game, a **stochastic** process, has been applied to the analysis of asset prices, particularly to see whether the rates of return to assets are such that asset prices and cumulated dividends at their present values are equal to the discounted value of a mutual fund.

Hall, P. and Heyde, C.C. (1980) *Martingale Limit Theory and its Applications*, New York: Academic Press.

Le Roy, S.F. (1989) 'Efficient capital markets and martingales', *Journal of Economic Literature* 27 (December): 1583–621.

Marx, Karl Heinrich, 1818–83 (030)

German-born philosopher, sociologist, journalist and leading classical economist. Born in Trier, the son of a prosperous lawyer, he was educated at the University of Bonn (briefly) and at the University of Berlin where he received a doctorate in 1841 for his research into post-Aristotelian Greek philosophy. His interest in socialism was first aroused by conversations with Baron von Westphalen, whose daughter Jenny he was later to marry; his taste for metaphysics was stimulated by involvement in the Young Hegelian Group from 1837. His career as a journalist began when he edited the liberal paper *Rheinsche Zeitung* from October 1842; his interest in economics dates from his residence in Paris in 1844 where he had migrated to study contemporary French socialism. It was to **Smith**, **Ricardo** and **James Mill** that he turned to obtain an analytical training to tackle what was to be his life-long research project, **capitalism**. Fortunately, in Paris he met Friedrich **Engels** who was to be until death his collaborator and, on many occasions, financial supporter. After a three-year sojourn in Brussels he visited England to see at first hand the most advanced industrial country; apart from short periods in Paris and Cologne 1848–9 to participate in the socialist movements which sprang up at the time of the 1848 European revolutions he spent the rest of his life in London financially precarious and incessantly acquiring in the British Museum Reading Room the masses of knowledge which fuelled his analysis of history and society.

His contribution to economics appears in *Grundrisse* (1857–8), *Das Kapital* (1867, 1885 and 1894) and *Theories of Surplus Value* (1905–10). Although many of the ideas in his works had long been discussed by classical economists, e.g. **value in use** and **value in exchange**, the decline in the rate of profit and labour as a basis of value, he was able to form them into a powerful new synthesis. This consisted of the Turgot–Smith **stages theory**, an analysis of the circulation of money and of commodities and his examination of the determinants of **surplus value** to expose the defects of capitalism in a way unparalleled in economics. But he has not been without his critics, particularly because many of his prophecies were unfulfilled with respect to the collapse of capitalism and the increasing **immiseration** of the working class. Marx realized that the **transformation problem** was a major challenge to his value and price theories: devotees since his death have tried to solve it but their proposed solutions usually require so many restrictive assump-

tions as to make their results trivial. Whatever may have been his defects as an economic theorist, his influence has been massive with thousands of academic disciples throughout the world determined to study economics in a sociological and ideological context.

Elster, J. (ed.) (1986) *Karl Marx: A Reader*, Cambridge: Cambridge University Press.
Freedman, R. (ed.) (1962) *Marx on Economics*, Harmondsworth: Penguin.
Junankar, P.N. (1982) *Marx's Economics*, Oxford: Philip Allan.
McLellan, D. (1973) *Karl Marx: His Life and Thought*, London: Macmillan.

Marxian economics (030)

The application of **Marx**'s theories of **value** and **exploitation** to price theory, **competition** and the working of modern **capitalist** economies. In recent years Marxian economists have attempted to provide an alternative to **neoclassical** analysis of most areas of economic theory and policy, including monetary and general macroeconomic theory as well as a study of **transnational corporations**, income distribution and the **business cycle**. Prominent Marxian economists in the twentieth century have included Paul **Baran**, Maurice **Dobb** and Ronald Meek.

Roemer, J.E. (1981) *Analytical Foundations of Marxian Economic Theory*, Cambridge: Cambridge University Press.

marzipan layer (310, 510)

The managers below the level of director or partner who are responsible for the operations of a financial institution such as a bank or brokerage house.

material balance (120)

The balance of demand and supply for a particular class of commodities. This balancing was a central feature of planning techniques in the **Soviet-type economy**. If there is excess demand when expected supply has been calculated, the planners can recommend the importation of extra quantities of the scarce resource or cut down the amounts requested by subordinate organizations.

material good (010)

A good which has the widest availability

because access to it is a function of absolute, not relative, real income.

See also: **positional good**.

mathematical economics (210)

'Economics, if it is to be a science at all, must be a mathematical science' (W.S. **Jevons**). Although the use of mathematics was to characterize the **marginalist** school, it was not until after 1950 that mathematical models, with increasing momentum, became so central to the formulation and exposition of economic theory. **Samuelson's** *Foundations of Economic Analysis* (1948) did much to show the power of mathematical tools and subsequent mathematical economists were to develop equilibrium and maximizing models. The mathematical techniques most frequently employed include calculus, differential equations, matrix algebra and **linear programming**.

Arrow, K.J. and Intriligator, M.D. (eds) (1981–4) *Handbook of Mathematical Economics*, Amsterdam: North-Holland.
Chiang, A.C. (1984) *Fundamental Methods of Mathematical Economics*, 3rd edn, Tokyo: McGraw-Hill.

Matif (310)

Marché à terme d'instruments financiers. French financial futures exchange, opened in Paris in February 1986.

mature economy (070)

A stagnant advanced **economy**; an economy at its peak making full use of available technology.

maturity (310)

The terminal date at which a **bond**, **bill** or debt is due to be paid.

See also: **term structure of interest rates**.

maturity mismatch (310)

A difference between the maturities of the assets and liabilities of banks. Banks, such as British banks in the past, never had this problem because of a policy of lending only short term; Germany and other European banks have traditionally permitted long-term lending, increasing the possibility of a mismatch.

maturity structure of debt (310)

An analysis of government debt according to the number of years to redemption of each government-issued **security**. The percentage of the total government debt in each category of years to maturity is stated, e.g. X per cent to mature within five years, Y per cent to mature in six to ten years. This analysis of the national debt is essential to debt management.

maturity transformation (310)

The activity of banks and building societies of borrowing short and lending long. This practice is possible because of the slow-changing habits of borrowers and the general law of averages which ensures little variation in the total amount deposited.

maximin (020)

Maximizing the gains to the worst-off.

See also: **Rawlsian justice**.

maximum likelihood estimator (210)

The value of a sample statistic which minimizes the squares of the differences between a regression line and actual data.

See also: **least squares method**.

Mayday (310)

The deregulation of the Wall Street securities industry on 1 May 1975. Price competition was increased by abolishing minimum commissions, a system which had existed on the New York Stock Exchange since 1792. A major effect of this change was a reduction in the number of securities firms.

See also: **Big Bang**.

MBO (510)

See: **management by objectives**.

MCA (710, 729)

See: **marginal cost of abatement**; **Monetary Compensation Amount**.

McFadden Branch Banking Act 1927 (310)

US federal statute which helped national banks to compete with state-chartered banks by allowing them the same power to open branches as the state banks in that area. An aim of the Act was to encourage banks to stay in the **Federal Reserve System**.

MCM (140, 210)

The multi-country econometric model used by the US Federal Reserve Board, covering the USA, Canada, Japan, the UK, Germany and the rest of the world.

Howe, H.E., Hernandez-Cata, E., Stevens, G., Berner, R., Clark, P. and Kwack, S.Y. (1981) 'Assessing international interdependence with a multi-country model', *Journal of Econometrics* 15: 65–92.

See also: **linkage models**.

MCT (320)

Mainstream **corporation tax**.

Meade, James E., 1907– (030)

British economist educated at Cambridge and Oxford universities. As Economics Fellow of Hertford College, Oxford, from 1930 to 1938 he contributed to the emerging macroeconomics of **Keynes** by participating in the **Cambridge Circus**. His subsequent career was spent at the League of Nations from 1940 to 1947, as professor of commerce at the London School of Economics from 1947 to 1957 and at Cambridge as professor of political economy from 1957 to 1967. He was awarded the **Nobel Prize for Economics** in 1977, with **Ohlin**, for his work on international trade. In wartime, with Richard Stone, he produced *National Income and Expenditure* (1944), a book which influenced much of post-war national income accounting. Subsequent books on international economics, especially *Theory of International Policy* (1951, 1955), clearly expounded the leading aspects of the subject, e.g. his examination of the relationship between a country's **internal** and **external balances** which has become a standard tool of macroeconomic analysis. Like the leading economists of the nineteenth century, he produced his *Principles of Political Economy* (four volumes, 1965–76). Numerous other works include those on **capital theory**, wealth distribution and **incomes policy**. In 1978 he chaired the Meade Commission on *The Structure and Reform of Direct Taxation*.

Howson, S. and Moggeridge, D. (eds) (1988–90) *The Collected Papers of James Meade*, vols I–IV, London: Unwin Hyman.

Johnson, H.G. (1978) 'James Meade's contribution to economics', *Scandinavian Journal of Economics* 80: 64–85.

mean (210)

A measure of the central tendency of a **population** or **sample**.

See also: **arithmetic mean; geometric mean; harmonic mean**.

mean deviation (210)

The sum of the differences between the numbers of a set and the **arithmetic mean** of the set, divided by the number of numbers in that set, e.g. for the set 3, 4, 5, 6, 7 whose arithmetic mean is 5, the mean deviation is $[(3 - 5) + (4 - 5) + (5 - 5) + (6 - 5) + (7 - 5)]$ divided by 5, i.e. 1.2, ignoring signs after the differences have been calculated.

means of payment (310)

A general function of money which enables it to be an immediate way of making a payment.

See also: **medium of exchange**.

measure of economic welfare (220)

Gross national product adjusted by the subtraction of 'bads' (which include pollution and services such as law and order) and the addition of 'goods' (which include household activities such as do-it-yourself (DIY) work) which are not conventionally measured in **national income** accounting. Nordhaus and **Tobin** introduced the term.

median (210)

The middle value (or **arithmetic mean** of the two middle values when there is an even number of values) of numbers arranged in order of magnitude, e.g. the median of 10, 15, 20, 25, 30 is 20.

See also: **mean; mode**.

medium of account (310)

A **numeraire** which is used for quoting prices and valuing the quantities used in accounts. It is usually but not necessarily a circulating currency, as in the case of guineas.

See also: **unit of account**.

medium of exchange (310)

A means of making a payment in the future; a form of credit which allows a transaction to proceed.

See also: **means of payment**.

medium of redemption (310)
Cash, or another type of money, into which banknotes are convertible.

Medium-term Financial Strategy (310, 320)
The UK policy for public borrowing and monetary growth first announced in May 1979 for the period 1979–84. The Strategy continues to be published annually in the UK budget report as a set of targets for public borrowing and monetary growth. Originally, it was argued that announcing the government's strategy gave everyone in the economy a firm basis for expectations. However, increasingly in the 1970s, the Strategy became a looser statement of intent.

See also: **Red Book**.

megacorp (510)
A large corporation controlled by its executives, not its shareholders. These corporations have been able to replace smaller competitive firms because technological change made possible production **economies of scale** and national and international markets. Also, the modernization of financial markets enabled the raising of capital to finance **mergers** and the expansion of existing firms and advances in accounting and management science removed managerial **diseconomies** as a barrier to growth. But continued expansion of megacorps is always threatened by the powers of tough governmental **competition policies** to break up firms that have acquired too much monopoly power.

Menger, Carl, 1840–1921 (030)
The founder of **Austrian economics** who, with **Jevons** in Manchester and **Walras** in Lausanne, is also credited with founding **marginalism** in the 1870s by using the idea of **diminishing marginal utility** as the foundation of a theory of value.

He was educated at the universities of Vienna, Prague and Cracow before becoming a journalist and civil servant. In 1871 he published his principal work, *Principles of Economics*, and became professor at the University of Vienna in 1879. He was also tutor to Crown Prince Rudolf.

Menger set the tone for much of later Austrian economics in that he objected to the use of mathematics (unlike Jevons) because it dealt with quantities, not essences, and led to arbitrary statements. He sought to enunciate laws based on simple elements, e.g. needs, satisfaction, goods, which were not influenced by time and space. Like many of his successors he had a libertarian attitude to economic policy.

Alter, M. (1990) *Carl Menger and the Origins of Austrian Economics*, Boulder, CO: Westview Press.
Hicks, J.R. and Weber, W. (eds) (1973) *Carl Menger and the Austrian School of Economics*, Oxford: Clarendon Press.

See also: **Hayek**; **Mises**; **Wieser**.

menu costs of inflation (150)
The costs of changing the prices on goods in an inflationary period, i.e. new price tags, catalogues and price lists.

Caplin, A. and Spulber, D. (1987) 'Menu costs and the neutrality of money', *Quarterly Journal of Economics* 102: 703–25.

See also: **shoe leather costs of inflation**.

mercantilism (030)
A system of ideas and government policies advanced by a series of writers of economic pamphlets, many of them merchants (hence the term), who in the period 1550–1750 advanced theories of international trade, money, prices and employment. The major writers of this school include Hales, Malynes, North, **Mun** and Child. The earlier writers emphasized the importance of keeping the **balance of payments** in surplus so that bullion could be accumulated. **Money** was not seen, initially, as being a factor of production, except to finance wars. **Tariffs**, **exchange controls** and monopoly trading companies were advocated to achieve these ends. Later writers developed more subtle theories looking at the balance of payments as a whole. Since the East India Company exported silver bullion to India to pay for imports from India, writers had to provide a more complex theory of international economics, moving from particular to general balances. In a sense, mercantilism was an

elaborate theoretical justification for tariffs, then a major source of government revenue. But sympathetic readers will note that all the writers of this school of economics wanted to advance policies which would create national strength and growth. As they were worried about unemployment (especially in England which was adjusting to the problem of provision for the poor after the dissolution of the monasteries and the decline in the wool industry) which prevented a nation from achieving its full output potential, they advocated public works and regional policies not dissimilar from many which have been used in Western countries in the twentieth century. The critiques of David **Hume** and Adam **Smith** – particularly Hume's assault in his price **specie-flow** model and Smith's discussion of the nature of money and of the desirability of free trade – relegated mercantilist doctrines to the sidelines of economics. But some nineteenth-century writers, including **List**, had ideas with a mercantilist tinge. The recent school of **neomercantilism** has kept these writers' ideas firmly on the agenda of economic policy discussions.

Heckscher, E.F. (1935) *Mercantilism*, trans. by M. Shapiro, ed. by E.F. Soderlund, London: Allen & Unwin.

McCulloch, J.R. (1954) *Early English Tracts on Commerce*, Cambridge: Cambridge University Press.

Viner, J. (1937) *Studies in the Theory of International Trade*, chs 1 and 2, London: Allen & Unwin.

merchandise balance of trade (430)

Visible balance of trade.

See also: **balance of payments**.

merchant bank (310)

A **secondary bank** which specializes in the finance of trade, portfolio management, **corporate finance** and **mergers**. As it does not receive deposits directly from the public, it obtains finance for lending from **wholesale money markets**. It has the exclusive right under the Companies Acts to transfer undisclosed sums from its profit and loss account to its hidden reserves. The more famous merchant banks include Morgan and Grenfell, Hill Samuel, Kleinwort Benson, Rothschilds, Hambros and Lazards.

Increasingly, in the USA 'merchant banking' refers to a high-risk form of investment banking which has extended the range of its services to include the provision of **bridging** finance and **equity** investment in firms purchased through a **leveraged management buyout**.

See also: **investment banking**.

merchant capitalism (040)

A system of wholesalers who advance funds to manufacturing workers to produce goods for the merchant's market. This stage of economic development was succeeded by **industrial capitalism**.

merger (520, 610)

An amalgamation of two or more firms into a new firm. Firms in industries at different stages of bringing a good to the final consumer, i.e. extractive, manufacturing or distribution, or in the same industry, can be merged: the former is a vertical merger and the latter a horizontal merger. A **conglomerate merger** is an amalgamation of firms with dissimilar activities. Mergers often come in waves, particularly in times of general economic depression as a way of reducing costs, e.g. in the USA in 1901–3 and in the UK in the 1920s. As a high proportion of conglomerate mergers fail to make efficiency gains in **research and development**, production or marketing, it is argued that they are without industrial logic; horizontal mergers have a better reputation for improving profitability and efficiency; vertical mergers make no significant difference. In the USA, e.g. in 1982 and 1984, guidelines for what are acceptable mergers have been published by the Antitrust Division of the Department of Justice.

See also: **horizontal integration**; **vertical integration**.

merger arbitrage (310)

Tactical use of the accumulated stocks of companies in takeovers, often practised by US investment banks. Arbitrageurs can determine the outcome of **takeover** bids, and often precipitate them.

See also: **greenmail**.

merit bad (010, 320)

A good or service disapproved of by a

central government on the basis of research into its bad effects. Drugs, tobacco and various unauthorized medical practices are major examples. Taxation and prohibition under the criminal law have been used as ways of preventing consumption of them.

merit good (010, 320)

A good provided by a government as it is regarded as desirable for consumption by the public. Thus education and libraries are often freely provided. It is argued that the superior wisdom of governments based on detailed research justifies them in assuming this paternalist role.

merit want (010, 320)

A demand for a good or service which the state decides should be supplied free, e.g. education, health care. Public expenditure is necessary to satisfy these wants.

See also: **merit bad**; **merit good**.

MES (520)

See: **minimum efficient scale**.

mesoeconomy (010)

That part of the **economy** run by big business. It is intermediate between households/small firms and national governments.

Holland, S. (1987) *The Market Economy from Micro to Mesoeconomics*, London: Weidenfeld & Nicolson.

mesokurtic (210)

See: **kurtosis**.

metallist (310)

Someone who believes that the value of a currency depends on the intrinsic value of the gold, silver or copper it is made of, or which backs a note issue.

See also: **cartalist**; **Currency School**.

Metropolitan Statistical Area (220, 840)

A large population centre of the USA which includes adjoining communities socially and economically integrated with it. In rural areas, except New England, MSAs refer to counties. This term replaced the 'Standard

Metropolitan Statistical Area' after June 1963.

See also: **Consolidated Metropolitan Statistical Area**; **Primary Metropolitan Statistical Area**.

MEW (220)

See: **measure of economic welfare**.

mezzanine finance (310)

An unsecured loan, often used to finance a **management buyout**, which ranks after secured loans but before equity in the event of a liquidation of a company. The interest charged on these loans is higher than for secured loans and linked equity is often given to the lender. This form of finance is used to supplement other sources to effect management buyouts.

MFA (420)

See: **Multi-Fibre Arrangement**.

MFN (420)

See: **most favoured nation**.

M-form (510)

A multidivisional type of enterprise organized so that the operating divisions are separated from those which make strategic decision-making. This structure, arranged as profit centres for different products, brands and geographical markets, was pioneered by Du Pont and General Motors.

Armour, H.O. and Teece, D.J. (1978) 'Organization, structure and economic performance: a test of the multidivisional hypothesis', *Bell Journal of Economics* 9: 106–22.

See also: **H-form**; **U-form**; **X-form**.

microeconomics (020)

The study of the economic behaviour of part(s) of an economic system, especially a household or a firm. To make this possible, **partial equilibrium analysis** (inaugurated by **Marshall**) and **general equilibrium** analysis (largely founded by **Walras**) is used. The major issues discussed are matters of pricing, distribution, investment, **welfare economics**, demand and supply. The **neoclassical economic** school was to make most of the microeconomic character of much of economics; **Keynesianism** had the opposite effect as its construction of macroeconomic models returned economics to the wider concerns which had been prominent in **classical**, and other, schools of economics. Increasingly economists have found it difficult in their construction of models to separate microeconomics from macroeconomics.

See also: **macroeconomics**.

microproduction function (210)
A firm's production function showing the maximum output which can be produced by its physical inputs, given the constraint of its technology.

See also: **production function**.

middle price (310)
The average of the buying and selling prices of securities on the **International Stock Exchange** which are quoted in the Stock Exchange Daily Official List. Prices quoted in the financial press usually approximate to the middle price.

MIGA (430)
See: **Multilateral Investment Guarantee Agency**.

migrant labour (810)
Foreign labour available in an economy for short periods of time – several months or a few years. This labour provides a national economy with what can be regarded as a secondary labour force. It is popular with employers as it increases the elasticity of labour supply and, being less unionized, can often be obtained at lower wage rates.

See also: **reserve army of labour**.

migration (810, 840)
Movement of population, labour or capital between countries or between regions. The most studied form of migration has been the international migration of labour, partly because of the large westward migrations of the nineteenth century to the USA. As part of the process of economic development of a country, there is rural–urban migration within it: this has happened in developed economies such as the USA and increasingly in less developed countries. Also, since 1960 attention has been paid to the movement of workers from the Mediterranean regions to more northern regions of **European Community** countries, of highly skilled workers to the USA and of New Commonwealth (i.e. the Indian subcontinent and Caribbean) workers to the UK.

Many explanations of migration are in terms of an analysis of factors pushing workers out of a country (unemployment, low incomes) and of factors pulling workers into a country (high growth, high pay and career advancement). The increasing provision of social services in advanced countries has contributed to demands for immigration controls. Ravenstein (1834–1913) distilled from British population censuses of 1861, 1871 and 1881 'laws' of migration which concluded that migration is largely caused by economic circumstances and is typically a step-by-step process of short movements from rural to urban areas.

Grigg, D.B. (1977) 'E.G. Ravenstein on the laws of migration', *Journal of Historical Geography* 3: 41–54.

Shaw, R.P. (1975) *Migration Theory and Fact: A Review and Bibliography of Current Literature*, Philadelphia, PA: Regional Science Research Institute.

See also: **brain drain; gravity model**.

migration-fed unemployment (130, 810)
A type of unemployment common to many Third World countries. Migration initially occurs because the urban wage rate is more than the **supply price** of rural workers and continues until deterred by urban unemployment. This type of unemployment seems near insoluble because any policy measures to create urban jobs will stimulate migration, causing labour supply to grow faster than demand and thus creating further unemployment.

military industrial complex (610)
The set of relationships between a defence ministry and the industries supplying weapons and other goods and services for the armed forces. It is argued that this complex is crucial to the functioning of many major capitalist economies as industrial output is to a large extent determined by defence requirements. **Galbraith** and several radical economists have discussed

the role of this complex in their analysis of modern Western economic systems. However, within the USSR there has also long been a close link between defence industries and the armed forces.

military Keynesianism (320)

The maintenance of a high level of **aggregate demand** by huge government expenditures on defence. This has been used as a description of the US economy post-1945.

Mill, James, 1773–1836 (030)

Father of John Stuart Mill and friend of **Bentham** and **Ricardo**. After failing to complete his theological training at Edinburgh University, he went to London where he maintained himself as a freelance journalist before becoming a clerk of the East India Company. He was deeply influenced by Ricardo in all of his economics.

Mill, John Stuart, 1806–73 (030)

English philosopher, political theorist and major classical economist. His father, James Mill, a close friend of **Bentham**, educated him at home in a rigorous programme which started with Greek at the age of three and reached political economy ten years later. John learned economics by making notes on **Ricardo**'s *Principles* which his father then published as *Elements of Political Economy* (1821). Following his father into a clerkship in the East India Company and engaging in the political reform movements of the day, John turned his attention to a range of philosophical and political issues, writing on women's rights, representative government, logic, **utilitarianism** and liberty. But he made an outstanding contribution to economics, being more than he modestly claimed – a clarifier of **Smith** and Ricardo's ideas.

In his brilliant *Essays on Some Unsettled Questions of Political Economy*, written when he was only 23 but not published until 1844, he developed the theory of **reciprocal demand** to explain the ratios at which nations would trade if they followed the principle of **comparative advantage**. Also he introduced the idea of a demand schedule, refined **Say's law** and expounded one of the earliest theories of the **trade cycle** which he attributed to price delusion. He returned to economics in his large *Principles of Political Economy with Some of their Applications*

to Social Philosophy, first published in 1848, republished seven times in his lifetime and the standard textbook on the subject in Britain until **Marshall**'s superseded it in 1890. Many features of the work were novel. He introduced a discussion of idealist **socialism** (St Simon and Fourier) – partly under the influence of Harriet Taylor, later to be his wife – and clearly expounded what have become key economic concepts. In the *Principles*, **opportunity cost**, **economies of scale**, the problem of **joint costs** and **sexual discrimination** in the labour market are some of his numerous innovations. His self-confident claim that he had finally sorted out the theory of value invited the ridicule of later writers, particularly **Jevons**, but Marshall can in many respects be regarded as a follower.

Hollander, S. (1985) *The Economics of John Stuart Mill*, Oxford: Basil Blackwell.

Mill, J.S. (1963) *The Collected Works of John Stuart Mill*, Toronto: University of Toronto Press; London: Routledge & Kegan Paul.

Ryan, A. (1974) *J.S. Mill*, London: Routledge.

Miller, Merton, 1923– (030)

Educated at Harvard and Johns Hopkins universities and professor of the University of Chicago from 1981. Along with **Modigliani**, he developed the study of corporate finance by examining the relationship between equity financing and borrowing and the relationship between the dividend policy of a firm and the firm's value. In 1990, he shared the **Nobel Prize for Economics** with **Markovitz** and **Sharpe**.

mineral-based economy (110)

An industrial **economy** using large machinery driven by a plentiful supply of energy, especially coal. This economy, less reliant on agricultural products, can sustain a higher **population density** than its predecessor, the **advanced organic economy**.

Wrigley, E.A. (1988) *Continuity, Chance and Change*, ch. 3, Cambridge: Cambridge University Press.

minimal state (320)

A state limited to a few functions, usually considered to be protection against force, theft, fraud and the enforcement of contracts. It is argued that as the price of promoting fairness is inefficiency and governments are fallible it is undesirable to give governments an extensive role. This notion of *laissez-faire* in modern clothes is attributable to **Nozick**.

Nozick, R. (1975) *Anarchy, State and Utopia*, Oxford: Basil Blackwell.

minimax (210)
Minimizing the maximum disadvantage; a **games theory** principle for choosing a course of action.

minimum efficient scale (520)
The level of output of a firm at which the **average cost** curve becomes a plateau of many minimum cost outputs. Such a concept is only applicable to L-shaped average cost curves. It is used to show the significance of **economies of scale**, e.g. by seeing the effect on costs of reducing the level of output to half the minimum efficient size or by comparing this level of production with the entire domestic demand for the products of that industry.

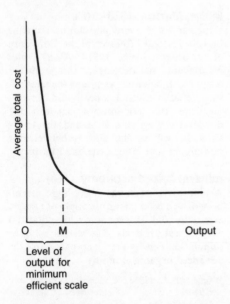

Level of output for minimum efficient scale

See also: **optimum firm**.

minimum lending rate (310)
The UK's successor to the **bank rate** used from October 1971 to August 1981 by the Bank of England for financing the money market when acting as **lender of last resort**. Unlike the bank rate, the minimum lending rate was usually tied to short-term money market interest rates, with the possibility of it being changed on the occasions when monetary policy demanded an administrative change.

See also: **federal funds rate**; **Lombard rate**; **prime rate of interest**.

minimum list heading (220)
Title of an industry or industrial group in UK production statistics.

minimum reserve requirements (430)
A form of exchange control which aims to reduce the impact on domestic liquidity of a foreign currency inflow.

minimum supply price of labour (820)
The lowest wage a worker will accept. Rather than accept less, a person will prefer to be either unemployed or out of the labour force.

See also: **reservation wage**; **voluntary unemployment**.

minimum wage (820)
The minimum rate of employee remuneration fixed by a government for an hour's work in a particular industry, region or whole economy. Many countries, including France and Australia, have long used this policy response to the problem of **low pay**. It is often argued that the imposition of a new minimum wage, or an increase in existing levels, will have an unemployment effect and will fuel inflation by increasing the entire **wage contour**; in the figure, setting a minimum wage W_m above the equilibrium wage W_e reduces employment by $Q_e - Q_m$. There are many countries where this has happened but detailed labour market analysis, especially where **monopsony** is present, is needed before such policies are wholly abandoned.

Starr, G. (1981) *Minimum Wage Fixing: An International Review of Practices and Problems*, Geneva: ILO.

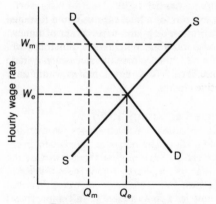

Employment measured in hours

DD demand for labour
SS supply of labour

Ministry of International Trade and Industry (610)

The key Japanese ministry for administering industrial policy. It acts primarily through giving administrative guidance rather than through controls and subsidization. It helps firms plan long term, giving advice on the appropriate level of investment to meet future demand and exporting. Its other tasks include the implementation of policies on the encouragement of small businesses, consumer protection and environmental policy. In the 1950s it took a major role in developing the steel and shipbuilding industries, in the 1960s electronics and heavy construction and in the 1980s advanced technologies.

Minsky, Hyman Philip, 1919– (030)

A prominent US **post-Keynesian** economist who was educated at Chicago and Harvard universities and has been professor of economics at Washington University, St Louis, MO. He has studied the flaws of capitalism, acknowledging the influence of **Schumpeter**. His post-Keynesian views were crucially influenced by meeting Joan **Robinson** and her circle in a visit to Cambridge, England, in 1968–9.

Minsky, H.P. (1975) *John Maynard Keynes*, New York: Columbia University Press.

MIRAS (320)

Mortgage Income Relief at Source. UK method of claiming tax relief on loans for housing. MIRAS replaces the previous system of declaring the amount of interest paid. This covers most interest payments to banks, insurance companies and local authorities where the interest payment qualifies for tax relief.

misaligned rate of exchange (430)

An exchange rate which persistently departs from its **fundamental equilibrium** level.

Mises, Ludwig Edler von, 1881–1973 (030)

A leading Viennese economist whose influential seminar conducted when he was professor of the University of Vienna from 1913 to 1936 included many famous economists, including **Machlup** and **Hayek**. He taught at the Graduate Institute of International Studies, Geneva, from 1934 to 1940 and was professor of economics at New York University from 1945 to 1969. As an economic liberal, he was a leading member of the **Austrian School**, which seemed to be eclipsed by **Keynesianism** until its powerful revival in the 1970s. Like his Austrian contemporaries, he began with **utility** theory and a study of **business cycles** but after the First World War attacked the nature of allocation in socialist societies and then investigated economic philosophy in great detail. In his *The Theory of Money and Credit* (1912) he was one of the first economists to integrate **microeconomics** and **macroeconomics** by founding his theory of money and credit on the individualistic approach of Austrian microeconomics. He also used a cash balance and **expectations** approach to money. His novel approach to the trade cycle based on the **specie-flow mechanism** with bank credit being crucial to the generation of booms and slumps was to be a major inspiration to Hayek.

Butler, E. (1988) *Ludvig von Mises*, Aldershot: Gower.

von Mises, L.E. (1912) *The Theory of Money and Credit*, trans. by H.E. Batson, London: Jonathan Cape.

—— (1937) *Socialism: An Economic and Sociological Analysis*, 2nd edn, trans. by J. Kahane, New York: Macmillan.

—— (1949) *Human Action, A Treatise on Economics*, New Haven, CT: Yale University Press.

—— (1962) *The Ultimate Foundation of Economic Science*, Princeton, NJ: Van Nostrand.

Moss, L.S. (ed.) (1976) *The Economics of Ludvig von Mises*, Kansas City, KS: Sheed and Ward.

misintermediation (310)

Mismatching the maturities of assets and liabilities by banks and other financial intermediaries who borrow short and lend long. The consequences of this are financial instability and the possibility of increased fluctuations in an economy.

McCulloch, J.H. (1981) 'Misintermediation and macroeconomic fluctuations', *Journal of Monetary Economics* 8 (July): 103–15.

See also: **disintermediation; intermediation; maturity mismatch; term structure of interest rates**.

missing market (010)

A market which at present does not exist but could be established to cope with an **externality**. The creation of these new markets is undertaken with the aim of reaching a social optimum. Often there is an absence of markets for **risk**, information and future goods and **home production**.

Hahn, F. (ed.) (1989) *The Economics of Missing Markets, Information and Games*, Oxford: Clarendon Press.

Mitchell, Wesley Clair, 1874–1948 (030)

A leading US **institutional economist** who laid the foundations for modern studies of the **business cycle**. Educated at Chicago University and professor at Columbia. His work *Business Cycles* (1927) began a long and dedicated investigation into economic fluctuations. Together with Arthur **Burns** he set up the **National Bureau of Economic Research**'s method of measuring of business cycles.

Burns, A.F. (ed.) (1952) *Wesley Clair Mitchell, the Economic Scientist*, New York: National Bureau for Economic Research.

MITI (610)

See: **Ministry of International Trade and Industry (Japan)**.

mixed bundling (530)

The sale of two or more goods or services either jointly in a package deal or separately.

See also: **bundling; pure bundling**.

mixed credit (430)

A mixture of a loan supplied by a financial institution at a commercial rate of interest and a **soft loan**. With a more generous form of credit, the volume of international trade and Third World development would have grown faster.

mixed economy (070)

An **economy** which combines the methods and goals of **capitalism** and **socialism**, particularly by encouraging the growth of the public sector. Partly under the influence of **Keynes**, there has been in many Western countries a commitment to **full employment** which encouraged the growth of the public sector and, hence, the mixed economy. In this type of economy, the basic capitalist model is augmented in a number of ways. To market principles are added some income redistribution through taxation and welfare benefits; to private sector firms, state-owned bodies; to pricing, a planning system, usually of no more than an **indicative** kind. Many West European economies, particularly Germany and Sweden, are of this kind. The British economy until 1979 was often described as being mixed but in the 1980s with the abandonment of **incomes policies**, the **privatization** of several **nationalized industries** and the attempt to apply **monetarism** the term is less applicable.

Lord Roll of Ipsden (ed.) (1982) 'The mixed economy', *Proceedings of Section F (Economics) of the British Association for the Advancement of Science Meeting*, London: Macmillan.

mixed good (320)

A good which has the characteristics of both **private** and **public goods**.

See also: **club good**.

MLE (210)

See: **maximum likelihood estimator**.

MLH (220)

See: **minimum list heading**.

MLM (530)

Multi-level marketing.

See also: **pyramid selling**.

MLR (310)
See: **minimum lending rate**.

MMC (310)
See: **money market certificate**.

MMDA (310)
See: **money market deposit account**.

MMMF (310)
See: **money market mutual fund**.

MNC (610)
See: **multinational corporation**.

mobility of labour (820)
Movements of members of the **labour force** between areas (geographical mobility), between industries (industrial mobility) or between occupations (**occupational mobility**). In the classical account of the labour market, mobility would continue until the net advantages of jobs were equalized (see **Smith**'s *Wealth of Nations*, Book I, ch. 10). However, increasingly labour economists became aware of the imperfections of the labour market which split it up into **non-competing groups**. Later, the cost of information and job search were emphasized as barriers to movement. The measurement of labour mobility depends greatly on the classification of areas, industries and occupations used: the broader the classification, the lower the amount of mobility. The right of labour to move freely within the **European Community** is granted by Article 48 of the **Treaty of Rome** and enforced by Article 49; the Council of Ministers by Regulation 1612 in 1968 gave effect to this principle.

See also: **motility**; **search cost**..

mobility status (810, 840)
A classification of the US population which compares the place of residence of an individual person at different dates.

mobility trap (840, 930)
An area of low house prices whose residents are prevented from moving to an urban area with higher property prices, e.g. from northeast England which has lower property prices than London.

mode (210)
The value of a set of numbers which most frequently occurs, e.g. 7 is the mode of 2, 3, 3, 4, 5, 6, 6, 7, 7, 7, 11, 11. Some distributions are without modes.

See also: **mean**; **median**; **unimodal distribution**.

modern economy (070, 110)
An **economy** which has reached an advanced stage of **development** with high per capita incomes, a full range of political and financial institutions, industries using the latest available technology and a large service sector. Although the shorthand measure of modernity is real **gross national product** per head, this is misleading because countries with different ranges of economic activity have been put on a par, e.g. China with India, Haiti with Mali, France with Libya. Increasingly, the overall level of technological diffusion has been chosen as a better indicator.

Modigliani, Franco, 1918– (030)
An Italian-born US economist who was educated at the University of Rome and the New School for Social Research. In his early career, he taught at the University of Illinois, Carnegie Institute of Technology and Northwestern University. From 1962 he has been a professor at the Massachusetts Institute of Technology. A major aspect of his work has been to relate **corporate finance** to **macroeconomics**, making it possible to see the impact of business finance on real variables. All students of economics are aware of his **life-cycle** approach to the **consumption function**. He was awarded the **Nobel Prize for Economics** in 1985.

Modigliani, F. (1980–9) *The Collected Works of Franco Modigliani*, 3 vols, Cambridge, MA, and London: MIT Press.

moments (210)
The sum of the deviations of the values of a variable from a point in a distribution divided by the number of values (first moment); for the second moment, the squares of the deviations have to be calculated; for the third moment, the cubes of the deviations etc.

monetarism (030, 310)

A modern revival of the **quantity theory of money**, making use of modern **neoclassical economics**. It regards the money supply as the most important determinant of aggregate money income and reasserts the relevance of price theory to macroeconomics. Central to monetarism are the concepts of a **transmission mechanism** to allow money to influence output, via relative prices, of normal output/employment instead of **full employment**, of the **natural rate of unemployment**, of monetary impulses between transitory and more permanent components of movements in price level and output, and of a political economy of society which analyses the role of government non-sociologically. **Friedman**'s works from the 1950s are the most famous writings on this subject. Popularly, monetarism is thought of as a tough **fiscal stance** and careful attention to monetary variables when targeting the economy. In practice, most monetarists use the gradualist approach of aiming for a rate of monetary expansion which will achieve long-term price stability. **Demand management** is avoided because of the belief that an economy will always tend to the **natural rate of unemployment**. It made headlines in the USA when the 1968 tax increase failed to curb inflation and when the monetarists at the Federal Reserve Bank of St Louis made striking predictions for 1969. From 1979 to 1981 in the USA and from about 1976 to the mid-1980s in the UK, with varying degrees of enthusiasm, the US and UK governments attempted to apply monetarist principles to their macroeconomic policy-making.

Friedman, M. (ed.) (1956) *Studies in the Quantity Theory of Money*, Chicago, IL: Chicago University Press.
—— (1969) *The Optimum Quantity of Money and other Essays*, London: Macmillan.
Laidler, D., Tobin, J., Matthews, R.C.O. and Meade, J.E. (1981) 'Conference papers on monetarism – an appraisal', *Economic Journal* 91: 1–57.
Stein, J.L. (ed.) (1976) *Monetarism*, Amsterdam: North-Holland.

monetarist approach to the balance of payments (430)

The view that **balance of payments** adjustments are made through capital movements and interest rate changes in capital markets. This is the alternative to the Keynesian approach of adjusting expenditure to achieve a balance of payments equilibrium.

monetary accommodation (310)

A discretionary change in the nominal money supply by central monetary authorities in response to a price change which has changed the real money supply.

monetary base (310)

Cash, banker's deposits with a central bank and short-term monetary assets which form the basis of bank credit; also known as **high-powered money**. Monetary policy sometimes takes the form of controlling the size of the monetary base as a means of restricting the growth of the money supply but it cannot simply hope that a change in the monetary base will ensure a corresponding change in total bank credit as there may be many portfolio adjustments, existing high-powered money in excess of reserve requirements and **disintermediation**.

Monetary Compensation Amount (710)

A payment under the European **Common Agricultural Policy**, adopted as a temporary measure in 1972, to compensate for divergences of the spot market currency rates of member states from **green currency** rates. Compensation takes the form of border taxes and subsidies on intra-**European Community** agricultural trade to achieve common farm produces. In 1984 it was agreed to phase out Monetary Compensation Amounts over four years.

Monetary Control Act 1980 (310)

The popular shortened title of the **Depository Institutions Deregulation and Monetary Control Act 1980**.

monetary inflation (150)

Inflation brought about by an increase in the **money supply**.

monetary overhang (310)

Accumulated savings which could cause future inflation. This overhang has long been a feature of Eastern European economies because shortages have meant that individuals could not spend as much of their incomes as they desired. This excess demand for goods and services when released pushes up prices.

monetary policy (310)

A governmental policy, for the most part implemented by a **central bank**, which influences **aggregate demand** by a variety of methods, including the changing of interest rates, **open market operations** and the setting of targets for the **money supply**. The least active of monetary policies is a long-term linkage between money supply growth and real gross domestic product (see **Friedman**); the most active, frequent changes to **fine tune** the economy. The earliest of monetary policies used interest rates as a means of controlling an economy, especially under the **gold standard**, then a range of methods to control the volume of bank deposits through required cash and reserve asset ratios was used. In the 1970s and 1980s in the USA and the UK, it was fashionable to adopt the **monetarist** view that the principal aim of monetary policy was to set targets for the rate of growth of key monetary aggregates: this proved so difficult that monetary policy reverted to using a variety of former methods.

Bain, A. (1980) *The Control of the Money Supply*, Harmondsworth: Penguin.

Chick, V. (1977) *The Theory of Monetary Policy*, Oxford: Basil Blackwell.

Dow, J.C.R. and Saville, I.D. (1988) *A Critique of Monetary Policy: Theory and British Experience*, Oxford: Oxford University Press.

Goodhart, C. (1989) *Money, Information and Uncertainty*, 2nd edn, London: Macmillan.

Great Britain Treasury (1980) *Monetary Control; A Consultation Paper*, London: HMSO, Cmnd 7858.

See also: **cheap money; monetarism; rules versus discretion**.

monetary veil (010, 310)

Money regarded as a veil which distracts attention from the real activities of the economy.

See also: **classical dichotomy**.

monetization (310)

The financing of government debt by increasing the money supply. This occurs when, at existing interest rates, it is difficult for a government to borrow by issuing bonds and has to resort to borrowing directly from the commercial banks and the money market, which in turn can expand their deposits and, hence, the money supply. The aim of monetization is to keep down interest rates and prevent **crowding out**. The extent of monetization in an economy is sometimes used as an indicator of economic **development**.

See also: **securitization**.

money (310)

1 Anything which is immediately and generally acceptable for the discharge of a debt or in exchange for a good or service.

2 In most cases, a liability of a government introduced into an **economy** by making transfer payments to firms and households or by purchasing assets.

To be used as a measure of value, it must be expressible in units and stable in value. It makes the **division of labour** possible, saving the time which would have to be spent on **barter**. As early as **Aristotle**, it was recognized that money serves as a medium of exchange, a unit of account and a store of value. What serves as money has varied from society to society and from time to time. In primitive societies commodities are used (even today tobacco is widely used in prisons), in societies of medium development coins and then **banknotes**, in modern economies the deposits of the leading **commercial banks**.

Friedman, B.M. and Hahn, F.H. (eds) (1990) *Handbook of Monetary Economics*, Amsterdam: North-Holland.

Galbraith, J.K. (1975) *Money. Whence it Came, Where it Went*, Boston, MA: Houghton Mifflin.

Harrod, R.F. (1969) *Money*, London: Macmillan; New York: St Martin's Press.

Jones, R.A. (1976) 'The origin and development of media of exchange', *Journal of Political Economy* 84: 757–75.

Laidler, D. (1969) 'The definition of money. Theoretical and empirical problems', *Journal of Money, Credit and Banking* 1: 508–25.

Newlyn, W.T. (1978) *The Theory of Money*, 3rd edn, Oxford: Clarendon Press.

See also: **call money; coinage; credit money; fiat money; high-powered money; inside money; IOU money; near money; outside** money; **paper money**; **plastic money**; **token money**.

money at call (310)

The most liquid of banks' assets, after cash. This money can be immediately recalled from the money market to which it is lent.

See also: **overnight money**.

money centre bank (310)

In terms of assets, one of the largest US banks. There are about eight or nine, mostly based in New York.

money gross domestic product (220)

The nominal value of all of the incomes arising from the economic activities within a country in a given period. This has often been a popular central target in macroeconomic policy-making.

money illusion (150)

Confusing money values with real values, a phenomenon of inflationary periods. Workers and consumers may be prepared to accept inferior bargains because they have not fully taken inflation into account. In collective bargaining, too much attention to money wage-rates can lead to workers not being compensated sufficiently for price changes; frequent product price changes make it difficult for consumers to be aware of the extent of inflation. Also known as inflation illusion.

See also: **price perception**.

money income (010)

Receipts expressed in money at the prices current when that income was paid; 'nominal income'.

See also: **real income**.

money laundering (310)

See: **laundering money**.

money market certificate (310)

A six-month US money market security, much used by **thrifts** for investing in US federal funds.

money market deposit account (310)

US retail bank deposit based on holdings of money market assets which was introduced in 1982.

money market mutual fund (310)

US **unit trust** consisting of money market securities. **Thrifts** have provided this means of allowing small investors to participate in short-term money markets; corporations find the funds useful for liquid investments.

money multiplier (310)

The change in the stock of money which results from a change in the **monetary base** by one unit, e.g. by one pound or one dollar. Thus if there is a change in a **reserve asset** by $1 million and the total volume of bank deposits increases by $5 million, the money multiplier has the value of 5. Any alteration in the desired **liquidity** ratio of the banking system will change the value of the money multiplier. The importance of this multiplier has been exaggerated as monetary authorities may make the level of interest rates a more important monetary target. Also, changes in the methods of monetary control and in the public's demand for currency require changes in reserve ratios.

money supply (310)

The total amount of **money** available within a country. It is variously measured in a narrow or broad way depending on which types of bank deposit are included and on whether bank deposits in other currencies are included.

Bank of England (1990) *Monetary Aggregates in a Changing Environment: A Statistical Discussion Paper*, 47.

See also: **M0**; **M1**; **M2**; **M3**; **M3c**; **M4**; **M5**; **sterling M3**.

monkey (310)

Five hundred units of a currency, e.g. of the dollar or pound sterling.

Monnet's law (120, 620)

People only accept change when they are faced with necessity and only recognize necessity when a crisis is upon them. This was first enunciated by Monnet, the father of French **indicative planning**.

monobank (310)

The single state-owned bank of a **Soviet-type economy** which functions both as a

central bank and as a **retail bank** throughout the economy. Although most capitalist economies have separate banking institutions which specialize in different banking functions, in the nineteenth century in several European countries there were banks with united functions.

mono-economics (020)
The type of economic theory regarded as applicable to every type of economic system and country, irrespective of its stage of development and economic conditions. **Classical** and **Marxist economics** emphasize the theoretical implications of different stages of development.

See also: **stages theory**.

Monopolies and Mergers Commission (610)
The UK body which investigates proposed mergers, monopoly situations and anticompetitive practices referred to it by the Director General for Fair Trading or the Secretary of State for Trade and Industry. Its predecessors were the Monopolies and Restrictive Practices Commission (1948 to 1956) and the Monopolies Commission (1956 to 1965): a change of name was necessary when the extra task of considering mergers was added to its remit. Its lack of power has often been noted: it cannot initiate its own inquiries, nor take action to remedy the situations it criticizes.

See also: **antitrust; competition policy; Federal Trade Commission**.

monopolistic competition (610)
A market structure first discussed by Edward **Chamberlin** in 1932. It is similar to **perfect competition**, apart from the crucial assumption of **product differentiation** which has the effect of introducing selling costs which create a **barrier to entry** with the effects of reducing the number of firms in the industry and creating a small amount of monopoly power for each producer. Since monopolistically competitive firms produce, in equilibrium, at a point of the average cost curve above the minimum, monopolistic competition is criticized for resulting in lower output and higher product prices than under perfect competition.

Chamberlin, E.H. (1933) *The Theory of Monopolistic Competition*, Cambridge, MA: Harvard University Press.

See also: **excess capacity theorem**.

monopoly (010, 610)
The sole producer of the entire output of goods and services of an industry. A monopoly usually has **inelastic** demand for its products, unless the industry is so narrowly defined that there are some near substitutes produced by other industries. Under monopoly, the demand curve for the firm is also the demand curve for the industry. If the monopoly follows the rule of profit maximization, i.e. it equates the **marginal revenue** and **marginal cost** of production, it has an opportunity to earn **supernormal profits**. In the past, the best examples of monopolies were chartered trading companies such as the East India Company; today, **public enterprises** are the best examples as in the private sector **competition policy** has opposed monopolization.

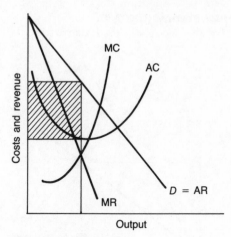

supernormal profits
D demand
AR average revenue · · · AC average cost
MR marginal revenue · · · MC marginal cost

See also: **concentration; Lerner index**.

monopoly capitalism (610)
1 An **economy** whose economic activities are dominated by **oligopolistic** industries so that a surplus, or **supernormal profits**, can be earned.

2 A centrally planned economy whose industry is run by huge state monopolies so that the task of coordinating economic activities is easier.

3 Transnational corporations who have behaved, according to Marxist economists, as economic imperialists.

Baran, P. and Sweezy, P. (1966) *Monopoly Capital*, New York: Monthly Review Press.

monopoly legislation (610)
See: **competition policy**.

monopoly power (010, 610)
The power of a dominant firm or firms over a particular market or economy. Proxy measures of this take the form of **concentration ratios**.

See also: **Herfindahl–Hirschman index**; **Lerner index**.

monopoly profit (010)
See: **supernormal profit**.

monopsony (010, 530)
The sole buyer in a particular market. In

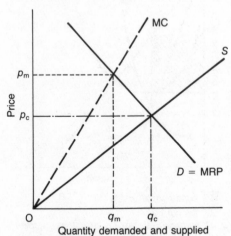

p_m	price under monopsony
p_c	price under perfect competition
q_m	quantity under monopsony
q_c	quantity under perfect competition
MC	marginal cost
MRP	marginal revenue product
D	demand
S	supply

product markets, public authorities are the major examples, e.g. the UK's National Health Service; in labour markets, any large firm, e.g. the National Coal Board in the British coal mining industry. As a monopsonist faces an upward-sloping factor supply curve, its **marginal cost** curve is above its **average cost** curve. Monopsonistic firms employ fewer workers at lower wages than competitive firms, if they are **profit maximizers**.

Mont Pelerin Society (010, 030)
A group of liberals who met in April 1947 at Mont Pelerin, sur Vevey, Switzerland to discuss liberalism, its decline and possible revival. Its original membership, dominated by **Hayek**, Karl Popper, Michael Polanyi, Lionel **Robbins** and von **Mises**, was later extended to include **Friedman** and **Stigler**. Its powerful political associates have included Adenauer, Arthur **Burns**, Enoch Powell, Sir Keith Joseph and Sir Geoffrey Howe.

moonlight economy (010, 820)
Part of a national **economy** which extensively uses cash for transactions to avoid records being kept which could be available to tax authorities.

See also: **cash economy**.

moonlighting (820)
The simultaneous holding of two jobs, one providing the main source of employment income and the other a supplement. This practice is widespread in low wage economies or sectors of economies.

moral hazard (010, 630)
A problem of **insurance**: by insuring property or one's life, the insured may indulge in more risky behaviour increasing the probability of the undesired event occurring. Thus an insurance system can cause **marginal social cost** to be in excess of **marginal private cost**, a sub-optimal situation. This encourages post-contractual optimism.

See also: **risk**.

moral suasion (310)
A method of the Bank of England to control commercial banks by negotiation, rather

than by **open market operations**.

See also: **jawbone**.

Morgan Stanley Capital International World Index (220, 310)

An index of stock market prices gathered from the world's leading stock exchanges covering about 60 per cent of their market capitalization.

Morgenstern, Oskar, 1902–77 (030)

A German-American mathematical economist, born in Silesia, Germany but educated at the University of Vienna. In his early career he was Director of the Austrian Institute for Business Cycle Research from 1931 to 1938 and professor of Vienna University from 1931 to 1938, in which period he was also a member of the Vienna Circle of philosophers and mathematicians. In 1938, the Nazi occupation of Austria led to his dismissal from the university and emigration to the USA. At Princeton University, he fruitfully collaborated with **von Neumann**, persuading him to apply **game theory** to economics: their collaboration resulted in *The Theory of Games and Economic Behaviour* (1944). His later work included books on economic prediction and aspects of US defence.

Morgenstern, O. (1965) *On the Accuracy of Economic Observations*, 2nd edn, Princeton, NJ: Princeton University Press.
— (1970) *The Predictability of Stock Market Prices*, Lexington, MA: Lexington Books.

Morishima, Michio, 1923– (030)

Japanese-born British professor of economics. He was born in Osaka, Japan, and graduated from Kyoto University. After teaching at Kyoto and Osaka and visiting Oxford and Yale, in 1968 he permanently emigrated to the UK where he was professor at Essex University from 1968 to 1970 and subsequently at the London School of Economics. He is a mathematical economist of note who has synthesized **general equilibrium** theory, **input–output analysis** and economic dynamics in his *Theory of Economic Growth* (1969). Also he has fruitfully applied mathematical economics to the study of **Marx**'s ideas in *Marx's Economics: A Dual Theory of Value and Growth* (1973) and in *Value, Exploitation and Growth*

(1978). His *Economic Theory of Modern Society* (1975) has popularized many results of mathematical economics, previously inaccessible to the non-mathematician.

Morishima, M. (1971) *Walras' Economics: A Pure Theory of Capital and Money*, Cambridge: Cambridge University Press.
— (1976) *The Economic Theory of Modern Society*, trans. by D.W. Anthony, Cambridge: Cambridge University Press.

mortgage (310)

Literally a 'dead pledge'; in practice a charge over property given to a lender so that a borrower can raise finance either to effect the original purchase of it or to acquire funds for other purposes. This centuries' old legal device has made possible the financing of mass house ownership throughout non-socialist economies.

See also: **adjustable rate mortgage**; **building society**; **collateralized mortgage obligation**; **equity-linked mortgage**; **mortgage bond**; **mortgage strip**; **thrift**.

mortgage bond (310)

A securitized form of a loan backed by a mortgage. These bonds have been created by investment institutions selling off their outstanding home loans to another company which finances the purchase by a bond issue (often a **Eurobond**). The borrower continues to pay interest to the original lender who then passes on the interest to service the **coupon** on the bonds which have been issued. Securitization increases the amount of mortgage lending, without the original lenders having to increase their capital. Also, **building societies** and housing loan associations become more competitive in the loans market, through securitization, as they are able to lend at lower interest rates. There are more examples of these bond issues in the USA than in the UK, despite more elaborate regulation of them. Mortgage bonds in sterling were first issued in 1987.

See also: **collateralized mortgage obligation**.

mortgage credit association (310)

An association owned by its members which raises finance by issuing bonds on a stock exchange. The interest payable on loans fixed over a five-year period is kept low by the relatively small costs of administration.

This type of association has flourished in Denmark.

See also: **building society; savings and loan association**.

mortgage strip (310)
The division of a mortgage into an interest-only part and a principal-only part to increase its marketability and to dispose of the assets of a **thrift** or other financial institution.

most favoured nation (420)
The status which accords a country the same trading privileges, e.g. exemptions from tariffs, as the other signatories to a commercial treaty or agreement. Under the rules of the **General Agreement on Tariffs and Trade**, all parties to the agreement are usually expected to accord this privilege to their fellow trading partners.

motility (820)
The tendency of a worker to be mobile in a labour market. This can be measured by a questionnaire concerning a worker's intentions. Determinants of motility include a person's level of education, type of occupation and financial ability to obtain housing in another area.

See also: **mobility of labour**.

moving averages (210)
A method of smoothing the fluctuations in a time series by calculating a series of **arithmetic means**. This is regularly used to eliminate seasonal fluctuations, e.g. a twelve-month moving average is calculated for January by dividing the sum of the values for January to December by 12, for February by dividing the sum of the values for the twelve months from February to the following January by 12 and so forth.

MPA (010)
See: **marginal principle of allocation**.

MPC (010)
See: **marginal propensity to consume**.

MPD (520, 720)
See: **marginal private damage**.

MPM (010, 420)
See: **marginal propensity to import**.

MPP (010)
See: **marginal physical product**.

MPS (010, 220)
See: **marginal propensity to save; Soviet Material Product System**.

MRP (010)
See: **marginal revenue product**.

MRR (310)
See: **minimum reserve requirements**.

MRS (010)
See: **marginal rate of substitution**.

MSA (220, 840)
See: **Metropolitan Statistical Area**.

MSD (010, 720)
See: **marginal social damage**.

MTFS (310, 320)
See: **Medium Term Financial Strategy**.

multicollinearity (210)
The state of an econometric relation such that some or all of the explanatory variables are highly correlated with each other.

See also: **autocorrelation**.

Multi-Fibre Arrangement (420)
A trade agreement covering textiles and clothing negotiated in 1973 between twenty-seven developing countries and sixteen developed countries which is a major exception to the **General Agreement on Tariffs and Trade**. It has been renewed three times, the last time in 1986. This quota scheme for producers was originally designed to provide gradual adjustment to international shifts in **comparative advantage** and to liberalize world trade gradually. In practice, it restricts the exports of fibres to consumer countries, e.g. the UK and USA. In 1986, the MFA was extended to more fibres (sisal, jute and ramie – a flax-like substance). A production limit is assigned to a country which then shares it out among individual producers: if one manufacturer wants to expand production then it can buy an enlarged quota on the open market. The General Agreement on Tariffs and Trade believes

that the MFA distorts the pattern of world trade as it impedes the expansion of low-cost producers. The MFA's effects have been to raise the cost of clothing and the profits of domestic producers in developed countries. It has curbed the exports of developing countries but has encouraged a shift to higher quality products amongst the established Third World producers.

Choi, Y.-P., Chung, H.S. and Marian, N. (1985) *The Multi-Fibre Arrangement in Theory and Practice*, London: Pinter.

multilateral aid (430)

Foreign aid which consists of the distribution to developing countries by an international agency, e.g. the **World Bank**, of the grants given by wealthier countries. Although it is argued that aid in this form is fairer than **bilateral aid**, it is still possible for there to be biases in the distribution policy of a major agency.

Multilateral Investment Guarantee Agency (430)

An offshoot of the **World Bank** created in 1988 to promote foreign investment by guaranteeing against many risks, including expropriation and currency transfer. It also offers advice to developing countries wanting to make their economies more attractive to the potential foreign investor.

multilevel marketing (530)

See: **pyramid selling**.

multimodal frequency curve (210)

A **frequency curve** with more than two maxima.

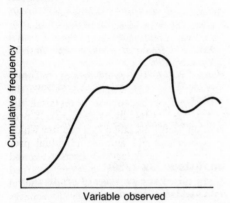

multinational corporation (510, 610)

An international firm that produces goods or services in several countries, without being concentrated in a single country. Although the term first became popular in the 1960s, by the late nineteenth century several US, British and Dutch firms had acquired such characteristics.

The advantages of production abroad, rather than export from the original country of operation, include a saving in transport costs, the adjustment of product design to make products more acceptable to local markets, a reduction, in many cases, in corporate taxation and access to local labour and capital which may be more abundant than at home. The immense success of this organizational form, prominent in many industries, including motor cars, computers, pharmaceuticals, food processing, oil and soap, has attracted envy and criticism: envy from national governments with less economic power and competence; criticism from Marxists who see the growth of multinationals as a sinister international expansion of **capitalism**. **Trade unions** complain about competition from cheap labour countries; science graduates lament the increased concentration of research and development activities in the United States to the detriment of other countries; national governments object to the loss of tax revenue and the difficulties of operating industrial and employment policies when much of their industrial sector is controlled by foreign-owned entities.

Many controls have been suggested to reduce what are seen to be the less attractive effects of multinationals: governments and trade unions lay down strict conditions for foreign countries wishing to invest, fiscal devices are used to maintain tax revenues and domestically owned multinationals are monitored. In extreme cases, exasperated national governments have nationalized the assets of foreign-owned subsidiaries: but in many cases this has been as sensible as cutting the hands off a worker and expecting the severed hands to do the same work as before – a subsidiary, unsupported by the services of the rest of the corporation is a poor shadow of its former self. Despite so many attempts to curb the activities of multinationals, they continue to grow,

311

enjoying all the benefits of **economies of scale** and retaining their status as major world economic institutions.

Caves, R.E. (1982) *Multinational Enterprise and Economic Analysis*, Cambridge: Cambridge University Press.

multiple correlation (210)

The extent to which there is a relationship between three or more variables, which is measured by the **coefficient of multiple correlation**.

See also: **linear correlation**.

multiple exchange rate (430)

An exchange rate with different values according to the nature of the international transaction. Often, **balance of payments** current account transactions are at a different rate from capital account transactions. Central banks allow these different rates because of the different pressures on parts of their balance of payments, e.g. needing imports of capital but not imports of luxury goods. Common examples of multiple rates are the existence of official and **black market** exchange rates in operation simultaneously and an official rate together with more favourable rates for industries being helped under an industrial policy.

See also: **dual exchange rate**.

multiplier (010)

The relationship between an increment in income and a change in **aggregate demand**; in particular, the ratio of extra expenditure to extra investment. There were hints of a multiplier concept as early as the seventeenth century by **Petty** but it was not until **Kahn** postulated an employment multiplier in 1930 that formal attempts were made to measure it, particularly by Colin **Clark**. It has become a central idea in macroeconomics. For a simple closed economy described by the equation

$$Y = C + I$$

where Y is national income, C is aggregate consumption and I is net investment, the multiplier is

$$\frac{1}{1 - MPC}$$

with MPC the marginal propensity to consume; for an open economy described by the equation

$$Y = C + I + (X - M)$$

where X is exports and M is imports, the multiplier is

$$\frac{1}{1 - (MPC + MPM)}$$

with MPM the marginal propensity to import.

Hansen, A.H. (1948) *Income, Employment and Public Policy: Essays in Honor of Alvin H. Hansen*, New York: Norton.

See also: **balanced budget**; **employment**; **foreign trade multiplier**; **money multiplier**; **regional multiplier**; **super multiplier**.

multiplier–accelerator model (140)

An economic model which attempts to explain **business cycles**: the **multiplier** makes income respond to investment and the **accelerator** ensures that changes in income will generate net investment. Given certain values in the basic equations, fluctuations will be generated but it is usual for there to be ceilings and floors to economic activity to cause turning-points in the national economy.

Goodwin, R.M. (1948) 'Secular and cyclical aspects of the multiplier and the accelerator', in *Income, Employment and Public Policy: Essays in Honor of Alvin H. Hansen*, New York: Norton.

Hicks, J.R. (1950) *A Contribution to the Theory of the Trade Cycle*, Oxford: Oxford University Press.

Samuelson, P.A. (1939) 'Interactions between the multiplier analysis and the principle of acceleration', *Review of Economic Statistics* 21: 75–8.

multistage tax (320)

A tax raised at each stage of production; a **value-added** or **turnover tax**.

multivariate analysis (210)

The examination of the relationship between several variables, usually a dependent variable and several independent variables. An example of this would be a study of the determinants of the unemployment rate (the dependent variable) and educational qualifications, age and previous work experience (independent variables).

See also: **regression**.

Mun, Thomas, 1571–1641 (030)

Director of the East India Company and leading **mercantilist** whose formulation of economic theory in *England's Treasure by Forraign Trade* (first published posthumously in 1664) represented the finest flowering of late mercantilist ideas. To justify the export of silver bullion by the Company, he extended the current idea of the balance of payments as being a particular balance between two countries to the concept of a general balance between one country and the rest of the world, permitting some individual balances to be in deficit. Adam **Smith**'s view of mercantilism was heavily influenced by Mun.

Appleby, J.O. (1978) *Economic Thought and Ideology in Seventeenth Century England*, Princeton, NJ: Princeton University Press.

Mundell–Fleming model (410)

An open economy model extending the IS–LM model on which an **FF curve** is imposed to show that the economy is in equilibrium when there are equilibria in its money and goods markets and its imports equal its exports. The **terms of trade** affect the positions of both the IS and FF curves.

Mundell, R.A. (1968) *International Economics*, New York: Macmillan.

See also: **IS–LM curves**.

muni (310)

US municipal bond.

Muth–Mills model (930)

A study of the relationship between the differential costs of commuting in an urban area and the differences in house prices. This model is used to explain the internal structure of cities. Lower house prices in the suburbs are sufficient to justify high commuting costs to the central business district.

Mills, E.S. (1967) 'An aggregative model of resource allocation in a metropolitan area', *American Economic Review* 57: 197–210.

Muth, R.F. (1969) *Cities and Housing*, Chicago, IL: Chicago University Press.

mutual fund (310)

US **unit trust**. There are many types: general equity funds which invest in a range of equities with the aim of outperforming the market as measured by, for example, **Standard & Poor's 500** index; index funds which are invested in the leading stocks which comprise the principal stock market price indices; strategic funds which are very diversified as they invest in all markets, including currency and futures markets; sector funds, which specialize in one sector of the stock market; overseas funds which consist of the stocks of a foreign country or a group of them, e.g. Japan or Europe; precious metal funds investing in gold, silver and other high value metals; tax-free funds which invest in tax exempt bonds of, for example, US states; funds of funds which spread risk by investing in several mutual funds; social conscience funds which avoid investments in morally criticized industries or countries.

See also: **investment trust**.

Myrdal, Gunnar, 1898–1987 (030)

A leading Swedish economist and sociologist. He studied at Stockholm University under **Wicksell**, **Cassel** and **Heckscher** in preparation for his notable academic and public career. In his varied life he was professor at Geneva from 1931 to 1932 and at Stockholm from 1933 to 1939 and 1961 to 1965, as well as being a senator of the Swedish parliament from 1934 to 1936 and from 1942 to 1946, Minister for Trade and Commerce from 1945 to 1947 and Executive Secretary of the UN Economic Commission for Europe from 1947 to 1957. He was awarded the **Nobel Prize for Economics**, with **Hayek**, in 1974; his wife, whom he married in 1924, gained the Nobel Peace Prize in 1982.

His major contribution to economics has been his work *Monetary Equilibrium*, a central work of the **Stockholm School**, in which he developed his 1927 doctoral thesis on price formation and change to show the importance of the *ex ante*, *ex post* distinction in macroeconomics. He is also famous for his contributions to methodological debates, particularly in his work *The Political Element in the Development of Economic Theory and Objectivity in Social Research* in which he advanced the idea of a value-free economics. His commitment to development economics is evident in his *Asian Drama*, as is his sociological ability in *American Dilemma*.

Kindleberger, C.P. (1987) 'Gunnar Myrdal, 1898– 1987', *Scandinavian Journal of Economics* 87: 393–403.

Myrdal, G. (1939) *Monetary Equilibrium*, London: W.M. Hodge.

—— (1944) *American Dilemma: The Negro Problem and Modern Democracy*, New York: Harper.

—— (Swedish edn 1930, English edn 1953) *The Political Element in the Development of Economic Theory*, trans. by P. Streeton, London: Routledge & Kegan Paul.

—— (1968) *Asian Drama: An Inquiry into the Poverty of Nations*, London and New York: Twentieth Century Fund.

—— (1970) *Objectivity in Social Research*, London: Duckworth.

N

N (220)

The quantity of employment. This notation was extensively used by **Keynes** and subsequent labour market theorists in their diagrams.

NAFA (310)

See: **net acquisition of financial assets**.

NAIC (310, 630)

National Association of Insurance Commissioners (USA) which includes regulators from the fifty state insurance commissions.

NAIRU (810)

Non-accelerating inflation rate of unemployment.

See also: **natural rate of unemployment**.

nanny state (910)

An economy which is a **welfare state** providing so many benefits as to take away much personal responsibility and create a **dependency culture**.

narcodollars (310)

Dollars which are used to launder the money of drug barons of the world.

See also: **laundering money**.

NASDAQ (310)

See: **National Association of Securities Dealers Automated Quotation System**.

NASDIM (310)

See: **National Association of Securities Dealers and Investment Managers**.

Nash bargaining (210)

A two-person economic game in which there is collusion between the players. Equilibrium is such that an individual's **marginal rate of substitution** = the **marginal rate of transformation**. This equilibrium is inefficient because the price facing the consumer is equal to the price of the **public good**, with some of the benefit accruing to others. This has been applied to **oligopoly** to show how a firm makes the best response to the decisions of its rivals.

National Association of Securities Dealers and Investment Managers (310)

UK association of insurance brokers and investment advisers, some of whom deal in over-the-counter shares.

See also: **over-the-counter market**.

National Association of Securities Dealers Automated Quotation System (310)

US securities market founded in 1938 which lists over-the-counter securities not listed on regular exchanges. By the end of the 1980s, it became the second largest securities market in the USA and the third largest in the world, making it the strongest stockmarket rival to the New York Stock Exchange, particularly because of its innovations in technology and market-making. The price quotations of its **market-makers** are the basis of competition in this electronic market; each stock has a minimum of two market-makers. From 1982, only stocks with at least 100,000 shares worth at least $5 each have been included, i.e. 2,500 stocks. It is also linked to the **International Stock Exchange** to provide a transatlantic market in 600 securities.

See also: **over-the-counter market**.

National Banking Act 1863 (310)

US federal statute whose provisions included the setting up of the **Comptroller of the Currency** to increase the supervision, and, therefore, the solvency of **commercial banks**. It restricted nationally chartered banks to operating only one branch.

See also: **branch banking**; **McFadden Branch Banking Act 1927**.

National Board for Prices and Incomes (820)

The British public board which administered a national prices and incomes policy from 1965 to 1972. Of its 170 reports, some were on whether particular price or wage increases were justified and others were concerned to relate these two aspects of inflation. The Board produced much applied microeconomic analysis which was in greater depth than the publications of many other public authorities of the day; the subsequent Pay Board produced less profound reports.

Fels, A. (1972) *The British Prices and Incomes Board*, Cambridge: Cambridge University Press.

Mitchell, J. (1972) *The National Board for Prices and Incomes*, London: Secker & Warburg.

See also: **incomes policy**; **prices policy**.

National Bureau of Economic Research (140)

Washington-based independent economics institute founded in 1920. Its famous research series includes the seminal work of **Kuznets** on **national income** and the studies by **Mitchell** and **Burns** of the business cycle. Its dominant concerns have been macroeconomic.

national debt (320, 430)

The total indebtedness of the central and local governments of a country at a particular time to its own public and foreign creditors which takes the form of short-term **bills** and long-term **bonds**. In most cases, such debt has accumulated because the country's public expenditure is more than its tax revenue. The burden of a national debt is usually measured by the ratio of national debt to gross national product. Long-term debt can be regarded as a burden to subsequent generations.

See also: **overlapping generations model**.

National Economic Development Council (120)

A tripartite council set up in the UK in 1962 consisting of representatives of the government, trade unions and employers which had the original aim of attempting to introduce **indicative planning** into Britain. Although some general economic forecasts were published, it soon, with the use of Economic Development Councils for particular industries, concentrated on producing detailed recommendations for improving sectors of the British economy. For much of its existence, it has been valued as a forum by all participants apart from in the 1980s when trade unions were in dispute with the government over deunionization of workers in intelligence establishments. In the 1980s, it moved from industrial policy measures to **supply-side economics**.

National Enterprise Board (610)

A British public corporation created by the Industry Act 1975 to encourage industrial investment and restructuring; in a sense a successor to the **Industrial Reorganization Corporation**. It used its funds to invest in private sector firms to bring about mergers. Also it had the task of managing existing government shareholders in major firms, especially British Leyland and Rolls Royce, helping small firms and allocating grants under regional policy. In 1980, the Conservative government considerably reduced its role by selling off many of its investments and by cutting its annual funds.

national income (010, 220)

1 The money value of the goods and services resulting from the economic activities of the residents of a country over a time-period, usually of a quarter or whole year.

2 A monetary **flow** showing net additions to wealth.

3 The sum of **factor incomes**.

4 The net national product (gross national product less depreciation) because income is a **flow concept** showing net additions to wealth over a time period.

Not all countries are agreed on what should be included in national income as different countries have varying views on what constitutes 'an economic activity' but there is conceptual accord that national income, national product and national expenditure are identical because there is in every economy a **circular flow** of income: an economic activity produces an output which, when sold, constitutes expenditure and creates incomes for the factors of production that have made it. The national income at market prices includes in the valuation of economic activities indirect taxes net of subsidies; the valuation at factor cost does not.

Rough estimates of the national income were made as early as the seventeenth century by **Petty** and Gregory King, but fairly accurate national income accounting is a product of the macroeconomic revolution in economic thinking in the 1930s: **Clark** and **Stone** in the UK and **Kuznets** in the USA laid the foundations for today's national accounting. International comparisons of different countries' national incomes should be treated with caution. Apart from different statistical conventions from country to country, there is also the problem of translating income estimates in one currency into those of another, often the US dollar. In general, measures of the national income usually exclude non-market activities, leisure and environmental social costs, making them inaccurate as measures of **economic welfare**.

Beckerman, W. (1966) *International Comparisons of Real Income*, Paris: OECD.

—— (1980) *An Introduction to National Income Analysis*, 3rd edn, London: Weidenfeld & Nicolson.

Kravrs, I.B. (1978) *International Comparisons of Real Product and Purchasing Power*, Baltimore, MD: published for World Bank by Johns Hopkins University Press.

United Nations International Comparison Project (1978) *Phase II*.

See also: **accounts; European system of accounts; measure of economic welfare; National Income and Product Accounts; net economic welfare; physical quality of life; purchasing power parity; System of National Accounts.**

National Income and Product Accounts (220)

The national income accounts of the USA which began in 1947; earlier estimates had been produced by the US Department of Commerce with the advice of **Kuznets** but they lacked an expenditure breakdown of the national product. The need for better economic information in the Second World War prompted the creation of this new accounting framework. The new accounts had the aims of providing a consistent and interrelated system, improving statistical procedures for estimating all series using the latest data and incorporating changes in basic aggregates to make the definitions used more useful.

The basic table is

gross national product =
personal consumption expenditures
+ gross private domestic investment
+ net exports of goods and services
+ government purchases.

Further tables present disaggregated statistics of the principal components.

Eisner, R. (1988) 'Extended accounts for national income and product', *Journal of Economic Literature* 26 (December): 1611–84.

Foss, M.F. (1983) *The US National Income and Product Accounts. NBER Studies in Income and Wealth*, vol. 47, Chicago, IL: University of Chicago Press.

US Bureau of Economic Analysis, *The National Income and Product Accounts of the United States, 1929–82. Survey of Current Business*, July issues.

See also: **European System of Accounts; national income; System of National Accounts.**

National Industrial Recovery Act 1933 (610, 830)

A major US federal statute of the **New Deal** which sought to promote industrial recovery. Under section 7, the codes of competition (statements of price and output policies) had to recognize the right of workers to organize collectively making this statute an important forerunner of the **Wagner Act.**

National Institute for Economic and Social Research (050, 140)

UK independent economics institute founded in 1938 to research into economic and social conditions. Apart from occasional pamphlets, it publishes an influential quarterly review and undertakes its own economic forecasting.

national insurance contribution (320, 910)

UK employment tax created in 1948. The contributions from employers, employees and the self-employed are kept in a separate fund to finance a range of benefits, including those for the unemployed, the sick and the retired. **Beveridge**, when devising this system, was inspired by the older social security system of Germany introduced by Bismarck.

nationalization (510)
The acquisition of privately owned enterprises by a government, with or without compensation.

See also: **nationalized industry**; **public enterprise**.

nationalized industry (610)
A publicly owned firm engaged in the production of goods and services. Although governments have been involved in the ownership of industrial concerns as early as the **mercantilists** and post offices have long been state-owned in many countries, it is in the twentieth century that large basic industries have been state-owned, e.g. in France and in the UK. In Britain, most of these were established by the Labour government of 1945 to 1950 as an implementation of clause four of the Labour Party constitution; private sector firms in the basic industries of transport, energy and steel, as well as the Bank of England, were purchased. The extension of public ownership gave Britain the character of a **mixed economy**. Other countries, particularly France, greatly extended public ownership in the 1930s; in the USA, the creation of AMTRAK was a rare US example of this organizational form. But in the 1980s, it became British government policy to 'privatize' the more profitable nationalized industries, including telecommunications, water, gas and electricity.

The trading position of a nationalized industry is affected by its monopoly position and the lack of market discipline, both by having public finance to supplement borrowings from capital markets and by being kept in existence when virtually bankrupt. As a consequence, a high proportion of government grants has been to subsidize wage bills, rather than to finance long-term investment. President Mitterrand of France in September 1981, one of the last to argue the case for nationalization, gave as reasons for taking into state ownership large industrial groups and banks, the elimination of monopoly and quasi-monopoly situations which provide a basis for political influence, safeguarding national sovereignty

and the provision of tools for industrial development in the future.

Chester, N. (1975) *The Nationalisation of British Industry, 1945–51*, London: HMSO.

Pryke, R. (1971) *Public Enterprise in Practice: The British Experience of Nationalisation over Two Decades*, London: MacGibbon & Kee.

—— (1981) *The Nationalised Industries: Policies and Performance since 1968*, Oxford: Robertson.

See also: **privatization**; **public enterprise**.

National Labor Relations Act 1935 (830)
See: **Wagner Act 1935**.

National Labor Relations Board (830)
US federal board created in 1933 and subsequently authorized by the **Wagner Act**. It attempts to prevent and remedy unfair labor practices to promote **collective bargaining** by conducting secret ballots to establish whether a labor organization can represent a group of workers.

national lottery (320)
A means of financing public expenditure by selling a large number of tickets and offering huge cash prizes to attract participants. These lotteries are conducted in many European countries, except the UK. In the USA, many states have lotteries to help to finance their expenditures.

National Plan (UK) (120)
An exercise in **indicative planning** which began in 1965 but, instead of lasting until 1970, terminated nine months later when the seamen's strike exacerbated a balance of payments problem necessitating deflation in place of the growth aims of the Plan. It was hoped that the British national income would increase by 25 per cent over five years. This was unlikely as many of the assumptions, e.g. those for export growth and labour mobility, were regarded as too generous; the Industrial Inquiry which provided a database for the planners was regarded as highly inaccurate. The essence of indicative planning – that government forecasts are sufficiently influential to encourage investment – was lacking: few believed in the ambitious schemes of the planners.

The National Plan, London: HMSO, Cmnd 2764, (1965).

national wealth (220)

The total **assets** owned by the residents of a country on a particular day. The most reliable estimates are for firms as they have to keep balance sheets. Many household assets are only valued on death so the sample of wealth statistics produced from probate sources is non-random. It could be argued that **human capital** estimates should be included in the national wealth as trained labour is a major national asset but few countries are statistically ambitious enough to attempt such a measure, although it is possible to produce an estimate if a **population census** asks questions about educational qualifications and training.

Goldsmith, R.W. (1985) *Comparative National Balance Sheets. A Study of Twenty Countries 1688–1978*, Chicago, IL and London: University of Chicago Press.
Revell, J.L. (1967) *The Wealth of the Nation: The National Balance Sheet of the United Kingdom, 1957–61*, Cambridge: Cambridge University Press.

See also: **balance sheet; stock and flow concepts; wealth**.

natural increase (840)

The increase in a human population which results from an excess of births over deaths. Natural increase rates are higher in the **Third** and **Fourth Worlds** than in the **First World**.

natural monopoly (010, 610)

An **industry** which, it is argued, should be run as a **monopoly**, usually to achieve the maximum amount of **economies of scale**. If a natural monopoly brought about by the technology of an industry were replaced by **competition**, there would be an increase in unit costs, as happens when a natural monopoly in energy distribution is split up, losing the advantages of technical scale economies. Another case for monopolies of this kind is that a good or service is not supplied by any private concern and can only be supplied by the government, e.g. national defence.

Shaked, A. and Sutton, J. (1983) 'Natural oligopolies', *Econometrica* 51: 1469–84.
Sharkey, W.W. (1982) *The Theory of Natural Monopoly*, New York and Cambridge: Cambridge University Press.

natural price (010)

The central long-run equilibrium product price around which market prices fluctuate. Adam **Smith**, in introducing this concept, said that the natural price would be the sum of the natural prices of land, labour and capital.

natural rate of growth (110)

The maximum long-term rate of **economic growth**. In the **Harrod–Domar** growth model it is measured as the sum of the rate of population growth and the rate of **technical** progress reflected in labour **productivity**: $G_n = n + t$, where G_n is the natural rate of growth, n is the rate of population growth and t is the rate of technical progress. Population growth leads to a growth of the **labour force**; technical progress increases labour productivity.

See also: **warranted rate of growth**.

natural rate of interest (010, 310)

Marginal product of capital.

See also: **market rate of interest; Wicksell**.

natural rate of unemployment (810)

1 The single rate of unemployment compatible with a constant rate of inflation.

2 The long-term rate of unemployment around which an economy fluctuates as expectations of wage and price changes are fully realized by the associated rate of inflation. Attempts to move the economy to a lower rate of unemployment by fiscal and monetary stimulation are unsuccessful as expectations increase leading to inflationary increases in prices and wages which push the unemployment rate back to the natural rate. The natural rate changes in response to changes in the composition of the labour force as flows in and out of the stock of the unemployed are affected. The natural rate is usually illustrated by a vertical **Phillips curve**.

Friedman, M. (1968) 'The role of monetary policy', *American Economic Review* 58 (March): 1–17.

natural resources (720)

Land, including soil, air, water, minerals,

animal and plant life. Environmental resources which support life and health and provide amenities and energy resources are included; human resources and physical capital are excluded.

Johnson, R.L. and Johnson, G.V. (eds) (1990) *Economic Valuation of Natural Resources. Issues, Theory, and Applications*, Boulder, CO: Westview Press.

Pearce, D. and Turner K. (eds) (1989) *Economics of Natural Resources and Environment*, Brighton: Harvester Wheatsheaf.

See also: **externality**; **pollution control**.

NAV (520)
See: **net asset value**.

NBER (140)
See: **National Bureau of Economic Research**.

NBPI (820)
See: **National Board for Prices and Incomes**.

near money (310)
Time deposits with financial institutions which, on notice, can be converted into money, e.g. **building society** deposits, **CDs**. These lack the essential characteristic of money – being immediately usable as a **medium of exchange** – but readily can be converted into money.

NEB (610)
See: **National Enterprise Board**.

NEDC (110)
See: **National Economic Development Council**.

NEDO (110)
National Economic Development Office (UK): the secretariat of the **National Economic Development Council**.

needs of trade (310)
A banking doctrine, advanced by the **Banking School**, that demand, rather than the amount of **specie** held by a bank, should determine the amount of banknotes in circulation.

needs standard (160)
A principle of **distribution** based on Louis Blanc's notion 'From each according to ability, to each according to needs'. It is difficult to implement this approach to income distribution as the concept of 'need' is subjective and it has the disincentive effect of discouraging more industrious and talented workers whose reward is diminished by the extra income given to the poor.

See also: **contribution standard**; **needs standard**; **subsistence**.

negative feedback (110)
The unfavourable effects of fast economic growth which make further growth difficult, e.g. because of diminishing returns in an agrarian economy.

See also: **diminishing returns law**.

negative income tax (320)
An income maintenance scheme which makes cash payments to persons with less than an arbitrary level of income (which is notionally related to **subsistence**). Advocates of such schemes argue that the **poverty trap** is eliminated, there is a reduction in administration costs and that the labour supply from low income households is increased because they would no longer be caught by high **marginal tax rates** when moving from welfare benefits to employment incomes under a discontinuous benefit-tax scale. Short-run US experiments of this kind have included urban schemes in New Jersey and rural projects in Iowa.

Parker, H. (1989) *Instead of the Dole: An Inquiry into the Integration of the Tax and Benefit Systems*, London: Routledge.

Pechman, J.A. and Timpane, P.M. (eds) (1975) *Work Incentives and Income Guarantees*, Washington, DC: Brookings Institute.

See also: **social dividend scheme**.

negative saving (310)
See: **dissaving**.

negotiable order of withdrawal (310)
See: **NOW account**.

negotiated coordination (120)
A form of democratic national planning, resembling French **indicative planning**, in which interest groups nationally, and within

each sector of an **economy**, reach agreement before their conclusions are reviewed by a national representative assembly. The principal issues in negotiations are investment and manpower.

Marquand, D. (1988) *The Unprincipled Society: New Demands and Old Politics*, London: Jonathan Cape.

neighbourhood effect (010, 720)

An **externality**, or spillover effect, which has a spatial impact. Industrial pollution provides many examples of costly effects; beautiful buildings and gardens increase the welfare of nearby residents.

neoclassical economics (030)

The school of economics which emerged in the UK and the USA in the late nineteenth century, after 'the Marginal Revolution', **Marshall**, **Edgeworth**, **Pareto**, **Wicksell** and **Walras** being its most prominent founders. Building on marginal analysis, it dominates much of US economics today, especially at Chicago University. It takes the view that an economy's equilibrium will occur after a disturbance because of a **tâtonnement** process with flexible wages and prices. As prices disseminate information and provide incentives for economic agents, economic plans and activities are coordinated.

This school of economics, emphasizing the roles of consumers, producers and savers, has shifted from a study of market allocation to the science of individual and institutional choices about resources in markets and other economic institutions. It provides little macroeconomic analysis, except in its aggregation of individuals' choices. **Hicks** and **Samuelson** have been the most brilliant theorists of the school in the twentieth century. Critics of neoclassicism reject the view of economic agents as being concerned with maximization of utility, profit or net income and want to dethrone the central principles of diminishing **marginal utility** and diminishing **marginal rates of substitution**. However, the neoclassicals continue to show the usefulness of the principles of maximization, equilibrium and substitution at the margin in their study of a host of modern problems, including job search, crime, time, marriage and housing, and the elegance of their theorizing.

Boland, L. (1982) *Foundations of Economic Method*, London: Allen & Unwin.
Henry, J.F. (1990) *The Making of Neoclassical Economics*, London: Unwin Hyman.

See also: **continuity thesis**; **marginalists**.

neo-Keynesians (030)

A modern refinement of Keynesian macroeconomics, particularly associated with **Hicks** and **Meade** in the UK and with **Tobin**, **Klein**, **Modigliani** and Blinder in the USA. To undertake this enhancement of Keynes's ideas, the **IS–LM** framework and the **Phillips curve** have been extensively used. This theoretical approach often refers to the failures of markets, particularly the labour market which does not clear because money wages are often inflexible downwards. A major policy prescription of this school of economics is demand management to keep an economy in equilibrium.

neo-Malthusians (840)

Followers of **Malthus** who in the nineteenth century advocated birth control as a means of checking population growth; in the twentieth century they have been more concerned to emphasize the conservation of natural resources, given limited technical progress.

Soloway, R.A. (1982) *Birth Control and the Population Question in England, 1877–1930*. London and Chapel Hill, NC: University of North Carolina Press.

See also: **Club of Rome**.

neo-Marxists (030)

A group of economists, especially Mandel and Sweezy, who have tried to re-interpret Marx in the light of more recent economists' thought, including Keynes's.

neo-mercantilism (030)

The modern advocacy of **protectionism** as a means to encouraging employment growth.

Johnson, H.G. (ed.) (1974) *The New Mercantilism: Some Problems in International Trade, Money and Investment*, Oxford: Basil Blackwell.

See also: **alternative economic strategy**; **infant industry argument**; **mercantilism**; **Smoot–Hawley**.

neo-Ricardian theory (020, 030)

A return to the **labour theory of value** of **Ricardo**, based on **Sraffa**'s seminal work of 1960 which attempted to solve the problems he raised, particularly the formulation of a satisfactory theory of a surplus-producing economy. A class analysis, rather than a **neoclassical** approach, is used to show how the surplus produced is divided into **profits**, **interest** and **rent**. Prices are not explained by labour time values but by a cost of production theory, stating the socially necessary conditions of production. Thus prices = physical quantities of machines and raw materials employed + wages paid to the workforce + a mark-up on those costs. The theory develops Marxian theory, discarding the view that the tendency of the rate of profit is to fall and the development tendencies of the capitalist mode of production. Neo-Ricardian analysis has been applied to specific aspects of twentieth-century capitalism, especially oligopoly.

Fine, B. and Harris, L. (1979) *Rereading Capital*, New York: Columbia University Press.
Steedman, I. (1977) *Marx after Sraffa*, London: New Left Books.

NEP (040, 060)

See: **New Economic Policy**.

net acquisition of financial assets (310, 540)

A set of sectoral balances used to analyse the overall state of an economy. These balances can be individually in deficit or surplus. The **Cambridge Economic Policy Group** used this approach a great deal in their analysis of the **public sector** borrowing requirement.

net asset value (520)

The value of the total assets of a company after deduction of all debts. It is expressed as X pence, or dollars, per share.

net barter terms of trade (420)

The ratio of an index of export prices to an index of import prices; the most commonly used measurement of the **terms of trade**.

net economic welfare (010, 910)

Gross national product adjusted by subtracting from it **'bads'** such as pollution and by adding the value of beneficial non-market activities, including leisure.

See also: **measure of economic welfare**.

net investment (010)

An addition to the stock of capital in a given time period. Net investment plus **replacement investment** constitute gross investment.

See also: **accelerator principle**.

net present value (520)

The discounted value of future income from a particular investment less the discounted value of expected costs. A positive net present value indicates that an investment project is worthwhile.

See also: **marginal efficiency of capital**.

net property income from abroad (430)

The receipts of rents, profits and interest arising from ownership of foreign assets, less the payments of the same to non-residents. Net property income from abroad is added to the **gross domestic product** to calculate the **gross national product**.

See also: **balance of payments**.

networker (810)

A person who works at home or at a local network office providing the head office with various services, e.g. marketing, research, training, financial analysis. These workers use computers linked by telephone to a main office. An obvious advantage of this system is a reduction in office accommodation costs but the social implications of isolated work and the effect on industrial relations of the geographical fragmentation of the labour force could be considerable in the long run.

See also: **homework**.

networking economy (610)

An **economy** consisting of many small specialist firms, or **networkers**, linked together by an information system, a **post-industrial society**.

net worth (540)

Total assets minus total liabilities; proprietors' capital employed in a business.

neutral budget (320)

1 A national financial budget with the **fiscal stance** of seeking to avoid stimulation or contraction of a national economy.

2 A national **structural deficit** equal to 0.

neutrality of money (310)

A money supply which can affect the price level but not real output and employment. This view of money is challenged by **neo-Keynesian** economists who argue that an increase in the money supply, by causing a shift in the LM curve, will bring down interest rates and increase real output.

See also: **classical dichotomy**.

neutral technical progress (620)

Inventions or **innovations** which do not affect the relative **productivities** of the **factors of production** used. **Hicks**, more precisely, defined this type of economic growth as progress which raises the marginal productivities of capital and labour in the same proportions for unchanged factor inputs, whereas **Harrod** sought to describe it as progress which does not change the **capital–output ratio** when there is a constant rate of interest and rate of profit on capital.

NEW (010, 910)

See: **net economic welfare**.

New Cambridge economics (030)

Some of the **Cambridge Economic Policy** group led by Wynne Godley who offered an **alternative economic strategy** for the British economy in the 1970s. Their views included the beliefs that inflation can be caused by trade union power, an increase in world commodity prices and devaluation and cured by an expansionary fiscal policy, that import quotas should be used to correct balance of payments problems and that tax rates should be set at a level which will bring about full employment and a balance of payments equilibrium.

Cuthbertson, K. (1979) *Macroeconomic Policy. The New Cambridge, Keynesian and Monetarist Controversies*, London and Basingstoke: Macmillan.

new classical economics (030)

A modern US and British school of economics which combines the use of the **rational expectations** hypothesis with **monetarism** and a **laissez-faire** approach to economic policy. All markets are assumed to be perfectly competitive in their behaviour and all unemployment is voluntary because it arises only when employers and employees make mistakes. Central to this technically sophisticated theory is the belief that markets clear. The principal proponents of these views in the USA are Lucas and Sargant; in the UK, Patrick Minford and Michael Beenstock.

Buiter, W.H. (1980) 'The macroeconomics of Dr Pangloss: a critical survey of the new classical macroeconomics', *Economic Journal* 90: 34–50.

Hoover, K.D. (1988) *The New Classical Economics*, Oxford: Basil Blackwell.

See also: **perfect competition**.

New Deal (320)

The US policies of President Franklin Roosevelt to revive the depressed US economy of 1933-7. Loosely called **'Keynesian'**, these policies included the creation of budget deficits. Financial stability was sought through **deposit insurance**, the setting up of the **Securities and Exchange Commission** and the extension of the powers to regulate banks. Collective bargaining was extended through the **Wagner Act** and through the codes of the National Recovery Administration. There was a new partnership between business and government which, in a sense, created a **mixed economy**.

Lippman, W. (1938) *The Good Society*, London: Allen & Unwin.

New Earnings Survey (220, 820)

An annual survey of British earnings published by the Department of Employment in 1968 and every year from 1970. It provides detailed statistics on the occupational, industrial and regional distributions of employment incomes.

New Economic Mechanism (120)

1 Hungarian economic reforms of 1968. Under this mechanism, the planning system was modified by replacing plan directives to a large extent by direct relationships between firms; price determination was more influenced by market forces through the linkage of domestic prices of exports and imports to world market prices and most investment decisions were decentralized.

2 Soviet economic reforms announced in 1987: changes to prices and wages were proposed in order to increase economic efficiency and improve economic incentives.

See also: **perestroika**.

New Economic Policy (040, 060)
The second phase of Lenin's economic policy for the Soviet Union in the 1920s which, in an attempt to increase production, replaced war communism with decentralization of industry and a measure of privately owned small-scale trade.

new federalism (320)
A view of the relationship between US federal and state governments announced by President Nixon in 1971 and revived by President Reagan in the 1980s, that there should be devolution of many federal activities to the states, including education and welfare programmes.

new industrial state (070, 120)
Galbraith's term for the modern economy which is dominated by a 'technostructure' of large firms dedicated to stable production and the creation of wants so that there is no deficiency of demand for their products. He argues that the planning system used can be practised by both **capitalist** and **socialist economies**.

Galbraith, J.K. (1967) *The New Industrial State*, London: Hamish Hamilton; Boston, MA: Houghton Mifflin.

new international division of labour (420)
Specialization, particularly by Third World countries, in a narrow range of exports, either because of the historical development of their industries or because of the global production planning practised by **multinational corporations**.

New International Economic Order (420, 430)
A proposal, popular amongst Marxian economists, to alleviate the problems of the Third World by changes in international trading arrangements and a writing-off of Third World countries' debts. Originally, it was hoped that this proposal, made in a resolution of the General Assembly of the United Nations in May 1974, would reduce, by international cooperation, the widening inequality between rich and poor countries. Marketing boards, similar to the **Organization of Petroleum Exporting Countries**, were proposed for many **primary products** so that income would be redistributed to poorer countries in the form of monopoly profits. Also, it was suggested that preferential treatment should be given for developing countries' exports to developed countries to enhance poorer countries' foreign trade earnings. The New International Economic Order provided a different approach to economic **development** as a means of raising living standards.

See also: **Brandt Commission; world debt problem**.

new issue (310)
The shares offered by a company when it is marketing its securities on a stock market for the first time or raising additional capital. The shares can be issued by **tender** or by prospectus.

See also: **placing; rights issue; stag**.

new Keynesian (030)
See: **neo-Keynesians**.

New Left (030)
See: **radical economics**.

newly industrialized country (050)
Spain, Brazil, Mexico, South Korea, Taiwan, Hong Kong and Singapore. These countries have acquired their status either because of the absolute size of their manufacturing sectors or through the rate of growth of their manufacturing industries. Some of these countries have used **tariffs** to protect their **infant industries**.

new microeconomics (030)
An examination of the microeconomic foundations of macroeconomics, particularly theories of **inflation** and the **natural rate of unemployment**. The School also

incorporates some of the ideas of the **post-Keynesians**.

Phelps, E.S., Alchian, A.A., Holt, C.C., Mortensen, D.T., Archibald, G.C., Lucas, R.E. Jr, Rapping, L.A., Winter, S.G. Jr, Gould, J.P., Gordon, D.F., Hynes, A., Nichols, D.A., Taubman, P.J. and Wilkinson, M. (1970) *The Microeconomic Foundations of Employment and Inflation Theory*, New York and London: Macmillan.

new protectionism (420)
See: **neo-mercantilism**.

New Right (030)
Political and economic thinkers who came to prominence in the 1980s in the USA and Western Europe through advocating **libertarian economics**. Their proposals include a minimal role for the State, little government intervention in the running of national economies, a market approach to production and distribution and **privatization**.

Thompson, G. (1990) *The Political Economy of the New Right*, London: Pinter.

See also: **economic devolution**; **laissez-faire**.

'news' (430)
Information about fundamental macroeconomic variables, e.g. unanticipated movements in interest rates, **national income** or a **balance of payments** current account which causes unanticipated changes in exchange rates.

Frenkel, J.A. (1981) 'Flexible exchange rates, prices and the role of 'news'. Lessons from the 1970s', *Journal of Political Economy* 89: 665–705.

new town (930)
Government-financed urban developments in the UK designed to reduce the population of the larger cities, especially London and Glasgow. The establishment of new towns occurred in two waves: in the late 1940s and the 1960s. All of these twenty-six towns have been run by separate corporations charged with the tasks of building sufficient housing and attracting industrial and commercial investment. Although the original planners of these towns hoped to integrate residential and industrial areas to reduce **commuting**, this has not happened as much as expected, partly because of a mismatch of jobs and workers. Increasingly these towns have found it difficult to grow as they have suffered, like the major old cities, from the decline of the British manufacturing sector. The utopian hopes for these towns have been dashed by rising unemployment and crime.

New York Mercantile Exchange (310)
The biggest market for energy futures and options; usually referred to as NYMEX.

New York Stock Exchange (310)
Established in 1792 when 24 brokers signed an agreement in Wall Street. It moved indoors in 1793 and took its present name in 1863. Every stock traded is assigned to a **specialist** who also acts as a broker. All of the Exchange's transactions are published daily. By 1987, the Exchange had 1366 members. In 1980, its subsidiary, the **New York Futures Exchange**, was opened.

See also: **American Stock Exchange**.

N-firm concentration ratio (220, 610)
The ratio of the sales of a group of firms of an industry to the sales of that industry as a whole. The number of firms most commonly chosen for industrial censuses is three, four, five, eight or sixteen and hence the ratios are sometimes called three-firm, four-firm, five-firm, eight-firm or sixteen-firm ratios. Also known as the leading firms ratio.

See also: **concentration**; **monopoly power**.

NIBM1 (220, 310)
See: **non-interest-bearing M1**.

NIC (050)
See: **newly industrialized country**.

niche bank (310)
1 A specialist bank which has a particular 'niche' in the financial sector. The consequence of this concentration on particular types of customer or financial service gives it higher profitability but the greater risk of not being diversified in its activities.

2 A **laser bank**.

niche trading (310)

Specializing in a particular form of trading, which is a characteristic of many securities markets.

NIDL (420)

See: **new international division of labour**.

NIEO (420, 430)

See: **New International Economic Order**.

NIESR (050)

See: **National Institute for Economic and Social Research**.

NIF (310)

See: **note issuance facility**.

Nikkei average (310)

The leading index of stock market prices used by the Tokyo Stock Exchange.

Nikkeiren (510)

Japanese Federation of Employers' Associations.

See also: **shunto**.

NIMBY (720)

'Not in my backyard': a frequently made objection to a detrimental environmental change nearby with the recommendation that someone else suffers. The sitings of many new buildings and waste dumps have met with this reaction.

NIPA (220)

See: **National Income and Product Accounts**.

NIT (320)

See: **negative income tax**.

Nobel Prize for Economics (030)

The 'Nobel Memorial Prize in Economic Sciences' awarded to distinguished economists and econometricians since 1969. Prominent in the list of prizewinners are persons from the USA, France, Scandinavia, the USSR and the UK:

1969 Ragnar Frisch; Jan Tinbergen
1970 Paul Samuelson
1971 Simon Kuznets
1972 Kenneth Arrow; John Hicks
1973 Wassily Leontief
1974 Friedrich von Hayek; Gunnar Myrdal
1975 Leonid Kantorovich; Tjalling C. Koopmans
1976 Milton Friedman
1977 James Meade; Bertil Ohlin
1978 Herbert Simon
1979 W. Arthur Lewis; Theodore Schultz
1980 Lawrence Klein
1981 James Tobin
1982 George Stigler
1983 Gerard Debreu
1984 Richard Stone
1985 Franco Modigliani
1986 James M. Buchanan
1987 Robert M. Solow
1988 Maurice Allais
1989 Trygve Haavelmo
1990 Harry Markovitz; Merton Miller; William Sharpe.

Breit, W. and Spencer, R.W. (1986) *Lives of the Laureates*, Cambridge, MA, and London: MIT Press.
Lindbeck, A. (1985) 'The prize in economic science in memory of Alfred Nobel', *Journal of Economic Literature* 23 (March): 37–56.

noise (210)

Random disturbances which distort a signal. The probability distribution of what is received depends on what is sent. This concept has been applied to econometric models.

See also: **white noise**.

nominal gross domestic product (220)

Gross domestic product at current prices. This is regarded as a suitable reference target for regulating public expenditure. In the UK it is available quarterly.

nominal income (010)

See: **money income**.

nominal tax rate (320)

The published rate of tax on a good, income or capital. The whole burden of such taxes is often reduced by tax allowances.

nominee account (310)

An arrangement for hiding the beneficial ownership of **shares**. Banks and other financial institutions buy shares in the name of a nominee account for persons or companies wishing to be anonymous. This is most useful to a company which is accumulating another company's shares with a view to making a takeover bid. Supporters of this system argue that its chief advantage is administrative convenience.

non-accelerating inflation rate of unemployment (810)
NAIRU.

See also: **natural rate of unemployment**.

non-basic commodity (010)
A commodity which affects the production of some, but not all, other commodities.

See also: **basic commodity**.

non-basic industry (930)
An industry which provides services to a complex of **basic industries**.

non-competing group (820)
An occupational group of the labour market separated from other groups by **barriers to entry**. John Stuart **Mill**, who first noted this market imperfection, likened the labour market to a hereditary caste system. Restricted access to education, union rules and discrimination separate the labour force into these groups, giving rise to occupational **wage differentials**.

non-employment (810, 840)
Being without a job. The unemployed, retired, sick, the rich living on investment income alone and carers for dependants make up this population category. Some of this underutilization of labour is associated with a lack of opportunity for paid employment or restricted access to employment.

non-goal equilibrium (210)
An **equilibrium** state which is the consequence of the interaction of economic forces and not the conscious pursuit of particular objectives by an economic agent. A major case is **national income** in a **market economy**.

See also: **goal equilibrium**.

non-interest-bearing M1 (220, 310)
A component of **M1** introduced because some banks changed the character of **current deposits** (**sight deposits**) by paying interest on them.

non-linear correlation (210)
The relationship between two variables which approximates in a diagram to a curve.

See also: **least squares method**; **linear regression**; **scatter diagram**.

non-linear pricing (010, 530)
See: **second degree price discrimination**.

non-market sector (010)
The part of an economy which does not sell its goods and services. The output of governments, households and farms (in the case of less developed economies) make up much of the activity of this sector.

non-pecuniary returns (010, 820)
The reward to a worker other than wages, salaries and fringe benefits. Personal satisfaction, power, status and continual happiness are amongst these returns.

non-profit enterprise (510)
An organization, other than a **firm**, whose members have no private **property rights** associated with it and, hence, no entitlement to profits. These enterprises, usually financed by donations, endowments or government grants, aim to maximize the quantity and quality of the service provided and to break even. In the public sector, most governmental institutions are NPEs; in the private sector, households, charitable foundations, mutual insurance companies and a variety of clubs are the major examples. The motives for establishing NPEs are various, including the provision of **merit goods**, the subsidization of religion and the arts and the commemoration of a major benefactor. A dislike of market mechanisms and altruistic attitudes have been fundamental to the growth of NPEs.

Gassler, R.S. (1986) *The Economics of Nonprofit Enterprise: a Study in Applied Economic Theory*, New York and London: University Press of America.

Holtman, A.G. (1988) 'Theories of non-profit institutions', *Journal of Economic Surveys* 2: 30–45.

Rose-Ackerman, S. (ed.) (1986) *The Non-Profit Sector: Economic Theory and Public Policy*, Oxford: Oxford University Press.

non-renewable resources (720)

Fossil fuels or metals which are exhaustible deposits of the earth's surface.

non-standard tax relief (320)

A reduction in the taxable income of a person on account of actual expenses incurred. These expenses are recognized by a tax authority as deductible.

non-tariff barrier (420)

A barrier to imports, other than an import tax. The non-tariff methods used include the imposition of rigid safety standards, strict administrative standards, global and bilateral quotas, orderly marketing arrangements and **voluntary export restraints**. Examples include the **Multi-Fibre Arrangement**, the USA's orderly marketing arrangement with Korea and Taiwan on non-rubber footwear, safety measures on colour TVs and CB radios, and the **European Community**'s import restrictions in 1981 on steel from Korea. The **General Agreement on Tariffs and Trade** approximately measures the extent of the application of restrictive measures as the ratio of restricted imports/ total imports. This measure is imprecise as a restriction will affect the total flow of imports. Non-tariff barriers can also be measured by calculating restricted imports as a share of the total consumption of manufactured goods, or, consumption of restricted manufactured goods as a share of the total consumption of manufactured goods.

See also: **protection; tariff.**

non-tradables (420)

Goods and services which do not enter into international trade. Many services of a personal kind, e.g. hairdressing, can only be sold within a country but most goods can be traded with the exception of those which cannot be preserved from perishing and those which are too heavy and fixed to remove, e.g. buildings (although there are exceptional cases of British buildings being shipped to the USA).

non-zero-sum game (210)

A situation in which the total amount to be distributed amongst the players is not equal to zero. The game may be a positive sum game, a negative sum game, or the sum may vary because of the strategies or decisions of the players, as in the **prisoner's dilemma** game.

See also: **zero-sum game.**

normal distribution (210)

A symmetric distribution shaped like a bell.

See also: **kurtosis.**

normal good (010)

A good which is increasingly demanded when income rises. For such a good, its **income elasticity of demand** will be positive.

See also: **inferior good.**

normal profit (010)

The minimum amount of **profit** which a firm must earn to remain in existence. The normal profit rate is the **opportunity cost** to the firm of employing capital in that industry. Since this profit is the minimum supply price of **entrepreneurship**, it will be included along with other costs in the total costs of a firm. When measuring **monopoly power**, normal profit is used as a benchmark: if a firm has profits in excess of normal profit, it is to some extent a monopolist.

normative economics (010)

Economics based on value judgments stating what should be the case, e.g. 'personal incomes should be equal'. This type of economics, which is contrasted with **positive economics**, raises issues which cannot be settled by appeals to facts. Much of **welfare economics** deals with normative issues.

Myrdal, G. (1954) *The Political Element in the Development of Economic Thought*, trans. by P. Streeten, London: Routledge & Kegan Paul.

See also: **economic methodology.**

Norris–La Guardia Act 1932 (830)

US federal statute which gave **labor unions** substantial relief from judicial interference. Under section 3 of the Act, **yellow dog contracts** were made unenforceable; under section 5 courts were prohibited from granting injunctions on the grounds of unlawful combination or conspiracy. Similar Acts were passed by several states.

See also: **Wagner Act 1935; Taft–Hartley Act 1947.**

note issuance facility (310)
Promises by banks to lend money to companies when they cannot raise it in short-term securities markets. This is a form of **off balance-sheet financing** or adjusted claim. Increasingly US banks are using NIFs as an alternative to traditional medium-term credit facilities, often arranged with a syndicate of banks.

See also: **revolving underwriting facility**.

no-trade equilibrium (010)
An equilibrium position with domestic demand equal to domestic supply for an autarkic state.

See also: **autarky**.

NOW account (310)
Negotiable order of withdrawal account; a **checking account** (US) which bears interest. Super-NOW accounts offer a higher rate of interest.

Nozick, Robert, 1938– (030)
US philosopher of the **New Right** famous for his notion of the 'minimal state'. He was educated at Columbia College and Princeton University. He has taught at Princeton 1962–5 and been a full professor of philosopher at Harvard since 1969. His libertarian view of the limited role of government is in accord with much of the thinking of **Friedman** and **Hayek**.

Nozick, R. (1974) *Anarchy, State and Utopia*, Oxford: Basil Blackwell.

See also: **forced labour**.

NPE (610)
See: **non-profit enterprise**.

NPV (520)
See: **net present value**.

NRV (540)
Net realizable value.

NSA (430)
Non-sterling area: it consisted particularly of countries linked to the US dollar.

See also: **sterling area**.

null hypothesis (210)
In statistics, the hypothesis that there are no differences between the characteristics of a population and a sample taken from it, or between two samples of that population.

numéraire (010)
A measuring rod for stating relative prices; Walras's term for a commodity used for this measurement purpose.

NV (510)
Naamlose venootschap: a Dutch public company.

NYMEX (310)
See: **New York Mercantile Exchange**.

NYSE (310)
See: **New York Stock Exchange**.

O

OASDHI (910)
See: **Old Age, Survivors, Disability and Health Insurance**.

objective function (210)
A statement in equation form of a dependent variable which has to be maximized or minimized by independent variables attaining optimal values. In the case, e.g. of a utility function, utility is the dependent variable to be maximized and quantities of different goods are the independent variables which have to be optimally combined.

objectives of firms (510)
What a **firm** has as its aim or target. **Profit maximization** is assumed in many theories of the firm to be the central aim of a firm but research since the 1930s has noted that managers have many other objectives, partly because they are not shareholders directly rewarded in proportion to profitability. Objectives which have replaced profit maximization include sales maximization, maintaining (or increasing) a market share and achieving a target rate of return on capital employed.

See also: **managerial models of the firm; theory of the firm**.

OBRA (320)
See: **Omnibus Budget Reconciliation Act**.

occupation (810)
The work activity of a person defined according to the education, skill, responsibility and experience demanded by an employer.

International Labour Organisation (1968) *The International Standard Classification of Occupations*, Geneva: ILO.

occupational mobility (820)
A worker's movement between one type of job and another. The amount of mobility depends greatly on the fineness of the occupational classification chosen. Since 1945, even with the broadest classification of occupations, a great shift from manual to white-collar jobs has been apparent in many advanced countries.

See also: **labour mobility**.

occupational segregation (810, 820)
An occupational distribution of a labour force such that men, or women, or different ethnic groups, are under-represented or over-represented in particular occupations compared with their proportions in the total labour force. An example of this would occur if overwhelmingly black males worked in domestic service. In many countries women are heavily concentrated in nursing, retailing, secretarial and domestic service jobs.

See also: **crowding hypothesis; discrimination**.

OCD (310)
See: **other checkable deposits**.

ODA (430)
See: **official development assistance; Overseas Development Administration**.

OECD (430)
See: **Organization for Economic Cooperation and Development**.

OEEC (430)
See: **Organization for European Economic Cooperation**.

off-balance-sheet financing (520, 540)
Funds raised for a business not shown in its **balance sheet**. This type of financing is resorted to when the company has borrowed near to the limit set by its Articles of Association or when it wants to avoid increasing its **gearing** and attracting an adverse stock market reaction. The appearance of a company's balance sheet can be improved by transferring liabilities to

associated companies or by using particular devices, e.g. the leasing of capital equipment, the artificial sale of stock to a financial company to acquire extra funds, mortgage **securitization**, **factoring**, sale and repurchase agreements and loan transfers. Increasingly, the bodies which supervise the accountancy profession are demanding fuller and more open financial reporting.

See also: **creative accounting**.

offer price (310)

1 The price at which a company offers to sell its shares to the public.

2 The selling price of **unit trust** units.

off-exchange instrument (310)

A financial product which is not traded on an official stock exchange but resembles officially recognized products. An example is a bank **certificate of deposit** linked to the performance of **Standard & Poor's 500** stock index.

Office of Fair Trading (610, 920)

UK body set up in 1973 to administer Britain's **competition policy**. Its tasks include examining monopoly situations, monitoring **anticompetitive practices** in the UK, regulating **consumer credit** and considering proposed mergers which might be referred to the **Monopolies and Mergers Commission**. It maintains the register of permitted restrictive trade practices.

Office of Management and Budget (320)

An office of the US President set up in 1970 in succession to the Bureau of the Budget (founded 1921) which is responsible for preparing the Executive's budget for presentation to Congress in January each year. After examination by House and Senate committees, a concurrent resolution on the Budget is announced by 15 April to be followed by legislation by 15 May. Once the budget is passed, the OMB supervises and controls its administration and provides data on programme performance.

official development assistance (430)

Aid granted by a national government to poorer countries either directly or through an international organization such as the **World Bank**.

See also: **foreign aid**.

official financing (430)

An item in the **balance of payments** of a country which is the amount of finance which has to be raised from overseas monetary authorities, by currency borrowing and drawing on official reserves to finance a deficit in the current and capital accounts.

offshore banking (310, 430)

Banking activities which are conducted abroad to evade domestic monetary controls. British financial institutions have resorted to small Commonwealth countries such as the Bahamas and a number of islands, including the Channel Islands and the Isle of Man. (The USA regards banking activities in every foreign country, including the UK, as 'offshore'.) The principal activities of offshore banks are the management of investment trusts and participation in Eurodollar and Eurobond markets.

off-the-job training (810, 850)

Formal training, usually away from the premises of one's employer, which takes the form of lectures, tutorials and practical sessions. A switch to this type of training has been necessary because of the haphazard nature of much **on-the-job training** and the increasing amount of technical knowledge required for many occupations.

See also: **general training**.

Ofgas (610)

Office of Gas Supply. This body was set up under the Gas Act 1986 to regulate the newly privatized British gas industry.

OFT (610, 920)

See: **Office of Fair Trading**.

Oftel (610)

Office of Telecommunications. This body was set up under the Telecommunications Act 1984 to regulate British Telecom.

Ohlin, Bertil, 1899–1979 (030)

Swedish international trade and macroeconomic theorist and a leader of the **Stockholm School**, who was educated at

331

Lund University, the Stockholm School of Business Administration, Harvard and at the University of Stockholm where he was a doctoral student of **Cassel**. He was a professor of economics from 1925 to 1930 at Copenhagen and at Stockholm from 1930 to 1965 (as successor to Heckscher). In a parallel political career, he was a member of the Swedish parliament from 1938 to 1970, leader of the Swedish Liberal Party from 1944 to 1967 and Minister of Trade from 1944 to 1945.

As a member of the **Stockholm School**, he in many ways anticipated **Keynesian** ideas by using the concepts of the **propensity to consume**, **liquidity preference** and the **multiplier** in articles of 1933 and 1934. In times of excess capacity, he argued (in 1934) that the government should undertake investment projects which would not compete with the private sector and would be deficit financed. He developed **Heckscher**'s factor price equalization theory of international trade to produce the **Heckscher-Ohlin trade theorem**. His most famous work is *Interregional and International Trade* (1933). His contribution to international trade theory earned him, with **Meade**, the **Nobel Prize for Economics** in 1977.

Samuelson, P.A. (1981) 'Bertil Ohlin (1899–1979)', *Scandinavian Journal of Economics* 83: 355–71.
Steiger, O. (1976) 'Bertil Ohlin and the origins of the Keynesian Revolution', *History of Political Economy* 8: 341–66.

OID bond (310)
See: **original issue discount bond**.

oil price increases (720)
Major supply shocks in 1973–4 caused by the **Organization of Petroleum Exporting Countries** raising the price of oil and in 1979–80 by a cutback in Iranian oil production and exports after the Iranian Revolution. In 1973–4, the price rose from $1.90 to $9.76; in 1979–80 from $17.26 to $28.67; in 1990, Iraq's invasion of Kuwait also led briefly to oil price inflation.

Okun, Arthur M., 1928–80 (030)
US economist and policy adviser who was educated at Columbia University and taught at Yale University from 1952 to 1963. He was a member of the **Council of Economic Advisers** from 1964 to 1968, the year in which he was chairman. His most influential work was with the **Brookings Institution** as its senior fellow from 1969, contributing to Brookings Papers on Economic Activity as joint editor. His fame largely rests with his *The Political Economy of Prosperity* (1970), *Equality and Efficiency – The Big Tradeoff* (1975) and his posthumous classic *Prices and Quantities – A Macroeconomic Analysis* (1981). His work as a macroeconomist had the major concern of attaining economic growth without inflation; the trade-off between equality and efficiency also interested him.

Gordon, R.J. and Hall, R.E. (1980) 'Arthur M. Okun: 1928–80', *Brookings Papers on Economic Activity* 1: 1–5.

See also: **discomfort index; invisible handshake; leaky bucket; Okun's law**.

Okun's law (110)
A rule of thumb, applicable to the US economy from 1960 to 1980, which states that when the ratio of actual to potential annual **gross national product** changes by 3 per cent (more recent estimates state 2 per cent), the observed unemployment rate changes in the opposite direction by 1 per cent. The potential gross national product is measured by extrapolating the US gross national product of 1950 (when there was full employment and full capacity) and adding to it the long-run trend of productivity improvements. A relationship noted by the US economist, Arthur **Okun**.

Okun, A.M. (1970) *The Political Economy of Prosperity*, Washington, DC: Brookings Institution.

Old Age, Survivors, Disability and Health Insurance (910)
The largest social insurance programme in the USA which was established by the Social Security Act 1935. It covers over 90 per cent of retired US citizens, although eligibility is based on age, not retired status. Employers, employees and self-employed persons finance it on a 'pay-as-you-go' principle through payroll taxes. The benefits granted are a percentage of average earnings over the period when a person could expect to have been in employment covered by the scheme. Since the Revenue Act 1942, it has been US

federal policy to encourage the expansion of private pension plans.

See also: **payroll tax; Social Security Act 1935**.

Old Lady of Threadneedle Street (310)
See: **Bank of England**.

old staples (630)
The heavy industries which used to form the basic industries of industrialized economies: coal, iron and steel and shipbuilding are the major examples.

See also: **commanding heights; heavy industry**.

OLG (020)
See: **overlapping generations model**.

oligopoly (610)
A **market** or **industry** consisting of a small group of sellers, often five or less. This term was originally coined by St Thomas More in his *Utopia* (1518). An oligopolistic type of market structure is usual in modern science-based industries, e.g. computer hardware, pharmaceuticals. Oligopolies can be collusive (firms make joint pricing and output decisions) or non-collusive. However, collusive oligopoly is less common because of competition laws which have outlawed it in many capitalist countries. Oligopoly price theory tries to explain the interaction of the decision-making of firms in non-collusive situations: the **kinked demand curve** is a major example of this approach, as are **price leadership** models. The most recent developments in oligopoly analysis have included the **Structure-Conduct-Performance**, strategic entry deterrence and **contestable** markets approaches.

Friedman, J.W. (1983) *Oligopoly Theory*, Cambridge, New York: Cambridge University Press.

See also: **kinked demand curve**

oligopsony (010, 530)
A market controlled by a few dominant buyers.

See also: **monopsony**.

OLS (210)
Ordinary least squares.

See also: **least squares method**.

OM (310)
The Options Market, Stockholm.

OMA (530, 610)
See: **orderly market agreement**.

OMB (320)
See: **Office of Management and Budget**.

Omnibus Budget Reconciliation Act (320)
US federal statute which both includes changes in tax laws and appropriations to various government spending programmes. An act of this kind removes the legislative work of passing several appropriation and revenue bills.

one-bank holding company (310)
US corporation with only one banking subsidiary and other subsidiaries which can be engaged in activities prohibited to banks.

one-club policy (310, 320)
Macroeconomic policy which chiefly uses one policy instrument, e.g. interest rates, to the exclusion of others.

one country, two systems (070)
A **centrally planned economy** which permits **capitalism** to operate in part of it. This arrangement has been proposed for Hong Kong after 1997 when it ceases to be a British colony so that capitalism will be permitted there, despite it being part of the Chinese economy.

one-crop economy (010, 110)
An **economy** whose production is largely concentrated on one **primary product** and hence is vulnerable to fluctuations in its **terms of trade** and major threats to production, e.g. bad weather. Economies producing copper, ground nuts, sugar and coffee have often been of this type.

one hundred per cent reserve banking (310)
A form of banking which maintains a bank's total volume of deposits (liabilities) equal to

reserve assets. Thus, under this system, a bank is unable to make **advances** through credit creation. Although banking of this kind enables banks to meet **runs on a bank**, it means that banks sacrifice profitability through not holding illiquid bills, bonds and loans.

See also: **fractional reserve banking**.

one-price law (010)
The market rule that only one price is produced by a market in equilibrium. The **Physiocrats** were the first economic writers to expound the view that internationally traded goods should be sold in the domestic market at the world equilibrium price.

one-tailed test (210)
A statistical significance test which is only concerned with the upper or the lower part of a distribution of a variable.

See also: **two-tailed test**.

One two three bank (310)
A fringe bank licensed by the UK Board of Trade under the Companies Act 1967, section 123. As there was lax control over these new banks and no supervision by the Bank of England, the banks were shown to be unstable during the **Barber boom** of the 1970s and the consequent **secondary banking crisis**.

on-the-job training (810, 850)
The acquisition of skills by copying the example of experienced workers who are continuously present to supervise the work attempts of the trainee. Most **apprenticeship** schemes are of this nature. **Becker** included this type of training in his concept of **human capital**.

See also: **off-the-job training**.

OPCS (220)
Office of Population Censuses and Surveys (UK).

OPEC (720)
See: **Organization of Petroleum Exporting Countries**.

open economy (070, 420)
An **economy** which engages in international trade. Open economies such as Britain, Holland and Belgium are, therefore, much affected by fluctuations in world trade. The smaller an economy, the more open it usually is, as it is unlikely to produce a full range of goods and services. The degree of openness of an economy can be measured by its imports or exports as a proportion of gross domestic product: for the most open of economies this can be over 60 per cent.

See also: **autarky**; **closed economy**.

open-ended fund (310)
A **unit trust** or **mutual fund** whose size is determined by the amount of units sold and hence is 'open'.

open market operations (310)
Purchases and sales of bills and government bonds by a **central bank** in order to change their prices and hence interest rates and the quantity of reserve assets held by the banking system. If a fall in interest rates is desired, the central bank will buy bonds to increase their price and hence their yields. This is a principal tool of **monetary policy** which can be used any day that markets are open and does not need legislative approval.

open population (840)
A population which experiences emigration of its residents and/or immigration from other areas.

open shop (830)
A firm which does not have an agreement with a trade union to employ only its members.

See also: **closed shop**; **union shop**.

Operation Twist (310)
Manipulation of the US **term structure of interest rates** in 1961 by the Kennedy Administration raising short-term rates and holding, or allowing to fall, long-term rates. The effects of this policy were hoped to be an improvement in the balance of payments through **hot money** flows attracted by higher short-term interest rates and some stimulus to investment by not raising the long-term rates.

Modigliani, F. and Sutch, R. (1966) 'Innovations in interest rate policy', *American Economic*

Review 56 (May) (Papers and Proceedings): 178–97.

opportunistic behaviour (010)
The action of a partner to an exchange who has an informational (or other) advantage, e.g. exclusive knowledge of the true quality of a good offered for sale.

See also: **asymmetric information; lemons market**.

opportunity cost (010)
The cost of the alternative foregone by choosing a particular activity. A major example of this is the choice of work rather than leisure, in which case the opportunity cost of working is the amount of leisure sacrificed. Such a cost arises from the scarce nature of resources. The economist uses opportunity cost as the central meaning of cost. The much-used expression, 'there's no such thing as a free lunch' reflects the fact that all goods and services have their opportunity costs.

See also: **accounting costs**.

optimal control (210)
The use of mathematical techniques to choose among alternative policies so that a system can be regulated or controlled. This approach is used increasingly to select a mixture of fiscal and monetary policies, as well as to manage a portfolio.

Pindyck, R.S. (1973) *Optimal Planning for Economic Stabilization: The Application of Control Theory to Stabilization Policy*, Amsterdam: North-Holland.

optimal peg (430)
A currency peg which aims to stabilize the prices of traded goods or the **balance of trade** or the **terms of trade** or the rate of **inflation** of a particular economy by attaching that economy's currency to a basket of other currencies in order to reflect the pattern of a country's trade. Pegging attempts to achieve an external balance continuously for that country.

Williamson, J.H. (1982) 'A survey on the literature on the optimal peg', *Journal of Development Economics* 11: 39–61.

optimal rate of pollution (720)
The rate of pollution at which the marginal social benefit of pollution control and marginal social cost of pollution are equal.

optimal tariff (420)
A **tariff** which increases a country's welfare by maximizing the return to its potential **monopoly** or **monopsony** power. This tariff must be set at that rate which equalizes the social benefit and social cost of the marginal import. Optimum tariffs have been recommended for less-developed countries with a substantial monopoly in their export trade. If the optimum tariff is zero, then there is a strong case for **free trade**.

Corden, W.M. (1974) *Trade Policy and Economic Welfare*, Oxford: Clarendon Press.

optimal taxation (320)
A tax structure which maximizes **social welfare**. As a taxation system uses a variety of taxes, optimal income taxes and optimal commodity taxes have to be determined simultaneously. Optimality is obtained by a correct **trade-off** between economic efficiency and distributional objectives.

See also: **Ramsey rule**.

optimal work effort (810)
The amount of work which equates the **marginal utility** of an hour's work with the marginal utility of another hour's leisure.

optimization problem (210)
The task of maximizing or minimizing an **objective function**. Major cases of optimization in economics include that of a consumer with a fixed income buying a combination of goods and services which will maximize his/her utility, the maximization of the wealth of **equity** shareholders by finding the best growth policy for a firm and minimizing the cost of producing a particular output by choosing the appropriate combination of factors of production. Different forms of programming are used to solve these problems.

Baumol, W.J. (1965) *Economic Theory and Operations Analysis*, 2nd edn, Englewood Cliffs, NJ: Prentice Hall.
Vajda, S. (1961) *Mathematical Programming*, Reading, MA: Addison-Wesley.

optimum city (930)
A large settlement which maximizes the

social welfare function of the households residing there.

Mirrlees, J. (1972) 'The optimum town', *Swedish Journal of Economics* 74: 114–35.

optimum currency area (430)

The group of countries ideally covered by one currency or by a number of linked currencies, e.g. the **European Monetary System**. The necessary conditions for an optimal area include wage and price flexibility and mobility of capital and labour. The social and political unity of the area is more important than its size. Setting up an area with a **common currency** brings about the adjustment costs of extra unemployment, reductions in residents' income and wealth and migration, which can be financed out of a joint **fiscal policy** for the area.

Ishiyama, Y. (1975) 'The theory of optimum currency areas: a survey', *International Monetary Fund Staff Papers* 22: 344–83.
Mundell, R.A. (1961) 'A theory of optimum currency areas', *American Economic Review* 51: 657–65.

optimum firm (010, 610)

A firm whose output is produced at minimum average cost. A unique optimum is only possible for firms with U-shaped average costs and only likely to exist in the short run.

See also: **minimum efficient scale**.

optimum population (840)

An ideal sized population which maximizes output per head. As this is not the maximum sized population which a country can support, the population can exceed such an optimum. Critics of this concept have noted that there is no consensus supporting the view that output per head should be maximized; for example, for military reasons a larger population may be preferred.

optimum quantity of money (310)

The growth in the quantity of money which reduces the nominal rate of interest to zero and aims to maximize the welfare of consumers. This can only be adopted as a policy if there is a model of how money is used in a national economy.

Bewley, T. (1983) 'A difficulty with the optimum quantity of money', *Econometrica* 51: 1485–1504.
Friedman, M. (1969) *The Optimum Quantity of Money and Other Essays*, Chicago, IL: Aldine.

option (310, 430)

The right to buy or sell a currency, commodity or financial asset at a specified price in a stated time period.

See also: **call option**; **put option**.

option demand (010)

Demand for a good or service which is usually not consumed by the person regarding it as desirable, e.g. private car users may desire there to be a public transportation service not for themselves but for those who cannot afford private transportation. A high option demand can reduce the price of the good or service in question: demand for insurance is of this kind – the more entering an insurance scheme, the lower the premia for insuring against a particular risk.

See also: **sponsor demand**.

options exchanges (310)

Options were first traded in 1973 with the opening of the Chicago Board Options Exchange (CBOE). Now option trading is offered by more than a dozen US exchanges and on the major European exchanges. On some exchanges more than one million contracts are traded daily in many products. Apart from equities and bonds, option trading is also available for precious metals, oil, agricultural commodities, foreign currencies and market indexes.

orderly market agreement (530, 610)

1 A restrictive trading agreement between the firms of an industry which is experiencing a decline in the total demand for its output. In response to this decline, voluntary quotas are agreed between firms to allow a more orderly adjustment to a lower level of sales, avoiding cut-throat price competition so that each firm can at least maintain its individual sales level. But there is limited scope for introducing these agreements as, if they are made by a group of firms without the approval of government, they are likely to violate national **competition policies**.

2 An agreement between countries to restrict exports to a country with trade deficits as a means of protecting its industries.

ordinalist revolution (030)

The major advance in welfare economics in the 1930s, particularly wrought by **Hicks**, which founded welfare theorems on the ordering of persons' utilities, not on the actual units of **utility** derived from consumption. The **indifference curve** was a major new tool of this analysis.

Cooter, R. and Rappoport, P. (1984) 'Were the ordinalists wrong about welfare economics?', *Journal of Economic Literature* 22 (June): 507–30.

Hicks, J.R. (1939) *Value and Capital*, ch. 1, Oxford: Clarendon Press.

See also: **revealed preference**.

ordinal utility (010)

Subjective satisfaction expressed as ordered preferences. This makes possible the ranking of satisfactions as first, second, third and so forth without having to state the amount by which one satisfaction is greater or less than another.

See also: **cardinal utility; util; utility**.

ordinary share (310)

A share of the capital of a British company which usually constitutes a major part of its issued capital. These shares will be paid a dividend if priority capital holders of debentures or preference shares have been paid and the directors decide to distribute the remaining earnings.

See also: **common stock**.

organic composition of capital (010)

A Marxian term for the ratio of constant to variable capital. Constant capital is the dead labour embodied in the means of production and variable capital the live labour, i.e. the labour required at that stage of production.

organic premium (530, 710)

The higher prices consumers are prepared to pay to obtain food which has been produced by an 'organic' farmer, i.e. someone using traditional agricultural methods and not artificial fertilizers and additives. To some extent the higher prices are justified by the higher costs associated with this small-scale farming.

organizational economics (020, 510)

A branch of microeconomics which has made use of psychology, sociology, political science, biology, ecology and anthropology to study the nature of organizations and phenomena associated with them. From early studies of power within organizations and the consequences of being dependent on outside resources, this form of economics has changed to using transaction cost, **team theory**, business strategy, **agency theory** and the **evolutionary theory of the firm**.

Barney, J.B. and Ouchi, W.G. (eds) (1986) *Organizational Economics*, San Francisco, CA and London: Jossey-Bass.

See also: **Williamson**.

Organization for Economic Cooperation and Development (430)

The group of rich industrialized countries founded in 1961 consisting of the 18 European countries of the **Organization for European Economic Cooperation**, USA and Canada. Later to join were Japan (1964), Finland (1969), Australia (1971) and New Zealand (1973), with the result that it now produces about two thirds of the world's output with only one sixth of its population. This Paris-based organization provides a forum for the discussion of policies for promoting economic growth, **free trade** and **foreign aid** to less developed countries and has an independent secretariat which produces tables of standardized economic data of member countries and economic forecasts (more accurate than many national forecasts because of the joint forecasting of linked economies). Its influential economic policy committee meets two or three times a year and is chaired by the chairman of the United States President's **Council of Economic Advisers**.

See also: **INTERLINK**.

Organization for European Economic Cooperation (430)

An international organization founded in

1948 to administer US aid to the 18 West European countries benefiting under the **Marshall Plan**. Its principal achievements were the creation of the European Monetary Agreement in 1956, its organization of the negotiations which established the **European Community** and its contribution to trade liberalization. The **Organization for Economic Cooperation and Development** succeeded it in 1961.

Organization of Petroleum Exporting Countries (720)

The major world oil producers' forum established by the Baghdad Conference of 1960, on the initiative of Venezuela, with aims which included the restoration of oil prices to their pre-September 1960 levels, the demand that oil companies keep their prices stable and the promise of countries not to agree to increase production if another country failed to reach an agreement with an oil company. The five founder members, Iraq, Iran, Kuwait, Saudi Arabia and Venezuela, were joined by Qatar in 1961, Libya and Indonesia in 1962, Abu Dhabi in 1967, Algeria in 1969, Nigeria in 1971, Equador in 1973 and Gabon in 1975. Its affairs were conducted in six monthly regular and further extraordinary meetings. Following years of turbulent negotiations with oil companies which failed to raise the incomes of the oil countries as much as they desired, the six Gulf oil producers in October 1973 unilaterally increased their oil price by 70 per cent and cut production by 5 per cent; in December 1973, there was a further price increase of 13 per cent. OPEC was able to agree on common prices and quotas until dual-pricing was introduced in 1976. Thus frustration with the oil companies made OPEC assume the role of price-fixing. However, the 1981 price increase was too great: Saudi Arabia dissented from the subsequent cut, leading to a price war and the weakening of the joint power of OPEC.

Ghanem, S. (1986) *OPEC. The Rise and Fall of an Exclusive Club*, London: KPI.

See also: **oil price increases**.

organization theory (510)

A modern **theory of the firm** which asserts that the goals and behaviour of a firm are the consequences of its organizational structure.

This theory challenges earlier theories based on **profit maximization**. A major example of this new approach is the assertion that managers are satisficiers, not maximizers.

See also: **managerial models of the firm**.

original issue discount bond (310)

A type of **junk bond** which is issued at a large discount below its par value with **coupon** rates below the market yields at the time of issue. After an initial period, the coupon rate is raised.

OSA (430)

See: **overseas sterling area**.

OTCM (310)

See: **over the counter market**.

other checkable deposits (310)

NOW accounts + **ATS** accounts (USA).

other things being equal (010)

See: *ceteris paribus*.

outlier (210)

A data point which is more than an arbitrary distance from a regression line.

outplacement agency (820)

An employment agency specializing in placing redundant executives. Financial sector **deregulation** in New York and London caused these agencies to flourish.

output budgeting (320, 520)

The division of an organization's budget into sub-budgets so that expenditures and output can be compared. Although this disaggregation is often arbitrary, it is a conscious attempt to improve the effectiveness of expenditure, particularly in the US public sector. Also known as the **planning, programming, budgeting** system.

outside lag (010, 310, 320)

The time between the implementation of an economic policy and the realization of all of the effects of the use of that policy instrument. As these instruments, e.g. tax rates, affect economic behaviour, it is unlikely that economic agents can or will change their decisions to buy, sell, invest, save, work or engage in leisure.

See also: **inside lag**.

outside money (310)

A monetary asset of the private sector which is a liability of a government, assuming government demand does not fall as its total debt rises in real terms. Gold coins under the **gold standard**, currency and bank reserves under a **fiat money** system and **high-powered money** are the major examples.

See also: **inside money**.

outsider wage setting (820)

The fixing of wages by the forces of an **external labour market** rather than by the personnel and labour policies of a particular firm.

See also: **insider wage setting**.

overaccumulation (010)

Investing too much so that current consumption has to be reduced; investing in projects with low rates of return.

over-award payment (820)

An addition to the Australian **basic wage** and **margins** awarded by the Arbitration Commission. It is the cause of **wage drift** in the Australian labour market.

overdraft (310)

See: **advance**.

overfunding (310)

The issue of more government bills and bonds than is necessary to finance government expenditure. A phenomenon of the UK in the 1980s.

See also: **Public Sector Debt Repayment**.

overhead capital (010)

See: **social capital**.

overhead costs (010)

Fixed costs mostly to pay for administration of an organization. These costs do not vary with the level of output.

overheating (010)

An over expansion in the level of economic activity of an economy, often as a result of the using of **demand management** to expand demand at a faster rate than the output potential of the economy permits. In some cases, a simplistic application of **Keynesianism** which poorly estimates sustainable growth and the amount of excess capacity in an economy is responsible. Overheating can be prevented by a control mechanism.

See also: **Medium Term Financial Strategy**.

overlapping generations model (020)

A general equilibrium model which examines the consequences of an economy being demographically structured such that each generation overlaps in time with its successor. This model has been used in the study of the rate of interest, business cycles, national debt and tax incidence.

Diamond, P.A. (1965) 'National debt in a neoclassical growth model', *American Economic Review* 55: 1126–50.

Kareken, J.M. and Wallace, N. (eds) (1980) *Models of Monetary Economics*, Proceedings and Contributions from Participants of a December 1978 Conference, Federal Reserve Bank of Minneapolis.

Samuelson, P.A. (1958) 'An exact consumption loan model of interest with or without the social contrivance of money', *Journal of Political Economy* 66: 467–82.

Wilson, C.A. (1981) 'Equilibrium in dynamic models with an infinity of agents', *Journal of Economic Theory* 24: 95–111.

overnight money (310)

Short loans of one to three days duration by banks to the money market. In London this is the major source of finance of the **discount houses**.

overseas assets (430)

The holdings by a country's government and residents of financial and other assets of other countries. The income from them, less payments overseas of the same nature, constitute the **net property income from abroad** item of the balance of payments. Short-term assets often accumulate through a difference in interest rates; long-term assets by the direct investment of **multinational corporations**.

overseas sterling area (430)

A group of countries connected with the UK which used sterling for international transactions as a principal currency reserve and linked the value of their currencies to the pound. It consisted principally of Commonwealth countries (except Canada), South Africa, Iceland, Ireland, Kuwait and Jordan and existed in its full form until June 1972, only Ireland and Gibraltar remaining until final abolition in October 1979 when British exchange controls ended. These countries acquired their sterling balances in several ways – by having a favourable current account surplus with the UK or by UK direct investment in them or by deposit in the UK of foreign currencies and gold earned by trade with countries outside the sterling area.

See also: **sterling**; **Sterling Area**.

overshooting price (010)
A price which in the short run overadjusts to changing market conditions and thus overshoots the long-run price.

Overstone, Lord (030)
See: **Loyd, Samuel Jones**.

over-the-counter market (310)
Trading in shares outside of a stock exchange by licensed brokers. A stock market of this type has existed in the USA since the 1870s.

overtime (810)
Work outside normal daily or weekly contractual hours, e.g. working longer than 8 hours per day or 40 hours per week. A **collectively bargained** agreement or a labour contract will clearly state what is normal and what is overtime working.

This work attracts a higher hourly rate of pay than normal hours working but can still be attractive to an employer when a temporary increase in production is necessary or when the non-wage labour costs are so high as to inhibit the recruitment of further workers. Despite the recessions of many countries in the 1970s and 1980s, much overtime working still occurs.

See also: **working hours**.

overtrading (520)
Operating a firm with a low **current ratio**, a shortage of working capital so that a shortage of cash makes payment of wages, taxes and sums due to trade creditors impossible on the date due.

See also: **undertrading**.

over-urbanization (110, 930)
The growth of a city at a higher rate than its creation of high wage employment, often brought about by the unrealistic expectations of persons in rural areas. There are many examples of such growth in less developed countries, especially in Africa.

Mills, E. and Becker, C. (1986) *Studies in Indian Urban Development*, New York: Oxford University Press.

owner occupation (930)
Housing occupied by the owner. In the UK, in 1914 10.6 per cent was owner occupied, in 1950 29.5 per cent but in 1985, 61.9 per cent. In the USA, 55 per cent of housing units were owner occupied in 1950 and 64 per cent in 1987. Tax relief on mortgage interest and the disappearance of much private sector housing available for renting have encouraged this growth.

own rate of interest (010, 310)
Sraffa's notion, used by **Keynes**, that for every durable commodity there is a rate of interest for it in terms of itself, e.g. a wheat rate of interest, a steel rate of interest. A steel rate of interest of 10 per cent means that 110 tons of steel in a year's time exchanges for 100 tons now. The money rate of interest is based on the same principle. The difference between market and spot prices is the basis for calculating own rates for particular commodities. Own rates show the relationship between the value of the future services of an asset and its present cost, expressed as a **yield** or a **rate of return**.

Keynes, J.M. (1936) *The General Theory of Employment, Interest and Money*, ch. 17, London: Macmillan.

P

Paasche index (210)

An index of output or prices which uses weights of the current year. The Paasche price index is

$$\frac{\Sigma p_i q_i}{\Sigma p_0 q_1}$$

where p_1 are the prices of the current year, p_0 are the prices of the base year and q_1 are the weights of the current year. The Paasche output index is

$$\frac{\Sigma p_1 q_1}{\Sigma p_1 q_0}$$

where q_1 are the quantities of the current year, q_0 are the quantities of the base year and p_1 are the prices of the current year.

Pacific Rim (110, 730)

The 34 countries and 23 islands around the Pacific which covers 70 million square miles and consists of 2.4 billion people (more than a half of the world's population). Since 1979 this world region has achieved more than a half of the world's economic growth. Future prospects for growth around the Pacific are considerable as the combination of Japanese production, innovation and marketing methods harnessed to Chinese resources is formidable.

Daly, M.T. and Logan, M.I. (1989) *The Brittle Rim*, Harmondsworth: Penguin.

package deal (010)

See: **interlinked transaction**.

PAF (310)

Percentage annual fixed (rate of interest).

panel data (220)

Data which is collected regularly over a period time from a randomly selected number of individuals. Many types of economic behaviour, including consumption, have been observed by this method.

paper gold (430)

See: **special drawing rights**.

paperless entry (310)

Electronic banking pioneered by the System Committee on Paperless Entry set up by the bank clearing houses of San Francisco and Los Angeles and the **Federal Reserve** in 1968. By 1978 a national network was set up.

See also: **dematerialization**.

paper money (310)

Banknotes which are generally acceptable in payment of a debt. Originally this paper derived its status from being convertible into gold or silver which were intrinsically valuable. Since 1931, banknotes have usually been inconvertible so paper money can act as a **medium of exchange** because of the financially sound character of the banking system which issues it. The status of paper money is recognized by making it 'legal tender'.

See also: **Banking School**; **gold standard**; **Thornton**.

paper profit (540)

An increase in the **book value** of an asset which is yet to be realized. This profit is expressed in nominal terms and does not take into account **inflation**.

paradox of thrift (010)

The contradictory effects of saving as it is both beneficial in providing funds for investment but detrimental to an underemployed economy. Adam **Smith** and other **classical** economists believed what is saved is invested so there cannot be excessive saving. However, **Keynes** and the leading Swedish economists of the 1930s believed that there could be an imbalance between *ex ante* saving and investment. Hoarding savings and not investing them contributes to a reduction in **aggregate demand** and the making of a recession. In the late twentieth century, many industrialized countries are worried by a deficiency in personal sector savings.

See also: **savings ratio; Stockholm School**.

paradox of value (010)

This states that goods with great usefulness, e.g. water, command a low price but those with little usefulness, e.g. diamonds, are expensive. Although this so-called paradox was known to the Greeks, especially **Plato**, it was **Smith**'s citing it in *The Wealth of Nations* which made it popular as a justification for cost of production, especially labour, theories of value. Despite his resolution of the paradox in his *Lectures on Jurisprudence* of 1762 to 1763 in terms of dearness being caused by scarcity, it was not until the **Marginalists** clearly set out the **diminishing marginal utility law** and distinguished total from marginal utility that the 'paradox' was put to rest. They asserted that water has a high total, but low marginal, utility and diamonds the reverse; price is proportional to marginal, not total, utility in **neoclassical economics**.

paradox of voting (020)

See: **impossibility theorem**.

parallel currency strategy (430)

The simultaneous use of a **common currency**, e.g. the **ecu**, and national currencies.

See also: **hard ecu**.

parallel loan (430, 520)

A two-way currency loan between two firms in different countries to protect them against exchange rate fluctuations, e.g. a British firm and an Italian firm may lend each other their own currency for six months after which time they repay that currency.

parallel market economy (060)

See: **second economy**.

parallel plants (510, 830)

Manufacturing plants or factories producing the same product for the same employer at different locations so that if a **strike** occurs in one, production can be switched to another, reducing the power of a **labor union**.

parallel pricing (530)

See: **price leadership**.

parameter (210)

A quantified characteristic of a statistical population, e.g. **mean, standard deviation**.

parasitic city (930)

A city which impoverishes the surrounding region by drawing into it capital and better quality labour. There are many cities in the **Third World** with this character.

See also: **generative city**.

parastatal (510)

A company at least 50 per cent owned by the state. As the state is responsible for any deficits made there is a tendency for such firms to have poor financial discipline and excessive labour forces. In Latin American countries parastatals have only been maintained by increases in the money supply with inevitable inflationary consequences for the national economy.

See also: **joint equity venture company; nationalized industry**.

Pareto, Vilfredo, 1848–1923 (030)

French-born Italian sociologist and economist who made a leading contribution to **welfare economics** by setting out the conditions for a welfare optimum, always known now as the 'Pareto optimum'. In his *Cours d'Economie Politique* (1896) he attempted a synthesis of economics, sociology and Marxist thought: economic **utility** was examined in a psychological and sociological context and Marxian class analysis was extended to a study of the nature of conflict between interest groups. Realizing the consequences for society of political democracy, he was reluctant to retain a socialist approach to conflict in his work *Les Systèmes Socialistes* of 1902.

Borkenau, F. (1936) *Pareto*, New York: Wiley.
Bucolo, P. (ed.) (1979) *The Economics of Vilfredo Pareto*, London and Totowa, NJ: Cass.

Pareto efficiency (010)

The efficiency of a system which cannot produce more of any product from the same level of inputs without reducing the output of another product by switching inputs between products or by changing techniques. This view of efficiency has been challenged because of the difficulties of valuing outputs and comparing them, its ambiguity in referring to many alternative allocations and the possibility that present allocations may produce different outputs in the future.

Pareto improvement (010)

Making at least one person in a community better off without anyone else being made worse off.

See also: **Pareto optimum**.

Pareto optimum (010)

An allocation of resources such that no one can be made better off without someone else being made worse off. The most famous notion of optimality in **welfare economics**.

Paris Club (430)

See: **Group of Ten**.

Parkinson's law (510)

'Work expands so as to fill the time available for its completion.' C. Northcote Parkinson postulated the law in 1955 after his observation of Admiralty staffing in the UK.

partial equilibrium analysis (020)

A technique of microeconomic analysis pioneered principally by **Cournot** and **Marshall** to analyse a market or other part of an economy by itself. Usually the relationship between only two variables is considered, with the assumption that anything which can influence that relationship remains unchanged. In demand analysis, the relationship between price and quantity demanded is analysed, assuming that 'other things being equal', i.e. that tastes, incomes, other prices, etc which could influence the quantity demanded do not change.

See also: *ceteris paribus*; **general equilibrium**.

partial unemployment (810)

See: **work sharing**.

participating security (310)

A security which entitles the holder both to a fixed amount of interest or dividends and to extra earnings above a pre-set level.

partnership (510)

A business jointly owned by two or more persons who are personally responsible for its debts and each share in its profits. This form of business has long been popular with professional persons, e.g. lawyers and accountants; banking often was organized in partnerships before the coming of joint stock companies.

See also: **limited company**.

par value (310, 430)

1 The nominal value of a share printed on a stock certificate at the time of issue.

2 The value of a currency under a fixed exchange rate regime.

See also: **Bretton Woods Agreement**.

patent (620)

A legally registered and protected invention which is the property of its inventor for a period of years. Patents create a formidable technological barrier to entry, establishing and maintaining monopoly power. Since patents allow monopoly profits to accrue to their inventors, they are a major private incentive to research and development. Non-patentholders can only use patented technical knowledge by licence. Although the patent system may encourage inventors, it has been criticized on the grounds that all scientific knowledge should be a free good and that the considerable legal costs of registering and protecting a patent exclude the poor inventor from using the system.

See also: **invention**; **product cycle**.

Patinkin, Don, 1922– (030)

A major Israeli monetary economist and interpreter of **Keynes** who was born in Chicago where he attended and taught at the University of Chicago. Since 1949 he has been lecturer and (from 1956) professor at the Eliezer Kaplan School of Economics and Social Sciences, Hebrew University of Jerusalem. From 1969, he has been Director of Research at the Maurice Falk Institute for Economic Research in Israel.

In *Money, Interest and Prices* (1956) he applied Hicksian **general equilibrium** analysis to Keynesian macroeconomics, brilliantly integrating the real and monetary economies by treating money as a commodity which renders services. However, in his other numerous writings he has had sharp words of criticism for central elements of **Keynes**'s *General Theory*, particularly the notion of **'involuntary unemployment'** and the absence of a supply function in Keynes's macro-model.

patrimonial industry (610)

An industry whose foreign ownership is limited to 49 per cent. This rule is applied in the Mexican economy to the industries which constitute the basic infrastructure.

See also: **joint equity venture company**; **parastatal**.

pattern settlement (820)

A wage agreement which follows the pay deal of a dominant bargaining group. Sweden and Japan both have coordinated bargaining of this kind, often with the bargain of the metal industries setting a pattern for other bargaining groups of **trade unions** and **employers' associations**. Lower inflation and higher levels of employment are associated with centralized collective bargaining of this kind.

See also: **wage round**.

pay-back method (540)

A method of **investment appraisal** which assesses a project by the length of time needed to repay that investment by its earnings. As a method, it has been criticized for bias against some projects which necessarily will yield earnings only in the long run.

PAYE (320)

Pay as you earn: the British method of deducting income tax from employees' pay automatically. It was introduced in 1944, partly on the advice of **Keynes**. In the USA, this is known as income tax withholding.

pay freeze (820)

A phase of an **incomes policy** in which no increase in wages and salaries is permitted. This can be used as an extreme measure by a national government in times of inflation or by an employer in serious financial difficulties. It is difficult to enforce a pay freeze for long as it usually entails workers suffering a fall in real incomes and prevents the labour market from being able to use changes in wage rates to adjust the supply of labour to changes in demand.

payment by results (820)

See: **incentive pay scheme**.

payment-in-kind bond (310)

A **junk bond** such that the issuer can issue more debt in lieu of a cash **coupon** payment over the early part of the bond's life.

See also: **original issue discount bond**.

pay-off (010)

The benefit derived from a course of action, net of cost.

See also: **minimax**; **regret**.

pay policy (820)

See: **incomes policy**.

payroll tax (320)

A tax on labour usually equal to a fixed proportion of the wage bill or of an individual employee's remuneration. In the USA, this tax became part of the federal revenue system by the Social Security Act 1935 when it was introduced to finance social security programmes. National insurance in the UK is based on this principle.

PCC (010)

See: **price consumption curve**.

PDI (010)

Personal disposable income.

P/E (310)

See: **price–earnings ratio**.

peace dividend (320)

The extra amount of revenue governments hope to have available for public expenditure or tax-cuts because of a reduction in defence expenditures resulting from the ending of the 'cold war' in 1989. However, the scope for turning guns into butter is limited by the political instability of several regions of the world.

peak-load pricing (010, 520, 720)

The charging of higher prices to consumers at times of peak demand to reflect the higher costs of supplying them then. There are many examples of this in the supply of energy and passenger transport, e.g. charging less for the electricity consumed by night storage heaters and lower rail fares on days with less traffic. Industries which need this type of pricing are characterized by a demand which fluctuates over the cycle of a day or a year and by a supply under conditions of high **fixed costs** and low **variable costs**. The higher prices charged to pay for extra capacity cannot be too great, otherwise consumers will shift their demand to other times which will make it increasingly difficult to raise sufficient revenue to cover the costs of peak-load special capacity.

Crew, M.A. and Kleindorfer, P.R. (1986) *The Economics of Public Utility Regulation*, Cambridge, MA: MIT Press.
Williamson, O.E. (1966) 'Peak load pricing and optimal capacity under indivisibility constraints', *American Economic Review* 56: 810–27.

See also: **two-part tariff**.

Pearson Report (130, 430)
The Report in 1969 of the Commission on International Development headed by Lester Pearson, a former Prime Minister of Canada. It recommended that developing countries should encourage **direct foreign investment**, that all developed countries should by 1975 devote at least 1 per cent of **gross domestic product** to **foreign aid** and that aid should not be tied to procuring goods in the donor's country.

World Bank Commission on International Development (1969) *Partners in Development: Report of the Commission on International Development*, New York and London: Pall Mall Press.

pecuniary economy of scale (010)
A reduction in the cost of purchasing inputs or obtaining investment finance as a result of operating at a higher output.

See also: **economy of scale**.

pecuniary external economy (010, 520)
A reduction in the average costs of a firm brought about by the financial actions of other firms. A major example of this is the simultaneous undertaking of several investment projects which reduce costs by reducing the **risk** of one of the projects failing.

See also: **economy of scale**.

pecuniary returns (010, 820)
Factor rewards in the form of money.

See also: **non-pecuniary returns**.

pegged exchange rate (430)
An exchange rate kept in the same relationship to another currency, or to gold, through using that country's central bank reserves or through borrowing from the **International Monetary Fund** or from other central banks. This is done to avoid unnecessary exchange rate fluctuations and because of the belief that central banks are more astute than private parties in setting exchange rates. Most pegging is done against the dollar. There are many examples of pegging. For almost 100 years, until 1934, the US dollar was 20.67 per fine ounce of gold. The UK pound was pegged at US$2.80 from 1948 to 1967; Haiti pegged the gourde at 5 gourdes to the dollar from 1907 onwards.

See also: **Exchange Rate Mechanism**; **gold standard**.

pendulum arbitration (830)
A system of arbitration under which the arbitrator has to choose either management or union proposals. As no compromise is possible, both sides are moderate in their stances. Although this was practised in the British coal industry as early as the period 1893 to 1914, it has been revived as a method of wage settlement: it is now popular in Japanese companies as a means of avoiding strikes. Arbitration is compulsory in 20 USA states for public sector industrial disputes, 8 using only pendulum arbitration and 2 using it to some extent. Perhaps such arbitration is most suitable when there is a general principle at stake, e.g. wage cuts or wage increases. Also known as flip-flop, final offer or straight-choice arbitration.

Davis, D. (1989) *The Power of the Pendulum*, London: Institute of Economic Affairs.
Treble, J.G. (1990) 'The pit and the pendulum: arbitration in the British Coal Industry, 1893–1914', *Economic Journal* 100: 1095–108.

penny share (310)
A share in a UK company worth less than 50p. The potential for capital growth is considerable for many of these securities.

See also: **heavy share**.

Penrose, Edith Tilton, 1914– (030)

After an education at Johns Hopkins University and various academic posts, including one in Baghdad, Penrose became Professor of Economics at the School of Oriental and African Studies, University of London, from 1964 to 1979. Her most famous contribution to economics is her theory of the growth of the firm which had the optimistic theme that the human and material resources managed by a firm can be used to achieve a limitless expansion of a firm through product and market diversification and the recruitment of additional high-level managers. Her other works include books on the international **patent** system, the international petroleum industry and Middle East oil.

Penrose, E.T. (1959) *The Theory of the Growth of the Firm*, Oxford: Basil Blackwell.

pension (910)

A replacement of employment earnings for retired persons. It can take the form of a flat-rate benefit or be related to previous earnings and be arranged by a government or firm or financial institution. Pensions can be financed from an insurance fund or on a 'pay-as-you-go' principle with contributions and government grants financing the pay-out of benefits.

pension fund (310, 910)

The accumulated contributions of an employer and employees of a firm, or other employing organization, which are used to finance the future payment of retirement pensions. In the UK, the largest funds are those of the long-established public corporations, major private sector firms and local governments. Pension funds since 1945 have become major **institutional investors** with the potential to have a great influence on the movement of share prices.

pension scheme (910)

An arrangement to pay a regular income to a person too old or too ill to work. By the late nineteenth century, many governments realized that some provision for the elderly was needed; in the twentieth century, the spread of **collective bargaining** brought a proliferation of private pension plans.

See also: **Old Age, Survivors and Disability Insurance**; **State Earnings Related Pensions Scheme**.

PEP (310)

See: **personal equity plan**.

percentage grant (320)

See: **grant in aid**.

percentile (210)

A value obtained by dividing data arranged in order of magnitude into one hundred equal parts. The first percentile, e.g. shows that value below which 1 per cent of the values of a variable lie. The **lower quartile** is the 25th percentile; the **median** is the 50th percentile; the **upper quartile**, the 75th percentile.

See also: **decile**; **median**.

perestroika (060, 120)

The reconstruction of the Soviet economy proposed in detail in 1987 consisting of granting greater independence to enterprises from many planning directives, even to the extent of being able to go bankrupt. As part of economic democratization, the rewards of all workers would depend on their contribution to the success of an enterprise; also, to improve economic efficiency, a more realistic structure of prices was proposed. The price structure in the 1980s was much in need of reform as rents had last been fixed in 1928, communal charges in 1946 and many food items, including bread, in 1954. This price rigidity prevented equilibrium between demand and supply from being reached in particular markets. The principal limitation on the freedom of enterprises was to be the requirement to meet state orders as a priority; the principal opposition is likely to come from unskilled workers with little to gain and surplus workers who will experience unemployment for the first time in their lives.

Gorbachev, M.S. (1987) *Perestroika: New Thinking for our Country and the World*, London: Collins.

Rapoport, V. (1989) *Perestroika: A Selection of Articles*, London: Overseas Publications Interchange.

See also: **Liberman**.

perfect competition (010, 710)

A market which has a large number of buyers and sellers engaged in the trading of a **homogeneous good**, with freedom of entry and exit for firms, no government intervention, no transport costs and a perfectly elastic supply of factors of production. Although few markets, apart from some securities and commodities markets even approach such a state of affairs, perfect competition is very important conceptually as an extreme case in the classification of markets. Many economic theories do not advance beyond the assumption of perfect competition.

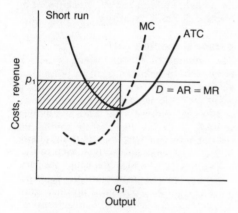

Short run

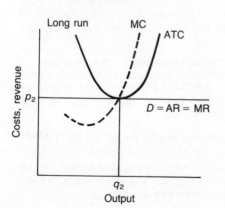

Long run

AR	average revenue
ATC	average total cost
D	demand
MC	marginal cost
MR	marginal revenue

Stigler, G.J. (1965) *Essays in the History of Economics*, ch. 8, Chicago, IL and London: University of Chicago Press.

perfect price discrimination (010, 530)

See: **first degree price discrimination**.

performance-related pay (820)

An **incentive pay scheme** which attempts to link all or part of an employee's remuneration to the achievement of output and output-related goals instead of to the amount of time supplied by an employee to a firm. It is hoped by firms with performance-related pay (PRP) schemes that turnover, profits, loyalty to the firm and quality of work done will increase and that industrial unrest and **absenteeism** will diminish.

See also: **profit-related pay**.

peripheral capitalism (070, 130)

The dependent **capitalism** of Third World countries. The gradual **industrialization** of less developed countries at the periphery raises their productivity and labour incomes and creates a surplus which is transferred to advanced countries at the 'centre'. The centre thus has a faster rate of capital accumulation and income growth than the periphery. Also, the centre is assumed to have greater technological progress than the periphery, as well as different income and price **elasticities** of demand for manufactures and primary products. The income and wealth disparities between centre and periphery which result have prompted the demand by **Prebisch** and others for a range of socialist policies to appropriate the surplus created at the periphery, to limit imports and to increase industrialization.

periphery firm (510, 610)

A small or medium-sized firm in a largely **oligopolistic** industry which is dominated by **core firms**.

perks (820)

See: **fringe benefits**.

permanent arms economy (070)

An **economy** which is able to continue its accumulation beyond the limit set by a fall in the rate of profit because more and more permanent value is diverted into unproductive consumption. A term coined by a British Marxist, Kidron to describe Western economies, despite being as applicable to many **Soviet-type economies**.

Kidron, M. (1968) *Western Capitalism since the War*, London: Weidenfeld & Nicolson.
Melman, S. (1974) *The Permanent War Economy*, New York: Simon & Schuster.

See also: **military industrial complex; military Keynesianism**.

permanent employment (810)

A Japanese practice of offering lifetime employment to workers when they join a firm from school or university. This became popular with firms short of labour in the 1950s and anxious about labour turnover. The system has rarely been applied to small firms and less to women than to men. Under this system, all employees, except senior management, retire at 55.

Taira, K. (1970) *Economic Development and the Labor Market in Japan*, New York: Columbia University Press.

permanent income hypothesis (020)

A theory of the **consumption function** that income can be divided into permanent income (expected lifetime income) and transitory income (e.g. **windfall gains**) so that permanent consumption is a function of permanent income and transitory consumption a function of transitory income. Before **Friedman**, the theory was suggested by several writers.

Friedman, M. (1957) *A Theory of the Consumption Function*, Princeton, NJ: Princeton University Press.

See also: **absolute income hypothesis; life-cycle hypothesis; relative income hypothesis**.

perpetuity (310)

A fixed interest bond with no redemption date.

See also: **consol**.

personal bank (310)

A bank with deposits from individual men and women and no commercial clients. Many savings banks were of this nature until extensive financial deregulation encouraged diversification.

personal capitalism (010, 610)

Ownership of industry by the families of the founders of major firms.

See also: **capitalism; merchant capitalism**.

personal equity plan (310)

UK fiscal arrangement introduced in 1987 which originally permitted individuals to invest up to £200 per month, or £2,400 per year, in equities, with the incentive of not having to pay income tax on dividends received from these investments. Plans can only be arranged by a 'registered manager', i.e. a bank, building society, stockbroker or licensed dealer in securities.

personal income (010)

The amount of **income** which a person receives from being engaged in productive activity or ownership of income-producing assets. It is determined by an individual's endowments (including abilities and **human capital**), tastes (for work, leisure, saving and risk-taking), and luck (windfall gains and losses). A person's income takes the form of wages, salaries, interest, dividends, gifts and rents. As all countries levy taxation, for most persons, **disposable income** is less than personal income.

personal income distribution (160)

The distribution of income between individuals; the **size distribution of income**. Statistics on this indicate what proportion of total household income is received by individuals in each income band, e.g. the top 5 per cent. Most studies show the stability of this distribution over time and considerable inequality.

Atkinson, A.B. (1983) *The Economics of Inequality*, 2nd edn, Oxford: Clarendon Press.
Phelps Brown, E.H. (1977) *The Inequality of Pay*, Oxford and New York: Oxford University Press.

personal sector liquid assets (310)

Savings deposits of persons with banks, building societies and state savings institutions. These deposits can be converted into cash at short notice.

per-unit tax (320)

A tax which increases the cost of producing a unit of a good by the amount of the tax; import **tariffs**, taxes on factors of production (e.g. the **Selective Employment Tax**), employer contributions to social security schemes and **value-added taxes**. Diagrammatically, such a tax is shown by an upward shift of the **marginal cost** curve by the amount of the tax. The extent to which producers and consumers pay the tax will depend on the **elasticity** of the demand and supply curves. A tax of this kind is usually contrasted with a **lump-sum tax**.

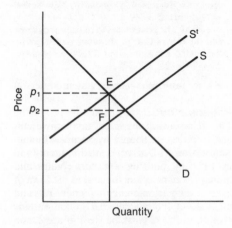

Quantity

EF   tax
p_1 price paid to producers
p_2 price paid by consumers
D   demand
S   supply before imposition of an indirect tax
S^t supply after the indirect tax has been imposed

perverse price (010)

A price which falls as a consequence of an increase in demand.

Broome, J. (1978) 'Perverse prices', *Economic Journal* 88: 778–87.

See also: **Giffen paradox**.

PESC (320)

See: **Public Expenditure Survey Committee**.

peso (430)

The name of separate national currencies of Bolivia, Chile, Colombia, Cuba, the Dominican Republic, Mexico, the Philippines and Uruguay.

Peter principle (510)

The hypothesis that in an organization with a hierarchy each person rises to the level of his/her incompetence and stays there. Poor information within internal labour markets is largely responsible for this. Professor Lawrence J. Peter (1920–90) of the University of Southern California sadly formulated this principle after extensively studying many organizations.

Peter, L. and Hull, R. (1969) *The Peter Principle: Why Things Always Go Wrong*, London: Souvenir Press.

petrocurrency (430, 720)

A **currency** whose value is influenced by the large part oil plays in that country's **balance of payments**.

petrodollars (310)

The surplus receipts of oil-producing countries which were invested abroad rather than spent on imports. Surpluses invested in Japan were termed petroyens, in Switzerland, petrofrancs.

petroleum revenue tax (320, 720)

British tax levied on the proceeds from selling oil and gas above a certain sales levy. Operating costs and royalties are deducted from sales revenue before the tax is charged. The exploitation of North Sea oil reserves brought about this tax which enabled British governments to share in the oil industry's prosperity.

Petty, Sir William, 1623–87 (030)

Described by **Marx** as the 'founder of political economy' and by **Keynes** as 'the father of modern economics'. He had an eventful life rising from being a cabin boy of humble origins to a chair of anatomy at Oxford, a chair of music at Gresham's College, London, Physician-General to Cromwell's army in Ireland, a founder of the Royal Society and an original thinker in economics, far surpassing most of his **mercantilist** contemporaries. His principal mentor was Thomas Hobbes, particularly in matters of taxation.

Most of his economic writings, dictated at night to his secretaries as he paced up and down his study munching raisins, were attempts to solve the policy problems posed by the Restoration of Charles II. His most comprehensive work was the first economic work on public finance, *A Treatise of Taxes* (1662); his posthumous *Political Arithmetick* (written 1671, pub. 1690) introduced the quantification of economic variables to political economy. He is credited with the first clear enunciation of many economic ideas, including **human capital**, the **labour theory of value**, **expenditure taxes**, **public works** as a cure for **unemployment**, the differential theory of **rent**, the **trade cycle**, the **circular flow** of income, the bank creation of **credit** and the **velocity of circulation**.

Hull, C.H. (ed.) (1899) *The Economic Writings of Sir William Petty*, Cambridge: Cambridge University Press. Reprinted 1963–4 New York: A.M. Kelley.

Roncaglia, A. (1985) *Petty: The Origins of Political Economy*, Cardiff: University College Cardiff Press.

Petty's law (630)

The tendency as an economy develops for the proportion of the labour force engaged in services to increase.

See also: **services**.

Phillips, Alban William Housego, 1914–75 (030)

New Zealand-born economist who invented in 1958 a major tool of macroeconomics, the 'Phillips curve', which originally showed the trade-off between wage inflation and unemployment and was subsequently applied to changes in the general price level. Also, in a series of articles he examined multiplier–accelerator relationships and did much to introduce the optimal control approach to stabilization policy.

In 1938, at the beginning of his career, he graduated as an electrical engineer, and then ran a cinema and hunted crocodiles in Queensland before acquiring a BA in sociology and economics (1949) and a PhD (1952) at the London School of Economics. As an undergraduate, he saw scope for applying his engineering knowledge to economics with the result that he was able to construct an analogue machine which applied dynamic control theory to a circular flow model of the economy; this met with the approval of leading economists such as James **Meade** and John **Hicks** and led to his first academic appointment. He was soon appointed to the Tooke Chair of Economic Science at the London School of Economics, which he held from 1954 to 1967. As a professor at the Australian National University from 1968 to 1970, he pursued his interest in the Chinese economy.

Blyth, C.A. (1975) 'A.W.H. Phillips, MBE', *Economic Record* 51: 303–7.

Phillips, A.W. (1950) 'Mechanical models in economic dynamics', *Economica*, New Series 17 (August): 283–99.

—— (1958) 'The relation between unemployment and the rate of change of money wage rates in the United Kingdom, 1861–1957', *Economica, New Series* 25: 283–300.

See also: **multiplier–accelerator model**.

Phillips curve (150, 810)

The relationship between unemployment and inflation so named by **Samuelson** and **Solow** after Phillips attempted to identify it in 1958 by plotting data on changes in money wage rates for the period 1861–1957 against the national unemployment rates (a measure of overall demand in the British economy). Later work on the Phillips curve sought to take into account incomes policies and inflationary expectations. The long-run Phillips curve is vertical at the **natural rate of unemployment**.

Phillips, A.W. (1958) 'The relationship between unemployment and the rate of change of money wage rates in the United Kingdom, 1861–1957', *Economica, New Series* 25: 283–99.

Santomero, A.N. and Seater, J.J. (eds) (1978) 'The inflation–unemployment trade-off: a critique of the literature', *Journal of Economic Literature* 15: 499–544.

Sawyer, M.C. (1991) *The Political Economy of the Phillips Curve*, Aldershot: Edward Elgar.

physical quality of life index (220)

A measure of **economic welfare** which is more sophisticated than **gross national product** per capita. This index, pioneered by the Overseas Development Council of Washington, DC, is based on the percentage of literacy in a population, infant mortality and life expectancy after age 1 (to avoid double

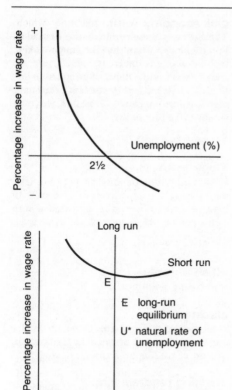

counting of infant deaths). Some countries rank much lower by this index than by per capita gross national product, e.g. oil-producing countries. Critics of the index are concerned about the narrowness of the index as there are so many other physical indicators of welfare.

Morris, M.D. and Alpin, M.B. (1980) *Measuring the Condition of the World's Poor: The Physical Quality of Life Index*, New Delhi: Promilla.

Physiocrats (030)

The leading French school of economic thought which was active in the 1760s and 1770s and whose members were the first to be called 'économistes'. **Quesnay**, Mirabeau, Dupont de Nemours and **Turgot** used the name Physiocrats to mean 'Lords of Nature' as they took the view that the economy should pursue its natural course, without the interference of government and that agriculture uniquely produces a surplus as plants and animals reproduce themselves but machines do not. Apart from presenting

one of the earliest models of the economy (in Quesnay's *Tableau Economique*), they also advocated a single tax based on agricultural rents and laid the foundations for classical price theory. Much of their work had been more clearly set out by **Cantillon**. But the high praise accorded to them by **Smith** and **Marx** ensures that they will never be forgotten.

Meek, R.L. (1962) *The Economics of Physiocracy: Essays and Translations*, London: Allen & Unwin.

PIBOR (310)

Paris Inter-Bank Offered Rate.

See also: **London Inter-Bank Offered Rate**.

picketing (830)

Verbal or physical persuasion of workers not to enter the premises of a firm where there is an **industrial dispute**. In the UK, only peaceful picketing to convey information by no more than six pickets assembled is legal.

piece rate (820)

A specific wage rate per unit of output which has often been used as an **incentive pay scheme**.

See also: **time rate**.

piecework system (830)

A wage system which rewards workers according to the number of pieces/units of a product they produce. This is the alternative to remunerating workers according to the time a worker contracts to offer an employer. Piecework was introduced to relate work to productivity. However, it has often been criticized for causing unstable earnings and causing stress to workers who over-exert themselves.

Pigou, Arthur Cecil, 1877–1959 (030)

The Cambridge economist who was fellow of King's College from 1902 to 1959 and professor of economics (in succession to **Marshall**) from 1908 to 1943. In *Wealth and Welfare* (1912), which was expanded into *The Economics of Welfare* (1920), he built upon Marshallian foundations a study of the size and distribution of national income and the case for government intervention. His other major works include *Industrial Fluctuations* (1927), *Public Finance* (1928) and *Employment and Equilibrium* (1941). Although he was initially critical of **Keynes**'s *General Theory*, by 1949 he was prepared to concede that it was an original contribution to economic analysis.

Casson, M. (1983) *Economics of Unemployment*, Oxford: Martin Robertson.
O'Brien, D.P. and Presley, J.R. (eds) (1981) *Pioneers of Modern Economics in Britain*, ch. 4, London: Macmillan.

Pigou effect (010, 320)

The effect on consumption of a change in the real value of cash balances brought about by a change in the money supply, e.g. an increase in the money supply which causes a rise in prices, a reduction in the purchasing power of cash balances which results in lower consumption. Diagrammatically, this effect can be shown as a shift in the IS curve. Also known as the 'real balance effect'.

See also: **IS–LM curves**.

Pigovian subsidy (320, 720)

A **subsidy** which encourages the production of goods and services which provide external benefits.

See also: **externality**; **Pigou**.

Pigovian tax (320, 720)

A tax which charges firms for the external costs which arise from their productive activities.

See also: **externality**; **Pigou**.

PIK bond (310)

See: **payment-in-kind bond**.

PIN (310)

1 Personal identification number: the number which gives the holder of a bank cash card or a credit card access to the cash or credit facilities of the financial organization concerned.

2 The Philippine Investment Note which is used by smaller banks to finance local investment.

Pink Book (430)

UK **balance of payments** accounts.

pink economy (610)

The business sector run for the benefit of homosexuals, often by the same. These include bars, restaurants, hotels, clothes shops and bookshops. Since so many homosexuals have no dependents, they have high disposal incomes available for consumption in this sector.

See also: **economy**.

Pippy (840)

Person inheriting parents' property: usually a middle-aged person living in an area with high property prices. The increased wealth of the person helps maintain the price level.

See also: **grey belt**.

Pittsburgh-plus (520)

See: **basing point pricing**.

placing (310)

A method of selling shares by which a seller and buyer privately arrange the transaction, instead of trading on a stock exchange.

planning programming budgeting (320)

A budgetary system which evaluates expenditure programmes in their entirety by taking into account the total costs and benefits of them, using **cost–benefit analysis**. This system, introduced into the US Department of Defense in the early 1960s, was extended to other US Departments in 1965.

Harberger, A.C. (1982) *Project Evaluation: Collected Papers*, London: Macmillan.

See also: **cost effectiveness**.

plastic money (310)

Credit cards and **debit cards** which are made with plastic and used instead of **banknotes**, **coins** and bank **cheques** to pay for consumer goods and services.

Plato, 428/7–348/7 BC (030)

Ancient Greek philosopher who was one of the first writers to discuss fundamental economic concepts, particularly in his *Republic* and *Laws* (Book V). He advocated a **division of labour** based on different natural abilities, discussed the role of **money** and advocated **exchange controls**, and common property amongst the guardians of his ideal republic.

See also: **Ancient Greeks; Aristotle**.

platykurtic (210)
See: **kurtosis**.

Plaza Agreement (430)
The agreement of the **Group of Five** meeting at the Plaza Hotel, New York, in September 1985 to intervene in exchange markets to bring down the value of the US dollar; within a year the US dollar was devalued by 22 per cent. $12 billion was spent by central banks in the first few weeks of the agreement. However, the US trade deficit continued to be large.

Plaza Two (430)
An agreement of the **Group of Five** in Paris in February 1987 to support the US dollar by attempting to increase Japanese and West German imports and to stabilize leading currency rates at the same levels.

plc (510)
Public limited company in the UK. Prior to the Companies Act 1980 the abbreviation used was 'Co. Ltd'; 'Ltd' now refers to private companies.

Plowden Committee (320)
See: **Public Expenditure Survey Committee**.

PMSA (220, 840)
See: **Primary Metropolitan Statistical Area**.

point elasticity (210)
The responsiveness of quantity demanded or supplied to an infinitely small price change. It is calculated, using differential calculus, as the product of two ratios. In the case of price elasticity of demand, it is given by

$$\text{point elasticity} = \frac{(\Delta Q_i / Q_i) \times 100}{(\Delta P_i / P_i) \times 100}$$

$$= \frac{\Delta Q_i P_i}{Q_i \Delta P_i}$$

See also: **arc elasticity; elasticity**.

point estimate (210)
An estimate of a **parameter** of a population which is given by one number.

See also: **interval estimate**.

point-input, point-output model (210)
An economic model which assumes that the output from a labour input takes one period to be produced.

polarization (310)
The rule of the Securities and Investment Board (UK) that banks and building societies must choose either to give independent advice on all life and **unit trust** products available on the market or to sell the products of only one company. Although the aim of the rule is to give consumers independent advice, it has resulted in less advice being offered in retail outlets.

polarization effect (420)
The cumulative and dynamic consequence to a country in an economic union of economic integration which can take the form of growing or diminishing prosperity. The countries which are more attractive as production centres grow at the expense of the others.

policy harmonization (420)
1 The aligning of the economic policies of one country with those of another. This form of economic integration can remove barriers to the movement of goods and services and factors of production. In the **European Community**, there have been many attempts to do this, especially between countries which are members of the **European Monetary System**.

2 Taxation treaties between countries which establish the rules for the taxation of incomes of individuals who receive incomes from countries of which they are not residents.

policy lag (010, 310, 320)
See: **inside lag; outside lag**.

policy variable (210)
See: **choice variable**.

political business cycle (140, 320)
Fluctuations in economic activity brought about by democratically elected governments seeking to win successive elections. It has been argued that political parties have a choice between unemployment and inflation

so that in the period before an election they will stimulate a boom to reduce unemployment at the expense of price rises but after the election will deflate when returned to power. This discretionary use of fiscal policy destabilizes an economy. The theory appears to be more applicable to some **Organization for Economic Cooperation and Development** economies, e.g. the USA and Germany, than others.

Lachler, U. (1982) 'On political business cycles with endogenous election dates', *Journal of Public Economics* 17: 111–17.

MacRae, C.D. (1977) 'A political model of the business cycle', *Journal of Political Economy* 85: 239–63.

Minford, P. and Peel, D. (1982) 'The political theory of the business cycle', *European Economic Review* 10: 253–70.

Nordhaus, W.D. (1975) 'The political business cycle', *Review of Economic Studies* 42: 169–90.

See also: **Phillips curve**.

political economy (010, 030)

The term used for **economics** in the eighteenth and nineteenth centuries and revived in recent years to reflect a policy-oriented view of the subject. Liberal political economy was founded by Adam **Smith** and was concerned then with the art of managing public finances and the advising of statesmen on revenue maximization. **Schumpeter**, in his *History of Economic Analysis* defined it as 'an exposition of a comprehensive set of economic policies that its author advocates on the strength of certain unifying normative principles, such as the principles of economic liberalism [or] . . . Socialism . . .'. **Robbins** asserted that political economy is concerned with policy prescriptions. Today, this applied view of economics rejects the of **perfect competition**, criticizes the uncertainties of free enterprise and makes use of **public choice** theory.

Lange, O. (1963 and 1971) *Political Economy*, New York and Oxford: Pergamon Press, 2 vols.

See also: **post-Keynesians**.

poll tax (320)

A tax of a fixed monetary amount levied on every member of a population. In feudal societies, the amount depended on rank so the same amount per head would be charged within a certain class but a different amount from class to class. The regressive nature of many poll taxes has often led to them being criticized. In the USA, poll taxes have been used by state and local governments. Until the 24th Amendment of the US Constitution of 1964 outlawed it, the payment of a poll tax was required of voters in the southern states, thus excluding the poor, many of whom were black. In the UK, a **'community charge'** which has some of the characteristics of a poll tax was introduced in 1989/90 to replace **'rates'**, the local property tax.

pollution charge (720)

This can take various forms including an **effluent fee** and a **user charge**.

pollution control (720)

Measures to reduce emissions of noxious gases and other wastes into the air, rivers and sea. Legislation, e.g. the US Clean Air Acts of 1970, 1977 and 1990 and the 1972 Amendments to the Federal Water Pollution Control Act, together with private actions and the orders of regulatory agencies are used to curb polluting activity and fine or sue the perpetrators of it. Pollution control programmes vary in effectiveness: often the control of the first and major emissions has a higher return to anti-pollution expenditure than further marginal expenditures. Increasingly it has been noted that pollution control measures reduce economic growth and profits.

Baumol, W.J. and Oates, W.E. (1975) *The Theory of Environmental Policy*, Englewood Cliffs, NJ: Prentice Hall.

pollution tax (320, 720)

A tax on firms responsible for emissions which should be equal to the marginal value of the damage caused. The aim of such a tax is to induce firms to follow optimal production techniques.

See also: **effluent fee**.

Poor Laws (040)

The succession of English statutes beginning with those of 1597 and 1601 which aimed to relieve poverty by providing welfare benefits or work within workhouses. This welfare programme was financed by levying a 'poor rate' on the landowners of each parish. The poor were confined to the parish of birth and separated into the able-bodied and 'impotent', i.e. infants, elderly persons, invalids and lunatics. Under an Act of 1722, the first 200 workhouses were erected for the aged and infirm; the able-bodied were given outdoor relief.

Growing rural poverty in the late eighteenth century prompted many economists of the day, including **Malthus**, to argue that the Poor Laws encouraged population growth and a magnification of the problem of poverty. **Smith** was opposed to arrangements which restricted geographical mobility by keeping the poor in the parishes of birth. A Royal Commission, which included Nassau **Senior**, was set up to investigate the administration of the Poor Laws. In its report of 1834, it recommended that relief should be confined to the 'indigent', i.e. the able-bodied pauper, the aged and the sick and available only within workhouses. Poor Laws, the Royal Commission argued, should not be available for the poor in general as that would include subsidizing low-paid workers. Other proposals in the period of classical economics included **Bentham**'s idea of profit-making industry houses into which the poor would be confined (*Pauper Management Improved*, 1798) and G. Poulett Scrope's insurance scheme financed by employers' contributions (*Principles of Political Economy*, 1832, ch. 12).

Boyer, G.R. (1990) *An Economic History of the English Poor Law*, Cambridge: Cambridge University Press.

Himmelfarb, G. (1984) *The Idea of Poverty. England in the Early Industrial Age*, New York: Alfred A. Knopf; London: Faber & Faber.

See also: **poverty; subsistence**.

popular capitalism (070)

An **economy** which allows a large proportion of the population to share in the profits which arise from private ownership under **capitalism**, usually through **wider share ownership**.

population (840)

1 All of the finite number of items from which a statistical sample is taken.

2 The total number of residents of a country or area within it. World population is dominated by China's population which constitutes about a quarter of the total. The major determinants of population growth are the birth rate, the death rate and international **migration**.

See also: **Malthus; statistics**.

population census (220, 840)

The counting of the number of persons within a country, or part of it, and the measurement of their characteristics. Most modern national censuses take place every five or ten years, the oldest continuous census being the USA's which started in 1791 (England and Wales has had a continuous census since 1801, apart from 1941); earlier limited censuses were conducted in several countries, e.g. in Iceland in 1703 but these were only occasional. The United Nations has played a major role in standardizing the categories of information sought by enumerators and in encouraging the universality of national censuses, which was achieved by 1983. Common to most censuses is data on age, sex, place of birth, marital status, normal residence and occupation. Increasingly planners have used the population census as a means of obtaining a broad range of socioeconomic data: this has met with some resistance as persons are sensitive about revealing many personal characteristics with the consequence that there can be underenumeration as the average person may suspect that the purpose of a census is to provide a statistical basis for conscription or increased taxation.

Benjamin, B. (1970) *The Population Census*, London: Heinemann.

Casley, D.J. and Lury, D.A. (1987) *Data Collection in Developing Countries*, 2nd edn, Oxford: Clarendon Press.

United Nations (1980) *Principles and Recommendations for Population and Housing Censuses*, New York: United Nations.

See also: *de facto* **population**; *de jure* **population**; **demographic accounting**; **demography**.

population density (840)

The number of persons per unit of land area. This is a major determinant of property prices, of much public expenditure, of many social costs and of productivity. Population densities vary greatly from country to country. Some less developed countries appear to have low population densities because a high proportion of their land areas are uninhabitable mountains, deserts or swamps.

population explosion (840)

The acceleration of the rate of population growth, especially after 1800 in industrialized countries, and in less developed countries in the twentieth century. A fall in the death rate as a consequence of the increased availability of public health measures and the slow spread of contraception in poorer countries have brought about this population growth. Famine is sadly likely to be the major curb to growth.

See also: **Malthus; neo-Malthusians**.

population policy (840)

Coordinated government measures to achieve a desired size, structure and rate of growth of population. Many population policies regard the birth rate as the key variable to be controlled as it is the major cause of rapid population growth or decline. If population growth is outstripping a country's economic development, as in China, birth control and rules on the maximum family size are introduced. If population decline is of concern to a country, e.g. because of a shortage of young men to maintain the size of a national army, fiscal inducements such as lower taxes are offered to increase average family size. Whatever the rate of growth of population, there are often policies to change the geographical distribution of population in order to equalize population density between regions, e.g. the creation of **new towns** in Britain.

United Nations (1982) *World Population Trends and Policies: 1981 Monitoring Report*, vols I and II, New York: United Nations.

See also: **regional policy**.

pork barrel legislation (320)

US federal legislation which grants federal money to projects non-essential in character and of benefit to small areas in the hope of maintaining voters' loyalty. As most of the taxpayers financing this expenditure do not benefit because of its connections with specific localities, it is usually only possible to pass such legislation by including it in wider bills of national appeal and by **logrolling**.

portfolio balance (020)

The distribution of a person's or a society's wealth among different assets according to the preferences of the portfolio holder. **Tobin** has, following **Keynes's** *General Theory*, used this approach to monetary theory. As yields vary from asset to asset, this approach has been used as an explanation of the structure of interest rates.

See also: **term structure of interest rates**.

portfolio investment (310)

Investment in securities.

See also: **foreign direct investment**.

portfolio selection (310)

The choice of the mixture of financial assets constituting the holdings of wealth of an individual or an institution. Available information, attitude towards risk and the income aims of the holder of the portfolio will all determine the selection. The resultant portfolio will often be a mixture of **risky** and **safe** assets.

Tobin, J. (1958) 'Liquidity preference as behaviour towards risk', *Review of Economic Studies* 25: 65–86.

portfolio trade (310)

The sale of the whole portfolio of a fund or other financial institution. The firm bidding for it knows the quality of the components of the portfolio but not the details of which securities are included.

positional good (010)

A good for which access depends on an individual's income relative to that of others. Many of these goods have this characteristic because they are fixed in amount, e.g. land available for leisure. When there is economic growth, the relative importance of positional goods increases because, as they are fixed in amount, access to them becomes more difficult thus limiting the benefits of that growth.

Hirsch, F. (1977) *Social Limits to Growth*, London: Routledge & Kegan Paul.

See also: **material good**.

position-risk capital (310)

The capital of a securities house which is used to guard against sudden downturns in markets. The past price volatility of a particular type of security will determine how much position-risk capital is needed to insure against a fall in stock market prices.

positive discrimination (820, 850)

Granting the minorities of society enhanced access to education and jobs in an attempt to reduce overall discrimination against minority groups. This approach to helping the disadvantaged is deeply resented by well-qualified applicants who are rejected and by minority groups who believe they are being patronized.

See also: **affirmative action**; **discrimination**; **reverse discrimination**.

positive economics (010)

Empirical, scientific economics based on a quantitative analysis of economic data. Although contrasted with **normative economics**, the distinction is often blurred, particularly because of the controversial nature of much of economic data. Positive economics has been criticized for the positivist philosophy from which it derives its methodology.

See also: **economic methodology**.

positive feedback (110)

The favourable consequences of economic growth generating further growth, e.g. because the first phase of growth includes the improvement of the infrastructure.

See also: **negative feedback**.

POS machine (310)

A register at the point of service (POS) in a shop which communicates directly with the customer's bank.

See also: **debit card**.

post-contractual optimism (010)

See: **moral hazard**.

posted price (720)

The price at which an oil company is willing to sell its crude oil. This term is derived from the practice of early oil producers of posting on their rigs their selling prices.

See also: **Gulf Plus**.

post-entry discrimination (820)

Setting the pay or promotion prospects of employed persons lower than could be expected on the basis of productivity and job performance. This has often occurred when a worker is a woman, non-white or old.

See also: **pre-entry discrimination**.

post-industrial society (010)

An economically advanced society with a declining manufacturing activity and expanding service sector. This inter-sectoral switch has coincided with the shrinking of the size of the working class, the growth of education and the growth of new industries based on **information technology**. With declining manufacturing activity, an economy becomes more decentralized as, increasingly, productive activities move from factories and offices back to the home, in some senses resembling the pattern of economic activity before the Industrial Revolution.

Bell, D. (1973) *The Coming of Post-Industrial Society*, Cambridge, MA: Harvard University Press.

Shelp, R.K. (1981) *Beyond Industrialization*, New York: Praegar.

See also: **de-industrialization**.

post-Keynesians (030)

Economists, including Sidney Weintraub, Joan **Robinson**, Paul Davidson, Al Eichner and Hyman **Minsky**, who tried to synthesize **Ricardo**, **Marx**, **Kalecki** and **Keynes** to incorporate a theory of income distribution into macroeconomics. The School believes that in goods, labour and money markets, demand determines supply, whatever the price level: this overthrows the entire classical theory of competition and price determination. The School has a stronger interest in macroeconomic relationships than in macroeconomic quantities, prefers to regard firms as using **mark-up** rather than market determination of prices and in its monetary theory believes that money creates speculative excesses which destabilize the economy. Empirical realities are preferred to the notion of equilibrium. The principal policy recommendations of this School are **incomes policies**, a new **international monetary system** and **indicative planning**.

Eichner, A.S. (ed.) (1979) *A Guide to Post-Keynesian Economics*, London and New York: Macmillan.

Kregel, J.A. (1972) *The Reconstruction of Political Economy: An Introduction to Post-Keynesian Economics*, London and Basingstoke: Macmillan.

Pheby, J. (1988) *New Directions in Post-Keynesian Economics*, Aldershot: Edward Elgar.

See also: **political economy**.

potential output (010)

The maximum output of an economy which will be achieved if all of its **factors of production** are fully employed. Actual output is often much less.

Okun, A.M. (1983) 'Potential GNP: its measurement and significance' in J. Pechman (ed.) *Economics for Policymaking*, Cambridge, MA: MIT Press.

See also: **full employment**.

potential surprise function (010, 210)

Shackle's view of **expectations** that the degree of surprise caused to us by the non-occurrence of a given outcome, assuming there has been no change in our relevant knowledge, is a function of the values of a continuous variable. The function is $y = y(x)$ where y is the degree of potential surprise and x is a continuous variable. Intensities of surprise lie between zero and the maximum intensity when what was believed impossible occurs. One of two hypotheses is more attractive if the potential surprise is nil and has a more desirable content than the other.

Shackle, G.L.S. (1949) *Expectations in Economics*, Cambridge: Cambridge University Press.

poverty (160)

1 Low income per person.

2 The state of being below an income level necessary for physical or social existence. As early as Adam **Smith** it was recognized that **subsistence** is defined not by physical needs

alone but also by the customs of society. However, when a society upgrades what it regards as minimal subsistence, it immediately statistically enlarges the poor sector of its population. In less developed countries, with large agricultural sectors, income and earnings figures are not always available so indirect measures, e.g. the rates of change of unemployment and food consumption and the lack of technical progress are used as poverty indicators.

Schiller, B.R. (1989) *Economics of Poverty and Discrimination*, 5th edn, Englewood Cliffs, NJ: Prentice Hall.

Sen, A. (1981) *Poverty and Famines: An Essay on Entitlement and Deprivation*, New York: Oxford University Press.

—— (1983) *On Economic Inequality*, Oxford: Clarendon Press.

Townsend, P. (1979) *Poverty in the United Kingdom*, Harmondsworth: Penguin.

poverty line (910)

The income level which is just sufficient to provide minimum **subsistence** for an individual or family. The social security legislation of a country usually defines it for the purposes of paying out benefits. There is always much controversy over the appropriate minimum. Even Adam **Smith** and **Ricardo** were reluctant to define it in terms of physical survival alone.

See also: **low pay; poverty; poverty trap**.

poverty trap (160, 320, 910)

1 Keeping low income groups at the same level of disposable incomes because of the rules of a country's tax and benefit system penalizing the shift from welfare to employment incomes.

2 Having no incentive to move from being a welfare recipient to an employed person. These people pay high **marginal tax rates** on their incomes because when they have an increase in income they both lose their cash welfare benefits and begin to pay income tax. The trap is calculated as the ratio of income tax + **national insurance contributions** + cash benefits lost/an extra increment of income.

See also: **unemployment trap**.

PPB (320)

See: **planning programming budgeting**.

PPF (010)
See: **production possibility frontier**.

PPI (220)
See: **producer price index**.

PPP (430)
See: **purchasing power parity**.

PQLI (220)
See: **physical quality of life index**.

praxeology (030)
A general theory of successful action which shows what can be deduced from the self-evident axiom that human beings act purposively. Von **Mises** used praxeology as the basis for explaining markets.

Prebisch, Raúl D., 1901–86 (030)
Argentinian economist, who virtually founded **UNCTAD**, being its first secretary-general from 1962 to 1969. He graduated from the University of Buenos Aires and was subsequently professor of political economy there. He held various jobs in the Ministry of Finance and was the first director-general of the Latin American Institute for Economic and Social Planning in 1948, a recognition of his status as a leading authority on Latin American economic problems. On the restoration of democracy to Argentina in 1984, he became an advisor to the new president. His policy proposals have influenced thinking on a **New International Economic Order**.

Prebisch–Singer thesis (420)
A thesis which argues that as the terms of trade have moved against developing countries protection and import substitution should be used to promote industrialization in such countries. This approach was advocated as a means of reducing income inequalities between nations.

Prebisch, R. (1950) *The Economic Development of Latin America and its Principal Problems*, New York: United Nations.
Singer, H.W. (1950) 'The distribution of gains between investing and borrowing countries', *American Economic Review* 40: 473–85.

precautionary demand for money (310)
The money which is needed to meet unforeseen expenditures. The expansion of credit facilities has reduced this demand.

See also: **speculative demand for money**; **transactions demand for money**.

predatory pricing (530)
Reductions in the prices of products below cost, usually in **oligopolistic** industries, to drive rival firms out of business. The increased output which usually results, with consequential **economies of scale**, makes it even more difficult for new firms to enter. To stop this practice, the charging of prices below short-run marginal cost is declared illegal, as has happened in several US **anti-trust** cases, e.g. the Standard Oil case of 1911.

Areeda, P.E. and Turner, D.F. (1975) 'Predatory pricing and related practices under section 2 of the Sherman Act', *Harvard Law Review* 88: 697–733.
McGee, J.S. (1958) 'Predatory pricing: the Standard Oil (NJ) case', *Journal of Law and Economics* 1: 137–69.

pre-emption right (310)
The right of existing shareholders, under company law and stock exchange listing requirements, to subscribe for new shares in proportion to their existing holdings.

pre-entry discrimination (820)
1 Discrimination in the educational system.

2 A refusal to hire because of the applicant's age, race or sex.

See also: **closed shop**; **discrimination**; **post-entry discrimination**.

preference share (310, 520)
Fixed interest shares which have first entitlement to a company's earnings after the payment of interest on **debentures**. Cumulative preference shares accumulate unpaid interest for payment at a later date.

preferred habitat theory (310)
A theory of the **term structure of interest rates** which asserts that the structure is governed by the desire of traders to equalize expected returns, adjusted for risk premiums taking into account that the

trader will have a preference for a short- or long-term investment 'habitat'.

Modigliani, F. and Sutch, R. (1966) 'Innovations in interest rate policy', *American Economic Review* (Papers and Proceedings) 56: 178–97.

premium (310)

1 An additional amount of money paid above a standard product or factor price.

2 The extent to which a market price of a security is in excess of its offer price (if the share is newly issued) or in excess of its asset value.

3 In insurance markets, the periodic amount (usually monthly or annually) an insured person has to pay to have a risk covered.

See also: **grey market; new issue; organic premium; stag.**

premium pay (820)

Additional pay for working outside normal hours (overtime) or in special circumstances, e.g. at night, or at a higher rate of **productivity.**

Premium Savings Bond (310)

A form of national savings introduced in the UK in 1956: there are weekly prizes of up to £250,000 instead of the payment of interest to all bondholders. They are redeemable on demand.

present value (210, 520)

The value now of future incomes or costs which is calculated by using the technique of **discounting**. This is central to much investment appraisal, especially when **cost–benefit analysis** is employed. **Keynes** gave this approach prominence by introducing the concept of the **marginal efficiency of capital.**

presumptive tax (320)

A tax based on an estimate of a taxpayer's income.

See also: **forfait system.**

price (010)

The amount of money, or something of value, requested, or offered, to obtain one unit of a good or service. Relative prices are not expressed in terms of money but in other goods or other services. Prices have been described as **signalling** devices: a price increase will indicate an excess of demand over supply encouraging producers to invest in increased productive capacity and the converse for a price fall.

price bunching (010, 520)

Synchronized price-setting by firms in the same or related markets.

See also: **price leadership; price staggering.**

price ceiling (150)

The maximum price set under a prices policy, or under specific legislation such as Rent Acts (UK), often set to help low-income households. As the price ceiling is characteristically below the equilibrium price, there will be excess demand and a need for rationing.

Price Commission (150)

British public body which administered prices policy from 1973 to 1980. It applied the rules of a Price Code which were enforced most rigorously against the largest companies, which had to gain approval in advance of price increases, whereas the smallest merely had to keep records available for inspection to show compliance with the Code. The rules included a statement of which cost increases could be passed on into product price increases and safeguards to maintain profits so that investment would not suffer. Many aspects of the code were similar to the French price policies in force in the 1950s and 1960s. The Competition Act 1980 abolished the Commission.

See also: **prices policy.**

price–consumption curve (010)

The relationship between changes in relative prices and the consumption of two goods. **Indifference curves** (I_1, I_2, I_3 and I_4) and **budget lines** are used to trace the path of consumption (the price–consumption curve PCC). From this curve can be derived a **demand curve** DD. The demand curve plots quantity demanded against price, which is the amount of money a consumer will give up to obtain one unit of a good. Thus at a consumption level of 1, a point on the demand curve can be obtained by measuring the distance between PCC and the top line, parallel to the horizontal axis, which encloses it. When two units of good B are demanded, a point on the demand curve is obtained by measuring half the distance between PCC and the top line, and so on.

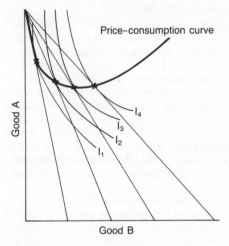

Price–consumption curve

Good A

Good B

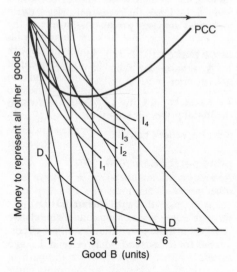

See also: **income consumption curve**.

price controls (150)
Governmental interference with the price mechanism to achieve prices which are not necessarily what a market would determine. These often take the form of either a **price ceiling** or a **price floor**.

Galbraith, J.K. (1952) *A Theory of Price Control*, Cambridge, MA: Harvard University Press.
Rockoff, H. (1991) *Price Controls*, Aldershot: Edward Elgar.

See also: **prices policy**.

price determination (010)
The method used by a market or administrators to fix a price. Increasingly many economists have noted that some important prices are not determined in the market by demand and supply but by herd instinct, social contract, negotiation, domination, politics, power and speculation: major examples of non-market determined prices are oil prices, the wage rate and the rate of interest.

See also: **administered pricing**.

price discrimination (010, 530)
1 The practice of charging different prices to different customers despite the cost of production being the same.

2 Setting different prices for different quantities of the same good.

Common ways of discriminating are according to consumers' incomes, e.g. charging students and retired workers less than others for entertainment, transport and professional services. This is possible because the **elasticity** of the demand curve changes from point to point on most downward sloping demand curves. For a monopolist, the incentive to discriminate arises from being able to increase profits through capturing some of the **consumer surplus** of the buyers. For the **profit maximizing** monopolist, the pricing rule to follow is to set prices such that the **marginal revenue** in each sub-market is equal to the marginal revenues in the others. It is essential for the monopolist to be able to prevent resale by customers in one sub-market to those in others.

See also: **discriminating monopoly**; **first degree price discrimination**; **second degree price discrimination**; **third degree price discrimination**.

price–earnings ratio (310)
The ratio of the market buying price of a share to its earnings per share. The *Financial Times* calculates this net of corporation tax

and unrelieved advance corporation tax. A ratio for a company higher than that of other companies in the same sector reflects the market's belief that its earnings are expected to grow more rapidly, and conversely if this ratio is low. It is difficult to use this ratio to make international comparisons of the value of companies as earnings are measured differently from country to country, e.g. more conservatively in Germany and Japan for taxation reasons.

See also: **cash-price–earnings ratio**.

price effect (010)
The effect on quantity demanded of a change in price. As changes in prices affect the relative ability to purchase particular goods and services and consumers' real incomes, the price effect can be analysed into **income and substitution effects**.

price elasticity of demand (010)
The responsiveness of quantity demanded to a change in price. It is measured crudely as the ratio of the percentage change in quantity to the percentage change in price; more accurately as **arc** or **point elasticity**. This basic tool of microeconomic analysis owes its precise formulation to **Marshall**, although the idea was present in the works of **Mun** and John Stuart **Mill**.

price flexibility (010)
Complete freedom of prices to move up and down in response to changes in demand and supply. Only in unregulated markets is this possible.

See also: **flexprice**.

price floor (010, 710, 820)
A minimum price which is usually set by a governmental order. The major examples of these are **minimum wages** and supported agricultural prices. The purpose of such intervention in markets is usually to maintain the income of certain groups, particularly of non-unionized workers or farmers.

price incentive (010, 110)
An inducement arising from goods and services having different prices. These incentives were regarded as crucial to generating economic growth by Adam **Smith** and his successors as they determine choices between work and leisure, between goods and labour, between present and future consumption (via the interest rate) and among goods.

price leadership (610)
The pricing practice of many **oligopolistic** industries which consists of the largest firm publishing its price list ahead of its competitors who closely follow the prices already announced. This anti-competitive practice has often been used as a substitute for **collusion**. Also known as parallel pricing.

price level (010)
The average of the prices of all the goods and services produced in an economy. This key macroeconomic concept is used in many models of an economy, e.g. **aggregate demand** and **aggregate supply** curves plot real income against the price level. Changes in the price level are measured by price indices, e.g. in the UK the **retail price index** and, in the USA, the **consumer price index** and **gross domestic product** deflator.

price maker (010, 310, 530)
1 A **monopolist** who can dictate the market price.

2 A member of a Stock Exchange who sets the initial prices for securities.

See also: **seller's market**.

price perception (010, 150)
Awareness of an actual price relative to other prices. When units of a currency are changed, e.g. through **decimalization** or through many price changes in a period of general **inflation**, consumers are often unable to understand what price is being stated.

See also: **money illusion**.

price rigidity (010)
The characteristic of **administered prices** which are constant over longish periods of time. Many **oligopolistic** industries provide examples of this.

See also: **fixprice**.

price-sensitive information (310)

Unpublished knowledge about a company, especially its current profitability and any takeover offers it has received, which can affect its **share** price. Dealing in such information is a major form of **insider trading**.

prices policy (150)

An anti-inflation policy often used in conjunction with incomes policies which sets rules for the determination of product prices. There has been a variety of such policies in France: price freezes, target average prices with freedom to vary individual prices in a product group, price fixing according to a formula stating which costs can be passed on into product prices. In the UK, there were such policies in the 1960s and the 1970s under the **National Board for Prices and Incomes** and the **Prices Commission**, whose rules were partially inspired by the prices policy of the Nixon Administration in the USA. The main problems of such policies are that they can cause a shrinkage of profit margins and net investment and reduce the responsiveness of price structures to changing market conditions.

price stabilization (130)

A scheme to maintain product prices at a constant price level in order to stabilize producer incomes. This is a method extensively used for **primary products**. Under such schemes, a **buffer stock** is established to adjust supply to fluctuations in demand and a price is set which, it is hoped, will avoid excessive accumulation or decline in the stocks held. Attempts by **Keynes** in 1942 to establish a global scheme were frustrated by governments opposed to state intervention in markets. Most schemes instituted by **UNCTAD** have been able to survive only a few years.

Newbery, D.M.G. and Stiglitz, J.E. (1981) *The Theory of Commodity Price Stabilization: A Study in the Economics of Risk*, Oxford: Clarendon Press.

price staggering (010, 520)

Price-setting which responds slowly to the other price decisions made in that market. An advantage of staggering is that a more carefully determined price is more sustainable.

Blanchard, O. (1987) 'Individual and aggregate price adjustment', *Brookings Papers on Economic Activity* 1: 57–109.

See also: **price bunching**.

price system (010)

A method of allocating goods and services or factors of production by the free movement of prices. The characteristics of this system are its economy in the amount of information needed for decision-making and its ability to bring about swift adjustments of supply to demand. **Excess demand** automatically pushes up prices, giving a direct signal to producers to increase their labour forces and capital stocks. However, the price system is criticized on the grounds that it ignores many **social costs** as these are rarely evaluated and charged to those responsible and can create income inequalities.

See also: **central planning**.

price taking (010)

A firm's acceptance of market prices as its own prices because it has no influence over market price determination. This occurs in markets in which each firm has only a small proportion of the total output or sales. Under **perfect competition**, all firms are price takers.

price twist (010)

The raising of one type of prices relative to another, e.g. of non-farm prices relative to farm prices.

See also: **Operation Twist**.

price war (530)

A ruthless campaign to drive rival firms from a market by repeatedly cutting prices. The only way an existing firm can escape the effects of such a conflict is to have some kind of price agreement with other firms, or to become the lowest cost firm.

See also: **destructive competition**.

primary capital (310)

The most secure form of bank capital. According to current US and UK definitions, it includes **common stock** or **equity**, retained earnings and minority interests in subsidiaries and excludes **intangible wealth** and investments in unconsolidated subsidiaries.

See also: **secondary capital**.

primary commodity prices (420)

World market prices of agricultural produce and minerals. As several Third World countries are greatly dependent on one or a few primary products for a very high proportion of their export earnings, they attempt to use international agreements to maintain price levels or, at least, prevent secular declines in prices. The most powerful international agreement is cartelization of production. Price stability will be always threatened by climate changes and the consequential variation in harvests.

See also: **commodity agreement**; **one-crop economy**; **primary product**.

primary dealer (310)

A **market-maker** in UK gilt-edged securities.

primary deficit (320)

The excess of a government's expenditure (excluding interest payments) over its income. Sometimes called the 'actual deficit'.

primary employment (010, 810)

See: **employment multiplier**.

primary labour market (820)

That part of a national labour market consisting of large firms whose workers have good pay, job security and training.

See also: **dual labour market**; **internal labour market**; **secondary labour market**.

primary market (310)

A financial market which is concerned with new issues of a particular bond, stock or other financial asset. Many markets combine primary and secondary functions.

See also: **secondary market**.

Primary Metropolitan Statistical Area (220, 840)

An individual component of a **Consolidated Metropolitan Statistical Area**.

primary product (010, 710)

An unprocessed agricultural product, particularly crops grown for food and textile manufacturing, as well as fossil fuels and metals. The production of primary products is the principal economic activity of many Third World countries, hence changes in primary product prices causes fluctuations in their national incomes. Changes in the **terms of trade** have often been to the disadvantage of less developed economies.

See also: **one-crop economy**.

primary ratio (540)

The ratio of operating profit to capital employed.

primary standard (720)

The legal limit permitted for pollutants in the air: beyond this limit, there is a danger to human health.

See also: **ambient standard**; **secondary standard**.

Prime-1 (310)

The top rating of creditworthiness of **commercial paper** made by Moody's Investors Service.

See also: **AAA**.

prime age worker (840)

In developed economies, a man or woman aged 25 to 55. This age classification is often used in studies of **labour force participation** as prime workers have a different attitude towards the labour market than other age groups with the consequence that their participation rates are higher than those of younger or older workers.

prime cost (010, 520)

The direct cost of running a business, particularly labour, energy and raw material costs; **variable costs**. A term used by **Marshall**.

See also: **supplementary cost**.

prime rate of interest (310)

The rate of interest that US commercial banks charge medium- and small-sized firms for borrowing. Historically, this was the interest rate the most creditworthy customers of banks were charged but with the development of the **commercial paper** market, the largest customers borrow below the prime rate.

See also: **base rate**.

primitive economy (010, 710)

A society which has not reached the stage of agriculture. It obtains its food through hunting animals and the gathering of wild crops, e.g. berries. Human needs are few and little work is required to obtain a simple subsistence livelihood. As there is no scarcity, economic problems do not arise. Adam **Smith** called this economy the 'rude society' and stated, with an example of the trading of deer for beavers, that value in this society would be determined by relative labour quantities.

principal (310)

A capital sum which is lent at a fixed rate of interest.

prisoners' dilemma (210)

The most famous of economic games. Two prisoners have a choice between confessing or not confessing to a crime. If both confess, they are sentenced to ten years; if both do not, they are sentenced to two years for being present at the scene of the crime; if one confesses and the other does not, he will get a one year sentence and the other twenty years. The matrix of alternatives is used to illustrate the principle that the pursuit of individual self-interest does not lead to a socially optimal result.

See also: **game theory**.

private cost (010)

The cost to an individual person, or a firm, of the resource(s) used, measured at market prices. In many cases, private cost approximates to the **opportunity cost** of employing such inputs.

See also: **social cost**.

private cost of unemployment (810)

Loss of employment income and unquantifiable personal stress.

See also: **social cost of unemployment**.

private enterprise (510)

1 The principal type of industrial or commercial firm in a capitalist or mixed economy.

2 The private sector of an economy.

Under private enterprise, the capital is owned principally by individuals or non-governmental organizations and its major decisions, particularly on investment, the scale of production and prices, are chosen by the firm itself, with government providing a framework for the activity of the enterprise rather than participating in the firm's decision-making. Increasingly, even in **Soviet-type economies**, private enterprises can operate alongside state-owned and state-run firms. In the late 1980s, increasingly in Eastern Europe and other communist countries private enterprise re-emerged, e.g. from 1987, in the USSR, simple service industries, e.g. taxi-driving, could be run as private concerns.

See also: **public enterprise**.

private enterprise system (070)

A decentralized **capitalist** economy which permits private ownership of business, much freedom of decision-making and the absence

Prisoner's dilemma

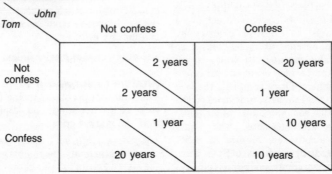

of most government direction except the regulation of **monopoly** and **public utilities** and corporate taxation.

See also: **economic devolution**.

private good (010)

A good which when consumed by one person cannot be consumed by another and whose supply can be restricted to one consumer. These properties of being 'rival' and 'exclusive' separate goods such as food from public goods.

See also: **club good; public good**.

private marginal benefit (010)
See: **marginal utility**.

private placement (310)

A direct method by which a firm can issue its shares by using the services of a financial institution to sell large blocks of the issue to institutional investors (pension funds, banks, insurance companies, etc.) The growth of **equity** investment by these institutions since 1945 has made large private placements possible.

See also: **institutional investor; underwriter**.

private rate of discount (310)
See: **discount rate**.

private sector (610)

The part of the economy which consists of firms which are owned by legal persons other than the state. In a **market economy** the private sector encompasses most economic activity.

privatization (320, 610)

The sale of publicly owned assets, especially industrial capital, to private investors. Many countries in the 1980s undertook this kind of reduction of the public sector to achieve a variety of aims: to improve industry by freeing it from bureaucratic state control, to augment public revenue, to widen share ownership, and to increase competition to benefit consumers. One example is the sale of several **UK nationalized industries** to the public, notably gas, steel, oil, water, electricity, telecommunications, the state airline, and airports. Examples in other countries include France's sale of St Gobain, Paribas and Suez, Japan's sale of its railways

and Hungary's sale of state firms to companies and individuals. Privatization has also taken the form of the sale of state and local authority housing.

In practice, the programme has not met all of its aims. Competition has not increased as much as was hoped because state monopolies in many cases have become private monopolies, instead of being split into competing companies. Also, some of the assets were sold at less than their market value thus reducing the amount of public revenue received from their sale.

Gayle, D.J. and Goodrich, J.N. (eds) (1991) *Privatisation and Deregulation in Global Perspective*, London: Pinter.
Swann, D. (1988) *The Retreat of the State: Deregulation and Privatisation in the UK and USA*, Brighton: Harvester Wheatsheaf.
Thompson, D., Kay, J.A. and Mayer, C. (eds) (1986) *Privatisation: The UK Experience*, Oxford: Clarendon Press.

See also: **economic devolution**.

probability (210)

The likelihood of an event occurring which is calculated as the total number of actual occurrences divided by the total number of possible occurrences. The value of a probability lies between 0 and 1.

probable error (210)

A quantity equal to 0.6745 **standard deviations** of the estimate of a population **parameter**.

producer price index (220)

US price index of commodities calculated by the Bureau of Labor Statistics; published since 1890. It uses sellers' prices by direct sale, or through an organized market, of the first considerable large volume commercial transactions of each commodity. By 1989, the producer price index was based on 3400 commodity price series.

See also: **consumer price index**.

producer's surplus (010)

The gain to a producer arising from selling some of his/her goods and services at more than the market price.

Marshall, A. (1920) *Principles of Economics*, 8th edn, appendix H, London: Macmillan; New York: St Martin's Press.

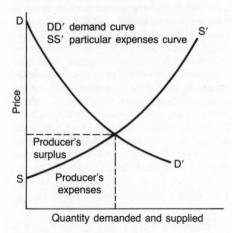

Quantity demanded and supplied

See also: **consumer's surplus**.

producer subsidy equivalent (710)
A method of providing agricultural support by which different types of aid to farmers are converted into this single measure which is the ratio of the cash value of government support to the value of agricultural produce. The **Organization for Economic Coope-ration and Development** devised this approach.

product compatibility (530)
Tying a product to another in order to reduce competition, e.g. through producing computer software which can be used only on a particular type of personal computer.

See also: **tying contract**.

product differentiation (010, 530)
A change in the appearance or presentation of a product to make consumers believe that it is different from similar products. This differentiation is undertaken to give the producer to some extent the power of a monopolist with a unique product. The concept is at the heart of the theory of **monopolistic competition** but in practice it occurs most frequently in **oligopolistic** industries.

production asymmetry (110)
A characteristic of a **dual economy** resulting from the traditional agricultural sector using a different combination of factors of pro-duction from the modern industrialized sector.

production function (210)
The statistical relationship between output and the factor inputs needed to produce that output which describes the technology of a process of production. The most famous of these functions are the **Cobb–Douglas** and **CES** functions.

Heathfield, D.F. (1971) *Production Functions*, London: Macmillan.

See also: **microproduction function**.

production possibility frontier (010)
A curve showing the maximum possible combinations of two goods that can be efficiently produced given a nation's resources. Each point on this curve shows the **trade-off** between the output of the two goods, or the **opportunity cost** of producing more of one good.

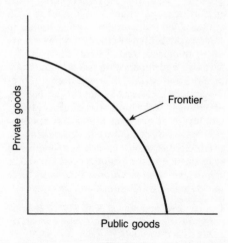

productive capital (010)
That portion of **social capital** invested in those sectors of the economy in which **surplus value** is created.

productive labour (010, 810)
A classification of labour first introduced by Adam **Smith** and later to be prominent in **Marxian** economics. Smith regarded labour as productive if it added value to the raw materials used, provided maintenance for

the labourer and profits for the employer and produced a vendible commodity; **Marx** regarded this type of labour as that which produces **surplus value**. The distinction between productive and unproductive labour has influenced the measurement of **national income**.

productive potential (110)
The maximum growth rate of a country, extrapolated from past trends. It is measured by considering both the growth rates of the supply of factors of production (labour and capital) and the **productivity** of those factors.

See also: **natural rate of growth**; **potential output**.

productivity (010, 110)
The amount of real output produced by one unit of a factor input. Labour and capital productivities have been extensively studied to understand the process of economic growth and the international trade performance of individual countries. US studies show that productivity is higher in more **capital-intensive** industries, which are also unionized and where the cost of turnover and supervision is lower and there is more industrial harmony. Labour productivity is measured as output per person, assuming that the quantities of other factors employed are constant (a difficult assumption in the case of capital). In general, labour productivity can be regarded as a function of investment and the **business cycle**, as well as the degree of supervision of the workforce and of salary differentials and incentives.

Davies, S.W. and Caves, R.E. (1987) *Britain's Productivity Gap – A Study Based on British and American Industries, 1968–77*, Cambridge: Cambridge University Press.
Denison, E.F. (1967) *Why Growth Rates Differ*, Washington, DC: Brookings Institute.
Kravis, I.B. (1976) 'A survey of international comparisons of productivity', *Economic Journal* 86 (March): 1–44.

productivity bargaining (830)
1   Wage bargaining which rewards workers for consenting to new working arrangements so that output can be increased. It was very popular in Britain in the 1960s under an **incomes policy** which allowed super-norm

increases if there was a genuine increase in productivity. Many difficulties arose, including the difficulty of separating labour from capital productivity, the resentment that workers who had long held back productivity growth by their **restrictive practices** were disproportionately rewarded and the difficulty of applying the principle to some sectors of the labour market, particularly the service industries. There was much less productivity bargaining in the USA in that period. Passing on productivity gains in higher wages, rather than in lower prices and higher output, it is argued, threatens the long-term employment prospects of workers.

2   **Collective bargaining** which uses productivity measures as a major determinant of increases in pay.

McKersie, R.B. and Hunter, L.C. (1973) *Pay, Productivity and Collective Bargaining*, London: Macmillan.

productivity shock (810)
A change in unemployment brought about by a labour-saving innovation or a general fluctuation in **productivity** levels.

product life cycle (620)
The life cycle of a product from when it is an innovation, often protected by **patents** and hence earning monopoly profits for its producer, through the stage when it is competing with substitutes to its final stage of maturity when its profitability is for the most part due to the **economies of scale** associated with a large output. This has been used to explain trade patterns and the behaviour of **multinational corporations**.

Vernon, R. (1971) *Sovereignty at Bay*, ch. 2, Harmondsworth: Penguin.

product moment formula (210)
For a **linear correlation** coefficient, this measure of the symmetry between X, the independent variable, and Y, the dependent variable, is calculated as the ratio of the sum of the products of the values of X and Y divided by the square root of the product of the sum of the squares of X values and the sum of the squares of Y values.

professional trader (310)
See: **specialist**.

profit (010, 540)

A surplus of revenue over cost. Economists, unlike accountants, include in total costs imputed **opportunity cost**. Until the **entrepreneur** was recognized as a factor of production, there was little debate about why profits were paid: reasons subsequently suggested by **classical** and later economists include that it is either a payment for supervising and coordinating land, labour and capital or a recompense for risk taking.

Knight, F.H. (1948) *Risk, Uncertainty and Profits*, London and New York: Harper Torchbooks.

profitability (520)

The rate of return to capital achieved by a firm. It is a function of managerial ability, resources available, the state of markets and the behaviour of trade unions (which can have a negative effect on the price/cost margin and on return to capital employed). Business analysts argue that 'profitability' is a vague concept as the data on profits is entirely dependent on accounting conventions and the nature of revenue/taxation law.

profit and loss account (540)

A financial statement of the revenue and expenditure of a firm and its consequential profit or loss. Unlike a **balance sheet**, it refers to a period of time, not a state of affairs at a point in time.

profit centre (520)

A part of a firm or other organization which has separate accounts so that costs and revenues can be attributed to it and its contribution to the total profits of that organization calculated. In **multinational corporations**, this form of decentralized accounting is essential to maintain efficiency.

profit maximization (010, 510)

Setting prices so that **marginal revenue** equals **marginal cost**; traditionally regarded as the central aim of the capitalist firm. When, at the margin, revenue is greater than cost, total profits could be increased by further output; when costs are greater than revenue, total profits decline. In the diagram the total profits curve is plotted by calculat-

ing the vertical distances between the total costs and total revenue curves. Up to output OM total profits are increasing as marginal revenue is greater than marginal cost; after output OM marginal cost is greater than marginal revenue and so total profits decline. At OM, where total profits are at a maximum, marginal revenue is equal to marginal cost.

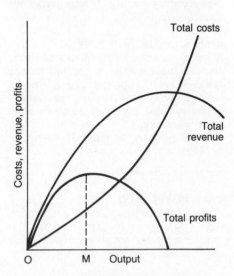

See also: **managerial models of the firm**.

profit motive (010)

The desire for personal gain which is the reason for a person engaging in an economic activity. This is regarded as the basic force which drives **capitalism**.

See also: **altruism**; **economic man**; **non-profit enterprise**.

profit-related pay (820)

Employee remuneration consisting of, or based on, **profits** as well as wages and salaries. This form of pay has the advantages of fluctuating with profits, so that a firm's wage bill falls in bad times and rises only in times of prosperity, and possibly influencing worker behaviour as the divide between ownership and employment is bridged by giving employees two types of factor income. There are long established examples of such an approach, e.g. granting Scottish fishermen shares of the proceeds from each catch of fish, and profit distributions to

Japanese workers. With fiscal encouragement and a managerial desire to reward increased performance without raising labour costs, there are likely to be more pay schemes related to profits. One disadvantage of this type of pay is that employees may resist further recruitment of staff as more employees will reduce per capita entitlements to profit. A scheme of this kind was introduced by the UK Chancellor of the Exchequer in 1987.

profit squeeze (010, 520)

A steady reduction in profits caused by the costs of labour or other factor inputs rising at a faster rate than product prices. This can occur at the level of the firm, the industry or the national economy. Squeezes often occur when prices are more severely controlled than wages, as in the UK from 1974 to 1979.

See also: **prices policy**.

profit taking (310)

A sale of shares which have risen in price, often by short-term speculators. This practice can cause temporary downturns in stock market price indexes.

programme deal (310)

Block portfolio switching by which a fund manager of an investment bank or stockbroking firm exchanges a bundle of unwanted securities for a portfolio with different characteristics. This popular US practice has spread to the London stock market. In most cases, the deals are based on the mid-price of the stocks on a particular day; the expected marketability of the stocks will determine the cost of the transaction.

programme trading (UK) (310)

See: **program trading**.

program trading (US) (310)

Wall Street, New York method of computer trading based on watching the relationship between the trend and fluctuations of stock market prices. A similar method is used in the UK. In favour of this system it is claimed that **institutional investors** benefit as they can tolerate large short-term losses but few individuals are rich enough to participate in this type of trading. However, the system can cause a high volume of sell orders to occur simultaneously bringing about massive declines in stock prices as took place in October 1987. As a result of the **Brady Commission**, the program trading of the **New York Stock Exchange** is prohibited whenever stocks fall by more than 50 points in any one trading day.

See also: **circuit breaker mechanism**.

progressive tax (160, 320)

A tax whose rate rises as income or expenditure rises. The principal examples of these are taxes on personal and corporate incomes. Some **indirect taxes**, e.g. **value-added** tax, are progressive if they exempt goods which constitute a higher proportion of the budget of lower income groups so that the tax falls more on higher income groups.

Progressive taxes aim to achieve a more equal distribution of income post-tax than pre-tax: this goal is central to the economic philosophies of some countries, particularly those with **social market economies** (e.g. Sweden). However, critics of tax progression are concerned about the impact of such tax structures on the supply of labour and the encouragement of a **brain drain**. Much of present-day **tax reform** severely challenges the progressive principle, despite its long ancestry. In the USA, e.g. the Tax Reform Act of 1981 reduced tax progression but the Tax Reform Act of 1986 increased it again. Rousseau argued that the wealthy because of having more property need more protection from the state so should pay more tax. **Smith** in his *Wealth of Nations* argued that tax contributions should be in proportion to ability to pay but did not indicate whether there should be an absolute or equal sacrifice. **John Stuart Mill** rejected the idea that taxation should be based on benefits received from the state as that would make taxation regressive. Vito di Marco justified progression in terms of the marginal **utility** of income being lower for a rich man than for a poor man, as **Bentham** had before him.

Boes, D. and Felderer, B. (1989) *The Political Economy of Progressive Taxation*, Berlin: Springer-Verlag.

See also: **benefit tax; canons of taxation; fiscal mobility; income tax; regressive tax.**

project appraisal (120)
The calculation of the total effects of an investment project on an economy, using both market prices and **shadow prices.**

Hansen, J.R. (1978) *Guide to Practical Project Appraisal: Social Benefit-Cost Analysis in Developing Countries*, Vienna: UNIDO.

Little, I.M.D. and Mirrlees, J.A. (1974) *Project Appraisal and Planning for Developing Countries*, London: Heinemann Educational.

See also: **cost–benefit analysis.**

proletariat (810)
The underprivileged class of society which has to sell its labour because it does not own the means of production. **Marx** regarded this class as exploited because **surplus value** from its output was appropriated by capitalists. He predicted that by social revolution the proletariat would achieve the economic justice the **bourgeoisie** denied it.

promissory note (310)
A signed promise in a document to pay a sum of money on demand or at a future specified date. These notes are often negotiable.

propensity to consume (010)
See: **average propensity to consume; marginal propensity to consume.**

propensity to save (010)
See: **average propensity to save; marginal propensity to save.**

property rights (010)
1 The exclusive rights to use, transform and transfer particular assets, goods and services. An analysis of property rights has enabled economists to develop a more realistic **theory of the firm**, rejecting the basic assumption of **profit maximization**, taking into account **transactions costs** and recognizing diverse patterns of property ownership. The behaviour of individuals, motivated by self-interest, within organizations is central to this new approach to microeconomics.

2 A privilege, power or immunity.

Carter, A. (1989) *The Philosophical Foundations of Property Rights*, New York and London: Harvester Wheatsheaf.

Furubotn, E.G. and Pejovich, S. (1972) 'Property rights and economic theory: a survey of recent literature', *Journal of Economic Literature* 10: 1137–62.

See also: **Coase.**

property tax (320)
A tax based on the value of property. The revenue from this tax is often the major source of local government finance.

See also: **rates; Tiebout hypothesis.**

proportional accounting (630)
A term in insurance for checking the total insurance cover to ascertain what percentage of claims and premiums are assigned to a particular insurance company.

proportional tax (320)
A tax which is fixed as a proportion of a **tax base**, e.g. income or expenditure generally or on a particular good or service. Although the revenue from the tax grows as the tax base expands, the marginal rate of tax continues to be equal to the average rate of tax. The US **payroll tax** is a proportional tax up to the ceiling on the tax.

See also: **flat rate tax; progressive tax; regressive tax.**

proportionate grant (320)
See: **grant-in-aid.**

Proposition 13 (320)
A proposition made binding on the State of California (USA) in 1978 to reduce the amount of taxation on residential property. It was believed that residential property owners were paying an unfair amount of taxation compared with business. The Proposition reduced the assessed values of property and limited future increases of those assessments to 2 per cent per annum and rate increases to 1 per cent per annum.

proprietors' income (220)
The net income of individual proprietorships and partnerships; an item in US **national income** accounts which separates income

of these types of firm on the grounds of their non-incorporation.

prospectus (310)
The document published by a company inviting the public to subscribe to a new issue of shares. It details the financial history, current trading, future prospects and multifarious activities of the company. A shrewd assessment of a prospectus enables the stock market to judge whether the shares when marketed will sell at a **premium**.

See also: **grey market; stag**.

prosperity indicators (220)
1 Changes in real income.

2 Increased consumption of superior goods and services.

Measures of these include the level of consumption of **consumer durable** goods, migration rates to suburbia, a rate of increase in enrolments in higher education greater than the rate of increase of real income and disproportionate increases in outlays for medical care.

protean economy (070, 110)
1 A changing **economy** which is moving from one pattern of economic activities and production methods to another.

2 An **economy** in which **entrepreneurs** are constantly transforming inputs, outputs, their relationships with each other and the nature of industries.

protection (420)
Barriers to the international flow of goods and services. The protectionist measures which are used include **tariffs**, import quotas and trade regulations (e.g. concerning quality). Because protection is a departure from **free trade**, after the **mercantilists** it was attacked by economists for its effect on the allocation of goods and services, but temporary protection has been conceded by many economists to be useful as a means of encouraging **infant industries**.

An analysis of the effects of protection on a national economy includes the changes in domestic production and consumption patterns and switches between foreign and domestic markets, with the consequence

that employment increases at the cost to consumers of having to spend more to purchase higher priced domestically produced goods. Developing countries with small export industries and thus fewer **economies of scale**, sometimes have lower **gross national products** as a consequence of protection.

It is measured by either the gross or net rate of protection, the latter taking into account both exports and imports. The cost of increasing employment through increasing domestic production can be measured as the 'cost per job' which is the increase in the amount of consumer expenditure to obtain the same amount of goods divided by the increased number of jobs in protected industries.

Although in times of recession, protectionist policies are popular, most lead to a reduction in world income. Despite many nations adhering to liberal trade policies, a variety of covert practices and agreements are used to protect domestic industries.

Belassa, B. and Associates (1971) *The Structure of Protection in Developing Countries*, Baltimore, MD: Johns Hopkins University Press.
Corden, W.M. (1971) *The Theory of Protection*, Oxford: Clarendon Press.
Kierzkowski, H. (ed.) (1987) *Protection and Competition in International Trade: Essays in Honor of W.M. Corden*, Oxford: Basil Blackwell.
Shutt, H. (1985) *The Myth of Free Trade: Patterns of Protectionism since 1945*, Oxford: Basil Blackwell.

See also: **effective rate of protection; Multi-Fibre Arrangement; non-tariff barrier; Smoot–Hawley; tariff; voluntary export restraint**.

proto-industrialization (040)
Domestic manufacture controlled by middlemen who use manufacturers as homeworkers, taking away their independence as sole proprietors.

Mendels, F.E. (1972) 'Proto-industrialization: the first phase of the industrialization process', *Journal of Economic History* 32: 241–61.

See also: **homework**.

proto-proletariat (910)
The very poor who scrape a living in the

informal **tertiary sector**. In a sense, they live like refugees.

See also: **low pay; poverty**.

Provisional Collection of Taxes Act (320)
UK statute which permits changes in **indirect taxes** to be made before that year's Finance Act has been passed. This Act reduces **implementation lags** in British **fiscal policy**.

proxy (310)
An agent of an absent voter empowered to cast his/her vote, e.g. a person attending a company meeting who votes on behalf of an absent shareholder.

PRP (820)
See: **performance-related pay; profit-related pay**.

PRT (320, 720)
See: **petroleum revenue tax**.

PSBR (310, 320)
See: **public sector borrowing requirement**.

PSDR (320)
See: **public sector debt repayment**.

PSE (820)
See: **public service employment**.

pseudo production function (020)
Joan **Robinson**'s term for a **production function** based on imaginary equilibrium positions which ignored the idea of production as a long-term accumulation process.

PSL (220, 310)
Private sector liquidity (UK). This broad measure of the money supply was much used in the 1980s and took two forms:

PSL1 = private component of sterling M3 excluding deposits of over two years' original maturity + private sector holdings of money market instruments + certificates of tax deposit

PSL2 = PSL1 + more liquid building society shares and deposits and other similar forms of liquid savings instruments + **SAYE** deposits + bank deposits with an original term longer than two years

See also: **M5**.

psychic income (010)
The subjective pleasures which flow to an individual person in a specified period. This can be the consequence of the receipt of money or of non-pecuniary rewards to employment (e.g. job satisfaction). **Bentham** and later **Jevons** and **Böhm-Bawerk** were to base much of economic theory on subjective sensations and experiences.

See also: **utility**.

psychological economy (070)
A capitalist economy which produces and administers the needs demanded by the system. This major view of the German-born US philosopher and social theorist Herbert Marcuse (1898–1979) influenced **New Left** writers in the 1960s.

Marcuse, H. (1964) *One Dimensional Man*, London: Sphere.

See also: **capitalism; needs standard; radical economics**.

psychology (020)
See: **economics and psychology**.

public choice theory (020, 320)
Explanation of policy-making in the public sector by analysis of the nature of policy selection. There are two approaches: the spatial analysis of political parties and their response to vote pressures (Downs) and the institutional approach (Brennan and **Buchanan**) which predicts the consequences of voters' choices in a specific institutional context. It is a form of applied **welfare economics** with libertarian assumptions.

Brennan, G. and Buchanan, J.M. (1980) *The Power to Tax*, Cambridge: Cambridge University Press.
Downs, A. (1957) *An Economic Theory of Democracy*, New York: Harper.
McLean, I. (1987) *Public Choice*, Oxford: Basil Blackwell.
Mueller, D.C. (1989) *Public Choice II*, Cambridge: Cambridge University Press.

public debt (310)
The total volume of government **bonds, bills** and other **securities** outstanding at a particular date. A large public debt accumulates by public borrowing over a number of years, especially to finance wars, infra-

structure investments and welfare programmes. The burden of this debt can be measured as the ratio of the cost of servicing it to that country's **gross domestic product**. The **Organization for Economic Cooperation and Development** provides information on government debt interest payments as a percentage of gross domestic product. The ratio rises when inflation and growth are low and real rates of interest are high and positive. Organization for Economic Cooperation and Development figures record currently high ratios for Greece and Italy and a lower ratio for the UK.

See also: **debt–service indicators**; **maturity**; **overlapping generations model**; **Third World debt problem**.

public economics (320)
A study of the economic decisions of government – taxation, public expenditure, **public goods** and public sector pricing.

Atkinson, A.B. and Stiglitz, J.E. (1980) *Lectures on Public Economics*, Maidenhead, London and New York: McGraw-Hill.

See also: **public finance**.

public enterprise (510)
An independent business organization owned by a government and subject to some political control. The name for these enterprises varies between countries, e.g. in the UK they are called **nationalized industries** or public corporations. The motives for taking firms into the public sector include the desire to achieve a better allocation of goods and services than the market can produce, to alter the distribution of income, to aid macroeconomic policy by having direct control over basic industries, to exploit for the country as a whole the benefits of **natural monopoly** and to advance **socialism**. In order to encourage public enterprises to be efficient, various goals are set for them, the most common being the requirement to achieve a minimum rate of return to capital employed and to price according to the **marginal cost** of producing their goods and services.

Borcherding, T.E., Pommerehne, W.W. and Schneider, F. (1982) 'Comparing the efficiency of private and public production: the evidence

from five countries', *Zeitschrift fur National-ökonomie* 42: 127–56.

Bös, D. (1986) *Public Enterprise Economics: Theory and Application*, Amsterdam: North-Holland.

Rees, R. (1984) *Public Enterprise*, 2nd edn, London: Weidenfeld & Nicolson.

See also: **private enterprise**.

public expenditure (320)
The expenditure of central, regional and local governmental organizations on intermediate and final goods and services. This is undertaken to achieve a variety of goals including the redistribution of benefits in kind, the provision of **public goods**, the correction of disequilibria in markets and the regulation of industry. In several countries, the increasing ratio of public expenditure to the national income has excited political debate. The ratio has, of course, increased when a collectivist ideology has influenced policy-makers or special interest groups have succeeded in obtaining public subsidization. But in many types of national economy the increase can be attributed to an expanding or ageing population, to public sector output being relatively more costly than production in the private sector, or to a greater use of bureaucratic methods.

public expenditure control (320)
A variety of administrative controls to keep the total of public expenditure within a certain limit, or to keep its rate of growth within a predetermined percentage of its present level. Before **Keynes**, the principal mechanisms for ensuring that public expenditure did not get out of hand were the **gold standard** and the practice of balancing budgets. Since 1945, more direct methods have been used in the periods when **fiscal policy** was used to reduce **aggregate demand** which had increased through the accumulation of large government deficits. In Britain in 1790, the total expenditure of the public authorities was about 12 per cent of **gross national product** and reached a peak of 60 per cent in 1975/6 and started rising again in the 1980s. The volume of public expenditure is determined by many factors which include the growth in per capita income (which increases the demand for both private and public goods), technical change (the advent of the motor car led to a demand for more

and better roads), population growth and change (more schools, hospitals and senior citizens' facilities), the relative cost of **public goods** and urbanization (the cause of congestion which requires an improved infrastructure to remedy it). As modern electorates expect governments to respond to all these changes, controlling public expenditure can be very difficult.

Buchanan, J.M. and Wagner, R. (1977) *Democracy in Deficit: The Political Legacy of Lord Keynes*, New York and London: Academic Press.

See also: **cash limit; Medium-term Financial Strategy**.

Public Expenditure Survey Committee (320)

The UK committee of officials from the Treasury and spending Departments charged with the task of updating public expenditure programmes. It was created as a result of the Plowden Committee's report in 1961 which recommended annual and five-year plans of public expenditure and the resources to finance it. This medium-term method of control extended the nature of expenditure control by the inclusion of figures for spending according to the functions of government.

Lord Plowden (1961) *The Control of Public Expenditure*, London: HMSO, Cmnd 1432.

public finance (320)

The study of the taxing and spending decisions of governments. Taxation is used instead of charging for government services or borrowing. Public expenditure is incurred because governments attempt to improve the distribution of income, to maintain **full employment** and to produce goods and services which the market would not produce (or not produce at low enough prices). At the macro-level, public finance examines the effectiveness of governmental attempts to achieve a tax-spending mix which will achieve simultaneously desired levels of employment, inflation and balance of payments surplus (deficit); at the micro-level, it examines the effects of public expenditure and taxation on allocation and economic behaviour (e.g. labour supply and saving). Although public finance has commanded the attention of writers as early as Hobbes, **Petty** and **Smith**, the subject has now expanded into a broad analysis of the public sector.

Atkinson, A.B. and Stiglitz, J.E. (1980) *Lectures on Public Economics*, Maidenhead, London and New York: McGraw-Hill.

Musgrave, R.A. (1959) *The Theory of Public Finance: A Study in Public Economy*, New York: McGraw-Hill.

—— (1969) *Fiscal Systems*, New Haven, CT: Yale University Press.

See also: **debt policy**.

public good (010, 310)

A commodity or service which is available to everyone in a particular catchment area, cannot be withheld from non-payers and is 'non-rival', i.e. one person's consumption does not diminish that of others. The main examples are national defence, sewerage, street-lighting, lighthouses, public health measures such as mass vaccination and scientific research. As individuals cannot be charged for goods and services collectively provided, it is usual to finance their production by taxation. Although the provision of public goods was small until the twentieth century, writers as early as **Petty**, **Smith** and John Stuart **Mill** argued for their existence. It is not always easy to distinguish between a public and a private good as some private goods gratuitously benefit third parties, e.g. maintaining a garden in a beautiful condition confers pleasure on many people in the vicinity.

See also: **club good; local public good; mixed good; private good**.

public interest company (510)

A proposed type of British **public enterprise** (e.g. telecommunications or gas) substantially owned by private shareholders who have no ultimate control as their shares are without voting rights. The public interest is chiefly represented by regulatory bodies, e.g. **Oftel**, which have the task of monitoring and controlling pricing, investment and standard of service. This form of public enterprise was proposed in the UK by the Labour Party in 1988 as a vehicle for reconverting privatized firms into public sector undertakings, without the expense of re-nationalization.

See also: **nationalized industry**.

public pricing (010, 530)

The pricing of the goods and services produced by **public enterprises**, or the governmental regulation of private sector pricing. Such government intervention is undertaken to prevent the **monopoly** exploitation of consumers, to stabilize **cobweb** markets (especially in agriculture), to provide **merit goods**, to prevent **merit bads** and to achieve a better distribution of incomes and benefits. The methods used include the setting of formulae to determine the prices of public enterprises and regulated **public utilities**, the setting of maximum prices (e.g. rent controls), the provision of free services (e.g. libraries and museums) and the establishment of financial rules (e.g. the interest rates and reserve requirements to be followed by banks).

See also: **prices policy**.

public sector (320)

All organizations at central and lower levels of government together with, in some definitions, firms in which there is at least majority ownership by state or municipal bodies. There is much debate about how to measure the size of the public sector. One method is to add up the number of activities undertaken by governmental organizations; another is to calculate the total volume of its output. But measuring output is a difficult and crude approach: in the case of non-marketed outputs, e.g. defence, it is usual to calculate output by measuring the sum of the value of inputs used which, by ignoring factor productivity, makes the bold assertion that an input increase leads to an output increase. Analysts of public policy increasingly demand more direct measures of output, e.g. in the case of health services, output can be measured directly using the number of patients treated rather than indirectly using the number of staff employed.

public sector balance sheet (320)

This consists of a range of assets (social overhead capital (non-marketable) + equity in public enterprises (partially marketable) + land and mineral assets + net foreign exchange reserves + present value of future tax programme + imputed net value of the government's cash monopoly) and balancing liabilities (net interest-bearing debts in domestic and foreign currencies + stock of high-powered money + present value of social insurance and other entitlements + public sector net worth).

public sector borrowing requirement (310, 320)

The excess of expenditure over receipts of central and local government. In more detail, it can be regarded as finance provided to the public sector by borrowing to provide for current and capital expenditure and for lending to the private sector and overseas. The public sector borrowing requirement (PSBR) is reduced by either cuts in public expenditure or by more stringent controls of existing spending programmes. The concept only became important to British economic policy-making in the 1970s, a period when the PSBR relatively increased: in 1975 it was 19 per cent of total government expenditure and 10 per cent of gross domestic product. Despite the central importance given to the PSBR by many Treasury ministers, it is difficult to achieve a target for it as there can be many changes in the components constituting both revenue and expenditure. British government saving in the 1980s caused the concept to be replaced by **public sector debt repayment**.

Peacock, A.T. and Shaw, G.K. (1981) *The Public Sector Borrowing Requirement*, Buckingham: University College at Buckingham.

public sector debt repayment (320)

UK budget surplus; a negative **public sector borrowing requirement**. A term coined by Chancellor of the Exchequer Nigel Lawson in his UK Budget speech in March 1988.

public service employment (820)

Jobs provided by national, state, regional or local governments to reduce the amount of unemployment. Some are of short duration, a temporary expedient to cope with a recession or to reintroduce to work long-term unemployed persons whose skills have diminished or become obsolete. But the increased role of the state in many countries has expanded the number of publicly financed jobs.

See also: **public works; workfare**.

public spending ratio (320)

Total governmental expenditure as a proportion of the **gross domestic product**.

See also: **public sector**.

public utility (610)
An industry or enterprise providing basic services to the public, such as energy, water, postal services or telephones, which is sometimes owned by the state but even if privately owned (as is often the case in the USA) is usually subject to public regulation. It is argued that because these industries are **natural monopolies** (at least in a local area), a special policy towards them is essential if the public is not to be exploited. Regulatory bodies pay great attention to the prices charge, safety standards and the quality of service of these utilities.

See also: **regulatory capture**.

public works (320)
Schemes financed by central or local government to create employment. Although such recommendations have long been associated with **Keynes**, they have a longer history: the **mercantilists** were in favour of them and the French Government set up national workshops as early as 1848.

See also: **crowding-out**; **Treasury view**.

pump priming (320)
See: **deficit financing**.

punt (430)
The currency of the Republic of Ireland.

purchase tax (320)
A tax levied on the sale of a commodity, often at different rates for different types of goods and services. Persons with a preference for the higher taxed goods suffer discrimination. In the UK, it was replaced by the **value-added tax** in 1973.

See also: **expenditure tax**.

purchasing power parity (430)
An equilibrium exchange rate such that two currencies purchase the same amount of goods and services in the two economies. This theory, first suggested by the **mercantilists**, then eloquently expressed by **Cassel** in 1916, asserts that monetary flows, affecting domestic prices, would continue until parity is achieved. This approach has been criticized for being unrealistic: many goods and services do not enter into international trade and there are many non-market determinants of exchange rates. However, PPP is a more useful way of comparing international living standards than market exchange rates which are more volatile.

Kravis, I.B., Heston, A. and Summers, R. (1978) *A System of International Comparisons of Gross Product and Purchasing Power*, Baltimore, MD: Johns Hopkins University Press.

pure bundling (530)
The sale of goods or services only as part of a joint package deal.

See also: **bundling**; **mixed bundling**.

pure competition (010)
Perfect competition without the assumptions of perfect knowledge and an absence of friction.

pure credit economy (070, 310)
An **economy** which finances all of its transactions with bank loans. An idea attributed to **Wicksell**.

Wicksell, K. (1935) *Lectures on Political Economy*, vol. 2, trans. by E. Classen, London: Routledge & Kegan Paul.

pure discretion (310, 320)
The conduct of an economic policy without following any policy rule.

See also: **rules versus discretion**.

pure economic rent (010)
The permanent return to a factor of production in excess of its **transfer earnings**. This arises from the unique nature of that factor which causes its supply to be **inelastic**. Examples of such factors include land, works of art exhibited at a charge to the public and exceptionally talented persons.

pure inflation (150)
An extreme case of **inflation** such that the prices of all products and **factors of production** are increasing at the same rate.

pure interest rate (310)
The **rate of interest** on a riskless investment.

pure monopoly (010)

A **monopoly** with a demand for its products equal to the whole of consumer expenditure.

pure profit (010)

Profit which is earned from the sale of a good or service after the full **opportunity cost** of employing all **factors of production**, including **normal profit** for the **entrepreneur**, is subtracted from sales revenue.

put option (310)

A right to sell a financial instrument or commodity at the current price within a specified period, normally of three months.

See also: **call option**.

put-through (310)

The simultaneous purchase and sale of a block of securities. This is a cheaper method of dealing for **institutional investors** as there is a smaller margin between buying and selling prices and a lower rate of broker's commission: the broker is prepared to carry out the transaction on more favourable terms because the risk of unsold stock is eliminated. Sometimes it is called a 'block trade'.

pyramiding (520)

Acquiring many small companies to build them into a large **holding company**.

pyramid selling (530)

The sale by companies of goods and services to individuals who then act as retailers, often in their own homes. Goods such as cosmetics and kitchen utensils have been sold in this way. This marketing method, which first appeared in the USA in the late 1940s and in the UK in the 1960s, has often been criticized because of the pressure applied by firms to persuade their agents to buy the goods themselves and to recruit others. Also known as multilevel marketing.

Q

QALY (910)
Quality-adjusted life years.

QR (420)
See: **quantitative restrictions**.

quadriad (310, 320)
The Treasury, the **Council of Economic Advisers**, the **Office of Management and Budget** and the **Federal Reserve**: the key formulators of the USA's economic policy.

quality-adjusted life years (910)
A measure of the efficiency of health services. For each type of medical intervention, e.g. a heart transplant or hip replacement, the cost of the operation/treatment is divided by the expected number of years the patient will benefit after the intervention. Using this approach to evaluating health care, to be efficient means switching resources to medical activities with low QALYs.

See also: **health economics**.

quality circle (830)
An alternative approach to **industrial relations**, enabling workers to participate more in the management of their enterprises.

quantitative restrictions (010, 420)
Quotas, especially on imports and foreign exchange, imposed to reduce a **balance of payments** deficit.

See also: **protection; tariff**.

quantity theory of money (020, 310)
A macroeconomic theory relating the stock of money to the price level. Although discussions of this theory are evident in **mercantilist** writings (especially in John Locke), it is to Irving **Fisher**, **Pigou** and Milton **Friedman** one looks for twentieth-century expositions. The Fisher or Yale equation is

$$MV = P_Y T$$

where T is the total volume of transactions, V is the weighted average velocity of circulation, P_Y is an index representing the weighted average of the prices of the commodities transacted and M is the total quantity of money.

The Cambridge equation, attributed to **Marshall** and **Pigou**, is

$$M = kP_C R$$

where M is the total quantity of money, R is the total resources enjoyed by the community, k is the proportion of those resources which the public desires to hold in the form of money and P_C is an index number which values resources in terms of consumption goods.

Friedman used a more multi-variate approach.

Laidler, D. (1991) *The Golden Age of the Quantity Theory. The Development of Neoclassical Monetary Economics 1870–1914*, Oxford: Philip Alan.
Fisher, I. (1911) *The Purchasing Power of Money*, New York: Macmillan.
Keynes, J.M. (1923) *A Tract on Monetary Reform*, London: Macmillan.
Locke, J. (1823) *Some Considerations of the Lowering of Interest and Raising the Value of Money. Collected Works*, vol. V, London. Original published in 1691.

See also: **monetarism**.

quartile deviation (210)
See: **semi-interquartile range**.

quasi-fixed factor (010)
Labour costs are fixed in that firms invest in hiring and training. Also, statutory protection of employment and changes in employment contracts have made it more difficult to vary the amount of labour employed in the short run, giving it a fixed character.

Oi, W.Y. (1962) 'Labor as a quasi-fixed factor', *Journal of Political Economy* 70: 538–55.

quasi-rent (010)

Marshall so described the income an owner receives from allowing others to use machines and other productive appliances made by man. This return is in excess of the **opportunity cost** of using that piece of **fixed capital**. Marshall proposed the concept as part of his explanation of **profits**.

Quesnay, François, 1694–1774 (030)

The French physician-cum-economist who founded the **Physiocratic** school of economics, the first French school of economics. His position as a court physician to Louis XV made him an influential person, but it was not until his sixties that he wrote on economics. He did so in *Encyclopédie* articles on 'Fermiers' (1756) and 'Grains' (1757) and in subsequent articles on 'Hommes' and 'Impot'. But his *Tableau Economique* (first edition 1758), showing the **circular flow** between landlords, farmers and manufacturers anticipated **input–output analysis** and was to be much admired by Adam **Smith** and **Marx**. Quesnay made economics a major talking point of the day: the salons were fascinated by 'les zigzags', their nickname for the *Tableau*.

Barna, T. (1975) 'Quesnay's Tableau in modern guise', *Economic Journal* 85: 485–96.

Meek, R.L. (1962) *The Economics of Physiocracy*, London: Allen & Unwin.

Vaggi, G. (1987) *The Economics of François Quesnay*, London and Basingstoke: Macmillan.

queuing system (010, 310)

A method of resource allocation which distributes resources on the principle of 'first come first served'. It is used to avoid congestion in many European bond markets and is an alternative to control by a central monetary authority. Potential issuers of bonds are placed in the queue according to the urgency of their financial need, their current credit worthiness and current monetary policy. Countries with this system include Germany and France. In general, queuing can be used as a method of allocation in any market.

quick assets ratio (520, 540)

Liquid assets divided by current liabilities; also known as the 'acid test ratio'. It should be at least 1.

quit rate (820, 830)

The proportion of workers who leave their jobs in a particular time period. This rate is used as a measure of labour turnover.

See also: **exit voice**.

quota (010, 420)

A restriction on the supply of a good or service. Import quotas are used to protect domestic industries; export quotas, to stabilize export earnings. Under any system of rationing, a quota will be the amount allocated to a particular person or organization.

See also: **non-tariff barrier**; **protection**; **tariff**; **voluntary export restraint**.

quoted company (310, 510)

See: **listed company**.

R

r (210)
See: **coefficient of correlation**.

racial discrimination (010, 810, 820)
Treating persons of another race unequally, especially with regard to wages and employment opportunities.

See also: **discrimination**.

Radcliffe Report (310)
A Royal Commission report, published in 1959, on the working of the UK monetary system. It promulgated the view that money is only one asset in the spectrum of **liquidity** and that as its **velocity of circulation** is unstable, the control of it is incidental to interest rate policy. Although opposed to the control of the money supply, given the sophistication of the post-war British financial system, from day to day it was recommended that interest rates should be used rather than credit controls as instruments of monetary policy: this was difficult to achieve given the need for stable interest rates to maintain an orderly **gilts** market.

Committee on the Working of the Monetary System (1959) *Report*, London: HMSO, Cmnd 827.

radical economics (030)
An application of Marxist and socialist theories to the analysis of the problems of advanced **capitalist** countries. The major concerns of radical economists are income inequality, international capitalism in the form of **multinational corporations, de-industrialization, unemployment, market failure**, defence expenditure and the low provision of many **public goods**. The humane concerns of these writers have influenced a great deal of policy-making but have yet to form the basis of a new society and economy in any major country.

Linder, M. (1977) *The Anti-Samuelson*, vols I and II, New York: Urizen Books.
Sawyer, M. (1989) *The Challenge of Political Economy: Radical Alternatives to Neo-Classical Economics*, Hemel Hempstead: Harvester Wheatsheaf.

Rambouillet summit (430)
Economic summit held in France in 1975 at which it was agreed that central banks would coordinate their policies to stabilize currencies. This was the first international monetary agreement after the collapse of the **Bretton Woods** system.

Ramsey prices (010)
Pareto-optimal prices which achieve a required level of profits. These prices maximize the sum of an industry's prices and its **producer's surplus**. The pricing rule Ramsey asserted was that, for a regulated firm (e.g. a **public utility** such as electricity), the excess of price over **marginal cost** will be highest for those goods which have low **elasticities** of demand. This is second-best pricing when first best is not available. It was adopted as a pricing rule by the **Interstate Commerce Commission** in 1985.

Baumol, W.J. and Bradford, D.F. (1970) 'Optimal departures from marginal cost pricing', *American Economic Review* 60: 265–83.

Ramsey saving rule (020)
The rate of saving multiplied by the marginal utility of money should always be equal to the amount by which the total net rate of enjoyment of utility falls short of the maximum possible rate of enjoyment.

Ramsey, F.P. (1928) 'A mathematical theory of saving', *Economic Journal* 38: 543–59.

Ramsey taxes (320)
Taxes which raise a given revenue from proportionate taxes on commodities with the decrease in utility being kept to a minimum. Ramsey suggested that the solution to this problem posed by **Pigou** was to increase tax revenue in the same proportion as the production of the taxed commodities.

Ramsey, F.P. (1927) 'A contribution to the theory of taxation', *Economic Journal* 37: 47–61.

Randall Commission (420, 430)

US commission which reported on foreign economic policy in 1954. It took the view that the policy of the USA should be to guide the world economy back to the liberal policies holding before 1914 – if not in trade, certainly in the movement of private long-term capital and in the convertibility of currencies. The main type of aid proposed by the Commission was technical assistance.

R&D (620)

See: **research and development**.

random variations (210)

Irregular movements in **time series** which can be calculated by dividing the original data by the **trend**, seasonal variations and **cyclical variations**.

random walk theory (310)

A theory concerning successive prices independent of each other in security or commodity markets which asserts that there are no trends in prices with the consequence that today's prices cannot be used to predict future prices. Bachelier was the first to note this, in 1900, in a study of French commodity markets.

Cootner, P.H. (ed.) (1964) *The Random Character of Stock Market Prices*, Cambridge, MA: MIT Press.

See also: **chartism**.

Randstad (730)

A continuous urban area of the Netherlands from Amsterdam to Rotterdam. For centuries, it has been noted for its high population density.

range (210)

The difference between the largest and smallest numbers in a set, e.g. 5 is the range of 2, 3, 4, 5, 6, 7.

See also: **semi-interquartile range**.

rank correlation (210)

The correlation between variables represented by the ranks they have in an ordered list, e.g. the relationship between cities ranked by population size and by average per capita income to see if the larger a city ranks, the greater the average income per capita.

See also: **Spearman's rank correlation formula**.

rank size rule (930)

This states that the population of a city or town in an urban hierarchy of a country is approximately the population of the largest city divided by the rank of the place concerned, e.g. if the largest city has a population of 2,000,000 then the fourth largest city will have 500,000 inhabitants.

Madden, C.H. (1956) 'On some indicators of stability in the growth of cities in the United States', *Economic Development and Cultural Change* 4: 236–52.

ratchet effect (010)

An upward shift in **aggregate demand**. This higher level of consumption and investment is permanent preventing an economy in recession from reverting to a level of output lower than at the beginning of the previous expansion. The **relative income hypothesis** asserts that when incomes are falling, consumption will not fall by the same amount as it will be difficult for households to make a swift adjustment to a new standard of living.

rate of excess demand (010)

See: **excess demand**.

rate of exploitation (010)

See: **surplus value**.

rate of interest (310)

1 The charge for borrowing money, usually measured as the percentage ratio between the sum payable to the lender and the amount borrowed, at an annual rate.

2 The bridge between income and capital.

3 The amount of money contractually promised at certain specified future dates.

Theories of the rate of interest have either explained this factor price as being determined by real forces (productivity and thrift) or monetary forces (the demand for and supply of money). Although **Keynes** took the latter approach, writers as early as the **mercantilists** tended towards monetary explanations. The Judaic, Islamic and Christian religions have often condemned interest charges for exploiting persons who borrow out of necessity. However, interest has been justified on the grounds that, as the lender has to abstain from current consumption to make the loan, he should be compensated.

See also: **Islamic banking; loanable funds theory; usury**.

rate of return (010, 520)

The ratio of the earnings from an asset to the value of that asset, usually expressed as a percentage. Companies calculate this as the ratio of pre-tax profit to the capital employed. Private and social rates of return of **human capital** and of major public investments are often calculated. An alternative measure is the **internal rate of return** which takes into account the timing of earnings.

rate of surplus value (010)

See: **surplus value**.

rates (320)

A tax on non-agricultural property long used in the UK to finance local government expenditure. Periodically, property was revalued on the basis of the expected rental income from property of that type to calculate for its rateable value. Each local authority decided, knowing the total rateable value of all properties in its area, what rate in the pound must be levied to obtain a desired level of revenue. Each property owner paid an amount equal to the rateable value of his property times the rate in the pound. As such local taxation has long been condemned for being full of anomalies, many proposals for reforming it have been made. In 1989 in Scotland and in 1990 in England and Wales, the domestic rate was replaced by the **community charge** (nicknamed 'the poll tax'); in 1990, the **uniform business rate** replaced business rates.

Foster, C.D., Jackman, R.A. and Perlman, M. (1980) *Local Government Finance in a Unitary State*, London: Allen & Unwin.

Layfield Committee (1976) *Local Government Finance. Report on the Committee of Inquiry*, London: HMSO, Cmnd 6453.

rate support grant (320)

An expenditure subsidy previously paid by the British government to local authorities which resulted in less having to be raised by rates (local property tax). This grant on average was equal to about one half of total local government expenditure. Central government, in order to ensure that minimum standards of services, e.g. in education, are maintained, has to provide this subsidy. After the domestic rates were replaced by the **community charge**, the rate support grant was replaced by a **revenue support grant**.

rating agency (310)

See: **bond rating agency**.

ratio analysis (520)

Percentages calculated in financial analysis to discover solvency, **overtrading** and profitability. Financial ratios, using balance sheet data, include **quick**, **current**, **stock** and capital (or earnings) ratios; operating ratios include **turnover** (or sales) ratios and cost ratios. The most important measure of overall profitability is the ratio of profit before tax to operating assets.

rational decision (010)

A choice which best serves a decision-maker in pursuit of a particular objective.

rational expectations (020)

A view of how individuals form their **expectations** of the future values of economic variables first advanced by Muth in 1961 and now a central pillar of **new classical economics**. Individuals when making decisions, it is assumed, have all relevant information, including knowledge of the structure of the economic system, and that any errors in the analysis of that information are attributable to random forces. This approach has been used to analyse asset markets, the **business cycle** and the **natural rate of unemployment**. There have been many criticisms of rational expectations, including questions about the assumption of rationality, the recurrence of economic processes and the adequacy of information.

Attfield, C.L.F., Demery, D. and Duck, N.W. (1985) *Rational Expectations in Macroeconomics*, Oxford: Basil Blackwell.

Begg, D.K.H. (1982) *The Rational Expectations Revolution in Macroeconomics: Theories and Evidence*, Oxford: Philip Alan.

Muth, J.F. (1961) 'Rational expectations and the theory of price movements', *Econometrica* 29: 315–35.

Pesaran, M.H. (1987) *The Limits to Rational Expectations*, Oxford: Basil Blackwell.

rationing (010)

A method of allocating a limited supply which consists of the person or organization in control of a fixed or given supply of a factor of production, good or service distributing parts of that supply to individual consumers, often on the basis of set criteria or queuing. Although the price system will ensure that a supply is assigned to the highest bidders, governments are reluctant to use such a method for essential goods. In socialist economies (and in other economies under the strain of conducting a war) extensive use is always made of rationing by the issue of vouchers and coupons which must be exchanged to obtain goods and services.

See also: **queuing system**.

raw data (210)

Data which has not yet been arranged in numerical order.

See also: **frequency distribution**.

Rawlsian difference principle (020, 160)

The toleration of inequalities only if it is to the advantage of the worse-off through making him/her as well off as possible in terms of rights, freedoms, opportunities, income and wealth. Also, inequalities must provide economic incentives to work harder and increase production.

See also: **egalitarianism**; **Rawlsian justice**.

Rawlsian justice (020)

1 A revival of social contract theory with general application to basic social and political institutions.

2 Anti-meritocratic **egalitarianism**.

3 A non-utilitarian approach to justice.

The view that justice is 'fairness' based on two principles. Firstly, that each person is entitled to the most extensive amount of liberty compatible with the liberty of others. Secondly, that the arrangement of social and economic inequalities is such that they are reasonably expected to be to everyone's advantage and attached to positions and offices open to all.

Daniels, N. (ed.) (1975) *Critical Studies on Rawls' 'A Theory of Justice'*, Oxford: Basil Blackwell.
Rawls, J. (1972) *A Theory of Justice*, Oxford: Oxford University Press.

See also: **utilitarianism**.

RD (310)

Reserve deposits of a bank.

RD and D (620)

Research, development and demonstration: the extension of **research and development** to the stage of producing a commercial prototype.

RE (010)

See: **rational expectations**.

reaction function (210)

This shows the preferences of decision-makers as revealed by an analysis of their actions. These functions have been used to study both economic policy-making by governments and the behaviour of non-collusive **oligopolists**.

Theil, H. (1964) *Optimal Decision Rules for Government and Industry*, Amsterdam: North-Holland; Chicago, IL: Rand McNally.

Reaganomics (320)

An application of **supply-side economics** to the running of the US economy in the 1980s which attempted to stimulate the economy. It consisted of a set of policies which included the reduction of taxes, of governmental regulation of business, of governmental interference in the market and a switch in federal expenditure so that more was spent on defense and less on social programs. The principles of Reaganomics were forcefully enunciated by the US **Council of Economic Advisers** in the *Economic Report of the President to the Congress* of February, 1982.

Boskin, M. (1989) *Reagan and the Economy*, San Francisco, CA: Institute for Contemporary Studies.
Niskanen, W.A. (1988) *Reaganomics: An Insider's Account of the Policies and the People*, New York: Oxford University Press.

See also: **Thatcherism**.

real balance effect (010)

A change in the aggregate demand for goods resulting from a change in the quantity of real money balances. This effect was noted by both **Pigou** and **Patinkin**. The effect asserts that unemployment causes a fall in prices, a rise in the real value of people's money holdings, a rise in aggregate demand and thus full employment. As this effect takes years to operate, the Keynesian 'unemployment equilibrium' is better regarded most of the time as disequilibrium. It should be contrasted with the **Keynes effect**.

Patinkin, D. (1956) *Money, Interest and Prices: An Integration of Monetary and Value Theory*, New York: Oxford University Press.

real bills doctrine (030, 310)
Adam **Smith**'s doctrine that there can never be an inflationary excess issue of **commercial bills** and other paper money because each bill represents a real transaction. Henry Thornton, in his *Paper Credit* (1802) criticized the doctrine for ignoring the fact that the same sum of money can support many bills.

See also: **Banking School; law of reflux.**

real economy of scale (010)
A reduction in the **average cost** of production as a result of an increase in output of the factory or enterprise.

real estate investment trust (310)
A trust which manages real estate assets in the form of equities and mortgages and is financed by stock, bond and bill issues and loans from financial institutions. The high **leverage** of these trusts led to many of them going bankrupt in the 1970s.

real exchange rate (430)
A **currency**'s value in terms of its real purchasing power. A basket of goods and services representative of an average consumer's purchasing is valued in the two currencies. This calculation is often made to show the relative cost of living for executives moving between the major cities of the world or to establish the real value of investment projects.

See also: **purchasing power parity**.

real growth (110)
An increase in the output of goods and

services measured at constant prices, i.e. after price changes have been eliminated.

real income (010)
1 Money income adjusted by the amount of inflation experienced by that person or organization over a given period. A **price index** is used to deflate money income. If, e.g. prices have risen by 10 per cent and money incomes by the same amount, real income will remain constant.

2 The amount of goods and services which can be purchased with a given money income.

real interest rate (310)
1 The money **rate of interest** adjusted by the rate of inflation. When there is a positive real interest rate, increased savings will be encouraged and investment discouraged; negative real rates will make borrowing more attractive. Real interest rates are zero when the money rate of interest is equal to the rate of inflation. The high real interest rates of the British and US economies in the 1980s were regarded as a major cause of low industrial investment in some years. Because of their effect on profit margins, high real interest rates are, in a sense, equivalent to administered price controls.

The real rate is calculated by the formula

$$\frac{100 + x}{100 \times y} \times 100 - 100$$

where x is the nominal rate of interest and y is the percentage rate of inflation.

2 The interest rate measured in goods.

See also: **own rate of interest.**

real price (010)
1 The nominal price of a good divided by a price index.

2 A relative price showing how much of one good exchanges for other goods. These prices show economic scarcity as they make possible a comparison between the price increases of particular commodities and of all commodities in general.

real property tax (320)
A tax based on the value of buildings and land. Such taxes are known as **rates** in the UK; in the USA as property taxes.

real rate of return (520)

The rate of return to capital assets after allowing for inflation. This rate, used as a target for British nationalized industries in a White Paper of 1978, was intended to be related to the real rate of return on private sector assets, taking into account the cost of finance, social time preference and the social objectives set for that particular industry.

real-wage hypothesis (020)

The view that real wages are inflexible downwards. This is a considerable expansion of Keynes's assumption that money wages are inflexible downwards.

real wages (820)

1 Money wages adjusted for inflation. Real wages can only increase if money wages rise faster than inflation.

2 The amount of goods and services a money wage can purchase.

recession (140)

A phase of the **business cycle** which succeeds a **boom** and precedes a trough; a six-month fall in **gross domestic product** according to the **National Bureau of Economic Research** of Washington, DC. The principal indicators of this are falling output and rising **unemployment**.

recessionary gap (010)

See: **deflationary gap**.

RECHAR (940)

'Reconversion charbon': a **European Community** scheme introduced in 1990 to help the revitalization of areas hit by coalpit closures.

reciprocal demand law (420)

A refinement of the law of **comparative advantage** which was used to determine the **terms of trade** between countries according to the relative demand measured in the amount of goods offered for the goods of another country. John Stuart **Mill** in his first essay of his collection *Essays on Some Unsettled Questions of Political Economy* (1844) and **Torrens** refined Ricardian international trade theory in this way.

Reciprocal Trade Agreements Act 1934 (420)

US federal trade statute of the Roosevelt Administration which attempted to undo the **protectionism** of the **Smoot–Hawley Tariff Act** by authorizing the President to negotiate bilateral, reciprocal trade agreements to reduce the tariffs introduced in 1930. The powers under this Act were regularly extended for further three-year periods by Congress.

recognition lag (010, 310, 320)

The length of time which elapses before an economic decision-maker is aware of a change in economic circumstances. This can occur because economic statistics take time to collect and are published less frequently than a decision-maker needs.

See also: **implementation lag**.

recognized professional body (310)

An institution regulating part of the UK financial sector, recognized by the **Financial Services Act** 1986. These are institutions, such as the Institute of Chartered Accountants, which are not involved in trading but in other investment services.

See also: **self-regulatory organization**.

reconciliation bill (320)

See: **appropriation bill**.

recontract (010)

Edgeworth's notion that buyers and sellers initially make provisional contracts at **disequilibrium prices** then subsequently, as a result of their exchange, make a new contract at, or approaching, an equilibrium price.

Walker, D.A. (1973) 'Edgeworth's theory of recontract', *Economic Journal* 83: 138–49.

See also: *tâtonnement*.

recovery (140)

The phase in a **business cycle**, after a **slump** and before a **boom**, in which output is rising and, often, unemployment is falling.

rectification (060)

Cuba's campaign for greater efficiency. This can be compared with the USSR's **perestroika**.

recurrent spot contracting (820)

See: **employment contract**.

recursive system (210)
A system of econometric equations such that if we know the values of variables up to the time $t-1$ we can obtain their values at time t. Systems of this kind demonstrate unilateral causal dependence.

recycling (430, 720)
The re-use of scarce raw materials, especially paper, glass and metals; the distribution of financial reserves from creditor to debtor countries. After the **Organization of Petroleum Exporting Countries'** price increases of 1973–4, the surpluses of the oil producers were lent on Euromarkets to poor countries, particularly of the Third World, helping to accelerate the **world debt problem**.

Red Book (320)
See: **Financial Statement and Budget Report**.

redemption date (310)
The date by which a fixed-term stock must be repaid by the government, company or corporation which has issued it.

redemption yield (310)
The yield on a stock repayable by a fixed date which includes both the interest on that stock and the capital gain if the current price is less than the redemption price. A net redemption yield adjusts the yield for income and capital gains taxes payable.

redlining (930)
1 Giving an area the status of a slum by making it ineligible for mortgage finance. Once this status has been given, redlining accelerates the decline of such areas. This has occurred in several US urban areas, including parts of New York City.

2 Refusing to grant credit because the lender cannot obtain a required return at any rate of interest.

reduced form equation (210)
An equation which has been manipulated to show each **endogenous** variable as the function of the set of **exogenous** and, if present, error terms.

reference cycle (140, 220)
The basic series of economic statistics, e.g.

gross national product or industrial output, which is chosen to indicate fluctuations in an economy.

See also: **coincident indicators**; **economic indicators**; **lagging indicator**; **leading indicator**.

refuge capital (430)
See: **capital flight**; **hot money**.

refunding (310)
Issuing new government securities to replace bonds or other securities which have matured.

See also: **overfunding**.

regional banking pacts (310)
US banking agreements used to overcome restrictive banking legislation which banned interstate commercial banking to create, in effect, interstate banks. The first pacts were between neighbouring states, e.g. in New England, excluding **money centre banks**.

regional economics (940)
The analysis of firms' location decisions and the causes of regional growth. Economists, with geographers, have the same analytical foundations in the works of von **Thünen** and Losch. It is mainly in times of high national growth that there can be a great deal of attention paid to regional imbalances.

Armstrong, H. and Taylor, J. (1985) *Regional Economics and Policy*, Oxford: Philip Allan.
Isard, W. (1965) *Methods of Regional Analyses: An Introduction to Regional Science*, Cambridge, MA: MIT Press; New York: Wiley.
Nijkamp, P. and Mills, E.S. (1986–7) *Handbook of Regional and Urban Economics*, 2 vols, Amsterdam and New York: North-Holland.

See also: **economic geography**.

regional employment premium (320, 940)
UK wage subsidy to firms in depressed regions which was in force from 1967 to 1977. Initially, it was a subsidy of £1.50 per man per week, with lower rates for women and juveniles.

regional multiplier (940)
The number of times the income or employ-

ment of a region will multiply as a consequence of an increase in autonomous expenditures.

Two approaches are often used: the economic base multiplier and the modified Keynesian approach. The economic base approach assumes that regional income can be divided into two parts – what arises from the **basic industries** of the region and what springs from other regional industries. This multiplier is then calculated as $1/(1-s)$ with s the ratio of income earned in the non-basic sector to total regional income, i.e. the regional multiplier is

$$\frac{1}{1 - (1 - t)(c - m)}$$

with t the income tax rate, c the marginal propensity to consume and m the marginal propensity to import. There are many problems in calculating this multiplier, including the fact that basic industries may vary greatly in the extent to which they export to other regions. The Keynesian approach merely applies a national multiplier formula to a region. A multiplier for a particular region is usually smaller than that for the national economy of which it is part as regions are more open, thus suffering from leakages of expenditures to other regions.

regional policy (940)

1 Measures to reduce the imbalance in prosperity between the regions of a particular country, particularly between the region around the capital city and the peripheral provinces.

2 Government aid to especially deprived cities, inner cities and other relatively small parts of a country.

Many countries have used incentives to encourage the location of expanding industries in the depressed regions and to reduce the **population density** of major cities, e.g. in the UK there has been a succession of measures since 1929 to subsidize the geographical mobility of labour, the building of factories, the training of workers and the payment of rates. Regional policies are measured by the number of jobs created in depressed regions and by the extent of convergence in interregional incomes, unemployment rates and rates of output growth. Regional policy is most active in times of

fast national economic growth as it is then easier to finance assistance to regions.

Diamond, D.R. and Spence, N.A. (1983) *Regional Policy Evaluation: A Methodological Review and the Scottish Example*, Aldershot: Gower Press.

Folmer, H. (1986) *Regional Economic Policy: The Measurement of its Effect*, Dordrecht and Lancaster: Nijhoff.

See also: **enterprise zone; growth pole**.

regional selective assistance (940)

UK government subsidization of capital and training costs of projects under the Industrial Development Act 1984, which aimed to create or maintain employment in designated depressed areas. As many projects were of a capital-intensive nature with little impact on local employment this programme has been managed increasingly carefully.

regional wage bargaining (830)

Wage negotiations for an industrial or occupational group covering workers in part, and not whole, of a country. This departure from national wage bargaining is popular with many employers as it enables pay to reflect more closely local labour market conditions; unions have often objected to this as it gives rise to regional wage differentials thus departing from the hallowed union tradition of setting the same pay for all workers of the same occupation or industry.

regression (210)

See: **least squares method; linear regression**.

regression curve (210)

See: **least squares method**.

regressive expectations (010)

Expectations that the value of an economic variable, e.g. the price level, will be a weighted average of its present and past values.

See also: **adaptive expectations; rational expectations**.

regressive tax (320)

One which falls disproportionately on lower income groups. As **income** decreases, the average rate of tax increases. Many **indirect taxes**, e.g. **excise duties** and sales taxes, are regarded as regressive but the extent to which they are depends on the consumption patterns of different income groups. **Poll taxes** are the simplest case of regression.

regret (020)

The difference between an actual **pay-off** and the pay-off which would have resulted from choosing the correct strategy when making decisions under **uncertainty**. Under a **minimax** strategy, the aim is to minimize the maximum regrets.

Loomes, G. and Sugden, R. (1982) 'Regret theory: an alternative theory of rational choice under uncertainty', *Economic Journal* 92: 805–24.

regulated firm (510)

A firm subject to detailed government regulation of its pricing and investment decisions. **Public utilities** are often controlled in this way because the goods and services they provide constitute a major part of the costs of all firms and a high percentage of the consumption expenditure of households.

regulation (010, 610)

Partial or complete intervention in the economic decision-making of a firm or other economic institution by the government or one of its agencies. The usual justification for this departure from free market principles is **market failure**. The major forms of intervention include **consumer protection**, the creation of **public enterprises** to run industries which are **natural monopolies** and the fixing of prices.

Bailey, E.E. (ed.) (1987) *Public Regulation: New Perspectives on Institutions and Policies*, Cambridge, MA: MIT Press.
Kahn, A.E. (1988) *The Economics of Regulation: Principles and Institutions*, 2 vols, New York: Wiley.
Stigler, G.J. (1971) 'The theory of economic regulation', *Bell Journal of Economics and Management Science* 2: 3–21.
Utton, M.A. (1986) *The Economics of Regulating Industry*, Oxford: Basil Blackwell.

See also: **regulatory capture**.

Regulation D (310)

An arbitrary rule of the US **Federal Reserve** System which classified bank deposits held for less than thirty days as **demand deposits**. This regulation was modified in 1980 when this classification of demand deposits conflicted with the new type of **time deposit** which has a minimum maturity of fourteen days. The regulation is subject to the requirement that banks keep to a required reserve ratio.

Regulation K (310, 430)

A regulation of the US **Federal Reserve System** which governs the international banking operations of US commercial banks and is reviewed every five years to ensure that these banks remain internationally competitive.

Regulation Q (310)

The ceiling to the rate of interest which US **commercial banks** could pay on deposits of less than thirty days maturity in the period 1933 to 1985. This maximum rate was fixed from time to time by the US **Federal Reserve System**. One of the aims of the regulation was to reduce the cost of housing finance as **thrifts** would be able to operate with low interest rates. As the regulation was evaded by bankers borrowing abroad to replace domestic deposits, the growth of the **Eurodollar** market was encouraged and much **disintermediation** occurred. In 1980, it was decided to phase out the regulation over a five-year period.

Regulation School (030)

A group of French economic thinkers founded in the 1970s and centred on Paris and Grenoble consisting of Michel Aglietta, Robert Boyer and Alain Lipietz. It derives its inspiration from the French philosopher Louis Althusser. Recognizing the success of **Fordism**, it advocates local government economic strategies to promote employment and revive industry.

Regulation U (310)

US banking regulation issued by the US **Federal Reserve System** under the Securities Exchange Act 1934 to limit the amount a commercial bank can lend to its customers for the purchase or holding of securities. The aim of this regulation was to reduce speculation in stock markets.

regulatory agency (610)
A governmental organization at national/federal or state/local level which has the task of supervising the decision-making of firms in a particular industry. These agencies approve price increases, as well as monitoring the quality of service and other matters of concern to consumers. There are many in the USA, especially for energy, water and transportation industries; in the UK, several ministries have the task of regulating public enterprises, e.g. the Home Office has powers over the British Broadcasting Corporation.

regulatory capture (010, 610)
The perversion of the aims of a regulatory agency by one of the organizations it is supposed to control, e.g. if a large corporation is able to evade **antitrust** policy. An organization can acquire power over the agency supposed to supervise it by using political influence, having superior technical knowledge or by the interchange of personnel.

reinsurance (630)
Spreading an insurance risk by making a treaty with other insurance companies to accept part of the risk in return for a share of premium income, hence this has been described as 'insuring the insurer'. Large assets such as ships and aircraft could not be insured if reinsurance were not available.

re-intermediation (310)
The return to the use of banks and other financial intermediaries after a period in which individuals and companies directly financed each other.

See also: **disintermediation**.

REIT (310)
See: **real estate investment trust**.

relative concentration (210)
A measure of the distribution of economic activity, or of values of an economic variable, using **Lorenz curves** and **Gini coefficients**. This is used to examine the distribution of the size of firms and the size of individual incomes.

relative income hypothesis (020)
Duesenberry's theory of the **consumption** function that consumption is a function of current income relative to income in preceding time periods and relative to the income of households which are regarded as models to follow. The theory was used to reconcile a conflict between time series and cross-section evidence.

Duesenberry, J. (1949) *Income, Saving and the Theory of Consumer Behavior*, Cambridge, MA: Harvard University Press.

relative price (010)
The price of one good expressed in terms of another, rather than money. The relative price of apples can be expressed in terms of oranges if a consumer has a choice between consuming either apples or oranges from a given income. Relative prices can be expressed by the slope of a **budget line**.

See also: **opportunity cost**; **price**.

relative surplus value (010)
See: **surplus value**.

remittance (130, 430)
A sum of money transferred to another person. A major type of remittance is a transfer to a relative or friend, often by a migrant worker to his/her family. For poor countries and poor agricultural regions, remittances can be a major source of income.

renewable resource (720)
A natural resource which, because of its biological nature, is self-renewing, e.g. game, fish, woodland. A greater yield can be obtained from it by growing it in an artificial environment as, e.g. in a fish farm.

See also: **non-renewable resource**.

Rengo (830)
Japanese labour union federation created in November 1987 through the merger of **Domei** and **Churitsuroren**. By 1989, it had 5.4 million members of whom 2.8 million were in manufacturing and 1 million were in transport.

See also: **enterprise union**; **Sohyo**.

rent (010, 710)
The charge made by the owner of property to another person who wishes to use it. From

Petty onwards, it was recognized that the amount of rent would vary according to the location and fertility of land: **Anderson** and **Ricardo** refined this view into a **differential theory of rent**. Without the private ownership of property, rent would not be paid – although in the public sector an imputed rent for the use of land and buildings is often charged in order to take into account the full cost of using factors of production.

See also: **economic rent**.

rental payment (010)
The payment for the use of a factor of production. Such payments are common in the hire of capital equipment but, in a sense, the concept applies to labour as wages are paid for labour services, not for the purchase of the worker as would be the case in slavery.

rentier (010)
A person whose income is entirely derived from the ownership of financial capital or other property. **Keynes** in his *General Theory* forecast the disappearance of this class of persons through an abundance of capital reducing its return to zero.

rent seeking (010)
Monopolizing activity. This is much criticized as it produces a social waste rather than a social surplus.

REP (320, 940)
See: **regional employment premium**.

repackaging (310)
Selling a portion of a bond issue by re-issuing it as a different type of security which will appeal to another part of the market, e.g. re-issuing a fixed rate bond as a **floating rate note**.

replacement cost (540)
The current value of an asset measured by how much it would cost to be replaced. This is a more accurate measure of the value of an asset than **historic cost**.

replacement investment (520)
Investment undertaken to keep a capital stock intact which is equal to the amount of capital which has depreciated. In **national income** accounting, net investment + replacement investment = gross investment.

See also: **depreciation; net investment**.

replacement labour force (810)
The use of migrant labour to fill job vacancies created by the movement of indigenous workers from areas of decline to the more prosperous regions of a country. In the UK, e.g. immigrant labour in the 1950s took up employment in declining areas, especially Northern England and the West Midlands, where inferior jobs existed as a consequence of the shift of British workers to the southeast of England.

replacement ratio (810, 910)
1 The ratio of welfare benefits paid to the unemployed to the average after-tax earnings of people in work.

2 The ratio of a pensioner's social security benefits and other **transfer incomes** to pre-retirement income. These ratios are measured to see either if they are so generous as to discourage persons from working or too low so that pensioners suffer a very large income loss.

REPO (310)
See: **repurchase agreement**.

representative firm (010, 610)
A term coined by **Marshall** to denote a firm which is characteristic of a particular industry or sector. It is the average firm, with 'a fairly long life, and fair success, which is managed with normal ability, and which has normal access to the economies, external and internal, which belong to that aggregate volume of production'. It is not to be equated simply with the **optimum firm** except, perhaps, in the sense of being the firm most likely to survive.

See also: **economy of scale**.

reproduction (010)
A new cycle of production created by a given amount of capital. Simple accumulation is a cycle with no accumulation; expanded reproduction, when accumulation is more than zero; contracted reproduction when accumulation is less than zero. This is a term popular with Marxian economists.

repurchase agreement (310)

A finance method used by the **Bank of England** and the **Federal Reserve Banks** of the USA to give banks and other financial institutions extra liquidity by buying government securities for a short period, usually a day, the borrower agreeing to repurchase at a stated price. It is very popular with financial institutions as a means of maintaining their inventories of securities at a low cost.

reputational equilibrium (150)

That rate of price **inflation** at which the benefit to a monetary authority from reneging from a monetary policy rule equals the cost of reneging, measured by future loss of reputation.

Backus, D. and Driffill, J. (1985) 'Inflation and reputation', *American Economic Review* 75: 530–8.

Barro, R.J. and Gordon, D.B. (1983) 'Rules, discretion and reputation in a model of monetary policy', *Journal of Monetary Economics* 12: 101–21.

reputation capital (520)

An intangible asset of a firm which is created by the making of implicit promises, e.g. to maintain a particular level of product quality or to give its workers permanent employment. A firm gains from not making such promises explicit terms of its contracts as it has the flexibility of not having to keep to that undertaking in extreme circumstances and from employees monitoring their own conduct because of the advantages to them of their firm having capital of this kind.

MaCaulay, S. (1963) 'Non-contractual relations in business', *American Sociological Review* 28: 55–69.

See also: **goodwill; intangible wealth**.

required rental on capital (010)

The rental which is equal to the **opportunity cost** of owning the capital.

required reserve ratio (310)

Ratio of reserve assets to total deposits of a bank or other regulated financial institution set by a central bank. For UK clearing banks the ratio was set at 12½ per cent in the period 1971–81, after which the proportion of reserves they have to hold is more at their own discretion.

resale price maintenance (530, 610)

A **restrictive practice** of manufacturers who insist on supplying goods subject to the condition that the goods are sold at recommended prices. By 1938 in the UK at least a third of consumer expenditure was on goods subject to this rule. In 1956, collective enforcement of RPM was outlawed by the Restrictive Trade Practices Act; in 1964, the Resale Prices Act made individual enforcement illegal, unless the class of goods was exempted by the Restrictive Practices Court. A major type of good still subject to RPM is books under the Net Book Agreement. As there was so much evasion of RPM before 1964 through discounting, stamp schemes and violation of manufacturers' recommendations by the large supermarket chains, it was difficult to measure the effects of abolishing RPM on retail distribution. In the USA, since 1940 it has been outlawed at the federal level as a violation of the **Sherman** and **Federal Trade Commission Acts** and also under state fair trade laws. The most that manufacturers legally can do is to 'suggest' to retailers an appropriate retail price and reinforce that suggestion by printing it on the packaging.

See also: **competition policy**.

rescheduling of debt (430)

The conversion of short-term debt into long-term debt negotiated by countries or companies finding it difficult to repay debt when payment is due. Countries reschedule their debt by applying to the Paris Club.

See also: **Group of Ten; Third World debt problem**.

research and development (620)

The activity of inventing new processes and products and applying them in industry, especially those which are science based and dependent for their survival and long-term growth on **innovation**. The study of this is often termed 'the economics of science'. Globally, much of R & D is concentrated in the USA because of large space and defence expenditures contracted out by federal agencies to private corporations and universities. Since 1890 larger industrial corporations, e.g. in the electrical industry, have conducted research in their own laboratories. Research based in Europe is on a much smaller scale, although many schemes are being introduced to increase Europe's R & D activity. In the **European Community**, to encourage R & D reciprocal arrangements are negotiated with the USA to open public purchasing to European cooperation; joint ventures are established and national government research grants are refused to non-European high technology companies in competition with European enterprises.

HMSO (annual) *Annual Review of Government Funded Research and Development* (UK).
Rosenberg, N. (ed.) (1971) *The Economics of Technological Change: Selected Readings*, Harmondsworth: Penguin.

research programme (030)

A cluster of interconnected theories constituting the principal ideas of a group of economists who have agreed on certain basic assumptions, e.g. **New Classical** economists. Lakatos is particularly associated with this approach to economic methodology.

Lakatos, I. and Musgrave, A. (eds) (1972) *Criticism and the Growth of Knowledge*, Cambridge: Cambridge University Press.

See also: **economic methodology**.

reservation price (010)

The minimum price a seller will accept; the maximum a buyer will offer. Reservation prices commonly occur in **auctions**.

reservation wage (820)

The minimum wage a worker is prepared to accept. The magnitude of this wage will depend on a worker's previous wages. In job search, a worker will continue to seek job offers until a job at or above the reservation wage is offered.

See also: **minimum supply price of labour**.

reserve army of labour (810)

The Marxian description of the unemployed portion of the labour force. It was **Marx**'s view that, under **capitalism, capital–labour** ratios would increase and that capitalists would need an excess supply of labour to keep down money wage rates. However, it is the experience of some countries, e.g. the UK, for both real wages and unemployment to rise.

reserve assets (310)

Cash and highly liquid monetary assets required to be held by financial institutions, especially banks, under the rules of a **central bank**. In the UK these have been defined as balances with the **Bank of England** (other than **special deposits**), **treasury bills**, company tax reserve certificates, some local authority and commercial bills and British government stocks with less than one year to maturity; in the USA required reserves take the form of vault cash and deposits with Federal Reserve Banks. From 1971 to 1981 in the UK, under the rules set out in the **Competition** and **Credit Control** statement of 1971, banks, and several other financial institutions, were required to observe a ratio of reserve assets of 12½ per cent. Reserve requirements can be imposed in the USA by the Board of Governors of the **Federal Reserve System**.

reserve base (310)

The high-powered money of the banking system. A central bank requires a certain proportion of cash or near-cash assets to be held: this forms the basis for the creation of bank deposits.

See also: **monetary base**; **money multiplier**.

reserve currency (430)

A **currency** widely used for the financing of international trade; it is held as an alternative to gold or **special drawing rights** of the **International Monetary Fund**. The most popular currency is the dollar: as a percentage of official holdings of foreign exchange of all countries in 1988, the US dollar accounted for 54.5%, compared to **sterling** 15%, the yen 6.7% and the DM 1.6%. In the past, the greater role of sterling as a reserve currency put a tremendous strain on the British economy as the volatility of sterling balances made it more difficult to keep the pound at its fixed parity.

Group of Thirty (1982) *Reserve Currencies in Transition*, New York: Group of Thirty.
Grubel, H. (1984) *International Monetary System*, 4th edn, Harmondsworth: Penguin Books.

reserve ratio (310)

See: **cash–deposits ratio**; **required reserve ratio**.

reserve requirements (310)

The proportion of the total assets of a **commercial bank**, or other deposit-taking institution, which a central bank insists should be kept in cash or short-term securities, usually with less than two years to maturity. Altering reserve requirements is a means of expanding or contracting the total money supply of an economy. In the USA, reserve requirements were instituted as early as the First Bank of the United States; in the twentieth century they were in force from 1913 to 1980. Reserves could be held in vault cash, a balance kept at a reserve bank or at a member bank which keeps reserves at the **Federal Reserve**.

In the USA after the implementation of the **Monetary Control Act** various reserve requirements have been set: for net transaction accounts, 3 per cent of deposits (12 per cent for deposits over \$40.4 million); for non-personal time deposits, 3 per cent if maturity of less than 1½ years (zero if greater maturity) and 3 per cent on Eurocurrency liabilities.

resident population (840)

See: *de jure* population.

residualization (930)

Downgrading the status of a public asset or part of a population so that only the poorest members of society can benefit. This can happen if health care and public sector housing are offered only to the lowest income groups of a nation.

Resolution Trust Corporation (310)

US federal government's liquidation agency set up in 1989 with the task of winding up hundreds of bankrupt **thrifts**. It is supervised by the **Federal Deposit Insurance Corporation** and funded by federal government grants and bond issues.

resource economics

The economic analysis of environmental issues, especially exhaustible resources, energy and pollution. As early as 1866 **Jevons** in writing of an impending coal shortage applied economic reasoning to the study of resources. However, it was particularly **Pigou**'s discussion of the costs of pollution in his pioneering work on **welfare economics** and Hotelling's seminal article on the principles concerning exhaustible resources which provided the analytical stimulus which set this subject going. Today, this branch of economics relies on the concept of **externalities** and **cost–benefit analysis** and provides recommendations for many forms of economic regulation.

Hotelling, H. (1931) 'The economics of exhaustible resources', *Journal of Political Economy* 39 (April): 137–75.

Norton, G.A. (1984) *Resource Economics*, London: Edward Arnold.

Peterson, F.M. and Fisher, A.C. (1977) 'The exploitation of extractive resources: a survey', *Economic Journal* 87: 681–721.

restrictive practice (610)

An anti-competitive practice of a firm, a group of firms or a **trade (labor) union** usually to restrict supply with a view to increasing that organization's income. Firms can do this in many ways, e.g. by practising **resale price maintenance**, by collusion to fix common prices and share out a market or by **price leadership**. **Trade unions**, particularly of the craft type, can restrict labour supply in the long term by agreeing with employers to limit the numbers of apprenticeships and in the short term by **strikes**. Labour restrictive practices can also take the form of minimum manning levels which, although increasing the number of hours of labour supplied, increase wages at the expense of profits. The **competition policy** of many industrialized countries has attacked firms carrying out these practices; trade union and industrial relations legislation has played a smaller role than employers in eliminating labour restrictive practices.

See also: **craft union**; **demarcation**.

reswitching (010)

Returning to the use of a production technique previously abandoned when its rate of return was too low because now the rate of return to the technique subsequently used has fallen lower. **Sraffa** in his *Production of Commodities by Means of Commodities*

(1960), identified this as a problem for capital theory arising from the heterogeneity of capital.

retail bank (310)
A bank attracting deposits from the general public and offering a wide range of services, including transfer of funds, personal loans, investment advice, insurance and foreign exchange. It is to be contrasted with a **wholesale bank**.

retail price index (220)
The British index of consumer prices, previously known as the cost of living index. By a monthly repricing of a bundle of goods and services representative of an average consumer's expenditure, it shows how much the price level has increased. The prices of more than 600 goods and services on sale in 180 towns are collected; data from the **Family Expenditure Survey** is also used. The **weights** used are 17.5 per cent for housing, 15.4 per cent for food and 4.2 per cent for local domestic taxation. Its emphasis on consumer prices makes it a crucial indicator of the welfare effects of inflation and is of central importance to wage negotiators. In the UK, there were changes of the base in 1974 and 1987. The inclusion of mortgage payments and local taxation is unusual by international standards.

See also: **consumer price index**; **headline rate of inflation**; **Laspeyres index**; **Paasche index**.

retained earnings (310, 520)
The **accounting profits** of a firm after tax and other charges which, instead of being distributed to shareholders or its other owners, are kept as an asset available for investment in working and fixed capital. When these earnings are used, the cost of using this form of finance is the rate of interest forgone by not employing them outside the firm.

retirement age (810, 840)
The age at which a person finally leaves the labour force. This is mainly determined by the employment and pensions legislation of a country. In developed countries it is between 60 and 65; in socialist countries 60 for males and 55 for females; in developing countries between 50 and 60 years. Uruguay has the most generous scheme: men can retire after thirty years of work and women after twenty-five, receiving a pension equal to 100 per cent of the wage rate received in the five years since reaching the age of 50. Equal opportunities legislation has led to a convergence between male and female retirement ages. Before 1900, the retirement age of workers was less of an issue as life expectancy was much lower and the provision of pensions unusual.

retrophobia (810)
Fear of going back to work and coping with the changes, including recently installed technology which have occurred during one's absence. This problem particularly afflicts women after a mid-career break.

returns to scale (010)
The change in output resulting from an increase in the quantities of factor inputs employed. Returns to scale can be shown by their effect on long-run average costs (LRAC). They can be increasing (output growing faster than inputs), constant (inputs and output increasing at the same rate) or decreasing (output growing at a slower rate than inputs). The returns which are most characteristic of a particular economy will determine whether it is growing, stationary or in decline. Central to **classical** economics was the assertion that there are diminishing returns to land. Allyn **Young**, **Sraffa** and Joan **Robinson** in their post-Marshallian study of the firm examined the implications of increasing returns.

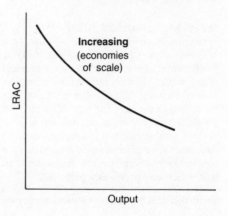

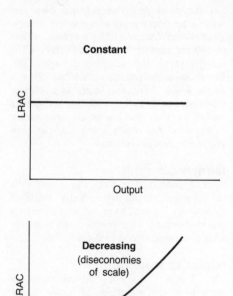

Young, A. (1928) 'Increasing returns and economic progress', *Economic Journal* 38: 527–42.

revalorization (010, 320)

Changing prices or tax rates, e.g. periodic increases in **excise duties** in line with **inflation** so that these **indirect taxes** are constant in real terms.

revaluation (430)

See: **currency revaluation**.

revealed preference (020)

An approach to consumer theory pioneered by **Samuelson** in place of **cardinal utility** or **indifference curve** methods; an empirical utility theory. It does not require complete information about a consumer's tastes but only knowledge of the combinations of goods actually purchased out of a consumer's total income. It is assumed that the consumer is consistent in never choosing a combination which is more expensive than that which was previously preferred.

Houthakker, H.S. (1950) 'Revealed preference and the utility function', *Economica, New Series* 27: 159–74.

Samuelson, P.A. (1938) 'A note on the pure theory of consumers' behaviour', *Economica, New Series* 5: 61–71, 353–4.

—— (1948) 'Consumption theory in terms of revealed preference', *Economica, New Series* 15: 243–53.

revenue (010)

The proceeds obtained by a firm during a given time period for the sale of its goods and services; the amount raised by a government from taxation and trading activities.

revenue economy (070, 060)

A non-market **economy** which extracts a surplus from the agricultural sector to provide sustenance for public servants. The **Physiocrats** in eighteenth-century France were the first to expound a theory concerning it. In the twentieth century, many socialist economies have been of this type.

revenue maximization (610)

See: **sales maximization**.

revenue neutral (320)

The characteristic of a **tax reform** which does not alter total tax revenue.

revenue sharing (320)

The division of the revenue from federal or central government taxes with state, county or local governments. In countries with federal constitutions, e.g. Australia, Canada, Germany or the USA, the principles for allocating revenues are set out in fundamental national constitutional documents. In the UK, revenue sharing in the form of the **rate support grant** and, later, the **revenue support grant**, has been decided within the framework of local government law.

Hunter, J.S.H. (1977) *Federalism and Fiscal Balance*, Canberra: Australian National University Press and the Centre for Research on Federal Financial Relations.

See also: **federal finance**.

revenue support grant (320)

UK central government grant to local authorities. It consists of a needs grant reflecting the needs of individual authorities and a standard grant on a per capita basis.

reverse causation hypothesis (020)

The view that the level of national income determines the size of the money stock, i.e. money has a passive role. This view, which was fervently advanced by **Kaldor** and Joan **Robinson**, is a frontal attack on the **quantity theory of money** and the use of the **transmission mechanism** in modern **monetarist** theory which asserts that money has an effect on real variables, particularly output and employment.

reverse discrimination (820)

Favouring a disadvantaged group by giving it better education or employment or wages to correct its social status and income rather than to reward its merit. This form of discrimination is evident when workers with different levels of productivity are paid the same wages.

See also: **affirmative action; discrimination; positive discrimination.**

reverse income tax (320)

See: **negative income tax.**

reverse J-shaped frequency curve (210)

A **frequency curve** with a negative slope.

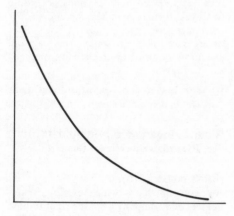

reverse takeover (310, 610)

A takeover of the firm which was originally the bidding company. A case of this would be if Alpha Products bids for Beta Products unsuccessfully and is then taken over by Beta Products.

See also: **merger; takeover.**

reverse yield gap (310)

See: **yield gap.**

reversionary bonus (310)

A bonus given by an insurance company to a policyholder for every year the policy is in force. It is paid out at the termination of the policy or on the death of the insured.

See also: **terminal bonus.**

revolving credit (310)

Credit which is available for an indefinite term for the same amount because the credit used is matched by regular payments from the debtor. An example is permitting credit cardholders to use the card up to a particular limit, $10,000: when that limit has been reached and the amount due paid, the credit is available again.

revolving underwriting facility (310)

An extended **note issuance facility** in the form of a conventional bank loan at low short-term interest rates offered because a money market has not purchased all of the short-term commercial paper offered.

rhetoric (030)

See: **economics as rhetoric.**

Rhinelands hourglass (730)

The belt of prosperous **European Community** cities of Europe stretching from the Benelux countries and West Germany to Northern Italy, with Paris as an offshoot. Also known as the Lotharingian axis.

Ricardian equivalence theorem (320)

This states that deficit finance has exactly the same economic impact as current taxation. This is because individuals take into account future taxes, e.g. the bonds created to finance a deficit can be given to one's children who can use them to pay future taxes. Thus, individuals increase their savings by an amount equal to tax cuts or the increases in government spending with the consequence that deficit finance does not stimulate the national economy. This form of **crowding-out** is named after **Ricardo** but formally explained by Barro.

Barro, R. (1974) 'Are Government bonds net wealth?', *Journal of Political Economy* 82: 1095–175.

See also: **overlapping generations model**.

Ricardian theory of value (020)
See: **Ricardo**.

Ricardo, David, 1772–1823 (030)
A leading English **classical economist** who came to economic study after a rigorous Talmudic education at the Portuguese Synagogue of Amsterdam, a lucrative career as a London stock jobber and a chance reading of **Smith's** *Wealth of Nations* at Bath in 1799. The great inflation of the Napoleonic Wars period brought him to write a pamphlet on monetary economics, *The High Price of Bullion*, in 1811; the **Corn Laws** controversy inspired *An Essay on the Influence of a Low Price of Corn on the Profits of Stock*, his first attempt to create a model of the economy using the **differential theory of rent**, the law of **diminishing returns** and the inverse relationship between wages and profits. James **Mill** encouraged him to expand it into the larger, and very influential, *Principles of Political Economy and Taxation*, first published in 1817. What originally had been a theory to show that restricting corn imports would lead to an extension of cultivation to marginal land and a fall in the rate of profit became an integrated theory of value, distribution, international trade and taxation. The most controversial aspect of it was, perhaps, his theory of **value** which was narrower than **Smith**'s in that it emphasized labour quantities as an explanation of relative values at all stages of society and was more concerned with the quest for an invariable standard of value, seen by contemporaries as important at a time when **index numbers** were not available to show the extent of inflation. Although many of his key theories were not original (e.g. **differential theory of rent**, the law of **comparative advantage**) his central model dominated the thinking of his day and was to be an important starting point for John Stuart **Mill**, **Marx** and **Marshall**. As a Member of Parliament from 1814 for a rotten borough, he was to be an influential debater on central issues, especially on monetary questions, later being a major inspiration for the **Currency School**. His home at Gatcombe Park, Gloucestershire (later the home of HRH The Princess Royal), was used as the venue of the Political Economy Club, the only forum for the leading economists of the time to discuss economics. He died, much admired, leaving the immense fortune of £775,000, including agricultural estates, despite having created an economic theory so despised by the landed interest.

Blaug, M. (1958) *Ricardian Economics: A Historical Study*, New Haven, CT: Yale University Press.
Hollander, S. (1979) *The Economics of David Ricardo*, Toronto: University of Toronto; London: Heinemann Educational Books.
Morishima, M. (1989) *Ricardo's Economics*, Cambridge: Cambridge University Press.
Sraffa, P. and Dobb, M.H. (eds) (1951–73) *The Works and Correspondence of David Ricardo*, Cambridge: Cambridge University Press.

See also: **neo-Ricardians**; **Sraffa**.

Ricardo effect (010)
Hayek's view of the effect of an increase in credit on **capital–labour** ratios which he dubiously attributed to **Ricardo** who had made the central determinant of capital-labour ratios the relative price of labour and machinery. When credit expands, according to Hayek, there is an increase in demand for consumer goods which leads to a rise in their prices and a fall in real wages. This wage fall encourages more labour-intensive methods to be adopted.

Hayek, F. von (1939) *Profits, Interest and Investment*, London: Routledge.

Ricardo invariance principle (010)
See: **Ricardian equivalence theorem**.

rights issue (310)
An issue of shares which existing shareholders of a company have the right to buy: this right can either be exercised or sold. The issue of these extra shares will bring about a fall in the existing share price.

See also: **bonus issue**; **scrip issue**.

right-to-work state (830)
US state which has made it illegal to require

a worker to join a labor union. Most of these twenty states are in the South.

See also: **US labor unions**.

ringfencing (320)
See: **earmarking**.

ringgit (430)
The currency of Malaysia.

risk (010)
The chance of an event occurring in accordance with a known probability. Actuarial calculations based on past experience make it possible to insure against the occurrence of such events. A person who is risk averse would require very favourable odds to make a bet; a **risk lover** would take a gamble even when the odds are unfavourable; a risk neutral person will be concerned not about the likelihood of particular bets being successful but that he, on average, makes a profit.

risk asset system (310)
A method of assessing the amount of **risk** a bank is taking which weights bank assets according to the length of time banks could lose profits on them. The **Federal Reserve System** recommends the adaptation of this system now in use in the **European Community** countries and suggests weights of 0 per cent for cash (and its equivalents), 30 per cent for money market assets, 60 per cent for moderate risk assets (e.g. local authority bonds) and 100 per cent for standard bank loans. Weighting the riskiness of bank assets makes it possible to ascertain the level of capitalization suitable for a particular bank. US and European adoption of this system is a step towards the international harmonization of banking standards.

risk aversion (010, 310)
Choosing **assets** with little risk of either capital loss or an uncertain return. Risk aversion can be expressed in different ways, including the choice of only very safe assets, e.g. government bonds, or the diversification of an investment portfolio. Many investors associate high risk with a high return.

Tobin, J. (1958) 'Liquidity as behaviour towards risk', *Review of Economic Studies* 25 (February): 65–86.

risk-based banking standards (310)
See: **risk asset system**.

risk-based premium (630)
An insurance premium which varies according to the riskiness of the subject of the insurance. The past record of the party insured and of persons with similar characteristics is the main determinant of the premium.

risk capital (310, 520)
1 Ordinary shares.

2 Common stock.

3 **Venture capital**. These constitute the part of long-term financial capital which has no claim on the **assets** of a firm and which will be lost if the enterprise goes bankrupt.

risk lover (010)
A person who will gamble even when a mathematical calculation shows the odds are unfavourable. Risk lovers will accept a lower expected income in the hope of obtaining a greater capital gain.

risk package (310)
The mixture of types of finance used to provide credit for a particular project, e.g. a fixed interest loan and an issue of ordinary shares.

risk pooling (010)
The adding together of the risks of many persons; a basic principle of **insurance**. Those who face the same risk are charged the same insurance premium.

risk sharing (010, 630)
A means of reducing the cost of **risk**. A major example of this is the underwriting system of **Lloyd's** insurance market in London.

See also: **reinsurance**.

risky asset (310)
An asset with an uncertain rate of return. Assessments of riskiness depend on consumption plans and the nature of other assets held by investors.

rival good (010)

A **good** which can only be consumed by one individual so his/her consumption prevents rivals from benefiting from it.

See also: **club good**; **private good**; **public good**.

riyal (30)

The currency of Saudi Arabia.

Rmb (310)

Renminbi (the currency of the People's Republic of China).

Robbins, Lionel (Lord), 1898–1984 (030)

The British economist who was educated at the London School of Economics where he subsequently became lecturer from 1925 to 1927, professor from 1929 to 1961 and Director and Chairman of the Court of the Board of Governors from 1968 to 1974. Before the Second World War he established his fame as an economic theorist through articles on the Marshallian **representative firm**, the **elasticity** of demand for income in terms of effort and the stationary equilibrium. His famous *Essay on the Nature and Significance of Economic Science* (1935) firmly separated **normative** from **positive economics** and asserted that economics was concerned with means and not ends: this greatly influenced the course of economics throughout the Western world. By bringing **Hayek**, with his knowledge of **Austrian economics**, to the London School of Economics in 1931 he was able to provide an alternative to the **Marshallian** economics of Cambridge. In his methodological works, he asserted that the propositions of economics are deductions from indisputable facts of experience, particularly the scarce nature of resources. The Austrian influence made him a strong opponent of **Keynesianism** in the 1930s but his work with the War Cabinet (for which he was Director of the Economic Section) led him to make peace with his academic enemies. After 1950, he wrote a series of elegant works on the history of economic thought, including studies of Robert **Torrens** and the classical theories of economic development and *laissez-faire*. The Robbins Report of 1963 on higher education in Britain helped to bring about a decade of university expansion.

Lord Robbins (1952) *The Theory of Economic Policy in English Classical Political Economy*, London: Macmillan.
—— (1958) *Robert Torrens and the Evolution of Classical Economics*, London: Macmillan; New York: St Martin's Press.
—— (1971) *Autobiography of an Economist*, London: Macmillan.

Robertson, Dennis Holme (Sir), 1890–1963 (030)

Major British economist of the twentieth century. He was educated at Trinity College, Cambridge, where he held a fellowship almost continuously from 1916, interrupted by a chair at the London School of Economics from 1939 to 1944. He succeeded **Pigou** as professor of economics at Cambridge from 1944 to 1957. His most famous works are *A Study in Industrial Fluctuations* (1915), *Money* (1922) and *Banking and the Price Level* (1926).

Until 1929 he worked closely with **Keynes** but the rupture of their friendship led to Robertson's severe criticisms of Keynes after 1936. Robertson disputed the use made of the **multiplier** concept and favoured a dynamic method, rather than Keynesian **comparative statics**. In the post-war period he championed traditional **monetary** policy and was suspicious of the use of **fiscal policy** to maintain **full employment**. From 1957 to 1959, he was one of the trio constituting the Cohen Council on Productivity Prices and Incomes, a body which attempted to restrain **inflation** by exhortation. Keynes was his supervisor.

He was a literary economist with an excellent writing style: he won the Chancellor's Medal for English Verse three times. He rarely used mathematics. *Banking and the Price Level* was his turning point, changing from the **quantity theory of money** approach to saving and investment, on the road to Keynes's **effective** demand. His wartime civil service work on the **balance of payments** led to collaboration with **Keynes** at **Bretton Woods**. Robertson thought that in the post-war world **Keynesianism** would be as rigid as the earlier tradition. The difference between Robertson and Keynes was, according to Hicks, 'a difference in point of view'; Robertson was interested in stabilizing the cycle and so wanted judicious encouragement at the right time. **Hicks**, assessing Robertson's life for the *Dictionary of National Biography* concluded: 'what Robertson feared was that Keynes's teaching would lead, in practice, to the over-use of encouragement and, in order to make that possible, at the same time to the over-use of restraint – an outcome which many people have felt that he was right to fear.'

Presley, J.R. (1979) *Robertsonian Economics: An Examination of the Work of Sir D.H. Robertson on Industrial Fluctuation*, London: Macmillan.

Robertsonian lag (010)

A **lag** lasting one period, e.g. a year or a quarter. **Robertson** applied this type of lag in his savings function: savings in one period were regarded as a function of the income of the previous period.

Robertson, D.H. (1926) *Banking Policy and the Price Level*, London: P.S. King. Reprinted New York: Augustus M. Kelly, 1949.

Robinson, Joan Violet, 1903–83 (030)

British economist, educated at Cambridge University where she met her husband Austin Robinson and taught in the Economics Faculty from 1929 to 1971, being appointed a professor in 1965.

A passionate theorist and socialist, she made major contributions to economics through her *Economics of Imperfect Competition* (1933) which influenced the teaching of microeconomics thereafter by producing independently of **Chamberlin** a theory of the firm for markets, both competitive and monopolistic. Her long guardianship of the **Keynesian** heritage began with *Introduction to the Theory of Employment* (1937). However, the influence of **Sraffa** and **Kalecki** led her to develop Keynesian theory from **comparative statics** to a dynamic growth theory, particularly in her *The Accumulation of Capital* (1956). Many of her works, especially *An Essay on Marxian Economics* (1942), attempted a synthesis of socialist and **Keynesian** economics.

Although trained in Marshallian analysis she became increasingly opposed to his time analysis: she moved from studying perfect competition to oligopoly, selling costs and product differentiation. In doing so, she provided a new box of tools in her theory of imperfect competition. Increasingly she saw her role as a developer of Keynesian theory but her attempt to do so in her *Accumulation of Capital* was not broad enough to achieve a satisfactory model of long-term development. Her interest in development was long-standing, dating back to her first visits to India in the 1920s and later including an on-the-spot study of Mao's China.

For the last thirty years of her life she was engaged in controversies with **Solow** and **Samuelson** about **capital theory**. The ferocity of her polemical and entertaining pen is evident in her *Collected Papers* (1951–79). In a supplementary *Times* obituary notice, her lodger of ten years' standing, Dr Carmen Blacker, wrote of 'her spartan way of life': 'A strict vegetarian, she slept all the year round in a small creeper-covered hut at the bottom of the garden. It was entirely unheated, and open on one side to all weathers, but no storm, deluge or frost could persuade her to sleep in the house. . . . In the early spring she was often woken by tits pecking at her hair for material for their nests.'

Gram, H. and Walsh, V. (1983) 'Joan Robinson's economics in retrospect', *Journal of Economic Literature* 21: 518–50.

Feiwel, G.R. (ed.) (1989) *Joan Robinson and Modern Economic Theory*, New York: New York University Press; London: Macmillan.

—— (1989) *The Economics of Imperfect Competition and Employment. Joan Robinson and Beyond*, London: Macmillan.

Harcourt, G.C. (1988) *Joan Robinson*, Brighton: Wheatsheaf.

Robinson, J. (1951–80) *Collected Economic Papers*, Oxford: Basil Blackwell.

—— (1969) *The Economics of Imperfect Competition*, 2nd edn, London: Macmillan.

—— (1969) *The Accumulation of Capital*, 2nd edn, London: Macmillan.

See also: **bastard Keynesianism**; **Cambridge controversies**; **quadriad**.

Robinson–Patman Act 1936 (610)

US federal statute which outlawed particular forms of **price discrimination** which were in favour of large purchasers. A discount to a larger buyer has to be based either on differences in cost or be justified as a price to meet the low price of a competitor.

See also: **antitrust**.

ROCE (540)
Return on capital employed.

See also: **rate of return**.

ROI (310)
Return on investment.

rolling settlement (310)
A system for investors paying a few days after the sale or purchase of securities, e.g. in the USA, five days. This method of settling accounts has been adopted by the **International Stock Exchange** (UK) as a successor to its long-established method of dividing the trading year into two or three week periods with accounts payable on settlement day.

rollover ratio (430)
The reciprocal of the value of the average **maturity** of a country's external debt which is used as a measure of a country's credit-worthiness.

See also: **debt–service indicators**.

'roof tax' (320)
Colloquial term for the property tax, adjusted by ability to pay, proposed in the UK by the Labour Party in 1990.

Rooker–Wise Amendment (320)
An amendment to Britain's 1975 Finance Bill requiring the government to raise tax allowances by the rate of increase of retail prices every March, unless parliament decided otherwise. In 1981 this principle was ignored. This attempted to reduce the depressing effect of **fiscal drag**.

Rostow, Walt Whitman, 1916– (030)
US economic historian and development economist, educated at Yale and Oxford, where he was a Rhodes Scholar. He has been professor of economic history at the Massachusetts Institute of Technology from 1951 apart from an interlude at the University of Texas from 1961 to 1969. His celebrated non-Marxian account of the process of industrialization in *The Stages of Economic Growth* (1960) was further developed in several works, including *The Economics of Take-Off into Sustained Growth* (1963), *The World Economy: History and Prospect*

(1978) and *Why the Poor Get Richer and the Rich Slow Down* (1980). His **neoclassical** approach to economic history was to inspire much of the later econometric analysis of long time series.

Rostow, W.W. (1971) *The Stages of Economic Growth: A Neo-communist Manifesto*, 2nd edn, Cambridge: Cambridge University Press.

See also: **industrial revolution; stages theory; take-off**.

rouble (430)
The currency of the USSR.

roundabout method of production (010)
A method of production which uses **capital** goods to increase the future **productivity** of factors of production. In a simple case such as fishing, the roundabout method would be used if labour was first expended on producing rods and nets, rather than attempting to catch fish with one's bare hands, so that fish can be caught in greater numbers in a given time period. This concept was central to **Böhm-Bawerk**'s capital theory.

See also: **capitalism**.

roundtripping (310)
Purchasing and reselling the same lot of securities or commodities or money when market prices are rising. An example would be if £X were borrowed for three months and interest rates rose before the end of that period, then the sum borrowed could be re-lent at a profit. This type of **arbitrage** is made possible by market distortions.

ROW (220)
Rest of the world; the countries other than those specifically mentioned in a table of trade or other statistics.

Royal Economic Society (010)
The leading British association of economists, founded in 1890 and known for its publication of the *Economic Journal*, which has always been edited by leading economists including **Edgeworth** and **Keynes**.

Hey, J.D. and Winch, D. (eds) (1990) *A Century of Economics: 100 Years of the Royal Economic Society and the Economic Journal*, Oxford: Basil Blackwell.

RPB (310)
See: **recognized professional body**.

RPI (220)
See: **retail price index**.

RPM (530, 610)
See: **resale price maintenance**.

RRR (520)
See: **real rate of return**.

RSA (940)
See: **regional selective assistance**.

RSG (320)
See: **rate support grant**.

RTC (310)
See: **Resolution Trust Corporation**.

ruble (430)
See: **rouble**.

RUF (310)
See: **revolving underwriting facility**.

rules versus discretion (310, 320)
Alternative approaches to economic policy, especially monetary policy. Rules necessitate predetermined responses to events; discretion, a response decided in the light of each economic situation requiring governmental action. There is a continuum of policy actions between, in the case of monetary policy, rigid rules such as the **Currency School**'s principle for the expansion of the note issue and **Friedman**'s idea of an **optimum quantity of money**, and the repeated discretionary use of **open market operations**, the **discount rate**, **reserve requirements** and **margin requirements** as practised on many occasions by the **Federal Reserve System**. **Tobin** has regarded it is an overworked dichotomy because if we incorporate new information for the determination of policy, the policy is bound to become discretionary. Other economists argue that rules are used in theoretical models, rather than in policy-making, as politicians and others are quick to deviate from their own rules.

runaway industry (630)
An industry which moves from its original location, often to benefit from reductions in costs, especially the lower costs of using non-unionized labour. Many US **multinational corporations** have chosen foreign countries for manufacturing as a means of avoiding the use of expensive labour.

runaway inflation (150)
See: **hyperinflation**.

runaway shop (830)
A workplace relocated from an area of high **unionization** to one of low unionization. This relocation is inspired by a desire to reduce labour costs and the incidence of industrial disputes.

running broker (310)
A London money market broker who 'runs a book' recording sales and purchases of short-term monetary assets.

run on a bank (310)
The simultaneous demands of the deposit-holders of a retail bank for their deposits to be paid. As it is difficult for banks to be sufficiently liquid to meet such concerted action against it without sacrificing the more profitable business of making loans, in the nineteenth and twentieth centuries **central banks** emerged to be the **lender of last resort** to maintain the liquidity of **domestic banking systems** as a whole and increasingly to supervise the operations of commercial banks. **Deposit insurance** is also a device to reduce bank runs as there is less point in the public demanding the return of their deposits in cash if there is a guarantee that their deposits will not be lost in a bank collapse.

See also: **financial crisis**; **financial panic**; **lifeboat operation**.

rupee (430)
The currency of India, Nepal, Pakistan and the Seychelles.

rustbelt (630, 730)
US geographical area in which the older manufacturing industries are located, especially Ohio, Michigan, Indiana and Illinois. As the labour forces of firms in that area are high cost and **unionized**, there are

many incentives for relocation of plants to the US South or to Mexico.

See also: **snowbelt; sunbelt**.

Rybczynski theorem (410)

The effect on production, consumption and the **terms of trade** of an increase in the quantity of one factor of production. As the same rates of substitution in production hold, when the quantity of the factor is increased there is an expansion in the production of the commodity using relatively more of it so that there is a deterioration in the relative price, or terms of trade, of that commodity.

Rybczynski, T.M. (1955) 'Factor endowments and relative commodity prices', *Economica, New Series* 22: 336–41.

See also: **Heckscher–Ohlin trade theory**.

S

SA (510)
Société anonyme (French, Belgian, Luxemburgese or Swiss public company).

sacrifice theory (320)
The assertion that taxation should be based on **ability to pay**. This approach to taxation can be traced back to Adam **Smith** and John Stuart **Mill**. It has been criticized for assuming that **interpersonal utility comparisons** are possible and for ignoring **disincentive effects** of taxation.

See also: **canons of taxation**.

SACU (420)
See: **South African Customs Union**.

SADCC (130)
See: **South African Development Coordination Committee**.

saddle point (210)
The determinate solution, in some games, in which all players follow a **maximin** strategy.

See also: **game theory**.

safe asset (310)
An asset with a fixed and certain rate of return, e.g. a bond of a reputable government.

saitori (310)
See: **specialist**.

sales maximization (510)
The aim of a firm to maximize its **total revenue**. Managers of large firms having this goal will continue to expand output to increase sales revenue, even if there is a reduction in total profits, provided that profits do not fall below a minimum level. This goal is thought to be attractive as sales revenue is more quickly and easily known than profits; also a larger volume of sales

indicates greater market power.

Baumol, W.J. (1967) *Business Behavior, Value and Growth*, rev. edn, New York: Harcourt, Brace & World.

See also: **managerial models of the firm**.

sales ratios (540)
Sales as a proportion of stock, debtors, fixed assets, share capital or working capital.

sales tax (320)
A tax on a good or a service at the point of sale. Some of these taxes are levied on specific goods, as is the case with **excise duties**; others are related to general categories of expenditure, e.g. the **value-added tax**.

See also: **expenditure tax**.

SAMA (310)
See: **Saudi Arabian Monetary Agency**.

sample (210)
A part of a **population** which is examined in order to ascertain the characteristics of the whole of that population. Random sampling (or probability sampling) is used to obtain unbiased estimates. Sampling can produce better evaluations by increasing the size of a sample or by stratification of the population to be sampled.

Kish, L. (1965) *Survey Sampling*, New York: Wiley.

Samuelson, Paul Anthony, 1915– (030)
The leading post-war US economist who graduated from the universities of Chicago and Harvard. He was fortunate in having as mentors men as distinguished as **Knight**, **Schumpeter**, **Viner**, **Leontief** and **Hansen**. Throughout his academic career he has been at the Massachusetts Institute of Technology where he became a full professor in 1947. He was awarded the **Nobel Prize for Economics** in 1970.

His vigorous rewriting of the theory

of many branches of economics began with his paper on **consumers' surplus** in 1938, deriving a demand curve from the **revealed preferences** of consumers. He published his doctoral dissertation as *Foundations of Economic Analysis* (1947), surveying economic theory in an attempt to move the subject towards comparative dynamics and showing how essential a mathematical approach is to economics. To the majority of economics students his fame rests on his highly successful textbook *Economics*, first published in 1948 and now jointly written with Nordhaus: to date it has sold over 10 million copies. It introduces students to a wide range of economic theory and its applications – over its twelve editions it has broadened its approach from an emphasis on the determinants of aggregate demand to a consideration of supply factors also. He is known to the economics profession as a theoretician of exceptional brilliance, with hundreds of technical papers attesting it. In many outstanding technical contributions he has provided a **multiplier–accelerator** theory of the **trade cycle**, a simplification of **general equilibrium** theory to make it applicable to concrete problems, a **revealed preferences** theory for **welfare economics**, a pure theory of public expenditure which takes into account both **private** and **public goods** and a rigorous factor–price equalization theorem. His eminence has made some describe this as 'the age of Samuelson'. But his **neoclassical** approach has aroused much opposition. His articulate expositions of current economic policy have long been available to the readers of *Newsweek* and the *New York Times*. His long distinguished career has done much to deal with the conclusion to his *Foundations*: 'Economics is a growing subject in which very much is left to be done.'

Brown, E.C. and Solow, R.M. (eds) (1983) *Paul Samuelson and Modern Economic Theory*, New York: McGraw-Hill.

Feiwel, G.R. (ed.) (1982) *Samuelson and Neo-Classical Economics*, Boston, MA: Kluwer.

Samuelson, P.A. (1965) *Foundations of Economic Analysis*, New York: Atheneum.

—— (1960, 1972, 1977) *The Collected Scientific Papers of Paul A. Samuelson*, vols I–IV, Cambridge, MA, and London: Harvard University Press.

samurai bond (310)

A bond issued in yen in Japan by a foreign concern and purchasable by non-residents of Japan.

Sandilands Report (150, 540)

UK report of 1975 of a committee on inflation accounting which recommended **current cost accounting**. It asserted that assets should be revalued at either their replacement or their economic value, as representative of their value to the business at the time; items in **profit and loss accounts** should be valued at their current cost at the time of the sale of the output. The main income measure used was **current operating profit**.

S&P 500 (220, 310)

See: **Standard & Poor 500**.

SarL (510)

Société à responsabilité limité: a private company in France etc.

satisficing (510)

Aiming to reach a satisfactory level of performance, rather than to maximize, for example, sales or profits. Modern theories, recognizing the complexity of managerial objectives, have noted that satisficing is a common aim.

See also: **managerial models of the firm**; **revenue maximization**; **sales maximization**.

Saudi Arabian Monetary Agency (310)

An Arab banking organization founded in 1952 to perform the functions of a **central bank** but called an agency because of the association between 'a bank' and payments for interest which is condemned by Islamic law. SAMA is now responsible for the coinage and note issue of Saudi Arabia, the supervision of commercial banks and the fiscal operations of the government.

Abdeen, A.M. and Shook, D.W. (1984) *The Saudi Financial System in the Context of Western and Islamic Finance*, Chichester: Wiley.

See also: **Islamic banking**; **usury**.

Saudi-ization (610)

A method of taking foreign businesses into

national ownership, not by **nationalization** but by demanding the sale of the majority of shares to private citizens. Saudi Arabia in 1977 used this approach to change the ownership of foreign-owned commercial banks.

See also: **multinational corporation**; **public enterprise**.

savings (010, 320)

The residue of **income** of the government, a firm or a household after all their expenditures have been incurred. There are many motives for saving. A government may do so to deflate the national economy, a firm to provide self-financing of investment, a household to provide for illness, retirement and the needs of descendants and favourite charities. In the long debate on the determinants of saving, it has been considered too simplistic to regard the **rate of interest** as the sole determinant because the level of prices is important too. Also, it has been noted that a strong personal motivation to save is independent of most macroeconomic variables. The **average propensity to save** of households varies from country to country.

See also: **life-cycle hypothesis**; **relative income hypothesis**.

savings and loan association (310)
See: **thrift**.

savings function (020)
The relationship between a nation's

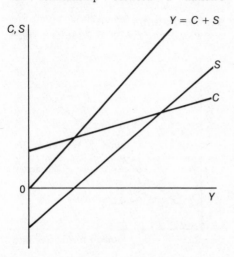

aggregate savings and its total disposable income. In the simplest models of an economy, in which national income (Y) is equal to consumption (C) plus savings (S), the savings function is, diagrammatically, the inverse of the **consumption function**.

savings ratio (010)

1 The **average propensity to save**.

2 Household savings as a proportion of its disposable income.

3 The proportion of a government's or firm's income retained. In the UK this ratio, in the case of households, fell from 14 per cent in 1980 to 4 per cent in 1987, much lower than Japan's 18 per cent and West Germany's 13 per cent. The fall in the British ratio in the 1980s is not entirely caused by the greater availability of **consumer** credit as the fall in the rate of inflation has reduced the incentive to save as a means of retaining the real value of assets. Also, the **life-cycle** effect of an ageing population has been to reduce savings. The extent to which low household saving is a problem has been exaggerated as there has been compensating increased saving in the corporate and governmental sectors. Movements in the savings ratio are always imprecise if there are deficiencies in **national income** statistics, e.g. non-recording of **black economy** activities (the black economy understates incomes but not consumer expenditure so official savings figures are depressed).

Say, Jean Baptiste, 1767–1832 (030)
Born in Lyons and trained in insurance in Croydon (London) and France, in the course of which his proprietor, Clavière, encouraged him to read **Smith**'s *Wealth of Nations*, the beginning of his interest in economics. During the French Revolution he was a journalist, secretary to Clavière, and rose to be Finance Minister and editor, from 1794 to 1800, of *La Décade Philosophique, Littéraire et Politique* which expounded Smithian doctrines. In 1803 he produced his major work *Traité d'économie politique*. Opposing Napoleon's policies he resigned his post as tribune and established a cotton mill. In 1814 he returned to Britain to report on its economic condition for the French Government, publishing a

pamphlet, *De l'Angleterre et des Anglais*. In 1819 he was appointed to a new chair of industrial economy at the Conservatoire des Arts et Métiers and in 1831 to the chair of political economy at the Collège de France. His *Traité* was expanded into *Cours complèt d'économie politique pratique* (1829), a larger work with many practical applications. **Keynes** revived the fame of Say by referring to **'Say's law'**, a law which ruled out permanent unemployment and had been largely accepted by **Ricardo** and many major classical writers although **Malthus** and John Stuart **Mill** disputed aspects of it. Say's supply and demand analysis, incorporating the concepts of **utility** and **scarcity**, make him one of the forerunners of neoclassical economics. Much of his economics was, in the French style, very abstract – as Malthus was quick to note.

SAYE (310, 320)
British savings scheme which consists of deductions from earnings, along with taxes.

Say's law (020)
A law of markets which is often summarized as 'supply creates its own demand'. This view of macroeconomics was based on the idea that production creates factor incomes which bring about a demand for the goods produced elsewhere in the economy. The consequence of this 'law' for **classical economics** was that there could never be a general and permanent 'glut', i.e. a deficiency in **aggregate demand**. Although this view is particularly attributed to Say by **Keynes** and others, many classical economists, e.g. James **Mill**, held to the same theory. The classical conclusion derived from this law is that through price flexibility an economy will always reach a full employment equilibrium in the long run.

Mill, J.S. (1877) *Essays on Some Unsettled Questions of Political Economy*, 3rd edn, No. 2, London: Longmans & Green.
Sowell, T. (1972) *Say's Law: An Historical Analysis*, Princeton, NJ: Princeton University Press.

SBA (510)
Small Business Administration (USA).

scalar principle (510)
Within organizations, this principle dictates that managerial authority and responsibility should flow continuously from the highest person to the lowest in the hierarchy.

scarcity (010, 720)
1 The limited quantity of a resource, factor of production or output.

2 Insufficient means to satisfy all of society's demands for resources. As population increased and there was competition for a fixed supply of natural resources, scarcity was viewed by many economists, including **Robbins**, as the principal economic problem: it raises all the major issues of allocation and pricing and is the reason why rent is paid. Because of scarcity, if goods or services are offered freely, a non-price method of allocation must be used, e.g. **rationing**. The importance of scarcity as a concept is challenged by Marxists who identify other concepts as central.

Robbins, L. (1935) *An Essay on the Nature and Significance of Economic Science*, London: Macmillan.

See also: **absolute scarcity**.

scarcity index (720)
The real cost of capital and labour inputs per unit of an extractive output which is expressed as an index of the prices of extractive outputs relative to non-extractive outputs.

Barnett, H.J. and Morse, C. (1963) *Scarcity and Growth: The Economics of Natural Resource Availability*, Baltimore, MD: Johns Hopkins University Press.

scatter diagram (210)
A scatter of points with *X*, *Y* values to which

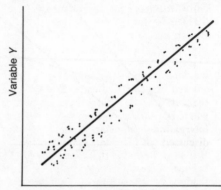

a curve is fitted as a means of making a preliminary study of the relationship between the variables X and Y.

See also: **least squares method**.

schedular tax (320)

1 A tax with different rates published in a schedule, especially a **progressive tax** on incomes.

2 A tax which is related to a particular schedule devised for that type of income rather than a global income tax on all types of income.

schilling (430)

The currency of Austria.

Schultz, Theodore William, 1902– (030)

Leading US authority on **human capital** theory. Educated in agricultural economics at South Dakota State College and the University of Wisconsin. Since 1943, he has been professor at the University of Chicago. His **Nobel Prize for Economics**, jointly awarded in 1980 with Arthur **Lewis**, was for his work in agricultural economics. Although he published a major work on this topic, *The Economic Organization of Agriculture* (1953), his major contribution to mainstream economics has been in leading the modern human capital movement, especially with his *The Economic Value of Education* (1963) and *Investment in Human Capital: The Role of Education and Research* (1971).

Schumacher, Ernst Friedrich, 1911–77 (030)

British economist and prophet who was born in Bonn and educated at Berlin, Bonn, Oxford and Columbia universities. When he was interned in Britain from 1940 to 1945, he worked first as an agricultural labourer and then at the Oxford Institute of Statistics where he worked on the problem of a new **international monetary system**, which he discussed with **Keynes**. He was naturalized British at the end of the war so that he could become a member (1946–50) of the British section of the Control Commission in Germany. From 1950 to 1970 he was econ-omic adviser and subsequently Director of Statistics to the National Coal Board. Increasingly he was attracted to Buddhism which gave his economics a distinctively ecological approach and led to his appointment as economic adviser to the government of Burma. He was the principal proponent of **intermediate technology** and of self-help to solve the rural poverty problems of less developed countries. His famous attack on materialism and consumerism was in his immensely popular set of essays *Small is Beautiful*: as its subtitle *A Study of Economics as if People Mattered* claimed, there can be an economics based on humanitarian considerations.

Schumacher, F. (1973) *Small is Beautiful: A Study of Economics as if People Mattered*, London: Blond & Briggs.
Wood, B. (1984) *Alias Papa: A Life of Fritz Schumacher*, London: Jonathan Cape.

Schumpeter, Joseph Alois, 1883–1950 (030)

A leading US economist who was educated at Vienna University where he was a pupil of **Böhm-Bawerk**, without becoming a wholehearted convert to the **Austrian School**. From 1911 to 1918 he held chairs at the universities of Czernowitz and Graz, was briefly Austrian Minister of Finance in 1920 and president of the Biederman Bank before moving to Bonn where he was professor from 1925 to 1932, completing his career as professor at Harvard from 1932 to 1950. His major contributions to economics were to study the nature of capitalist development and industrial fluctuations and to accumulate a vast knowledge of the history of economic theory. He emphasized the role of **entrepreneurs** and **innovation** in a number of works: *Capitalism, Socialism and Democracy* (1942), *The Theory of Economic Development* (1951; original German edition, 1912) and his monumental *Business Cycles* (1939). His wife posthumously completed his colossal *History of Economic Analysis* (1954), a work which in a schoolmasterly fashion separated economists of many centuries into the sheep and the goats.

Frisch, H. (ed.) (1981) *Schumpeterian Economics*, New York: Praeger.

Schwartz, Anna Jacobson, 1915– (030)

Leading US monetary historian and economist. Educated at Barnard College, New York, and Columbia University. Apart from some academic posts, she has been a research associate of the **National Bureau of Economic Research** since 1941. Her collaboration with Milton **Friedman** in the analysis of long time series to examine monetary changes and their effects is very well known.

Schwartz, A. and Bordo, M.D. (1980) *A Retrospective on the Classical Gold Standard*, Chicago, IL: University of Chicago Press.
Schwartz, A. and Friedman, M. (1963) *A Monetary History of the United States 1867–960*, Princeton, NJ: Princeton University Press.
—— and —— (1970) *Monetary Statistics of the United States*, New York: Columbia University Press.

Scitovsky, Tibor, 1910– (030)

Hungarian, educated at Budapest and the London School of Economics where he also taught before emigrating to the USA in 1946. From 1958 to 1968 he worked at the **Organization for Economic Cooperation and Development**, at Yale from 1968 to 1970, at Stanford from 1970 to 1976 and back at the London School of Economics from 1976 to 1978. He is particularly famous for his **welfare economics**, *Welfare and Competition* (1951) being his principal work on that subject. His numerous other interests include international economics, e.g. *Economic Theory and Western European Integration* (1958), and an interesting work which uses behavioural psychology to challenge **consumer sovereignty** theory: *The Joyless Economy* (1976).

Scitovsky reversal test (010)

A development of the **Kaldor–Hicks** compensation test which enlarges it by the condition that there is no increase in social welfare by a return to the original situation on the part of losers. **Scitovsky**'s consideration of changes in real income took into account its distribution.

Scitovsky, T. (1941) 'A note on welfare propositions in economics', *Review of Economic Studies* 9: 77–88.
—— (1952) *Welfare and Competition: The Economics of a Fully Employed Economy*, London: Allen & Unwin.
—— (1976) *The Joyless Economy: An Inquiry into Human Satisfaction and Consumer Dissatisfaction*, New York: Oxford University Press.

See also: **welfare economics**.

SCOPE (310)

System Committee on Paperless Entry.

See also: **dematerialization; paperless entry**.

SCP (510)

See: **structure–conduct–performance model**.

screening (820)

An explanation of the higher pay of more educated workers used as an alternative to **human capital** theory. It is asserted that firms choose graduates on the basis of their qualifications as these indicate natural abilities and training potential rather than particular skills. Also applied to the study of **unemployment**.

scrip issue (310)

Shares which are offered as an alternative to dividends.

See also: **bonus issue; rights issue**.

S-curve (110)

The path of long-term growth.

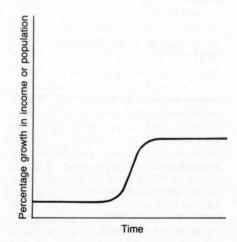

SDR (430)
See: **special drawing rights**.

SEAQ (310)
See: **Stock Exchange Automated Quotation System**.

search cost (010, 820)
The costs to the buyers and sellers of a market of acquiring information about prices and quantities available. Some markets, particularly the labour market, have suffered for a long time from imperfections such as **asymmetric information**: both employers and workers have to incur many costs (e.g. of advertising, travel, time taken from other activities) to come into contact with each other. Search costs are a form of investment by a worker, with higher wages being the return to such expenditure. If buyers and sellers are rational profit maximizers in their search activities, they will continue seeking for what they desire until the marginal cost of search equals the marginal benefit derived from it. **Stigler** was a pioneer in his application of search theory to labour markets.

Lippman, S. and McCall, J.J. (1976) 'The economics of job search: a survey', *Economic Inquiry* 14: 115–89, 347–68.
Pissarides, C.A. (1976) *Labour Market Adjustment*, Cambridge: Cambridge University Press.
Stigler, G.J. (1962) 'Information in the labor market', *Journal of Political Economy* 70 (October Supplement): 94–105.

search good (010)
A good infrequently purchased, e.g. a major consumer durable, legal services; hence the consumer has to search for information about its quality.

See also: **experience good**.

search unemployment (810)
Frictional unemployment; being without a job during a period of looking for another one. Many workers will endure lower incomes during periods of unemployment in the hope of increasing lifetime earnings.

See also: **unemployment spell**.

seasonal adjustment (210)
The elimination of seasonal fluctuations from a **time series**, often by the method of **moving averages**.

seasonal unemployment (810)
The state of being without a job for a few months of a year because of the month to month fluctuations in demand for labour of a particular industry. The hotel and agricultural industries are major sectors with this type of unemployment.

SEC (310)
See: **Securities and Exchange Commission**.

secondary action (830)
Industrial disputes organized by a **trade (labor) union** against an employer or employers who are not in dispute with the union with the aim of making the original industrial action more effective. This form of action can take the form of strikes and boycotts of goods of related firms so that consumers have no other supplier of the goods they require. Both US and UK union legislation restricts the range of actions.

secondary bank (310)
A wholesale bank obtaining its funds from other banks and not from the general public, as is the case with **retail** or **commercial banks**.

See also: **investment bank; merchant bank**.

secondary banking crisis (310)
A crisis in 1973–4 amongst UK **merchant banks** who had made loans to finance property speculation in the early 1970s and then suffered from many bad debts when the property market collapsed. Some of these banks survived by being rescued by a 'lifeboat operation' mounted jointly by the Bank of England and leading clearing banks.

secondary capital (310)
Bank capital consisting of limited-life preferred stock, bank-subordinated notes and debentures and unsecured long-term debt of the parent company and its non-bank subsidiaries.

See also: **primary capital**.

secondary employment (010, 810)
See: **employment multiplier**.

secondary labour market (820)

That part of a national labour market consisting of small firms employing workers at low wages and offering them little training.

See also: **external labour market; primary labour market**.

secondary market (310)

A financial market for trading in securities already in existence, which usually takes the form of a stock exchange. The growth of the number of types of tradable financial asset has led to the creation of new markets.

See also: **primary market**.

secondary standard (720)

A standard for pollution levels which is necessary to protect vegetation, buildings and visibility. It is assumed that pollution control is already sufficient to protect human health.

See also: **ambient standard; primary standard**.

second best (010)

An allocation which falls short of being **Pareto** efficient by not fulfilling all of Pareto's conditions for optimality.

Lipsey, R.G. and Lancaster, K. (1956) 'The general theory of the second best', *Review of Economic Studies* 24: 11–32.

second-degree price discrimination (010, 530)

Setting different prices for different quantities, e.g. offering discounts for purchasing larger quantities, but subjecting all customers to the same price schedule.

See also: **price discrimination**.

second economy (060)

The market-oriented part of a **socialist economy** run by private persons. It can be legal or illegal; increasingly, private enterprise has been permitted in the service sector in Eastern Europe.

Grossman, G. (1977) 'The second economy of the USSR', *Problems of Communism* 26: 25–40.

See also: **first economy**.

second generation product (620)

A product which is in many respects similar to an existing product and captures its market from it. In science-based industries, e.g. pharmaceuticals, a new drug is often supplanted by a related compound. The cost and riskiness of industrial research has increased because of the need to extend a product range to replace supplanted products.

second market (310)

Unlisted securities market (UK). In France, a second market was established in 1983 to allow smaller companies to go public with lower costs and small share issues.

second price auction (530)

A method of selling consisting of potential buyers submitting sealed written bids for an item with the item being sold to the highest bidder at the second highest price offered. The London stamp auctions are conducted in this way.

See also: **auction**.

Second World (070, 730)

Centrally planned economies of the **Soviet type**. These were chiefly the economies of Eastern Europe from 1948 to 1990.

See also: **First World; Fourth World; Third World**.

sector adjustment lending (940)

An aid-assisted loan given to improve the performance of a specific sector of an economy. As such targeting neglects some sectors of an economy, it reduces the number of linked benefits of providing finance more generally, e.g. the advanced sectors by receiving finance could bring about a general improvement through **spillover effects**.

See also: **soft loan**.

Securities and Exchange Commission (310)

US regulatory body set up in 1933 with the task of regulating US securities markets, the offer of securities to the public, mutual funds, investment companies, public utility securities and investment advisers.

See also: **blue-sky laws**.

Securities Association (310)

The UK body which regulates stock market and related **securities** firms, having taken over from the Stock Exchange its regulatory function. This is the largest of the **self-regulatory organizations** set up by the **Financial Services Act**. It covers a larger securities industry than did the Stock Exchange Council and vets both member firms and staff who have dealings with the public.

Securities Exchange Act 1934 (310)

Basic US federal statute which regulates securities exchanges and **over-the-counter trading**, set up the **Securities and Exchange Commission** and sets out the information which corporations have to provide to have their securities listed on an exchange.

securities house (310)

A financial firm dealing in a wide range of governmental and corporate securities.

securities market (310)

A market in which new or existing stocks and shares are sold. **Primary markets** are concerned with new issues, **secondary markets** with maintaining a market in bills, bonds, stocks and shares already issued; securities markets often combine both functions. In recent years, the principal developments in these markets have been to move from the use of specialist trading to **financial conglomerates** and to devise methods of regulation appropriate to markets which have been transformed by internationalization and rapid electronic communication.

securitization (310)

The conversion of bank loans into tradable securities. Borrowers, instead of raising loans, request merchant or investment banks to raise money for them by the issue of **shares**. The collapse of stock markets in 1987 made it more difficult to raise finance by new issues.

Bonsall, D.C. (1990) *Securitisation*, London: Butterworth.

Henderson, J. and Scott, J. (1988) *Securitisation*, Cambridge: Woodhead Faulkner.

See also: **monetization**.

security (310)

A financial instrument in bearer form or registered form, i.e. its ownership is the bearer or the person listed in a register for that security. Securities take many forms, including **bonds**, **stocks** and **shares**.

See also: **bearer bond**; **bearer share**.

seed capital (310, 520)

A form of **venture capital** used to finance entrepreneurs attempting to set up businesses. In the **European Community**, the European Seed Capital Fund Network coordinates the provision of this capital in several European Community countries.

segmented labour market theory (820)

The supposition that the labour market is divided into a number of subgroups with little mobility between them and different rules for determining wages and allocating labour within them. The best example is **dual labour market** theory.

seignorage (310, 430)

1 The levy charged by states for converting precious metals into coins (the UK abolished the charge in 1666).

2 The power of a country whose **currency** is a **reserve currency** (the best example is the USA which can use its dollars to pay for its imports) or the revenue, net of the cost of production, gained from issuing banknotes or another form of currency.

3 The profit which arises from issuing a currency. Seignorage is a major source of government revenue in high inflation **economies** as a government can finance its deficits by creating more money.

See also: **free banking**.

selection bias (210)

A deviation from the random selection method of sampling. Although selections which depart from the random method of selection fail to provide an accurate description of the population sampled, models of self-selection have often been used in economics, e.g. to study occupational choice, the returns to training and the returns to schooling.

Roy, A.D. (1951) 'Some thoughts on the distribution of earnings', *Oxford Economic Papers, New Series* 3: 135–46.

Selective Employment Tax (320)

A tax designed by **Kaldor** and in force in the UK from 1966 to 1973 which sought to encourage the movement of workers from **service** industries to manufacturing industries by imposing a **payroll tax** on the former. It led to a decline in service sector employment but did not noticeably revive manufacturing industry which had more severe problems than a shortage of labour.

Reddaway, W.B. (1970) *Effects of the Selective Employment Tax. First Report. The Distributive Trades*, London: HMSO.

self-insurance (320, 520)

The absorption of unusual losses by an organization itself, without resort to insurance companies and markets. Many governmental organizations follow this principle.

self-regulation (310)

Control of a profession or a market by the members of it, rather than by the government. In the UK, the Stock Exchange has the **International Securities Regulatory Organization**, **IMRO**, **Lautro**, **Fimbra** and **AFBD**; in the USA, the American Medical Association is a prominent case of self-regulation. If such a form of regulation is unsuccessful in preventing and prosecuting offenders, there is usually a call for governmental control.

self-regulatory organization (310)

An organization set up by a profession or group of specialist financial traders to regulate the conduct of its members; a form of regulation which is an alternative to a governmental regulatory organization. In the UK, examples of these organizations include **Lloyd's**, the **Securities Association**, **AFBD**, **Fimbra**, **IMRO** and **Lautro**.

See also: **Financial Services Act**; **regulation**.

self-sufficient economy (070)

An **economy** in which the domestic supply and domestic demand are equal for all goods and services. This is a notional state which some US policy-makers see as an optimal goal for the US economy.

See also: **autarky**.

sellers' market (530)

A market in which sellers have a dominant influence on price because of excess demand.

See also: **buyers' market**.

selling short (310)

See: **short selling**.

SEM (810)

See: **special employment measures**.

semi-colonial country (070)

A politically independent country whose economy is dominated by international imperialist **capitalists**: a Marxian concept.

semi-interquartile range (210)

The **upper quartile** minus the **lower quartile** divided by two, for a particular data set.

Sen, Amartya K., 1933– (030)

Leading **social choice** theorist, born in Bengal and educated at the Presidency College, Calcutta, and Trinity College, Cambridge. His academic posts have been professor at the Jadavpur University, Calcutta, fellow of Trinity College, Cambridge, from 1957 to 1963, professor at Delhi from 1963 to 1971, professor at the London School of Economics from 1971 to 1977, Drummond Professor of Political Economy at Oxford from 1977 to 1986 and subsequently professor at Harvard. His distinguished career has embraced **social choice theory** and **development economics**. His rigorous works *Collective Choice and Social Welfare* (1971) and *On Economic Equality* (1973) show his ability to wrestle with the **impossibility theorem** and to cast doubt on **Pareto optimality**. As a noted contributor to development economics, he has offered practical advice in *Choice of Techniques* (1960) and *Employment, Technology and Development* (1975) as well as illuminating the poverty problem in *Poverty and Famines: An Essay on Entitlement and Deprivation* (1981) which looked at poverty in terms of a lack of income, not of food supply.

Senior, Nassau William, 1790–1864 (030)

Leading **classical economist** educated at Magdalen College, Oxford, and Lincoln's Inn where he was called to the Bar in 1819. His first literary work was as a reviewer for the *Quarterly Review* which included commenting on the usage of key economic terms and the **Corn Laws**. As Drummond Professor of Political Economy at Oxford University from 1826 to 1830 and from 1847 to 1851 he published lectures on precious metals, population, money and wages. His views on the **Poor Laws** and the Factory Acts made him a prominent adviser to governments. His **abstinence** theory of savings and his inclusion of **marginal utility** as a cause of value established his originality as an economic theorist.

Levy, S.L. (1970) *Nassau W. Senior 1790–1864*, Newton Abbot: David & Charles.
Senior, N.W. (1831) *Three Lectures on the Rate of Wages*, London: Murray; reprinted New York: Augustus M. Kelley.
—— (1836) *An Outline of the Science of Political Economy*, London; reprinted New York: Augustus M. Kelley, 1965.
—— (1966) *Selected Writings on Economics: A Volume of Pamphlets 1827–1852*, New York: Augustus M. Kelley.

senior debt (310)

A debt secured by collateral which has to be repaid before any other stockholders or creditors in the event of liquidation.

See also: **junior debt**.

seniority principle (820)

A feature of the structure of pay, benefits, promotion and redundancy procedures. Although in the USA this 'wage for age' principle has its strongest effects on the pay of non-unionized workers and on the **fringe benefits** of **unionized** workers, in general it is most visible as the underlying principle of pay determination under **trade (labor) unions**. In Japan, **enterprise unions** use seniority as the basis for sharing out increases to the total wage bill. As an economic justification for this approach to wages and salary policy, it is argued that experience should be rewarded. Also, a worker aware that this principle underlies the pay structure will be more reluctant to move to another employer, thus increasing the private return to the employer of any investment in training.

See also: **human capital**.

SEPON (310)

Stock Exchange Pool Nominees; a company part of the **Talisman** system.

sequential externality (010)

An economic activity which affects the productivity of another activity in a later time period, e.g. chemical production which reduces the effectiveness of fishing through pollution.

See also: **contemporaneous externality**.

sequestration (320, 830)

1 Spending cuts in the US Federal Budget imposed under the **Gramm–Rudman–Hollings** law.

2 Temporary seizure of assets under a court order, e.g. of union funds under British employment legislation.

serial correlation (210)

See: **autocorrelation**.

SERPS (320, 910)

See: **State Earnings-Related Pensions Scheme**.

service industry (630)

An industry not producing goods but performing various tasks, including transportation, distribution, professional advice, finance. This sector has expanded rapidly in Western countries since 1950, partly as the result of firms becoming more specialized and buying in services which were previously provided within their own organizations and partly through rises in consumers' real incomes making possible the purchase of others' labour.

services (010)

The non-physical output which flows from the employment of a **factor of production**. The major example is labour services which can be menial, e.g. cleaning, or as demanding as the provision of professional advice. As an economy reaches an advanced stage of development its activities are increasingly of this nature.

See also: **Petty's law**.

servicing a debt (310)
Repaying the interest due on a debt.

See also: **debt–service indicators; world debt problem**.

set aside (710)
A payment to farmers to take land out of agricultural production. The success of farmers in increasing productivity in Europe in recent decades has made necessary this approach to reducing mountains of stored produce.

SET index (310)
The price index of leading shares traded on the Bangkok stock exchange.

settlement day (310)
Account day on the **International Stock Exchange** when payments for purchases of securities must be made.

See also: **rolling settlement**.

Sex Discrimination Acts 1975, 1986 (820)
UK legislation which requires equal treatment of men and women.

sexual discrimination (010, 810, 820)
The unfavourable treatment of one sex, usually women, in matters of wages, recruitment or promotion. In the USA federal legislation first addressed itself to this in civil rights legislation of the 1960s; in the UK under the **Equal Pay Act** 1970 and **Sexual Discrimination Acts** 1975 and 1986; in the **European Community** under Article 119 of the **Treaty of Rome**. The economic analysis of discrimination dates back to John Stuart **Mill**'s writings on the wages of women in his *Principles*.

See also: **crowding hypothesis; occupational segregation**.

sexual division of labour (810)
The division of occupations into two groups: those predominantly carried out by men and those where women are in the majority. As early as **John Stuart Mill** it was recognized that female employment was crowded into comparatively few occupations. This concentration arose from the belief that women are only capable of doing jobs similar to their household tasks, i.e. cleaning, cooking, nursing, bringing up young children and secretarial tasks. **Barriers to entry** created by male-dominated **trade unions**, e.g. in printing, perpetuated this concentration. Legislation such as the UK's **Sex Discrimination Act** of 1975 have sought, as a major aim, a higher proportion of women in each occupational group.

Mill, J.S. (1948) *Principles of Political Economy*, Book II, ch. XIV, section 5.

See also: **crowding hypothesis; occupational segregation**.

Shackle, George Lennox Sharman, 1903– (030)
British economist noted for his works on **expectations**. After an education at New College, Oxford, and the London School of Economics, he worked at the Oxford Institute of Statistics and, during the war, in the Economic Section of the Cabinet Secretariat before being appointed Reader in Economic Theory at Leeds University from 1950 to 1951 and Brunner Professor of Economic Science at the University of Liverpool from 1951 to 1969. He has delved deeply into the central issues of **Keynes**'s *General Theory*, **expectations** and **uncertainty**, e.g. in his *Expectations, Investment and Income* (1938) and *Expectations in Economics* (1949). A lively account of the renaissance of economics in the 1930s is detailed in *The Years of High Theory* (1967). The principal questions he examines are the significance of time, the meaning and process of human choosing and the role of information in choosing.

Ford, J.L. (ed.) (1990) *Time, Expectations and Uncertainty. Selected Essays of G.L.S. Shackle*, Aldershot: Edward Elgar.

See also: **potential surprise function**.

shadow economy (010)
The activities of the **black economy** and of households and voluntary organizations. The value of all the goods and services produced in this way do not enter into the official **national income** accounts.

Brezinsti, H. (1991) *The Shadow Economy*, Boulder, CO: Westview Press.
Smith, S. (1986) *Britain's Shadow Economy*, Oxford: Basil Blackwell.

shadow price (010)

An imputed price used where a market price does not exist. Prices of this type are used by large firms for their internal transactions, by central planners for accounting purposes and in **cost–benefit analysis** to measure the effects of a particular investment. There are shadow rates of interest, shadow exchange rates and shadow wage rates. The purpose of such pricing is to correct distortions introduced by monopoly, taxes and unemployment. The concept has many applications in both developed and less developed countries (because they tend to overvalue their labour and undervalue their foreign exchange).

Little, I.M.D. and Scott, M.F.G. (eds) (1976) *Using Shadow Prices*, London: Heinemann Educational.

shallow market (010)

A market with little trading with the consequence that an individual transaction can have a great influence on the market price.

sham trading (010, 310)

Buying or selling not backed by goods. This type of trading is central to the idea of a **futures** market.

Shapley value (210)

The utility that a participant in an *n*-person game with an uncertain outcome, e.g. a lottery, expects to obtain. The game assumes that utility is transferable between the players and that it is a **zero-sum game**. Shapley values have been used in models of taxation, the allocation of joint costs and the study of voting systems.

Shapley, L.S. (1953) 'A value for *n*-person games', in H.W. Kuhn and A.W. Tucker (eds) *Contributions to the Theory of Games*, Princeton, NJ: Princeton University Press.

share (310)

A portion of the financial capital of a limited company which gives the holder an entitlement to a fixed return, in the case of preference shares, or, in the case of ordinary shares, a variable dividend decided by the board of directors. Ordinary shares are also known as **equities**.

share borrowing (310)

The borrowing of **shares**, usually from the holdings of large **institutional investors**, by **market-makers** in order to effect delivery of shares more speedily. This enables payment to be received immediately, at the low fee of about 2 per cent of the value of the borrowed shares. This practice was previously permitted for **jobbers** who wanted to sell short, i.e. sell shares they did not own and then borrow to effect delivery. In the UK, the Stock Exchange restricts the practice now to **market-makers** to encourage more firms to undertake that role. Stock borrowing has long been permitted in US markets.

share buy-back (310, 520)

Purchase by a company of its own shares, if permitted by its Articles of Association. This practice, which aims to enhance the earnings per share of a company, is more prevalent in the USA than in the UK.

sharecropper (710)

A tenant farmer who pays his rent in kind as a percentage of his crops. In return the landlord provides seed, fertilizers, implements and other non-labour inputs. This type of joint venture is a common feature of agriculture in less developed countries and regions. The relative shares of landlord and tenant will depend on the scarcity of labour relative to capital and local culture. The landlord's share is much larger in Middle Eastern countries than in southern Europe. In developed countries, unlike Third World countries, sharecroppers will be compensated for permanent land improvements and will be granted longer leases to encourage the development of agriculture.

Byres, T.J. (ed.) (1983) *Sharecropping and Share-croppers*, London: Cass.

shared monopoly (610)

See: **oligopoly**.

share economy (070)

1 An economy in which industry is widely owned through the distribution of **equity**

shares to employees and other small share-holders.

2 The sharing of the revenues of a firm with its employees.

See also: **wider share ownership**.

share fisherman (820)
A fisherman whose remuneration is a proportion of the profits from each catch. This method of pay has long been used in Scotland.

share support operation (310, 520)
The purchase of the shares of a company by its directors and their associates which is intended to boost the share price, especially during a **takeover**.

See also: **share buy-back**.

Sharpe, William, 1934– (030)
Educated at the University of California, Los Angeles, and professor of economics at Stanford University since 1970. He has developed the **capital asset pricing model** to examine portfolio risk into its systematic and unsystematic elements. In 1990 he shared the **Nobel Prize for Economics** with **Markovitz** and **Miller**.

See also: **beta**.

shekel (430)
The currency of Israel.

shelf registration (310)
A company or government **bond** which is approved prior to issue. When the market is favourable, the bond is issued at short notice. This method of issue was introduced in the USA in 1982.

shell company (310, 510)
A company which has ceased to engage in its original activities, has few assets and earnings but usually has a stock market quotation. Some former plantation companies are of this kind. These companies provide an easy way for a new company to acquire a stock market quotation by a 'shell operation'.

shell operation (310)
Acquisition of a **shell** company as a means of obtaining a stock market quotation.

sheltered employment (810)
Employment specially provided for disabled persons. In the UK, the firm Remploy was set up in 1945 under the Disabled Persons (Employment) Act as a principal way of implementing the Act but other firms were expected to offer at least 3 per cent of their jobs to the disabled. Remploy by using a fine subdivision of labour is capable of providing more technically simple jobs than other employers.

Sherman Act 1890 (610)
The founding statute of the US federal antitrust legislation. This Act prohibits 'all contracts, combinations and conspiracies in restraint of trade' (section 1) and monopolization in interstate and foreign trade (section 2). The Act was followed by further federal legislation.

Bork, R.H. (1978) *The Antitrust Paradox*, New York: Basic Books.

See also: **antitrust**; **Celler–Kefauver Antimerger Act**; **Clayton Act**; **Federal Trade Commission Act**; **Robinson–Patman Act**.

shifting of taxes (320)
Passing the burden of a tax from the person who originally pays it to another. A principal example is the shifting of a tax on commodities from producers to consumers (forward shifting); there can also be backward shifting, e.g. when an *ad valorem* tax has to be paid by a producer because the final prices are the same pre- and post-tax.

See also: **tax incidence**.

shift share analysis (940)
A technique in regional analysis for analysing the effects on a region's growth of its share of national industrial activity, usually measured by employment, being structurally different from that of the country as a whole. Thus, for example, if region X were growing faster than the country of which it was part, this analysis would indicate how much of that regional growth could be attributed to it having a higher proportion of rapidly growing industries than the country as a whole. The shift can be split into a proportional shift, reflecting differences in

the mix of industrial sectors at national and regional levels, and a differential shift caused by different employment growth rates in a region and the nation of which it is part.

shifts in demand or supply curves (010)

An upward or downward movement of a whole demand or supply curve because a variable, other than price, has changed. A change in consumer tastes, in consumer incomes or in the prices of other goods can move a demand curve; a change in technology or governmental regulation can move a supply curve. These shifts are always the result of a failure of the *ceteris paribus* condition.

See also: **identification problem**.

Shinsanbetsu (830)

National Federation of Industrial Organizations: this Japanese national-level trade union federation had a membership of 56,000 persons in October 1988 at the time of its dissolution.

See also: **Rengo**.

shock inflation (150)

A once-and-for-all change in the price level which may be caused by a change in **indirect tax** rates or import prices or a major change in the supply of a major commodity, e.g. oil.

See also: **oil price increases**.

shoe leather costs of inflation (150)

Costs in time and effort to carry out economic transactions because the falling value of money in times of inflation brings about a reduction in money holdings.

See also: **menu costs of inflation**; **transactions cost**.

shop steward (830)

An elected official of a trade union who represents a group of workers within an establishment or factory. He/she participates in local bargaining on pay, conditions of work and disciplinary procedures. It was argued in the 1960s by the **Donovan Commission** that in Britain they were central actors in an informal system of factory-level industrial relations.

short (430)

A deficit: a foreign exchange dealer is 'in short' when he has a deficit in a particular currency.

See also: **long**.

shortage economy (070)

An **economy** which is characterized by **excess demand** for many goods and services for substantial periods of time. This often happens because for welfare reasons prices of basic necessities are kept below their market clearing levels. Under a **centrally planned economy**, there is a tendency to adhere to the same set of prices for many years, not raising them as demand rises. Also, if the prices set by a government reflect its priorities and not those of consumers excess demand can easily develop.

See also: **Soviet-type economy**.

short selling (310)

Selling a security which is not owned by the seller who subsequently buys sufficient volume of that security to effect delivery. Such behaviour, the activity of a **bear**, is popular when markets are falling in price.

See also: **share borrowing**.

short-termism (310, 320)

Preferring the short to the long term in economic decision-making, particularly preferring to spend current income rather than invest long term. This attitude is manifest in the low proportion of total expenditure on research and development, inadequate investment in technology and poor control over the total wages bill. UK Chancellor of the Exchequer Nigel Lawson coined the term in 1986 to characterize much of the thinking of industrialists and financiers. Also, it has been argued that major **institutional investors**, e.g. pension funds, despite their ability to make long-term investments, are too interested in capital gains from short-term market movements.

short-term money market (310)

A market in financial securities which have a lifespan of several months at most; it is based in a major financial centre. Since 1970, many new markets of this kind have been established in the City of London, New York and European financial capitals. The items traded include **certificates of deposit**, **treasury bills**, **commercial bills**, local authority bills, discount house deposits, local authority deposits, **ecus** and **special drawing rights**.

See also: **discount market**.

short-time working (820)

Working fewer hours than the standard working week, as defined by a collectively bargained agreement or an individual employment contract. This is a method of making a short-term adjustment to a fall in demand for labour; it often precedes redundancies.

See also: **working hours; overtime**.

Shoup Mission (320)

A mission of inquiry headed by the US economist Carl S. Shoup who recommended in 1949 a complete overhaul of the **Japanese taxation system**, bringing it closer to the US system than to Western Europe's.

Bronfenbrenner, M. and Kogiku, K. (1957) 'The aftermath of the Shoup tax reforms', *National Tax Journal* 10: 236–54.

Shoup Mission (1949) *The Report on Japanese Taxation*, Tokyo: General Headquarters, Supreme Commander for the Allied Powers.

shunto (830)

The Japanese Spring Wage Offensive. Since 1955, the union federations have presented simultaneous wage claims to employers with one union being chosen to advance the first wage and conditions claim which acts as a pacemaker for other unions. The system gives more power to a trade union movement which is characterized by 34,000 small unions mostly at the enterprise level and provides macroeconomic guidelines for enterprise bargaining.

See also: **enterprise union; pattern settlement; wage round**.

shutdown price (010)

A minimum price equal to the short-run average **variable cost**. Below this price, firms would prefer to shut down rather than

accept a lower price and incur losses, including payments needed to cover **fixed costs**.

SIB (310)

Securities and Investments Board.

SIBOR (310)

Singapore Inter-Bank Offered Rate.

See also: **London Inter-Bank Offered Rate**.

SIC (220)

See: **Standard Industrial Classification**.

SICAV (310)

A French **unit trust**.

siege economy (070)

A national **economy** cut off from economic relationships with the rest of the world, usually through war or **economic sanctions**. To maintain the availability of a wide range of goods, such economies have to diversify into activities new to them. It has been argued in favour of tariffs that some high cost industries should be protected from international competition in case a country is under siege in the future and needs the output from those industries.

See also: **autarky; open economy**.

sight deposit (310)

A bank deposit which is immediately payable on demand.

See also: **current account; time deposit**.

signal jamming (010)

A type of **barrier to entry** which 'jams', or prevents, a potential entrant from gaining information about the profitability of the existing firms of an industry.

Fudenberg, D. and Tirole, J. (1986) 'A "signal jamming" theory of predation', *Rand Journal of Economics* 18: 211–31.

signalling (010)

Providing information for economic decision-making, particularly by the price mechanism. Changes in prices 'signal' to producers and potential producers a change in the relationship between demand and supply in that market. If prices rise, producers will be aware of a supply deficiency and encouraged to increase their output and, if necessary, their capital stock. Similarly in labour markets an increase in occupational pay will encourage persons to acquire the appropriate training and to apply for jobs of that kind.

significance test (210)
A procedure which calculates a statistic to ascertain whether an observed deviation from the **null hypothesis** is real or the product of chance.

See also: **chi-squared distribution**; *F*-test; **Student's *t* distribution**.

silver ring (310)
The two or three City of London discount houses who principally run the books which determine the discount market.

SIMEX (430)
Singapore International Monetary Exchange.

Simon, Herbert Alexander, 1916– (030)
US theorist of corporate behaviour who was educated at Chicago University. He taught at the Illinois Institute of Technology from 1942 to 1949 and at the Carnegie Institute of Technology from 1949. Subsequently, he has taught at Carnegie-Mellon University, as professor of administration and psychology from 1949 to 1955 and since then as holder of the chair of Computer Science and Psychology. His eclectic knowledge of psychology, computer science and economics has enabled him to write extensively on administrative behaviour and corporate decision-making. His famous textbook *Administrative Behavior* was first published in 1947. His celebrated contribution to economics has been the concept of **bounded rationality**. He was awarded the **Nobel Prize for Economics** in 1978.

Simons, Henry Calvert, 1899–1946 (030)
Educated at the University of Michigan and professor successively at Iowa, 1920–7, and Chicago, 1927–46. He was a founder of the **Chicago School**, a prominent tax theorist whose ideas underlie the US federal individual income tax and a noted libertarian in his attitude to economic policy.

Simons, H.C. (1938) *Personal Income Taxation: The Definition of Income as a Problem of Fiscal Policy*, Chicago, IL: University of Chicago Press.
—— (1948) *Economic Policy for a Free Society*, Chicago, IL: University of Chicago Press.
—— (1950) *Federal Tax Reform*, Chicago, IL: University of Chicago Press.

simulation model (210)
A model of economic reality which concentrates on the main and crucial features of an economy and attempts to estimate the relationships between those features with a view to estimating the effects of changing the values of those variables. Such models have been used in the study of cyclical fluctuations and in corporate decision-making and national economic planning.

Bonini, C.P. (1963) *Simulation of Information and Decision Systems in the Firm*, Englewood Cliffs, NJ: Prentice Hall.
Duesenberry, J.S., Eckstein, O. and Fromm, G. (1960) 'A simulation model of the United States economy in recession', *Econometrica* 28: 749–809.

single-capacity trading (310)
The method of trading that separated **jobbers** from brokers on the London Stock Exchange which was in force from 1908 to 1986. London's deregulation, usually termed **Big Bang**, gave stock exchange members the right to combine both functions and be **market-makers**.

single currency (430)
The only currency which is acceptable as **legal tender** in a particular country or countries; different from a **common currency**.

Single European Act 1986 (420)
An amendment to the **Treaty of Rome** which has changed the nature of decision-making in the **European Community** by permitting majority voting instead of unanimity, limited the harmonization of policies to essential standards, granted the European Parliament a greater role in the creation of legislation, reaffirmed the need to increase the **European Community**'s economic and social cohesion in labour and scientific matters and added to the Treaty a recognition of organizations, such as the **European Monetary System**, which have been created since 1958. The features of the Act are

derived from Lord Cockfield's report *Completing the Internal Market* (1985) which listed 300 changes which would have to be implemented by 1992 to remove barriers to movement and trade.

single factorial terms of trade (420)
Net barter terms of trade multiplied by a **productivity** change index for the export trades. This enables a nation to calculate what its factors of production earn in foreign goods.

See also: **terms of trade**.

single market (420)
The internal market of the **European Community** to be created by 1992 as a consequence of the **Single European Act** of 1986. The European Community market will be unified by the removal of all barriers to movement and trade, as well as unifying the financial market. The European Community has estimated that member countries could gain to the extent of 4¼–6½ per cent of **gross domestic product** through the institution of this internal market because of the removal of barriers affecting trade and production and through the exploitation of **economies of scale** and the efficiency which arises from increased competition. This stage of removing the final barriers to trade in the European Community concerns the removal of remaining differences between the technical regulations between countries, waiting at frontiers to conform with customs regulations, the restriction of competition for public contracts to the nationals of one country and the restriction of competition in financial, transport and some other service industries. This liberalization will have an impact on industrial costs, efficiency and innovation, bringing about increased specialization based on **comparative advantage**. Increased market integration is estimated to bring about a cost reduction of 1–7 per cent of the costs of one-third of European industry worth 60 billion ecu and a gain in the gross domestic product of the European Community of 4¼–6½ per cent (i.e. 175 to 255 billion ecu for the twelve member states). These gains will be realized in a period of five or six years; how they will be divided between countries and their regions is difficult to estimate. Post-1989 developments in Eastern Europe and the reunification of Germany could not be taken into account.

Emerson, M., Anjean, M., Catinat, M., Goybet, P. and Jacqueman, A. (1988) *The Economics of 1992*, Oxford: Oxford University Press.

single tax movement (320)
The campaign in the USA by Henry **George** for existing taxes to be replaced by a single tax on land, which would absorb all pure rents. This view was based on the observation that landlords have an unearned income arising from land as it rises in value through being fixed in supply but increasingly demanded as the population grows. A century before, the **Physiocrats**, too, proposed a single tax on land. For such a change in taxation to be fair to all factors of production, **economic rent** wherever it occurs, including a portion of the earnings of talented performers, would have to be taxed.

George, H. (1879) *Progress and Poverty*, New York: J.W. Lovell.
—— (1918) *Single Tax – What It Is and Why We Urge It*, Los Angeles, CA: Golden Press.

See also: **Turgot**.

single union deal (830)
An agreement between an employer and a **trade union** which excludes other unions from organizing workers in that firm or in a workplace within it. This simplification of **industrial relations** has increasingly been requested by firms setting up new plants and is accepted by trade unions who fear that the alternative is a non-union plant. Japanese-owned companies have been major pioneers of this approach in the UK where it was deeply resented by the trade unions which often were rejected as recognized representatives of workers. Countries with **industrial unions**, e.g. Germany, or **enterprise unions**, e.g. Japan, have long accepted the principle of one union in charge of worker representation.

Bassett, P. (1986) *Strike Free: New Industrial Relations in Britain*, London: Macmillan.

SIP (720)
State implementation plan (USA) for pollution control.

See also: **Environmental Protection Agency**.

SITC (220)
See: **Standard International Trade Classification**.

size distribution (160, 210)
A frequency distribution which classifies an economic entity according to size classes. Personal incomes can be classified to show what proportion falls into each range of income; likewise, data on firms can be presented in this way. Endowments of human and non-human capital are major determinants of the size distribution of income.

Champernowne, D.G. (1953) 'A model of income distribution', *Economic Journal* 63: 318–51.
Meade, J.E. (1964) *Efficiency, Equality, and the Ownership of Property*, London: Allen & Unwin.

See also: **personal income distribution**.

size of an economy (070)
A national **economy's gross national product**. This is used as a measure because **national income** accounting attempts to measure all the output from all economic activities in a given time period. Land areas and populations are used to measure the size of a country.

skewed frequency curve (210)
A **frequency curve** whose maximum is near the beginning (skewed to the right, positively skewed) or near the end (skewed to the left, negatively skewed) of the range of values of a variable (see figures below).

skewness (210)
The degree of asymmetry of a distribution. This is measured as the **arithmetic mean** minus the **mode** divided by the **standard deviation**.

skill differential (820)
See: **wage differentials**.

skimming (530)
A pricing policy for new products which sets prices at a high level to 'skim' the expenditure of higher income customers. These high prices are intended to cover the costs of **research and development**.

sleeping economy (310)
Forgotten bank deposits and savings certificates.

See also: **monetary overhang**.

sliding parity (430)
A small frequent change in a **fixed exchange rate**.

SLM (820)
Segmented labour market theory.

See also: **dual labour market**.

slump (040, 140)
A long period of low national output and high unemployment, e.g. the early 1930s.

See also: **depression; recession**.

slumpflation (150)
Friedman's assertion that rising levels of **unemployment** and rising rates of price **inflation** occur simultaneously. Dia-

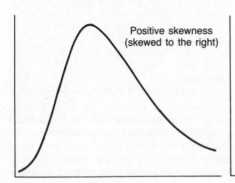
Positive skewness (skewed to the right)

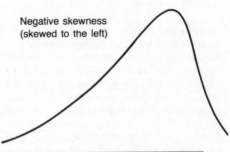
Negative skewness (skewed to the left)

grammatically this is shown by a positively sloped **Phillips-curve**.

See also: **stagflation**.

Slutsky effect (020)

A consumer's reaction to a change in price. **Hicks** in *Value and Capital* attributed this to the Soviet mathematician and statistician Eugen Slutsky (1880–1948) who contributed, to economics, suggestions about consumer theory. This fundamental equation of price theory splits the effect of a price change into an **income effect** and a **substitution effect**. The effect can also be applied to the effect on the labour supply of a **lump sum tax**.

Slutsky equation (010)

This states that a **price effect** is equal to the sum of the **income and substitution effects**.

small firm (610)

A **firm** often defined as having less than 200 employees and managed by its owner. Despite the growth in the size of firms in the twentieth century, there is still a role for small businesses where the market is limited in size, **economies of scale** do not exist (e.g. in craft industries) or larger firms prefer to subcontract out many operations (e.g. in Japanese shipbuilding). In the UK many incentives are offered to small firms as there is the belief that they are a major source of **innovation** and will be tomorrow's large employers. In the UK, 25 per cent of firms are small, but in the USA, France and FRG 60 per cent of firms are small.

Bannock, G. (1981) *The Economics of Small Firms*, Oxford: Basil Blackwell.
Curran, J., Stanworth, J. and Watkins, D. (eds) (1986) *The Survival of the Small Firm*, vols I and II, Aldershot: Gower.

smart card (310)

A **credit card** with a built-in store of information about the holder and his/her financial state. The information is stored in a wafer-like microchip embedded in the plastic. These were pioneered in France, where 3 million had been issued by the end of 1986. Banks and credit companies are prepared to pay the greater production cost of these as they are less likely than earlier types of card to be fraudulently misused. They could be the dominant card for financial transactions in the USA and many **Organization for Economic Cooperation and Development** countries in the near future.

See also: **carte à mémoire**.

smart money (310)

The short-term volatile deposits of very rich persons which in times of national crisis are moved to safer havens overseas.

See also: **capital flight**.

Smith, Adam, 1723–90 (030)

Scottish economist and philosopher who was the founder and leader of the classical school of economics. He was born in Kirkcaldy, a Fife town to the north of Edinburgh, the only son of a Customs Commissioner who died before his birth leaving his mother to be a major influence throughout 61 years of his life. He was educated at the local burgh school and at Glasgow University from 1737 to 1740 under Francis Hutcheson, professor of moral philosophy, whose utilitarian ideas were to influence the early stage of Smith's economic theorizing. An unhappy period as Snell Exhibitioner at Balliol College, Oxford, from 1740 to 1746 enabled him to spend long solitary hours in acquiring the basis of his erudition. Returning to Scotland, he was successively professor of logic, 1751–2, and professor of moral philosophy from 1752 to 1764 at Glasgow University. His wide duties as a professor included lecturing on jurisprudence which he broadly interpreted to include economics, as the police in France had the task of regulating markets. In his extant *Lectures on Jurisprudence* for the winter of 1762 to 1763 there is an early sketch of the ideas which were to appear in *The Wealth of Nations*: the **division of labour**, the distinction between **value in use** and **value in exchange**, the importance of **free trade** and the stages of economic development are discussed. More importantly for his career, he produced in that period his *Theory of Moral Sentiments* (1759; republished five times in his lifetime) which was based on the Stoics' view of the natural order and provided an exposition of his concept of the **invisible hand** which was to play an important role in the theoretical framework of *The Wealth of Nations*. A leading government minister, Charles Townsend, was so impressed by the *Theory* that he persuaded Smith to abandon his Glasgow professorship and become travelling tutor to his stepson, the young Duke of Buccleuch. This Grand Tour to France and Switzerland in the years 1764–6 enabled Smith to meet **Quesnay** and **Turgot**, the prominent **Physiocrats** who were perhaps the most important economists of the day: not surprisingly, their influence is evident in *The Wealth of Nations*.

The Grand Tour, cut short by the death of the Duke's brother, brought Smith back to Kirkcaldy where, supported by his continued stipend of £300 per annum from the Duke, he spent six years preparing his great work on economics. In London, from 1773 to 1776, he completed it, as well as giving government ministers advice on major policy issues, including the problem of the American colonies. His highly acclaimed *Wealth of Nations* (1776 and four more editions in his lifetime) provided a powerful theory of **economic growth** (built upon the division of labour principle and the consequence of man's desire for betterment which leads to savings which are productively invested), theories of value and distribution and an exposition of libertarian economic policy which, although sharing much with *laissez-faire* economists, permits many exceptions, e.g. on the grounds of national defence the navigation laws which excluded foreign ships from carrying British trade are permissible. From 1778 to his death he resided as a Commissioner of Customs in Edinburgh – perhaps a strange occupation for a propounder of free trade but a useful £600 per annum addition to his income. Also, this post was a major mark of government approval and an opportunity to undertake empirical research into the mercantile system he so forcefully attacked. Any reader of his works is soon impressed by their breadth, humanity and fundamental arguments. Justifiably, he was then and is now regarded as one of the world's greatest thinkers and economic theorists.

Hollander, A. (1973) *The Economics of Adam Smith*, Toronto: University of Toronto Press.
Skinner, A.S. and Wilson, T. (eds) (1975) *Essays on Adam Smith*, Oxford: Oxford University Press.
Smith, A. (1976–7) *Collected Works*, ed. by A.S. Skinner and T. Wilson, Oxford: Oxford University Press.

See also: **Adam Smith Institute; classical economics; mercantilism;** *Wealth of Nations*.

Smithsonian Agreement (430)

A realignment of major world **currencies** by the **Group of Ten** in December 1971 at the Smithsonian Institute, Washington, DC. This agreement was forced on the international financial community by President Nixon when he ordered the US Treasury to suspend their gold sales in August 1971. Wider fluctuations of 4.5 per cent against the US dollar were permitted, the US dollar was devalued against gold by 7.9 per cent and the official gold price was raised from $35 to $38 per fine ounce. The subsequent floating of currencies, e.g. of sterling in June 1972, quickly abrogated the principal terms of the agreement.

See also: **Bretton Woods Agreement**.

smokestack American stocks (310)

The **common stock** of basic US industries.

Smoot–Hawley Tariff Act 1930 (420)

The major US federal statute to establish **protectionism** in the twentieth century. It included **tariff** schedules for over 20,000 products, proposing increases in many cases. It led to **beggar-my-neighbour** policies which some economists claim was a major cause of the worldwide depression in the 1930s.

See also: **Reciprocal Trade Agreements Act**.

SMSA (220, 840)

See: **Standard Metropolitan Statistical Area**.

SNA (220)

See: **System of National Accounts**.

snake in the tunnel (430)

The exchange rate regime which was part of the **Smithsonian Agreement** and existed from December 1971 to March 1973. The 'tunnel' was the permitted range of 4.5 per cent fluctuations around the dollar; the 'snake', the band of 2.25 per cent to which the participating currencies were confined at a particular time. It also applies to the **European Monetary System**'s currency movements since 1979.

SNB (310)
Swiss National Bank; the central bank of Switzerland.

SNIG (110)
Sustained non-inflationary growth.

snowbelt (940)
An older industrial area – in the USA, the Midwest and Northeast.

See also: **rustbelt**; **sunbelt**.

snugging (310)
The tightening of US **monetary policy** by pushing up interest rates and thereby lowering bond prices. An expression introduced by Paul Volcker when he was Chairman of the **Federal Reserve System** In the 1980's.

social accounting (220)
See: **national income**.

social adjustment cost (010, 410)
The social production cost, i.e. producer's welfare loss, brought about by increased competition from imports. A major cost of this kind is the unemployment caused by imports replacing domestic production.

See also: **Trade Act**.

social capital (010)
Fixed investment created for and used by the community as a whole, e.g. roads, hospitals and schools.

See also: **infrastructure**.

social choice theory (020)
An attempt to provide a normative rationale for social decisions in societies where individuals have different preferences about the options available. **Bernoulli** was the first to discuss individual decision-making systematically. This theory is based on **utilitarian welfare economics** and assumes that full information is available to a decision-maker who is then in a position to maximize **social welfare**. As there are so many methodological problems in aggregating individual preferences, social choice theory has made an extensive examination

of **voting procedures** as a means of creating aggregated social preferences. This complex theory is criticized for its unrealistic assumption of full information and for the dictatorial method of decision-making it proposes. A major application of it is the study of the appropriate extent of the public sector and the mechanism for controlling it.

Arrow, K. (1966) *Social Choice and Individual Values*, 2nd edn, New York: Wiley.
Hoag, G.C. and Hallett, G. (1940) *Proportional Representation: The Key to Democracy*, New York: National Municipal League.
Rothenberg, J. (1961) *The Measurement of Social Welfare*, Englewood Cliffs, NJ: Prentice Hall.

social compact (830)
See: **social contract**.

social conscience fund (310)
A **mutual fund** whose portfolio does not include investments in morally criticized corporations and companies. Tobacco, alcohol, arms and South African investments have all been candidates for exclusion.

social contract (830)
An agreement, also known as the 'social compact', which lasted from March 1974 to July 1975 between the UK Labour government and trade unions to grant various social benefits, pro-labour union laws, price controls and higher public expenditure in return for union-organized restraint of wages. The government kept its promises; the unions failed to restrain pay which rose in twelve months by 32 per cent. Rather different from Rousseau's celebrated philosophy of that name.

social cost (010)
The **opportunity cost** to society of the resources which it uses. This is equal to all the costs incurred by a society in producing a good or service. In most cases of production there is a divergence between private and social costs.

Pearce, D.W. (ed.) (1978) *The Valuation of Social Cost*, London: Allen & Unwin.

See also: **private cost**.

social cost of monopoly (010)
The welfare losses which result from the

restriction of output and higher prices under monopolistic production. There is also the social cost which occurs through striving to attain a monopoly position.

social cost of unemployment (810)
The reduction in national output resulting from an economy operating at a production level less than **full employment**.

See also: **private cost of unemployment**.

social credit (030, 320)
A scheme advanced by Major C.H. Douglas in the 1920s to advance discounts to retailers, and dividends to citizens, to solve the problem of under-consumption. This attempt to cure unemployment in the interwar years (based on a theory of the **trade cycle)** was partially implemented in Alberta, Canada, in 1935 when a scheme to distribute to all citizens social dividends based on the real wealth of the country was introduced.

Douglas, C.H. (1933) *Social Credit*, 3rd edn, London: Eyre & Spottiswoode.

social democracy (070)
A national economy whose economic policies are conducted within the framework of a **social contract** between labour and capital.

social dividend scheme (320)
An integration of income maintenance with income taxation. The state fixes an income maintenance payment related to household size in order to prevent dire poverty. Income above this is subject to progressive taxation but income below it is supplemented by 'dividends' in the form of a cash sum. Although long advocated by many political parties, such schemes are difficult to implement.

See also: **negative income tax; poverty trap**.

social good (010)
See: **public good**.

socialism (070)
A way of organizing an **economy** so that the society owns productive capital and distributes the **national income** for the benefit of all. It is the alternative to uncontrolled **capitalism** and to some extent a rejection of market mechanisms. Early idealistic forms of socialism, often based on the idea of producers' **cooperatives**, were suggested by Owen, Fourier and St Simon and were soon analysed in John Stuart **Mill**'s *Principles of Political Economy* (1848). Later socialist writings departed from the cooperative principle and based their theories on wider premises. **Marx, Engels** and their followers were more ambitious in their theorizing, and provided a long-term analysis of the emergence of capitalism (mythically described by **Turgot** and **Smith)** and late **classical** theories of **value** and **distribution**.

Today, socialism for a whole economy is often associated with **planning** (as in **Soviet-type economies**); economies which have modified their type of central planning by combining planning with market mechanisms (e.g. Hungary and Yugoslavia) are examples of what is termed **market socialism**. As socialism coincided with the rise of **trade unions** in the countries first to industrialize, it is not surprising that there has often been an intimate association between labour and socialist parties. The remaining idealists who desire to live in societies which follow strict **egalitarian** principles would be best to choose sub-economies such as the Israeli kibbutzim or the US Hutterite communities.

See also: **egalitarianism; guild socialism; industrial democracy; market socialism**.

socialist economy (070)
A national **economy** which attempts to achieve a fairer distribution of income and to use a method of allocation other than the market. There are many types, including **market socialism** and **state capitalism**.

Kantorovich, L.V. (1965) *The Best Use of Economic Resources*, Oxford and New York: Pergamon.

social liberalism (030)
The political philosophy which advocates that collective action increases individual welfare and liberty. It is argued that this type of **mixed economy** preserves both markets and political freedom, as well as giving a greater role to government. **Keynes** and **Beveridge** were the chief proponents of this view.

socially necessary labour time (810)

The amount of time a worker devotes to the production of a particular good under normal conditions of production at the current standard of labour **productivity**. **Marx** found it necessary to refine the notion of labour quantity in this way to avoid the implication of his theory – that laziness increases **value**.

social market economy (070)

An **economy** which combines private ownership of industry and market methods of allocation with high welfare expenditures and industrial policies. Germany has long been a major example of this type of economy.

social opportunity cost of foreign exchange (430)

The effective local currency cost to a country of the foreign exchange it spends plus the effective local currency yield to it of the foreign exchange it generates by exporting and by **import substitution**.

social overhead capital (010, 640)

See: **social capital**.

social ownership (610)

A form of public ownership similar to **nationalization**. It is different from the type of British nationalization introduced in the 1940s in that members of the public hold non-voting shares and there is a greater degree of **workers' participation** in management.

See also: **cooperative**; **industrial democracy**.

social product (220)

The national product of a particular country or community.

See also: **national income**.

social profit (010)

The total return to an economy of an investment project which includes both money profit and the achievement of other aims, including, for example, a fairer income distribution.

See also: **cost–benefit analysis**.

social rate of discount (010)

1 The rate at which society transfers resources between periods.

2 The rate at which a government makes an intertemporal transfer as representing the wishes of society. The concept is central to **cost–benefit analysis**.

See also: **private rate of discount**.

social security (320, 910)

Transfer incomes, especially retirement pensions and unemployment benefits. The provision of such benefits varies greatly from country to country, being particularly generous in Scandinavian countries and Germany. The ratio of employer and employee contributions (used to finance social security) to wages is high in countries such as the Netherlands but much lower in countries such as Japan and the USA. Many studies show that an increase in social security charges is shifted to the wage earner if he/she regards the corresponding benefits as part of his/her wage. Social security schemes increase distortions in the labour market by increasing the cost of labour to the firm without increasing it to wage earners who do not regard the benefits as a full addition to their incomes. Social security can be financed in two ways. It can be fully funded so that investments are accumulated to produce an income for future recipients of social security grants, or it can be financed on a 'pay-as-you-go' basis, i.e. by current contributions, mainly by present members of the labour force.

Social Security Act 1935 (910)

US federal legislation which established a system of welfare payments financed by the contributions of employers and employees. Initially it was set up to finance retirement and survivor benefits but subsequently it has been extended to cover disability benefits and the cost of medical care.

social spending (320)

Public expenditure on health, education and the provision of transfer incomes. After excluding expenditure on defence and grants to industry, most of a nation's public expenditure is now of this type.

See also: **peace dividend**.

social time preference rate (010)

The rate at which society trades consumption of one time period with consumption of another. A positive rate means that the present is preferred to the future. Although the market rate of interest has been used as a proxy for this rate, it is not in all cases suitable because there is a variety of markets and rates according to the term, purpose and other aspects of the loan, the preferences of persons, including children, who neither borrow nor lend at interest are ignored and market rates can be pushed up by the monopoly power of banks and by the risk of non-repayment and the shorter life expectancies and time horizons of the poor, especially in less developed countries.

social wants (010, 320)

Services wanted by the community as a whole to increase its welfare. An individual does not desire these solely for his/her own consumption and as they are collectively supplied they cannot be charged to individuals. Prominent examples of such wants include **pollution control** and expenditure on law and order.

See also: **merit want**.

social welfare (010)

The economic well-being of a society as a whole, often measured in terms of the total volume of goods and services becoming available to it over a given period, i.e. **real income**. There is much dispute about an appropriate measure as **national income** accounting does not cover all **goods** and **bads** of an economy and total income measure ignores income distribution. As changes in social welfare are used to judge the efficacy of economic policies, a variety of tests have been used to see whether there has been an unambiguous increase in welfare. The stark **Pareto** approach has been challenged and replaced by other approaches, notably by **Scitovsky** and Rawls, to deal with the problem of the extent to which losers' reduction in welfare is more than compensated for by gainers' increase, after redistribution of real income. Much of **welfare economics** is concerned with this difficult problem which, as Little has shown,

reflects the value-loaded nature of many welfare discussions.

Little, I.M.D. (1957) *Critique of Welfare Economics*, 2nd edn, Oxford: Oxford University Press.

See also: **measure of economic welfare**.

social welfare function (020)

The total well-being of a society as a function of its resource allocation. Originally this was regarded as the sum of individual utilities but **Arrow** showed the impossibility of this when individuals have divergent opinions as the four conditions of collective rationality, the Pareto principle, non-dictatorship and independence of any alternative in an environment other than where the social choice is made cannot simultaneously be satisfied.

See also: **Arrow; Bergson; impossibility theorem**.

Society for Worldwide Interbank Financial Telecommunications (310, 430)

A private network established in 1973 in Brussels and operational from 1977 by European banks for the transfer of funds; by 1988 this financial information service had been extended to Asia, Australia and Latin America.

soft budget (120, 320)

A budget with a flexible limit. In **centrally planned economies**, the budgets of many firms are 'soft' because loss-making firms are kept in business by subsidies, tax concessions and credits.

soft commission (310)

Commission for a stockbroker's services based on actual services supplied, thus lower than standard commissions.

soft commodity (710)

An agricultural product such as coffee, cotton or sugar.

See also: **primary product**.

soft currency (430)

A **currency** which few want to hold as it is continuously depreciating, except in the periods when the inducement of high interest rates encourages foreigners to hold deposits of it. The currencies of Italy, Iceland and Mexico have been of this kind for many years.

See also: **hard currency**.

soft landing (310, 320)
Reaching a desired macroeconomic position for a country painlessly. Usually a landing of this kind makes possible the reduction of inflation without causing a recession.

soft loan (310, 430, 610)
A loan on easy terms, i.e. at a lower than market rate of interest and to be repaid over a longer period of time than is customary. This easing of the terms of credit has often been used to encourage the development of Third World countries and the depressed regions of industrialized countries.

soft modelling (210)
A form of factor analysis using as few **parameters** as possible. This approach is used to build socioeconomic models where there is little information on the place of each variable in a causal chain.

Joreskog, K. and Wold, H. (1982) *Systems under Indirect Observation*, Amsterdam: North-Holland.

sogo bank (310)
A Japanese mutual bank set up after the Second World War to finance small and medium-sized local firms with a minimum capital of 400 million yen (compared with 1 billion yen for commercial banks). When faced with the competition of deregulated **commercial banks** and of local **credit unions**, many sogos have turned to very risky lending; others have converted into commercial banks.

sogo shosha (530)
Japanese transnational trading company.

Sohyo (830)
General Council of Trade Unions of Japan: this national federation of trade unions had a membership of 3.9 million by 1989, of whom 1.2 million worked in the government sector, 1.1 million in services, 0.84 million in transport and communications and 0.52 million in manufacturing.

See also: **enterprise union**; **Rengo**.

sole proprietor (510)
A person who is both the sole owner and the manager of a firm, receiving all its post-tax profits and entirely responsible for its liabilities. The growth of self-employment is some indication of the increasing popularity of this form of enterprise.

See also: **partnership**; **small firm**.

Solow, Robert M., 1924– (030)
A leading US capital and growth theorist, at **Samuelson's** side in the **Cambridge controversies**. After a university education at Harvard, since 1950 he has spent his entire academic career at the Massachusetts Institute of Technology. Some of his contributions to growth theory are evident in his text *Growth Theory: An Exposition* (1969). His neoclassical position in capital theory emerges in his *Capital Theory and the Rate of Return* (1963). Later works included research into the economics of non-renewable resources. His major contributions to **macroeconomics** earned him the **Nobel Prize for Economics** in 1987.

Solow residual (110)
That part of economic growth which cannot be explained by the growth of the labour force or the stock of capital.

Solow, R.M. (1957) 'Technical change and the aggregate production function', *Review of Economic Studies* 39: 312–20.

South African Customs Union (420)
A customs union of Botswana, Lesotho, Swaziland and the Republic of South Africa set up in 1969.

South African Development Coordination Committee (130)
An organization formed in April 1980 to coordinate the transport, trade and development of Angola, Botswana, Lesotho, Malawi, Mozambique, Swaziland, Tanzania, Zambia and Zimbabwe.

sovereign loan (310)
A commercial loan to a sovereign state. Collateral is not offered with such loans and so there is little redress in the case of default. Much of the large foreign debts of Third

World countries today are of this nature. The only way of enforcing repayment of capital and interest is by negotiation and by refusing further credit facilities.

See also: **senior debt; world debt problem**.

Soviet Material Product System (220)

The distinctive system of **national income** accounting used in the USSR which, for the most part, regards goods, but not services, as constituting production. Government services and many private services are excluded. This attitude to national income accounting, so different from that used by Western countries, is founded on the distinction between **productive** and **unproductive labour** used by **classical economists**.

Soviet-type economy (070, 120)

A **centrally planned economy** of the kind set up under the five-year plans of the 1920s and 1930s which was adopted by most East European economies after 1948 and increasingly abandoned after 1989. This economy was based on a one-party state, largely organized in state-owned enterprises reporting in vertical hierarchies to industrial ministries which handed down detailed orders on every aspect of production within the framework of five-year and annual operational plans. Trade unions, also organs of the state, were given the tasks of overseeing the welfare of workers and contributing to the audit of individual enterprises. When the system failed to be efficient and supply the needs of consumers, reforms were attempted: these included devolving more decision-making to individual enterprises, allowing them to trade directly with each other and with foreign enterprises, allowing more incentives to managements and workers to encourage better use of resources, and more flexible pricing including **marginal cost pricing**.

Ellman, M. (1979) *Socialist Planning*, Cambridge and New York: Cambridge University Press.

spaceman economy (720)

An **economy** which aims to minimize the amounts of inputs needed to produce a stable stock of goods, consistent with a stability of life-supporting environmental systems. **Boulding** devised this notion in keeping with the idea of a 'Spaceship Earth'

with finite resources and fragile biological life-support mechanisms.

See also: **cowboy economy**.

Spanish customs/practices (820)

Restrictive labour practices, often unauthorized, which result in a worker being paid for doing little work, e.g. the ways of avoiding work which were for a long time rife amongst Fleet Street (London) printers, merchant seamen and television technicians in the UK. These customs are 'Spanish' in the sense of making possible a siesta-like existence.

See also: **featherbedding; restrictive practice**.

spatial benefit limitation (320)

The benefits derived from **local public goods**.

See also: **Tiebout hypothesis**.

spatial duopoly (730)

Two firms located at different places competing for the same group of dispersed customers.

spatial equalization (940)

The reduction in interregional inequalities in incomes or another economic variable.

See also: **regional policy**.

spatial monopoly (730)

A dominant firm which controls a market because of its distance from others. The growth of transport systems in the twentieth century has caused the disappearance of most monopolies of this type.

spatial oligopoly (730)

Several firms of the same industry located at different places competing for the same group of dispersed customers.

Spearman's rank correlation coefficient (210)

This measures the interrelatedness of the ranks of two variables. The coefficient is given by:

$$r_s = 1 - \frac{6 \sum_{i=1}^{N} (X_i - Y_i)^2}{N (N^2 - 1)}$$

where X and Y are the two variables and N is the number of pairs of values of X and Y.

special bracket firm (310)

An **investment bank** or similar financial institution which is at the top of a list of a syndicate of **underwriters** on a **tombstone**.

special deposit (310)

An additional cash deposit by commercial banks required on occasions by the Bank of England. The purpose of these deposits has been to reduce the total volume of bank deposits and hence the money supply by a shrinkage of the liquid assets of banks. This UK technique of credit control was first used in 1958; in 1971 it was also applied to the larger finance houses.

See also: **'corset'**.

special drawing rights (430)

International **reserve assets** under the control of the **International Monetary Fund** available for settling inter-country indebtedness since 1968. This 'paper gold' was created after the Washington Communiqué of March 1968 closed the Gold Pool because leading countries saw no need for more official holdings of official gold. Special drawing rights have a gold guarantee and carry a small amount of interest; they are 70 per cent wholly owned and 30 per cent credit. Over a five-year period each participant country must keep, on average, 30 per cent of its reserves in special drawing rights to avoid a few countries having all. On 1 January 1970, $3,500 million were distributed, followed by $3,000 million on 1 January 1971 and $3,000 million on 1 January 1972. A country can use its special drawing rights to finance a **balance of payments** deficit or to support its **exchange rate**. When drawing on them, a country informs the managing director of the International Monetary Fund who finds a partner to swap special drawing rights for currency. Special drawing rights grew to about one-twentieth of world reserves within twenty years of their creation. Without the large US balance of payments deficit and the resources of the **Eurodollar** market, a larger volume of special drawing rights would be needed.

special employment measures (810)

A variety of UK schemes to reduce unemployment of particular types. The Job Release Scheme aims to cut labour supply; the Community Programme and Enterprise Allowance aim to create jobs, especially for the long-term unemployed; and the Youth Training Scheme and Young Workers Scheme aim to cut youth unemployment.

specialist (310)

A stockbroker who creates a continuous market in stocks assigned to him/her by a particular stock exchange and corrects imbalances in supply and demand. This system is used by both the New York and Toronto stock exchanges (in the latter, the specialist is called a 'professional trader' or 'pro'). Also, on these exchanges, the specialists are permitted to deal on their own account. On other exchanges there are similar but government-appointed stockbrokers, e.g. at Frankfurt the Kursmakler and at Paris l'agent de change; similarly, on the Tokyo exchange, the saitori.

specialization (010)

1   Subdivision of labour.

2   A reduction in the number of economic activities of a country with a view to reducing costs and maximizing output. One of the major examples of specialization is in international trade, first justified by the doctrine of **absolute advantage** and subsequently by **comparative advantage**. Advocates of specialization always point out the general increase of real incomes which results from factors of production being employed in their best uses.

See also: **division of labour**.

specie (310)

Gold or silver coins.

specie-flow mechanism (430)

The automatic means under the **gold bullion standard** which brought about a **balance of payments** equilibrium. An outflow of gold lowered the prices of domestic production, thereby improving that country's balance of trade and inducing an inflow of **bullion** (the reverse would happen when there is an inflow). David **Hume**, one of the earliest proponents of this view, used this argument to refute **mercantilist** views that a country should, and can, have a permanent balance of payments surplus. Although this approach is appropriate to **fixed exchange rate** systems, it has inspired modern theories of the balance of payments which concentrate on the supply of, and demand for, money.

specification (210)

An initial stage in **regression** analysis in which an econometrician obtains assumptions by making inferences from data. These assumptions can be selected by examining the data or by repeated attempts using one assumption after another to ascertain what inferences follow.

Leamer, E.E. (1978) *Specification Searches*, New York: Wiley.

See also: **identification problem**.

specific duty (320)

An **indirect tax** which is the same whatever the value of the good or service taxed. Taxes on spirits and tobacco are often taxed in this way so that the duty levied does not change with producers' prices. Many import duties are specific in nature. The opposite of a specific duty is an *ad valorem* tax.

specific egalitarianism (020, 160)

The allocation of certain goods to ensure equal distribution of them to groups regarded as being most in need. A major example is **rationing** in wartime.

See also: **egalitarianism**.

specific training (810, 850)

Training which is of use to only one employer because of its specialized nature, e.g. knowledge of a particular production process. Employers are encouraged to invest in training of this kind as they, and not others, will receive the return from it.

See also: **general training; human capital**.

speculation (310, 430)

Buying and selling in commodity or financial markets, which are subject to many price fluctuations, in order to make a capital gain. It has been described as 'arbitrage through time'. Although much condemned as an unreal activity for private gain, it does contribute to price stability.

speculative demand for money (310)

The **demand for money** which arises from

stock market speculators leaving the market because of their expectation that no further capital gain can be obtained from investing their cash holdings. As bond prices and interest rates are inversely related, when bond prices are thought to have reached a peak, interest rates will be at their minimum – the **liquidity trap**. There is thus an inverse relationship between the rate of interest and the speculative demand for money.

spillover effect (830)

The indirect effect on another person(s) of a gain or loss to the original person(s). In British **collective bargaining** in which an increase in wages granted to **unionized** workers is given to non-unionized workers, this effect is commonplace. Other spillover effects in the labour market include unemployment amongst unionized workers because of pay increases and a shrinkage of **wage differentials** when there is an increased supply of less skilled workers (e.g. through mass immigration). In some markets injurious spillover effects can be compensated for by actions in tort/delict. But in the labour market the extent to which those responsible pay for the indirect effects of their actions is often restricted under labour relations legislation.

See also: **externality; insider wage setting; secondary action; social cost**.

sponsor demand (010)

A demand for a good or service which is paid for by a person other than the consumer, e.g. the commercial financing of sporting events.

See also: **market demand; option demand**.

spot market (310, 430)

A market in which currencies or commodities are traded for immediate delivery. In currency markets, the spot market is linked to a **forward market** by interest rate differences between countries, by **speculation** and by **hedging**.

spot price (010)

The present price of an asset, currency or commodity for immediate delivery.

See also: **future; option**.

spot rate (310, 430)
The price for a currency, security or commodity to be immediately delivered.

spread (310)
The range of a share price between its buying and selling prices. Spreads are lower the more **liquid** and efficient a stock market.

spread effect (940)
The transmission of economic growth in one region to another.

See also: **backwash effect**.

spreading (310)
Price **arbitrage** over time, often practised in commodity markets. It involves the purchase of a contract in one delivery month and the selling of a contract for a related commodity in a different delivery month. In option markets, 'spreading' is buying a **call option** at one striking price and selling it at another.

Sraffa, Piero, 1898–1983 (030)
Born in Turin, the son of a law professor and educated at Turin University he was a professor at the universities of Perugia and Cagliari from 1924 to 1926 before his long and influential Cambridge, UK, career successively at King's and Trinity Colleges from 1927 to his death. His move to Cambridge was made possible by an article attacking the Marshallian **theory of the firm** published by the *Economic Journal* (1926), the first indication of his theoretical brilliance. His greatest contribution to economics was his edition of the works of **Ricardo** from 1951 to 1973 and his most controversial a short book, *Production of Commodities by Means of Commodities* (1960), which began a critique of economics that founded the **neo-Ricardian** school. **Leontief** and Pasinetti saw his work more as another example of linear production theory.

Roncaglia, A. (1977) 'The Sraffian revolution', in S. Weintraub (ed.) *Modern Economic Thought*, Oxford: Basil Blackwell.

Steedman, I. (1988) *Piero Sraffa*, Brighton: Wheatsheaf.

——(ed.) (1989) *Sraffian Economics*, vols I and II (Schools of Thought in Economics No. 4) Aldershot: Edward Elgar.

SRD (310)
See: **Statutory Reserve Deposit**.

SRO (310)
See: **self-regulatory organization**.

SSAP (540)
See: **Statements of Standard Accounting Practice**.

stabex system (420, 710)
A scheme which assists **ACP** countries to make up the shortfalls in their agricultural export earnings.

stabilization policy (140)
See: **countercyclical policy**.

stable equilibrium (010)
An **equilibrium** state which is maintained by the rules of the system concerned.

Stackelberg duopoly model (020)
A model of duopoly in which one firm is the price leader and the other the price follower. Market equilibrium is reached only if one firm is the leader and one the follower; there is disequilibrium if both want to be price leaders or price followers.

stag (310)
A speculator who attempts to make a profit from subscribing to new issues of **shares** and selling them immediately they are marketable. For the stag to be successful, the offer price has to be lower than the market price. Stagging is encouraged by financial press reports which attempt to assess the true value of the issuing company and predict the market price when trading starts.

See also: **grey market**.

stages theory (110, 130)
A theory of economic development which shows the transition of an economy from its most primitive state to modern capitalism. **Turgot** and **Smith** independently advanced such views in 1750 but the late classical use of it in the hands of **Marx** immortalized it. Smith divided history into four ages – hunters, shepherds, agriculture and commerce. More recently **Rostow** has suggested a five-stage theory which is as ambitious as Marx's but without a theory of

class conflict incorporated into it. Rostow's theory has been regarded as being essentially an account of a **Walrasian** moving equilibrium.

stagflation (150)

An unhappy combination of high price **inflation**, high unemployment and low economic growth. Although the phenomenon was first extensively discussed in the 1960s, it was present in Western economies before the First World War. It was regarded as an indication of the failure of **Keynesian-style** demand management and led to a call for **incomes policies**, including a **tax-based incomes policy**.

Cornwall, J. (ed.) (1984) *After Stagflation: Alternatives to Economic Decline*, Oxford: Martin Robertson.

Helliwell, J.F. (1988) 'Comparative macroeconomics of stagflation', *Journal of Economic Literature* 26 (March): 1–28.

Okun, A.M. (1981) *Prices and Quantities*, Washington, DC: Brookings Institution; Oxford: Basil Blackwell.

Weitzman, M.L. (1984) *The Share Economy*, Cambridge, MA: Harvard University Press.

See also: **infession**.

Stakhanovite (810)

A worker with very high productivity. This paragon is named after Alexei Stakhanov (1906–77) who is reputed to have mined 108 tons of coal in the USSR in 1935.

Siegelbaum, L.H. (1988) *Stakhanovism and the Politics of Productivity in the USSR, 1935–41*, Cambridge and New York: Cambridge University Press.

stand-alone cost (010, 610)

The cost of production which is equal to a simulated market price that is the maximum which can be charged without buyers going to a rival firm.

See also: **constrained market pricing**.

Standard & Poor 100 (220, 310)

A stock market index derived from the Standard & Poor 500 stock index: it covers about 60 per cent of the value of stocks traded on the New York Stock Exchange on most days. Its base date is 1976.

Standard & Poor 500 (220, 310)

This stock index represents 80 per cent of the value of stocks traded on the New York Stock Exchange and is one of the twelve leading indicators used by the US Department of Commerce to gauge economic performance. The index, with a base date of 1941–3, consists of 400 company stocks, 40 financial stocks, 20 transportation stocks and 40 public utility stocks, each weighted in the index by the number of shares issued.

standard commodity (010)

Composite commodity whose price does not change when there is a change in the distribution of income. The components of the standard commodity are in the same proportions as in aggregate production. This concept was introduced by **Sraffa** to solve **Ricardo**'s search for an invariant standard of **value**.

Sraffa, P. (1960) *Production of Commodities by Means of Commodities: Prelude to a Critique of Economic Theory*, Cambridge: Cambridge University Press.

standard deviation (210)

A measure of the dispersion of values of a variable about its **arithmetic mean** which is calculated as the square root of the sum of the differences between each of those values and the arithmetic mean divided by the number of values minus 1.

See also: **mean deviation; variance**.

standard error of estimate (210)

A measure of the scatter of values about a regression line of Y on X which is measured by the square root of the sum of deviations of Y values from the estimated value of Y divided by the number of values.

See also: **linear regression**.

Standard Industrial Classification (220)

A way of arranging economic data according to the major divisions of a country's industrial structure, using industry codes. In the USA, the classification used eleven divisions:

A agriculture, forestry and fishing
B mining
C construction

D   manufacturing
E   transportation, communication, electric, gas and sanitary services
F   wholesale trade
G   retail trade
H   finance, insurance and real estate
I   services
J   public administration
K   non-classifiable establishments

Each division is divided into major groups and each industry is assigned a four-digit classification.

In the UK, the revised 1980 classification also has a divisional structure:

0   agriculture, forestry and fishing
1   energy and water supply industries
2   extraction of minerals and ores other than fuels, manufacture of metals, mineral products and chemicals
3   metal goods, engineering and vehicles industries
4   other manufacturing industries
5   construction
6   distribution, hotels and catering, repairs
7   transport and communication
8   banking, finance, insurance, business services and leasing
9   other services.

CSO (1979) *Standard Industrial Classification*, London: HMSO, revised 1980.

Executive Office of the President, Office of Management and Budget (1987) *Standard Industrial Classification Manual 1987*.

Standard International Trade Classification (220)

A classification of commodities and manufactured goods almost universally employed to describe imports and exports. The ten principal sections are as follows:

0 food and live animals
1 beverages and tobacco
2 crude materials, inedible, except fuels
3 mineral fuels, lubricants and related materials
4 animal and vegetable oils, fats and waxes
5 chemical and related products not elsewhere specified
6 manufactured goods, classified chiefly by material
7 machinery and transport equipment
8 miscellaneous manufactured articles

9 commodities and transactions not classified in the previous sections

These sections are further subdivided into two-digit sections and subsequently into three-, four- and five-digit sections.

Standard Metropolitan Statistical Area (220)

A term used in the wage statistics of the Bureau of Labor Statistics (USA). This concept was introduced into the US census in 1950 to describe a metropolitan labour market in which **commuting** connected cities and the surrounding areas.

See also: **local labour market**.

Standard Statistical Metropolitan Area (220, 840)

An urban area of the USA. This concept was used until June 1963 when it was replaced by the **Metropolitan Statistical Area**.

staple export (420)

A product internationally traded which is based on the exploitation of natural resources; a **primary product**. In some developing countries, the performance of this sector has a crucial effect on the development of the economy as a whole.

See also: **one-crop economy**.

Star Chamber (320)

Popular name for the UK governmental committee which has been chaired by the Deputy Prime Minister. It considers the public expenditure proposals of the spending ministers with a view to reducing their aggregate to the planning total. The name derives from an English court of justice, abolished in 1640, noted for its arbitrary procedure.

state capitalism (060)

A transitional stage to **communism**, as typified by the original Soviet economic system. The state owns almost 100 per cent of industrial capital and agricultural land, using a hierarchy of industrial ministries, agencies and enterprises to run the productive sector of the economy.

See also: **Soviet-type economy**.

State Earnings-Related Pension Scheme (910)

UK state **pensions scheme** introduced in 1975 and intended to be fully implemented by 1998. It originally entitled employees to 25 per cent of indexed qualifying earnings during the best twenty years of indexed earnings in a working life. The size of the pension would be within the range of a flat rate for a single person to an upper limit of 6.5–7.5 times the minimum level. Contracting out was permitted, provided that a guaranteed minimum pension was paid.

When reviewed in 1985, the State Earnings-Related Pension Scheme was criticized for its costs, for not targeting on the needy, for giving too large a role to the state and for discouraging private schemes. It was initially proposed then to replace the scheme with the requirement that at least 4 per cent of earnings be contributed to an occupational or private scheme to purchase an **annuity**; subsequently this was modified to the recommendation to reduce contributions by setting pension levels lower so that they would only replace 20 per cent of employment earnings.

See also: **Old Age, Survivors, Disability and Health Insurance**

state enterprise (610)

A firm owned by the state. These have often been founded because of the lack of private initiative and capital to establish them, e.g. Dutch state mines in Holland around 1900 and various enterprises in Turkey in 1923. It was John Stuart **Mill** who argued that there should be state enterprises where an undertaking was necessary but no private concern would establish or run it.

There are various ways of organizing state enterprises, e.g. the British method of creating separate public corporations and the Italian method of creating holding companies (IRI and ENI). In Germany, the government has major or majority stakes in 900 businesses, including Lufthansa and Volkswagen. As many state enterprises make trading losses, it is unlikely that they would be able to raise capital without government help. Since 1978, China has allowed a variety of enterprises, e.g. collective, individual (two helpers can be employed plus five apprentices) and joint ventures between state-owned and individual enterprises with profits distributed as dividends.

See also: **public enterprise**.

Statements of Standard Accounting Practice (540)

Accounting standards issued by the Accounting Standards Committee for the British and Irish institutes of chartered accountants in 1975 and subsequently revised. The goal of these statements is to ensure that accounts provide a **true and fair view** of the financial position of the organization described in a set of accounts.

The standards cover the treatment of accounting policies, the results of associated companies, earnings per share, government grants, extraordinary items and prior year adjustments, changes in the purchasing power of money, taxation under the imputation system, stocks and work in progress, source and application of funds, deferred taxation, depreciation, current cost accounting, post-balance-sheet events, contingencies, investment properties, foreign currency translation, leases and hire purchase contracts, goodwill, acquisitions and mergers, and research and development.

state monopoly capitalism (070)

A type of economic system, particularly the **Soviet-type economy** in which the state owns all the means of production (except for a few minor services and agricultural enterprises) and exploits scale economies by running each branch of production as a state-owned monopoly. **Marx** regarded such a stage of economic development the prelude to full communism when the state itself would wither away.

Cowling, K. (1982) *Monopoly Capitalism*, London: Macmillan.
Fine, B. and Marfin, A. (1984) *Macroeconomics and Monopoly Capitalism*, Brighton: Wheatsheaf.

See also: **monopoly capitalism**.

state theories (320)

Explanations of government behaviour in terms of voting systems, the goals of bureaucrats and class interests. All these involve conflict – between different voters' wishes or between bureaucrats and legislators or between labour and capital. The relative power of each group will be influenced by the amount of information possessed.

state trading organization (420)

An agency of an East European economic ministry which in the past had the task of importing and exporting on behalf of domestic industrial enterprises. In recent economic reforms, e.g. in Hungary, enterprises have been given a limited power to engage directly in international trade. Since the beginning of 1987, in the USSR twenty ministries and seventy large factories have been allowed to deal directly with their foreign customers and suppliers and to retain up to 50 per cent of their foreign currency earnings (in practice a smaller percentage is actually released).

static model (210)

An equation, or equations, describing economic relationship(s) with all the constituent variables measured at the same time.

See also: **comparative statics; dynamic economics**.

stationary state (110)

The position of an **economy** with zero output growth, the rate of profit at a minimum and only **subsistence** wages. Classical economists, with economic **development** as one of their central concerns, feared the movement of an economy towards this state, with the major exception of John Stuart **Mill** who welcomed an economy which was not concerned with ruthless expansion and could instead pay attention to income distribution and the quality of life.

Mill, J.S. (1965) *Principles of Political Economy: With Some of Their Applications to Social Philosophy*, ed. by J.M. Robson, Book IV, ch. VI, Toronto: University of Toronto Press.

See also: **steady state economy**.

statistical population (210)

A group, finite or infinite in size, of persons or things with at least one common characteristic. Statisticians attempt to learn about the nature of a population by taking samples.

statistics (210)

A set of methods for the collection, present-ation, summary and analysis of data with a view to the drawing of valid conclusions.

Hughes, A.J. (1971) *Statistics: A Foundation for Analysis*, Reading, MA: Addison-Wesley.

statutory incidence (320)

See: **tax incidence**.

statutory minimum wage rate (820)

The minimum wage set in the UK by a **wages council** for the group of workers covered by that council. Trade union and employer representatives sit with independent members of a council to make the recommendation of a new minimum wage rate to the Secretary of State for Employment. The reduction in the number of such councils in the 1980s reduced the number of these wage rates.

See also: **minimum wage; wages council**.

Statutory Reserve Deposit (310)

An account of an Australian trading bank at the Reserve Bank which must be equal to 7 per cent of the bank's total deposits.

steady state economy (010, 110)

An economy with a constant size of population and stock of capital goods. The number of births and immigrants is equal to the number of deaths and emigrants; investment is only undertaken to maintain the existing capital stock.

See also: **stationary state**.

steady state equilibrium (010, 210)

An **equilibrium** whose stability is such that the market to which it refers returns to its original state after a temporary change in an **exogenous variable**, or moves to a new equilibrium after a permanent change in an exogenous variable.

steady state growth (110)

Growth such that capital, labour, total consumption and output change at the same rate or remain constant in amount over time. As the rate of growth of capital depends upon savings, steady state growth requires the savings function to have stable characteristics: debt policy can promote stability by keeping the rate of interest constant. Steady state growth does not entail **full**

employment as it is compatible with various levels of unemployment.

step cost (540)
A cost which is fixed over a range of output and then rises to a new level, or plateau, over a range of larger output. Fixed costs have to be paid at output 0.

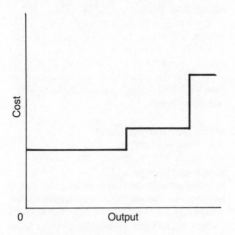

stepped bond (310)
A bond with an interest rate which increases over its lifetime. This method of financing a company pushes up the company's rate of profit in the short term as it reduces its interest charges.

sterilization (310, 430)
Isolating the domestic money supply from the effects of **balance of payments** deficits and surpluses. This is achieved by a central bank's **open market operations**, e.g. in the case of a balance of payments deficit it will buy bonds from domestic bond-holders to increase the amount of cash available. Under the **gold standard**, sterilization required preventing an inflow of gold from increasing the quantity of money domestically in circulation.

sterling (430)
Britain's domestic **currency** which is extensively used internationally as a unit of account (e.g. in the invoicing of trade), as a means of payment (e.g. an intervention currency) and as a store of value (especially as a reserve currency).

See also: **sterling area**.

sterling area (430)
The group of countries, mainly of the Commonwealth, defined in the Exchange Control Act 1947 of the UK, which pegged their currencies to sterling and held their foreign exchange balances in sterling. It arose out of the dominance of the British economy before 1914 but declined in the 1950s when many of these countries diversified their reserves, much to the relief of Britain which was often threatened with the sale of such sterling holdings and a consequential attack on the pound. To cope with these sterling balances, British governments successively negotiated dollar guarantees in Basle in 1968 and 1977. Today, few countries can be said to be in the sterling area.

Strange, S. (1971) *Sterling and British Policy: A Political Study of an International Currency in Decline*, Oxford: Oxford University Press.

See also: **overseas sterling area**.

sterling commercial paper (310)
Commercial bills of exchange denominated in sterling which are short term and negotiable. These are popular with firms seeking an additional source of finance for **working capital** and with institutional investors wanting a short-term investment.

sterling M3 (220, 310)
Broad definition of the **money supply** now known as M3. It is measured as **M1** plus private sector sterling time bank deposits plus private sector holdings of sterling bank **certificates of deposit**. Overshooting of targets for its growth has made it less useful for policy-making.

See also: **M3c**.

sterling warrant into gilt-edged stock (310)
An option to buy or sell a specific **gilt** stock which was introduced in July 1987 in London. They have a life of up to twelve months. They are popular with securities houses as a **hedging** device. Gilt options are also traded by the **London International Financial Futures Exchange** and the **International Stock Exchange**.

sticky price (010)

A price with limited flexibility. The principal examples of these are money wage rates which are inflexible downwards and interest rates which have a minimum level. Prices of this kind are fundamental to the **Keynesian** macroeconomic model.

Barro, R. and Grossman, H. (1976) *Money, Employment and Inflation*, Cambridge and New York: Cambridge University Press.

See also: **fixprice**; **liquidity trap**.

Stigler, George Joseph, 1911– (030)

A leading twentieth-century US microeconomist. After an education at Washington, Northwestern and Chicago universities, he became a professor at Brown University in 1946 and then was professor at Columbia from 1947 to 1959 and subsequently at Chicago. Also, he worked for the **National Bureau of Economic Research** from 1943 to 1959. He was awarded the **Nobel Prize for Economics** in 1982 for his theory of economic regulation. His PhD thesis, supervised by Frank **Knight** and published as *Production and Distribution Theories* (1941), began his extensive writings on the history of economic thought, as is evident in his *Essays in the History of Economics* (1965). But his eminence is derived from a lifetime of work on microeconomics, beginning with *The Theory of Price* (1942) and continuing with more specialized topics, e.g. his empirical refutation of the **kinked demand curve** (*Journal of Political Economy*, October 1947) which challenged many writers on the subject. An article on information in labour markets (*Journal of Political Economy, Supplement*, October 1962) inspired much work on search models of unemployment. His contribution to the economics of regulation is notable: controversially, he has held that regulatory agencies act in the producer's, and not the consumer's, interest.

stochastic process (210)

A distribution with random probability which can be analysed statistically.

stochastic term (210)

A random variable.

See also: **disturbance term**.

stock adjustment principle (010, 520)

The adjustment made to the **accelerator principle** to allow for unused capacity. The accelerator equation would produce too high a prediction of the required level of net investment if the amount of excess capacity were not subtracted.

stock and flow concepts (210, 220)

A stock (e.g. wealth) is measured at a point in time; a flow (e.g. income) is measured over a period. A **balance sheet** uses stock concepts; a **profit and loss account**, flow concepts. This distinction, crucial to **macroeconomics**, is increasingly used in the analysis of **unemployment**.

stock borrowing (310)

See: **share borrowing**.

stock exchange (310)

A physical and electronic market in which government **bonds** and the **securities** of companies are regularly traded. The world's leading exchanges are usually compared in terms of the volume and dollar value of stocks traded, the range of financial products marketed and the number of members entitled to trade.

Goldenberg, S. (1986) *Trading inside the World's Leading Stock Exchanges*, London: Sedgwick & Jackson.

See also: **International Stock Exchange**; **NASDAQ**.

Stock Exchange Automated Quotation System (310)

A screen-based dealing system which allows all **market-makers** in a particular security to display their buying and selling prices to all users simultaneously. For a screen price quotation, there must be a minimum of 1,000 shares; the system is open from 9 am to 5 pm Monday to Friday. This system had to be introduced in London in 1986 after **deregulation** of the Stock Exchange.

stockholder diffusion (310)

The extent to which ownership of a company/corporation is spread amongst several investors.

See also: **wider share ownership**.

Stockholm School (030)

A group of Swedish economists, particularly **Myrdal, Ohlin**, Lindahl and Hammerskold, who developed their own macroeconomic theory and policy in the 1920s and 1930s. Although there are certain similarities with the work of **Keynes**, this school was particularly noted for its use of the dynamic method, introducing the distinction between *ex ante* and *ex post* values of variables. They recommended the use of **fiscal policy** as a means of reducing unemployment. They were the lineal descendants of **Wicksell**.

Hansson, B.A. (1982) *The Stockholm School and the Development of the Dynamic Method*, London: Routledge.
Sandelin, B. (ed.) (1991) *The History of Swedish Economic Thought*, London and New York: Routledge.

See also: *ex ante* **variables**; *ex post* **variables**.

stock index arbitrage (310)

An investment strategy to gain from the difference between the prices shown in stock indices on the futures market and the underlying cash value of stocks.

stock index futures market (310)

US market for hedging and arbitrage to minimize risks and maximize returns in the stock market. This Chicago-based market, inspired by Chicago commodity futures, started in 1980; New York now has a similar market. The item traded, stock indices, can be regarded as baskets of shares. Institutions and corporations have found them attractive as portfolio insurance.

stock market price index (220, 310)

An indicator of the change in value of the stocks and shares traded on a particular stock exchange. This is calculated by added together the price changes in the leading stocks. The principal indices include the **Affärsvälden General, All Ordinaries, Barclays, CAC, CBS Tendency, Comit, composite, Credit Suisse, DAX, Dow Jones Industrial Average, Financial Times Stock Exchange, Hang Seng, Nikkei, SET, Standard & Poor's** and **Straits Times Industrial**.

stock–output ratio (520)

The ratio of stocks of raw materials, compo-

nents and semi-finished goods to the output of a firm. Stocks are held during the period of production to safeguard against late delivery of supplies which could hold up production schedules.

stock ratios (540)

1 Raw material stock divided by total turnover.

2 Work-in-progress divided by total turnover.

3 Raw material stock divided by purchases.

4 Finished stock divided by total turnover.

stocks (310)

1 Fixed interest **securities** issued by governments or companies.

2 Accumulated raw materials, semi-finished goods and unsold finished goods. Changes in such stocks can be very volatile, being responsible for much of the annual change in the **national income** and the **balance of payments**.

See also: **common stock**.

Stolper–Samuelson theorem (420)

An international trade theorem which states that, when the relative price of one of two commodities increases, the factor of production used more intensively in its production has an increased real rate of return and the factor less intensively used has a lower rate of return. Sometimes called 'a magnification effect'.

Stolper, W. and Samuelson, P.A. (1941) 'Protection and real wages', *Review of Economic Studies* 9: 58–73.

Stone, John Richard Nicholas, 1913– (030)

Cambridge economist and statistician who pioneered much of **national income** analysis. He was educated at Cambridge University and a member of the Central Statistical Office of the UK War Cabinet from 1940 to 1945 before returning to Cambridge to be Director of the Department of Applied Economics, 1945–55, and Professor of Financial Accounting, 1955–80. His first work, an article on costs, appeared in

Econometrica as early as 1936. Not only national income accounting but demand analysis, **input–output analysis** and aggregate consumption and savings functions have been central to his research. He was awarded the **Nobel Prize for Economics**.

Deaton, A. (ed.) (1981) *Essays in the Theory and Measurement of Consumer Behaviour in Honour of Sir Richard Stone*, Cambridge: Cambridge University Press.
Stone, R. (1954–66) *The Measurement of Consumers' Expenditure and Behaviour in the United Kingdom, 1920–38*, Cambridge: Cambridge University Press.
—— (1959) *Social Accounting and Economic Models*, London: Bowes & Bowes.

stop-go (310, 320)

British macroeconomic policies of the 1950s and 1960s which alternately deflated and stimulated the economy. The expansion was often with a view to winning an imminent general election; the retrenchment, a recognition that the economy had become so overheated that the balance of payments was suffering. When **fine-tuning** became increasingly unsuccessful, stop–go policies disappeared.

See also: **Butskellism**; **political business cycle**.

store of value (310)

A function of **money** which makes it possible to defer the use of income received. In times of high **inflation** money ceases to have this use and non-monetary assets are preferred to money.

storming (120, 510)

Leaving most of a required amount of work to the weeks or days immediately preceding a production deadline. This was a common practice under Soviet central planning.

St Petersburg paradox (020)

A paradox of **game theory** identified by **Bernoulli** and so-called because of its first being stated in the *Commentarii* of the St Petersburg Academy. This paradox in a game of chance is that the mathematical expectation of gain is infinite but the fair price to the player is finite. Bernoulli's approach to this problem was to replace mathematical expectation (probabilities of winning multiplied by monetary prices) by moral expectation (probabilities of winning multiplied by personal utilities).

Samuelson, P.A. (1977) 'St Petersburg paradoxes: defanged, dissected and historically described', *Journal of Economic Literature* 15: 24–55.

straddle (310)

Buying a futures contract in one market and simultaneously selling it in another.

straight bond (310)

A bond carrying a set rate of interest, redeemable over a set period at the price on the bond.

straight choice arbitration (830)

See: **pendulum arbitration**.

Straits Times Industrial Index (310)

The price index of the leading shares traded on the Singapore stock exchange.

strategic tax planning (320)

The use of tax avoidance schemes to reduce tax liability.

streaker (310)

See: **zero coupon bond**.

strike (830)

A work stoppage by a group of workers undertaken to enforce a particular demand, in most cases a wage increase. The legalization of **trade unions** and, in some countries, the protection of them by making them immune from actions in tort/delict for the losses caused by the strike has increased the incidence of strikes in the twentieth century.

International comparisons of strikes are difficult because of different definitions of strikes (e.g. whether to include political strikes and very small stoppages) but it does seem that some countries, e.g. Switzerland and Norway, have few strikes, but others, e.g. Australia and Italy, have recorded a high level of strike activity in many years. Determinants of strike activity include a country's industrial structure as some industries (e.g. mining and transport) are particularly strike-prone, the **collective bargaining** system, the phase of the **trade cycle** and the extent of industrial **concentration** in large organizations. In Britain in the 1960s and

1970s there were many strikes in general election years as these invariably coincided with the breakdown of an **incomes policy**. The effects of strikes are difficult to calculate as there has to be a comparison between output on a 'normal day', which may be rare, and output on a day that there was a stoppage; also the allocation of fixed costs may be too arbitrary to identify the extent of losses caused by strikes. Some would view strikes as an inevitable frictional cost of a collective bargaining system. Certainly, in a few industries it is a well-tried tool in wage bargaining. Strikes can be **Pareto optimal** *ex ante* in that not striking would make the employer or trade union worse-off, despite the strike being suboptimal *ex post*.

Hayes, B. (1984) 'Unions and strikes with asymmetric information', *Journal of Labor Economics* 2: 57–83.

Hyman, R. (1972) *Strikes*, London: Fontana Collins.

Jackson, M.P. (1988) *Strikes: Industrial Conflict in Britain, USA and Australia*, Hemel Hempstead: Harvester Wheatsheaf.

Knowles, K.G.J.C. (1952) *Strikes: A Study in Industrial Conflict*, Oxford: Basil Blackwell.

See also: *ex ante, ex post*.

strike-free deal (830)

A legally enforceable employment contract under which a **trade union** promises to refrain from striking for a period of time. This can take the form of a **collective bargain** explicitly stated as being enforceable under section 18 of the **Trade Unions and Labour Relations Act** or an individual contract with an employee.

See also: **strike**.

strike price (310)

A pre-fixed price to buy or sell an **option**.

stripped security (310)

A mortgage-backed **security** which is separated into two securities – the principal and the interest. These have the attractions of being guaranteed by the US federal government and having a higher yield than treasury bonds. Changes in the rate of prepayments causes a fluctuation in their value.

See also: **mortgage strip**.

strong equilibrium (210)

An **equilibrium** such that there is no coalition of players which can gain by a simultaneous deviation from it.

structural adjustment policy (310, 320)

An attempt to effect a major change to an economy, often after an external shock. This policy aims to get the economy back to its pre-shock growth path, improving its **balance of payments** over the medium term, i.e. about five years. The main policy instruments used are incentives to increase production, saving and investment in the public and private sectors, together with supporting monetary and budgetary policies. Also, there are often specific policies for energy and agriculture. The oil price increases of 1973 made policies of this kind an urgent priority in many economies.

structural deficit (320)

The excess of a government's expenditure over its income when that economy is at **full employment**.

structural inflation (150)

Inflation caused by supply shortages especially in the agricultural and exporting sectors of an economy. This type of inflation was thought to be the main cause of inflation in several Latin American economies.

Seers, D. (1962) 'A theory of inflation and growth in underdeveloped economies based on the experience of Latin America', *Oxford Economic Papers, New Series* 14: 173–95.

structural model (210)

A set of equations based on an economic theory which shows **endogenous variables** as equal to a mixture of **exogenous variables** and constants. For example, if one of the equations is a **consumption function**, then $C = a + cY$, i.e. aggregate consumption C is equal to a constant a plus national income Y multiplied by the marginal propensity to consume c.

structural unemployment (810)

Unemployment caused by a difference between the structure of employment vacancies and the structure of unemployment, usually brought about by technological change. Unemployed persons have different skills from those being demanded by employers or are located in a different place from a potential employer. Critics of this concept regard it as only a case of extreme **frictional unemployment**.

structure–conduct–performance model (610)

An approach to industrial economics, often applied to the study of **oligopoly**, which shows how tastes, technology and institutions produce market structures which dictate a firm's conduct and subsequent performance. The aspects of 'structure' considered include **concentration, branding** and **barriers to entry**; 'conduct' includes deciding what to produce and at what prices and carrying out all the functions of a firm; 'performance' is measured by efficiency, profitability, technical progress and employment creation. A policy conclusion of this model has been the demand for tougher **antitrust** policy.

Mason, E.S. (1939) 'Price and production policies of large-scale enterprises', *American Economic Review, Papers and Proceedings* 29: 61–74.
Reid, G.C. (1987) *Theories of Industrial Organization*, Oxford: Basil Blackwell.

stub equity (310)

Part of the equity of a company which is retained by the vendor of that company when it is sold. A stake of this kind expresses confidence in the new management.

See also: **vendor finance**.

Student's *t* distribution (210)

A statistical distribution (named after Gosset who used the pseudonym 'Student') which is calculated as follows:

$$t = \frac{X - \mu}{s} \sqrt{(N - 1)}$$

where X is the sample mean; μ is the population mean; s is the sample standard deviation; and N is the sample size. These t statistics are calculated for the testing of hypotheses.

See also: **chi-squared distribution; null hypothesis**.

stylized fact (210)

A fact of the real world simplified and made more abstract to be usable in an economic model. Each school of economics has its favourite stylized facts, e.g. that there are steady long-term capital–output ratios and

Kuznets's view that the **average propensity to consume** is relatively constant over long periods.

Kaldor, N. (1961) 'Capital accumulation and economic growth', in F. Lutz (ed.) *The Theory of Capital. Proceedings of a Conference held by the IEA*, London: Macmillan.

subsidiarity (320)

The principle of limiting the higher levels of government and devolving economic decision-making as far as possible to the lowest levels of local government so that those affected by governmental actions have the maximum amount of control over them. Subsidiarity is constantly mentioned as a goal for the **European Community**.

See also: **economic devolution.**

subsidy (320)

A negative tax, i.e. a payment by the government to a firm or household. In most cases these are payments to a firm to reduce the cost of the labour or capital it employs. Subsidies can distort the pattern of production and, if used for a long period of time, will become increasingly expensive as the economy's output will diverge more and more from the pattern of demand. Households can also be subsidized to reduce the cost of goods and services they purchase: many countries have subsidized food to increase the welfare of lower income households. The **Soviet-type economy** made extensive use of subsidies.

See also: **corrective subsidy; export subsidy; Pigorian subsidy; wage subsidy**.

subsistence (820, 910)

The minimum amount of resources, particularly food, that a worker needs to survive. By the time of Adam **Smith**, the idea of subsistence in physiological terms had been replaced by psychological subsistence, which takes into account differences in custom, the nature of societies and time periods. Social policy-makers emphasize today that subsistence must include sufficient income to function in that society.

Townsend, P. (1979) *Poverty in the UK*, Harmondsworth: Penguin.

See also: **poverty; iron law of wages**.

subsistence theory of wages (820)
See: **iron law of wages**.

substitute (010)
A good or service which a consumer regards as providing as much utility as an alternative. The character of being a substitute can be established by measuring the **cross price elasticity of demand** between the two goods (services). If that elasticity measure is positive, then the goods (services) are substitutes.

substitution effect (010)
See: **income and substitution effects**.

sucre (430)
The currency of Equador.

sunbelt (940)
An area of a country with new growing industries, e.g. California or the UK belt from Cambridge through Berkshire and Hampshire to Bristol. The expansion of such an area often poses a threat to the prosperity of an older industrial area.

See also: **snowbelt**.

sunk cost (010)
Costs incurred by a firm which remain even if it leaves that industry.

sunk cost fallacy (010)
The mistaken view that a firm should take into account the fixed costs it has incurred when deciding whether to continue with production. Concern for sunk costs rejects the marginal approach to decision-making and ignores the notion of **shutdown price**.

sunrise industry (630)
An industry based on new technology, e.g. a computer software industry. In the USA, these industries are concentrated in California and around Boston; in the UK, around Cambridge and in the Thames Valley.

See also: **sunbelt**.

sunspot theory (140)
1 A **trade cycle** theory first enunciated by **Jevons** which asserted that fluctuations in an **economy** are caused by periodic spots over the sun which cause bad weather, poor harvests, output decline and commercial crises.

2 Random phenomena, an extrinsic uncertainty which has no effect on tastes, endowments or production possibilities.

Cass, D. and Shell, K. (1983) 'Do sunspots matter?', *Journal of Political Economy* 91: 193–227.

Jevons, W.S. (1884) *Investigations in Currency and Finance*, London: Macmillan.

super-multiplier (010)
The double effect of investment as investment increases income and the level of investment raises the equilibrium level of income.

Hicks, J.R. (1950) *The Trade Cycle*, Oxford: Oxford University Press.

superneutrality (310, 320)
Economic policies which have no real effects as they only bring about nominal changes in an economy.

supernormal profit (010)
Profits in excess of **normal profit**. This can occur under **perfect competition** in the short run but is often a permanent feature of many **monopolistic** and **oligopolistic** firms.

supplementary cost (010, 520)
The general expenses of running a firm which are incurred even if output is zero; a term used by **Marshall**.

See also: **fixed cost**; **prime cost**.

Supplementary Financing Facility (430)
The provision by the **International Monetary Fund** in February 1979 of $7.8 billion of special drawing rights to add further financial help when a country is suffering from a structural problem with its balance of payments.

supplementary special deposits scheme (310)
See: **'corset'**.

supply control (710)
A reduction in production undertaken to maintain or increase prices and producers' incomes. This policy, much used in the agricultural sectors of a number of economies, has been criticized for its effects on efficiency and land values.

See also: **Common Agricultural Policy**; **set aside**.

supply curve (010)

The relationship between product prices and quantities supplied in a product market, holding all other factors constant, or between amounts of a **factor of production** and its peculiar factor price – wage rate, **rent** or **rate of interest**. It shows how much is supplied at each price. Under **perfect competition** there is a supply curve that is independent of the demand curve because price is equal to marginal cost and the market supply curve is the aggregation of individual firms' marginal cost curves. Under **monopoly**, demand and supply are interdependent because, when a monopolist decides how much to produce, both marginal revenue and **marginal cost** have to be considered as both are affected by output. This usually upward-sloping curve was first devised by **Marshall**.

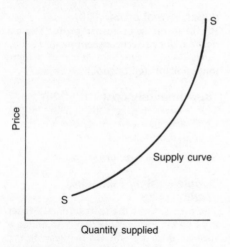

Quantity supplied

supply function (010)

The relationship between the amount of a good or service produced and its price.

See also: **aggregate supply**.

supply price (010, 820)

The minimum price at which a factor of production, especially labour, is willing to be employed.

See also: **reservation wage**.

supply-side economics (030, 320)

A major US school of economics which inspired the economic policies of the USA under President Reagan and of the UK under Prime Minister Thatcher. Opposing the **Keynesian** view that **aggregate demand** is central to determining the level of economic activity, supply-siders place emphasis on **aggregate supply**. Thus there has been a revival in the respectability of **Say's law** and a concern for the **disincentive effects** of taxation. The **Laffer curve** has been a major innovation of the school. The adherents of supply-side economics and **monetarism** often coincide. The **New Classical economists** have formalized many of their insights.

Bartlett, B. and Roth, T.P. (1983) *The Supply-side Solution*, Manhattan Institute for Policy Research; London and Basingstoke: Macmillan (1984).

Minford, P. (1991) *The Supply Side Revolution in Britain*, Aldershot: Edward Elgar.

See also: **Reaganomics**; **Thatcherism**.

supply-side shocks (010)

Events external to an economy which affect its production of goods and services. Major recent shocks have been the **Kennedy Round** of tariff reductions in 1968–70, the oil price increases of 1973 and 1979 and the **information technology** revolution.

suppressed inflation (150)

Inflation which is restrained by price controls; the state of an economy with excess demand which has not yet brought about factor and product price increases.

surplus approach (020, 030)

A view of classical theories of **value** and **distribution** as being dependent on there being a surplus above the necessary inputs required for production. This approach was most emphasized in **Marx**'s analysis of capitalist economies.

Marx, K. (1969–72) *Theories of Surplus Value*, trans. by E. Burns, London: Lawrence & Wishart.

See also: **Physiocrats**; **surplus value**.

surplus economy (020, 070)

An economy that produces a surplus product above what is necessary to maintain that society. **Quesnay** in his *Tableau économique* postulated that the agricultural sector had the unique characteristic of producing a *produit net* (surplus). Classical economists, especially **Smith** and **Ricardo** in their use of the concept of profit in their **distribution** theory, extended the notion of 'a surplus' to all sectors of a national economy.

See also: **surplus value**.

surplus value (010)
The value produced by labour in excess of the amount needed to maintain it which is used as a measure of the extent of exploitation of workers in Marxian economics.

Absolute surplus value arises from the lengthening of the working day or the increased speed of the production process so that a worker works more hours than required to provide **subsistence**; relative surplus value is the result of decreasing the amount of labour needed to produce subsistence for the worker, i.e. increasing labour productivity. In early stages of capitalist development, surplus value is absolute in nature but it is largely relative in later stages. The rate of surplus value, also known as the rate of **exploitation**, is measured by the ratio of surplus value to **variable capital**.

survival process (020)
An application of Darwinism to the price system. Alchian asserted that the price system selects firms as fit to survive according to their ability to make greater profits than their competitors.

Alchian, A.A. (1950) 'Uncertainty, evolution and economic theory', *Journal of Political Economy* 58:211–21.

sustainable development (110)
Long-term development which includes the establishment of the basic social and economic institutions necessary for continuing economic growth. The conservation of plant and animal species is recommended for the sake of future generations. Sustainable development is more difficult if there are trade-offs to be considered between different economic activities.

See also: **Brundtland Report**.

sustainable economic growth rate (110)
The annual rate of growth of real gross domestic product which is in line with the

growth of productivity and the present level of capacity utilization. A growth rate in excess of this leads to inflation and/or an increase in a balance of payments current account deficit.

swap market (310)
The market for the exchange of debt obligations in order to take advantage of conditions in different financial markets.

swap network (430)
An arrangement in the USA between the **Federal Reserve System** and fourteen foreign central banks, together with the **Bank for International Settlements**, which permits short-term currency swaps between the Federal Reserve System and other central banks.

sweated trade (810)
An arduous set of occupations with long hours, tedious work and low pay. Most common examples are in the clothing industry. Often the trade is characterized by small firms and a lack of **unionization**.

Swedish budget (320)
A budget which is not balanced annually but over a period of years. This principle was originally followed by British **nationalized industries**.

Swedish School (030)
See: **Stockholm School**.

sweetener (010, 520)
An amount of cash given to encourage an economic agent to agree to an economic transaction, e.g. the purchase of a state-owned company. Also known as a 'kickback'.

sweetheart contract (830)
An employment contract whose terms are fixed by management.

SWIFT (310, 430)
See: **Society for Worldwide Interbank Financial Telecommunications**.

SWING (310)
See: **sterling warrant into gilt-edged stock**.

swing producer (610)
A producer who agrees with the other

producers of an industry to absorb the fluctuations in demand for the industry's products by producing whatever is required above the output level set for the other producers. Saudi Arabia agreed to assume this role for the **Organization of Petroleum Exporting Countries** in the 1980s.

SWOT (510)
Strengths, Weaknesses, Opportunities, Threats. These aspects of a business are examined to assess its past and present performance and prospects.

symmetallism (310)
Marshall's plan for an international currency based on gold and silver. This **bimetallic** version of **Ricardo**'s plan was proposed by Marshall to the Gold and Silver Commission, 1888. The international currency was based on a gold bar of 100 grammes and a silver bar of 2,000 grammes.

Marshall, A. (1923) *Money, Credit and Commerce*, Book I, ch. VI, London: Macmillan.

symmetrical frequency curve (210)
A **frequency curve** with the shape of a bell with one-half the mirror image of the other. This symmetrical curve is also called 'bell-shaped'.

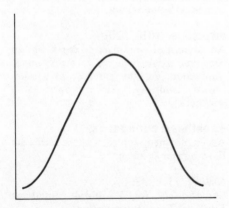

syndicalism (830)
Cooperative worker control of industry brought about by direct strike action. This extreme form of trade unionism has attracted more support in France than elsewhere.

Sorel, G. (1941) *Reflections on Violence*, trans. by T.E. Hulme, New York: P. Smith.

See also: **industrial democracy; workers' participation**.

syndicated loan (310)
A loan which is underwritten or managed by a syndicate of financial institutions. Since 1970, there have been many cases of these in Euromarkets and through the recycling of the revenues of the **Organization of Petroleum Exporting Countries**.

synergy (510)
The extra dynamic which comes from merging two organizations together. The new larger organization is more effective than the sum of the two previous firms, particularly because of a variety of types of **economy of scale**. This principle has often been appealed to as a justification for **mergers**.

System of Material Product Balances (220)
The framework for the national income statistics of centrally planned economies used by the United Nations. It uses as basic sectors the socialist sector and the private sector. The principal tables of these statistics are as follows:

1 Net material product by use
2 Net material product by kind of activity
3 Primary incomes by kind of activity in the material sphere
4 Primary incomes from net material product
5 Supply and disposition of goods and material services
6 Capital formation
7 Final consumption
8 Personal consumption
9 Total consumption of the population

The differences between this national income accounting system and the **System of National Accounts** include different methods of treating depreciation, different definitions of residents for the purposes of recording external transactions and the exclusion of non-material services.

Standing Statistical Commission, Council of Mutual Economic Assistance (1969) *Basic Methodological Rules for the Compilation of the Statistical Balance of the National Economy*, Moscow.

System of National Accounts (220)

A set of accounting conventions drawn up by the United Nations. This provides a framework for the systematic recording of transaction flows in a national economy. The sectors in the accounts are as follows:

- General government
- Corporate and quasi-corporate enterprises
- Households and private unincorporated enterprises
- Non-profit institutions serving households
- Rest of the world

For each country, the flows are defined as follows.

1 Total supply of goods and services
    Gross output of goods and services
    Imports of goods and services
2 Disposition of total supply: intermediate and final uses
    Intermediate consumption
    Government final consumption expenditure
    Private final consumption expenditure
    Gross capital formation
    Exports of goods and services
3 Cost components and income shares
    Value added and gross domestic product
    Compensation of employees
    Operating surplus
    Consumption of fixed capital
    Indirect taxes
    Subsidies
    Withdrawals from quasi-corporations
    Property income
4 Taxes and unrequited transfers
    Casualty insurance transactions
    Taxes and other government receipts
    Household transfer receipts
    Transfers received by private non-profit institutions
    Other current transfers
5 Finance of gross accumulation
    Net saving
    Surplus of the nation on current transactions
    Purchases of land, net
    Purchases of intangible assets, net
    Capital transfers
    Net lending
6 Financial assets and liabilities
7 Other assets
    Reproducible tangible assets
    Non-reproducible tangible assets
    Non-financial intangible assets

These flows are recorded in tables divided into four parts.

1 Summary information
2 Final expenditures on gross domestic product: detailed breakdowns and supporting tables
3 Institutional sector accounts: detailed flow accounts
4 Production by kind of activity: detailed breakdowns and supporting tables

This accounting framework is used for all national income statistics of United Nations countries except for **centrally planned economies** which use the **System of Material Product Balances**.

A System of National Accounts, Studies in Methods, Series F, No. 2, New York: United Nations, 1968.

T

Tableau économique (030, 210)
See: **Quesnay**.

tacit knowledge (620)
See: **locked-in knowledge**.

Taft–Hartley Act 1947 (830)
'The Labor–Management Relations Act', a major US federal labor statute which amended the **Wagner Act** particularly by attempting to balance the rights and responsibilities of labor and management. Section 8(c) listed six unfair labor practices by unions: (1) restraining/coercing employees in their rights to engage in or refrain from collective bargaining; (2) causing an employer to discriminate against non-union workers; (3) refusing to bargain with an employer despite being the representative of its workers; (4) engagement in or inducement of workers to engage in strikes, refusals to work and boycotts when, for example, union recognition has not been certified by the **National Labor Relations Board**; (5) charging an excessive or discriminatory fee to enter a union under a union shop clause; and (6) extorting a payment from an employer for services not performed or about to be performed.

Taft–Hartley also banned the **closed shop**, authorized states to have right-to-work laws, gave the US President the power to direct the Attorney-General to petition for an eighty-day injunction against a strike or lockout which constituted a national emergency, attacked communist infiltration of labor unions by requiring union officials to swear anti-communist affidavits before they could use the National Labor Relations Board and banning unions and corporations from political expenditures. Many of these new prohibitions could be enforced under the criminal law. For years, the labor movement attacked Taft–Hartley for creating 'slave labor' as organizing labor became more difficult.

Getman, J.G. and Blackburn, J.D. (1983) *Labor Relations: Law, Practice and Policy*, Mineola, NY: Foundation Press.
Morris, C.J. (ed.) (1983) *The Developing Labor Law*, vols 1 and 2, Washington, DC: Bureau of National Affairs.

See also: **Norris–La Guardia Act**; **right-to-work state**; **US labor union**.

taka (430)
The currency of Bangladesh.

take-off (110, 130, 620)
The crucial stage of economic **development** when an economy 'takes off' into steady growth because its capital–output and savings ratios rise to at least 10 per cent of national income. This first occurred in the older industrialized countries – in Britain in the 1780s, in the USA in the 1820s, in France and Germany in the 1850s. Critics of this approach to development have asserted that it ignores the interplay between economic, social and technological determinants. However, the proponent of this theory, **Rostow**, argued from an examination of economic trends that there are five stages of growth: the traditional society, preconditions for take-off (e.g. **inventions**, the rise of **entrepreneurs**), take-off, the drive to maturity and the age of mass consumption.

Rostow, W.W. (1960) *Process of Economic Growth*, 2nd edn, Oxford: Clarendon Press.
—— (1971) *The Stages of Economic Growth: A Non-communist Manifesto*, 2nd edn, Cambridge: Cambridge University Press.

takeover (610)
A method of merging two firms by which one firm bids for another and, if successful, 'takes it over'. Takeover by the stealthy purchase of shares in public companies is now outlawed under the strict rules of major stock exchanges.

See also: **merger**.

take-up rate (320)
The proportion of those eligible for a particular benefit who claim it. Pecuniary

and psychic costs (including embarrassment) cause the rate always to be less than 100 per cent. Many voluntary organizations attempt to publicize benefits available to claimants, thereby increasing the take-up rate and making it more difficult to maintain the present rate of benefit.

Talisman (310)
'Transfer Accounting, Lodging for Investors and Stock Management': the computerized settlement system of the **International Stock Exchange**.

tangible net worth (520)
Shareholders' equity minus intangible assets.

tangible wealth (010, 540)
The **fixed capital** and **inventories** of firms.

See also: **intangible wealth**.

TAPS (310, 430)
Transatlantic Payment System.

tap stock (310)
A government bond issued, e.g. in the UK or USA, at a fixed price but not sold in its entirety as some of it is held back 'on tap' to be released gradually when market conditions are favourable. Other government stocks are sold by **tender**.

targeting (310, 320)
The use of specific policy instruments to reach particular targets, e.g. a low rate of inflation. This principle of macroeconomic policy-making is suboptimal if there are side effects from targeting which create distortions in allocation.

target price (710)
The price of an agricultural product of the **European Community** which is annually fixed by the agricultural ministers of member countries. This is higher than an **intervention price**.

See also: **Common Agricultural Policy**.

target variable (210)
A quantified policy goal, e.g. 5 per cent unemployment.

tariff (010, 320, 420)
1 A **price**.

2 An import tax. The superiority of a tariff to import licensing arises from its lower administrative costs and the production of revenue; few tariffs succeed in excluding all imports and so they earn revenue. As a form of taxation, tariffs have been used from earliest recorded history as in primitive economies they had the advantage of involving fewer valuation problems than taxes on income or on capital. In the post-war period, tariff reductions aimed to reduce the protectionism of the 1930s; most of these had withered away before the **Dillon**, **Kennedy** and **Tokyo Rounds**.

In the figure, DD is the demand curve, SS is the supply curve, $p_1 - p$ is the tariff and $p_2 - p$ is a prohibitive tariff which excludes all imports. QQ_1 is the protective effect, i.e. an increase in domestic production, Q_2Q_3 is the consumption effect, i.e. the reduction in total consumption and QQ_3 are the imports at price p before a tariff is imposed. a is the redistribution effect, i.e. additional economic rent to domestic producers continuing in production and economic rent to new domestic producers, b and d are deadweight losses of the tariff and c is the revenue effect, i.e. the tax revenue obtained by the government by imposing the tariff $p_1 - p$.

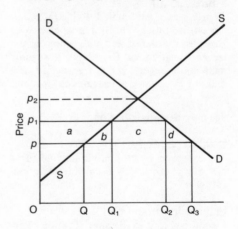

Ratner, S. (1972) *The Tariff in American History*, New York: Van Nostrand.
Scott, M.F., Corden, W.M. and Little, I.M.D. (1980) *The Case Against General Import Restrictions*, London: Trade Policy Research Centre.

See also: **free trade**; **protection**.

tarification (310)
The introduction of charges for services which were previously free. A recent example has been the introduction of bank charges for many client transactions.

taste (010)
The view of an individual of the relative merits of two or several things or possibilities. Assumptions about tastes are crucial to the analysis of choice in economics and are usually represented by **indifference curves**. In the study of consumer behaviour, tastes are depicted as a choice between goods with different **utilities**; in labour market analysis as a choice between work and leisure; in the analysis of risk as a choice between outcomes with different probabilities. Assumptions about tastes are central to **neoclassical economics**.

tâtonnement (010)
A process of market clearing in which, by bargaining, an **equilibrium** is reached between buyers and sellers. **Walras** introduced this term, meaning 'groping', into economics with his example of an **auction**.

Taurus (310)
Transfer and Automated Registration of Uncertified Stock. This system of electronic paperless transfer of securities is used by the **International Stock Exchange**. Electronic handling of every share transaction will make the processing of **bargains** cheaper and faster.

See also: **dematerialization**.

taxable capacity (320, 520)
The extent to which households and firms can pay a tax and a fiscal authority can collect it.

taxable income (320)
Income subject to income taxation. Personal and other allowances are deducted from total pre-tax income to ascertain what is taxable.

taxation (320)
A method of raising revenue for a government by levies on persons and firms. Taxes can be direct or indirect and can be raised centrally or locally. A government will choose its taxation policy with reference to its effects on income distribution post-tax, on incentives and on investment and economic growth. Also, the taxation raised will be decided as part of its **fiscal stance**. Instead of taxation, a government can finance its activities by charging for the services it offers or by borrowing.

Blinder, A.S., Solow, R.M., Break, G.F., Steiner, P.O. and Netzer, D. (1974) *The Economics of Public Finance*, Washington, DC: Brookings Institution.

Kay, J.A. and King, M.A. (1990) *The British Tax System*, 5th edn, Oxford: Oxford University Press.

Pechman, J. (1977) *Federal Tax Policy*, 3rd edn, Washington, DC: Brookings Institution.

See also: **canons of taxation**.

tax avoidance (320)
A taxpayer's careful arrangement of his/her activities and business affairs to minimize liability to taxation.

See also: **tax evasion**.

tax base (320)
That which is taxed, e.g. income, wealth, property, expenditure or consumption. A government can raise its total tax revenue by using several tax bases. Originally little was taxed because of problems of valuation and collection; gradually, there has been a movement from **indirect taxes** on imports and various types of consumption to **income tax** and **property tax**.

See also: **taxable capacity**.

tax-based incomes policy (320, 820)
A method of controlling the growth of wages and salaries by increasing the taxation of firms which have paid more than the prescribed norm. Firms would be liable for taxation on the unauthorized addition to their average wage bills. In the USA, this policy has frequently been advocated on the grounds of its supposed administrative simplicity. The version of this policy suggested by **Okun** was to offer an anti-inflationary tax credit of 1½ per cent of salary (on salaries up to $20,000 per annum) in return

for the employer not increasing pay by more than 6 per cent.

Seidman, L.S. (1978) 'Tax-based incomes policies', *Brookings Papers* 2: 301–48.

See also: **market anti-inflation plan**.

tax bracket creep (320)
See: **bracket creep**.

tax buoyancy (320)
The relationship between total revenue and income and output such that as the **tax base** grows so does total tax revenue.

See also: **tax elasticity**.

tax burden (320)
1 The ratio of the total tax revenues of a country to its **gross domestic product**.

2 The total effects of a country's taxes on all its residents or on certain sectors or types of taxpayer, e.g. firms or households.

Although objectively this burden is the transfer to government of part of taxpayers' resources, many taxpayers would subjectively regard the burden as greater. Governments impose taxes primarily to finance expenditure but they can unintentionally inhibit the growth of incomes and the capital stock. A guide to tax burdens in **Organization for Economic Cooperation and Development** countries is published annually in the May issue of *Economic Trends (UK)*. The tax burden is high in industrialized Europe but low in less industrialized Europe, e.g. Portugal and Turkey. An approximate measure of the tax burden often used is the **average rate of tax**. More elaborate assessments of a tax burden take into account collection costs, the effect on productivity of a tax structure, the extent to which taxpayers can plan because the tax system is stable, and the degree of equity, horizontally and vertically.

Pechman, J.A. and Okner, B.A. (1974) *Who Bears the Tax Burden?*, Washington DC: Brookings Institution.

tax capitalization (320, 930)
The effects on the price of a taxed good, e.g. a house, of the discounted present value of future tax payments. Thus if a house is expected to be liable to high property taxes in the future, a present valuation of it will take that into account. As high local property taxes lower property values, residents are encouraged by this capitalization effect to move to other areas.

See also: **fiscal mobility; Tiebout hypothesis**.

tax credit (320)
An amount which is subtracted from the taxes owed to a government.

tax effort (320)
The extent to which a tax revenue collection service collects the amount of tax which can be raised from a particular tax base.

See also: **taxable capacity**.

tax elasticity (320)
The responsiveness of tax revenue to an increase in income or output. An elastic tax is such that revenue from it grows faster than the tax base.

See also: **tax buoyancy**.

tax erosion (320)
The reduction in tax revenues brought about by exemptions from the comprehensive taxation of income, e.g. capital gains allowances and the tax exemption of **fringe benefits**.

tax evasion (320)
Reduction of one's tax burden by inaccurate statements of income and other circumstances relevant to tax liability. The amount of evasion depends on the probability of being detected in such conduct and the penalties for such offences.

Allingham, M.G. and Sandmo, A. (1972) 'Income tax evasion: a theoretical analysis', *Journal of Public Economics* 1: 323–38.

Ehrlich, I. (1973) 'Participation in illegitimate activities: a theoretical and empirical investigation', *Journal of Political Economy* 81: 521–65.

See also: **income tax; tax avoidance**.

Tax Exempt Special Savings Account (320)
The savings incentive scheme, known as 'Tessa', introduced by the British Government in 1990 and effective from January 1991. Tax on interest is exempt provided that capital is not withdrawn for five years

and no more than £9,000 is accumulated; if interest is withdrawn it is taxed at the basic rate of income tax. Savings will be accumulated in either bank or building society accounts.

tax expenditure (320)

A tax incentive or tax subsidy, a departure from the normal tax structure, e.g. credit against tax, deductions and deferrals of tax liabilities. This loss of a government's tax revenue is allowed in order to reach various social goals, e.g. raising the post-tax income of the lower paid, encouraging education or promoting residential investment. This concept was introduced in the USA by the Treasury in 1968 and is now a spending programme of the US Internal Revenue Service.

Surrey, S.S. and McDaniel, P.R. (1985) *Tax Expenditures*, Cambridge, MA, and London: Harvard University Press.

tax farming (320)

Delegation of the right to collect taxes to private tax collectors who then have the freedom to raise more than the quota requested by government. This ancient system is open to much exploitation of taxpayers.

See also: **goal system**.

taxflation (150, 320)

See: **wage–tax spiral**.

tax harmonization (320)

The standardization of tax rates, tax rules and tax definitions throughout a number of countries. Usually, in a harmonization exercise the existing practice which is most common is adopted as the standard. Sometimes harmonization is necessary to achieve other policy goals, e.g. in the **European Community** the harmonization of **indirect taxation** is necessary if the goal of unimpeded movement of goods is to be achieved.

European Parliament (1990) *The Economic Consequence of Fiscal Harmonization in Europe*, Luxemburg: Office for Publications of the European Communities.
Shibata, H. (1969) *Fiscal Harmonization under Freer Trade: Principles and their Applications*

to a Canada–US Free Trade Area, Toronto: University of Toronto Press.

tax haven (320)

A country with very low rates of taxation which attracts companies and individuals wishing to minimize tax liability. The countries benefit from the influx of currency and the consequential commercial activity. Most of these havens are small islands or countries off the USA, e.g. the Bahamas and the Virgin Islands, or in and around Europe, e.g. Monaco and the Channel Islands. Larger countries would find it difficult to finance public expenditure if they adopted such a low tax policy.

tax incidence (320)

Reduction of personal or corporate income caused by the imposition of a tax. Incidence is classified according to the group or sector on which a tax falls. These groups can be producers or consumers, those with a particular size of income, regions, industries, countries or generations.

The incidence is shifted forward to the consumer if the price of the final good rises because of the tax; backward, if there is a decline in demand for final goods and the price of intermediate goods falls. The incidence is shifted to future generations if current public expenditure is financed by incurring debts. Tax incidence can be analysed with a **partial equilibrium** approach as is the case when taxes on goods are analysed and the demand and supply **elasticities** are calculated or with a **general equilibrium** approach when, e.g. with a **corporation tax**, the effects on output and on **capital–labour ratios** are examined. Statutory incidence shows liability under tax laws. Economic incidence shows how taxation affects economic behaviour, e.g. the number of hours worked or the amount saved: such incidence traditionally concentrated on the effect of taxation on the **functional income distribution**; now it is looked at more in the context of the **size distribution of income**. Tax incidence was discussed as early as the eighteenth century by the **Physiocrats**.

Harberger, A.C. (1962) 'The incidence of the corporation income tax', *Journal of Political Economy* 70: 215–40.
Pechman, J.A. (1985) *Who Paid the Taxes, 1966–85?*, Washington, DC: Brookings Institution.

—— (1989) *Tax Reform: The Rich and the Poor*, Brighton: Harvester Wheatsheaf.

Shoven, J.B. (1976) 'The incidence and efficiency effects of taxes on income from capital', *Journal of Political Economy* 84: 1261–84.

See also: **absolute tax incidence; differential tax incidence**.

tax reform (320)

A change in a tax system which attempts to improve allocation, efficiency and **equity**. Tax reform usually takes the form of reducing the number of separate rates of tax and abolishing many tax allowances. Because tax reform is motivated by a desire to reduce administrative costs, as well as to reduce **tax avoidance**, there have to be fewer tax allowances, a simpler progression of tax and the abolition of certain types of tax, e.g. on capital.

Tax reform is high on the political agenda of many countries, including the UK, Canada, New Zealand, France, Japan and Sweden. Common to many of these proposals is a switch from income to **expenditure taxes** and a reduction of the top marginal income tax rates. Indexation of personal allowances is often removed, thus increasing tax yields in times of inflation. In the UK, the top marginal rate of income tax was reduced in 1979 from 83 per cent to 60 per cent and value-added tax was raised from two rates of 8 per cent and 12.5 per cent to a single rate of 15 per cent; in stages, corporation tax has been reduced from 52 per cent to 35 per cent. But in the Budget of 1988 income tax was simplified by the reduction in the number of bands to two – at 25 per cent and 40 per cent. In the USA, the Reagan Administration quickly reduced the top marginal rate of income tax from 70 per cent to 50 per cent and in 1986 the top rate was cut to 28 per cent. Japan reduced the top income tax rate from 85 per cent to 65 per cent; great reductions in corporate tax rates are envisaged and to maintain tax revenue a value-added tax at 5 per cent and a withholding tax of 20 per cent on postal savings and bank accounts are to be introduced. West Germany also cut income tax and corporation tax rates: the top income tax rate from 56 per cent to 53 per cent, minimum rates from 22 per cent to 19 per cent and corporation tax from 56 per cent to 50 per cent with cuts in many allowances. Australia proposed cutting top income tax rates from 60 per cent to 49 per cent in harness with an incomes policy. Tax cuts to a top rate of 50 per cent have no redistributive effect but a cut below 50 per cent does. Curiously some countries, e.g. Japan, have both high economic growth and high marginal tax rates.

The transition to a new system can produce undesired effects, e.g. a decline in the capital value of assets. To implement a tax reform, either a gradualist approach of dealing with a particular tax at a time or a package approach of widespread change can be adopted. Civil servants prefer the former but it leads to more confrontation with lobbies; there is likely to be support for the package approach only if there is widespread discontent with the current system.

Aaron, H.J. and Galper, H. (1985) *Assessing Tax Reform*, Washington, DC: Brookings Institution.

Ballantine, J.G. (1986) *Tax Reform in Japan and the United States – A Stimulus to New Economic Vitality?*, New York: Japan Society.

Feldstein, M.S. (1976) 'On the theory of tax reform', *Journal of Public Economics* 6: 77–104.

Kay, J.A. (1990) 'Tax policy: a survey', *Economic Journal* 100: 18–75.

Pechman, J. (1989) *Tax Reform: The Rich and the Poor*, London: Harvester Wheatsheaf.

See also: **US tax reform**.

Tax Reform Act 1986 (320)

US federal statute which undertook the sweeping reform of the US tax system beginning in January 1987 that simplified the structure of taxation by introducing two rates of individuals' tax at 28 per cent and 15 per cent instead of the fifteen rates previously in force; given the loss of previous allowances, in practice the top **marginal tax rate** became 33 per cent. The corporate rate was cut from 46 per cent to 34 per cent with a minimum rate of 21 per cent. To compensate for the loss of revenue from cutting tax rates, many tax deductions have been phased out, e.g. consumer interest on debt (except for housing), lower tax rates for capital gains, pension plans, real estate investments; even business meals and entertainment are only 80 per cent and not 100 per cent deductible.

Davies, D.G. (1986) *United States Taxes and Tax Policy*, Cambridge: Cambridge University Press.

See also: **tax reform**.

tax revenue (320)

The yield from a particular tax, or of the tax system as a whole. The amount of revenue depends on the **tax base** chosen, the tax rates set and the amount of compliance with tax legislation. In some countries, there is a heavy reliance on one particular tax, e.g. the USA uses an individual income tax to raise a high proportion of federal government revenues. The growth in tax revenue can be measured by **income elasticity of demand**, i.e. the responsiveness of tax revenues to the growth of nominal gross national product.

See also: **Laffer curve**.

tax structure (320)

The set of tax rates applying to a particular tax base, e.g. different rates of **income tax** or different rates of **value-added tax**. For income taxes, the simplest tax structure is based on the principle of a constant average tax rate; this is rare as so many tax structures are **regressive** or **progressive**. In a diagram the tax structure is apparent by plotting post-tax income against pre-tax income (OC is changes in income in the absence of an income tax, OA is income exempt from tax, OBD shows the course of income when there is a constant marginal tax rate on incomes above OA and OBEFG shows the course of income under a progressive income tax with higher marginal rates on higher income bands).

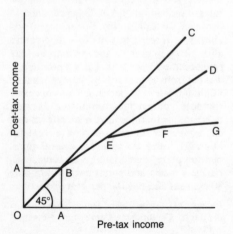

See also: **direct–indirect taxes ratio**.

tax threshold (320)

The income level at which **income** becomes liable to taxation.

tax unit (320)

The person or group subjected to taxation, e.g. a single person, a married couple or a household.

tax wedge (320)

1 The difference between the **marginal cost** of producing a good and the marginal benefit from consumption in the case of indirect taxes.

2 The difference between the marginal value of leisure sacrificed by a worker and the marginal value to society of another hour of work in the case of personal income taxes.

3 The difference between gross and net, after tax, rates of return in the case of investors.

Tax wedges produce a distortion in welfare.

Taylorism (510)

The US creed of scientific management suggested by F.W. Taylor (1856–1915) who applied at the Bethlehem Steel Company the principle of work study and a greater subdivision of labour as a means of achieving increased efficiency.

Merkle, J.A. (1980) *Management and Ideology: The Legacy of the International Scientific Management Movement*, Berkeley, CA: University of California Press.

Taylor, F.W. (1911) *The Principles of Scientific Management*, New York: Harper.

TDP (720)

See: **tradable discharge permit**.

team briefing (830)

Direct communication between managers and employees as an alternative to indirect contact with workers via trade unions. Although it reduces the role of trade unions, it sometimes exists in unionized firms.

team theory (020)

A study of the efficient joint choices of several persons. A team has common interests and beliefs and performs various tasks.

The theory is concerned with the optimal allocation of tasks and information within the team.

Marshak, J. and Radner, R. (1972) *Economic Theory of Teams*, New Haven, CT: Yale University Press.

technical efficiency (010)
Production using a method which maximizes production from given quantities of factor inputs.

See also: **allocative efficiency**.

technical progress (620)
The use of new techniques and/or the introduction of new products. Historically, technical progress has taken the form of the saving of labour and raw materials, mechanization and the use of inventions; in most cases, changes in the capital stock are necessary to achieve it. Technical progress can be measured by considering changes in the proportion of output using a particular technique, e.g. of steelmaking, by increases in speed or by improvements in product quality. Technical progress is a major determinant of economic growth.

Heertje, A. (1977) *Economics and Technical Change*, trans. by Z. St-Gallay, London: Weidenfeld & Nicolson.

See also: **disembodied technical progress; embodied technical progress; diffusion rate; invention; innovation; labour-augmenting technical progress; research and development**.

technological rent (010)
Part of monopoly profits which have been created by **technical progress**.

telecommuting (820)
Working for a firm at home, connected by telephone lines to supply work from a personal computer. This is a major development in the small-firm sector.

See also: **homework; networker**.

telework (620)
Office work using decentralized information and communication technology carried out in households. A new form of work organization made possible by developments in **information technology**.

temporary equilibrium (010)
Hicks's idea that over a short period of a 'week' variations in prices can be neglected. During this period both current prices and expected prices are allowed to influence plans for consumption and production. The stability of this equilibrium depends on the **elasticity** of price expectations. This concept of equilibrium is crucial to Hicksian dynamic analysis.

Hicks, J.R. (1939) *Value and Capital*, chs 10, 11, 12, Oxford: Oxford University Press.

tender (010, 310)
1 A method of selling shares by which prospective buyers specify the price at which they are willing to buy.

2 Direct sale of government securities.

3 A method of fixing the price of a contract often used in the construction and heavy engineering industries.

See also: **tap stock**.

1040 ('ten forty') (320)
1 The basic tax form used in the USA for individuals and families to report their personal incomes. A taxpayer first calculates his/her adjusted gross income, then subtracts a standard deduction (personal exemptions) and then deducts tax credits, e.g. expenditure on child care when both parents are working. Persons with lower incomes and no deductions against tax use a simplified version of this form.

2 A US government bond which is redeemable at the option of the government after ten years but only has to be paid up after forty years.

Tennessee Valley Authority (610)
A public corporation established in 1933 and owned by the US federal government. Its tasks include flood control, wholesale power supply to parts of seven states, economic development of tourism and natural resources, and job training. Apart from its power programme which is self-financing, it receives appropriations from Congress to finance its activities.

terminal bonus (310)
A bonus given by an insurance company to

the policyholder at the time that an insurance policy matures.

See also: **reversionary bonus**.

term premium (310)

The difference between the **yields** of fixed income securities of different maturities not attributable to current or anticipated future levels of short-term interest rates. Expected returns on exogenous securities, the quantity of extant securities, the distribution of asset holdings and the flows of new wealth across different classes of investors, classified according to their attitude to risk, have all been suggested as determinants of these premia.

terms of trade (410, 420)

1 The ratio of the values of the goods and services traded between countries.

2 The weighted or unweighted ratio of export price indices to import price indices.

Since changes in the terms of trade have so great an effect on the **gross national product** of **open economies** there are many policy responses to deteriorating terms: these include changing the underlying bargaining relations in international trade, the collective self-reliance of less developed countries in trade and investment, import substitution and changes in types of exports. Some studies suggest that the deterioration in the terms of trade has been more the result of the characteristics of countries than of commodities.

The best measures calculated have been the **International Monetary Fund**'s index of thirty primary commodities exported by less developed countries deflated by the United Nations' index and the World Bank's indicators of market prices divided by a unit value index of total manufactures exported from developed market economies to less developed countries.

See also: **commodity terms of trade; double factorial terms of trade; factorial terms of trade; income terms of trade; net barter terms of trade; single factorial terms of trade**.

term structure of interest rates (310)

The relationship between interest rates on securities of different maturities, particu-

larly the relationship between short- and long-term interest rates. Economists, including **Hicks**, have attempted to explain this structure in terms of **expectations**; others have attributed the structure to the attitudes of borrowers and lenders to **liquidity** and **risk** or to market segmentation that prevents funds being shifted from short-term to long-term markets. Long-term interest rates are often more than short-term rates as many investors cannot lend long term and so have to be paid a premium to be encouraged to lend.

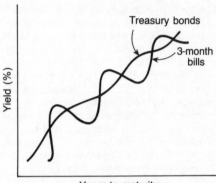

Meiselman, D. (1962) *The Term Structure of Interest Rates*, Englewood Cliffs, NJ: Prentice Hall.

Nelson, C.R. (1972) *The Term Structure of Interest Rates*, New York: Basic Books.

tertiary sector (630)

That part of an **economy** which produces services. The formal part of this sector is dominated by schools, hospitals, retailing, banks and insurance; the informal part is dominated by self-employed persons in the **black economy**. In the USA and the UK, as a consequence of **de-industrialization**, it has become, as measured by employment, the major sector of the economy.

See also: **services**.

Tessa (320)

See: **Tax Exempt Special Savings Account**.

test rate of discount (520, 610)

The real rate of return that UK public sector investments are expected to achieve at the margin. The UK government, in its continuing attempts to improve investment appraisal in **nationalized industries**, proposed this rate in a White Paper of 1967; it was originally set at 8 per cent, to represent 'the minimum rate of return to be expected in a marginal low-risk project undertaken for commercial reasons' with the hope that there would be greater consistency in the granting of approval for projects. It has subsequently been changed to reflect market changes in interest rates.

The Chancellor of Exchequer (1967) *Nationalized Industries: A Review of Economic and Financial Objectives*, London: HMSO, Cmnd 3437.

test statistic (210)
The distribution of a standardized variable, also known as a z score. For a normal distribution the z score is the statistic minus the mean of the sample all divided by the **standard deviation** of the sample.

Thatcherism (010, 320)
An attitude of frugality towards public expenditure and a belief in the supremacy of market forces. Mrs Margaret Thatcher in 1970 as UK Secretary of State for Education, by abolishing free school milk, gained the former reputation; as Prime Minister of the UK from 1979 to 1990, her emphasis on monetary control (instead of extensive government intervention backed by public funds), on the **privatization** of nationalized industries and on the removal of **labour market rigidities** expressed her desire for the release of free market forces. She has frequently used the analogy of good household management for such policies and is thus the contemporary expounder of Gladstonian finance. Sir Geoffrey Howe in his first Budget speech of 1979 outlined the programme of Thatcherism in his four principles: the strengthening of economic incentives, the reduction of the burden of financing the public sector, the reduction in the role of the state to increase freedom of individual choice and increased responsibility in collective bargaining.

Johnson, C. (1991) *The Economy under Mrs Thatcher: 1979-90*, Harmondsworth: Penguin.
Thompson, G. (1986) *The Conservatives' Economic Policy*, London: Croom Helm.

Walters, A.A. (1986) *Britain's Economic Renaissance: Margaret Thatcher's Reforms, 1979-84*, Oxford and New York: Oxford University Press.

theonomy (020)
Literally, government or rule by God, but now used to mean the application of theology, especially the theology of the Bible, to economics; the use of Biblical law in the study of the reconstruction of society.

Rushdoony, R.S. (1973) *The Institutes of Biblical Law*, Nutley, NJ: Craig Press.

theory of clubs (020, 320)
An explanation of the nature of **club goods** which share some of the characteristics of **public goods** without non-excludability. This theory can be traced back to **Pigou** and **Knight**; recent writers on this subject include **Buchanan** and Tiebout.

Buchanan, J.M. (1965) 'An economic theory of clubs', *Economica, New Series* 32: 1–14.
Sandler, T. and Tschirhart, J. (1980) 'The economic theory of clubs: an evaluative survey', *Journal of Economic Literature* 18: 1481–521.

theory of the firm (020, 610)
An explanation of how the aims of a firm are related to its decision-making. Since **Marshall**, economists have studied the rationale for managerial decisions on pricing, product mix, output, advertising and investment. Earlier theories were built on the assumption of **profit maximization**; later theories have attempted to incorporate wider theories of managerial behaviour and to recognize different organizational forms. The theory of the firm constitutes a major part of microeconomics.

Baumol, W.J. (1967) *Business Behavior, Value and Growth*, New York: Harcourt, Brace & World.
Clarke, R. and McGuinness, T. (eds) (1987) *The Economics of the Firm*, Oxford: Basil Blackwell.
Marshall, A. (1920 *Principles of Economics*, 8th edn, London: Macmillan.
Stigler, G.J. (1952) *The Theory of the Firm*, rev. edn, New York: Macmillan.
Williamson, O.E. (1963) *Economics of Discretionary Behavior: Managerial Objectives in a Theory of the Firm*, Englewood Cliffs, NJ: Prentice Hall.

See also: **Coase**; **structure–conduct–performance model**.

third age (840)

The period of a person's life after middle age from 50 years onwards. This age group has a dominant role in many consumer markets of industrialized countries in the late twentieth century.

third degree price discrimination (010, 530)

Charging different prices to different customers. This is the most common form of price discrimination. Discrimination is often on the basis of the income, age, student or unemployed status of the consumer.

See also: **price discrimination**.

third market (310)

The UK stock exchange founded in January 1987 to allow the trading of small companies' securities. The first and second markets consist of the main list of the **International Stock Exchange** and the **Unlisted Securities Market**. As the companies using this market are small, and often new, investment in their shares is very risky. Nevertheless, it is a market with great growth potential, partly because of the companies promoted by the **Business Expansion Scheme**.

third-party effect (010)

See: **externality; spillover effect**.

third way (070)

See: **market socialism**.

Third World (070, 730)

Developing economies which, with the exception of oil producers, have low per capita incomes, large agricultural sectors and a shortage of most kinds of capital. Some have defined the Third World as those countries in receipt of **foreign aid**.

Reitsma, H.A. and Kleinpenning, J.M.G. (1985) *The Third World in Perspective*, Assen and Maastricht: Van Gorcgum.
Reynolds, L.G. (1985) *Economic Growth in the Third World, 1850–1980*, New Haven, CT, and London: Yale University Press.
Worsley, P. (1967) *The Third World*, 2nd edn, London: Weidenfeld & Nicolson.

See also: **First World; Second World**.

Third World debt problem

See: **world debt problem**.

Thirty Share Index (310)

See: **Financial Times Industrial Ordinary Share Index**.

Thomson Report (940)

Report on the Regional Problems in the Enlarged Community, a report of a **European Community** Commissioner in 1973 which surveyed the economic and social problems of the member countries on the eve of the first oil crisis.

Thornton, Henry, 1760–1815 (030)

London banker and leading monetary theorist of the early nineteenth century who was a member of the Clapham Sect, a group of Evangelical social reformers who succeeded in abolishing British participation in the slave trade, and Member of Parliament for Southwark from 1782 to 1815. His famous book *Paper Credit* (1802), much praised by **Schumpeter**, **Hayek** and **Hicks**, defended the issue of inconvertible banknotes, showed the relationship between interest rates and international gold flows, analysed the market for loanable funds, defined the nature of inflation and presented a definition of full employment.

Hicks, J.R. (1967) *Critical Essays in Monetary Theory*, ch. 10, Oxford: Clarendon Press.
Thornton, H. (1939) *An Enquiry into the Nature and Effects of the Paper Credit of Great Britain*, ed. by F. von Hayek, London and New York: George Allen & Unwin.

threat effect (830)

Effect on the wages of a non-unionized labour force of the threat of a **trade (labor) union** organizing to raise wages. A non-unionized employer wanting to prevent unionization raises wages to the union level. Threat effects contribute to the spread of wage inflation.

three-digit industry (610)

An **industry** defined according to a fine classification such that the economy's industrial structure is broken down into as many as 999 industries.

See also: **two-digit industry**.

three-stage least squares (210)

A rewriting of **two-stage least squares** estimators and the application of generalized least squares to all the relations in the model to obtain a simultaneous estimate of all parameters.

Zellner, A. and Theil, H. (1962) 'Three-stage least squares: simultaneous estimation of simultaneous equations', *Econometrica* 30: 54–78.

threshold population (840, 930)
The minimum size that a population must be to carry out the functions of a town or city. A major determinant of this size will be **agglomeration economies**.

See also: **central place theory**.

thrift (310)
Saving; hence in the USA it refers to a savings and loan association, similar to a British **building society** in having the task of providing mortgages. In the 1980s, the US thrifts went further into insolvency as a consequence of financial deregulation, including the ending of **Regulation Q** and the diversification of their investments; lax supervision and the guaranteeing of deposits contributed to poor financial control.

In **Keynesian** economics thrift is attacked because it has the effect of lowering **aggregate demand** if savings are hoarded.

See also: **paradox of thrift; Resolution Trust Corporation**.

Thünen, Johann Heinrich von, 1783–1850 (030)
A Prussian landlord who can be credited with creating **marginalism** and managerial economics and presenting one of the first general equilibrium models and models of location.

Samuelson, P.A. (1983) 'Thunen at two hundred', *Journal of Economic Literature* 21 (December): 1469–88.

TIBOR (310)
Tokyo Inter-Bank Offered Rate.

See also: **London Inter-Bank Offered Rate**.

tick (310)
One thirty-secondth of a percentage point, especially of the interest rate on UK **gilts**.

Tiebout hypothesis (320, 930)
The view that there should be small local government areas in order to increase the amount of citizen choice between different combinations of facilities and local taxes. Individuals would be able to obtain the combination closest to their preferences by moving between these small areas.

Mieszkowski, P. and Zodrow, G.R. (1989) 'Taxation and the Tiebout model: the differential effects of head taxes, taxes on land rents, and property taxes', *Journal of Economic Literature* 27 (September): 1098–146.

Oates, W.F. (1969) 'The effect of property taxes and local public spending on property values: an empirical study of tax capitalization and the Tiebout hypothesis', *Journal of Political Economy* 77: 957–71.

Tiebout, C. (1956) 'A pure theory of local government expenditures', *Journal of Political Economy* 64: 416–24.

See also: **fiscal mobility**.

tied aid (430)
Foreign aid which is given on condition that the recipient purchases the exports of the donor country. This has been called 'devalued aid' as the recipient may have to purchase goods higher in price and lower in quality than is available on international markets; in extreme cases the aid is supplied in physical amounts, e.g. food and medicines. However, many donor countries with their own **balance of payments** problems would give little aid at all if it were not in this form.

See also: **bilateral aid; multilateral aid**.

tied cottage (910)
A house provided to a worker holding a particular job, especially in the agricultural sector. When the worker ceases to hold that job, he/she has to seek alternative accommodation.

tied house (630)
In the British brewery industry, a public house (inn) which can only sell the products of the brewery to which it is connected, usually by ownership.

tight fiscal policy (320)
Low government expenditure, high taxation or both.

tight monetary policy (310)
A strict **monetary policy** which attempts to curb the growth of the money supply and

raises interest rates. This policy is often employed by economies with an unacceptable rate of inflation and/or balance of payments problems. These goals are sought by reducing **aggregate demand** and inducing capital inflows from other countries.

till money (310)

The cash which UK **clearing banks** have on their premises for payments to customers. Until 1971 it could be included in the **reserve assets** of these banks: it was excluded then as cash needed for transactions purposes could not be regarded as a reserve.

time budget survey (810)

An investigation into the allocation of time between paid work, unpaid work (e.g. household cleaning) and leisure which aims to discover the range of a person's activities. Data are collected from the diary entries of volunteers. Surveys of this kind have been used to assess the extent of the **informal economy** and to measure **labour force participation rates**.

Birdsall, N. (1980) 'Measuring time use and non-market exchange', in W.P. McGreevy (ed.) *Third World Poverty: New Strategies for Measuring Development Progress*, Lexington, MA: Lexington Books.
Stafford, F.P. (1985) *Time, Goods and Well-Being*, Ann Arbor, MI: Survey Research Center, Institute for Social Research, University of Michigan.

time deposit (310)

A sum of money that the depositor does not have the right to withdraw within six days of making the deposit, unless the deposit is subject to an early withdrawal penalty of at least seven days' simple interest.

time rate (820)

A wage rate per unit of time, often an hour.

See also: **piece rate**.

time series (220)

A collection of data showing the values of an economic variable at different dates, e.g. expenditure on clothing for each year of a decade. Movements of time series can be divided into secular (long-term), cyclical, seasonal and random changes.

Box, G.E.P. and Jenkins, G.M. (1970) *Time Series Analysis: Forecasting and Control*, San Francisco, CA: Holden-Day.

See also: **cyclical variations; random variations; seasonal adjustment trend**.

timeshare (930)

The property right to use a house or apartment, usually for holiday purposes, for specified weeks of a year, either over a fixed term of years or in perpetuity. The right can be bought and sold. Timesharers often have to pay an annual maintenance charge to the firm organizing the timeshares.

time span (810)

The amount of time an employee can work without reporting to his/her immediate superior. These spans have been used as a proxy measure of all the attributes of a job which can give rise to occupational pay differentials. Elliott Jaques has extensively applied this to the rationalization of organizations' pay structures, e.g. at Glacier Metals (UK) and Honeywell Computers (USA).

Jaques, E. (1956) *Measurement of Responsibility*, Cambridge, MA: Harvard University Press.
—— (1964) *Time-span Handbook*, London: Heinemann.

See also: **wage differentials**.

TINA (310, 320)

There Is No Alternative; the perpetual war-cry of tough Thatcherite **monetarists** since 1979.

See also: **Thatcherism**.

Tinbergen, Jan, 1903– (030)

Prominent Dutch econometrician who, after studying physics at Leiden University and gaining a PhD for extremum problems in economics and physics, did research into the **business cycle** from 1929 to 1945 at the Dutch Central Bureau of Statistics. He was Director of the Netherlands Central Planning Bureau from 1945 to 1955, Professor of Development Planning at Erasmus University, Rotterdam, from 1955 to 1973 and Professor of International Cooperation at Leiden from 1973 to 1975. With **Frisch**, he won the first **Nobel Prize for Economics** in 1969; four years later his brother shared the Nobel Prize for Biology. His skills as an econometrician have yielded many books, directly arising from the jobs he has held. His first works were on **business cycles** but his experience with the Central Planning Bureau produced renowned works on economic policy which asserted that government policy must have the same number of instruments as it has quantified targets. Later he turned to **development economics** and the study of income distribution.

Tinbergen, J. (1952) *On the Theory of Economic Policy*, Amsterdam: North-Holland.
—— (1956) *Economic Policy: Principles and Design*, Amsterdam: North-Holland.
—— (1968) *Statistical Testing of Business Cycle Theories*, New York: Agathon Press.

TIP (320, 820)
See: **tax-based incomes policy**.

TNC (610)
See: **transnational corporation**.

Tobin, James, 1918– (030)
US economist educated at Harvard University and an economics professor at Yale University since 1947; in 1981 he was awarded the **Nobel Prize for Economics**. A prominent **Keynesian** who has attacked the narrowness of **monetarism** with his wider **portfolio selection** theory. In a paper on **liquidity preference** in 1958, he extended Keynesian analysis by asserting that **liquidity preference** is a response to the risk associated with the probability distribution of interest rate expectations. In many papers, he has repeatedly used a **general equilibrium** approach to a study of financial **intermediation** and flow of funds analysis. In 1961–2 he served on President Kennedy's **Council of Economic Advisers**. His wideranging interests include **stabilization policies**, growth policies and the poverty problem. He originated the **Tobit model** method.

Purvis, D. and Myhrman, J. (1982) 'James Tobin's contribution to economics', *Scandinavian Journal of Economics* 84: 61–88.
Tobin, J. (1974 and 1975) *Essays in Economics*, vols I and II, Cambridge, MA: MIT Press.
—— (1974) *The New Economics: One Decade Older*, Princeton, NJ: Princeton University Press.

See also: **flow of funds account**.

Tobin tax (320)
A proposed uniform tax levied by all countries of the world on all foreign exchange transactions with the aim of making short-term **hot money** movements unprofitable.

Tobit model (210)
An econometric model which copes with the problem of missing data in the form of a shortage of observations beyond a limit point, e.g. zero, so that there are no negative values. **Tobin** was the first to tackle this problem in his analysis of household expenditure on a durable good.

Amemiya, T. (1984) 'Tobit models: a survey', *Journal of Econometrics* 24: 3–61.
Tobin, J. (1958) 'Estimation of relationships for limited dependent variables', *Econometrica* 26: 24–36.

token money (310)
Anything accepted as **money**, not because of its intrinsic value, but because of custom or legal enactment. Thus banknotes are token money and gold coins are not. Token money costs less to produce than its face value, e.g. a pound note in the UK costs only several pence.

See also: **fiat money**.

Tokyo Round (420)
A series of tariff cuts arranged under the auspices of the **General Agreement on Tariffs and Trade** in the period 1973–9. Tariff reductions were to be implemented in equal annual amounts from 1980 to 1987. A duty of 20 per cent was reduced by 59 per cent, a 10 per cent duty by 42 per cent and a 5 per cent duty by 26 per cent. The **European Community** and Japan made advance reductions; other countries made them by 1990. It was the intention that in this Round tariff averages weighted by total imports of manufactured goods would decline by 30 per cent in the USA, 28 per cent in the European Community and 46 per cent in Japan. Smaller reductions in tariffs of goods from developing countries (as in the **Kennedy Round**) were agreed as they are sensitive products, e.g. textiles. At the end of the round, tariffs on manufactured goods, weighted by total imports, were to be cut by 4.9 per cent in the USA, 6 per cent in the

European Community and 5.4 per cent in Japan.

See also: **General Agreement on Tariffs and Trade; Uruguay Round**.

toll (010)

The charge for the use of a service; in some cases an excessive charge. Major examples of tolls are those for the use of highways and a telephone system to make long-distance calls.

toll model (820)

Okun's model of a labour market in which a firm hiring a worker has to pay a 'toll' to cover the costs of training and initiation. This model is used to explain cyclical variations in employment and unemployment.

Okun, A.M. (1981) *Prices and Quantities: A Macroeconomic Analysis*, ch. 2, Washington, DC: Brookings Institution; Oxford: Basil Blackwell.

tombstone (310)

A press advertisement recording the details of a new issue or loan. The names on the tombstone are the managers and underwriters (or syndicate members) to the issue. The amount of the loan and the listing terms are also given.

tontine (310)

A scheme, invented by Lorenzo Tonti, a Neapolitan banker, in 1653, consisting of several subscribers advancing the same amount to a borrower who pays the same amount of interest in total to all the subscribers until the survivor receives all the interest on the amount advanced. Thus if there are 100 subscribers receiving £50 each in interest, when there are only 50 left each subscriber will obtain £100 each and the survivor will receive £5,000 per annum. This popular method of raising funds in the eighteenth and nineteenth centuries was last used by the British government to raise a loan in 1789. One of the most amusing accounts of a tontine is given in the short novel *The Wrong Box*.

Stevenson, R.L. and Osbourne, L. (1889) *The Wrong Box*, London: Longman.

top-down linkage model (940)

A regional model which shows the local reaction to national economic change, e.g. cyclical fluctuations in **national income**. It usually ignores the feedback of economic activity upwards from the region.

Klein, L.R. (1969) 'The specification of regional econometric models', *Papers of the Regional Science Association* 23: 105–15.

top-level efficiency (010)

An increase in the total collection of goods available to a society which makes everyone better off. This type of efficiency combines both production and exchange efficiencies.

See also: **Pareto optimum**.

top-sided federalism (320)

A description of US federalism of the 1968–78 period in which federal aid and state spending grew faster than local spending. One way in which this occurred was through the **Comprehensive Employment and Training Act 1973** which replaced thirteen separate manpower training programmes to channel additional federal aid to local governments.

See also: **fiscal federalism**.

Torrens, Robert, 1780–1864 (030)

A prolific English **classical economist** who was in the Royal Marines from 1797 to 1835 and Member of Parliament from 1831 to 1835. In a long series of publications from 1808, he participated in the major economic debates of the day, particularly on monetary questions, switching from being an anti-bullionist in the 1820s to membership of the **Currency School**. He also formulated the law of **comparative advantage** independently of **Ricardo** and the law of **reciprocal demand** independently of John Stuart **Mill**.

Fetter, F.W. (1962) 'Robert Torrens: Colonel of Marines and political economist', *Economica, New Series* 29: 152–65.
Robbins, L. (1958) *Robert Torrens and the Evolution of Classical Economics*, London: Macmillan.

total costs (010)

All the costs of producing a good or service. In the short run the total is divisible into **fixed** and **variable costs**, but in the long run all costs are variable.

total fertility rate (840)

A measure of the average number of live

births throughout a woman's child-bearing period. It is calculated by adding the average number of live births of all age-specific groups (15–44 years) together.

total public debt (310)

All the bonds and bills issued by the central and local governments of a country which are outstanding at a particular time. In the USA this consists only of borrowings by the US Treasury. It is limited in size by the **Gramm–Rudman–Hollings Act**.

See also: **gross federal debt; public sector borrowing requirement**.

total revenue (010)

All the proceeds from selling a particular amount of output, i.e. total quantity sold multiplied by price. Maximizing total revenue is a rule of thumb objective of some firms.

See also: **managerial models of the firm**.

town clearing (310)

Same day clearing of a cheque with a value of more than £10,000 within a specified central area of the City of London after over-the-counter trading has closed for the day.

tradable discharge permit (720)

A permit which permits the holder to discharge a specified amount of a pollutant. As this permit can be sold to another person, the permission can be transferred.

tradable emission permit (720)

See: **marketable discharge permit**.

Trade Act 1974 (420)

US federal statute which regulates the foreign trade of the USA. Under an escape clause, industries can apply for **tariffs** and other trade restrictions to be erected in their favour if it can be proved that the industry concerned has suffered from foreign competition as seen in a fall in employment, output or profits. Under the Act, workers unemployed or threatened with unemployment as a consequence of imports can be given income support, relocation allowances, job search allowances and training.

trade balance (430)

A sub-balance of a country's balance of payments showing the relationship between total exports and total imports. It is usually divided into a visible balance, referring to goods, and an invisible balance, referring to services. The balance is in surplus if exports exceed imports; in deficit if imports are in excess of exports.

See also: **current account**.

trade bill (310)

A **bill of exchange** payable in one, two, three or six months.

trade creation (420)

The effect of a **customs union** which increases the volume of trade through the elimination of previous trade barriers between members.

See also: **trade diversion**.

trade credit (520)

1 Loans between non-financial firms, e.g. a wholesaler's financing of a new retailer by allowing payment months after the delivery of supplies.

2 Credit offered by a firm to its customers.

In times when monetary stringency is brought on by a **tight monetary policy**, trade credit often replaces bank credit.

trade cycle (140)

Fluctuations in the level of national economic activity over a period of years. Although first observed by **Petty**, it was not until **Malthus**, John Stuart **Mill** and **Marx** that there were serious attempts to explain such oscillations. As most trade cycle theories explain fluctuations in terms of changes in investment, the length of the cycle depends on the durability of the capital good: the shortest are inventory cycles, the longest are infrastructure investment cycles, e.g. in transport systems.

Haberler, G. (1964) *Prosperity and Depression*, 5th edn, London: Allen & Unwin.
Matthews, R.C.O. (1959) *The Trade Cycle*, Cambridge: Cambridge University Press.

See also: **business cycle; Juglar cycle; Kitchin cycle; Kondratieff cycle; Kuznets cycle**.

trade deficit (430)

An excess of imports over exports.

See also: **trade balance**.

trade diversion (420)
The effect of a **customs union** in changing the flows of goods and services between countries with increasing volumes going to other members of the union.

See also: **trade creation**.

traded option (310)
An **option** which can be bought and sold until its expiry date; at expiry, the last holder can exercise the option.

Trade Expansion Act 1962 (420)
US federal trade statute concerned with the liberalization of trade.

See also: **Kennedy Round**.

trade-off (010)
The relationship between two inversely connected variables such that more of one means less of another. Trade-offs occur in many parts of both microeconomics and macroeconomics, e.g. the trade-off between work and leisure, between consumption of one good and of another of a consumer with a fixed income, between high wages and high employment, between efficiency and equity. Famous trade-offs include **Ricardo's** between wages and profits and **Phillips's** between unemployment and inflation. The conflicting aims of individuals and of governments make trade-offs inevitable; scarcity necessitates choice between competing alternatives.

See also: **opportunity cost**.

trade policy (420)
See: **commercial policy**.

trade regime (420)
A country, or countries, following a particular trade policy of **protection** or **free trade**. Within the policy there can be different rules for various industries and products, e.g. import substitution for some and export promotion for others.

trade strategy (420)
The balance between production for domestic and foreign markets. An outward-oriented strategy would leave to domestic producers only those goods which cannot be more cheaply produced abroad; an inward-oriented strategy follows the principles of **import substitution** and **protection**. As **protection** invites retaliation, a country which is inward looking is likely to enjoy fewer economies of scale and to be more monopolistic. Outward-oriented economies, e.g. Singapore, Hong Kong and South Korea, have experienced higher rates of growth in real national income per head than inward-oriented countries.

trade surplus (430)
See: **trade balance**.

trade threat (420)
A trade restriction designed to change non-trade policies of a government, e.g. concerning human rights or the cleanliness of the environment. A **boycott** is the most common form of threat.

See also: **economic sanctions**.

trade union (830)
An association of workers or employers, especially the former. Trade unions have always been concerned with both the short- and the long-term welfare of their members – with varying degrees of success. These unions have been analysed as monopolists in the labour market, creating market imperfections. Unions are often criticized for opposing technical change but they can raise productivity by encouraging cooperation between management and labour. Many models of wage bargaining assume that the employer unilaterally selects the level of employment and that the union can only influence the wage level, but there are models which assume that unions can bargain about both employment and wages. The world's largest labour organization is I.G. Metall of West Germany which has 2.5 million members.

Hirsch, B.T. and Addison, J.T. (1986) *The Economic Analysis of Unions: New Approaches and Evidence*, Boston, MA: Allen & Unwin.
MacDonald, I.M. and Solow, R.M. (1981) 'Wage bargaining and employment', *American Economic Review* 71: 896–908.

See also: **closed shop; labor union; right-to-work state; strike; union shop; yellow dog contract**.

Trade Union Act 1984 (830)

UK industrial relations statute which imposed a duty on unions to hold secret ballots of their memberships for the election of the officers of the principal executive committee every five years. Also, ballots are required every ten years for the setting up of union political funds. Political dues cannot be collected from union members who are certified as exempt from contributing or object to doing so.

See also: **Employment Act 1980**.

Trade Unions and Labour Relations Act 1976 (830)

An act which consolidated UK labour legislation.

trade-weighted exchange rate (430)

The exchange rate of one country's currency for another's adjusted to reflect the composition of the exports of each country.

trading on the equity (520)

The effect on the earnings of a company with **preference shares** and **debentures** as well as **ordinary shares** of high **gearing**. A disproportionate amount of an increase in earnings will be available for distribution to holders of ordinary shares.

transaction cost (010, 510)

The running costs of an economic system; the cost of effecting an exchange or other economic transaction. These costs, which vary in magnitude from one economic system to another, include those of negotiating and drafting contracts and the subsequent costs of adjusting for misalignments. This concept is fundamental to the analysis of economic **regulation**, labour market hiring, **vertical integration** and competition in the capital market.

Coase, R. (1937) 'The nature of the firm', *Economica, New Series* 4: 386–405.
Commons, J.R. (1934) *Institutional Economics: Its Place in Political Economy*, Madison, WI: University of Wisconsin Press.
Demsetz, H. (1968) 'The cost of transacting', *Quarterly Journal of Economics* 82: 33–53.
Williamson, O.E. (1975) *Markets and Hierarchies: Analysis and Antitrust Implications*, New York: Free Press.

See also: **Commons**.

transaction cost economics (020)

A branch of economics which makes 'the transaction' the fundamental concept of economics and analyses problems as contracting problems. This approach to economics considers institutional alternatives and uses as its assumptions **bounded rationality**, opportunism and **asset specificity**. One of the first economists to emphasize the importance of transactions was **Commons**.

Williamson, O.E. (1985) *The Economic Institutions of Capitalism*, New York: Free Press; London: Collier Macmillan.

transactions demand for money (310)

The amount of money an individual wishes to hold in order to finance current purchases of goods and services. No monetary theorist disputes that such a demand exists.

See also: **demand for money**.

transferable discharge permit (720)

See: **marketable discharge permit**.

transfer earnings (010)

The minimum income of a **factor of production** which will keep it in that employment rather than another, measured by the earnings of that factor in the best alternative employment. Any part of a factor's earnings in excess of transfer earnings is **economic rent**.

See also: **opportunity cost**.

transfer income (010, 220)

The income of a person or a firm which does not arise from productive activity but, often, from a governmental grant. The principal examples of these are retirement pensions, student maintenance grants and subsidies to farmers. If such transfer incomes were included in the **national income** there would be double counting of **factor incomes** – when originally received and when redistributed as a transfer.

transfer pricing (520)

The pricing of goods and services which are transferred within large organizations, especially **multinational corporations**. As many of these goods and services are not marketed outside that organization, arbitrary pricing rules, often of a cost-plus type, are used. It is argued that transfer pricing can be unfair and used as a device to avoid corporate taxation in high tax countries. Increasingly tax codes have insisted on corporations following rules which produce fair prices. Transfer pricing also has a major impact on the value of international trade as a high proportion of it consists of trade between subsidiaries of large international enterprises.

transfer problem (430)
The difficulty of transferring capital in large quantities from one country to another, e.g. the reparation payments Germany had to make after the First World War. Students of the problem have been concerned with the imposition of a second burden on countries having to make the transfer as transfers would change the **terms of trade**; whether this happens depends on the relative size of the **marginal propensities to consume** of the recipient and donor countries for a particular product.

transformation curve (210)
See: **production possibility frontier**.

transformation problem (020)
The problem stated in Marx's *Das Kapital* of deriving prices from values and of deriving profits from surplus value. Solutions offered by mathematical economists have attracted criticism on account of their restrictive assumptions.

Böhm-Bawerk, E. von (1949) *Karl Marx and the Close of his System*, New York: Augustus Kelly.
Junankar, P.N. (1982) *Marx's Economics*, ch. 3, Oxford: Philip Alan.
Roemer, J. (1981) *Analytical Foundations of Marxian Economic Theory*, Cambridge: Cambridge University Press.

transitory income (010)
Unexpected income which is an addition to permanent income. Legacies and wins from gambling are prominent examples.

transmission mechanism (310)
The means by which changes in the money supply have an effect on output, employment and prices. The change in the money supply leads to a change in interest rates in different markets which, in turn, brings about a change in expenditures and output. However, the speed of reaction to monetary changes depends on the nature of **lags** in the economy. This mechanism can be regarded as portfolio adjustment as a growth in the money supply faster than the growth in output will push up the prices of non-monetary assets, e.g. property and durable goods, and stimulate output of them. There has always been controversy about the mechanism because of the two-way causality between money supply and expenditure changes.

See also: **Friedman**; **monetarism**.

transnational corporation (510, 610)
A firm with substantial operations in many countries but controlled from its original home base. This location of activities in many countries is a response to the worldwide distribution of resources, governmental constraints, market opportunities and technology. A firm with this wide geographical base is able to benefit from increased **economies of scale**, full utilization of its management and greater returns to its **research and development** expenditures. The first examples of transnationals are probably the large overseas trading monopolies advocated by the **mercantilists**, e.g. the East India Company.

See also: **multinational corporation**.

transport economics (930)
The study of the demand for transport and the relative merits of different systems for carrying persons and goods. This requires applications of consumer theory to determine demand for what is both an intermediate and a final service, and an analysis of transport industries to understand supply problems. Over the past twenty years increasing use has been made of **cost–benefit analysis** to appraise investments in roads and transport systems. Transport economics has been a close partner of **urban economics**. Early transport economists attempted to set out the rules for optimal pricing, investment, cost allocation; later there was more interest in the impact of government regulation on resource allocation and distribution, congestion and the multiproduct nature of transportation firms.

Glaister, S. (1981) *Fundamentals of Transport Economics*, Oxford: Basil Blackwell.

Winston, C. (1985) 'Conceptual developments in the economics of transportation: an interpretive survey', *Journal of Economic Literature* 23: 57–94.

traveller's cheque (310)

A **cheque** which is denominated in a major **currency** and widely accepted throughout the world for the purchase of local goods and services and for exchange into local currencies. American Express invented this financial instrument in 1891.

traverse (110)

The route which an economic system takes as it moves from one equilibrium to another. In a sense, an economy is in **disequilibrium** as it proceeds along the traverse.

Hicks, J.R. (1965) *Capital and Growth*, ch. 16, Oxford: Oxford University Press.

treasury (320, 520)

A government or corporation department in charge of finance.

treasury bill (310)

A short-term means of government borrowing following the model of a commercial bill of exchange which was invented by **Bagehot** in 1877. In the UK treasury bills effect borrowing for ninety-one days, in the USA for three, six, nine or twelve months.

Treasury model (140)

The economic forecasting model used by the UK Treasury.

'Forecasting in the Treasury', *Economic Progress Report*, June 1981.

Treasury view (320)

The attitude towards the management of the British economy in the 1920s and 1930s attacked by **Keynes**. The Treasury believed in balanced national budgets and attacked **public works** schemes on the grounds that they would not stimulate aggregate economic activity because of '**crowding-out**'. This view was abandoned in 1937 when the Treasury at last conceded the role of public works as part of a **countercyclical policy**.

Middleton, R. (1985) *Towards the Managed Economy: Keynes, the Treasury and the Fiscal Policy Debate of the 1930s*, London: Methuen.

Peden, G.C. (1984) 'The "Treasury View" on public works and employment in the interwar period', *Economic History Review* 37: 167–81.

treat effect (820, 830)

A deliberate increase in the wages of non-union employees of a firm undertaken by a management to show that **unions** confer no benefit on workers. This tactic has been used as a means of reducing the **unionization** of a firm's labour force.

See also: **threat effect**.

Treaty of Rome (420)

The treaty which set up the **European Economic Community** in 1958. The signatories were France, West Germany, Italy, the Netherlands, Belgium and Luxemburg. Subsequent treaties have enlarged the Community: in 1973 Britain, Ireland and Denmark joined, in 1981 Greece and in 1986 Spain and Portugal. The treaty establishes the Community as a **customs union** with mobility of capital and labour within it.

trend (210)

The general direction in which a **time series** is moving in the long term; the secular change. This is often measured by the **least squares method** where the variable examined is the dependent variable and time is the independent variable.

trend periods (140)

See: **Kondratieff cycle**.

TRF (840)

See: **total fertility rate**.

trickle-down theory (110)

A theory of economic **development** which asserts that development should follow traditional growth patterns with prosperity gradually coming to the least deprived members of society. This theory has also been applied to advanced free-market economies in which the richer members of society through their spending raise the real incomes of the poor. The extent of trickling down is usually measured by an increase in the real incomes of the poor, rather than by the removal of all income inequality which would need a 'flood'.

See also: **dual economy**.

trigger mechanism (310)

A method of **program trading**: this method of mathematical analysis uses as key market indicators a cash index to indicate present values and a futures index to indicate future values.

truck (820)

A wage payment in goods or in vouchers to obtain goods at the shops of the employer. In the UK, the Truck Acts of 1831, 1887 and 1896 made the truck system illegal, replacing it with wage payments in the current coin of the realm.

See also: **Wages Act 1986**.

true and fair view (540)

An auditor's opinion that a set of accounts are both devoid of fraud and in conformity with measurement conventions regarded by professional accounting institutes as accurate for portraying the current state of a business. A major concern since 1970 has been to ensure that the values used in statements of accounts have been adjusted to eliminate the effects of inflation.

See also: **current cost accounting**; **Statements of Standard Accounting Practice**.

trust fund (320, 910)

1 A fund managed by a group of trustees for the benefit of others.

2 The US Federal Government Fund which receives the revenue from a particular tax in order to finance a particular welfare payment. The best known is the **Old Age, Survivors, Disability and Health Insurance** (founded in 1935 and extended to cover disabled persons in 1956) which is financed out of the revenue from the payroll tax. Other trust funds include the Hospital Insurance Fund and the Unemployment Insurance Fund. In the USA the balance of a trust fund is either held as a cash balance with the US Treasury or invested in US securities.

Truth in Lending Act 1968 (920)

US **consumer protection legislation** requiring lenders of money to inform borrowers of the true rate of interest on their loans. The British parallel is the **Consumer Credit Act**.

TSA (310)

The Securities Association (London): a **self-regulatory organization**.

Turgot, Anne-Robert Jacques, 1727–81 (030)

French Physiocrat. Educated at a Paris seminary and the Sorbonne, he abandoned careers in the church and the law to become a tax administrator as intendant, Limoges, 1761–74, and Contrôleur Général of France, 1774–6. His celebrated *Réflexions sur la Formation et la Distribution des Richesses* (1766) anticipated many of the central themes of **Smith**'s *Wealth of Nations* in that it discussed **free trade**, a *laissez-faire* approach to industry, the effects of the **division of labour**, **value** and price theory, a **stages theory** and the determinants of factor prices.

Groenewegen, P.D. (1977) *The Economics of A.R.J. Turgot*, Dordrecht and Lancaster: Martinus Nijhoff.

turnkey contract (520)

A construction and engineering contract to build and equip a factory, a power station or other large capital project so that it is completely ready for use. The purchaser merely has to turn the key in the front door to start using the capital asset. Contracts of this kind are popular in Third World countries.

turnover ratios (540)

See: **sales ratios**.

turnover tax (320)

A tax levied on the value of the sales revenue of a firm. It is distortionary in that the total tax paid will be higher for goods which pass through several firms to their final sale than for those which do not.

turnpike theorem (110)

A proposition in the theory of economic growth for providing an optimal programme over a finite horizon to reach a particular objective. These theorems make different assumptions about the quantities and relative prices of factor inputs required to follow a particular growth path.

Dorfman, R., Samuelson, P.A. and Solow, R.M.

(1958) *Linear Programming and Economic Analysis*, New York: McGraw-Hill.

TVA (320, 610)

1 Tennessee Valley Authority.

2 Taxe sur la Valeur Ajoutée: the French **value-added tax**.

twenty-four-hour trading (310)

Trading at any time of day on the world's stock exchanges because of their being located in different time zones and often allowing **after-hours dealings**.

two-digit industry (610)

An **industry** defined according to a broad classification such that an economy's industrial structure is divided into no more than ninety-nine industries. This is usually contrasted with a **three-digit industry**.

two-dollar broker (310)

An independent broker on the **New York Stock Exchange** who executes orders to buy and sell on behalf of commission brokers.

two-gap development model (110)

A planning model which takes into account a savings gap (domestic savings less than the level needed to reach a growth target) and a foreign exchange gap (between expenditure needed on imports to achieve target growth and earnings from exports).

Chenery, H.B. and Bruno, M. (1962) 'Development alternatives in an open economy: the case of Israel', *Economic Journal* 72: 79–103.

two-part tariff (010)

A price consisting of two parts: one part pays for **fixed costs**, the other for **variable costs**. A major example of this is the charging of a telephone rental to cover fixed costs and the separate charging for calls to pay for variable costs.

Feldstein, M. (1972) 'Equity and efficiency in public sector pricing: the optimal two part tariff', *Quarterly Journal of Economics* 86: 175–87.

See also: **price discrimination**.

two-stage least squares (210)

An econometric method which makes use of all predetermined variables in an econometric model so that the parameters of a single relation can be estimated. The independent variable is replaced by a matrix of least squares regressions of that variable on all the predetermined variables. The final stage is to apply least squares again to the variables of the equation.

See also: **three-stage least squares**.

two-tailed test (210)

A statistical test to show that a **null hypothesis** lies between a plus or minus range of a statistic. If a 95 per cent **confidence interval** is used, then the null hypothesis is rejected if it lies in the +2.5 or −2.5 per cent tails.

See also: **one-tailed test**.

tying contract (530)

A sales contract which specifies that a particular good or service will only be supplied if an associated one is purchased, e.g. that oxygen will only be supplied if ancillary equipment is ordered. Under US and UK law this **restrictive practice** is outlawed.

Type I error (210)

The rejection of a null hypothesis which should be accepted.

Type II error (210)

The acceptance of a null hypothesis which should be rejected.

U

UBR (320)
See: **uniform business rate**.

UDEAC (420)
See: **Union Douanière et Economique de l'Afrique Centrale**.

U-form (510)
The unitary form of business enterprise organized in the traditional way of dividing it up according to function. This is an appropriate structure for smaller enterprises; for larger organizations, this form imposes high communication costs.

See also: **H-form**; **M-form**; **X-form**.

U hypothesis (110, 160)
A view of the income distribution of less developed countries advanced by **Kuznets** and others that the share of **national income** going to the poorest part of the population declines at the start of economic development and rises only in the later stages of development, often because of a change in government policies to help the poor. The income distribution often changes over time in this way because development has taken the form of industrialization of benefit to only a small part of the economy.

Adelman, I. and Marris, C.T. (1973) *Economic Growth and Social Equity in Developing Countries*, Stanford CA: Stanford University Press.
Kuznets, S. (1966) *Modern Economic Growth: Rate, Structure and Spread*, New Haven, CT: Yale University Press.

See also: **Kuznets curve**.

UK economic forecasting (140)
The work of organizations which regularly produce detailed independent forecasts of the UK economy. Apart from the Treasury and the Bank of England, forecasting is also undertaken by Henley Forecasting, the **National Institute of Economic and Social Research**, London Business School, Liverpool University, Oxford Economic Forecasting, Phillips and Drew, the Con-federation of British Industry, James Capel, Simon and Coates, Hoare Govett, Goldman Sachs, Shearson Lehman, Laing and Cruickshank, Wood Mackenzie and the **Organization for Economic Cooperation and Development**.

Laury, J.S.E., Lewis, G.R. and Ormerod, P.A. (1978) 'Properties of macroeconomic models of the UK economy: a comparative study', *National Institute Economic Review* 83: 52–72.

See also: **economic forecasting**; **linkage models**.

UK gilts market (310)
Market in British government bonds. About 150 government securities are traded in this British market. After the London market was deregulated twenty-nine **primary dealers** established themselves in the market, using the USA as a model: with this number of dealers no firm will have a vital proportion of the market. The Central Gilts Office acts as the clearing house for transactions in **gilts**.

UK stock exchanges (310)
See: **International Stock Exchange**.

UK taxation (320)
A mixture of taxation on households (income tax and national insurance contributions), on firms (corporation tax), on wealth (capital gains and capital transfer taxes) and on goods and services (VAT and excise duties) with offsetting allowances at the national level. Local government currently has the revenue from the **community charge** and **uniform business rate**. Recent statistics indicate both the relative yield of these taxes, and the switch from direct to indirect taxation since 1979.

Kay, J.A. and King, M.A. (1990) *The British Tax System*, 5th edn, Oxford: Oxford University Press.
HMSO, *Economic Trends*, monthly.

umbrella fund (310)
A fund set up abroad to evade restrictions on

investment imposed by a domestic government.

unbiased estimator (210)

A **parameter** of a population which is the same as the corresponding statistic for a sample taken from it, e.g. the **arithmetic means** are the same.

unbundling (520, 530)

1 The separate charging for the services provided by a bank or other financial institution.

2 A de-merger which involves the selling off of the component parts of a firm.

uncertainty (010)

A state of affairs with an unknown outcome which is not subject to a probability distribution. In economics, there are many states of uncertainty e.g. of demand, of returns to investment. Uncertainty imposes many costs, e.g. the holding of higher inventories to safeguard against an irregular supply of raw materials and components. The forms of uncertainty are as various as its determinants – competition, technological change, the **business cycle**, and change of government or governmental policies.

Borch, K.H. (1968) *The Economics of Uncertainty*, Princeton, NJ: Princeton University Press.

See also: **risk**.

unconditional grant (320)

Australian federal grant to an individual state which is a means of sharing tax revenues to provide public services at the same level throughout Australia. As the use of these grants is not stipulated, it is possible for them to be used to reduce taxes rather than to maintain services.

See also: **Commonwealth Grants Commission; federal finance**.

UNCTAD (420)

See: **United Nations Conference on Trade and Development**.

Unctad Liner Code (630)

The set of rules of the **United Nations Conference on Trade and Development** (UNCTAD) allowing shipping conferences to fix cargo rates and to share out routes between the ports of UNCTAD members.

undepletable externality (720)

An **externality** with collective effects so that if one person is affected by it the effect on others will not be diminished, e.g. smog.

See also: **pollution control**.

underemployment (810)

Work with a low **productivity**, e.g. agricultural labour on small farms; part-time employment of workers who want full-time jobs. The extent of underemployment is reflected in low wages and in a lower output per person than that of workers in the most efficient enterprises of that industry. Much underemployment occurs in the **secondary sector** of the labour market.

underground economy (010)

The economic activities of a nation which are not officially recorded and are sometimes illegal.

Geige, E.L. (ed.) (1989) *The Underground Economies*, Cambridge: Cambridge University Press.

See also: **black economy; informal economy**.

underlying inflation rate (150, 220)

The adjusted **retail price index** with seasonal food prices, the **community charge** and mortgage interest payments removed.

See also: **core inflation; headline rate**.

undertrading (520)

Operating a firm with **excess capacity** because of a low demand for its products.

See also: **overtrading; X-efficiency**.

underwriter (310)

1 A financial institution which promises to take up the unsold shares of a new issue.

2 An **insurance** company or **Lloyd's** syndicate which accepts an insurance risk.

UNDP (130)

See: **United Nations Development Programme**.

unemployment (810)

1 The state of being part of a labour force,

wanting to work, but without a job.

2 A **disequilibrium** phenomenon arising from inflexible prices.

Unemployment can take many forms – **voluntary**, **involuntary**, **frictional**, **structural**, **demand deficient**. It has been measured both as a **stock** and as a **flow**, using as statistical sources registers of persons declaring themselves to be unemployed and household surveys. In **classical economics**, unemployment is viewed as a temporary phenomenon until price flexibility restores an economy to full employment. **Keynes** challenged the classical view and later economists have been sceptical about the clearing of markets.

Layard, R. (1986) *How to Beat Unemployment*, Oxford: Oxford University Press.
Minford, P. (1983) *Unemployment: Cause and Cure*, Oxford: Basil Blackwell.
Sinclair, P. (1987) *Unemployment: Economic Theory and Evidence*, Oxford: Basil Blackwell.

See also: **natural rate of unemployment**.

unemployment causes (810)

A method of classifying the types of **unemployment**, based on the theory of employment held by a particular labour economist. **Classical economists**, with their belief that all markets ultimately clear, believed that unemployment was a short-term phenomenon of a **frictional** type; if it was longer it could be attributed to a change in the structure of industry. **Keynes** insisted that unemployment could be **involuntary**, as a consequence of a deficiency in demand. Thus, it became popular to classify unemployment as **frictional**, **structural** or **demand deficient**. The rapid pace of technological change and the growth of welfarism in many countries in the post-1945 period suggested new causes of unemployment. Changes in the relative cost of capital and labour and the relationship between the level of unemployment benefits and the pay of jobs at the bottom of the earnings league have also been noted as causing unemployment.

Sachs, J.D. (1983) 'Real wages and employment in the OECD countries', *Brookings Paper on Economic Activity.*

unemployment compensation (910)

An insurance payment to unemployed people. This benefit is a usual provision in developed countries, but it is as rare in developing countries as it was in the Soviet-type economies. In those countries offering this form of compensation, payments have become more generous over time: after 1973, the unemployment benefit rate reached 75 per cent of after-tax incomes in major European countries.

unemployment spell (810)

A completed period of **unemployment**. Spells are likely to be longer at higher levels of benefit, when workers have savings and when the overall rate of unemployment is high. The number of spells has been increasing in both the US and UK labour markets.

Akerlof, G.A. and Main, B.G.M. (1980) 'Unemployment spells and unemployment experience', *American Economic Review* 70: 885–93.

unemployment statistics (220, 810)

Data on the total numbers within a country's labour force without a job but seeking employment. It is customary to subdivide this information by sex, age, industry, occupation and duration of unemployment. European unemployment statistics are regularly published in the Eurostats Labour Force Survey; US statistics are published by the Bureau of Labor Statistics (USA) and UK statistics by the Department of Employment (UK). Governmental bodies charged with the task of collecting these data constantly attempt to refine their definition of unemployment to obtain a more accurate measure: by doing so, they invite the accusation that they are distorting the figures. In the UK, for example, there were fifteen changes in the statistical conventions used in the period 1979–86 which some critics have claimed illegitimately reduced the numbers unemployed by 400,000.

unemployment trap (810, 910)

The barrier to employment caused by unemployment benefits. If these benefits are greater than the wages of low paid workers, job search and accepting jobs are often discouraged. The extent of this trap is measured by the ratio of benefits to income, the **replacement ratio**.

See also: **poverty trap**.

unequal exchange (430)

Trading which is systematically biased

against one party because of a movement in the **net barter terms of trade** or because of an unequal distribution of productive assets.

unfair labour practice (830)

Conduct of an employer or an employee which can attract penalties under labour relations legislation. It was possible for employers to commit such practices under the National Labor Relations Act (**Wagner Act**) of 1935 in the USA; in 1947, the **Taft–Hartley Act** extended this to labor unions also. The short-lived Industrial Relations Act of 1971 in the UK made use of this concept.

UNIDO (130, 610)

See: **United Nations Industrial Development Organization**.

uniform business rate (320)

British property tax on businesses levied at the same rate throughout England from April 1990 with separate Scottish and Welsh business rates to replace business **rates** previously fixed by local authorities. By making this form of local taxation uniform, rates rose in the more prosperous south of England and fell in the less prosperous north. Transitional arrangements over a five-year period cushioned the effects of the change.

See also: **community charge; rates**.

Uniform Commercial Code (310, 510)

A legal code enacted in 1952 in Pennsylvania and then copied, with some variations, by all other US states and territories except Louisiana and Puerto Rico. It provides a flexible approach to the formation and performance of contracts.

uniformity assumption (020)

Chamberlin's assumption that under **monopolistic competition** each firm of an industry has identical cost and demand curves.

uniform price (010)

A price which is the same for all groups of consumers because no **price discrimination** is being practised.

unimodal distribution (210)

A distribution of numbers with only one **mode**.

unintended investment (010)

Investment which occurs despite not having been planned. It chiefly takes the form of an accumulation of stocks (inventories) because sales are less than predicted.

union (830)

See: **international union; local union; trade union; US labor union**.

union density (830)

See: **unionization**.

Union Douaniére et Economique de l'Afrique Centrale (420)

A **customs union** with a common central bank set up in 1966 between Cameroon, the Central African Republic, the Congo and Gabon.

unionization (830)

The proportion of a **labour force** in membership of **trade (labor) unions**. Unionization varies greatly from country to country, being very high in Scandinavia, Israel and Eastern Europe but low in the USA. Between regions of a country it varies because of differences in the industrial structure and in state laws if the country has a federal constitution (e.g. in the USA, southern states with '**right-to-work**' legislation have lower levels of unionization). Unionization is higher in most large and **oligopolistic** firms as the **marginal cost** of recruiting an extra member is lower in those firms than in scattered small firms. Before the growth of **white-collar** trade unions it was thought that technical change would reduce unionization and also that increases in female labour force participation would reduce overall participation. These fears have not been entirely fulfilled. However, the pattern of increasing unemployment, particularly the decline of heavy industries with many manual jobs, has reduced overall unionization. Unionization is also known as union density.

Union of National Economic Associations in Japan (830)

Founded in 1950 as the only nationwide

Japanese federation of associations of scholarly economics, commerce and business adminstration organizations. Its thirty-five groups include societies for accounting, agricultural economics, economic sociology, economic geography, the history of economic thought, planning, public utility economics and socialist economies. It is based at Waseda University, Tokyo.

union shop (830)

A firm which requires all employees to be members of a **labor union**, which has been recognized to have **collective bargaining** rights in that firm, within a short specified time of taking up employment. The US equivalent of the British post-entry **closed shop**. The looser meaning of a union shop is a workplace with unionized workers.

See also: **agency shop**; **right-to-work state**.

union wage effect (820, 830)

The difference between the wages of unionized and non-unionized workers. In the figure, the union raises wages from W_0 to W_1 by restricting employment to N_1. As the principal concern of unions is wage negotiations, this effect is an indicator of their success. US studies suggest that the effect is about 30–40 per cent when union and non-union wages are compared. The effect is larger for young than for older workers, for non-whites than for whites. It is greater in industries with monopoly power and in sector-wide bargaining. It was greater in the interwar depression, and in the late 1970s, because the unionized sector could fight wage cuts. In the UK, the effect is measured by comparing wages under **collective bargaining** agreements with those elsewhere in the economy, for the most part with their minimum pay determined by **wages councils** orders; the effect can vary from 10 to 25 per cent. Pure union wage effects are difficult to measure as there may be a difference in the quality of unionized and non-unionized workers.

Lewis, H.G. (1963) *Unionism and Relative Wages in the United States*, Chicago, IL: University of Chicago Press.
—— (1983) 'Union relative wage effects: a survey of macro estimates', *Journal of Labor Economics* 1: 1–27.

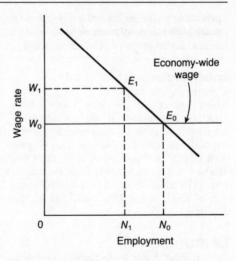

Mulvey, C. (1978) *The Economic Analysis of Trade Unions*, Oxford: Martin Robertson.

union wage policy (820, 830)

The course of action of **labor** or **trade unions** in wage negotiations, usually with the aims of obtaining the same pay for the same job within an establishment and the equalization of pay for similar workers across establishments. **Dunlop** treated the union as a firm with the overall aim of maximizing the total wage bill of its members – a view regarded as too simplistic by Ross who encouraged labour economists to examine more facets of union behaviour in **collective bargaining**. The greatest achievement of union wage policy is the standardization of wage rates for workers in the same occupational group, thus preventing labour from competing against itself.

Dunlop, J.T. (1950) *Wage Determination under Trade Unions*, 2nd edn, New York: Augustus M. Kelly; Oxford: Basil Blackwell.
Ross, A.M. (1948) *Trade Union Wage Policy*, Berkeley, CA: University of California Press.

unitary elastic (210)

Elasticity equal to +1. If a demand curve is of this elasticity throughout, then it will take the shape of a rectangular hyperbola. Over the part, or whole, of a demand curve which is of unitary elasticity, there will be constant **total revenue** associated with each point on the curve because the percentage change in quantity demanded will be matched by a percentage change in price of the same magnitude in the opposite direction.

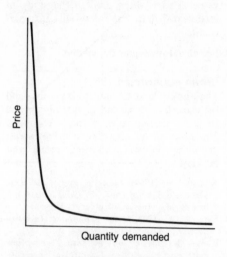

Quantity demanded

Unitas all share index (310)
The stock market index of Helsinki, Finland.

unit banking (310)
A domestic banking system with single banks each operating from only one location. US retail banking was originally of this form but gradually in the twentieth century **branch banking** throughout a county or a state was permitted and **bank holding** companies were permitted.

See also: **correspondent bank**; **McFadden Branch Banking Act 1927**.

unit cost (010)
The cost of producing one unit of a product. This is calculated as the **average cost** of producing a batch or a standard unit for that type of production, e.g. a book or a barrel of beer, or the **marginal cost** of producing the last unit.

United Nations Conference on Trade and Development (420)
An organ of the General Assembly of the United Nations which has the aim of improving the trade of less developed countries, particularly through international commodity agreements. After its first meeting in 1964, it has met subsequently in 1968, 1972, 1976, 1979, 1983 and 1987; all members of the United Nations and its specialized agencies belong to it.

Its efforts have been less than successful: in the 1980s, international agreements on rubber, coffee, cocoa and tin were incapable of protecting Third World countries from falls in prices and the great increase in their foreign debts; the tin agreement failed in 1985 with the bankruptcy of the buffer stock; coffee producers found it increasingly difficult to come to an agreement. Success is unlikely until developed countries reflate their economies to provide bigger markets for primary products and less developed countries diversify their economies.

United Nations Development Programme (130)
A United Nations organization formed in 1965 to render technical assistance to developing countries. It undertakes the work previously done by the UN Expanded Programme of Technical Assistance and the UN Special Fund. It offers **soft loans** for development.

United Nations Industrial Development Organization (130, 610)
A Vienna-based organization created in 1967 to promote Third World industrialization by advising on industrial strategy and evaluating projects.

unitization (310)
The division of real property into tradable portions, providing a new form of investment. Thus a large building can be sold in portions which are regularly traded like shares in companies.

See also: **timeshare**.

unit of account (310)
A **medium of account** which is used as a measure or standard of value because of the stability of its value. **Hard currencies** are particularly used for this purpose.

See also: **medium of account**; **numeraire**.

unit pricing (520)
Quoting prices per unit of weight, e.g. X cents per ounce, so that goods produced in different standard sizes can be compared.

unit tax (320)

A tax per unit sold which usually takes the form of a **sales** or **purchase tax**.

unit trust (310)

A trust which purchases stock exchange securities and sells unit portions of the portfolio acquired to the general public. Many unit trusts have specialized portfolios, e.g. concentrating on property shares or Japanese securities, on the yield of a portfolio or the rate of growth of its capital value. The trust managers charge the unit-holders for their investment management. This investment device, introduced in the UK from the USA in 1931, is attractive to the small investor as a means of diversifying risk.

See also: **investment trust; mutual fund**.

unit value index (150, 220)

A price index which is calculated by dividing the total value of a good by the total quantity of it. Since technical progress involves the substitution of light goods for heavy goods, unit value indices underestimate the magnitude of price changes.

Unlisted Securities Market (310)

The second tier of the **International Stock Exchange**, created in November 1980, to enable a director unwilling to apply for a full listing on the Exchange to deal in his company's shares. For a listing on the USM a company needs a three-year record of successful business and the directors must sell at least 10 per cent of the company, whereas for a full listing the company needs a five-year record and a minimum sale of 25 per cent. In 1980 thirty-five companies were given a listing on the USM; in 1985 ninety-eight companies joined, and so about 350 companies were listed by 1987. The attraction of a listing on this market is the lower cost compared with being listed on the Stock Exchange. In the first five years of its existence, the USM raised £882.6 million.

Bannock, G. and Doran, A. (1987) *Going Public: A Report on Unlisted Securities*, London: Economist Intelligence Unit.

unproductive labour (010, 810)

See: **productive labour**.

upper quartile (210)

The value of a set of numbers such that three-quarters of the numbers are lower in value. This is often used in the study of income distributions. The seventy-fifth **percentile**.

See also: **lower quartile; median**.

urban economics (930)

The study of land use, location decisions and the growth of cities and towns. This broad subject encompasses the economic dimension of all activities in urban areas, including industry, housing, crime and **poverty**.

Alonso, W. (1964) *Location and Land Use: Toward a General Theory of Land Rent*, Cambridge, MA: Harvard University Press.
Evans, A.W. (1985) *Urban Economics: An Introduction*, Oxford: Basil Blackwell.
Fujita, M. (1989) *Urban Economic Theory*, New York and Cambridge: Cambridge University Press.
Mieszkowski, P. and Straszheim, M. (eds) (1979) *Current Issues in Urban Economics*, Baltimore, MD, and London: Johns Hopkins University Press.

See also: **land economy**.

Uruguay Round (420)

The **General Agreement on Tariffs and Trade** (GATT) negotiations of 1986–91 in which ninety-two countries participated. The principal features of the Round were an attempt to reduce the protectionism of developed countries, without full reciprocity from less developed countries, and to reduce US and **European Community** subsidies to agriculture to cut surpluses and make world agricultural markets work more smoothly. This is the first time a policy to deal with agricultural products has been the subject of GATT negotiations – even reductions in agricultural sanitary regulations have been proposed as they can act as a barrier to trade. Trade-related investment, **intellectual property** rights and trade services were also covered.

See also: **Dillon Round; Kennedy Round; Tokyo Round**.

user charge (320, 720)

1 A charge per quantity of an emission discharged into a sewerage system,

2 A charge for a service provided by a central or local government or by a public enterprise, e.g. a ticket for admission to a swimming pool. These charges are based on the **average cost** or **marginal cost** of providing the service.

user cost (520)
The cost of capital depreciation attributable to one unit of output; the price a firm should pay for using its own capital stock.

use value (010)
See: **value in use**.

US federal finance (320)
Finance raised by taxes and borrowing to finance the activities of the federal government of the United States. The power to tax is derived from Article 1, section 8, of the US Constitution which gives the Congress power to levy and collect taxes and duties in order to pay debts and provide for common defence and the general welfare of the USA. This Article also requires that the rates of taxation should be uniform throughout the states of the union. Most of tax revenue at the federal level comes from the individual income tax and is used both to finance federal expenditures and to give grants to state governments.

See also: **federal finance**.

U-shaped frequency curve (210)
A **frequency curve** which is the shape of the letter 'U' with maxima at both ends of it.

US labor union (830)
A voluntary association of employees with the major aim of **collective bargaining** for improvements in wages and other conditions. These are either **locals** (restricting membership to a local area) or **internationals** (covering the whole of the USA). Although unions have existed in the USA for two hundred years, they have not achieved the same levels of **unionization** as in many other countries, including the UK; this can be explained partly by anti-union legislation in some of the southern states.

Freeman, R.B. and Medoff, J.L. (1984) *What Do Unions Do?*, New York: Basic Books.

See also: **right-to-work state**.

USM (310)
See: **Unlisted Securities Market**.

US tax reform (320)
See: **Tax Reform Act 1986**.

US Trade Representative (420)
An office set up in 1963 as part of the Executive Office of the US President to direct trade negotiations and formulate trade policy. It now operates under the authority of the Omnibus Trade and Competitiveness Act 1988.

US treasury bond market (310)
US bond market which, until 1986, had only thirty-five **primary dealers**. Its daily dealings of $100 billion or more make it one of the most influential financial markets in the world, as does the prices it sets of US Treasury bonds which influence the cost of capital throughout the world because of the importance of the dollar. Entry to the market is difficult. As a dealer must have 0.75 per cent of daily turnover, excluding trades among dealers, to qualify, entry means either attracting business away from existing dealers or purchasing an existing dealer, as some British and other banks are now attempting. The margins have to be very small, sometimes as low as 1/64 of a point, to be competitive.

US Treasury market (310)
US securities market in which 35,000 different bonds, bills and notes issued by governmental agencies are traded. Dominant in the market is the Federal Reserve Bank of New York which does 25 per cent of the clearing.

usury (310)
An exploitative **rate of interest**; formerly the term for 'the rate of interest' as the Judaic, Islamic and Christian religions condemned any rate of interest as wrong. Usury laws were common either to outlaw the charging of interest or to impose a ceiling rate. Economists as far back as the **mercantilists** realized that a maximum rate of interest is often unenforceable. There are still laws in the UK and USA governing the maximum rate of interest that moneylenders can

charge. Usury is a major issue in **Islamic banking** today.

util (010)

One unit of satisfaction. If it were possible to measure **cardinal utility** then the amount of satisfaction would be expressed in utils. Most economists have regarded it as impossible to count utils as **utility** is a subjective valuation.

See also: **ordinal utility**; **revealed preference**.

utilitarianism (020, 030)

An approach to moral philosophy popularized by **Bentham** and originally devised by Beccaria and Helvetius and later used by Godwin and **John Stuart Mill**. It is concerned to show that the rightness of an action is to be judged by its consequences in terms of pain and pleasure, using a 'balance sheet' approach to see whether there is a net advantage. The goal of utilitarians is to achieve 'the greatest happiness for the greatest number'. Critics of utilitarianism have pointed out the difficulties of reducing values to utilities and of aggregating the happiness of individual persons.

Halevy, E. (1934) *The Growth of Philosophic Radicalism*, trans. by M. Morris, London: Faber & Faber.
Lyons, D. (1965) *Forms and Limits of Utilitarianism*, Oxford: Oxford University Press.
Smart, J.J.C. and Williams, B. (1974) *Utilitarianism: Pro and Con*, Cambridge: Cambridge University Press.

See also: **cardinal utility**; **felicific calculus**.

utility (010)

The satisfaction derived from an activity, particularly consumption. The total amount of such satisfaction is total utility; the satisfaction from the last unit is **marginal utility**. **Bentham** in his suggested calculus of pleasure and pain was influential in introducing this notion into **economics** but the **marginalists** were the first economists to make it the central concept of economic theory. The measurement of utility has provoked long debates between cardinal utility (utility measured in units) and ordinal utility (utility revealed through preferences). Without this concept, much of **neoclassical** economic theory would not be possible. Earlier economic writers, especially those of the **classical school**, used 'utility' in the objective sense of the inherent worth of something.

Majumdar, T. (1961) *The Measurement of Utility*, London: Macmillan.
Page, A.N. (ed.) (1968) *Utility Theory: A Book of Readings*, New York: Wiley.
Robertson, D., Sir (1956) *Economic Commentaries*, ch. II, London: Staples Press.

utility function (020, 210)

This is generally expressed in the form $U = f(x_1, x_2, x_3, x_4, x_5, \ldots)$. It shows a consumer's **utility** as a function of the quantities of goods and services 1, 2, 3, 4, 5, . . . that he/she consumes.

Green, H.A.J. (1972) *Consumer Theory*, Harmondsworth: Penguin.

utility possibility frontier (010)

This connects the **Pareto-efficient** combinations of the **utilities** of two individuals. A movement from B to A is Pareto efficient as both Adam and Eve are better off; a movement from A to C increases Eve's utility but reduces Adam's.

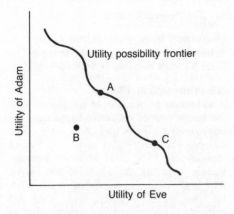

Utility possibility frontier

UVI (150, 220)

See: **unit value index**.

V

valorization (010)
The process by which **capital** increases its own value. In **Marxian** economics, it is asserted that this occurs because capital increases its own value by the production of **surplus value**.

value (010)
Intrinsic worth or **price** of a good or service. Earlier economic writers from **Aristotle** made the distinction between **value in use** and **value in exchange** (prices) with, in many cases, the objective use value being measured by the cost of production of that article. **Cantillon**, **Smith**, **Ricardo** and John Stuart **Mill** agonized over the determinants and measure of different types of value, often using the so-called 'water and diamonds paradox': the **paradox of value**. Apart from **Marx** and his disciples, interest in the concept of **intrinsic value** waned and attention was concentrated on prices, except inasmuch as intrinsic value can be equated with long-term equilibrium prices.

value added (010)
1 The contribution to total production made by an industry, a firm or a worker. In the case of a firm, it is calculated by subtracting from its sales its purchases from other firms. It is used to measure the **national income** by the output method and is a frequently used base for indirect taxation.

2 An amount equal to the sum of factor incomes at one stage of production.

value-added network service (630)
A service electronically produced, e.g. electronic mail and computerized information. The provider of the service adds value to the transmission and switching provided by the telephone company.

See also: **networker**.

value-added tax (320)
A tax levied on the **value added** by a firm. As 'value added' can be variously measured, different tax bases are possible. The tax can be a percentage of the income of a firm (its wage payments and return to capital net of depreciation), or the value of what it produces (its income not allowing depreciation) or the value of what is consumed by its customers minus the firm's purchases of inputs and expenditure on capital goods.

The sales of small firms and the sale of basic goods, e.g. food and children's clothing, are often excluded from the tax – as are export sales (unlike import purchases). The principal method of tax collection is the invoice method of examining the sales invoices of all taxable traders, which checks the accuracy of both intermediate and final sales simultaneously. It is argued that taxing most goods is more equitable than a more selective tax but the regressive effects of value-added tax on all goods and services at a single rate have long been debated. As a proportion of the revenue from value-added taxes in member countries of the **European Community** constitutes the major source of European Community revenue, there are pressures for higher and standard rates through the European Community.

Aaron, H.J. (ed.) (1981) *The Value-Added Tax: Lessons from Europe*, Washington, DC: Brookings Institution.

value discrepancy hypothesis (610)
The theory that a firm will only bid for another if it values it higher than its present owners do. This attempt to explain **mergers** is based on there being imperfect information and **uncertainty** in the private industrial sector.

Gort, M. (1969) 'An economic disturbance theory of mergers', *Quarterly Journal of Economics* 82: 624–42.

value in exchange (010)
The price of a good or service. **Classical economists** contrasted this with **value in use**.

value in use (010)

The intrinsic value, or usefulness, of a good. **Classical economists** contrasted this value with **value in exchange**.

value share (220)

The expenditure on a particular commodity or factor of production divided by total expenditure.

value subtractor (610)

An enterprise with negative **value added** as a result of its activities. Such a firm has such high labour and capital costs that it cannot even cover the cost of the raw materials it uses: thus the value of the inputs it uses is greater than the revenue it obtains from its sales. Many **Soviet-type economies** were discovered to have a substantial number of value subtractors at the end of the 1980s.

VAN (630)

See: **value-added network service**.

Vanek, Jaroslav, 1930– (030)

A Czech who obtained degrees in statistics, mathematics and economics at Sorbonne (1952) and at Geneva (1954). He emigrated to the USA in 1955, gaining a PhD at the Massachusetts Institute of Technology in 1957 and spending most of his academic career as a professor at Cornell University. He is a leading theorist of labour-managed enterprises. His major work, *The General Theory of Labour-Managed Market Economies* (1970), was modified by the concessions to consumers in his *The Participatory Economy: An Evolutionary Hypothesis and a Development Strategy* (1971). The development of his ideas is apparent in his *The Labor-Managed Economy: Essays by Jaroslav Vanek* (1977).

VAR (210)

See: **vector autoregression**.

variable capital (010, 820)

The **Marxian** term for the **wages fund**.

See also: **organic composition of capital**.

variable cost (010)

A cost which varies with the level of output. In the short run, it is distinct from a **fixed cost** which is the same at all levels of output;

in the long run all costs are variable. Labour, the favourite example of such a cost, has become more fixed in nature in recent years as a result of employment legislation and a change in labour contracts.

See also: **quasi-factor fixed cost**.

variance (210)

The average of the sum of the squares of deviations of data from their **mean**, calculated for a **statistical population** or a sample taken from it; the square of a **standard deviation**.

VAT (320)

See: **value-added tax**.

vault cash (310)

Money kept by US commercial banks on their premises which is included in the banks' reserves.

Veblen, Thorstein Bunde, 1857–1929 (030)

A leading US **institutionalist economist**, famous for his analysis of **conspicuous consumption**. He was educated at Carleton College and Yale University, subsequently teaching economics at Chicago, Stanford, Missouri and New York. Inspired by a Darwinian evolutionary approach to the social sciences, he took a multidisciplinary view of economics, linking it to anthropology and sociology. His biting analysis of modern industrialism in *The Theory of the Leisure Class* (1899), *The Theory of Business Enterprise* (1904), *The Higher Learning in America* (1918) and *Absentee Ownership* (1923) provided a non-Marxist critique of contemporary **capitalism**. In some senses he was an inspiration for **Galbraith**.

Diggins, J.P. (1978) *The Bard of Savagery: Thorstein Veblen and Modern Social Theory*, Brighton: Harvester Press.

Veblen good (010)

A good for which there will be a fall in demand if the price falls because of the belief that the quality has fallen.

See also: **conspicuous consumption**; **Giffen good**.

vector autoregression (210)

An econometric methodology used as the

alternative to large structural models of national economies which forecasts the joint movements of principal macroeconomic variables, ignoring their microeconomic determinants. An application of vector autoregression has been the study of the independence of real macroeconomic variables from nominal variables. Critics have noted that the economic hypotheses used are very broad.

Sims, C.A. (1980) 'Macroeconomics and reality', *Econometrica* 48: 1–45.

vegetative control (010)
A mechanism for organizing economic activity in a modern **economy** with much **division of labour** which uses quantity adjustments rather than price **signals**. It is characterized by simple behavioural rules, e.g. the rule that production is increased if output stocks fall or the sales of other firms increase and the rule that more inputs are purchased if production increases. This control is exercised bilaterally between single pairs of buyers and sellers; price signals have no influence on the level of production. A major example of this mechanism was the West German economy from 1946 to 1948.

Kornai, J. (1980) *The Economics of Shortage*, vols A and B, Amsterdam: North-Holland.

velocity of circulation (310)
The number of times a stock of money circulates to finance a level of expenditure/income/output. Thus if the money supply is £100 million and national expenditure/income is £500 million, the velocity of circulation will be 5. Erratic changes in the money supply since 1970 have made velocities unstable and the relationship between changes in the money supply and changes in output more difficult to predict.

See also: **monetarism**.

velocity of money (310)
See: **velocity of circulation**.

vendor finance (310)
Finance provided by the seller of a company in the form of deferred payment for it or retained equity in the company.

See also: **stub equity**.

vent for surplus (410)
An explanation for international trade. Adam **Smith** asserted that trade arises because the domestic market is too small to purchase all of an economy's output and so trade is necessary. This reflected his view that the **division of labour** is limited by the extent of the market. The view was challenged by John Stuart **Mill** who wondered why a surplus was initially created. But more recently it has been applied to the study of economic development, e.g. by Myint in the 1950s.

Myint, H. (1958) 'The "Classical theory" of international trade and the underdeveloped countries', *Economic Journal* 68: 317–37.

venture capital (310, 520)
Finance for new high risk companies. There are large venture capital industries in the USA, the UK and Canada. **Investment banks**, **merchant banks** and governmental agencies all supply this capital in the hope that new businesses have a potential for long-term growth.

See also: **seed capital**.

VER (420)
See: **voluntary export restraint**.

Verdoorn's law (110)
The dynamic relationship between the rate of growth of output and the growth of **productivity** because of increasing returns. This is named after the Dutch economist who first noted the relationship in 1948. It was applied to the UK economy by **Kaldor** in the 1960s and 1970s and was the theoretical justification for his recommendation of the **Selective Employment Tax** in 1966 which was designed to shift the labour force increasingly into manufacturing (which was alleged to have labour shortages); a higher rate of growth of employment was expected to stimulate manufacturing productivity.

vertical discrimination (820)
The different treatment of persons at different levels of an employing organization, e.g. new entrants and persons holding the top jobs. A much quoted example is the easy entry of women and minority races to less skilled and lower paid jobs and the difficulties they experience in gaining promotion. Vertical discrimination is less

susceptible to legislative treatment than **horizontal discrimination** as there are fewer records of promotion processes than there are of earnings.

See also: **discrimination; horizontal discrimination**.

vertical equity (160, 320)
The treatment of persons in different income groups according to the **ability to pay** principle. This principle is used to justify a progressive tax system.

See also: **horizontal equity; progressive tax**.

vertical expansion (510)
The expansion of a firm's activities into another or other stages of production, e.g. the setting up of a firm which is both a manufacturer and a retailer. This form of internal expansion usually takes the form of the creation of new subsidiaries; not a **vertical merger**.

vertical formation (510)
The creation of a firm with several stages of production.

vertical integration (610)
The joining together of two or more stages of production either through a **vertical merger** or **vertical expansion**.

vertical merger (610)
A **merger** of firms at different stages of production, e.g. a merger between a manufacturer and a retailer. The search for economies in marketing, production and finance motivates such integration.

villa economy (010, 040)
An **economy** consisting of an extended household, as in Ancient Rome and Ancient Greece. The villa was the centre of the economic activities of a rural area, receiving and processing raw produce, including the milling of corn and the pressing of grapes.

See also: **agricultural household; Ancient Greeks; economics**.

Viner, Jacob, 1892–1970 (030)
Canadian economist, born in Montreal and educated at McGill and Harvard universities. He was a professor at Chicago University from 1925 to 1946 (also editor of the *Journal of Political Economy*, 1928–46) and at Princeton from 1946 to 1960. His career began in international economics as a postgraduate student of Frank W. Taussig: he published his doctoral thesis *Dumping: A Problem in International Trade* in 1923. Then he tested the classical theory of balance of payments adjustments in *Canada's Balance of International Indebtedness, 1900–13* (1924). Before **Keynes** published his *General Theory*, he was an advocate of budget deficits and increased public spending to stimulate the economy. Also, he anticipated many of the ideas of **monopolistic competition**. He made many outstanding contributions to the history of economic thought, e.g. his critique of **mercantilism** in *Studies in the Theory of International Trade* (1937) and his detailed biographical essay on Adam **Smith** which formed the introduction to the reprint of John Rae's *Life of Adam Smith* (1965).

vintage effect (110)
The effect on **productivity** of a capital stock being old.

visible hand (010)
A non-market method of allocation, e.g. as happens in the US economy through the activities of dominant large corporations.

Chandler, A.D., Jr (1977) *The Visible Hand: The Managerial Revolution in American Business*, Cambridge, MA: Belknap Press.

Vision (610)
A long-term plan of **MITI** (Japan).

vital revolution (840)
See: **demographic transition**.

voice (010, 830)
See: **exit voice**.

volume ratio (540)
Actual hours worked divided by budgeted hours for that productive activity all multiplied by 100.

voluntary export restraint (420)
A non-tariff form of **protectionism**. A country whose domestic industry is suffering from high levels of imports negotiates with

the principal supplying country/countries the maximum amount traded. Western countries have entered into such agreements with Japan, particularly to limit car imports.

See also: **Multi-Fibre Arrangement**.

voluntary unemployment (810)

Unemployment, at a given wage rate, caused by members of the labour force refusing to take jobs offered.

See also: **involuntary unemployment**.

von Neumann, John, 1903–57 (030)

A leading mathematical economist who pioneered games theory and made major contributions to cybernetics. After an education at Budapest, Zurich and Berlin universities, he emigrated to the USA and became a professor at Princeton University in 1933. His famous collaboration with the economist Oskar Morgenstern resulted in *Theory of Games and Economic Behavior* (1944).

Morgenstern, O. (1958) 'Obituary. John von Neumann, 1903–57', *Economic Journal* 68: 170–4.
Taub, A.H. (1961) *Collected Works of John von Neumann*, New York and Oxford: Pergamon.

von Neumann–Morgenstern stable set (210)

A set of outcomes of a game which is not dominated by one of its outcomes. This concept has been applied to the analysis of parliaments and **cartels**.

von Neumann, J. and Morgenstern, O. (1944) *Theory of Games and Economic Behavior*, Princeton, NJ: Princeton University Press.

voodoo economics (320)

President Bush's view of the claim of **Reaganomics** that cutting taxes would improve the fiscal position of the US federal government.

voting procedures (010)

A democratic method of choosing between different persons or policies in an election. The simplest method is the majority principle of choosing whoever or whatever gains 50 per cent of the votes plus one. Other systems include the plurality rule in which a candidate is chosen for receiving the largest number of votes of all the other candidates.

More complicated systems include using the **Condorcet criterion**.

Mueller, D.C. (1989) *Public Choice II*, chs 4–11, Cambridge and New York: Cambridge University Press.

voucher system (010, 910)

A method for consumers of government-provided goods and services to choose between alternatives. Instead of a government agency deciding who gets what, individuals are given vouchers which entitle them to purchase up to a particular cash amount. This has been used in the USA under the food stamp scheme; in both the USA and the UK it has been suggested as a means of parental choice between schools, tenants' choice between various forms of rented accommodation and adults' choice in health care. As these schemes can be expensive to administer, they have not flourished as much as expected.

See also: **Lindahl price**.

Vredeling directive (830)

The 'Draft Directive on Procedures for Informing and Consulting Employees' proposed by the Dutch Commissioner Vredeling of the **European Community** in 1980. It proposed that companies with more than 1,000 employees should keep their workers fully informed about all the activities of the company concerned, except for secret and confidential matters. At least annually a report would be given to workers' representatives about the structure of the company and plans for employment and investment. Workers in subsidiary companies would be informed about changes in activities, output and working methods with thirty days to express an opinion before a change was made. Trade unions welcomed the directive but there was much opposition from employers' organizations, including the **Confederation of British Industry**.

See also: **industrial democracy; workers' participation**.

vulgar economists (030)

Marxian term for economists who are very specialized in only one part of the discipline.

W

wage (820)
See: **wages**.

wage contour (820)
The connected wage rates offered by firms with **internal labour markets** to persons in the **external labour market**. These are the '**key rates**' for the few jobs at which a person can enter a firm; they are connected into a contour because competing firms in the external labour market cannot get out of line with other employers' wage offers.

Dunlop, J.T. (1957) 'The task of contemporary wage theory', in G.W. Taylor and F.C. Pierson (eds) *New Concepts in Wage Determination*, pp. 117–39, New York: McGraw-Hill.

wage differentials (820)
Differences in employment income which reflect the segmented nature of the labour market. The labour force has several structures – geographical, industrial, occupational, sexual and racial – which create corresponding wage differentials. Regional wage differentials exist because of the relative prosperity of capital regions and peripheral areas as well as a traditional ranking of regions in terms of pay. In the USA, the most famous regional difference is between northern and southern states. Industrial differentials reflect the degree of concentration and productivity of particular industries. Occupational differentials arise from differences in bargaining ability and the amounts of education necessary to enter each occupation. Many differentials have been stable for long periods of time because of the forces of custom but the skill differential (the ratio of the pay of skilled to unskilled workers in the same trade), which was constant for many centuries prior to 1914 in many capitalist countries, has subsequently shrunk because of an increasing amount of publicly financed education and a declining supply of unskilled labour.

Sexual and racial differentials reflect different levels of investment in **human capital** and **discrimination**.

Phelps Brown, E.H. (1977) *The Inequality of Pay*, Oxford and New York: Oxford University Press.

wage diffusion (150, 820)
The transmission of wage increases in the leading sector of a national labour market, or major bargaining group, to other workers in a national economy. This can occur because of the established wage leadership of an industrial or occupational group, or because of traditional **wage differentials** in a national wage structure.

See also: **pattern settlement**; **shunto**; **wage round**.

wage drift (820)
The difference between the percentage increase in earnings and the percentage increase in basic wage rates agreed under a **collective bargaining** procedure. An example would be if earnings grow in a year by 10 per cent and basic wage rates by 6 per cent, then wage drift is 4 per cent. This major labour market phenomenon of the UK in the 1950s and 1960s was largely attributed to a two-tier **collective bargaining** system with the national level determining basic wages and the local level responsible for supplements to basic pay. Wage drift often occurs under **piecework systems**.

See also: **Donovan Commission**.

wage flexibility (820)
A policy advocated by **classical** and **new classical** economists to restore an economy to **full employment**. **Keynes** challenged wage flexibility as a feasible policy as he believed that money wages are inflexible downwards. Later economists argue in favour of flexibility because workers have 'priced themselves out of a job'; opponents of

flexibility assert that the free movement of wages contributes to the problem of **low pay**.

wage gap (830)

The relative wage differential between **unionized** and non-unionized labour brought about by a trade union exercising its bargaining rights.

Mincer, J. (1983) 'Union effects: wages, turnover, and job training', in J.D. Reid, Jr (ed.) *New Approaches to Labor Economics: A Research*, Annual Supplement 2, Greenwich, CT: JAI Press.

wage–price spiral (150)

A self-sustaining inflationary process: higher wages lead to increased product prices which lead to more wage claims and higher wages. Wage **indexation** is a major cause of such spirals.

wage-push inflation (150)

Price inflation initiated by increases in wages brought about by powerful trade unions and not by an excess demand for labour. This is a type of **cost-push inflation**.

wage–rental ratio (620)

The ratio of the wage cost to the rental cost of using a particular technique of production, which is dependent on the capital-labour ratio chosen, which is in turn dependent on the relationship between wages and rental costs.

wage rigidity (010, 820)

The phenomenon of wages remaining at the same level absolutely or relative to other rates of pay in the same wage structure. At the national level wage rigidity occurs if **labour's share of the national income** is constant, as it has been in some countries for long periods of time.

See also: **labour market rigidities**.

wage round (820)

An annual set of pay negotiations by the major bargaining groups, usually with one industry (often engineering) making a settlement which becomes a pace-setter for other groups. Particularly true of Britain in the 1950s and 1960s and, even more so, in Japan under **shunto**.

See also: **pattern settlement**; **wage diffusion**.

wages (820)

Payment to workers for supplying their services for a particular amount of time, or for producing a defined amount of output. To avoid the abuse known as the **truck** system, wages have had to be paid in the UK in cash unless workers consent to direct payment into a banking account. The Wages Act 1986 has removed the right to payment in cash unless that is already the method of payment.

See also: **wage differentials**; **wage theory**.

Wages Act 1986 (820)

UK statute which repealed the **Truck** Acts of 1831–1940, abolishing the requirement for wages to be paid in the **coin** of the realm. The Act also limited the powers of remaining **wages councils**.

wages council (820)

A tripartite council with union, employer and independent representatives (appointed by government) given the task of recommending (in the case of the UK, to the British Employment Secretary) minimum wage rates and hours for the low paid workers covered by a particular council. This innovation of the state of Victoria, Australia, was introduced into the UK in 1909; wages councils still deal with about a tenth of the UK labour force, particularly in agriculture and catering. Their popularity with **trade unions** arises from the difficulty unions experience in organizing workers in sectors with many small firms and from their approval of the inspectorate set up to monitor the wages actually paid by employers. In the 1980s, the UK government wanted to abolish all these councils as it was believed that the minimum wage rates set were too high, especially for young workers, thus contributing to unemployment.

wages fund theory (820)

The classical theory of the demand for labour. Each employer needs a fund of **circulating capital** to finance the period until products are sold; an economy will have a wages fund which is the aggregate of each firm's fund and will be the maximum amount which can be paid out nationally in wages. The average wage rate of the economy is simply the wages fund divided by the employed labour force. The rigid adherents of this theory used it as a justification for resisting union demands for higher remuneration, pointing out that a higher average wage rate would cause unemployment. The idea of the wage fund ignores other methods of financing production, exaggerates the degree to which the total fund is fixed and does not consider how a capitalist will allocate his income between different types of investment and consumption.

Taussig, F.W. (1896) *Wages and Capital: An Examination of Wages Fund Doctrine*, London: Macmillan.

wage subsidy (320)

A payment to a firm of a grant equal to a proportion of its wage bill or of its wage rates to encourage higher levels of employment in a particular sector, e.g. manufacturing, or throughout the economy. In the 1960s in the UK, the labour cost of employing workers in manufacturing was subsidized and service sector employers more heavily taxed under the **Selective Employment Tax**. Wage subsidies are often paid only for employing additional staff as the aim of wage subsidization is usually to increase employment.

See also: **regional employment premium**.

wage–tax spiral (150, 320)

An explanation of **inflation** in terms of the effects of government taxation and social security charges on the labour market. It is argued that a widening gap between pre-tax and post-tax employment incomes (i.e. an increase in **average tax rates**) encourages **trade unions** to ask for higher money wages which in turn leads to general inflation. Also known as 'taxflation'.

Jackson, D., Turner, H.A. and Wilkinson, F. (1972) *Do Trade Unions Cause Inflation?*, Cambridge: Cambridge University Press.

wage theory (820, 830)

Explanations of the determination of wages at the macro and micro level. The earliest theories, of the **just wage**, were normative in character. In the eighteenth century, **Cantillon** and **Smith** discussed the determinants of **wage differentials** and the idea of a

wages fund was used to explain the average level of wages in an economy. In **neoclassical** economics, the concept of **marginal productivity** was used to explain wage rates. With the growth of **collective bargaining**, wage theory paid more attention to institutional influences on wages, especially **union wage effects**: **Hicks**, **Pigou** and **Dunlop** all made early contributions to bargaining theories. The exploration of the distinction between **internal** and **external labour markets** constituted a further attempt to make wage theory more realistic, as has the discussion of **insider** and **outside wage setting**.

wage unit (820)

The money-wage of a unit of labour, i.e. the wages and salaries bill divided by the quantity of employment. **Keynes** relied greatly on this method of measurement in his *General Theory*, by measuring **national income** in wage units.

Wagner Act 1935 (830)

US federal labor statute (also known as the Wagner–Connery Act) which sought to establish collective bargaining in interstate commerce through dealing with the problems of union recognition, of employers who refuse to bargain and **company unionism**. The **National Labor Relations Board** was established as an independent administrative agency to enforce the provisions of the Act. It succeeded the National Labor Board set up in 1933 to hear complaints against employers who refused to bargain.

Unfair labor practices which could be committed by management were listed in section 8 of the Wagner Act: (1) interfering with the rights of employees to organize themselves; (2) interfering in the affairs of a labor union; (3) discriminating in the hiring of workers to affect union membership; (4) discriminating against or discharging workers who had complained under the Act; and (5) refusing to bargain with chosen representatives of employees.

The Act was criticized for being too pro-union. It was a major cause of the great expansion in US labor union membership from 3.7 million members in 1935 to 14.8 million in 1945.

See also: **Taft–Hartley Act**.

Wagner's law (320)

Adolph Wagner's assertion in 1883 that public expenditures would expand as industrial society developed. He prophesied that pressures for social progress would entail a continuous growth of the public sector and an expanding share of public expenditure in the national income. The assertion of this law reflected the foundation of a **welfare state** in the Germany of his day.

Musgrave, R.A. and Peacock, A. (eds) (1958) *Classics in the Theory of Public Finance*, pp. 1–16, London and New York: Macmillan.

Walras, Marie Esprit Léon, 1834–1910 (030)

French-born economist who, with **Menger** and **Jevons**, was a founder of the **marginalist** school and the first to use **general equilibrium** analysis. His father, Auguste Walras, had already made use of the concept of marginal utility (or *rareté*, as he termed it) to explain the basis of value. His son, with the mathematical help of a professor of mechanics, was to extend its application powerfully. From 1870 to 1892, Léon Walras was professor of economics at the University of Lausanne, Switzerland (to be succeeded by **Pareto**). In an ambitious writing programme he sought to expound political economy in a threefold manner – as pure, applied and social. The first branch of his theory was published as *Eléments d'Economie Politique Pure* (1874–7; English translation, 1953): it is his chief claim to be regarded as one of the world's greatest economic theoreticians. In the *Eléments* he uses **general equilibrium** analysis to present an integrated theory of exchange, production, capital and money.

Hicks, J.R. (1934) 'Léon Walras', *Econometrica* 2: 338–48.
Morishima, M. (1977) *Walras' Economics. A Pure Theory of Capital and Money*, Cambridge: Cambridge University Press.
Walker, D.A. (ed.) (1983) *William Jaffe's Essays on Walras*, Cambridge: Cambridge University Press.
Walras, L. (1954) *Elements of Pure Economics or The Theory of Social Wealth*, trans. by W. Jaffe, London: Allen & Unwin.

Walrasian stability (010)

The dynamic stability of a market or the economy as a whole: this is possible because prices respond with infinite velocity to **disequilibrium** situations. Positive **excess demand** (demand greater than supply) causes price rises; negative excess demand (demand less than supply) causes price falls.

Walras's law (010)

A **general equilibrium** law that, if the first $n-1$ markets are in equilibrium, then the last market is also in equilibrium. This is so because the **aggregate demand** for goods, including money, must equal their **aggregate supply**.

Walsh–Healy Act 1936 (820)

US federal statute which provided that **minimum wage** standards be observed in all government contracts worth over $10,000.

See also: **Fair Wages Resolution**.

warehouse economy (420)

An **economy** which imports most of the manufactured goods it consumes, rather than making them itself. A description applied to the UK economy during the 1980s.

warehouse receipt (310)

The receipt issued to the depositor of inventories with a warehouse company. This receipt can be a negotiable security and act as collateral for a loan. This arrangement is a popular method of finance in the US agricultural sector.

warranted rate of growth (110)

The rate of growth of national income which maintains the equality of planned saving and planned investment. In the **Harrod–Domar** growth model it is measured as $G_w = s/v$ where G_w is the warranted rate of growth, s is the **marginal propensity to save** and v is the **incremental capital–output** ratio. It was described as a fruitful tautology by **Harrod**.

See also: **natural rate of growth**.

warranty (530)

The right of a buyer to get a seller to rectify or compensate for the failure of a product to meet its stated level of performance. The US Magnuson–Moss Warranty – Federal Trade Commission Improvement Act 1975 requires explicit warranties for all products selling for more than $15. A warranty is different from a service contract (which is not related to the product's performance). Products carrying warranties are more attractive to consumers as the risk to buyers of non-performance is eliminated.

Warsaw Convention (630)
The Air Warsaw Convention of 1929 which standardized passenger tickets, luggage tickets and carrier liability. All members of the **International Air Travel Association** are bound by it.

waste (010)
1 The undesired costs resulting from a particular economic activity; a major **externality**.

2 Transactions which do not create **wealth**, e.g. **rent-seeking** behaviour.

3 Waste can also occur because of the peculiar nature of certain types of economic organization, e.g. **barter** economies waste time through the need of buyers and sellers to search for each other; competitive economies are wasteful in needing advertising and other selling expenditures.

water and diamonds paradox (010)
See: **paradox of value**.

wealth (010)
The stock of assets held by a person, a firm or a country. Wealth is measured at a particular date, e.g. 31 December, and not over a period as is the case with **income**. Wealth statistics are subject to much error because of valuation problems and owners' concealment, especially if wealth and inheritance taxes are in force. Many forms of income, e.g. rent and profits, are a return to the wealth a person holds.

See also: **human capital; national wealth**.

wealth distribution (160, 220)
The interpersonal distribution of **asset** holdings, often quoted in the form of what proportion of national wealth is held by the top 5 per cent, or some other portion of the population.

Atkinson, A.B. and Harrison, A.J. (1978) *The Distribution of Personal Wealth in Britain*, Cambridge: Cambridge University Press.
Wolff, E.N. (ed.) (1987) *International Compari-*

sons of the Distribution of Household Wealth, Oxford: Clarendon Press.

wealth effect (010)
The effect of a change in interest rates and the price level on aggregate demand, particularly consumption.

See also: **Pigou effect**.

Wealth of Nations (030)
Adam **Smith's** masterly treatise on economics first published in 1776. Although **Cantillon** had previously produced a general work on economics as a whole, it was Smith's which was to provide a comprehensive statement of the subject and to found the school of **classical economics**. The unity of this work, divided into five parts, is provided by his central concern – an inquiry of the causes of wealth, i.e. **economic growth**. The two important determinants of growth were declared to be the **division of labour** and the ratio between **productive** and unproductive labour (a less important cause of the growth process). As a leader of the Scottish Enlightenment, he saw the growth process as being founded on the desire for betterment which leads to saving, which is then invested making possible the division of labour. As the specialization of economic activity inherent in the division of labour principle requires large markets, he fervently supported **free trade**. Like the **Physiocrats** before him, the government was to be limited to a few basic functions and taxation was to be levied according to strict principles. Just as **Cantillon** had given a perceptive account of international finance because of his experience as a banker, Smith, acutely aware of the great advances in banking in his native Scotland, could set out many of the issues for the subsequent classical debate on monetary theory.

See also: **absolute advantage; canons of taxation; economic growth**.

wealth tax (320)
A tax levied on the amount of capital a person owns. Although there are different schemes from country to country, the tax is usually levied on the net value of assets. It should be distinguished from a tax on capital income.

See also: **capital gains tax; capital tax**.

weight (210)

An amount by which the values of an economic variable are multiplied so that the relative significance of each variable in an index, particularly a price index, is taken into account.

See also: **Laspeyres index; Paasche index**.

welfare economics (020)

The branch of economics which sets out the rules for maximizing the welfare of society by considering both the size of social welfare and its distribution. As normative issues are its concern this is one of the most abstract and theoretical branches of economic science. The subject has advanced much from **Pigou**'s *Economics of Welfare* (1919) which defined economic welfare as 'that part of social welfare that can be brought directly or indirectly into relation with the measuring-rod of money' and then examined the relationship between private and social products, discussed **Pareto optimality** and considered in detail welfare problems raised by **monopoly** and wages. As so many attempts are made to increase social welfare through income redistribution, it was inevitable that the principles for compensation were rigorously discussed – particularly in the **Kaldor-Hicks compensation principle**, the **Scitovsky reversal test** and in Rawls's **maximin** principle. Other approaches include the attempt to devise a **social welfare function**, seemingly sunk by **Arrow's impossibility theorem** and the general theory of the **second best**. Despite so many false theoretical starts, welfare economics has inspired a great number of empirical studies, some using **cost–benefit analysis**, in matters as diverse as health, transport and energy economics.

Just, R.E., Hueth, D.L. and Schmitz, A. (1982) *Applied Welfare Economics and Public Policy*, Englewood Cliffs, NJ, and London: Prentice Hall.

Little, I.M.D. (1957) *A Critique of Welfare Economics*, 2nd edn, Oxford: Oxford University Press.

Sugden, R. (1981) *The Political Economy of Public Choice: An Introduction to Welfare Economics*, Oxford: Martin Robertson.

See also: **normative economics**.

welfare state (910)

A state which provides for basic needs by using taxation to finance benefits for low income groups and to provide free personal services, especially health care. Germany provides one of the earliest examples of a welfare state; Sweden, one of the most comprehensive amongst **mixed economies**. Since 1945 it was thought that a mixed economy with a welfare state was the natural way for Western industrialized economies to evolve but the problems of controlling inflation in the 1970s brought many to criticize the extent of state welfare provision. Welfare states are becoming increasingly expensive because of the ageing of the populations of advanced countries and rising expectations of increased welfare benefits and improved health care. Inevitably, there are vigorous debates on means testing and alternative methods of finance and a crusade in favour of greater economic efficiency.

Barr, N. (1987) *The Economics of the Welfare State*, London: Weidenfeld & Nicolson.

Barry, N. (1990) *Welfare*, Milton Keynes: Open University Press.

Hills, J. (ed.) (1990) *The State of Welfare. The Welfare State in Britain since 1974*, Oxford: Oxford University Press.

Marsh, D. (1970) *The Welfare State*, London: Longman.

Ringen, S. (1988) *The Possibility of Politics. A Study in the Political Economy of the Welfare State*, Oxford: Clarendon Press.

welfare trap (160, 320, 910)

See: **poverty trap**.

Werner Report (430)

European Community report of 1970 which set out the conditions for monetary union as (1) total and irreversible convertibility of currencies, (2) complete liberalization of capital transactions and a complete integration of banking and other financial markets and (3) the irrevocable locking of exchange rate parities to end margins of fluctuation.

See also: **Delors Plan**.

Wharton model (110, 210)

A quarterly model of the US economy which has been used for forecasting purposes since 1963. Originally it was based on Keynesian principles of income determination, but increasingly in the 1980s it had a monetary content.

Klein, L.P., Friedman, E. and Able, S. (1983) 'Money in the Wharton quarterly model',

Journal of Money, Credit and Banking 15: 237–59.

white-collar worker (810)

A non-manual worker employed in an office, laboratory or shop; a manager, professional worker, clerk, technician or sales assistant. There has been an increasing proportion of workers of this type in the labour force as a result of technological change, the growth of the public sector and the increasing bureaucratization of firms in oligopolistic industries. It was feared in the 1950s that this shift in the occupational structure would lead to the demise of **trade unions** but instead new trade unions specializing in the organization of white-collar workers have emerged. This upgrading of the labour force has contributed to rising labour costs.

white good (010, 630)

1 A consumer durable, such as a washing machine, cooker or refrigerator, which is usually painted white.

2 Household linen (the original meaning of the term).

See also: **brown good**; **consumer durable**.

white market (010)

A legal market which does not contravene any governmental regulation; the opposite of a **black market**.

white noise (210)

A time series which is completely random, all lagged correlations being zero; its spectrum density is constant.

white revolution (710)

An agricultural revolution, particularly promoted in India, which encouraged the growth of herds of dairy cattle.

wholesale bank (310)

A bank acquiring its deposits from corporations and the interbank market.

See also: **retail bank**.

wholesale money market (310)

An interbank market in which banks offer or obtain large deposits from each other. This is an important way for **merchant, invest**ment and other **secondary banks** to obtain deposits as they do not receive deposits directly from the public.

wholesale price index (220)

UK index of the group of commodities bought and sold by wholesalers. Changes in this index precede and indicate likely changes in the **retail price index**.

See also: **coincident indicators**.

Wicksell, Knut, 1861–1926 (030)

Leading Swedish economist whose ideas were to inspire the **Stockholm School** and form a basis for a macroeconomic theory which was an alternative to **Keynesianism**. Educated at Uppsala University in mathematics, Wicksell soon showed himself to be a courageous liberal, especially in propagating **neo-Malthusian** views – like John Stuart Mill he was arrested for doing so. Income from journalism and various grants enabled him to undertake independent study from 1885 to 1900; he came under the influence of **Böhm-Bawerk** and acquired a great admiration for his theory of capital. This influence was clear in his celebrated *Value, Capital and Rent* (1893, original German edition) and *Interest and Prices* (1898, original German edition). A major theme of his work was the relationship between **natural** and **market rates of interest** which, he believed, are at the heart of cumulative processes of expansion and contraction in the economy. His work, as indicated by his lectures at Lund University (where he was a professor from 1901), shows that he was eager to synthesize the capital theory of the **Austrian School** with Walrasian **general equilibrium** notions and other **neoclassical** insights.

Gardlund, T. (1958) *The Life of Knut Wicksell*, Stockholm: Almqvist & Wiksell.

Uhr, G.C. (1960) *The Economic Doctrines of Knut Wicksell*, Berkeley, CA: California University Press.

See also: **pure credit economy**.

wide monetary base (220, 310)

Notes and coins in circulation with the public plus banks' till money plus bankers' balances with the Bank of England.

wider share ownership (310)

Widespread ownership of the **shares** of

public companies throughout the population. It is argued that encouragement of this, as in the UK, makes private capitalism more acceptable throughout the country and that companies are less vulnerable to **takeover** as private shareholders retain their shares longer than **institutional investors** do. In the UK, **privatization** has increased the number of persons holding shares.

widget (010)
A convenient term for a non-specified product or service used in discussions of the principles of costing or industrial processes.

widow's cruse (110)
1 The Cambridge expression, used by **Kahn** and Joan **Robinson**, to refer to an economy which continues at the same level of output, neither expanding nor contracting as any spending of entrepreneurs' profits leads to an equal creation of other profits elsewhere in the economy.

2 The money-creating process of continually increasing money through bank lending.

Williamson, Oliver Eaton, 1932– (030)
Educated at MIT, Stanford and Carnegie-Mellon universities. Apart from a time as assistant professor at Berkeley, University of California from 1963 to 1965, he has been a professor at the University of Pennsylvania from 1965. His work on **transaction costs**, organizational hierarchies and **antitrust** policy have made him a leader of the revived school of **institutional economics**.

Williamson, O.E. (1970) *Corporate Control and Business Behavior*, Englewood Cliffs, NJ: Prentice Hall.
—— (1975) *Markets and Hierarchies*, New York: Free Press.
—— (1986) *Economic Organization: Firms, Markets and Policy Control*, Brighton: Harvester Wheatsheaf.

windfall gain or loss (010)
An unexpected increase or decrease in **ex post** income; if it had been expected, it would have been included in **ex ante** income. These windfalls are part of **transitory income** but not of **permanent income**.

windfall profit (010)
An unexpected **profit** arising from a circumstance not controlled by a **firm** or an individual. These profits constitute **transitory income** and can give rise to unusual consumer behaviour.

window dressing (310)
Interbank borrowing to improve the appearance of a bank's balance sheet. This was abandoned by British **clearing banks** in 1946 but is still practised in some banking systems, e.g. in France.

WIPO (620)
See: **World Intellectual Property Organization**.

withdrawal (010)
Not spending income on domestically produced goods and services but using it to buy imports, pay taxes or make savings with the consequence that the value of the **multiplier** is reduced. The **circular flow of income** distinguishes withdrawals from **injections**. Also known as a **leakage**.

withholding tax (320)
A tax on earnings, interest or dividend payments deducted at source. This tax is designed to simplify the collection of tax and to ensure that tax is not evaded. By taxing dividends due for repatriation, it is hoped that foreign-owned companies will be encouraged to invest in the country where its subsidiary is located.

women economists (030)
See: **female economists**.

won (430)
The currency of North and South Korea.

Wootton, Barbara, 1897–1988 (030)
Economist and social scientist noted for her works on **incomes policy**, **planning** and criminology. She was educated at Girton College, Cambridge where she originally read classics before a reading of **Marshall**'s *Principles of Economics* turned her to economics as her principal academic concern. Although being awarded first class honours with distinction, university regulations prevented her, as a woman, from taking her

degree. Soon she was made a fellow of Girton and Director of Studies in Economics. In 1922, she became a research officer of the Trades Union Congress. From 1926–8 she was Principal of Morley College for Working Men and Women, then Director of Studies for Tutorial Classes in the University of London (1928–45), Professor of Social Studies (1945–52) and at the end of her career a Nuffield research fellow.

Her achievements have been recognized by the award of many honorary degrees, a life peerage and being made a Companion of Honour. Throughout her works there is a practical utilitarian concern to relate problems to reality. Her attack on Lionel **Robbins**'s definition of economics in her *Lament for Economics* and her approach to planning and wage policy all indicate her desire to influence policy-makers by using an empirical approach. Much of her knowledge of economy and society came from membership of many committees and commissions on leading public issues covering topics ranging from criminal statistics, hallucinogens and broadcasting to taxation, shop hours and the civil service. She married John Wesley Wootton when she was 20; he was killed five weeks later in the First World War. She was married a second time in 1934 to a student, George Wright.

Bean, P. and Whynes, D. (eds) (1986) *Barbara Wootton. Social Science and Public Policy. Essays in her Honour*, London and New York: Tavistock Publications.

Wootton, B. (1934) *Plan or No Plan*, London: Gollancz.

—— (1938) *Lament for Economics*, London: Allen & Unwin.

—— (1945) *Freedom under Planning*, London: Allen & Unwin.

—— (1959) *Social Science and Social Pathology*, London: Allen & Unwin.

—— (1964) *The Social Foundations of Wage Policy: A Study of Contemporary British Wage and Salary Structure*, 2nd edn, London: Allen & Unwin.

—— (1967) *In a World I Never Made: Autobiographical Reflections*, London: Allen & Unwin.

workable competition (010, 610)

Competition which fulfils only some of the conditions for **perfect competition**; an absence of **anticompetitive practices**. It is a **second best** situation. The criteria suggested to see whether an industry is in a state of workable competition are its level of profits relative to normal profits, its costs relative to those of the most efficient scale, the extent of its product variation and selling costs and its rate of technical progress relative to what is considered satisfactory; this list shows at once how **normative** the concept is. The notion is central to the implementation of US **antitrust** policy and increasingly used in British **competition policy**.

Clark, J.M. (1961) *Competition as a Dynamic Process*, Washington, DC: Brookings Institution.

Sosnick, S.H. (1958) 'A critique of concepts of workable competition', *Quarterly Journal of Economics* 72: 380–423.

Utton, M.A. (1986) *The Economics of Regulating Industry*, Oxford: Basil Blackwell.

work classification (810)

A method of classifying work requirements which is an alternative to job description. The elements in the classification are the work range, the work structure (how changeable work goals are), work control (how much discretion is involved) and the cognitive effort required. This classification has been applied to knowledge-intensive **white-collar** work.

worker compensation insurance (910)

Sickness and accident benefits financed by employers' premiums. In the USA the amount of such insurance varies from state to state and according to the accident record of the firm.

workers' participation (830)

The participation of employees in the management of the firms where they work. In Europe, a major example since 1950 has been Germany. There, two basic laws govern such schemes: the works constitution law (*Betriebsverfassungsgesetz*) and co-determination law (*Mitbestimmungsgesetz*). Under the former, works councils, which can determine several matters including working hours and vacations, can be formed if more than five workers are regularly employed. Co-determination law deals with the structure of the supervisory board which exists in addition to an executive board and has worker representatives. The law, originally applied only to the iron, steel and coal industries, stipulated an equal number of employee and shareholder representatives on supervisory boards. Gradually, this type of workers' participation has spread to private sector firms. In 1976, the law was extended to all companies with over 2,000 employees, an extension to smaller companies being strongly resisted by employers. The chairman, a shareholders' representative, has a second (casting) vote and the representation of senior staff on the supervisory board has, it is argued, weighted the composition in favour of the management.

See also: **industrial democracy**.

workfare (910)

US schemes of community work which qualify the unemployed for social security benefits. The idea was first used by the Roosevelt Administration in the 1930s. The US Federal Act of 1981, the Omnibus Budget Reconciliation Act, forced all recipients of federal or state aid to register for work or job training and gave the states the powers to require such persons to participate in work incentive, job search or work experience programmes. These schemes have been criticized for creating slave labour, for displacing existing workers, for adding to administrative costs and for reducing the chance of the unemployed seeking good jobs. The most enthusiastic implementation of the scheme has been in West Virginia. Other countries, e.g. Sweden, have versions of such schemes to keep down the level of unemployment.

working capital (520)

Current assets minus current liabilities; capital available to provide short-term financing for a firm. Classical economists regarded this as mainly the raw materials and the **wages fund**. Today it is often regarded as a measure of the **liquidity** of a firm.

working capital ratio (540)

See: **current ratio**.

working hours (810)

The total number of hours a person works per day or per week. The recommendation which is often made to reduce them as a means of increasing workers' welfare and chances of employment is based on too simplistic an analysis: a reduction in hours often raises unit labour costs which, in turn, reduces international competitiveness and profit margins on traded goods leading to lower economic growth and employment. If reduced working hours raise **productivity**, no extra demand for labour results. In France, working hours were reduced from forty to thirty-nine per week, with full compensation, in January 1982; in West Germany, the Metalworkers Union demanded in 1984 a reduction from forty to thirty-five hours with partial compensation.

Marx made the length of the working day a key issue: he argued that working hours longer than those necessary to produce subsistence for workers created **surplus value**. Paradoxically, working hours have been longer in socialist countries, being forty-two to forty-five hours per week. But in the developing countries of Africa and Asia, weekly working hours are often as much as fifty or fifty-five. Japan which has industrialized only recently still has long average working hours, about forty-eight per week (three-quarters of the labour force works a six-day week).

working population (810)

See: **labour force**.

work sharing (810)

A method of reducing unemployment by splitting a full-time job into two part-time jobs. Parents sometimes do this in order to share in domestic duties and child rearing. Occupations which have introduced this form of sharing include school teaching and social work.

See also: **job sharing**.

World Bank (430)

Popular name for the International Bank for Reconstruction and Development which was conceived at **Bretton Woods** in 1944 and started business in 1947; it was intended that it should be linked to the **International Monetary Fund** by member countries belonging to both. It aims to encourage the provision of private, rather than public, investment. Of its initial authorized capital of 10 milliard dollars, one-tenth was paid in dollars and gold. Federal and state bonds of the Bank issued in the USA raised a substantial amount of the original capital. At different phases of its life, it has been a bank of reconstruction, a development bank and a policy reformer.

Current aims suggested for the bank include the major provision of funds and technical advice to Third World borrowers, the coordination of aid to less developed countries and theoretical leadership in development policy. Some people in the USA regard the World Bank as a means of spreading US political philosophy and monetarism, but the financial rise of Japan as the world's major lender has increasingly diminished US influence. In recent years, the Bank has lent about 90 per cent of its advances for infrastructure projects, e.g. education, health, irrigation and telecommunications. Currently, recipient countries are being asked to adopt price reforms and market-related trading reforms.

World Bank classification of countries (730)

Industrial market economies (mainly the leading **Organization for Economic Cooperation and Development** countries), East European non-market economies, high income oil exporters, low income developing countries (with gross national product per capita less than US$400 in 1984) and middle income developing countries (with gross national product per capita in 1984 over US$400).

world debt problem (430)

The consequences of the large debts of less developed countries accumulated since 1970. The magnitude of this indebtedness has given rise to problems of debt servicing and the stability of the banking system. The significance of the debts has often been measured by the debt–gross national product or debt–service ratios but it has been asserted that a better measure is the comparison of the rate of growth of export earnings with the rate of interest. Several approaches have been suggested to reduce this indebtedness, e.g. in 1986 the World Bank suggested **sector adjustment lending** as a means of reducing the indebtedness of certain **Third World** countries. Some coun-

tries have reduced their indebtedness by a policy of exchanging debt for equity but there are limits to such conversions as many national governments are alarmed to see more foreign ownership of domestic companies. Major Western banks have gradually written off these loans as bad debts.

Griffith-Jones, S. (ed.) (1988) *Managing World Debt*, Brighton: Harvester Wheatsheaf.
Holley, H.A. (1987) *Developing Country Debt: The Role of the Commercial Banks*, London: Routledge.

See also: **debt–service indicators**.

world inflation (150)

The rates of **inflation** country by country around the world, measured by annual rates of increase of consumer or producer prices. Countries with high postwar inflation records include Argentina, Brazil, Israel, Mexico and Yugoslavia; countries with low inflation records include Japan, Switzerland, the USA, and West Germany before reunification.

Brown, A.J. (1985) *World Inflation since 1950*, Cambridge: Cambridge University Press.
Horsman, G. (1988) *Inflation in the Twentieth Century*, Brighton: Harvester Wheatsheaf.

World Intellectual Property Organization (620)

A Geneva-based body which is concerned with upholding international conventions on protected ideas and with harmonizing national laws concerning such property.

See also: **intellectual property**.

world monetary reserve assets (430)

The total of the assets of all the countries of the world, in the form of **special drawing rights**, **gold** and **reserve currencies**.

See also: **reserve assets**.

world monetary system (430)

The institutional mechanism for settling inter-country indebtedness and for providing loans to increase the liquidity of countries in need. After the **gold standard**, there was a world institutional gap until the **Bretton Woods** system was devised. Although the arrangements for pegging exchange rates ended in 1971, the **International Monetary Fund** and the **World Bank** remain as pillars of a world system.

world systems perspective (110)

A method of analysing economic development which uses a structural approach to put **foreign aid** in the context of being part of the world economy and measures that country's relationship with the rest of the world economy.

world trade (420)

The total volume of exports or imports of all world economies. The growth of trading within **multinational corporations**, much of which is measured at artificial **transfer prices**, has made it more difficult to gain a precise idea of the value of exports of particular countries. The volume of world trade fluctuates according to the state of major economies, especially the USA, and grows at different rates within particular trading blocs and between them.

writer (310)

A **call** seller in an option market who sells **options** against shares he already owns in order to improve their performance.

X

X (420)
Exports.

XD (310)
Ex dividend.

X-efficiency (020, 520)

Leibenstein's concept of efficiency which rejects the technical efficiency notion of profit maximizing and cost minimizing. He argued that individual workers are free to choose their effort level and interpret their own jobs. The equilibrium position for a firm will be when every individual is in his/her 'inert area', an effort point which, if moved away from, would reduce utility. This level of 'efficiency' and associated cost is comfortable for a firm's individuals. Prices are fixed using conventional formulae.

Leibenstein, H. (1976) *Beyond Economic Man: A New Foundation for Macroeconomics*, Cambridge, MA: Harvard University Press.
—— (1978) *General X-Efficiency Theory and Economic Development*, New York and London: Oxford University Press.
—— (1980) *Inflation, Income Distribution and X-Efficiency Theory*, London: Croom Helm; New York: Barnes & Noble.

Xenophon, 430–354 BC (030)

At an early age a follower of Socrates before embarking on military campaigns, including the expedition of Cyrus. The three works attributed to him which are most relevant to economics are *Ways and Means to Increase the Revenues of Athens*, perhaps the first work on **public finance** in which he argued for state intervention to expand silver mining, *Oeconomicus* which included a discussion of the nature of wealth and income differentials and *Cyropaedia* which explains that the **division of labour** is limited by the extent of the market.

See also: **Ancient Greeks**; **Aristotle**; **Plato**.

X-form (510)

A hybrid type of business enterprise which is a mixture of the **H-** and **M-forms**.

Williamson, O.E. (1986) *Economic Organization: Firms, Markets and Policy Control*, ch. 4, Brighton: Harvester Wheatsheaf.

See also: **U-form**.

xr (310)

Ex rights.

See also: **rights issue**.

Y (010)
Income; in many cases, real disposable income.

Yankee bond (310)
A bond issued in the US securities market by a non-US concern.

yearling (310)
A British local government stock which matures in a year.

See also: **government bond**.

yellow dog contract (830)
An individual employment contract under which a worker promises not to join a **trade (labor) union**. This standard practice of many US firms in the 1920s was used to impede the growth of union membership. It was outlawed by the **Norris–La Guardia Act**.

yellow stripe price (310)
A stock market price shown on a screen of the **Stock Exchange Automated Quotation System** which refers to large **bargains** of a particular stock.

yield (310, 710)
1 Return to an investment measured by dividend or interest receivable divided by price of that **security**.

2 The annual produce from cultivating a piece of land.

See also: **redemption yield**.

yield curve (310)
The relationship between the percentage yield of a bond and the number of years to its maturity. An inverse yield curve is downward sloping, a positive yield curve upward sloping and a flat yield curve horizontal. In most cases the yield, determined in a secondary market, is for a previously issued bond. The yield is also a guide to the pricing of new bond issues. The **term structure of interest rates** determines the

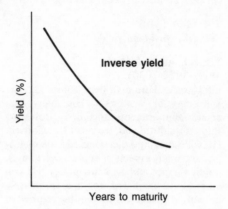

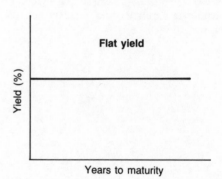

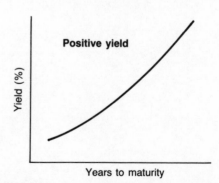

curve, e.g. if short-term rates are higher than long-term, there will be an inverse yield curve.

See also: **term structure of interest rates**.

yield gap (310)
The **yield** on equities minus the yield on bonds. Inflation after 1959 depressed the capital values of bonds, raising their yields in both the UK and the USA: this created a 'reverse yield gap' which has fluctuated between about 1 per cent and 9 per cent.

Y'ld Gr's (310)
See: **gross dividend yield**.

Young, Allyn Abbott, 1876–1929 (030)
Educated at Hiram College, Ohio, and the University of Wisconsin. His many academic appointments included professorships at Stanford and, from 1913, at Cornell. His wide-ranging articles included demography and many aspects of applied economics, public finance and antitrust policy. He will long be remembered for his immensely influential article on **increasing returns to scale** which both advanced the theory of economic growth and challenged the Marshallian **theory of the firm**. Tragically, he died of influenza in London.

Young, A.A. (1928) 'Increasing returns and economic progress', *Economic Journal* 38: 527–42.

yuan (430)
Standard monetary unit of China.

yumpie (840)
Young upwardly mobile professional.

See also: **yuppie**.

yuppie, yuppy (840)
A young urban professional. Most of these aggressive young graduates are employed in financial centres such as New York and London. These health-conscious workaholics firmly believe in free-market economics. Their high salaries have made it possible for them to contribute to the **gentrification** of inner city areas.

See also: **yumpie**.

Z

zaibatsu (510)
A Japanese group of large companies owned by a family-controlled holding company.

See also: **chaebol**.

zai teku (520)
Financial management (Japanese).

ZBB (320)
See: **zero base budgeting**.

zero base budgeting (320)
A method of governmental budgeting which begins with an appraisal of all spending projects on their merits and then, by aggregation, produces a budget total. It was intended, when it was introduced by the Carter Administration in the USA in the 1970s, to replace the traditional budget method of deciding first on an expenditure total and then allocating that sum among different programmes. In practice, it is questionable whether this method can be implemented as project analysis is long, costly and difficult – and not applicable to all parts of a budget.

Sarant, P.C. (1978) *Zero-base Budgeting in the Public Sector: A Pragmatic Approach*, Reading, MA: Addison-Wesley.

zero coupon bond (310)
A bond which bears no interest. As the bond is issued at a discount, it has a **redemption yield**.

zero growth (110)
The characteristic of an economy in a **stationary state**. This has been suggested as a goal for modern advanced economies. It is advocated on the grounds that growth of the **gross national product** generates social costs in the form of pollution, congestion and more arduous labour and that such growth necessitates too rapid a use of non-renewable resources. This view is often expressed as a condemnation of all growth rather than an attack on particular undesirable economic activities. Changes to more environmentally friendly production techniques make economic growth more acceptable.

See also: **Club of Rome**.

zero population growth (840)
The goal of many twentieth-century disciples of **Malthus** which usually takes the form of advocating birth control. In many Western European countries the use of contraceptive pills since the 1960s has brought the natural rate of increase below the replacement level.

See also: **neo-Malthusians**.

zero priced (010)
Free. This term enables the prices of everything to be placed on a continuum from zero to a considerable sum. Many goods and services provided by the public sector are given freely to consumers, e.g. most of the health care provided by Britain's National Health Service. Although goods can be free to a consumer, they are not costless because of the scarcity of factor inputs.

zero profit (010)
The absence of **supernormal profits** in the long run, under conditions of **perfect competition**, as firms earn only **normal profits** which are included in average costs.

zero-rated good (320)
A good not subject to value-added tax. Exemptions from value-added tax vary from country to country but the principal items excluded in some countries have been food, clothing and educational materials.

zero real interest (310)
A nominal rate of interest equal to the rate of inflation of that country.

zero-sum game (020, 420)
Economic activities in which the gains to the winners equal the losses to the losers. There

are many examples of these games, e.g. the attempt of all major trading countries to have export surpluses.

Zeuthen, Frederik Ludvig Baug, 1888–1959 (030)

Danish mathematical economist who graduated from Copenhagen University in 1912 and was employed by the Danish social security system from 1912 to 1930 before beginning his academic career. He developed a theory of **collective bargaining** based upon the possible outcomes of expected conflict, as perceived by management and labour, and developed the theory of **duopoly** by expanding the notion of **product differentiation**.

Zeuthen, F.L.B. (1930) *Problems of Monopoly and Economic Welfare.*
—— (1959) *Economic Theory and Method*, Cambridge, MA: Harvard University Press.

zloty (430)

The currency of Poland.

zone franc (430)

The currencies of France, its overseas territories and some African countries which are tied to the French franc.

See also: **CFA franc**.

zone of freedom (630)

A price range of the tariffs set by major airlines. The 'zone' is the range below and above a single reference level within which an air tariff must be set.

zoning (710)

A local government method of regulating land use. By the prohibition of certain types of building in particular areas, land values and the nature of economic activity are affected.

ZPG (840)

See: **zero population growth**.

Z-score (310)

A measure of the overall performance of a company which takes the form of a weighted index. The index is $a + b \times$ profitability $- c \times$ gearing. In this equation, a is a constant and b and c are coefficients reflecting the relative importance of each ratio. The score for an individual company is compared with a test score to judge whether the company is a financial failure or a success.

Subject classification index

Throughout the *Dictionary*, entries have been classified numerically by subject matter using the *Economic Journal* subject classification system given below. The Index lists entries classed under each heading of the system, and will help the user to find entries or bibliographies relating to particular areas of economic activity or research. The *Economic Journal* system is used by kind permission of its editors and Blackwell Publishers.

000 General economics; Theory; History; Systems

010 General economics
020 General economic theory
030 History of economic thought; methodology
040 Economic history
050 Single country studies; industrialized economies; capitalist
060 Single country studies; industrialized economies; socialist
070 Comparative economic systems

100 Economic growth; Development; Planning; Fluctuations; Inflation

110 Economic growth
120 Planning theory and policy
130 Economic development studies
140 Economic fluctuations; forecasting; stabilization
150 Inflation
160 Income distribution, theory, measurement and policy

200 Quantitative economic methods and data

210 Econometric, statistical and mathematical methods and models
220 Economic and social statistics

300 Domestic monetary and fiscal theory and institutions

310 Domestic monetary and financial theory and institutions
320 Fiscal policy and theory; public finance

400 International economics

410 International trade theory
420 Trade relations; commercial policy; international economic integration
430 Balance of payments; international finance

500 Administration; Business finance; Marketing; Accounting

510 Administration
520 Business finance and investment
530 Marketing
540 Accounting

600 Industrial organization; Technological change; Industry studies

610 Industrial organization and public policy
620 Economics of technological change
630 Industry studies
640 Economic capacity

700 Agriculture; Natural resources

710 Agriculture
720 Natural resources; energy economics
730 Economic geography

800 Manpower; Labour; Population

810 Manpower training and allocation; labour force and supply
820 Labour markets; public policy
830 Trade unions; collective bargaining; labour–management relations

(*The Economic Journal* 100 (June 1990): 662)

010 General economics

abatement
absolute surplus value
abstinence
accounting profit
accrued expense
accrued income
Adam Smith Institute
adaptive expectations
additional-worker hypothesis
adjustment cost
adverse supply shock
agency cost
agglomeration economy
aggregate demand
aggregate output
aggregate supply
agricultural household
alienation
allocative efficiency
altruism
American Economic
    Association
amortization
anarchism
animal spirits
arbitrage
asset
asset specificity
asymmetric information
atomistic competition
auction
auctioneer
autarky
autonomous consumption
autonomous expenditure
autonomous investment
average incremental cost
average propensity to consume
average propensity to save
average total cost
axioms of preference
bad
balanced budget multiplier
bargaining
barrier to entry
barter
barter economy
basic commodity
behaviour line
Bergson social welfare function
bilateral monopoly
binomial charge
bioeconomics
black economy
black market
bliss point
bottleneck
bounded rationality

branding
breakeven level of income
Brookings Institution
brown good
bubble
budget constraint
budget line
bundled deal
C
capital
capital intensive
capital–labour ratio
capital–output ratio
capital reswitching
capture theory
cardinal utility
cash economy
catallactics
Centre for Policy Studies
ceteris paribus
change in demand or supply
charge circular flow
circulating
capital
classical dichotomy
clearing
clearing market
club good
cobweb
cognitive consonance
cognitive dissonance
collective good
commodity
commodity fetishism
common cost
common ownership
comparative advantage
comparative statics
compensated demand curve
competition
competitive trading
complement
compliance cost
composite commodity
compulsory savings
concentration economy
Condorcet criterion
conspicuous consumption
constant capital
constant returns to scale
constrained market pricing
consumer durable
consumer sovereignty
consumer's surplus
consumption externality
consumption function
contemporaneous externality
contingent fee
contingent market
contract curve

contracting
contractual savings
controlled market
core economy
cornucopia
corridor
countervailing power
cross price elasticity of demand
cross-trading
deadweight loss
decision cycle
decreasing returns
deflation
deflationary gap
demand
demand curve
demerit good
Dennison's law
depression pole
derived demand
destructive competition
devalorization
differential theory of rent
differentiated good
differentiated product
diminishing marginal rate of
    substitution
diminishing marginal utility law
diminishing returns law
direct cost
directly unproductive profit-
    seeking activities
discount market
discount rate
discriminating monopoly
diseconomy of scale
disequilibrium
disequilibrium price
distortion
distribution
disutility
diversification
division of labour
division of thought
domestic absorption
double switching
DRY
dumping
duopoly
economic agent
economic cost
economic devolution
economic good
economic journals
economic man
economic profit
economic rent
economics
economic system
economic welfare

economism
economy
economy of scale
economy of scope
economy of size
effective demand
effectual demand
efficient market
egalitarianism
eigenprices
elasticity
elasticity of demand
elasticity of expectations
elasticity of substitution
elasticity of supply
employment
Employment Act 1946
employment multiplier
Engel coefficient
entrepreneur
envelope curve
environmental determinism
equality
equal product curve
equilibrium
equilibrium GNP
equilibrium price
ex ante, ex post
ex ante variables
excess capacity
excess demand
excess supply
exchange efficiency
exclusion principle
exit-voice
exogenous expectations
expectations
experience good
explicit contract
explicit cost
ex post variables
external economy of scale
externality
extrapolative expectations
factor cost
factor endowment
factor market
factor of production
factor productivity
fad
felicific calculus
final demand
final good
financial journalism
firm
firm consumption
first best economy
first degree price
  discrimination
fixed cost

fixprice
flexprice
floor price
forced saving
foreign trade multiplier
formal economy
free good
free market
full employment
future goods
futures
gender discrimination
general equilibrium
generalized medium
gestation period
Giffen good
glut
good
Haig–Simons definition of
  income
hedonic output
hedonic price
Hicks charts
Hicksian income measure
hiding hand
hold-up
home production
homo economicus
homogeneous good
homo sovieticus
household behaviour
household decision-making
i
I
illth
implicit marginal
  income
imputed income
incentive compatible
income
income–consumption curve
income elasticity of demand
increasing opportunity costs
  law
increasing returns to scale
incremental cost
indecomposability
indifference curve
indirect cost
indivisibility
inducement good
industry
inelasticity
inequality
inferior good
inflationary gap
information cost injection
inside lag
Institute of Economic Affairs
insurance

intangible wealth
interest
interest elasticity of savings
interest risk
interlinked transaction
intermediate good
internal balance
internal economy of scale
internalizing an externality
interpersonal utility
  comparisons
intrinsic value
inverse elasticity rule
investment
invisible hand
IS
IS–LM curves
isocost
isoproduct
isoquant
joint cost
joint demand
joint products
just price
K
Kaldor–Hicks compensation
  principle
Keynes effect
Keynesian cross diagram
Keynesian equilibrium
kickback
kinked demand curve
labour
labour power
lacking
lag
law of satiable wants
law of value
law of variable proportions
leakage
learning curve
lemons market
Lerner effect
limit price
linkage
long period
Lundberg
lag
luxury
M
macroeconomic demand
  schedule
magic quadrilateral
malleable capital
marginal cost
marginal cost of abatement
marginal efficiency of capital
marginal efficiency of
  investment
marginalism

marginal physical product
marginal principle of
  allocation
marginal private cost
marginal product of labour
marginal propensity to
  consume
marginal propensity to import
marginal propensity to save
marginal rate of substitution
marginal rate of
  transformation
marginal revenue
marginal revenue product
marginal social cost
marginal social damage
marginal utility
market
market adjustment
market clearing
market clearing price
market demand
market discrimination
  coefficient
market distortion
market economy
market equilibrium
market failure
market forces
market power
Marshallian demand curve
Marshallian long period
Marshallian short period
Marshallian stability
material good
merit bad
merit good
merit want
mesoeconomy
missing market
monetary veil
money income
monopoly
monopoly power
monopoly profit
monopsony
Mont Pelerin Society
moonlight economy
moral hazard
multiplier
national income
natural monopoly
natural price
natural rate of interest
neighbourhood effect
net economic welfare
net investment
nominal income
non-basic commodity
non-linear pricing

non-market sector
non-pecuniary returns
normal good
normal profit
normative economics
no-trade equilibrium
numéraire
oligopsony
one-crop economy
one-price law
opportunistic behaviour
opportunity cost
optimum firm
option demand
ordinal utility
organic composition of capital
other things being equal
outside lag
overaccumulation
overhead capital
overhead costs
overheating
overshooting price
own rate of interest
package deal
paradox of thrift
paradox of value
Pareto efficiency
Pareto improvement
Pareto optimum
pay-off
PDI
peak-load pricing
pecuniary economy of scale
pecuniary external economy
pecuniary returns
perfect competition
perfect price discrimination
personal capitalism
personal income
perverse price
Pigou effect
policy lag
political economy
positional good
positive economics
post-industrial society
potential output
potential surprise function
price
price bunching
price–consumption curve
price determination
price discrimination
price effect
price elasticity of demand
price flexibility
price floor
price incentive
price level

price maker
price perception
price rigidity
price staggering
price system
price taking
price twist
primary employment
primary product
prime cost
primitive economy
private cost
private good
producer's surplus
product differentiation
production possibility frontier
productive capital
productive labour
productivity
profit
profit maximization
profit motive
profit squeeze
property rights
psychic income
public good
public pricing
pure competition
pure economic rent
pure monopoly
pure profit
quantitative restrictions
quasi-fixed factor
quasi-rent
queuing system
quota racial discrimination
Ramsey prices
ratchet effect
rate of return
rational decision
rationing
real balance effect
real economy of scale
real income
real price
recessionary gap
recognition lag
recontract
regressive expectations
regulation
regulatory capture
relative price
relative surplus value
rent
rental payment
rentier
rent seeking
representative firm
reproduction
required rental on capital

507

020 General economics theory

absolute income hypothesis
AD–AS
adding-up controversy
agency theory
agio theory of interest
Arrow–Debreu model
Bertrand duopoly model
Cambridge
  controversies
capital theory
characteristics theory of
  consumer demand
classical savings theory
class savings theory
Coase theorem
Cobb–Douglas production
  function
compensation principle
consumer equilibrium
contestable markets thesis
core
corn model
Cournot's duopoly model
dependency theory
disequilibrium economics
dual-decision hypothesis
dynamic
economics
economics and psychology
economics of law
employment function
Engel's law
evolutionary theory of the
  firm
excess capacity theorem
expenditure function
full-cost pricing
game theory
general equilibrium
grants economics
impact multiplier
implicit contract theory
impossibility theorem
income and substitution
  effects
Keynes expectations
labour disutility theory
labour process theory
labour theory of value
law and economics
life-cycle hypothesis
Lucas supply function
macroeconomics
managerial models of the firm
marginal cost pricing
marginal productivity theory
maximin

microeconomics
mono-economics
neo-Ricardian theory
organizational economics
overlapping generations model
paradox of voting
partial equilibrium analysis
permanent income hypothesis
portfolio balance
pseudo production function
public choice theory
quantity theory of money
Ramsey saving rule
rational expectations
Rawlsian difference principle
Rawlsian justice
real-wage hypothesis
regret
relative income hypothesis
revealed preference
reverse causation hypothesis
Ricardian theory of value
savings function
Say's law
Slutsky effect
social choice theory
social welfare function
specific egalitarianism
Stackelberg duopoly model
St Petersburg paradox
surplus approach
surplus economy
survival process
team theory
theonomy
theory of clubs
theory of the firm
transaction cost economics
transformation problem
uniformity assumption
utilitarianism
utility function
welfare economics
X efficiency
zero-sum game

030 History of economic thought; methodology

Abramovitz, Moses, 1912–
Allais, Maurice, 1911–
Ancient Greeks
Anderson, James, 1739–1808
Aquinas, St Thomas, 1225–74
Aristotle, 384–322 BC
Arrow, Kenneth Joseph, 1921–
Austrian School
Ayres, Clarence Edwin, 1891–
  1972
Bagehot, Walter, 1826–77
Bailey, Samuel, 1791–1870
Bain, Joe Staten, 1912–
Banking School
Baran, Paul, 1910–64
bastard Keynesianism
Bauer, Peter Thomas, 1915–
Baumol, William Jack, 1922–
Becker, Gary Stanley, 1930–
behavioural economics
Bentham, Jeremy, 1748–1832
Bergson, Abram, 1914–
Bernoulli hypothesis
Beveridge, William Henry (Lord),
  1879–1963
Blaug, Mark, 1927–
Böhm-Bawerk, Eugen von, 1851–
  1914
Boulding, Kenneth Ewart, 1910–
Buchanan, James McGill, 1919–
Bullionist controversy
Burns, Arthur Frank, 1904–87
Cambridge Circus
Cambridge Economic Policy
  Group
Cambridge School
Cantillon, Richard, c.1680–c.1734
Cassel, Karl Gustav, 1866–1945
Chamberlin, Edward Hastings,
  1899–1967
Chenery, Hollis Burnley, 1918–
Chicago School
Child, Sir Francis, 1642–1713
Clark, Colin Grant, 1905–89
Clark, John Bates, 1847–1938
classical dichotomy
classical economics
classical savings theory
class savings theory
Coase, Ronald Harry, 1910–
Commons, John Roger, 1862–
  1945
comparative statics
continuity thesis
corn model
Cournot, Antoine Augustin,
  1801–77

Schumacher, Ernst Friedrich, 1911–77
Schumpeter, Joseph Alois, 1883–1950
Schwartz, Anna Jacobson, 1915–
Scitovsky, Tibor, 1910–
Sen, Amartya K., 1933–
Senior, Nassau William, 1790–1864
Shackle, George Lennox
Sharman, 1903–
Sharpe, William, 1934–
Simon, Herbert Alexander, 1916–
Simons, Henry Calvert, 1899–1946
Smith, Adam, 1723–90
social credit
social liberalism
Solow, Robert M., 1924–
Sraffa, Piero, 1898–1983
Stigler, George Joseph, 1911–
Stockholm School
Stone, John Richard Nicholas, 1913–
supply-side economics
surplus approach
Swedish School
Tableau économique
Thornton, Henry, 1760–1815
Thünen, Johann Heinrich von, 1783–1850
Tinbergen, Jan, 1903–
Tobin, James, 1918–
Torrens, Robert, 1780–1864
Turgot, Anne-Robert Jacques, 1727–81
utilitarianism
Vanek, Jaroslav, 1930–
Veblen, Thorstein Bunde, 1857–1929
Viner, Jacob, 1892–1970
Von Neumann, John, 1903–57
vulgar economists
Walras, Marie Esprit Léon, 1834–1910
Wealth of Nations
Wicksell, Knut, 1861–1926
Williamson, Oliver Eaton, 1932–
Wootton, Barbara, 1897–1988
Xenophon, 430–354 BC
Young, Allyn Abbott, 1876–1929
Zeuthen, Frederik Ludvig Baug, 1888–1959

040 Economics history

Bank Charter Act 1844
bimetallism
Canal Age
chartism
Colbertism
Combination Acts
Corn Laws
cottage industry
Cultural Revolution
domestic system
feudalism
Great Depression
industrial capitalism
industrial revolution
late capitalism
logistic cycle
Long Boom
Luddite
Manchester School
merchant capitalism
New Economic Policy
Poor Laws
proto-industrialization slump
villa economy

050 Single country studies; industrial economies; capitalist

capitalism
catching-up hypothesis
English disease
Gang of Four
National Institute for Economic and Social Research
newly industrialized country

511

060 Single country studies; industrial economies; socialist

communism
Cultural Revolution
development planning
first economy
Gosplan
Gossnab
Great Leap Forward
New Economic Policy
parallel market economy
perestroika
rectification
revenue economy
second economy
state capitalism

070 Comparative economic system

altruism
Asiatic mode of production
auto-economy
autogestion
blue economy
bootblack economy
branch economy
capitalist class
capitalist imperialism
centrally planned economy
closed economy
command economy
communal economy
consumer society
convergence hypothesis
corporate state
corporatism
cowboy economy
decentralized market economy
dual economy
economic institution
economic system
economy
enclave economy
financial economy
First World
Fourth World
hansom cab economy
imperialism
informal economy
institution
interdependent economy
international comparisons
international comparisons of
    the cost of living
international wage levels
inter-nation equity
lemonade stand capitalism
liberal collectivism
managerial revolution
market economy
mature economy
mixed economy
modern economy
new industrial state
one country, two systems
open economy
peripheral capitalism
permanent arms economy
popular capitalism
private enterprise system
protean economy
psychological economy
pure credit economy
revenue economy
Second World
self-sufficient economy

semi-colonial country
share economy
shortage economy
siege economy
size of an economy
social democracy
socialism
socialist economy
social market economy
Soviet-type economy
state monopoly capitalism
surplus economy
third way
Third World

110 Economic growth

AC
advanced organic economy
antagonistic growth
backward linkage
balanced growth
big push
blocked development
Brundtland Report
Buddhist economics
capital accumulation
capital deepening
capital widening
class savings theory
Club of Rome
Cobb–Douglas production
   function
debt-led growth
Denison residual development
development economics
development policy
do-able
economic development
economic growth
engine of growth
factor-augmenting technical
   progress
First Development Decade
forward linkage
fundamental contradiction of
   capitalism
Gerschenkron effect
golden age
golden rule
growth
growth accounting
Harrod–Domar model
immiserizing growth
incremental capital–output
   ratio
inducement mechanism
industrialization
Kaldor's laws
Kuznets curve
Lewis–Fei–Ranis model
linkage
Long Boom
malleable capital
mineral-based economy
modern economy
natural rate of growth
NEDO
negative feedback
Okun's law
one-crop economy
over-urbanization
Pacific Rim
positive feedback
price incentive

production asymmetry
productive potential
productivity
protean economy
real growth
S-curve
SNIG
Solow residual
stages theory
stationary state
steady state economy
steady state growth
sustainable development
sustainable economic growth
   rate
take-off
traverse
trickle-down theory
turnpike theorem
two-gap development model
U hypothesis
Verdoorn's law
vintage effect
warranted rate of growth
Wharton model
widow's cruse
world systems perspective
zero growth

120 Planning theory and policy

centrally planned economy
Chinese modernization drive
collectivization of agriculture
command economy
economic methods
economic planning
filière concept
five-year plan
Gosplan
Gossnab
guild socialism
indicative planning
Mahalanobis model
market socialism
material balance
Monnet's law
National Economic
   Development Council
   National Plan (UK)
negotiated coordination
New Economic Mechanism
new industrial state
perestroika
project appraisal
soft budget
Soviet-type economy
storming

130 Economic development studies

ACP
Chinese modernization drive
cost–benefit analysis
dependency theory
development economics
development planning
dual economy
ECA
enclave economy
estate economy
Food and Agriculture
   Organization
import substitution
less developed country
Lomé Convention
migration-fed unemployment
Pearson Report
peripheral capitalism
price stabilization
remittance
South African Development
   Coordination Committee
stages theory
take-off
United Nations Development
   Programme
United Nations Industrial
   Development Organization

140 Economic fluctuations; forecasting stabilization

accelerator principle
active fiscal policy
boom
Brookings Institution
business cycle
ceiling
coincident indicators
COMET
Council of Economic Advisers
countercyclical policy
countervailing power crisis
cyclical unemployment
depression
diffusion index
economic climate
economic forecasting
economic indicators
economic weather
EPA expectations
floor
German economic institutes
hedging
hog cycle
INTERLINK
inventory cycle
investment reserve system
Juglar cycle
Kitchin cycle
Kondratieff cycle
Kuznets cycle
lagging indicator
large-scale models
leading indicators
linkage models
logistic cycle
long wave
manpower forecasting
MCM multiplier–accelerator
   model
National Bureau of Economic
   Research
National Institute for
   Economic and Social
   Research
political business cycle
recession
recovery
reference cycle
slump
stabilization policy
sunspot
theory
trade cycle
Treasury model
trend periods
UK economic forecasting

150 Inflation

administered inflation
core inflation rate
cost-push inflation
demand-pull inflation
demand-shift inflation
Fisher theorem
galloping inflation
GDP deflator
hyperinflation
indexation
inertial inflation
infession
inflation
inflation illusion
inflationist
inflation tax
Katona effect
market anti-inflation plan
menu costs of inflation
monetary inflation
money illusion
Phillips curve
price ceiling
Price Commission
price controls
price perception
prices policy
pure inflation
reputational equilibrium
runaway inflation
Sandilands Report
shock inflation
shoe leather costs of inflation
slumpflation
stagflation
structural inflation
suppressed inflation
taxflation
underlying inflation rate
unit value index
wage diffusion
wage–price spiral
wage-push inflation
wage–tax spiral
world inflation

160 Income distribution, theory, measurement and policy

absolute poor
access differential
contribution standard
distributional/social weights
egalitarianism
equality
equality standard
factor income
functional income distribution
horizontal equity
income differential
inequality
inheritance tax
intergenerational distribution
  of income
intergenerational equity
invisible foot
Lorenz curve
low pay
needs standard
personal income distribution
poverty
poverty trap
progressive tax
Rawlsian difference principle
size distribution
specific egalitarianism
U hypothesis
vertical equity
wealth distribution
welfare trap

210 Econometric, statistical and mathematical methods and models

activity analysis
adaptive expectations
aggregation problem
analysis of variance
arc elasticity
ARIMA
arithmetic mean
arithmetic progression
ARMA
autocorrelation
average
Bayesian method
bidding technique
bimodal frequency curve
boundary constraint
Box–Jenkins
breakeven analysis
bunch map
butterfly effect
CA
catastrophe theory
chain index method
chaos theory
chartism
chi-squared distribution
choice variable
classical model
cliometrics
Cobb–Douglas production
  function
cobweb
coefficient of correlation
coefficient of determination
coefficient of multiple
  correlation
coefficient of multiple
  determination
coefficient of variation
COMET
compensated demand curve
confidence interval
confidence level
confluence analysis
constant elasticity of
  substitution production
  function
consumption function
contingency table
continuous variable
core
corner solution
correlation
cost–benefit analysis
cost-effectiveness analysis
Cowles Commission

critical value
cyclical variations
data-mining
decile deflation
degrees of freedom
demometrics
depreciation
derivative
difference equation
differentiation
diffusion index
discomfort index
discounting
discrete variable
distributional/social weights
disturbance term
domain
dummy variable
Durbin–Watson statistic
econometrics
economic life
economic model
efficient estimator
eigenprices
empirics
endogenizing the exogenous
endogenous variable
EPA error
Euler's theorem
exogenous variable
ex post variables
extremum
FIFO
FIML
first best economy
flow
flow of funds account
frequency curve
frequency distribution
frequency polygon
frequency table
F test
game theory
generalized least squares
general market equilibrium
geometric mean
geometric progression
Gerschenkron effect
Gini coefficient
goal equilibrium
goal variable
growth accounting
harmonic mean
Herfindahl–Hirschman index
heteroscedasticity
histogram
homoscedasticity
identification problem
impact multiplier

income elasticity of demand
indexation
index number
indicator variable
information theory
input–output analysis
instrument variable
INTERLINK
intermediate target
interval estimate
isolated market equilibrium
J-shaped frequency curve
Keynesian cross diagram
kurtosis
lagged variable
large-scale models
Laspeyres index
least squares method
leptokurtic
level of significance
LIML
Lindahl equilibrium
linear correlation
linear programming
linear regression
linkage models
longitudinal data
Lorenz curve
loss function
lower quartile
Markov chain model
martingale
mathematical economics
maximum likelihood estimator
MCM
mean
mean deviation
median
mesokurtic
microproduction function
minimax
mode
moments
moving averages
multicollinearity
multimodal frequency curve
multiple correlation
multivariate analysis
Nash bargaining noise
non-goal equilibrium
non-linear correlation
non-zero-sum game
normal distribution
null hypothesis
objective function
OLS
one-tailed test
optimal control
optimization problem
outlier

parameter
percentile
platykurtic
point elasticity
point estimate
point-input, point-output
  model
policy variable
potential surprise function
present value
prisoners' dilemma
probability
probable error
production function
product moment formula
random variations
range rank correlation
raw data
reaction function
recursive system
reduced form equation
regression
relative concentration
reverse J-shaped frequency
  curve
saddle point
sample scatter diagram
seasonal adjustment
selection bias
semi-interquartile range
serial correlation
Shapley value
significance test
simulation model
size distribution
skewed frequency curve
skewness
soft modelling
Spearman's rank correlation
  coefficient
specification
standard deviation
standard error of estimate
static model
statistical population
statistics
steady state equilibrium
stochastic process
stochastic term
stock and flow concepts
strong equilibrium
structural model
Student's *t* distribution
stylized fact
symmetrical frequency curve
Tableau économique
target variable
test statistic
three-stage least squares
Tobit model

transformation curve
trend
two-stage least squares
two-tailed test
Type I error
Type II error
unbiased estimator
unimodal distribution
unitary elastic
upper quartile
U-shaped frequency curve
utility function
variance
vector autoregression
Von Neumann–Morgenstern
  stable set
weight
Wharton model
white noise

220 General economics

aggregate output
augmented-GNP
Blue Book
Bureau of Economic Analysis
capital consumption
CBM Census of Manufactures
Census of Retail Trade
coincident indicators
Consolidated Metropolitan
    Statistical Area
constant prices
Consumer Expenditure Survey
consumer price index
cost, insurance and freight
cost of living index
CPI-U
CPI-W
cross-section data
CSO current prices
data
DC Divisia money index
double counting
economic indicators
Engel coefficient
establishment
ETAS
European system of accounts
factor cost
Family Expenditure Survey
flow
flow of funds account
General Household Survey
gross domestic fixed capital
    formation
gross domestic product
gross national product
gross social product
gross state product
headline rate of inflation
implicit price deflator
INSEE
international comparisons
international comparisons of
    the cost of living
international competitiveness
K
labour's share of national
    income
lagging indicator
leading indicators
M0
M1
M2
M3c
M4
M5
market prices
measure of economic welfare

Metropolitan Statistical Area
MEW
minimum list heading
money gross domestic product
Morgan Stanley Capital
    International World Index
N
national income
National Income and Product
    Accounts
national wealth
New Earnings Survey
N-firm concentration ratio
nominal gross domestic
    product
non-interest-bearing M1
OPCS
panel data
physical quality of life index
population census
Primary Metropolitan
    Statistical Area
producer price index
proprietors' income
prosperity indicators
PSL reference cycle
retail price index
ROW
social accounting
social product
Soviet Material Product
    System
Standard & Poor 100
Standard & Poor 500
Standard Industrial
    Classification
Standard International Trade
    Classification
Standard Metropolitan
    Statistical Area
Standard Statistical
    Metropolitan Area
sterling M3
stock and flow concepts
stock market price index
System of Material Product
    Balances
System of National Accounts
time series
transfer income
underlying inflation rate
unemployment statistics
unit value index
value share
wealth distribution
wholesale price index
wide monetary base

310 Domestic monetary and financial theory and institutions

AAA
acceleration clause
accepting house
accommodating credit
account
account days
accrual interest rate
activist
adjustable-rate mortgage
adjusted claim
administration lag
advance
AFBD
Affärsvälden General Index
affinity card
after-hours dealings
aftermarket
agency broker
agent bank
agent de change
AHC Banks
All Ordinaries Index
allotment letter
All Share Index
alpha stock
alternative economic strategy
American Depository Receipt
American Stock Exchange
angel
announcement effect
annual percentage rate (of
    interest)
annuity
APACS
arb
arbitrage
A share
asset motive
asset sweating
Association of International
    Bond Dealers
ATM
ATS Australian Loan Council
automated clearing house
Automated Real-time
    Investment Exchange
automated teller machine
backwardation
BACS bank capital
bank charges
Bank Charter Act 1844
bank deposits
bank efficiency
banker's turn
bank holding company
Bank Holding Company Act 1956

DAX days of grace
DDD
debasing a currency
debenture
debit card
debt
debt contract
debt–equity swap
debt policy
debt ratio
debt restructuring
debt service indicators
debt trap
decimalization
deep discount bond
delta stock
demand deposit
demand for money
demand management
dematerialization
denationalized money
deposit account
deposit base
deposit insurance
Depository Institutions
Deregulation and Monetary
    Control Act 1980
deposit-taking business
depression pole
deregulation
derivative
development bank
discounted share price
discount house
discount market loans
discount rate
discount window
disequilibrium money
disinflation
disintermediation
dissaving
dividend
dividend net
dividend yield
Divisia money index
dollarization
domestic banking system
domestic credit expansion
Douglas Amendment 1965
Dow Jones average
drug economy
DTB
dynamically inconsistent
    policy
earmarked gold
earnings per share
earnings yield
easy money policy
Edge Act corporation
EFT

eftpos
eligible liability
endowment effect
eps
equity
equity joint venture
equity-linked mortgage
equity warrant
ethical unit trust
Eurobank
Eurobond
Eurocheque
Eurodollar
Eurodollar market
Euroequity
Eurofranc
Euromarket
Euromoney deposit
ex ante, ex post
Exchequer
Exchequer White
ex dividend
Exim
expedited funds availability
expensive easy money
Export Import Bank
Farm Credit System
Fed
Federal Deposit Insurance
    Corporation
federal funds
federal funds market
federal funds rate
Federal Home Loan Board
Federal Open Market
    Committee
Federal Reserve Bank
Federal Reserve Note
Federal Reserve System
Federal Savings and Loan
    Insurance Corporation
Fed funds
fiat money
fiduciary issue
Fimbra
financial asset
financial capital
financial conglomerate
financial crisis
'financial engineering'
financial intermediary
financial investment
financial journalism
financial panic
Financial Services Act 1986
financial supermarket
financial system
Financial Times Actuaries All-
    Share Index
Financial Times Industrial

Ordinary Share Index
Financial Times Stock
    Exchange 100 Share Index
fine-tuning
first price auction
Fisher effect
Fisher theorem
fix
flight from money
floating rate note
floor
flooring
floor planning
flotation
football pool
Footsie
forfaiting
fountain pen money
fractional reserve banking
fraud
free banking
fringe banking crisis
front-end loading
fronting loan
funding
fungible asset
futures market
gamma stock
gap analysis
Garn St Germain Depository
    Institutions Act 1982
gearing
general government net worth
generalized medium
gilt-edged security
gilts
Ginny Mae
giro
Glass–Steagall Act
global deregulation
golden parachute
golden share
gold market
gold reserves
goldsmith banking system
Goodhart's law
government bond
government broker
Government National
    Mortgage Association
government security
gradualist monetarism
green stripe price
Gresham's law
grey market
grey Monday
gross dividend yield
gross federal debt
Hang Seng Index
heavy share

helicopter money
hidden reserves
high-leveraged takeover
high-powered money
high-yield financing
hire purchase
HOBS home banking
Humphrey–Hawkins Act
	1978
Hunt Commission
hybrid auction
IBF
ICFC
implementation lag
IMRO
index-linked gilt
index-tracking fund
Industrial and Commercial
	Finance Corporation
industrial share
in-home banking
inside lag
inside money
insider trading
instant monetarism
institutional investor
insurance market
inter-dealer broker
interest-bearing eligible
	liabilities
interest elasticity of savings
interest rate cartel
interest rate swap
interest risk
interlocking directorship
Intermarket Trading System
intermediation
International Banking Act
	1978
International Investment Bank
International Monetary
	Market
International Securities
	Regulatory Organization
International Stock Exchange
investment banking
investment trust
IOU money
IPMA
Islamic banking
IS–LM curves
issuing house
jawbone
jobber
junior debt
junk bond
kursmakler
L
labour standard
laser banking

laundering money
Lautro
law of reflux
LBO
legal tender
lender of last resort
lending rate
letter of credit
leverage
leveraged management buyout
lifeboat operation
liquid assets and government
	securities
liquid assets ratio
liquidity
liquidity preference
liquidity trap
listed bank
listed company
listed security
Lloyd's loanable funds theory
loanshark
loan stock
locked-in effect
Lombard rate
London Discount Market
	Association
London Inter-Bank Offered
	Rate
London Traded Options
	Market
long-term credit bank
loyalty bonus
M
M0
M1
M2
M3
M3c
M4
M5
Macmillan Gap
macroeconomic policy
managed currency fund
management buyout
margin call
margin requirements
margin trading
market-maker
market rate of interest
marking
marzipan layer
Matif
maturity
maturity mismatch
maturity structure of debt
maturity transformation
Mayday
McFadden Branch Banking
	Act 1927

means of payment
medium of account
medium of exchange
medium of redemption
Medium-term Financial
	Strategy
merchant bank
merger arbitrage
metallist
mezzanine finance
middle price
minimum lending rate
misintermediation
monetarism
monetary accommodation
monetary base
Monetary Control Act 1980
monetary overhang
monetary policy
monetary veil
monetization
money
money at call
money centre bank
money market certificate
money market deposit
	account
money market mutual fund
money multiplier
money supply
monkey
monobank
moral suasion
Morgan Stanley Capital
	International World Index
mortgage
mortgage bond
mortgage credit association
mortgage strip
muni
mutual fund
NAIC
narcodollars
National Association of
	Securities Dealers and
	Investment Managers
National Association of
	Securities Dealers
	Automated Quotation
	System
National Banking Act 1863
natural rate of interest
near money
needs of trade
negative saving
negotiable order of withdrawal
net acquisition of financial
	assets
neutrality of money
new issue

New York Mercantile
  Exchange
New York Stock Exchange
niche bank
niche trading
Nikkei average
nominee account
non-interest-bearing M1
note issuance facility
NOW account
NYFE
offer price
off-exchange instrument
offshore banking
OM
one-bank holding company
one-club policy
one hundred per cent reserve
  banking
One two three bank
open-ended fund
open market operations
Operation Twist
optimum quantity of money
option
options exchanges
ordinary share
original issue discount bond
other checkable deposits
outside lag
outside money
overdraft
overfunding
overnight money
over-the-counter market
own rate of interest
PAF
paperless entry
paper money
participating security
par value
payment-in-kind bond
penny share
pension fund
perpetuity
personal bank
personal equity
plan personal sector liquid
  assets
petrodollars
PIBOR
PIN
placing
plastic money
polarization
policy lag
portfolio investment
portfolio selection
portfolio trade
position-risk capital

POS machine
precautionary demand for
  money
pre-emption right
preference share
preferred habitat theory
premium
Premium Savings Bond
price–earnings ratio
price maker
price-sensitive information
primary capital
primary dealer
primary market
Prime-1
prime rate of interest
principal
private placement
private rate of discount
professional trader
profit taking
programme deal
programme trading (UK)
program trading (US)
promissory note
prospectus
proxy
PSL
public debt
public good
public sector borrowing
  requirement
pure credit economy
pure discretion
pure interest rate
put option
put-through
quadriad
quantity theory of money
queuing system
Radcliffe Report
random walk theory
rate of interest
rating agency
RD
real bills doctrine
real estate investment trust
real interest rate
recognition lag
recognized professional body
redemption date
redemption yield
refunding
regional banking pacts
Regulation D
Regulation K
Regulation Q
Regulation U
re-intermediation
repackaging

repurchase agreement
required reserve ratio
reserve assets
reserve base
reserve ratio
reserve requirements
Resolution Trust Corporation
retail bank
retained earnings
reverse takeover
reverse yield gap
reversionary bonus
revolving credit
revolving underwriting facility
rights issue
risk asset system
risk aversion
risk-based banking standards
risk capital
risk package
risky asset
riyal
Rmb
ROI
rolling settlement
roundtripping
rules versus discretion
running broker
run on a bank
safe asset
saitori
samurai bond
Saudi Arabian Monetary
  Agency
savings and loan association
SAYE
SCOPE
scrip issue
secondary bank
secondary banking crisis
secondary capital
secondary market
second market
Securities and Exchange
  Commission
Securities Association
Securities Exchange Act 1934
securities house
securities market
securitization
security
seed capital
seignorage
self-regulation
self-regulatory organization
selling short
senior debt
SEPON
servicing a debt
SET index

settlement day
sham trading
share
share borrowing
share buy-back
share support operation
shelf registration
shell company
shell operation
short selling
short-termism
short-term money market
SIB
SIBOR
SICAV
sight deposit
silver ring
single-capacity trading
sleeping economy
smart card
smart money
smokestack American stocks
SNB
snugging
social conscience fund
Society for Worldwide
    Interbank Financial
    Telecommunications
soft commission
soft landing
soft loan
sogo bank
sovereign loan
special bracket firm
special deposit
specialist
specie
speculation
speculative demand for money
spot market
spot rate
spread
spreading
stag
Standard & Poor 100
Standard & Poor 500
Statutory Reserve Deposit
stepped bond
sterilization
sterling commercial paper
sterling M3
sterling warrant into gilt-edged
    stock
stock borrowing
stock exchange
Stock Exchange Automated
    Quotation System
stockholder diffusion
stock index arbitrage
stock index futures market

stock market price index
stocks
stop–go
store of value
straddle
straight bond
Straits Times Industrial Index
streaker
strike price
stripped security
structural adjustment policy
stub equity
superneutrality
supplementary special deposits
    scheme
swap market
symmetallism
syndicated loan
Talisman
TAPS
tap stock
targeting tarification
Taurus
tender
terminal bonus
term premium
term structure of interest rates
third market
Thirty Share Index
thrift
TIBOR
tick
tight monetary policy
till money
time deposit
TINA
token money
tombstone
tontine
total public debt
town clearing
trade bill
traded option
transactions demand for
    money
transmission mechanism
traveller's cheque
treasury bill
trigger mechanism
TSA
twenty-four-hour trading
two-dollar broker
UK gilts market
umbrella fund
underwriter
Uniform Commercial Code
Unitas all share index
unit banking
unitization
unit of account

unit trust
Unlisted Securities Market
US treasury bond market
US Treasury market
usury
vault cash
velocity of circulation
vendor finance
venture capital
warehouse receipt
wholesale bank
wholesale money market
wide monetary base
wider share ownership
window dressing
writer
XD
xr
Yankee bond
yearling
yellow stripe price
yield
yield curve
yield gap
zero coupon bond
zero real interest
Z-score

320 Fiscal policy and theory; public finance

ability to pay
abortive benefits
above the line
absolute tax incidence
Accelerated Cost Recovery
  System
accelerated depreciation
accession tax
active fiscal policy
activist
actual budget
administration lag
administrative cost
ad valorem tax
Advance Corporation Tax
alternative economic strategy
announcement burden of a tax
announcement effect
appropriation bill
automatic stabilizer
Autumn Statement
average tax rate
backward shifting
balanced budget
Balanced Budget and
  Emergency Deficit Control
  Act 1985
balanced budget multiplier
Barber boom
basic relief
below the line
benefit approach to taxation
benefit tax
bloc grant
blue return
bracket creep
budgetary policy
budget cutting
budget incidence
Budget Resolution
budget year
built-in stabilizer
buoyant tax
Bureau of the Budget
Butskellism
cadastral survey
canons of taxation
Cantillon effect
capital gains tax
capital income tax
capitalization effect of a tax
capital tax
capital transfer tax
capitation tax
carbon tax
carry-back, carry-forward
  system

cash limit
cash transfer
catalytic policy mix
categorical grant
CBO
Chancellor of the Exchequer
clear income
collective good
commodity tax
Commonwealth Grants
  Commission
community charge
compensatory finance
compliance cost
composite rate tax
compulsory competitive
  tendering
Condorcet criterion
Congressional Budget and
  Impoundment Control Act
  1974
Consolidated Fund
Consolidated Fund standing
  services
consumption tax
contract compliance
cooperative federalism
corporate income tax
corporation income tax
corporation tax
corrective subsidy
corrective tax
cost-effectiveness analysis
Council of Economic
  Advisers
council tax
creative federalism
crowding out
CTD
cumulative multistage
cascade system
daisy-chain scheme
debt
debt neutrality
debt policy
decelerator
decision cycle
dedicated budget
deemed tax
deficit financing
demand management
differential tax incidence
direct and indirect taxation
direct–indirect taxes ratio
direct labour organization
direct tax
disincentive effect
disinflation
disposable income
distortionary tax

double taxation of savings
double-taxation relief
dual federalism
dynamically inconsistent
  policy
earmarking easy rider
economic incidence
effective tax rate
emission charge
environmental tax
equity taxation
ex ante, ex post
excess burden of a tax
excise duty
excise tax
expenditure tax
export subsidy
external debt
factor tax
federal finance
final income
Financial Statement and
  Budget Report
fine-tuning
fiscal approximation
fiscal crisis
fiscal dividend
fiscal drag
fiscal federalism
fiscal illusion
fiscal incidence
fiscal indicators
fiscalist
fiscal mobility
fiscal neutrality
fiscal policy
fiscal rectitude
fiscal stance
flat grant
flat rate tax
flat tax
flypaper effect
forced labour
forfait system
formal indexation
free depreciation
free rider
full employment budget
functional financing
funding gap
FY
General Accounting Office
general fund
general sales tax
gifts tax
global deregulation
goal system
government intervention
government role
graduated income tax

graduate tax
Gramm–Rudman–Hollings
Act
grant in aid
head tax
high employment surplus
horizontal equity
Humphrey–Hawkins Act 1978
hybrid income tax
hypothecation
implementation lag
implicit marginal
income
impure public good
imputed income
incentive contract
incentive effect
income splitting system
income support
income tax
indirect tax
individual income tax
inertial effect
inflation-adjusted deficit
inflation tax
inheritance tax
in-kind transfer
inside lag
Institute of Fiscal Studies
interest equalization tax
intergenerational equity
internal debt
Internal Revenue Service
inter-nation equity
invisible foot
Islamic fiscal policy
IS–LM curves
Japanese tax system
Laffer curve
lag
laissez-faire
leaky bucket
Lerner effect
leverage
lifetime averaging
Lindahl equilibrium
Lindahl price
line item veto
local government finance
local public good
logrolling
long-term income averaging
lump-sum tax
macroeconomic policy
marginal tax rate
marriage allowance
MCT Medium-term Financial
Strategy
merit bad
merit good

merit want
military Keynesianism
minimal state
MIRAS
mixed good
multistage tax
national debt
national insurance
contribution
national lottery
negative income tax
neutral budget
New Deal
new federalism
nominal tax rate
non-standard tax relief
Office of Management and
Budget
Omnibus Budget
Reconciliation Act
one-club policy
optimal taxation
output budgeting
outside lag
PAYE
payroll tax
peace dividend
percentage grant
per-unit tax
petroleum revenue tax
Pigou effect
Pigovian subsidy
Pigovian tax
planning programming
budgeting
Plowden Committee
policy lag
political business cycle
poll tax
pollution tax
pork barrel legislation
poverty trap
presumptive tax
primary deficit
privatization
progressive tax
property tax
proportional tax
proportionate grant
Proposition 13
Provisional Collection of
Taxes Act
public choice theory
public economics
public expenditure
public expenditure control
Public Expenditure Survey
Committee
public finance
public sector

public sector balance sheet
public sector borrowing
requirement
public sector debt repayment
public spending ratio
public works
pump priming
purchase tax
pure discretion
quadriad
Ramsey taxes
rates
rate support grant
Reaganomics
real property tax
recognition lag
reconciliation bill
Red Book
regional employment premium
regressive tax
revalorization
revenue neutral
revenue sharing
revenue support grant
reverse income tax
Ricardian equivalence theorem
ringfencing
'roof tax'
Rooker–Wise Amendment
rules versus discretion
sacrifice theory
sales tax
savings
SAYE
schedular tax
Selective Employment Tax
self-insurance
sequestration
shifting of taxes
short-termism
Shoup Mission
single tax movement
social credit
social dividend scheme
social security
social spending
social wants
soft budget
soft landing
spatial benefit limitation
specific duty
Star Chamber
state theories
statutory incidence
stop–go
strategic tax planning
structural adjustment policy
structural deficit
subsidiarity
subsidy

superneutrality
supply-side economics
Swedish budget
take-up rate
targeting tariff
taxable capacity
taxable income
taxation
tax avoidance
tax base
tax-based incomes policy
tax bracket creep
tax buoyancy
tax burden
tax capitalization
tax credit
tax effort
tax elasticity
tax erosion
tax evasion
Tax Exempt Special Savings
  Account
tax expenditure
tax farming
taxflation
tax harmonization
tax haven
tax incidence
tax reform
Tax Reform Act 1986
tax revenue
tax structure
tax threshold
tax unit
tax wedge
1040 ('ten forty')
Tessa
Thatcherism
theory of clubs
Tiebout hypothesis
tight fiscal policy
TINA
Tobin tax
top-sided federalism
treasury
Treasury view
trust fund
turnover tax
TVA
UK taxation
unconditional grant
uniform business rate
unit tax user charge
US federal finance
value-added tax
vertical equity
voodoo economics
wage subsidy
wage–tax spiral
Wagner's law

wealth tax
welfare trap
withholding tax
zero-base budgeting
zero-rated good

**410 International trade
theory**

absolute advantage
autarky
comparative advantage
comparative costs
domestic resource cost
Edgeworth box
factor endowment
factor price equalization
  theorem
FF curve
gains from trade
Heckscher–Ohlin trade
  theorem
international trade theory
law of reciprocal demand
Leontief paradox
Mundell–Fleming model
Rybczynski theorem
social adjustment cost
terms of trade
vent for surplus

420 Trade relations; commercial policy; international economic integration

alternative economic strategy
Andean Common Market
Arab Common Market
Arab Maghreb Union
Association of South East
  Asian Nations
availability thesis
barter
beggar-my-neighbour policy
BERD
border trade
'British problem'
buffer stock
Caribbean Basin Initiative
Caribbean Community
CARIFTA
CEC
Centre for International
  Studies
centre–periphery system
CEPAL
CEPGL
closed economy
Cocom
Comecon
commercial policy
commodity agreement
commodity terms of trade
commodity trade structure
Common Agricultural Policy
common external tariff
common market
Communauté Economique de
  L'Afrique de l'Ouest
compensating common tariff
core economy
Council for Mutual Economic
  Aid
counterpurchase
countertrade
customs union
cyclical trade
delinking
Delors Plan
dependent economy
Dillon Round
directly unproductive profit-
  seeking activities
double factorial terms of trade
dumping
Economic Community of the
  countries of the Great Lakes
Economic Community of
  West African States
economic integration

economic sanctions
economic union
effective rate of assistance
effective rate of protection
European Communities
European Community
European Economic
  Community
European Free Trade
  Association
European Monetary Union
export
export promotion
export subsidy
external shock
factorial terms of trade
fair trading
Food and Agriculture
  Organization
foreign trade organization
foreign trade zone
free on board
freeport
free trade
free-trade area
FTZ
General Agreement on Tariffs
  and Trade
generalized system of
  preferences
geographical trade structure
Group of twenty-four
Group of seventy-seven
Havana Charter
import
import penetration ratio
import substitution
in-bond manufacturing
income terms of trade
infant industry argument
Institute for International
  Economics
interdependent economy
inter-industry trade
internal market
International Trade
  Organization
intra-industry trade
invisible trade
Jackson Amendment
Kennedy Round
Latin American Free Trade
  Association
Lomé Convention
M
marginal propensity to
  import
most favoured nation
Multi-Fibre Arrangement
net barter terms of trade

new international division of
  labour
New International Economic
  Order
new protectionism
non-tariff barrier
non-tradables
open economy
optimal tariff
polarization effect
policy harmonization
Prebisch–Singer thesis
primary commodity
prices protection
quantitative restrictions
quota
Randall Commission
reciprocal demand law
Reciprocal Trade Agreements
  Act 1934
Single European Act 1986
single factorial terms of trade
single market
Smoot–Hawley Tariff Act
  1930
South African Customs Union
stabex system
staple export
state trading organization
Stolper–Samuelson
  theorem
tariff
terms of trade
Tokyo Round
Trade Act 1974
trade creation
trade diversion
Trade Expansion Act 1962
trade policy
trade regime
trade strategy
trade threat
Treaty of Rome
Union Douanière et
  Economique de l'Afrique
  Centrale
United Nations Conference on
  Trade and Development
Uruguay Round
US Trade Representative
voluntary export restraint
warehouse economy
world trade
X
zero-sum game

430 Balance of payments; international finance

absorption approach
accommodating credit
accounting balance of
  payments
additional facilities
adjustable peg
African Development Bank
aid
Aid and Trade Provisions
Andean Common Market
arbitrage
artificial currency
Asian Development Bank
baht
Baker plan
Balance for Official Financing
balance of payments
balance of payments
  equilibrium
balance of trade
balancing item
bancor
Bank for International
  Settlements
Basle Concordat on Banking
  Supervision
bear
bilateral aid
bill of exchange
Brandt Commission
Bretton Woods Agreement
bull
butterfly effect
cable
capital account
capital flight
Cedal
CFA franc
chaos theory
chart point
clean float
colon
Committee of Twenty
commodity reserve currency
commodity stabilization
  schemes
common currency
compensatory financial facility
convertible currency
cost, insurance and freight
crawling peg
credit rating
credit reserves
credit tranche facility
currency
currency appreciation
currency basket

currency depreciation
currency devaluation
currency reform
currency revaluation
currency stabilization scheme
currency swap
current account
DAC
debt–equity swap
debt-led growth
debt service indicators
depreciation
devaluation
dinar
direct foreign investment
dirham
dirty float
divergence indicator
divergence threshold
dollar
dollar overhang
dollar standard
domestic credit expansion
dong
dual exchange rate
Economic and Social Council
economic sanctions
economic summits
ecu
effective exchange rate
ERP
Eurobond market
Euroclear
Eurocurrency market
Eurodollar
Eurodollar market
Eurofed
Eurofranc
Euromoney deposit
European Bank for
  Reconstruction and
  Development
European Cooperation
  Administration
European currency unit
European Investment Bank
European monetary
  cooperation
European Monetary
  Cooperation Fund
European Monetary System
European Monetary Union
European Recovery Program
European Unit of Account
exchange controls
exchange cross rate
Exchange Equalization
  Account
exchange rate
exchange rate agreement

Exchange Rate Mechanism
exchange rate regime
exchange rate target zone
exchange risk
extended fund facility
external account
external balance
external debt
external shock
fixed exchange rate
flexible exchange rate
floating exchange rate
foreign aid
foreign direct investment
foreign exchange
foreign exchange market
foreign trade multiplier
forex
forex trading
forint
forward market
franchise gap
free alongside
fundamental equilibrium
futures market
General Agreement to Borrow
gliding rate
global deregulation
global monetarism
goldbug
gold bullion standard
gold demonetization
gold exchange standard
gold franc
gold market
gold reserves
gold shortage
gold standard
green currency
green pound
Group of Five
Group of Seven
Group of Ten
Group of Thirty
guilder
hard currency
hard ecu
hedging
hot money
IBF
ICCH
Institute for International
  Finance
Inter-American Development
  Bank
International Bank for
  Economic Cooperation
International Bank for
  Reconstruction and
  Development

510 Administration

AG
agency cost
agency theory
AGM
batch production
bourgeoisie
business organization
business studies
chaebol
chartered company
chief executive officer
company
conglomerate
cooperative
core firm
corporation
cowboy
crisis management
direct labour organization
economic programming
enterpriser
entrepreneur
evolutionary theory of the
    firm
executive leasing
expense preference
firm
flexible firm
Fordism
forward integration
GmbH
going concern
golden parachute
growth theory of the firm
H-form
hierarchical decomposition
    principle
holding company
industrial democracy
information cost
intrapreneur
joint stock company
just-in-time production
Keidanven
keiretsu
labour-managed firm
limited company
management by objectives
managerial models of the firm
managerial revolution
managerial utility function
maximization
marzipan layer
megacorp
M-form
multinational corporation
nationalization
Nikkeiren

non-profit enterprise
NV
objectives of firms
organizational economics
organization theory
parallel plants
parastatal
Parkinson's law
partnership
periphery firm
Peter principle
plc
private enterprise
profit maximization
public enterprise
public interest company
regulated firm
SA
sales maximization
SarL satisficing
SBA scalar principle
shell company
sole proprietor
storming
SWOT
synergy
Taylorism
transaction cost
transnational corporation
U-form
Uniform Commercial Code
vertical expansion
vertical formation
X-form
zaibatsu

520 Business and investment

above the line
Accelerated Cost Recovery
    System
accelerated depreciation
accelerator principle
acid-test ratio
adjustment speed
administered pricing
administrative cost
adverse selection
amortization
animal spirits
anticipatory pricing
arbitration
A share
asset stripping
asset sweating
bankruptcy
basing point pricing
below the line
bonding cost
breakeven pricing
B share
Business Expansion Scheme
capital accumulation
capital consumption
cash flow
ceiling price
circulating
capital
commercial paper
conglomerate merger
corporate finance
costing margin
credit
cross-subsidization
current assets
current liabilities
current operating profit
debt
debt restructuring
Delphi method
depreciation
direct product profitability
discounted cash flow
divestment
earnings
economic life
employee ratios
equipment trust bond
escalator clause
factoring
financial capital
'financial engineering'
financial leverage ratio
financial policy
fixed capital

fixed cost
franchise financing
fraud
free depreciation
front end loading
gearing
general fund
Giffen good
goodwill
greenmail
holding gain
hurdle rate of return
implicit cost
incentive contract
Industrial and Commercial
  Finance Corporation
insolvency
internal rate of return
inventory
investment appraisal
investment climate
kickback
LBO
leverage
leveraged management buyout
liquid assets
long fraud
Ltd
Macmillan Gap
management buyout
marginal cost pricing
marginal efficiency of capital
marginal efficiency of
  investment
marginal private damage
mark-up pricing
merger
minimum efficient scale
net asset value
net present value
off-balance-sheet financing
output budgeting
overtrading
parallel loan
peak-load pricing
pecuniary external economy
Pittsburgh plus
preference share
present value
price bunching
price staggering
prime cost
profitability
profit centre
profit squeeze
pyramiding
quick assets ratio
rate of return
ratio analysis
real rate of return

replacement investment
reputation capital
retained earnings
risk capital
seed capital
self-insurance
share buy-back
share support operation
stock adjustment principle
stock–output ratio
supplementary cost
sweetener
tangible net worth
taxable capacity
test rate of discount
trade credit
trading on the equity
transfer pricing
treasury
turnkey contract
unbundling
undertrading
unit pricing
user cost
venture capital
working capital
X-efficiency
zai teku

advertising
auction
badge engineering
black market
branding
brand loyalty
bundling
buyers' market
characteristics theory of
  consumer demand
churning
consumer sovereignty
contracting
customize
differentiated good
differentiated marketing
differentiated product
differentiation
direct sale
Dutch auction
English auction
first degree price
  discrimination
first price auction
franchise loss leader
market concentration
market share
mixed bundling
monopsony
multilevel marketing
non-linear pricing
oligopsony
orderly market agreement
organic premium
parallel pricing
perfect price discrimination
predatory pricing
price discrimination
price maker
price war
product compatibility
product differentiation
public pricing
pure bundling
pyramid selling
resale price maintenance
second-degree price
  discrimination
second price auction
sellers' market
skimming
sogo shosha
third degree price
  discrimination
tying contract
unbundling
warranty

540 Accounting

above the line
accounting
accounting costs
accounting cycle
accounting identity
accounting profit
accrual accounting
accrued expense
accrued income
acid-test ratio
activity ratio
APB
balance sheet
below the line
book value
bottom-line accounting
BOY
CA
capacity ratio
capital budgeting
capital value
cash budgeting
cash flow accounting
cost ratio
creative accounting
current cost accounting
current purchasing power
current ratio
deprival value
discounted cash flow
double counting
Du Pont formula
earnings ratio
economic value
efficiency ratio
expense ratio
FIBS
FIFO
financial accounting
Financial Reporting Council
first in, first out
historic cost
income statement
inflation accounting
intangible wealth
last in, first out
LIFO
management accounting
margin of safety
net acquisition of financial
    assets
net worth
NRV
off-balance-sheet financing
paper profit
pay-back method
primary ratio
profit

profit and loss account
quick assets
ratio replacement cost
ROCE
sales ratios
Sandilands Report
Statements of Standard
    Accounting Practice
step cost
stock ratios
tangible wealth
true and fair view
turnover ratios
volume ratio

610 Industrial organization and public policy

absolute concentration
administrative costs of
    regulation
aggregate concentration
agribusiness
anarchism
anticompetitive practices
antitrust
artificial barrier to entry
Australian Industries
    Preservation Acts 1906–50
Averch–Johnson effect
barometric firm leadership
barrier to exit
behavioural economics
bucket shop
capacity charge
capital intensive
capitalist imperialism
capture theory
cartel
Celler–Kefauver Antimerger
    Act 1950
Clayton Act 1914
Colbertism
collusion
commanding heights
common ownership
commune
competition policy
competitive fringe
competitive process
concentration
concentration ratio
Confederation of British
    Industry
conglomerate merger
constrained market pricing
cooperative
core firm
corporate morality
cost leader
cottage industry
countervailing power
David Hume Institute
de-industrialization
department
deregulation
dirigisme
divestment
dominant firm
Dutch disease
economics of law
equity joint venture
establishment
external economy of scale

630 Industry studies

brown good
cabotage
churning
composite insurance company
contingent market
CTN
Davignon Plan
domestic system
DTP
expert system
footloose industry
in-bond manufacturing
Insurance Ombudsman
   Bureau
International Air Travel
   Association
locked-in industry
moral hazard
NAIC
old staples
Petty's law
proportional accounting
reinsurance
risk-based premium
risk sharing
runaway industry
rustbelt
service industry
sunrise industry
tertiary sector
tied house
Unctad Liner Code
value-added network service
Warsaw Convention
white good
zone of freedom

640 Economic capacity

absorptive capacity
capacity
capacity charge
capacity utilization
capital utilization
carrying capacity
excess capacity
gestation period
social overhead capital

710 Agriculture

adjustment gap
agribusiness
Agricultural Adjustment Act
   1933
agricultural household
agricultural policy
Asiatic mode of production
Brundtland Report
buffer stock
cadastral survey
Cairn's Group
cash crop
cobweb
collectivization of agriculture
Commodity Credit
   Corporation
common access resources
Common Agricultural Policy
deficiency payment
differential theory of rent
diminishing returns law
Farm Credit System
floor price
Food and Agriculture
   Organization
food chain
green revolution
intervention price
land
land economy
land ownership
Monetary Compensation
   Amount
organic premium
perfect competition
price floor
primary product
primitive economy
producer subsidy equivalent
rent
set aside
sharecropper
soft commodity
stabex system
supply control
target price
white revolution
yield zoning

720 Natural resources, energy economics

abatement
absolute scarcity
ambient standard
bad
b/d
best available technology
bid vehicle
bioeconomics
black gold
Brundtland Report
bubble policy
carbon tax
Clean Air Act Amendments
    1970
Coase theorem
command and control
    regulation
contingent valuation
cowboy economy
depletable externality
effluent fee
emission charge
emission fee
emission reductions banking
environmental determinism
environmental issues
Environmental Protection
    Agency
environmental tax
exploitation factor endowment
green conditionality
Gulf Plus
hard commodity
integrated pollution control
International Energy Agency
IPE
marginal cost of abatement
marginal private damage
marginal social damage
marketable discharge permit
natural resources
neighbourhood effect
NIMBY
non-renewable resources
oil price increases
optimal rate of pollution
Organization of Petroleum
    Exporting Countries
peak-load pricing
petrocurrency
petroleum revenue tax
Pigovian subsidy
Pigovian tax
pollution charge
pollution control
pollution tax
posted price

primary standard
recycling
renewable resource
resource economics
scarcity
scarcity index
secondary standard
SIP
spaceman economy
tradable discharge permit
tradable emission permit
transferable discharge permit
undepletable externality
user charge

730 Economic geography

Benelux
bottom-up linkage model
core region
economic geography
First World
Fourth World
freeport
free-trade area
frostbelt
FTZ
geographical trade structure
Golden Triangle
gravity model
grey belt
infrastructure
LDC
little dragons
local monopoly
location theory
Lotharingian axis
Pacific Rim
Randstad
Rhinelands hourglass
rustbelt
Second World
spatial duopoly
spatial monopoly
spatial oligopoly
Third World
World Bank classification of
    countries

810 Manpower training and allocation; labour force and supply

abstract labour
activity rate
apprenticeship
backward-bending labour
   supply curve
blue-collar worker
casualization
central occupation
community programme
Comprehensive Employment
   and Training Act 1973
   (USA)
concrete labour
cyclical unemployment
demarcation
discouraged workers
   hypothesis
disguised unemployment
downsizing employment
Employment Act 1946
Employment Institute
Equal Employment
   Opportunity Commission
ergonomics
frictional unemployment
full employment
gender discrimination
general training
hidden unemployment
home production
homework
household decision-making
hysteresis
industrial training grant
International Standard
   Classification of
   Occupations
involuntary employment
involuntary unemployment
island
job security
job sharing
labour
labour force
labour force participation rate
labour mobility
labour power
labour supply
last in, first out
LIFO
LTU
manpower forecasting
manpower policy
migrant labour
migration
migration-fed unemployment

mobility status
NAIRU
natural rate of unemployment
networker
non-accelerating inflation rate
   of unemployment
non-employment
occupation
occupational segregation
off-the-job training
on-the-job training
optimal work effort
overtime
partial unemployment
permanent employment
Phillips curve
primary employment
private cost of unemployment
productive labour
productivity shock
proletariat
racial discrimination
replacement labour force
replacement ratio
reserve army of labour
retirement age
retrophobia
search unemployment
seasonal unemployment
secondary employment
Sex Discrimination Acts 1975,
   1986
sexual discrimination
sexual division of labour
sheltered employment
social cost of unemployment
socially necessary labour time
special employment measures
specific training
Stakhanovite
structural unemployment
sweated trade
time budget survey
time span
underemployment
unemployment
unemployment causes
unemployment spell
unemployment statistics
unemployment trap
unproductive labour
voluntary unemployment
white-collar worker
work classification
working hours
working population
work sharing

820 Labour markets; public policy

affirmative action
ageism
annualized-hours system
asymmetric information
bargaining theory of wages
basic wage
boycott
Civil Rights Act 1964
COLA
comparable worth
compensating wage differential
contingency claims contracting
contract compliance
contracting
cost of living adjustment
crowding hypothesis
discrimination
dual labour market
earnings
efficiency real wages
efficiency wage
efficient job mobility
employment contract
employment multiplier
equalizing wage differential
Equal Pay Act 1963
Equal Pay Act 1970
Equal Pay Directive
escalator clause
European Social Charter
external labour market
Fair Wages Resolution
featherbedding
floor price
fringe benefits
gender discrimination
going rate
golden handcuffs
golden handshake
golden hello
golden parachute
golden rate
hedonic wages
horizontal discrimination
incentive pay scheme
incomes policy
inertial effect
insider wage setting
internal labour market
internal labour market
   contracting
internal search
international wage levels
invisible handshake
iron law of wages
jawbone
job acceptance schedule

535

International Labour
  Organization
International Miners'
  Organization
international union
international union federation
job control unionism
Labor Management Relations
  Act 1947
Labor Management Reporting
  and Disclosure Act 1959
labor union
labour-managed firm
labour process theory
Landrum–Griffin Act 1959
local union
lockout
National Industrial Recovery
  Act 1933
National Labor Relations Act
  1935
National Labor Relations
  Board
Norris–La Guardia Act 1932
open shop
parallel plants
pendulum arbitration
picketing
piecework system
productivity bargaining
quality circle
quit rate
regional wage bargaining
Rengo
right-to-work state
runaway shop
secondary action
sequestration
Shinsanbetsu
shop steward
shunto
single union deal
social compact
social contract
Sohyo
spillover effect
straight choice arbitration
strike
strike-free deal
sweetheart contract
syndicalism
Taft–Hartley Act 1947
team briefing
threat effect
trade union
Trade Union Act 1984
Trade Unions and Labour
  Relations Act 1976
treat effect
unfair labour practice

union density
unionization
Union of National Economic
  Associations in Japan
union shop
union wage effect
union wage policy
US labor union
voice
Vredeling directive
wage gap
wage theory
Wagner Act 1935
workers' participation
yellow dog contract

840 Demographic economics

ageing population
brain drain
carrying capacity
chain migration
circular migration
closed population
Consolidated Metropolitan
  Statistical Area
crude population rate
current population survey
de facto population
de jure population
demographic accounting
demographic transition
demography
demometrics
dependency ratio
Dinks
empty nester
GLAM
gravity model
grey belt
grey society
immigration
Malthus, Thomas Robert,
  1766–1834
Markov chain model
Metropolitan Statistical Area
migration
mobility status
mobility trap
natural increase
neo-Malthusians
non-employment
open population
optimum population
Pippy
population
population census
population density
population explosion
population policy
Primary Metropolitan
  Statistical Area
prime age worker
resident population
retirement age
Standard Statistical
  Metropolitan Area
third age
threshold population
total fertility rate
vital revolution
yumpie
yuppie, yuppy
zero population growth

850 Human capital

age–earnings profile
apprenticeship
factor endowment
general training
human capital
off-the-job training
on-the-job training
positive discrimination
specific training

910 Welfare, health and education

abortive benefits
absolute poor
Aid to Families with
    Dependent Children
cash transfer
contractual savings
dependency culture
dependency ratio
deserving poor
dole bludger
early retirement scheme
economic crime
economics of crime
European Social Charter
Great Society
health economics
human capital
immiseration
implicit marginal income
income support
IRA
nanny state
national insurance
    contribution
net economic welfare
Old Age, Survivors, Disability
    and Health Insurance
pension
pension fund
pension scheme
poverty line
poverty trap
proto-proletariat
QALY
quality-adjusted life years
replacement ratio
social security
Social Security Act 1935
State Earnings-Related
    Pension Scheme
subsistence
tied cottage
trust fund
unemployment compensation
unemployment trap
voucher system
welfare state
welfare trap
worker compensation
    insurance
workfare

920 Consumer protection

annual percentage rate (of
    interest)
consumer credit
Consumer Credit Act 1974
consumer durable
consumerism
consumer protection
    legislation
consumer society
Office of Fair Trading Truth
    in Lending Act 1968

930 Urban economics

agglomeration diseconomy
agglomeration economy
anchor tenant
basic industry
bid rent
Building Societies Association
CBD
central place theory
commuting
company town
concentration economy
council housing
economic rent
enterprise zone
filtering
gazumping
generative city
gentrification
homeless
ideal limit
land economy
mobility trap
Muth–Mills model
new town
non-basic industry
optimum city
over-urbanization
owner occupation
parasitic city
rank size rule
redlining
residualization
tax capitalization
threshold population
Tiebout hypothesis
timeshare
transport economics
urban economics

940 Regional economics

assisted area
backward linkage
backwash effect
branch economy
core region
economic base multiplier
European Investment Bank
European Regional
    Development Fund
forward linkage
growth pole
isolated state
RECHAR
regional economics
regional employment premium
regional multiplier
regional policy
regional selective assistance
sector adjustment lending
shift-share analysis
snowbelt
spatial equalization
spread effect
sunbelt
Thomson Report
top-down linkage model